AF662983

GOYLE'S

Law of Specific Performance

Specific performance, with its genesis in Equity and progression with contemporary desideratum, has come to pervade the domain of Civil Law, in particular, where the contractual obligations are flouted by way of breach of contractual stipulations. It prescribes the remedies to make good the loss suffered for the transgression of the terms of contract. *'Ease of doing business'* is the catchphrase in the business world today where contractual relationships play a crucial role. But, the relief of 'specific performance' in vogue prior to the amendments in the Act, being a discretionary relief, was not sufficient enough to infuse confidence in the business community to do business in India. Therefore, the framework of entire law of specific performance was needed to be overhauled to make the specific performance *'a certainty'* rather than *'a discretionary relief'*. The recent amendments by the Specific Relief (Amendment) Act 2018 are the attempts in this regard to keep pace with the contemporary needs of the business world to strengthen the enforcement of contractual relationship for smooth flow of trade and commerce and for boosting the confidence of investors. The introduction of the concept of *'substituted performance of contract'* in the Specific Relief Act 1963 in 2018 has now altered the nature of relief from *discretionary* to *distinct and certain*. Thus, the law has developed from *specific performance* to *substituted performance* of contract.

The essence of specific performance of contract has its pervasive presence in almost every sphere of life. Despite its origin in the hoary past, it has managed to march with the changing society. The instant edition of this book is a thoroughly revised and up to date one incorporating recent legislative changes and judicial pronouncements of Supreme Court and High Courts, in addition to the cases from American and English laws to make the book practically useful. Relevant and contemporary topics, such as Equity, Estoppel, Damages, Compensation, Restitution, Fraud, Pre-emption, Injunction, to mention a few, have been thoroughly revised and updated, where need be.

It goes without saying that law is a dynamic subject. Therefore, recent changes, both legislative and judicial, have necessitated the inclusion of new topics touching upon the core of law of specific performance to make the present edition more pragmatic and effectively useful for the readers. Numerous topics, such as, *substituted performance of contract, objective theory of contract, doctrine of mitigation, doctrine of mutuality, vicarious performance, concept of right to recover, power to engage expert by the court*, to name but a few, have been discussed extensively to make the book more practical and useful.

To make the book up to date and comprehensive, the Specific Relief (Amendment) Act 2018 has been extensively dealt with. Different topics of practical utility have been incorporated in the light of the recent amendments in the Act. The impact of the Jammu and Kashmir Reorganisation Act 2019 has got proper treatment.

Kolkata
Eastern Law House Private Ltd.
54 Ganesh Chunder Avenue
Kolkata 700 013

New Delhi
Eastern Law House Private Ltd.
36 Netaji Subhash Marg, Daryaganj
New Delhi 110 002

GOYLE'S

Law of Specific Performance

FIFTH EDITION

by

S.K. Pathak LLM
West Bengal Judicial Service

Kolkata New Delhi
EASTERN LAW HOUSE

Published and processed by
EASTERN LAW HOUSE PRIVATE LTD.
54 Ganesh Chunder Avenue
Kolkata 700 013
Tel: (033) 2215-1989
Email: mail@elh.co.in
www.elh.co.in

First Edition 1984
Second Edition 1992
Third Edition 2003
Fourth Edition 2014
Fifth Edition 2020

©
EASTERN LAW HOUSE PRIVATE LTD.
AND THE ESTATE OF L.C. GOYLE
2020

Whilst all reasonable care has been taken to ensure accuracy of the contents of this book, no person associated with the creation or publishing of this book shall have responsibility for any loss or damages that may be caused to any person due to errors or omissions which may have crept in inadvertently in this publication. Disputes, if any, are subject to Kolkata jurisdiction.

ISBN 978-81-7177-359-6

Printed at
Dey's Offset, Kolkata

Preface to the Fifth Edition

The Specific Relief Act 1963, provided for specific performance as a discretionary and equitable relief. Wide discretion was conferred upon the Courts to decide the cases of specific performance. With the passage of time, discretionary jurisdiction exercised by the courts made award of damages a general rule and grant of specific performance an exception in cases concerning breach of contract. However, since after the enactment of the Act in 1963, massive economic development has taken place all around ushering in a new era of commercial activities including foreign direct investments, public private partnership, public utilities infrastructure developments, to name just a few. The changed economic scenario required speedy resolution of dispute and expediting enforcement of contracts. However, the Act appeared to be deficient in catering to the newly-evolved needs of the business world because of the contemporary economic growth. The Parliament, therefore, felt the need of amending the Act to fine-tune the legal regime given the rapid economic growth taking place in the country and expansion of infrastructure activities. As such, the Act has been subjected to many a change by way of the Specific Relief (Amendment) Act 2018. The most remarkable aspect of the recent changes made in the Act is the removal of the discretionary and equitable jurisdiction of the court in cases involving specific performance.

According to the Annual Report of Ease of Doing Business Ranking released by the World Bank,[1] India is ranked 163 in enforcing contract and 100 in '*ease of doing business*'. In order to improve the position in contract enforcement and ease of doing business in India, numerous changes have been brought out by the Parliament by amending the Specific Relief Act 1963 by way of the Specific Relief (Amendment) Act 2018. Sections 6, 10, 11, 14, 15, 16, 19, 20, 21, 25 and 41 have been amended and ss. 20A, 20B

1 http://www.doingbusiness.org/data/exploreeconomies/india.

and s. 20C have been newly inserted to provide a time-bound and speedy disposal of disputed initiated under the Act. For that purpose, s. 20C provides for disposal of the cases under the Act within a maximum period of 18 months notwithstanding the provisions in the Civil Procedure Code. Section 20B has contemplated for the Special Courts to try the suit relating to contracts of infrastructure projects.

Section 11 of the Act has now removed the discretion of court by replacing "*may, in the discretion of the court, be enforced*" with "*shall be enforced by the court*," thereby making specific performance a statutory remedy, subject to the provisions contained in the Act. Prior to its amendment, s. 14 provided for specific performance where compensation was not provided as adequate relief. But, now the provision has been deleted making specific performance a relief in generality. Section 20 of the Act has been completely changed by the Specific Relief (Amendment) Act 2018 thereby introducing a new concept of "*substituted performance of contract*" and removing the discretion of the Court in granting specific performance.

The recent amendments have been made in the Act with a view to keeping pace with the needs of a new era of economic activities where the speedy enforcement of contract and creation of an environment for doing business must be a priority and existing legal framework must be effective enough to resolve the disputes expeditiously.

To make the book practically useful, different aspects of the newly-introduced amendments in the Act have been elaborately and critically discussed. While revising the book, due care has been taken to incorporate all the recent amendments to make the book up-to-date and useful to the readers. To add to the utility of the book, recent case laws of the Supreme Court and the different High Courts up to December 2019 have been included and discussed on different areas relating to specific performance.

I am grateful to my friends, colleagues and family members for the support and encouragement I received while revising the book. I am particularly grateful to Shri Asok De, Director, Eastern Law House, who entrusted this work to me for revision. I am also thankful to the editorial team of the Eastern Law House for the painstaking efforts they have taken to complete the book.

Kolkata
10th January 2020

S.K. PATHAK

Preface to the First Edition

Portia— A pound of that same merchant's flesh is thine;
The court awards it, and the law doth give it.
—*The Merchant of Venice,* IV. I. 297-298.

Specific Performance is with us for centuries. Pollock & Maitland tell us "that the oldest actions of the common law aim for the more part, not at 'damages' but at what we call 'specific relief'. By far the greater number of the judgments that are given in favour of plaintiffs are judgments which award them seisin of land, and these judgments are executed by writs that order the sheriff to deliver seisin. But even when the source of the action is in our eyes a contractual obligation, the law tries its best to give specific relief. Thus, if a lord is bound to acquit a tenant from a claim for suit of court, the judgment may enjoin him to perform this duty and may bid the sheriff distrain him into performing it from time to time. In Glanville's day the defendant in an action on a fine could be compelled to give security that for the future he would observe his pact. The history of Covenant seems to show that the judgment for specific performance (*quod conventio teneatur*) is at least as old as an award of damages for breach of contract. We may find a local court decreeing that a rudder is to be made in accordance with an agreement, and even that one man is to serve another."[1]

But there came a time when, the older forms having been neglected, an action for damages, an action which traced descent from *breve de transgressione,* seemed to be almost the only remedy offered by the common law.

An 'action for damages' was a novelty; but in later days it came to be looked upon as the common law's panacea. At the same time, it was this inability of older courts to give specific relief that paved the way for the evolution of an 'equitable jurisdiction' in the Chancery.[2]

1 *The History of English Law,* 2nd Ed., vol. II, p. 595.
2 *Op. Cit.*, p. 523.

With reference to this equitable remedy, Lord Justice Fry wrote, "If a contract be made and one party to it makes default in performance, there appears to result to the other party a right at his election either to insist on the actual performance of the contract, or to obtain satisfaction for the non-performance of it. It may be suggested from this that it follows......... that it ought to be assumed that every contract is specifically enforceable until the contrary be shown. Be so board a proposition has never, it is believed, been asserted by the judges of the Court of Chancery or their successors in the High Court of justice, though if prophecy were the function of a law writer, it might be suggested that they will more and more approximate to such a rule."[3]

Unfortunately, this prophecy has not been wholly realised. But the Courts are now more and more inclined to grant this relief.

How to compel the other party to the contract to perform his contractual obligations, or to secure an order of specific performance against him, is the central theme of this book. Specific performance, as is well known, is an equitable remedy and no one can claim it as a matter of right. What are the principles that govern the exercise of the equitable jurisdiction? What are the types of contracts that can be specifically enforced? Who can claim specific performance?

What are the personal bars on persons claiming relief? Against whom the Order can be made? What are the defences to an action for specific performance are some of the major questions that arise while claiming this remedy as against the common law remedy of damages.

The book seeks to answer these questions on the basis of statutory provisions and the principles extracted from over 650 cases determined by Courts in India, Great Britain and the Dominions during the last 300 years.

The book is divided into five Chapters. Chapter 1 deals with eligible and non-eligible contracts, Chapter 2, with parties, Chapter 3, with defences, Chapter 4, with jurisdiction and powers of courts, and Chapter 5, contains extracts from relevant statutes.

I apologise for not following the usual pattern of sectionwise commentary. Instead, I have chosen to deal with the subject topicwise. I hope that the reader will find the treatment interesting.

Delhi High Court
31st July 1984 L.C. GOYLE

3 *Specific Performance of Contracts*, 6th Ed., p. 21.

Contents

PAGE

Part Two

Specific Performance of Contract

Table of Cases

Part One

Specific Performance

Introduction

Ubi jus, ibi remedium In the days of yore, the source of most of the rights and liabilities could be traced to the common law. Then statutory enactments were few. Even such enactments only created rights or liabilities but seldom provided forums for remedies. The result was that any person having a grievance that he had been wronged or his right was being affected, could approach the ordinary civil court on the principle of law that where there is a right there is a remedy—*ubi jus, ibi remedium.*[1] This equitable maxim means that there is no wrong without a remedy. *Jus* signifies "the legal authority to do or to demand anything" and *remedium* is defined as the right of action or the means given by law for the recovery or assertion of a right. Thus, whenever the common law gives a right or prohibits an injury, it also gives a remedy.[2] The maxim *ubi jus, ibi remedium* is considered to be so valuable that it led to the invention of the form of action called an action on the case. The common law lives and grows, but when there is no precedent, the common law will judge according to the law of nature and the public good.[3] Where there is a wrong there is a remedy. Equity will not suffer a wrong to go without a remedy. In *Ashby* v *White,*[4] where a qualified voter was not allowed to vote and who therefore sued the Returning Officer, it was held that if the law gives a man a right, he must have "a means to vindicate and maintain it and a remedy if he is injured in the exercise of and enjoyment of it. It is indeed a vain thing to imagine a right without a remedy,

1 *Shiv Kumar Chadha* v *Municipal Corpn. of Delhi* (1993)3 SCC 161.
2 Broom's *Legal Maxims,* 12th Ed., p. 134.
3 Jauk Cent 117.
4 [1703]2 Ld Raym 938; [1703]92 ER 126.

for, want of right and want of remedy are reciprocal". It was argued that the candidate for whom the plaintiff wanted to vote was elected and that there was no precedent for such an action, and if it was allowed that would lead to multiplicity of proceedings. But the contention was rejected and Lord Holt observed that if man will multiply injuries, action must be multiplied too, for every man that is injured ought to have his recompense. The ancient Roman jurisprudential maxim[5] *ubi jus, ibi remedium* is not an empty formality or a mere tautological proposition.[6]

This maxim has a human right aspect also, since access to justice is a human right and, therefore, a party having a grievance must have a remedy.[7] Thus, if a man has a right, he must have the means to vindicate and maintain it, and also a remedy, if he is injured in the exercise and enjoyment of the said right, and that it is indeed, a vain thing to imagine a right without a remedy, for the want of a right and the want of a remedy, are reciprocal.[8] However, such right can be excluded by substantial legislation expressly extinguishing the same.[9] Therefore, where the remedy is barred, the right is rendered unenforceable.[10]

In India, the jurisdiction of the civil court[11] as enacted in s. 9 of the Code of Civil Procedure exemplifies the doctrine.[12] As a matter of fact, s. 9, CPC is in enforcement of the fundamental principles of law laid down in the maxim *ubi jus, ibi remedium*. A litigant, thus having a grievance of a civil nature has a right to institute a civil suit in a competent civil court unless its cognizance is either expressly or impliedly barred by any statute.[13]

This maxim has been applied to different cases by the Supreme Court. The doctrine of necessity is a common law doctrine and is applied to tide over the situations where there are difficulties. Law does not contemplate a vacuum, and a solution has to be find out rather than allowing the problem to boil over.[14] In *Shiv Shankar Dal Mills* v *State of Haryana*[15] the Supreme Court held that social justice is a pervasive presence; and so, save in special situations it is fair to be guided by the strategy of equity by asking

5 *Anita Kushwaha* v *Pushap Sudan* (2016)8 SCC 509.
6 A. Dicey, *Law of the Constitution*, 7th Ed. 1908, pp. 199-200.
7 *Bhagubhai Dhanabhai Khalasi* v *State of Gujarat* (2007)4 SCC 241.
8 *Dhannalal* v *Kalawatibai* (2002)6 SCC 16; AIR 2002 SC 2572.
9 *Rajender Bansal* v *Bhuru* (2017)4 SCC 202.
10 *Mithilesh Kumari* v *Prem Behari Khare* (1989)2 SCC 95; AIR 1989 SC 1247.
11 *Dhruv Green Field Ltd.* v *Hukam Singh* (2002)6 SCC 416; AIR 2002 SC 2841.
12 *Swamy Atmananda* v *Sri Ramakrishna Tapovanam* (2005)10 SCC 51; AIR 2005 SC 2392.
13 *Rajasthan SRTC* v *Bal Mukund Bairwa* (2009)4 SCC 299.
14 *Lalit Kumar Modi* v *Board of Control for Cricket in India* (2011)10 SCC 106.
15 (1980)2 SCC 437; AIR 1980 SC 1037; see *Ashish Ranjan* v *Anupma Tandon* (2010)14 SCC 274; *Atma Linga Reddy* v *Union of India* (2008)7 SCC 788; *Makhan Singh Tarsikka* v *State of Punjab* AIR 1964 SC 381.

those who claim the service of judicial process to embrace the rule of distributive justice, while moulding the relief by consenting to restore little sums, taken in little transactions, from little persons to whom they belong. Thus, writ cannot be turned down on the negative plea of alternative remedy, and must be sustained on the basis of rule "*ubi jus, ibi remedium*" and equity.

He who seeks equity must do equity This equitable doctrine means that the plaintiff who seeks equity must himself be prepared to do equity. In other words, he must recognize and submit to the right of his adversary, because the principle is—*you must do unto your neighbour what you wish him to do unto you.* A court of equity would not allow the plaintiff to say, "*Give me the equitable relief that I seek, but I am not prepared to make any allowances for the claim or right of the other party. Let him enforce it by a separate suit.*" As Maitland puts it, "he who expects a benefit under a deed or will or other instrument, must adopt the whole content of that instrument and must conform to all its provisions and renounce all rights that are inconsistent with it".[16] According to Snell,[17] "to obtain equitable relief the plaintiff must be prepared to do 'equity', in its popular sense of what is right and fair to the defendant. This is a rule of 'unquestionable justice' which, however, "decides nothing in itself; for you must first inquire what are the equities which the Defendant must do and what the Plaintiff ought to have". Thus, a court of equity acts upon the rule that he who seeks equity must do equity. By this it does not mean that the court can impose arbitrary conditions upon a plaintiff simply because he stands in that position on the record. The rule means that a man who comes to seek the aid of a court of equity to enforce a claim must be prepared to submit in such proceedings to any directions which the principles of a court of equity may make it proper to give. He must do justice to the matters in respect of which the assistance of equity is asked. In a court of law it is otherwise; when the plaintiff is found to be entitled to judgment, the law must take its own course and no terms can be imposed. The rule of this maxim was probably the foundation of the doctrines of the consideration and tacking of mortgages.[18]

In India, law is replete with the instances of statutory provisions, albeit scattered in different enactments, founded on the principle contained in the maxim "*one who seeks equity must do equity*". For example, ss. 19A, 64 and 65 of the Indian Contract Act 1872 are based upon the principle contained in the maxim. Moreover, ss. 30 and 33 of the Specific Relief Act

16 F.W. Maitland, *Equity: A Course of Lectures*, 2nd Ed. 1936, p. 287 (Cambridge University Press); *V.S. Palanichamy Chettiar Firm* v *C. Alagappan* (1999)4 SCC 702; AIR 1999 SC 918.

17 *Principles of Equity*, 26th Ed., p. 34.

18 Halsbury's *Laws of England*, 4th Ed., vol. 16, paras 1303, 1304.

1963 are also founded on the principle "one *who seeks equity must do equity*". Even, ss. 35 and 51 of the Transfer of Property Act 1882 are enacted on the similar line. The same principle may also be noticed in ss. 62 and 86 of the Indian Trusts Act 1882.

He who comes to equity must come with clean hands It is aptly said that "he that hath committed an inequity, shall not have equity." It is well known that *ex turpi causa non oritur actio,* i.e. no cause of action arises from a wrongful consideration.

Clean hands are thus a principal condition to invoke the aid of equity. A party who does not come to court with clean hands cannot seek such an indulgence.[19] In application of the principle underlying the maxim a person will not be allowed to assert his title to property which he has dealt with so as to defeat his creditors or evade tax, for he may not maintain an action by setting up his own fraudulent design. The maxim does not mean that equity strikes at depravity in a general way. The cleanliness required is to be judged in relation to the relief sought and the conduct complained of must have an immediate and necessary relation to the equity sued for. It must be depravity in a legal as well as in a moral sense.[20]

In Spry on *Equitable Remedies,*[1] referring to *Moody* v *Cox*[2] and *Meyers* v *Casey* [3] it is stated,"... that the absence of clean hands is of no account 'unless the depravity, the dirt in question on the hand, has an immediate and necessary relation to the equity sued for'. When such exceptions or qualifications are examined it becomes clear that the maxim that predicates a requirement of clean hands cannot properly be regarded as setting out a rule that is either precise or capable of satisfactory operation."

Thus, for instance, a person who entered into the service by producing a false caste certificate and obtained appointment for the post meant for a Scheduled Caste, thus depriving a genuine Scheduled Caste candidate of appointment to that post, does not deserve any sympathy or indulgence of the court since a person who seeks equity must come with clean hands. He, who comes to the court with false claims, cannot plead equity nor would the court be justified to exercise equity jurisdiction in his favour. Equity jurisdiction cannot be exercised in the case of a person who got the appointment on the basis of a false caste certificate by playing a fraud.[4] The legal maxim *jure naturae aequum est, neminem cum alterius detrimento, et injuria fieri*

19 *J.H. Patel* v *Subhan Khan* AIR 1996 SC 3439; (1996)5 SCC 312.
20 Halsbury's *Laws of England,* 4th Ed., vol. 16, p. 1305.
1 4th Ed., p. 5.
2 [1917]2 Ch 71; [1916-17] All ER Rep 548 (CA).
3 [1913]17 CLR 90; [1913] HCA 50.
4 *Ram Saran* v *IG of Police, CRPF* (2006)2 SCC 541; *R. Vishwanatha Pillai* v *State of Kerala* (2004)2 SCC 105; *Bank of India* v *Avinash D. Mandivikar* (2005)7 SCC 690.

locupletiorem, means that it is a law of nature it is just that, no one should be enriched to the detriment and injury of another.[5] Similarly, persons invoking the equitable extraordinary jurisdiction under Art. 226 of the Constitution should come with clean hands and should not conceal material facts.[6]

The principle underlying the maxim has been recognised in different statutory provisions. Sections 25 and 28 of the Specific Relief Act 1963 and s. 23 of the Indian Trusts Act 1882 embody the said principle.

Equity treats as done what ought to be done As between two persons where one of them had incurred an obligation and undertaken upon himself to do something for the other, courts of equity looks on it as done and as producing the same result as if the obligation or undertaking had been actually performed.[7] Equity treats a contract to do a thing as if the thing was already done, though only in favour of persons entitled to enforce the contract specifically and not in favour of volunteers.[8] This equity creates a personal obligation which compels the transferor to perform his contract when he is able to do so on the acquisition of the subsequent interest. The principle underlying it was very fully stated in *Holroyd* v *Marshall*[9] where Lord Westbury, LJ, observed:

> "It is quite true that a deed which professes to convey property which is not in existence at the time is as a conveyance void at law simply because there is nothing to convey. So in equity a contract which engages to transfer property which is not in existence cannot operate as an immediate alienation because there is nothing to transfer. But if a vendor or mortgagor agrees to sell or mortgage property, real or personal, of which he is not possessed at the time and he receives the consideration for the contract and afterwards becomes possessed of property answering the description in the contract, there is no doubt that a court of equity would compel him to perform the contract and that the contract would in equity transfer the beneficial interest to the mortgagee or purchaser immediately on the property being acquired. This of course assumes that the supposed contract is one of that class of which a court of equity would decree the specific performance. If it be so, then immediately on the acquisition of the property described the vendor mortgagor would hold it in trust for the purchaser or mortgagee, according to the terms of the contract."

In the application of this equity, it is immaterial that the promisee or transferee knew the truth namely that the promissor or the transferor had

5 Black's *Law Dictionary*, 10th Ed.
6 *Ramjas Foundation* v *Union of India* AIR 1993 SC 852; 1993 Supp (2) SCC 20.
7 Story, *Commentaries on Equity Jurisprudence*, 3rd Ed., pp. 37, 38.
8 Snell's *Principles of Equity*, 26th Ed., p. 435.
9 [1861]10 HLC 191; [1861]11 ER 999.

no authority to transfer the interest which he purported to transfer.[10] Thus, in *Gaya Din* v *Kashi*,[11] the plaintiff was suing for pre-emption, and in order to raise money for the litigation, in anticipation of a decree, mortgaged the property in suit. After he obtained a decree and got possession, equity treating that as done which ought to be done, gave the mortgagee a charge on the property and placed him in the position of a mortgagee. Similarly, in *Deb Nath Moral* v *Sashi Bhusan Moral*,[12] a landlord made a settlement of a non-transferable holding (now, a plot of land). The settlement was invalid at the time it was made because the *raiyat* had not abandoned the holding (now, a plot of land). But the subsequent abandonment of the holding (now, a plot of land) by the *raiyat* validated the settlement.

When possession is held under an agreement for a lease, of which specific performance would be ordered, the parties are treated in equity as being in the same position with regard to their respective rights as if a lease has been granted.[13] Similarly, money which would have been payable under a contract if the defendant had not wrongfully prevented anything from becoming due will be treated as a debt in equity, although it is not a debt in law.[14]

Delay defeats equity [*Vigilantibus non dormientibus, jurasubvenient* = equity aids the vigilant and not the indolent].

Delay which is sufficient to prevent a party from obtaining an equitable remedy is technically called "laches".[15] It is now a well-recognized principle of jurisprudence that a right not exercised for a long time is non-existent. Even when there is no limitation period prescribed by any statute relating to certain proceedings, in such cases courts have coined the doctrine of laches and delays as well as doctrine of acquiescence and non-suited the litigants who approached the court belatedly without any justifiable explanation for bringing the action after unreasonable delay. Doctrine of laches is in fact an application of maxim of equity "delay defeats equities".[16] The leading case on this subject is *Allcard* v *Skinner*.[17] Ms. Allcard wanted to devote her life for the good and charitable works and became a member of the Society of Sisters for the Poor. Within a few days of becoming a member, Ms. Allcard made a will bequeathing all her properties to Ms. Skinner, Lady Superior of the Sisterhood and in the succeeding years made several gifts to the value of

10 *Seth Parma Nand* v *Champa Lal* 1956 All LJ 1; AIR 1956 All 225.
11 ILR (1907)29 All 163.
12 37 CWN 1144; AIR 1934 Cal 82.
13 *Gray* v *Spyer* [1922]2 Ch 22 (CA).
14 *London, Chatham and Dover Rly. Co.* v *South Eastern Rly. Co.* [1892]1 Ch 120 (CA); [1893] AC 429.
15 Snell's *Principles of Equity*, 33rd Ed., para 5-011.
16 *Prabhakar* v *Sericulture Deptt.* (2015)15 SCC 1; AIR 2016 SC 2984.
17 [1887]36 Ch D 145 (CA).

£7000 to Ms. Skinner. Ms. Allcard left the Sisterhood about 8 years later and immediately revoked her will, but waited for a further period of 6 years before commencing the action to recover what was left of the money given by her to Ms. Skinner. The trial court dismissed her action. The Court of Appeal consisting of Cotton, Lyndley and Bowan, LJJ were of the opinion that at the time of the gifts the relationship between the donor and the donee was such that in the absence of independent competent advice from others the gifts could not stand. According to the learned Judges, Ms. Allcard was not a free agent at the time of making the gifts and she was therefore entitled to set aside the transfers when she left the Sisterhood in 1879. On the question whether the plaintiff was entitled to recover possession of the gifts, there was a difference of opinion. Justice Lyndley and Justice Bowan were of the opinion that Ms. Allcard's inaction for six years after she left the Sisterhood indicated her intention to confirm the gift. Laches and acquiescence thus disentitled her from claiming back the property. Cotton, LJ held otherwise in his dissenting judgment. This maxim that "*delay defeats equity*" has been well recognized and followed in a number of cases in India.[18] Under the maxim *caveat emptor* courts of justice require that each party to a contract shall exercise a due degree of vigilance and caution. On the subject of limitation of actions the general policy of law is to use legal diligence and it shall never turn to the disadvantage of the creditor. In ancient possessory actions there was a time of limitation settled beyond which no man should avail himself of the possession of himself or his ancestors, or take advantage of wrongful possession of his adversary; for if he were negligent for a long and unreasonable time, the law refused afterwards to lend him any assistance to recover the possession.[19]

Thus, equity favours a vigilant rather than an indolent litigant. The discretionary relief can be had provided one has not by his act or conduct given a go-by to his rights.[20] Delay defeats discretion and loss of limitation destroys the remedy itself. Delay amounting to laches results in benefit of discretionary power being denied on principles of equity. Loss of limitation resulting into depriving of the remedy, is a principle based on public policy and utility and not equity alone.[1]

It is now well settled principle of law that "delay defeats equity" has its fullest application in the matter of grant of relief under Art. 226 of the

18 *Sahdeo Jha* v *Union of India* (1992)3 SCC 190; JT 1992(1) SC 568; *Union of India* v *Kishorilal Bablani* (1999)1 SCC 729; AIR 1999 SC 517; JT 1998(8) SC 428; *Delhi Development Authority* v *Ravindra Mohan Agarwal* (1999)3 SCC 172; AIR 1999 SC 1256; JT 1999(2) SC 368.

19 Broom's *Legal Maxims*, 12th Ed., p. 555.

20 *Municipal Council, Ahmednagar* v *Shah Hyder Beig* (2000)2 SCC 48.

1 *Board of Secondary Education of Assam* v *Mohd. Sarifuz Zaman* (2003)12 SCC 408.

Constitution. It is correct that no period of limitation is provided to invoke writ jurisdiction under Art. 226 of the Constitution but the same does not mean that the machinery of writ jurisdiction can be set in motion at any time at the whims and fancies of a party. It is also settled that there may be cases where even the delay of shorter period would be considered sufficient to decline relief under Art. 226 of the Constitution while in certain cases the court may be persuaded to condone the long delay if sufficient reasons are disclosed by such party.[2]

The law of Specific Relief is, thus, founded on the principles of equity enunciated by the courts of equity in England. The principles and rules of equity were worked out in the Court of Chancery during centuries, in accordance with the demands of "conscience".[3] One of the leading general principles of equity jurisdiction was to give relief where there was no remedy or where no adequate remedy was granted by the common law.[4] The earliest instance of specific performance in India may be traced to s. 192 of the Code of Civil Procedure 1859.[5] However, the Specific Relief Act 1877 was passed in British India to define and amend the law relating to certain kinds of specific relief. It was drafted on the lines of the Draft New York Civil Code 1862 and its main provisions embodied the doctrines evolved by the Courts of Equity in England, which had previous to the Act been applied in India as principles of equity, justice and good conscience.[6] The Act was repealed and replaced by the Specific Relief Act 1963 after the independence on the recommendation of the Law Commission of India.

Though the Parliament passed the Specific Relief Act 1963 replacing the old Act of 1877, yet it has been held by the Supreme Court that the Act is not exhaustive enough to cover the entire gamut of law relating to specific performance in India. It does not consolidate the whole law on the subject. As the preamble would indicate, it is an Act "to define and amend the law relating to certain kinds of specific relief". It does not purport to lay down the law relating to specific relief in all its ramifications. Although

2 *Delhi Transport Corporation* v *Maya* (2007)137 DLT 96.

3 Potter, Harold, *An Historical Introduction to English Law and its Institutions*, 3rd Ed. 1948, p. 550. See Sir James O'Connor, *Thoughts about the Common Law*, 3 Camb LJ (1928) 161, 164.

4 Walsh, William F, *A Treatise on Equity*, 1930, p. 24.

5 Section 192. 'When the suit is for damages for breach of contract, if it appears that the defendant is able to perform the contract, the Court with the consent of the plaintiff may decree the specific performance of the contract within a time to be fixed by the Court and in such case shall award an amount of damages to be paid as an alternative if the contract is not performed.' See G.C. Rankin, *Background to Indian Law*, 1946, p. 77.

6 Law Commission of India, 9th Report, 1958, p. 1.

a matter on which the Act defines the law it might generally be exhaustive, the Act as a whole cannot be considered as exhaustive of the whole branch of the law of specific performance.[7] At the same time, it is not restricted to specific performance of contracts as the statute governs powers of the court in granting specific reliefs in a variety of fields.[8]

Though the Specific Relief Act is based on English law,[9] there is difference between English and Indian laws so far as the specific performance is concerned. In England the relief of specific performance pertains to the domain of equity; in India, to that of statutory law. In England there is no period of limitation for instituting a suit for the said relief and, therefore, mere delay—the time lag depending upon circumstances—may itself be sufficient to refuse the relief; but, in India mere delay cannot be a ground for refusing the said relief, for the statute prescribes the period of limitation. If the suit is in time, delay is sanctioned by law; if it is beyond time, the suit will be dismissed as barred by time; in either case, no question of equity arises.[10] Be that as it may, the provisions may be interpreted in the light of the principles recognized by the English Courts unless the provisions in the Act expressly diverge from that law, in which case the provisions of this Act shall prevail.[11]

Specific relief is relief in specie. It is a remedy which aims at the exact fulfilment of an obligation. It directs the party in default to do or forbear from doing the very thing, which he is bound to do or forbear from doing.[12] It is the actual execution of the contract according to its stipulations and terms, and the courts direct the party in default to do the very thing which he contracted to do.[13] Specific performance compels a person to perform his contract or statutory obligation. The word "specific" requires careful scrutiny. The word "specifically described" came on the anvil of two English cases. Having quoted the case[14] Lopes, LJ observed "specifically described" means described with such particularity as is used in an ordinary business

7 *Hungerford Investment Trust Ltd.* v *Haridas Mundhra* (1972)3 SCC 684; AIR 1972 SC 1826; (1972)3 SCR 690; *Kishore Chand Shiva Charan Lal* v *Bhoodhan Electric Supply Company* AIR 1944 All 66; *Ramdas Khatau & Co.* v *Atlas Mills Co.* AIR 1931 Bom 151; *A. Pramila* v *G.V. Rathaiah* (1998)3 AP LJ 130; (1998)4 ICC 91; (1998)5 ALT 719; (1999)1 CCC 377.

8 *Ashok Kumar Srivastav* v *National Insurance Co. Ltd.* (1998)4 SCC 361.

9 *Rahmath Unnissa Begum* v *Shimoga Cooperative Bank Ltd.* AIR 1951 Mys 59.

10 *Mademsetty Satyanarayana* v *G. Yelloji Rao* (1965)2 SCR 221; AIR 1965 SC 1405.

11 *Akshaya Lingam Pillai* v *Avayambala Ammal* AIR 1933 Mad 386; *Rahmathunnissa Begam* v *Shimoga Co-op. Bank Ltd.* AIR 1951 Mys 59; *R.D. Areshwar Hmana* v *Flora Sasoon* AIR 1928 PC 208.

12 *Adhunik Steels Ltd.* v *Orissa Manganese and Minerals (P) Ltd.* (2007)7 SCC 125; AIR 2007 SC 2563.

13 *Mayawanti* v *Kaushalya Devi* (1990)3 SCC 1.

14 *Carpenter* v *Deen* [1989]23 QBD 566 (CA).

inventory of such chattels. Fry, LJ said in that case "In considering the meaning of the words 'specifically described' we should look at the scope and object of the section. They are in my opinion plain. I think they are to facilitate the identification of the articles enumerated in the schedule with those found in the possession of the grantor that is to say, to render the identification as easy as possible, and to render any dispute as to the intention of the parties as rare as possible, and to shut the door to fraud and controversy, which almost always arise when general descriptions are used. That is to be done as far as possible; by which I mean, as far as reasonably possible so far as a careful man of business trying to carry the object of the Act into execution could and would do without going into unreasonable particulars."[15] As laid down by the Supreme Court the word 'specific' is specific enough to avoid being vague and general. What is precise, exact, definite and explicit is specific. Sometimes what is specific may also be special, yet they are distinct in semantics.[16]

However, the jurisdiction of the court in specific performance is discretionary, and the discretion must of course be not arbitrary or capricious but judicial. In this connection, Fry[17] observes:

> "There is an observation often made with regard to the jurisdiction in specific performance which remains to be noticed. It is said to be in the discretion of the court. The meaning of this proposition is not that the court may arbitrarily or capriciously perform one contract and refuse to perform another, but that the court has regard to the conduct of the plaintiff and to circumstances outside the contract itself, and that the mere fact of the existence of a valid contract is not conclusive in the plaintiff's favour. 'If the defendant', said Plumer V.C., 'can show any circumstances *de hors,* independent of the writing, making it inequitable to interpose for the purpose of a specific performance, a Court of Equity, having satisfactory information upon that subject, will not interpose'."

It also needs to be mentioned that in view of statutory provisions contained in the Specific Relief Act 1963, the discretion is governed by statutory provisions.[18] Moreover, the Specific Relief Act is an adjective law. It is, in its essence, a part of law of procedure.[19] The substantive law must be looked for elsewhere.[20]

15 *Davidson* v *Carlton Bank Ltd.* [1983]1 QB 82 (CA).
16 *Maru Ram* v *Union of India* 1980 CrLJ 1440 (1455); AIR 1980 SC 2147; 1981 Cr LR (SC) 1; (1981)1 SCR 1196.
17 Fry, *A Treatise on the Specific Performance of Contracts*, 6th Ed., p. 19.
18 *Gunwantbhai Mulchand Shah* v *Anton Elis Farel* (2006)3 SCC 634.
19 *Jaya Sen* v *Sujit Kr. Sarkar* AIR 1998 Cal 288; *Radheshyam Kamila* v *Kiran Bala Dasi* AIR 1971 Cal 341.
20 *Moulvi Ali Hossain Mian* v *Rajkumar Halder* AIR 1943 Cal 417 (426).

Specific performance—meaning of Specific performance is an equitable relief, given by the court to enforce against a defendant the duty of doing what he agreed by a contract to do. In traditional sense, the term "specific performance" means the remedy available in equity to compel a person actually to perform a contracted obligation. In modern sense, specific performance is an equitable relief granted by the court in certain cases of contract in the form of judgments. Section 10 of the Specific Relief Act 1963 states the cases in which specific performance of contract is enforceable in a court of law. But s. 10 has been amended in 2018 after its amendment s. 10 provides that the specific performance of a contract shall be enforced by the court subject to the provisions of ss. 11(2), 14 and 16 of the Act. Besides, ss. 11, 12 and 13 of the said Act deal with the powers of court to pass decree of specific performance. Specific performance is an equitable relief and he who seeks equity can be put on terms to ensure that equity is done to the opposite party even while granting the relief. The final end of law is justice, and so the means to it too should be informed by equity. That is why he who seeks shall do equity.[1] In broader sense specific performance includes also compulsive performance of specific statutory duty, e.g. restoration of possession to person dispossessed of immovable property otherwise than in due course of law by a suit within six months from dispossession (*vide* s. 6, Specific Relief Act), restitution *vide* s. 144, CPC, specific performance is, now available by statutes.

When a contract is not duly performed on one side, the normal rule is an action at law to recover damages for breach of contract, but if this were the only remedy, it would always be at the option of the defaulting party either to perform his contract or to pay damages. In many cases damages are adequate remedy and the exercise of this option does no injury to the other party, but in cases where the remedy of damages was not adequate, equity in very early times assumed jurisdiction to deprive the defaulting party of this option and to compel him to carry his contract into effect. The remedy of specific performance is peculiar to equity, but it is exercised in respect of contracts which form a subject that is equally within the cognizance of courts of "Common Law" and the foundation of the equitable jurisdiction is that the remedy at law is inadequate.[2] Latter-day common law, however, so far as specific performance of contract is concerned, spurned the idea. Its edict is compensation, not compulsion, when the damages were adequate, *caditquestio*. But there were cases where either there was no standard for assessing the damage or the damages were inadequate. It was here that equity stepped in and in its bid to do 'complete and more perfect justice' evolved the

1 *K. Kalpana Saraswathi* v *P.S.S. Somasundram Chettiar* (1980) 1 SCC 630; AIR 1980 SC 512; *H.V. Vebavyasachar* v *Shivashankar* AIR 2010 SC (Supp) 394.

2 Halsbury's *Laws of England*, 4th Ed., vol. 16, p. 1216.

remedy of specific performance. Specific performance is equitable relief, given by the court to enforce against a defendant, the duty of doing what he agreed by contract to do; a plaintiff may, therefore, obtain judgment for specific performance although there has not, in the strict sense, been any default by the defendant before the issue of the writ.[3]

Pre-requisites for a suit of specific performance English and American lawyers are so familiar with the jurisdiction of equity in enforcing the specific performance of contracts, that it probably occurs to very few of them that there is anything extraordinary in this remedy of the Courts of Chancery. The doctrine of specific performance is, however, one of the paradoxes of legal history. Only in the United States and the British Empire, the two countries in which popular government has attained its highest development, is it permitted so far to invade the liberty of the individual as to compel him specifically to perform his contracts upon pain of imprisonment. '*Nemo potest praecise cogi ad factum*' was a rule of the Roman law.[4] In common law jurisdictions, the expression 'specific performance' has a well understood meaning. A good description was given by Maitland in his lectures on Equity:[5]

> In granting a decree for specific performance — or a judgment for specific performance — the Court in effect says to the defendant, You must perform specifically the contract into which you entered — that is to say you must do the very thing that you promised to do on pain of going to prison.

Existence of contract Before a court passes a decree of specific performance there must be a valid binding and concluded contract between the parties to the suit. The existence of a valid contract is the basis for consideration of legal proceedings in a suit for specific performance. The court cannot make a contract for the parties and then proceed to pass decree for specific performance of a contract it has itself made. It cannot require the performance of any contract other than the one which the parties themselves have made.[6]

In early times a Court of Equity assumed jurisdiction to compel a party to a contract for breach of which damages recoverable at law were not an adequate remedy, to perform his part of the contract. The remedy of specific performance is this in contrast with the remedy by way of damages for breach of contract, which gives pecuniary compensation for failure to carry

3 Chitty on *Contracts*, 32nd Ed., vol. 1, para 27-004.
4 James Barr Ames, *Lectures on Legal History and Miscellaneous Legal Essays,* 1913, Ch XXII, p. 248 (Cambridge Harvard University Press).
5 F.W. Maitland, *Equity: A Course of Lectures*, 2nd Ed. 1936, p. 30 (Cambridge University Press).
6 *Corpus Juris Secundum*, vol. 81, § 35.

out the terms of the contract. The remedy is special and extraordinary in its character, and the court has discretion to grant it, or to leave the parties to their rights at law. The discretion is, however, not an arbitrary or capricious discretion; it is discretion to be exercised on fixed principles in accordance with the previous authorities. The judge must exercise his discretion in a judicial manner. If the contract is valid in form and has been made between competent parties and is unobjectionable in its nature and circumstances, specific performance is in effect granted as a matter of course, even though the judge may think it involves hardship. The mere existence however, of a valid contract is not in itself enough to bring about the interference of the court; the conduct of the plaintiff, such as delay, acquiescence, breach on his part, or some other circumstance outside the contract, may render it inequitable to enforce it, or the contract itself may, for example, on the ground of misdescription, be such that the court will refuse to enforce it.[7] Specific performance of contract thus being an equitable remedy, no one can claim it as a matter of right and the grant of relief is in the sole discretion of the court, though the discretion has to be exercised on well-settled principles. The remedy is available to both the parties and either party may file a suit even before the due date of completion. A party also need not wait till the other breaks its promise, for the breach of the contract is not an essential part of the cause of action in equity.[8] Further since it is a remedy *in personam,* the subject matter of the contract also need not be within the jurisdiction of the court.[9]

However, under Indian law, no decree for specific performance may be passed by the court in the absence of any subsisting agreement between the parties.[10] The contract between the parties is the foundation of obligation and the specific performance is the enforcement of that obligation. The contract at the same time should be valid and enforceable. Therefore, specific performance cannot be ordered if the contract itself suffers from some defect which makes the contract invalid or unenforceable.[11] However, the discretion of the court will be there even though the contract is otherwise valid and enforceable and it can pass a decree of specific performance even before there has been any breach of the contract. After all, the contract, being the foundation of the obligation, must be found to be valid and enforceable.[12] Thus, a plaintiff cannot maintain a suit for specific performance after the contract is determined.[13]

7 *Words and Phrases Legally Defined*, 2nd Ed., vol. 5, p. 100.
8 *Hasham* v *Zenab* [1960] AC 316; *Marks* v *Lilley* [1959]2 All ER 647.
9 *Richard West and Partners (Inverness) Ltd.* v *Dick* [1969]1 All ER 943.
10 *Municipal Council, Udaipur* v *Mahendra Kumar* (2008)12 SCC 771.
11 *Mayawanti* v *Kaushalya Devi* (1990)3 SCC 1.
12 *Mayawanti* v *Kaushalya Devi* (supra).
13 *Percept D'Mark (India) (P) Ltd.* v *Zaheer Khan* (2006)4 SCC 227.

Good faith, diligence and equitable conduct An aggrieved person who comes to court for relief or specific performance must show that he has acted in good faith with due diligence and with clean hands. There are cases in which courts of equity will insist on the maxim that he who seeks equity must do equity with more rigor than in suits for the specific performance of contracts. The facts and circumstances of each case must control the court in determination of the question of complainant's good faith.[14] Specific performance should not be granted to plaintiff unless his course of conduct relating to the transaction has been one that merits the approval of a court of equity and unless he has complied with all statutory requirements. Specific performance will be denied where the plaintiff is guilty of fraud, false representations or failure to disclose information. However, specific performance does not in any way supplant the ordinary remedy of damages and it is open to a plaintiff to claim either specific performance with or without damages or damages alone. In an appropriate case, even if the plaintiff fails in getting an order of specific performance, the court may award him compensation in lieu of specific performance (See *post*). If the contract cannot be specifically enforced, it is also open to the plaintiff to pray in the alternative for the cancellation of the contract by rescission or delivered up to be cancelled of the contract;[15] and where the court gives such a direction, it may order the plaintiff to restore the benefit that he may have received from the other party or to pay him compensation.[16]

In certain cases, it may be possible to get the same relief indirectly, for instance, through an injunction restraining the defendant from committing breach of a negative obligation or from interfering with the rights of the plaintiff or mandating the defendant to perform an act with a view to preventing the breach of those rights. To put it differently, injunction is a form of specific relief. It is an order of a court requiring a party either to do a specific act or acts or to refrain from doing a specific act or acts either for a limited period or without limit of time. The two principal varieties of specific relief are decree of specific performance and the injunction.[17] [See, for example, *Sky Petroleum Ltd.* v *VIP Petroleum Ltd.*[18] (injunction restraining the defendant from withholding the supplies of fuel oils, when the plaintiff could not have his supplies from elsewhere); *Greenwell* v *Porter*[19] (injunction restraining shareholders from voting contrary to their undertaking); *Hill* v *C.A. Parsons & Co. Ltd.*[20] (injunction restraining the company from terminating the

14 *Corpus Juris Secundum,* vol. 81, § 947–948.
15 Section 29 of the Specific Relief Act 1963.
16 Section 30, *ibid.*
17 *Adhunik Steels Ltd.* v *Orissa Manganese and Minerals (P) Ltd.* (2007)7 SCC 125; AIR 2007 SC 2563.
18 [1974]1 All ER 954.
19 [1902]1 Ch 530.
20 [1971]3 All ER 1345.

services of its engineer); *Puddephatt* v *Leith*[1] (injunction directing a shareholder to exercise his voting rights in accordance with his contractual undertaking)]. In fact in certain cases, the relief through injunction is more effective, in that injunction can be sought even at the interlocutory stage; [see *Astro Exito Navegacion SA* v *Southland Enterprise Co. Ltd.*[2] (mandatory injunction to compel execution of contractual obligations)]. Thus, remedy through injunction is so efficacious that even after the death of the judgment-debtor, the decree of injunction may be enforced against the legal representative of the deceased judgment-debtor.[3]

In *Zarina Siddiqui* v *A. Ramalingam*,[4] the Supreme Court observed that remedy for specific performance is an equitable remedy. The equitable discretion to grant or not to grant a relief for specific performance also depends upon the conduct of the parties. Grant of a decree for specific performance of contract is a discretionary relief and it has to be exercised judiciously and not arbitrarily. The courts ordinarily would not grant any relief in favour of the person who approaches the court with a pair of dirty hands.[5]

General considerations for remedy of specific performance The rule that the remedy of specific performance is not generally available to enforce contracts relating to personal property is subject to many exceptions. These are partly founded on the principle of inadequacy of the remedy at the common law in particular case and partly on the special and peculiar nature and value of the subject matter of the contract. Specific enforcement of contractual obligations was available only in equity. For the plaintiff this was a more advantageous remedy than the Common Law remedy of damages. Fry, LJ wrote on *A Treatise on the Specific Performance of Contracts*[6] with regard to equitable remedy as follows:

> "If a contract be made and one party to it makes default in performance, there appears to result to the other party a right at his election either to insist on the actual performance of the contract, or to obtain satisfaction for the non-performance of it. It may be suggested from this that it follows ..... that it ought to be assumed that every contract is specifically enforceable until the contrary be shown. But so broad a proposition has never, it is believed, been asserted by the judges of the Court of Chancery or their

1 [1916]1 Ch 200.
2 [1982]3 All ER 335 (CA).
3 Section 50 of the Code of Civil Procedure 1908; *Prabhakara Adiga* v *Gowri* (2017)4 SCC 97.
4 (2015)1 SCC 705.
5 *Mohammadia Co-op. Building Society Ltd.* v *Lakshmi Srinivasa Co-op. Building Society Ltd.* (2008)7 SCC 310.
6 6th Ed., p. 21.

successors in the High Court of Justice, though if prophecy were the function of a law writer, it might be suggested that they will more and more approximate to such a rule."

This prophecy has not been wholly fulfilled, because the scope of the remedy remains subject to many limitations.[7] The basic limitations are the following: (1) The "heavy-handed nature of enforcement mechanism". (2) Specific performance of certain contracts, such as sale of goods or share having market to mitigate loss by making substitute contract. Certain limitations on the scope of specific enforcement are justifiable, but others are more open to controversy. The House of Lords[8] has thrown some light on the restrictive view of the scope of the remedy of specific performance.

In India, the relevant provisions relating to specific performance of a contract are contained mainly in ss. 9 to 25 and 28 of the Specific Relief Act 1963. Sections 10 to 14 deal with eligible and non-eligible contracts. Sections 15 to 19 enumerate the person for and against whom contracts may be specifically enforced. Section 9 provides for defences in suits for relief based on contracts. Sections 20 to 24 specify the jurisdiction and the powers of the court regarding grant of relief. Section 25 extends the scope of the relief to certain awards and directions contained in a Will. Section 28 provides for post-decree reliefs.

As to specific performance by statute, s. 6, Specific Relief Act mandates that a person dispossessing the plaintiff on immovable property without the consent of the plaintiff without recourse to law should be compelled to restore possession to plaintiff if the suit is instituted within six months from the date of dispossession. The object of this provision is to restore the "*status quo ante*". As held by the Supreme Court in *Nagar Palika* v *Jagat Singh*,[9] provision of s. 6 is a reproduction of provision of the Roman Law, under which by an "*inter dictum de vi*" a person wrongfully dispossessed from property should recover by proving previous possession without being required to prove his title.

Again s. 144 of CPC is an instance of specific performance of a statutory obligation. A person who has obtained a benefit under an order of court or judicial verdict which is subsequently found to be wrong cannot be allowed to retain the benefit. And he must restore the benefit to the aggrieved person. It is based upon the principle of *unjust enrichment*.[10] The principle is embodied in the dictum "*restitutio in integrum*". The principle provides

7 Chitty on *Contracts*, 2nd Ed., vol. II, p. 1962.

8 *Co-operative Insurance Society Ltd.* v *Argyll Stores (Holdings) Ltd.* [1998]1 AC 1; [1997]2 WLR 898.

9 AIR 1995 SC 1377; (1995)3 SCC 426; JT 1995(3) SC 281.

10 *Allahabad Bank* v *Bengal Paper Mills Co. Ltd.* (2004)8 SCC 236.

that a person entitled to damages should, as nearly as possible, get that sum of money which would put him in the same position as he would have been if he had not sustained the wrong.[11]

A statutory obligation [here Governmental duty under s. 10, Contract Labour (Regulation and Abolition) Act 1970] can be secured by a writ of *mandamus* under Art. 226 of the Constitution.[12]

A contract of employment can also be specifically enforced, subject to certain exceptions. Unless governed by a statute or statutory rules the provisions of the Indian Contract Act would be only applicable at the formulation of the contract as also the determination thereof. Subject to certain just exceptions even specific performance of contract by way of a direction for reinstatement of a dismissed employee is also permissible in law.[13] Thus, when the court grants the relief of reinstatement or back wages, the courts, in fact, grants specific performance of contracts of service.[14] However, a contract for personal service will not be enforced by an order for specific performance nor will it be open for a servant to refuse to accept the repudiation of a contract of service by his master and say that the contract has never been terminated. The remedy of the employee is a claim for damages for wrongful dismissal or for breach of contract. But, when a statutory status is given to an employee and there has been a violation of the provisions of the statute while terminating the services of such an employee, the latter will be eligible to get the relief of a declaration that the order is null and void and that he continues to be in service, as it will not then be a mere case of a master terminating the services of a servant.[15]

Pre-emption is provided in some statutes and in Muslim personal law similarly pre-emption compels the defendant to deliver possession to the pre-emptor decree-holder.

Mandatory injunction too is a form of specific performance. Specific performance presupposes an executory, as distinct from an executed agreement, something remaining to be done, such as the execution of a deed or conveyance, in order to put the parties in the position relative to each other in which by the preliminary agreement they were intended to be placed.[16]

11 *Livingstone* v *Rawyards Coal Co.* [1880]5 AC 25 (HL); reiterated in *Malay Kumar Ganguly* v *Dr. Sukumar Mukherjee* (2009)9 SCC 221.

12 *A.K. Chowdhury* v *State of W.B.* 91 CWN 212.

13 *Bank of India* v *O.P. Swarnakar* (2003)2 SCC 721; 2003 SCC (L&S) 200.

14 *Integrated Rural Development Agency* v *Ram Pyare Pandey* 1995 Supp (2) SCC 495; 1995 SCC (L&S) 881.

15 *Executive Committee, U.P. State Warehousing Corpn.* v *Chandra Kiran Tyagi* (1969)2 SCC 838.

16 *Wolverhampton & Walsall Ry. Co.* v *London & North Western Ry. Co.* [1873] LR 16 Eq 433.

Principles underlying specific performance The principle underlying the specific performance remedy is the jurisdiction of the court of equity to grant relief where the damages as remedy at law is inadequate. This branch of equity jurisdiction was evolved in England on the presumption of uniqueness of land which led to the conclusion that damages at law could never be adequate compensation for the breach of contract to transfer an interest in land. Hence, resort to specific performance was the ultimate in such kind of transaction. Pomeroy[17] said that in applying the doctrine of specific performance the courts have established further rule that in general the legal remedy of damages is inadequate in all agreements for the sale or letting of land, or of any estate therein. Therefore, in such class of contracts the jurisdiction is always exercised, and a specific performance granted unless prevented by other and independent equitable considerations which directly affect the remedial right of the complaining party. The mutuality of remedy concept has been the prop which has supported equitable jurisdiction to grant specific performance in actions by vendors of real estate. Where the vendor asks to receive the price stipulated to be paid at the hands of a court, the remedy is mutual. The modern view is that the rules of mutuality of remedy is satisfied if the decree of specific performance operates effectively against both parties and gives to each the benefit of a mutual obligation.

Doctrine of mutuality The doctrine of mutuality is a conventional rule evolved gradually by the decisions of the English Courts of Equity.[18] The doctrine is stated as follows in Lord Justice Fry's *A Treatise on Specific Performance of Contracts*:[19]

> "A contract to be specifically enforced by the Court must, as a general rule, be mutual, that is to say, such that it might, at the time it was entered into, have been enforced by either of the parties against the other of them. Whenever, therefore, whether from personal incapacity to contract, or the nature of the contract, or any other cause, the contract is incapable of being enforced against one party, that party is equally incapable of enforcing it against the other, though its execution in the latter way might in itself be free from the difficulty attending its execution in the former."

17 *Equity Jurisprudence and Equitable Remedies: A Treatise on Equity Jurisprudence*, 5th Ed., § 221(*b*).

18 *Minor Ramalingam Reddi* v *Babanambal Ammal* AIR 1951 Mad 431; (1950)2 MLJ 597.

19 3rd Ed., p. 215; A similar statement was made by Pomeroy, *A Treatise on the Specific Performance of Contracts*, 2nd Ed., p. 229; see also, J.B. Ames, *Mutuality in Specific Performance*, Columbia Law Review, vol. 3, No. 1, January 1903, pp. 1-12.

In *Waring* v *Manchester Co.*,[20] the rule was stated as under:

> "The Court does not give relief to a plaintiff, although he be otherwise entitled to it, unless he will, on his part, do all that the defendant may be entitled to ask from him; and if that which the defendant is entitled to, be something which the Court cannot give him, it certainly has been the generally understood rule that that is a case in which the Court will not interfere."

Thus, the rule of mutuality says that a contract is specifically enforceable only if, as a general rule, there is mutuality between the parties thereto; or in other words, if it might have been enforced by either of the parties against the other at the time it came into existence.[1] The doctrine as evolved and developed by the Equity Courts in England was imported in India by the decision of the Judicial Committee in *Mir Sarwarjan* v *Fakhruddin Mohammed Chowdhuri*[2] by Lord Macnaghten. However, this *doctrine of mutuality* which found its place in English decisions rather from a desire for symmetry than from its inherent utility was discarded by the Specific Relief Act which defined and amended the law relating to Specific Relief in India.[3] The Law Commission of India did not favour the continuance of this doctrine in India. The Commission[4] suggested as under:

> "We do not consider it necessary to import the doctrine of mutuality into our codified law of specific performance. On the contrary we could do away with the doctrine in *Sarwarjan's* case (39-I.A. 1) by inserting in s. 22, a provision embodying the law as stated in American Restatement as follows:
>
> "The fact that the remedy of specific enforcement is not available to one party is not a sufficient reason for refusing it to the other party."

The recommendation of the Law Commission has been incorporated in s. 20(4) of the Specific Relief Act 1963. However, Madhya Pradesh High Court opined that the doctrine of mutuality or lack of mutuality has not been completely discarded by Indian Legislature. Referring to s. 20(4) of the Specific Relief Act 1963, the High Court[5] observed as under:

> "The use of the word "merely" in this sub-section clearly goes to show that on this ground alone a relief of specific performance cannot be refused. This clearly goes to show that if there are other circumstances which could

20 [1849]7 Hare 482 (492). The same view was expressed by Wood, V.C. in *Stocker* v *Wedderburn* [1857]69 ER 1163; [1857]3 K&J 393 (404) and by Lord Cranworth in *Blackett* v *Bates* [1865] LR I Ch Ap 117 (124).

1 *A. Venkatasami Naidu* v *Annamailai Goundar* AIR 1964 Mad 474.

2 ILR (1912)39 Cal 232 (PC); (1911-12)16 CWN 74.

3 Whitley Stockes, *Anglo-Indian Codes*, vol. I, p. 931.

4 *Law Commission of India*, 147th Report, p. 9, 1993.

5 *Than Singh* v *Barelal* AIR 1974 MP 24.

be considered for refusal of specific performance along with them this doctrine also could be considered. In our view, therefore, the only interpretation possible of this sub-section appears to be that merely on the ground of want of mutuality a suit for specific performance cannot be thrown out."

It is submitted that the doctrine of mutuality has not been consistently followed by courts in India. The courts in India have not specifically dealt with the doctrine of mutuality in many cases except some cases relating to minors. Reference to such cases would show that the doctrine of mutuality was used by the courts in India to decide the cases relating to the benefit and interest of minors. As a matter of fact, the term has been used in Indian cases as a catch phrase to find out a solution in respect of agreements which on enforcement were likely to bring out unjust result. Now, s. 20 of the Act provides for substituted performance of contract instead of discretionary relief of specific performance of contract. The discretion of the court has now been done away with in the matter of granting relief under the amended provision of s. 20 of the Act.

No specific performance by writ Ordinarily, a specific performance of contract would not be enforced by issuing a writ of or in the nature of *mandamus* particularly when keeping in view the provisions of the Specific Relief Act 1963 under which damages may be an adequate remedy for breach of contract.[6] Thus, where a breach of contract is complained of, a party complaining of such breach may sue for specific performance of the contract, if contract is capable of being specifically performed, or the party may sue for damages. Such a suit would ordinarily be cognizable by the civil court. The High Court in its extraordinary jurisdiction would not entertain a petition either for specific performance of contract or for recovering damages. A right to relief flowing from a contract has to be claimed in a civil court where a suit for specific performance of contract or for damages could be filed.[7] Therefore, a writ petition is not an appropriate remedy for impeaching contractual obligations.[8]

Conduct of party Where conduct of vendee is not *bona fide*, for vendee having made false plea of payment of sale consideration, vendee is not entitled to equitable relief of specific performance.[9]

Specific performance as supplementary to Common Law remedy By an order of specific performance the court directs the defendant to perform

6 *Noble Resources Ltd.* v *State of Orissa* AIR 2007 SC 119; see also *United India Insurance Co. Ltd.* v *Manubhai Dharmasinhbhai Gajera* (2008)10 SCC 404.
7 *Divl. Forest Officer* v *Bishwanath Tea Co. Ltd.* (1981)3 SCC 238; AIR 1981 SC 1368.
8 *Har Shankar* v *Deputy Excise & Taxation Commissioner* (1975)1 SCC 737; AIR 1975 SC 1121.
9 *Chodi Mahalakshmi* v *Koppada Sathiraju* AIR 2011 AP 125.

the contract in accordance with its terms. The jurisdiction to order specific performance is supplementary to the Common Law remedy or damages. The court will not pass an order of specific performance in the following cases according to English Law:[10] (*a*) Specific performance will not be granted where damages provide adequate relief. (*b*) In considering whether or not to entertain a claim for specific performance, the court will take into account whether "mutuality" exists between the parties. (*c*) The court will not generally compel the performance of contracts which involve personal service. (*d*) The obligations in an agreement which it is sought to enforce ill defined and in such circumstances the specific performance will be an unsuitable remedy. (*e*) An order for specific performance would not be granted if the court is required to constantly supervise the execution of the contract. (*f*) Specific performance is a discretionary remedy. The court can take into account that the conduct of the claimant is tricky or unfair. (*g*) The court will also refuse specific performance where the interest to be transferred is merely transitory.

No specific performance through power of attorney To succeed in a suit for specific performance, the plaintiff has to prove: (*a*) that a valid agreement of sale was entered into by the defendant in his favour and the terms thereof; (*b*) that the defendant committed breach of the contract; and (*c*) that he was always ready and willing to perform his part of the obligations in terms of the contract. If a plaintiff has to prove that he was always ready and willing to perform his part of the contract, that is, to perform his obligations in terms of the contract, necessarily he should step into the witness box and give evidence that he has all along been ready and willing to perform his part of the contract and subject himself to cross-examination on that issue. A plaintiff cannot obviously examine in his place, his attorney holder who did not have personal knowledge either of the transaction or of his readiness and willingness. Readiness and willingness refer to the state of mind and conduct of the purchaser, as also his capacity and preparedness on the other. One without the other is not sufficient. Therefore a third party who has no personal knowledge cannot give evidence about such readiness and willingness, even if he is an attorney holder of the person concerned. Law in this regard may be summarised as under:

(*a*) An attorney holder who has signed the plaint and instituted the suit, but has no personal knowledge of the transaction can only give formal evidence about the validity of the power of attorney and the filing of the suit.

(*b*) If the attorney holder has done any act or handled any transactions, in pursuance of the power of attorney granted by the principal, he

10 Anson's *Law of Contract*, 29th Ed., pp. 575-581.

may be examined as a witness to prove those acts or transactions. If the attorney holder alone has personal knowledge of such acts and transactions and not the principal, the attorney holder shall be examined, if those acts and transactions have to be proved.

(*c*) The attorney holder cannot depose or give evidence in place of his principal for the acts done by the principal or transactions or dealings of the principal, of which principal alone has personal knowledge.

(*d*) Where the principal at no point of time had personally handled or dealt with or participated in the transaction and has no personal knowledge of the transaction, and where the entire transaction has been handled by an attorney holder, necessarily the attorney holder alone can give evidence in regard to the transaction. This frequently happens in case of principals carrying on business through authorised managers/attorney holders or persons residing abroad managing their affairs through their attorney holders.

(*e*) Where the entire transaction has been conducted through a particular attorney holder, the principal has to examine that attorney holder to prove the transaction, and not a different or subsequent attorney holder.

(*f*) Where different attorney holders had dealt with the matter at different stages of the transaction, if evidence has to be led as to what transpired at those different stages, all the attorney holders will have to be examined.

(*g*) Where the law requires or contemplated the plaintiff or other party to a proceeding, to establish or prove something with reference to his "state of mind" or "conduct", normally the person concerned alone has to give evidence and not an attorney holder. A landlord who seeks eviction of his tenant, on the ground of his "*bona fide*" need and a purchaser seeking specific performance who has to show his "readiness and willingness" fall under this category. There is however a recognised exception to this requirement. Where all the affairs of a party are completely managed, transacted and looked after by an attorney (who may happen to be a close family member), it may be possible to accept the evidence of such attorney even with reference to *bona fides* or "readiness and willingness". Examples of such attorney holders are a husband/wife exclusively managing the affairs of his/her spouse, a son/daughter exclusively managing the affairs of an old and infirm parent, a father/mother exclusively managing the affairs of a son/daughter living abroad.[11]

11 *Man Kaur* v *Hartar Singh Sangha* (2010)10 SCC 512.

Specific performance on oral contract It is possible that a decree for specific performance can be granted on the basis of an oral contract.[12] Way back in 1945, Lord Du Parcq in a case[13] observed, while deciding a suit for specific performance, that an oral contract is valid, binding and enforceable. A decree for specific performance could be passed on the basis of oral agreement. This view of a Privy Council was also followed by the Supreme Court in *Kollipara Sriramulu* v *T. Aswatha Narayana*[14] and held that an oral agreement with a reference to a future formal contract will not prevent a binding bargain between the parties. However, in such a case, heavy burden lies on the plaintiff to prove that there was *consensus ad idem* between the parties for the concluded agreement for sale of immovable property. But, whether there was such a concluded contract or not would be a question of fact to be determined in the facts and circumstances of each individual case.[15]

Suit for specific performance vis-a-vis suit under s. 77 of the Registration Act 1908 Section 77 of the Registration Act contemplates a remedy for the enforcement of a right to get a document registered by filing a civil suit, if the registration is refused. The purchaser can resort to proceedings under the Registration Act and the special statutory remedy under s. 77 of that Act to obtain registration of executed document. But, if for any reason it becomes impossible to obtain registration after resort to such proceedings or because of other circumstances which prevent any resort to such proceedings under the Act, then undoubtedly the vendee is entitled to bring a suit for specific performance of the agreement to sell in his favour.[16] Thus, the lesser remedy provided under s. 77 of the Act cannot take away the larger remedy provided for under the Specific Relief Act and that the Act does not touch or affect the equitable jurisdiction possessed by the civil courts to pass a decree, for specific performance where circumstances exist entitling the plaintiff to pass a decree, and that if the remedy under s. 77 of the Act is not available and even if available, is not effective and it is futile to initiate proceedings under the Act, the vendee may have his remedy for specific performance.[17]

The provisions of the Specific Relief Act and the Registration Act may to a certain extent cover the same field but so that one will not supersede the other. Where the stage indicated in s. 77 of the Act has reached and

12 *K. Nanjappa* v *R.A. Hameed* (2016)1 SCC 762.
13 *Shankarlal Narayandas Mundade* v *New Mofussil Co. Ltd.* (1945-46)73 IA 98; AIR 1946 PC 97.
14 AIR 1968 SC 1028.
15 *K. Nanjappa* v *R.A. Hameed* (2016)1 SCC 762.
16 *Manicka Goundan* v *Elumalai Goundan* (1956)2 MLJ 536; AIR 1957 Mad 78.
17 *K. Veeran Ambalam* v *Vellaiammal* AIR 1960 Mad 244; *Ellammal* v *Rangaswamy Koundar* (1982)95 LW 546; (1982)2 MLJ 41.

no other relief except a direction for registration of the document is really asked for, s. 77 of the Act may be an exclusive remedy. However, in other cases it has no application, inasmuch as a suit for specific performance is of wider amplitude and is primarily one for enforcement of a contract and other consequential or further relief. If a party is seeking not merely the registration of a sale deed, but also recovery of possession and *mesne profits* or damages, a suit under s. 77 of the Act is not an adequate remedy.[18]

Specific performance of Government contract and Art. 299 of the Constitution

Before 1947 even in England, the King was not liable to be sued for contractual liability in any ordinary court. But, the scenario changed with the passage of the Crown Proceedings Act 1947. In India, the Indian Contract Act 1872 does not prescribe any form for entering into contracts. It may be oral or in writing. The Government can also enter into a contract. Just as any individual is governed by the Indian Contract Act 1872 in respect of any contractual liability, the Government or the State is similarly regulated by the provisions of the Act, though the Government contract has been given constitutional status.[19] As regards its enforceability of performance, it need be noted that in pure contractual matters the extraordinary remedy of writ under Art. 226 or Art. 32 of the Constitution cannot be invoked. However, in a limited sphere such remedies are available only when the non-Government contracting party is able to demonstrate that it is a public law remedy which such party seeks to invoke, in contradistinction to the private law remedy simpliciter under the contract. Deciding the question as to whether the specific performance of contract in the civil court or writ remedy in the High Court would be the proper remedy in the matter of Government entering into contract with private parties, the Supreme Court has laid down the following principles of law:[20]

(I) At the stage of entering into a contract, the State acts purely in its executive capacity and is bound by the obligations of fairness.

(II) State in its executive capacity, even in the contractual field, is under obligation to act fairly and cannot practise some discriminations.

(III) Even in cases where question is of choice or consideration of competing claims before entering into the field of contract, facts have to be investigated and found before the question of a violation of Art. 14 of the Constitution could arise. If those facts are disputed and require assessment of evidence the correctness of which can only be tested satisfactorily by taking detailed evidence, involving

18 *Kalavakurti Venkata Subbaiah* v *Bala Gurappagari Guruvi Reddy* (1999)7 SCC 114.
19 *See*, Articles 298 and 299 of the Constitution of India.
20 *Joshi Technologies International Inc.* v *Union of India* (2015)7 SCC 728.

examination and cross-examination of witnesses, the case could not be conveniently or satisfactorily decided in proceedings under Art. 226 of the Constitution. In such cases the Court can direct the aggrieved party to resort to alternate remedy of civil suit, etc.

(IV) Writ jurisdiction of the High Court under Art. 226 of the Constitution cannot be intended to facilitate avoidance of obligation voluntarily incurred.

(V) Occurrence of commercial difficulty, inconvenience or hardship in performance of the conditions agreed to in the contract can provide no justification in not complying with the terms of contract which the parties had accepted with open eyes.

(VI) Ordinarily, where a breach of contract is complained of, the party complaining of such breach may sue for specific performance of the contract, if contract is capable of being specifically performed. Otherwise, the party may sue for damages.

(VII) Writ can be issued where there is executive action unsupported by law or even in respect of a corporation there is denial of equality before law or equal protection of law or if it can be shown that action of the public authorities was without giving any hearing and violation of principles of natural justice after holding that action could not have been taken without observing principles of natural justice.

(VIII) If the contract between private party and the State/instrumentality and/or agency of the State is under the realm of a private law and there is no element of public law, the normal course for the aggrieved party, is to invoke the remedies provided under ordinary civil law rather than approaching the High Court under Article 226 of the Constitution of India and invoking its extraordinary jurisdiction.

(IX) The distinction between public law and private law element in the contract with the State is getting blurred. However, it has not been totally obliterated and where the matter falls purely in private field of contract, the writ petition is not maintainable. The dichotomy between public law and private law rights and remedies would depend on the factual matrix of each case and the distinction between the public law remedies and private law field, cannot be demarcated with precision. In fact, each case has to be examined, on its facts whether the contractual relations between the parties bear insignia of public element. Once on the facts of a particular case it is found that nature of the activity or controversy involves public law element, then the matter can be examined by the High Court in writ petitions under Article 226 of the Constitution of India to see whether action of the State and/or instrumentality or agency of the State is fair, just and equitable or that relevant factors are taken into consideration and irrelevant factors have not gone into the decision-making process or that the decision is not arbitrary.

(X) Mere reasonable or legitimate expectation of a citizen, in such a situation, may not by itself be a distinct enforceable right, but failure to consider and give due weight to it may render the decision arbitrary, and this is how the requirements of due consideration of a legitimate expectation forms part of the principle of non-arbitrariness.

(XI) The scope of judicial review in respect of disputes falling within the domain of contractual obligations may be more limited and in doubtful cases the parties may be relegated to adjudication of their rights by resort to remedies provided for adjudication of purely contractual disputes.

Part Two

Specific Performance of Contract

CHAPTER 1

Contractual Obligations

Objective theory of contract[1] A contract is "a promise that the law will enforce". The law will not enforce all promises that are not "supported by consideration". For example, if *A* says "I promise to give you my car", that is not a promise and the law will not enforce. But if *A* says "I will sell you my car for Rupees five lakh", the law will enforce it if the offer is accepted. The requirement for consideration is sometimes referred to as the *bargain requirement*. It is said that the law does not enforce gratuitous promises; it only enforces bargain. But this statement, while generally true, is subject to exceptions.[2] An offer is defined as "the manifestation of willingness to enter into a bargain so made as to justify another person in understanding that his assent to that bargain is invited and will conclude it." According to this definition the main elements of an offer are the following: (1) It is a "manifestation" (written, verbal, conduct by internet posting, etc.); (2) "of willingness to enter into a bargain"; (3) "so made as to justify another"; (4) "in understanding that" (*a*) "his assent to the bargain is invited"; and (*b*) "will conclude it". The objective theory of contract is concerned with the statement addressed to a person who reasonably believes that it is an offer.[3]

The objective theory of contract provides that mutual assent to a contract is determined by reference to external acts and manifestations, not by

1 For origin and historical development of the theory, see Joseph M. Perillo, *The Origins of the Objective Theory of Contract Formation and Interpretation*, 69 Fordham L Rev 427 (2000).

2 George W. Kurney and Robert M. Lloyd, *Contracts: Transactions and Litigation*, 3rd Ed., p. 1.

3 *Ibid*, p. 2.

evidence of subjective, internal intention.[4] Stated simply, formation of contract depends on what is communicated, not on what is merely thought.[5] Contrary to the objective theory is the subjective or will theory of contract. As stated earlier, the objective theory is based on what the parties communicated, and the subjective theory is based on what the parties thought. By the end of the nineteenth century the objective approach to the mutual assent requirement had become predominant, and courts continue to use it today.[6]

Meaning and ingredients of contract A contract is an agreement which is enforceable by law [s. 2(*h*), Contract Act] and becomes void when it ceases to be enforceable [s. 2(*j*), Contract Act]. Section 10 enumerates the ingredients of a contract. It provides that all agreements are contracts if they are made by the free consent of parties competent to contract, for a lawful consideration and with a lawful object, and are not hereby expressly declared to be void. It is also made clear that this will not affect any law in force in India and not expressly repealed by the Contract Act, by which any contract is required to be made in writing or in the presence of witnesses, or any law relating to the registration of documents. Some of the contracts which have to be reduced to writing are the contracts mentioned in s. 25 of the Indian Contract Act, in s. 19 of the Copyright Act, in ss. 6 and 7 of the Carriers Act and in ss. 12, 30 and 109 of the Companies Act 1956 (now repealed and replaced by the Companies Act 2013 and those sections are correspond to ss. 3, 7 and 56 of the Companies Act 2013 respectively). A Will must be executed in the presence of the witnesses or the attesting witnesses have received a personal acknowledgement from the testator that he did execute the document. It requires no registration. Nor it falls within the domain of contract. Its specific performance is out of question. Documents requiring registration are enumerated in s. 17 of the Registration Act.

Ingredients of contracts are that (1) there must be a consideration (unless it is by deed); (2) the parties must have an intention to create legal relations; (3) the parties must have capacity to contract; (4) the agreement must comply with any formal requirements; (5) the agreement must be legal; (6) the agreement must not be rendered void either by some Common Law or by some statutory rule or by some inherent defect, such as operative mistake.[7]

Evidently, before any contract is enforced, it is essential that the terms of the contract must be clear, definite, certain and complete and the contract

4 Oliver Wendell Holmes, Jr., *The Common Law*, Ed. 1991, p. 309, (Dover Publications, Inc.).

5 Duncan Kennedy, *From the Will Theory to the Principle of Private Autonomy: Lon Fuller's "Consideration and Form"*, 100 Colum L Rev 94, 129-30 (2000).

6 E. Allan Farnsworth, *Contracts* § 3.6, at 114 (1982).

7 *Oxford Dictionary of Law*, 8th Ed.

must be free from doubt, vagueness and ambiguity so as to leave nothing to conjecture or to be supplied by the court.[8]

Is execution of a formal agreement necessary? English Courts[9] have consistently followed the rule laid down by The Court of Appeal in *Pagnan S.P.A.* v *Feed Products Ltd.*[10] as follows:

> "It is sometimes said that the parties must agree on the essential terms and that it is only matters of detail which can be left over. This may be misleading, since the word 'essential' in that context is ambiguous. If by 'essential' one means a term without which the contract cannot be enforced, then the statement is true: the law cannot enforce an incomplete contract. If by 'essential' one means a term which the parties have agreed to be essential for the formation of a binding contract, then the statement is tautologous. If by 'essential' one means only a term which the Court regards as important as opposed to a term which the Court regards as less important or a matter of detail, the statement is untrue. It is for the parties to decide whether they wish to be bound and, if so, by what terms, whether important or unimportant. It is the parties who are, in the memorable phrase coined by the Judge, 'the masters of their contractual fate'. Of course, the more important the term is the less likely it is that the parties will have left it for future decision. But there is no legal obstacle which stands in the way of the parties agreeing to be bound now while deferring important matters to be agreed later. It happens every day when parties enter into so-called 'heads of agreement'."

In India, the law has developed more or less on the same line. It has been held by Lord Du Parcq that unless an inference can be drawn from the facts that the parties intended to be bound only when a formal agreement had been executed, the validity of the agreement would not be affected by its lack of formality.[11] An agreement even if not signed by the parties can be spelt out from the correspondence exchanged between the parties. However, the duty of the court in this regard is to find out from the correspondence as to whether the parties were *ad idem* to the terms of contract.[12] Terms of registered agreement to sale cannot be varied by an unregistered document which is to be executed in future. An agreement cannot be enforced in respect of varied terms.[13]

8 *Nair Service Society* v *R.M. Palat* AIR 1966 Ker 311 at p. 313 (DB).

9 *Mamidoil-Jetoil Greek Petroleum Co. SA* v *Okta Crude Oil Refinery AD* [2001]2 All ER (Comm) 193; [2001]2 Lloyd's Rep 76 (CA)]; Lloyd's *Law Reports* at p. 89; *Wilson Smithett & Cape (Sugar) Ltd.* v *Bangladesh Sugar and Food Industries Corpn.* [1986]1 Lloyd's Rep 378; Lloyd's *Law Reports* at p. 386.

10 [1987]2 Lloyd's Rep 601 (CA).

11 *Shankarlal Narayandas Mundade* v *New Mofussil Co. Ltd.* AIR 1946 PC 97; see also *Trimex International FZE Ltd.* v *Vedanta Aluminium Ltd.* (2010)3 SCC 1.

12 *Govind Rubber Ltd.* v *Louids Dreyfus Commodities Asia (P) Ltd.* (2015)13 SCC 477.

13 *Shanti Mishra (Smt.)* v *Samual* AIR 2018 All 242.

Five principles of interpretation of contract Lord Hoffmann in *Investors Compensation Scheme Ltd.* v *West Bromwich Building Society*[14] has summarized five principles of interpretation of contracts. These are as follows:

(1) Interpretation is the ascertainment of the meaning which the document would convey to a reasonable person having all the background knowledge.

(2) The background means "matrix of fact".

(3) The law excludes from the admissible background, the previous negotiations of the parties and their declarations of subjective intent.

(4) The meaning which a document (or any other utterance) would convey to a reasonable man is not the same thing as the meaning of its words.

(5) The rule that words should be given their "natural and ordinary meaning reflects the common sense proposition that is not easily acceptable that people have made linguistic mistakes, particularly to formal documents."

These five principles of interpretation of contract are adopted by the courts in Hong Kong,[15] New Zealand[16] and Australia[17] with a cautious approach. In India, however, the Supreme Court has taken recourse to the rule of purposive interpretation for construing the terms of contract. It has been held by the Supreme Court that the purpose of a contract is the interests, objectives, values, policy that the contract is designed to actualize. It comprises the joint intent of the parties. Every such contract expresses the autonomy of the contractual parties' private will. It creates reasonable, legally protected expectations between the parties and reliance on its results. Consistent with the character of purposive interpretation, the court is required to determine the ultimate purpose of a contract primarily by the joint intent of the parties at the time the contract so formed. It is not the intent of a single party; it is the joint intent of both the parties and the joint intent of the parties is to be discovered from the entirety of the contract and the circumstances surrounding its formation.[18] Even in international commercial contract, the purposive interpretation rule has been followed.[19] Thus, each contract has to be interpreted on its own terms taking into

14 [1998]1 WLR 896; [1998]1 All ER 98.

15 *Jambo King Ltd.* v *Faithful Properties Ltd.* [1999] HKCFAR 279.

16 *Boat Park Ltd.* v *Hutchinson* [1999]2 NZLR 74.

17 *Royal Botanic Gardens and Domain Trust* v *South Sydney City Council* [2002]76 AJLR 436; [2002] HCA 5.

18 *DLF Universal Limited* v *Director, Town and Country Planning Department, Haryana* (2010)14 SCC 1.

19 *Sumitomo Heavy Industries Ltd.* v *ONGC Ltd.* (2010)11 SCC 296; AIR 2010 SC 3400.

account the conduct of the parties,[20] and the object and entire terms of the contract.[21]

Classification of contracts Contracts may be classified according to (*i*) their subject matter, (*ii*) their parties, (*iii*) their form (whether contained in deed or in writing, whether express or implied), (*iv*) their effect (whether bilateral or unilateral, whether valid, void or unenforceable).

Five conditions for implied terms of contract According to Chitty,[1] contracts may be either express or implied. Contracts are express when their terms are stated in words by the parties. They are often said to be implied when their terms are not so stated, as, for example, when a passenger is permitted to board a bus: from the conduct of the parties the law implies a promise by the passenger to pay the fare, and a promise by the operator of the bus to carry him safely to his destination.[2] In construing a contract, a term or condition not expressly stated may, under certain circumstances be implied by the court, if it is clear from the nature of the transaction or from something actually found in the document that the contracting parties must have intended such a term or condition to be a part of the agreement between them. Such an implication must in all cases be founded on the presumed intention of the parties and upon reason, and will only be made when it is necessary in order to give the transaction that efficacy that both parties must have intended it to have, and to prevent such a failure of consideration as could not have been within the contemplation of the parties.[3] In *B.P. Refinery (Westernport) Pty. Ltd.* v *Shire of Hastings*[4] the Privy Council has laid down five conditions which are to be satisfied for an implied term of contract. These are: (1) It must be reasonable and equitable. (2) It must be necessary to give business efficacy to the contract. (3) It must be so obvious that "it goes without saying". (4) It must be capable of clear expression. (5) It must not contradict any express term of the contract.

Four elements of a contract under the Indian Contract Act 1872 Basically, every contract involves four elements, *viz.*

(1) Competency of the parties;

(2) Consensus;

(3) Consideration and object; and

(4) Certainty.

We shall deal with these elements in brief.

20 *Udaipur Sahkari Upbhokta Thok Bhandar Ltd.* v *CIT* (2009)8 SCC 393.

21 *Bihar State Electricity Board* v *Green Rubber Industries* (1990)1 SCC 731.

1 Chitty on *Contracts*, 23rd Ed., pp. 9-10, para 12.

2 *Haji Mohd. Ishaq* v *Mohd. Iqbal and Mohd. Ali & Co.* (1978)2 SCC 493.

3 Halsbury's *Laws of England*, vol. 8, 3rd Ed., p. 121.

4 [1978]52 ALJR 20 (PC); [1997]180 CLR 266.

(1) ***Competency of the parties*** Sections 11 and 12 of the Indian Contract Act deal with it. Section 11 provides that every person is competent to contract who is of the age of majority according to the law to which he is subject and who is of sound mind and is not disqualified from contracting by any law to which he is subject. Section 12 defines what is a sound mind for purposes of contracting. The word "person" is a word of wide import and includes any company or association or body of individuals whether incorporated or not [s. 3(42) of the General Clauses Act]. The age of majority is fixed at 18 years, unless a guardian has been appointed in respect of that person, in which case, it is 21 years.

Section 11 of the Indian Contract Act provides that who are competent to contract. This section lays down the rule of three kinds of disqualifications, namely, those arising from (*i*) minority; (*ii*) insanity; (*iii*) disqualified by some provisions of the personal law. The incapacity of a minor under the Indian law to bind himself or his estate by a contract is more complete than that under the English law.[5] Under the Guardians and Wards Act 1890, a District Court and a High Court have power (*a*) to appoint and declare guardians, (*b*) to remove guardians and (*c*) to control guardians of a person or property or both of a minor (s. 39 of the Guardians and Wards Act). Under the Hindu Minority and Guardianship Act 1956 the powers of a natural guardian are conferred in s. 8 of the Act. Section 11 of the Act bars a *de facto* guardian to deal with the property of a Hindu minor. The object of the Act is the protection of minor. The legislature has thought it fit to confer a right of suit in certain circumstances not only on the minor but also on a person to whom the minor has transferred his right.[6] A contract for sale of immovable property belonging to a private deity is specifically enforceable if it is for legal necessity.[7] A contract by a mentally ill person like that of a minor is void.[8]

Section 12 of the Indian Contract Act 1872 explains what a sound mind means for the purpose of contracting. It follows that if a person lacks the essential element of sound mind, the agreement becomes void. Under the English law the contract will be void if the plaintiff was aware of the fact.[9] Minor though disqualified from entering into contract is capable of receiving property by way of gift.[10] Similarly, if a person puts himself into a position of alcoholic addiction executes contracts after accepting money from third parties and creating rights, the law would be extremely slow in allowing such a party to escape the consequences of the contract unless it is

5 *Ramanathan* v *Palanippa* AIR 1939 Mad 776.
6 *Amirtham Kudumbah* v *Sarnam Kudumban* AIR 1991 SC 1256.
7 *Durga Thakurani Bije Nijigarh* v *Chintamani Swain* AIR 1982 Ori 158.
8 *Johri* v *Mahila Draupati* AIR 1991 MP 340.
9 *Imperial Loan Co.* v *Stone* [1872]1 QB 599.
10 *K. Balakrishnan* v *K. Kamalam* AIR 2004 SC 1257.

demonstrated to the hilt that the executant virtually did not know what he was doing when the contract takes place.[11] The avoidance of a contract is not only exceptional but is a very special exception which would be permitted in the rarest of rare cases.[12] Even if a man is suffering from schizophrenia, in the absence of a positive statement made by a doctor that he was treating a person of unsound mind, it cannot be treated that such a person was lunatic. In other words, merely a proof that a person long ago at one stage of his life suffered from schizophrenia would not result into an inference that he is a person of unsound mind.[13] Section 12 of the Contract Act 1872, therefore, does not go to the extent of declaring a contract void, if at the time of making the contract he was capable of understanding the contract and forming a rational judgment as to its effect upon his interest.[14]

HINDU LAW A *karta* can dispose the property of the family, only if it is for the benefit of the family. It is true that for a transaction to be regarded as of benefit to the family, it need not be of defensive character in order to be binding on the family. In each case the court must be satisfied from the material before it that it was, in fact, such as conferred, or was reasonably expected to confer, benefit on the family at the time it was entered into. Where adult members are in existence, the judgment is to be not that of the manager of the family alone but that of all the adult members of the family including the manager.[15] The joint Hindu family by itself is a legal entity capable of acting through its *karta* and other adult members of the family in its management. Since there is no need for any natural guardian for the minor's undivided interest in the joint Hindu family property, as provided under ss. 6 and 12 of the Hindu Minority and Guardianship Act, the previous permission of the court under s. 8 of the said Act for disposing of the interest of the minor in the joint Hindu family is not required.[16]

POWER OF NATURAL GUARDIAN OF A HINDU MINOR TO TRANSFER THE MINOR'S IMMOVABLE PROPERTY Prior to the enactment of the Hindu Minority and Guardianship Act 1956, a natural guardian of a Hindu minor could do all acts which were reasonable and necessary for the protection of the minor's property.[17] He

11 *S. Basavaraj* v *V.N. Adilakshmamma* ILR (1998) Kar 2220; 1998 AIHC 4008.
12 *Ibid.*
13 *Mst. Lakshmi* v *Dr. Ajay Kumar* AIR 2006 P&H 77.
14 *Ibid.*
15 *Balmukand* v *Kamla Wati* AIR 1964 SC 1385; (1964)6 SCR 321 (*held* on facts sale was not for the benefit of the family) affirming *Balmukand* v *Pindi Dass* AIR 1958 Punj 267 and relying on *Jagatnarain* v *Mathura Das* AIR 1928 All 454 (FB); *Sital Prasad Singh* v *Ajablal Mander* AIR 1939 Pat 370; *A.T. Vasudevan,* in re AIR 1949 Mad 260.
16 *Sri Narayan Bal* v *Sridhar Sutar* AIR 1996 SC 2371; (1996)8 SCC 54; JT 1996(1) SC 711.
17 *Padma Krishna Chettiar* v *Nagamani Ammal* ILR (1916)39 Mad 915; *Sonu* v *Dhondu* ILR (1904)28 Bom 330.

could transfer any portion of the minor's property by mortgage or sale in the case of need or for the benefit of the estate, as laid down by the Judicial Committee of the Privy Council in *Hanooman Prasad Pandey* v *Mst. Babooee Munraj Koonwaree.*[18] For the first time, the rights of a natural guardian to make alienation of the minor's property have been curtailed and statutorily regulated by the Hindu Minority and Guardianship Act 1956.[19] Even under this Act, the position is not departed from except with reference to the transfer of minor's immovable property by the guardian and in the case of such transfer, the previous permission of the court is insisted on. Section 8 of the said Act entitles the guardian to do all acts which are (1) necessary (2) reasonable and proper for the minor's benefit; or (3) for the realisation, protection or benefit of the minor's estate.[20] It is not necessary to take the prior permission of the court where the guardian wants to transfer the movable property of the minor and such transfer by the guardian will be governed by general test already obtained under the Hindu Law *viz.*, the transfer is for the benefit or necessity of the minor. Though the language of sub-secs. (1) and (2) of s. 8 of the Hindu Minority and Guardianship Act 1956 is peremptory, sub-sec. (3) of s. 8 lays down that any alienation made by the natural guardian in contravention of sub-secs. (1) and (2) is only voidable at the instance of the minor or any person claiming under him. In other words, such an alienation is not void, but only voidable.

Next to the question of natural guardian's power to enter into an agreement for the sale or purchase of the immovable property for and on behalf of the minor. If the guardian of a Hindu minor entered into a contract either for sale or purchase of immovable property, the contract was one which was not binding upon the minor and consequently neither the minor nor the other party to the contract can specifically enforce the contract.[1] The learned Judges relied on a judgment of the High Court of Madras in *Sitaram Rao* v *Venkatnarayana.*[2] No permission of the court was necessary for the purchase of a property for the minor if such an act was necessary, reasonable and proper for the benefit of the minor unless such act bind the minor personally or imposes a personal liability on him.[3] The point is now set at rest by the decision of the Supreme Court in *Manik Chand* v *Ramachandra*[4] which went up on appeal from the judgment of the

18 (1854-57)6 MIA 393.

19 *Sursati Devi* v *Joint Director of Consolidation* 1982 All LJ 1473.

20 *Manik Chand* v *Ramachandra* AIR 1981 SC 519; (1980)3 SCR 1104; (1980)4 SCC 22.

1 *Ramachandra* v *Manik Chand* AIR 1968 MP 150.

2 AIR 1956 Mad 1035 (FB); *Mir Sarwarjan* v *Fakruddin Md. Chowdhury* (1912)39 IA 1 (PC).

3 *Radheyshyam Kamila* v *Kiran Bala Dasi* AIR 1971 Cal 341; relying on *Subrahmanyam* v *Subba Rao* AIR 1948 PC 95; *Suryaprakasam* v *Ganga Raj* AIR 1956 AP 33.

4 AIR 1981 SC 519; (1980)3 SCR 1104; (1980)4 SCC 22.

High Court of Madhya Pradesh in *Ramachandra* v *Manik Chand.*[5] Their Lordships pointed out, reversing the judgment of the High Court of Madhya Pradesh that the power conferred by s. 8 of the Hindu Minority and Guardianship Act was in no way restricted than that was recognised under the Hindu Law. It applied even to a contract for purchase of immovable property. As it is within the competence of the guardian, the contract is entered into effectively on behalf of the minor and the liability to pay the money is the liability of the minor under the Transfer of Property Act. It cannot be said that in a contract for purchase of a property, the guardian would be binding the minor by his personal covenant. Thus the contract entered into by the guardian on behalf of the minor is enforceable.[6] A minor may be sued through his natural guardian, who has obtained the requisite permission of the court under s. 8 of the Hindu Minority and Guardianship Act, even though he has not been appointed as a guardian *ad litem* as provided for in Or. 32, r. 3 of the CPC.

The crux of the matter is that it has to be seen whether the minor was effectively represented in the litigation. Non-compliance with the provisions of Or. 32, r. 3, CPC which are mandatory would not render the decision void. But if the non-compliance has caused prejudice to the minor or he was not effectively represented, the decision will be void, that is, the minor can either ignore it or avoid it. This approach is in consonance with justice because where the matter has been properly contested and no prejudice has been caused to the minor, it will be sheer injustice to the other side to reopen the matter again.[7]

If a contract by competent guardian of a Hindu minor for sale or purchase is for necessity or for the benefit of the minor, it would be valid and enforceable, though in this case the court would not lose its discretionary power to refuse to enforce the agreement if the supervening circumstances affect the interests of the minor and the circumstances have changed to his detriment at the time the contract is sought to be enforced.[8]

However, where the contract has been signed by the *karta* of the joint Hindu family in his personal capacity, the contract will not be binding on the family.[9] Similarly, where it is not proved that the contract was entered into by the *karta* or manager of the family, as such, the contract will not be enforced against other members.[10]

5 AIR 1968 MP 150 referred to above.
6 *Chatterbhuj Goel* v *Gurpreet Singh* AIR 1983 P&H 406.
7 *Amrik Singh* v *Karnail Singh* AIR 1974 P&H 315 (FB); see also *Walian* v *Banke Behari Pershad Singh* (1903)30 IA 182; ILR (1903)30 Cal 1021; *Nirmal Chandra Ray* v *Khandu Ghose* AIR 1965 Cal 562.
8 *Bhupal* v *Mam Chand* AIR 1973 All 543 at p. 545.
9 *Khali Panigrahi* v *Kamala Devi* AIR 1967 Ori 100 (DB).
10 *Jogesh Chandra Hota* v *Bibhuti Bhusan Sahani* AIR 1967 Ori 95 (DB).

Where the mother of minors, though their father was alive, sold their property and the father attested the sale deed, it was held that such sale of minor's property by mother is not voidable but void. Explaining the position of law, the Supreme Court held that the provisions of s. 8 are devised to fully protect the property of a minor, even from the depredations of his parents. Section 8 empowers only the legal guardian to alienate a minor's immovable property provided it is for the necessity or benefit of the minor or his estate and it further requires that such alienation shall be effected after the permission of the court has been obtained. It is difficult, therefore, to hold that the sale was voidable, not void, by reason of the fact that the mother of the minors signed the sale deed and the father attested it.[11]

But where a member of the joint family holding a general power of attorney from other members, except his widowed mother, sold the property on behalf of all the members including the mother, it was held that the omission of the mother's name in the general power-of-attorney was not fatal to the plaintiff's suit, when she had neither set up any adverse title nor had come forward to raise any objection.[12]

Agreements were not based on any decision of a Board of Management of Society which alone was competent to take decision for sale and acquisition of property for the Society. The Secretary who has signed the agreement on behalf of the Society on the basis of the resolution of the general body was not competent or authorised or entitled to execute such an agreement on behalf of the Society. So the agreement is not binding on the society. Hence the decree of specific performance is not unsustainable.[13]

Power of de facto guardian of a Hindu minor to transfer the minor's immovable property It was pointed out by the Privy Council in *Hunoomanpersaud Panday*'s case that a *de facto* guardian had the same power of alienating the property of his ward as a natural guardian.[14] But, the enactment of the Hindu Minority and Guardianship Act 1956 has done away with such power of the *de facto* guardian. Section 11 of the Act provides that after the commencement of the Act, no person shall be entitled to dispose of, or deal with, the property of a Hindu minor merely on the ground of his or her being the *de facto* guardian of the minor. In *Madhigowda* v *Ankegowda*[15] the Supreme Court observed that s. 11 of the Act brings about a material change in the law relating to *de facto* guardians or *de facto* managers of a Hindu minor's estate by enacting in express terms that after

11 *Panni Lal* v *Rajinder Singh* (1993)4 SCC 38.
12 *Basruddin Khan* v *Gurudarshan Das* AIR 1970 Pat 304 at p. 308 (DB).
13 *Durga Education Society, Chhattisgarh* v *Shakti Pictures Circuit Ltd., Amravati, Maharashtra* AIR 2018 Chh 102.
14 *Hunoomanpersaud Panday* v *Babooee Munraj Koonweree* (1854-57)6 MIA 393; 18 WR 81 (PC).
15 (2002)1 SCC 178.

the commencement of the Act, no person has the right or authority to do any act as a *de facto* guardian of such minor. Although the expression "*de facto* guardian" is often used in judgments, there is in law nothing like a *de facto* guardian. The statute recognizes a natural guardian or a testamentary guardian or a guardian appointed by the court. In law a person who is not a guardian as aforementioned who takes interest upon himself, the general management of the estate of a minor can be more appropriately described as "*de facto* manager". Any alienation by a *de facto* guardian will be governed by the provisions in s. 11 of the Act. The alienation, being against the statutory prohibition, would be void *ab initio* and the alienee would not acquire any title to the property.

AGREEMENT FOR SALE ON BEHALF OF PRIVATE DEITY: SPECIFIC PERFORMANCE Deity is not a minor,[16] for the purpose of enjoyment of any priviledge other than any other artificial person and a sale of property of private deity by its *marfatdar* (trustee) is specifically enforceable.

CONTRACTS BY MENTALLY ILL PERSON AND INTOXICATED PERSONS A mentally ill person or a person *non compos mentis* is one incapable of understanding the contract and of forming a rational judgment as to its effect upon his interest. In England, the contract of a lunatic is voidable at his instance. But in India, a contract by a mentally ill person is void *ab initio*. In *Mohoribibi* v *Dharmodas Ghose*,[17] by parity of reasoning it should be held that a contract by a mentally ill person is also governed by s. 11 and is void *ab initio*. So, the Indian law diverges from the English law on this point. But both in England and in India a lunatic may enter into a valid contract during a lucid interval. In a lucid interval the mentally deranged regains his sanity and hence he regains his contractual capacity during the said interval.

In England a drunken person's contract is voidable,[18] but in India, the contract by a drunken person is void.

DRUNKENNESS In India, contract entered by a drunken person is said to be void.[19] However, the law on the issue of contract during drunkenness has in recent years been elucidated by the courts. It has been held that s. 12 of the Contract Act which defines as to when a person can be said to possess a sound mind for entering into a contract, seems to suggest, especially under *illustration* (*b*) thereto, that intoxication can render a person incapable of making a contract; however, the drunkenness envisaged thereunder is of severe variety—as can be gauged from the expression "so drunk" used in the

16 *Gopal Shridhar Mahadeb* v *Shasheebhushan Sarkar* AIR 1933 Cal 109; *Sri Durga Thakurani Bije Nijigarh* v *Chintamoni Swain* AIR 1982 Ori 158.
17 ILR (1903)30 Cal 539 (PC).
18 *Mathews* v *Boxten* [1873] LR 8 Exch 132; *Surrey* v *Gibson* [1845]13 M&W 623.
19 *Kamala* v *Karuna* 15 IC 404; *Kotumal* v *Dur Mohammad* 136 IC 525.

aforesaid illustration—it must have the effect of crippling a person's ability to form a rational judgment. Moreover, such inebriation should be shown to affect the cognitive capacity of the person at the precise time when the contract is executed as the section recognises that a person who is usually of unsound mind may make a contract when he is of a sound mind, as is also well brought out by illustration (*a*) appended to the section. Intoxication has several gradations—which may be beneficial or detrimental—and law permits only such drunkenness which is severe and capable of destroying the mental faculty of a man to set aside a contract. Further, at the cost of repetition, it must be emphasised that such inebriation has to be proved to exist at the time the contract is entered into, in order to successfully bail the maker out of a contractual obligation.[20] The High Court of Karnataka[21] dealing with the question of a alcohol-addict entering into a contract and the resultant consequences observed that though under normal circumstances if it is established that the executant was not only given to the consumption of alcohol but what one may categorize as a long term addict, a court would take judicial notice of the fact that such a person would for the greater part sink to a very weak mental condition, but stated however that one cannot generalize with regard to such situations because there may be lucid breaks when the party is perfectly and completely sober and it is for this reason that even in the case of such a person that the law requires that there must be strict factual proof of the fact that the infirmity was present at the point of time when the contract was being executed. The court relying upon the minority judgment of the High Court of Australia in *Bromley* v *Ryan*[1] further pointed out that unlike other forms of mental illnesses depriving a party of exercise of a sound mind, alcohol addiction is virtually a self-induced condition and therefore such defense should be very sparingly upheld and that too in extremely rare cases. It observed that there is a well-settled principle of jurisprudence which postulates that a party cannot take advantage of its own wrong and in this view of the law, if a person puts himself into a position of alcoholic addiction, executes contracts after accepting money from third parties and creates rights, the law would be extremely slow in allowing such a party to escape the consequences of the contract unless it is demonstrated to the hilt that the executant virtually did not know what he was doing when the contract took place.

Thus, in law, *mere drunkenness* is not sufficient to dislodge a contract which is otherwise binding.

Senile dementia In order to gauge impact of senile dementia on the enforcement of a suit of specific performance of contract, what is essential

20 *Yogendra Singh* v *Prem Lata* RFA36/2005, dated 27.09.2013, Delhi High Court (Unreported Judgment).

21 *S. Basavaraj* v *V.N. Adilakashmamma* MANU/KA/0324/1998.

1 (1956)99 CLR 362.

to look into is that the court must be satisfied (*i*) that there is a concluded contract which would be binding at law if all proper formalities had been observed, and in particular that the parties have agreed, expressly or impliedly, on all the essential terms of the contract; and (*ii*) that the terms are sufficiently certain and precise that the court can order and supervise the exact performance of contract. However, the grounds on which specific performance will be refused do not fall into rigid categories. There is a general jurisdiction to deny specific performance if the court, on the particular facts, considers it just to do. The most familiar specific ground is the legal incapacity. The legal incapacity of the defendant to bind himself by contract is a defence to an action for specific performance.[2] Mental health of the person entering into a contract is facet of legal capacity or incapacity.

CONTRACT BY A PERSON SUFFERING FROM SENILE DEMENTIA Where senile dementia in the case of an old man is proved to have existed on a particular date, it is more reasonable to presume its continuance than its discontinuance, and the onus will be upon persons who wish the court to uphold transactions entered into by him subsequent to that date to prove that they were not vitiated on the ground of his incapacity. Where a person is under delusion that he possesses thousands of acres of land when in fact he has about a hundred acres, he cannot be said to be in a position to form a rational judgment as to the effect on his interests of a transaction entered into by him.[3]

MUSLIM LAW Legal guardian of a Muslim minor is only his father, or, if he is not alive, his executor, failing whom his paternal grandfather or great paternal grandfather or their respective executors, and so any contract entered into by the mother as a *de facto* guardian would be void irrespective of whether the transaction is for the benefit of the minor,[4] and this applies equally to contracts of sale, lease, mortgage or any other transfer.[5] Such a transaction is not merely voidable but void.[6] No other relation except as noted above can be a legal guardian of Muslim minor as regards his property. Even a brother of a minor, for example, cannot be a legal guardian.[7] In default of legal guardians a duty of appointing guardian for the protection and preservation of the minor's property is of the court on proper application.[8]

2 Halsbury's *Laws of England*, 4th Ed., vol. 44(1), p. 489, paras 840, 841.
3 *Govindaswami Naicker* v *K.N. Srinivasa Rao* AIR 1940 Mad 73.
4 *K.M. Jaina Beevi* v *M.K. Govindaswami* AIR 1967 Mad 369 at p. 372 (DB) relying on *Imambandi* v *Mutsaddi* AIR 1918 PC 11; *Md. Amin* v *Vakil Ahmed* AIR 1952 SC 358; 1952 SCR 1133; 1952 SCJ 539; *Md. Zafir* v *S.K. Amiruddin* AIR 1963 Pat 108.
5 *Govinda Karup* v *Beekhu* AIR 1931 Mad 147; see also *Fathima Bivi* v *Sadhakatalla* AIR 1977 Mad 215 at p. 216.
6 *Md. Rahimuddin* v *Aish Begam* (1978)2 Andh WR 84.
7 *Syed Shah Ghulam Ghouse Mohiuddin* v *Syed Shah Ahmed Mohiuddin Kamisul Quadri* (1971)1 SCC 597.
8 *Syed Shah Ghulam Ghouse Mohiuddin* v *Syed Shah Ahmed Mohiuddin Kamisul Quadri* (1971)1 SCC 597.

However, the law on this point has further developed in different cases. In *Mohamad Amin Shah* v *Mst. Ateeka Banu*[9] the court faced a very peculiar situation where the father of two girls above the age of puberty had died while their mother had remarried. The High Court considering the various options best suited for the said two girls and appointed an elderly male step-cousin as their guardian but regarding their property, joint guardianship was given to girl's father's sister along with the said male step-cousin of the girls. In *Ali Mohammad* v *Ramnivas*,[10] a *de facto* guardian, who signed a mortgage deed, was declared to be unfit to transfer any right or interest in immovable property of the minor and such transfer was held to be void. Thus, it is submitted, as it appears from the trends of the recent cases on the subject, that the Supreme Court[11] laid emphasis on protecting the property interests of minors and even rejected the case of adverse possession against the minor's property after the sale of minor's property by her mother. This activist approach of the court is not only in sync with the principle of 'welfare of child' but it also aims at protecting the rights of the weaker sections of the society, among whom children have a definite place.

A *de facto* guardian gets no recognition under Muslim law which considers him to be without any legal authority to deal with the minor's property and any such dealing is wholly void.[12] A transfer by a *de facto* guardian can't even be ratified by the minor on attaining majority.[13] But alienation of any property by a *de facto* guardian of a Muslim minor can be ratified by a minor on attaining majority.[14] It is respectfully submitted that this view of the Kerala High Court is not correct. When the transaction entered into by a *de facto* guardian of a Muslim minor is void *ab initio*, no question of ratification arises. To hold that quondam Muslim minor can ratify the transfer of immovable property by his *de facto* guardian would undo Muslim law which regards the *de facto* guardian of a Muslim minor as a mere interloper. But if any such contract has been executed, it is not open to the minor to claim the assets of the estate and at the same time to repudiate the liability of the estate, where the sale proceeds have been applied for the discharge of the debts of the estate.[15]

9 AIR 1963 J&K 32.
10 AIR 1967 Raj 258.
11 *Mahboob Sahab* v *Syed Ismail* AIR 1995 SC 1205; *Meethiyan Sidhiqu* v *Md. Kunju Pareeth Kutty* AIR 1996 SC 1003.
12 *Salma Bibi* v *Nazimuddin* (1994)1 KLT 974; *Meethiyan Sidhiqu* v *Md. Kunju Pareeth Kutty* AIR 1996 SC 1003; (1996)7 SCC 436; JT 1996(1) SC 578.
13 *Ali Mohammed* v *Ramniwas* AIR 1967 Raj 258; *Anto* v *Reoti Kumar* AIR 1936 All 837; *Karam Chand* v *Vali Mohamed* AIR 1937 Sind 157.
14 *Lakshmi Ammal* v *Saidutty* ILR (1967)1 Ker 631.
15 *Fathima Bivi* v *Sadhakatalla* AIR 1977 Mad 215 at p. 217.

Transfer of an immovable property by a *de facto* guardian of a Muslim minor is void not only *qua* the minor but also *qua* those who are *sui juris.*[16] This view, it is respectfully submitted, is not correct. In *Maimunnisa Bibi* v *Abdul Jabbar,*[17] the deed of sale was executed by the mother and her three sons of whom two were minors represented by their mother. Veerasamy, J (as he then was) held that the sale was void only as regards the minors and was valid as regards the mother and the major son. Reference is also invited to the decision of the Privy Council in *Matadin* v *Sheikh Amhed Ali.*[18] In that case, three out of the four grandsons of a Muslim testator sold certain properties on their own behalf and as guardian of their minor brother to the defendant who held a mortgage over the said properties executed by the testator. The fourth grandson, on attaining majority, instituted the suit for redemption of his share of the mortgage. The Privy Council allowed the claim of the quondam minor. The implication of this decision is that the sale is valid as regards the other brothers. It may however be pointed out that where the minor is represented by a *de facto* guardian in a family settlement or family arrangement or family partition, the entire transaction is void *qua* all parties including those who were then *sui juris.*[19] To sum up, it is respectfully submitted that the concept of *de facto* guardian is completely out of vogue in modern Muslim law, in as much as equating the powers of *de facto* guardian with those of a legal guardian would wipe out altogether one of the most important safeguards provided by the Muslim law for the protection of interests of infants.

POWER OF THE LEGAL GUARDIAN Under the Muslim law, a legal guardian of the properties of a minor has no power to sell the immovable property of the minor except in the following cases *viz.*,

(1) where he can obtain double its value;
(2) where the minor has no other property and the sale is necessary for his maintenance;
(3) where there are debts to be discharged and no other means of paying them;
(4) where there are legacies to be paid, and no other means of paying them;
(5) where the expenses exceed the income of the property;
(6) where the property is falling into decay; and

16 *Ali Mohammed* v *Ramniwas* AIR 1967 Raj 258.
17 AIR 1966 Mad 468.
18 (1912)39 IA 49 (PC).
19 *Pratap Singh* v *Sant Kumar* AIR 1938 PC 181; *Mohd. Amin* v *Vakil Ahmed* AIR 1952 SC 358; 1952 SCR 1133; 1952 SCJ 539.

(7) where the property has been usurped and the guardian has reason to fear that there was no chance of fair restitution.[20]

In *Sara Banu* v *Asmatulla (died) by his LRs*,[1] the question whether the alienation made by a *de jure* natural guardian of a Muslim minor which was beyond the powers conferred on him by and under the Muslim law is void or voidable came up for consideration before a Bench of the Madras High Court. In that case, the father of a Muslim minor girl alienated her property which was found by the High Court to be beyond his powers as natural guardian under the Muslim law. The question was whether the alienation was void or voidable. The suit for partition and recovery of the property was filed by quondam minor three years after she attained majority but within 12 years from the date of alienation. If the transaction is held voidable, the suit was barred by time under Art. 60 of the Limitation Act and if it was void, the suit was in time. Ibrahim Khalifulla, J speaking for the Bench, dealt at length with the law on the matter and has come to the conclusion that alienation made by the minor's father was against the principles of Muslim law relating to the sale of immovable property of the minor and was void *ab initio*. The suit for partition was found to be in time.

HUSBAND AND WIFE Husband has no implied authority to act on behalf of his wife in the matter of sale of her property. His implied authority does not extend to acts which are outside the ordinary course of business and which are neither necessary nor incidental to his authority. If a sale is beyond such authority, it will not bind the wife.[2] But when a married couple is living together and the husband acts alone in dealing with the joint property, the presumption is that he is acting as the wife's agent in respect of her interest as well as his own, though the presumption is rebuttable.[3]

So, also, a purchase of property by the husband in the name of his wife unexplained by other proved or admitted facts is to be regarded as a benami transaction by which the beneficial interest in the property is in the husband, although the ostensible title is in the wife.[4] Before passing of the Benami Transactions (Prohibition) Act 1988 (now Prohibition of Benami Property Transactions Act 1988), a property purchased by a person in the name of his wife or unmarried daughter, was held to belong to him. The English doctrine of advancement had no application in India. Under the English doctrine, where the purchase is made by a person in the name of his wife or child, the presumption was that the transaction had been made by way

20 Mulla's *Mohammedan Law*, 21st Ed., p. 459; *Imambandi* v *Muthsadi* ILR (1918)45 Cal 878 (PC); (1918)45 IA 73.

1 (2001)2 LW 387.

2 *Phuljhari Devi* v *Mithai Lal* AIR 1971 All 494 at pp. 498-99.

3 *Ma Lon Ma* v *Ma Shwe Byu* (1911)10 Ind Cas 919 (Rang).

4 *Sara Lakshmiah Chetty* v *Kothandrama Pitlai* AIR 1925 PC 181.

of advancement or gifts to the wife or child. Courts in this country consistently held that the doctrine had no application in India and there was no presumption of gift in the case of purchase or transfer in the name of one's wife or child. The burden of providing the advancement or the gift was therefore on the person alleging it.[5] The Prohibition of Benami Property Transactions Act 1988 totally prohibits benami transactions [*vide* s. 3(1)].

CO-OPERATIVE SOCIETY A co-operative society becomes a legal person after it is registered and it is after registration that it acquires the capacity to enter into contracts. Moreover, s. 37 of the Gujarat Co-operative Societies Act 1961 clearly says that after registration it can enter into contracts. The principle of estoppel cannot operate against a person who was non-existent at the date when the transaction took place.[6]

(2) *Consensus* "To consent" is to agree upon the same thing in the same sense (s. 13 of the Contract Act). Therefore where the consent is itself lacking, or the consent leaves something further to be done before the agreement will be complete there is no contract. In order to create a valid contract there must be consensus *ad idem*, i.e. agreement upon the same thing in the same sense.

Section 13 of the Indian Contract Act 1872 defines what is meant by consent and s. 14 of the said Act relates to free consent which is necessary for a valid contract. This principle is based on the following observation in *Smith* v *Hughes*:[7] "It is essential to the creation of a contract that both parties should agree to the same thing in the same sense." If the parties are not *ad idem* on the subject matter about which they are negotiating, there is no real agreement between them.[8] When their minds are directed to different objects or they attach different meanings to the language which they use, there is no agreement. "The cases in which this may occur are the following: (1) When the misunderstanding relates to the identity of the other party to the agreement; (2) When it relates to the nature or terms of the transaction; and (3) When it relates to the subject matter of the agreement." A party may be taken to have assented if he has so conducted himself as to be estopped from denying that he has so assented.[9]

However, it may often be that the parties may realize, after having entered into the agreement or after having signed the contract, that one of the matters which was essential to the agreement, was not understood by them in the same sense and that both of them were carrying totally different

5 *Smt. Parvathy Gangaram Agarwal* v *Firm Jayramdas Bhagat* AIR 1962 Punj 188.
6 *Shri Ramji Mandir Narsinhji* v *Narsinh Nagar Co-operative Housing Society Ltd., Navgari* AIR 1979 Guj 134 at pp. 138, 139 (DB).
7 [1871] LR 6 QB 597 at p. 609.
8 *India Meters Ltd., Madras* v *P.S.E.B.* (1993)1 SCC 230; 1992(2) Scale 372.
9 Halsbury's *Laws of England*, 4th Ed., vol. 9, para 288.

impressions of that matter at the time of entering into the agreement or executing the document. Such realization would have the effect of invalidating the agreement under s. 20 of the Act. On such realization, it can be legitimately said that the agreement was "discovered to be void". The words "discovered to be void", therefore, comprehend a situation in which the parties were suffering from a mistake of fact from the very beginning but had not realized, at the time of entering into the agreement or signing of the document, that they were suffering from any such mistake and had, therefore, acted *bona fide* on such agreement. The agreement in such a case would be void from its inception, though discovered to be so at a much later stage.[10]

Where the parties agree that the agreement will not be final unless reduced to writing, the earlier agreement is merely a provisional agreement. In the event of dispute between the parties the question will have to be determined by ascertaining the true intention of the parties.[11]

Where a document is proposed to be executed by several parties and only some of them execute the document while others do not, the question whether the document is binding on at least those who have executed it, depends upon the intention of the parties, and the intention that the document would not be enforceable even against the executing parties has to be established by the executing parties by showing that they would not have executed the agreement if the other party had not joined in the agreement, or that they did not intend to be bound by the agreement until and unless the others who were proposed to be parties to the agreement joined in the execution.[12]

Factors which vitiate free consent of parties are:

(*a*) "coercion" as defined in s. 15 of the Indian Contract Act;

(*b*) "undue influence" as defined in s. 16 of the Indian Contract Act;

(*c*) "fraud" as defined in s. 17 of the Indian Contract Act;

(*d*) "misrepresentation" as defined in s. 18 of the Indian Contract Act; or

(*e*) "mistake" subject to the provisions of ss. 20, 21 and 22 of the Indian Contract Act.

Section 14 of the Indian Contract Act defines free consent when it is not caused by coercion, or undue influence, or fraud, or misrepresentation,

10 *Tarsem Singh* v *Sukhminder Singh* (1998)3 SCC 471; AIR 1998 SC 1400.

11 *Golab Ray* v *Murlidhar Modi* AIR 1964 Ori 176 relying on *Harichand Mancharam* v *Govind Laxman* AIR 1923 PC 47; *Shankarlal Narayandas Mundade* v *New Mofussil Co. Ltd.* AIR 1946 PC 97.

12 *Viswasam* v *E. Ramachandran Nadar* AIR 1972 Mad 221 at p. 227.

or mistake. Section 19 of the Indian Contract Act provides voidability of agreement without free consent.

(A) Coercion Section 15 of the Indian Contract Act 1872 defines coercion as committing or threatening to commit, any act forbidden by the Indian Penal Code 1860 or the unlawful detaining or threatening to detain, any property, to the prejudice of any person whatever, with the intention of causing any persons to enter into an agreement. In *Andhra Sugars Ltd.* v *State of A.P.*[13] it has been held that the compulsion of law is not coercion as defined in s. 15 of the Indian Contract Act 1872.

(B) Undue influence A transaction may be vitiated on account of undue influence where the relations between the parties are such that one of them is in a position to dominate the will of the other and he uses his position to obtain an unfair advantage over the other. It manifests that two conditions are ordinarily established by the person seeking to avoid the transaction. He has to prove (1) that the other party to a transaction was in a position to dominate his will; and (2) that the other party had obtained an unfair advantage by using that position.

Sub-section (2) of s. 16 of the Indian Contract Act lays down a special presumption that a person is deemed to be in a position to dominate the will of another (*i*) where he holds a real or apparent authority over the other, or (*ii*) where he stands in a fiduciary relation to the other, or (*iii*) where he enters into a contract with a person whose mental capacity is temporarily or permanently affected by reason of age, illness or mental or bodily distress.

Sub-section (3) of s. 16 has manifestly a limited application. The presumption will arise if it is established by evidence that the party who had obtained the benefit of a transaction was in a position to dominate the will of the other and that the transaction is shown to be unconscionable. If either of these two conditions is not fulfilled, the presumption of undue influence will not arise and the burden will not shift.[14] The law in India as to undue influence as embodied in s. 16 of the Indian Contract Act is based on the English Common Law.[15] According to Halsbury's *Laws of England*,[16] "where there is no relationship shown to exist from which undue influence is presumed, that influence must be proved". There is no presumption of undue influence in the case of a gift to a son, grandson, or son-in-law, although made during the donor's illness and a few days before his death.[17]

13 AIR 1968 SC 599.
14 *Ladli Parshad Jaiswal* v *Karnal Distillery Co. Ltd.* AIR 1963 SC 1279.
15 *Subhas Chandra Das Mushib* v *Ganga Prasad Das Mushib* (1967)1 SCR 331; AIR 1967 SC 878.
16 3rd Ed., vol. 17, p. 673.
17 Halsbury's *Laws of England*, 3rd Ed., vol. 17, p. 679.

Thus, the relation of solicitor and client, trustee and *cestui que* trust, spiritual adviser and devotee, medical attendant and patient, parent and child are those in which such a presumption arises. Section 16(2) of the Contract Act states that such a situation can arise wherever the donee stands in a fiduciary relationship to the donor or holds a real or apparent authority over him.[18] Sub-section (3) contains a rule of evidence.[19]

Undue influence requires to be separately pleaded with specificity, particularity and with precision. A general allegation in the plaint that the plaintiff is a simple old man of ninety who reposed great confidence in the dependent is wholly insufficient to amount to an averment of undue influence.[20] Merely because the parties are nearly related to each other or merely because the donor was old or of weak character, no presumption of undue influence can arise.[21] Thus, inference or possibility of undue influence must be proved with sufficient materials and attending circumstances.[1]

(C) Undue influence and coercion In cases of fraud, undue influence and coercion, the parties pleading it must set forth full particulars and the case can only be decided on the particulars as laid. There can be no departure from them in evidence. General allegations are insufficient even to amount to an averment of fraud of which any court ought to take notice however strong the language in which they are couched may be, and the same applies to undue influence and coercion. There is no presumption of imposition merely because a donor is old and weak. Mere close relation also is insufficient to presume undue influence.[2]

(D) Fraud A fraud is an act of deliberate deception with the design of securing something by taking unfair advantage of another. It is a deception in order to gain by another's loss. It is a cheating intended to get an advantage.[3] A fraudster has been likened to Milton's sorcerer, Comus, who exulted in his ability to, '*wing me into the easy-hearted man and trap him into snares*'. Fraud is proved when it is shown that a false representation has been made (*i*) knowingly, or (*ii*) without belief in its truth, or (*iii*) recklessly, careless whether it be true or false.[4] Thus, fraud has a wider meaning. A decree may be set aside on the ground of fraud. Fraud is classified under

18 *Subhas Chandra Das Mushib* v *Ganga Prasad Das Mushib* (1967)1 SCR 331; AIR 1967 SC 878.
19 *Afsar Sheikh* v *Soleman Bibi* (1976)2 SCC 142; AIR 1976 SC 163.
20 *Ibid.*
21 *M. Rangasamy* v *Rengammal* AIR 2003 SC 3120.
1 *D.N. Jeevaraj* v *State of Karnataka* (2016)2 SCC 653.
2 *Raja Ram* v *Jai Prakash Singh* (2019)8 SCC 701.
3 *S.P. Chengalvaraya Naidu* v *Jagannath* (1994)1 SCC 1; AIR 1994 SC 853.
4 *Derry* v *Peek* [1886-90] All ER Rep 1; [1889]14 AC 337 (HL).

five heads in a leading case.[5] The intention to deceive is not necessarily an intention to injure or to cheat.[6] When it is proved that the statement is false, it must be further shown that the plaintiff has acted upon it and has sustained damage by so doing.[7] If facts proved fraud the question of fraudulent intention or motive is immaterial. In action for fraud not only should fraud be established that this fraud was the inducing cause of the contract for misrepresentations which do not deceive, do not amount to fraud. The plaintiff must prove that the contract was induced by fraud and the plaintiff was damnified. Fraud without damage or damage without fraud, gives no cause of action, but when these two concur an action lies.[8] The following are the ingredients of fraud as contemplated by s. 17 of the Act: (*a*) There should be a suggestion as to a fact. (*b*) The fact suggested should not be true. (*c*) The suggestion should have been made by a person who does not believe it to be true. (*d*) The suggestion should be found to have been made with intent either to deceive or to induce the other party to enter into, that is the contract in question.[9] Fraud, which vitiates the contract, must have a nexus with the acts of the parties prior to entering into the contract. Subsequent breach of contract on the part of a party would not vitiate the contract itself.[10] Fraud like any other charge of criminal offence whether made in civil or criminal proceedings must be established beyond reasonable doubt. A finding as to the fraud cannot be based on suspicion and conjecture.[11] Fraud vitiates every solemn act. Fraud and justice never dwell together.[12]

DOCTRINE OF NON EST FACTUM This doctrine postulates that a person who is induced by the false statement of another, and who has signed a written contract that is fundamentally different in character from the one which he envisaged, then such a person is competent to say that it is not his document.[13] The doctrine was evolved to help the people who were blind and illiterate from the consequences of the contract which they had entered but were unable to read its stipulations due to their natural infirmities or the content of the contract was not fully explained to them. The doctrine had its genesis in English law. The leading case on the point was *Thoroughgood* v *Cole*.[14] The case was before the Court of Common Pleas.

5 *Chesterfield* v *Janssen* 26 ER 191.
6 *United Motor Finance Co.* v *Addison* AIR 1939 PC 21.
7 *Hansraj Gupta* v *DET Co.* AIR 1940 PC 98.
8 *Smith* v *Cladwick* [1884]9 AC 187; [1881-85] All ER Rep 242.
9 *R.C. Thakkar* v *Gujarat Housing Board* AIR 1973 Guj 34.
10 *Reliance Salt Ltd.* v *Cosmos Enterprises* (2006)13 SCC 599.
11 *Senenska Handels' Banken* v *Indian Charge Chrome* (1994)1 SCC 502; AIR 1994 SC 646.
12 *State of A.P.* v *T. Suryachandra Rao* (2005)6 SCC 149.
13 *Harmesh Kumar* v *Maya Bai* AIR 2006 P&H 1.
14 [1584]2 Co Rep 9a; 76 ER 408 (KB).

In that case one William Chicken was in arrear of the rent. He preferred to Mr. Thoroughgood, the landlord a deed by which he was relieved from 'all demands whatsoever' which Mr. Thoroughgood had against him. Obviously, the exclusion comprised not only arrears of rent, but also the right to recover the land. Thoroughgood was illiterate, but a bystander picked up the deed and explained "that you do release to William Chicken all the arrears of rent that he doth owe you and no otherwise, and thus you shall have your land back again." Thoroughgood signed the deed, after replying. "If it be no otherwise, I am content". Subsequently, Mr. Chicken sold the land to an innocent purchaser. Mr. Thoroughgood sued in trespass and recovered his land. It was held by the Court of Common Pleas that the defendant was a layman and illiterate and that he had been defrauded of a misrepresented recital of the contents of the deed. The rule so laid down was further expounded by Biles, J in *Foster* v *Mackinnon*[15] in the following words:

> "...if a blind man, or a man who cannot read, or who for some reason (now implying negligence) forbears to read, has a written contract falsely read over to him, the reader misreading to such a degree that the written contract is of nature altogether different from the contract pretended to be read from the paper which has blind or illiterate man afterwards signs; then, at least if there be in negligence, the signature so obtained is of no force. And it is invalid not merely on the ground of fraud, where fraud exists, *but on the ground that the mind of the signer did not accompany the signatures; in other words, that he never intended to sign, and therefore, in contemplation of law never did sign, the contract to which his name is appended........ He was deceived, not merely as to the legal effect, but as to the actual contents of the instrument."* (Emphasis supplied)

In India, the rule was followed in *Sanni Bibi* v *Munshi Siddik Hossain*.[16] In the said case, plaintiffs asked for cancellation of a sale-deed of land on the ground that they had signed it on the representation that it was *jimba nama* for their maintenance for a term of three years. Following the rule laid down in *Thoroughgood*'s case, it was held that the document was *void ab initio*, as there was no consent at all to the sale deed. The Supreme Court in *Smt. Bismillah* v *Janeshwar Prasad*,[17] explained that the application of the doctrine was not limited to cases of illiteracy or physical infirmities but it was extended much beyond. The court observed as under:

> "The common law defence of *non est factum* to actions on specialties in its origin was available where an illiterate person to whom the contents of a deed had been wrongly read executed it under a mistake as to its nature

15 [1869] LR 4 CP 704.
16 AIR 1919 Cal 728.
17 (1990)1 SCC 207; AIR 1990 SC 540.

and contents, he could say that it was not his deed at all. In its modern application, the doctrine has been extended to cases other than those of illiteracy and to other contracts in writing. In most of the cases in which this defence was pleaded the mistake was induced by fraud; but that was not perhaps, a necessary factor, as the transaction is "invalid not merely on the ground of fraud, where fraud exists, but on the ground that the mind of the signor did not accompany the signature; in other words, that he never intended to sign, and therefore, in contemplation of law never did sign, the contract to which his name is appended".

However, the limitation of the doctrine in modern times has been underlined by the House of Lords in *Saunders* v *Anglia Building Society.*[18] It was held that the plea of *non est factum* could not be available to anyone who signed without taking the trouble to find out at least the general effect of the document. Nor could it be available to a person whose mistake was really a mistake as to the legal effect of the document. There must be a radical or fundamental difference between what he signed and what he thought he was signing. Commenting on *Saunders*, *Chitty*,[19] however, observed that the defence of *non est factum* was not lightly to be allowed where a person of full age and capacity had signed a written document embodying contractual terms. In exceptional circumstances the plea was available so long as the person signing the document had made a fundamental mistake as to the character or effect of the document. It was further observed that their Lordships appeared to have concentrated on the disparity between the effect of the document actually signed, and the document as it was believed to be (rather than on the nature of the mistake) stressing that the disparity must be "redical", "essential", "fundamental", or "very substantial". It is, therefore, submitted that the doctrine has its own limitation. The 'distinction-test' based on the character of the document and the contents of the document did not find favour in all cases. Practically speaking, the true test may be based on resolving the issue from case to case basis having regard to its factual setting and without giving any dogmatic attachment to any fixed principle of universal application.

(E) MISREPRESENTATION Where a person makes a positive assertion relying upon the statement of another that a certain third party would become a director, he is not warranted in making that assertion.[20] A representation may be untruthful by reason of suppression and concealment of truth, not untruthful in the sense of direct falsehood, but untruthful because it is intended to convey to the public an impression different from the reality, because it is known by the person who conveys it, or ought to be known by

18 [1971] AC 1004; [1970]3 All ER 961.
19 *Contracts (General Principles)*, 25th Ed., p. 194.
20 *Niaz* v *Parsottam* 29 ALJ 153.

him, to be materially different from that which was the real state of the case.[1] Sub-section (2) of s. 18 of the Indian Contract Act is intended to meet all those cases of "constructive fraud" where the circumstances are such as to make the party who derives a benefit from the transaction equally answerable in effect as if he had been actuated by motives of fraud.[2] Falsehood vitiates a transaction, it is no defence to say that the same thing might have resulted if the truth had been known. The injury must be the immediate and not the remote consequence of the representation.[3]

According to sub-sec. (3) of s. 18 of the Indian Contract Act a party is entitled to rescind a contract to which he is induced to enter by fraudulent representation regarding the thing bargained for. But where there is innocent misrepresentation or misapprehension, it does not authorise a rescission unless it is such as to show that there is a complete difference in substance between what was supposed to be and what was taken, so as to constitute a failure of consideration.[4] Where a deed is executed by a party is alleged by him to be vitiated by misrepresentation, the onus is upon that party to establish the plea of misrepresentation.[5] Statement about the existing state of the law innocently made cannot constitute misrepresentation if it is later found that the statement was erroneous.[6] A vague promise included in salary structure in the employment agreement does not amount to misrepresentation.[7]

(F) MISTAKE A contract is not voidable where the mistake is not mutual, but only one of the parties labours under mistake as to matter of fact.[8] A unilateral mistake could, in the absence of fraud, only afford ground for rescission if the mistake was induced by some innocent misrepresentation made by or on behalf of a party or by some misleading conduct on his party.[9]

(I) *MUTUAL MISTAKE* A mutual mistake on a matter of fact which is essential to the agreement, would make the agreement void. There may be some defect that is unknown to both the parties whereby the contract is so fundamentally affected that there is good ground for holding the contract void because of mutual mistake of fact.[10] Section 20 of the Contract Act

1 *Nokhia* v *State of H.P.* AIR 1985 HP 88.
2 *Oriental Bank Corporation* v *John Fleming* ILR (1879)3 Bom 242.
3 Chitty on *Contracts,* 30th Ed., vol. 1, paras 27-054–27-055.
4 *Bell* v *Lever Brothers Ltd.* [1931]1 KB 557; [1931] All ER Rep 1.
5 *Kuppuswami Chettiar* v *ASPA Arumugam Chettiar* AIR 1967 SC 1395.
6 *Ganga Retreat & Towers Ltd.* v *State of Rajasthan* (2003)12 SCC 91.
7 *Gayatri Balaswamy* v *ISG Novasoft Technologies Ltd.* (2014)6 CTC 602.
8 *Hazi Abdul Rahman Allarakhia* v *Bombay & Persia Steam Navigation Co.* ILR (1892)16 Bom 561.
9 *Hasham* v *Zenab* [1960] AC 316; *Riverlata Properties Ltd.* v *Paul* [1974]2 All ER 657 (CA); [1975] Ch 133.
10 *Nursing Dass Kothari* v *Chutto Lal Misser* ILR (1923)50 Cal 615.

is enacted on the said principle. It provides that an agreement would be void if both the parties to the agreement were under a mistake as to a matter of fact essential to the agreement. The mistake has to be mutual and in order that the agreement be treated as void, both the parties must be shown to be suffering from mistake of fact. Unilateral mistake is outside the scope of this section.[11]

(II) *MISTAKE DUE TO IGNORANCE OF PARTY* A person cannot plead a mistake when his ignorance of facts is due to his own negligence. In such a case he is treated as if he had the knowledge.[12]

(III) *COMMON MISTAKE* A common mistake is there where both the parties are mistaken about the same vital fact although both parties are *ad idem*, e.g. the subject matter of the contract has already perished. A common mistake is made or shared alike by both, where mutual mistake made or entertained by each of the person towards or with regard to each other.[13]

(IV) *TEST TO DETERMINE FUNDAMENTAL MISTAKE* The test for determining fundamental mistake is that both parties would give the same answer to the question "what are you contracting about"? If they would give different answers, the mistake whatever else its effect may be, will not nullify consent.[14] Unlike the case of common mistake the question of consent is directly involved in case of fundamental mistake.

(V) *MISTAKE BY ONE PARTY* A contract cannot be avoided by the purchaser when he has knowledge of the defect in title or when ignorance of the defect has not been established by evidence.[15] The mistake of one party, therefore, inducing him to enter into a contract is of no consequence if the other party is not implicated in the mistake. Where a plaintiff alleged that he had paid in excess of what was due under a contract of purchase and asked for refund of the excess under s. 20 of the Indian Contract Act he could have the contract avoided on the ground of mutual mistake or under s. 31 of the Specific Relief Act, he could apply to have the instrument rectified.[16]

(VI) *MISUNDERSTANDING OF TERMS* A contract based on misunderstanding of its terms is not enforceable between the parties. Where the memorandum upon an insurance policy was framed under a mistake, and not in accordance with the terms verbally agreed upon, there could be no agreement, the premium paid must be refunded.[17] Where it is agreed that a building

11 *Tarsem Singh* v *Sukhminder Singh* (1998)3 SCC 471.
12 *Tamplin* v *James* [1880]15 Ch D 215.
13 *I.T.C. Ltd.* v *George Joseph Fernandes* (1989)2 SCC 1; AIR 1989 SC 839.
14 Treitel, *Law of Contract*, 11th Ed., p. 298; see Anson's *Law of Contract*, 29th Ed., pp. 288-289.
15 *Secretary of State for India* v *Dewan Bahadur Yellapeddi* AIR 1925 Mad 859.
16 *U. Shwe Thaung* v *Kyaw* AIR 1930 Rang 12.
17 *Fowler* v *Scottish Society* 28 LJ Ch 684.

contractor will be paid on his bills being certified by an architect and the contractor submits the bill so certified, the employer can impeach it only on the ground of fraud or collusion, it cannot be impeached for mere negligence or mistake for which the employer may have remedy against the architect, but the contractor is bound to be paid.[18]

(VII) *MISTAKE AS TO LAW IN INDIA* A mistake as to law in India resulting in the payment by one person to another, and making an inequitable that the payee should retain the money, is no ground for relief. Where a mortgagee took a mortgage with a full knowledge of a prior unregistered mortgage under a mistaken impression that on registration his mortgage would have priority, the contract was not voidable as it was caused by mistake as to law in force in British India.[19] An error of law, therefore, does not vitiate contract, much less will it annul a conveyance after many years.[20] Where parties at the time when they entered into an agreement believed that a certain kind of lease carried with it mineral rights, but the Privy Council in two subsequent decisions threw grave doubts on the title of the lessee to the mineral rights, the mistake having been discovered, it was held that the agreement could not stand.[1]

(VIII) *RELIEF AGAINST MISTAKE OF LAW* It has been said that the court has power to grant relief against mistakes in law if it be satisfied that the consent of a party has been induced by those mistakes.[2] But a compromise in a family agreement entered into, in which all the parties acted under the advice of a professional man cannot be set aside at the instance of one of the parties, because he was ignorant of his rights, in the absence of fraud or explanation to the parties of what their rights were, or unless the matter involved a question of foreign law.[3] What would be the remedy if someone has paid money under a mistake of law? Summarizing the position in English Law, it was said that as a general rule, it is well established in equity as well as at law, that money paid under a mistake of law, with full knowledge of the facts, is not recoverable, and that even a promise to pay, upon a supposed liability, and in ignorance of the law, will bind the party.[4] In India, the relief is provided under s. 72 of the Contract Act 1872. It provides that a person to whom money has been paid, or anything delivered, by mistake or under coercion, must repay or return it. In this connection, it has been observed by the Supreme Court that the word 'mistake' used under s. 72 of the

18 *Alimahomed Rahimtullah* v *Pandurang Laxman* 18 Bom LR 156; 33 Ind Cas 701.
19 *Jawand* v *Sawan* AIR 1933 Lah 836.
20 *Vishnu Sakharam Phatak* v *Kashinath Bapu Shankar* ILR (1886)11 Bom 174.
1 *Ram* v *Ganesh* 21 CWN 404.
2 *Jagadish Prosad Pannalal* v *Produce Exchange Corpn.* AIR 1946 Cal 245.
3 *Stewart* v *Stewart* 6 Cl & F 911; In re, *Roberts* [1905]1 Ch 704.
4 *STO* v *Kanhaiya Lal Makund Lal Saraf* AIR 1959 SC 135; Kerr on *Fraud and Mistake*, 7th Ed., p. 140.

Contract Act is not in limited sense, rather it refers to both the mistake of law and the mistake of fact. The principle enunciated is that if one party under a mistake, whether of fact or law, pays to another party money which is not due by contract or otherwise that money must be repaid. The mistake lies in thinking that the money paid was due when in fact it was not due and that mistake, if established, entitles the party paying the money to recover it back from the party receiving the same.[5] Further, a contract is not voidable because it was caused by a mistake as to any law in force in India.[6] The contract would not be void also on the ground that it was made under mistake of law.[7] It needs mention that 'mistake of law' would also cover 'mistake of bye-laws'.[8] Thus, if any benefit is derived upon mistaken application of law the party cannot be allowed to be unjustly enriched and in that case the party who has been affected must be restituted.[9]

(3) *Consideration and object* An agreement without consideration is void unless (1) it is in writing and registered and is made on account of natural love and affection between the parties standing in a near relation to each other; or (2) it is a promise to compensate wholly or in part a person who has already voluntarily done something for the promissor or something which the promissor was legally compelled to do; or (3) it is a promise made in writing signed by the person charged therewith or his agent to pay wholly or in part debts barred by time. Where a contract for sale does not contain any stipulation fixing the amount of consideration, the contract is void and is not enforceable in law. It is a mere *nudum pactum.* If the consideration is not fixed for the agreement, it will only amount to an agreement to agree and is not a binding contract.[10] It is well settled that inadequacy of consideration is not a ground to affect a contract. But inadequacy of consideration may be taken into account by the court in determining the question whether the consent of the promissor was freely given. It may also be pointed out that under the Indian Law, unlike English Law, past consideration is valid and consideration need not move from promisee himself. Even a stranger to the consideration can sue upon the contract in India.

For the validity of the contract, the consideration and object should be lawful. The consideration and object of an agreement are not lawful if:

(*a*) it is forbidden by law; or

5 *STO* v *Kanhaiya Lal Makund Lal Saraf* 1959 SCR 1350; AIR 1959 SC 135.
6 Section 21 of the Contract Act 1872; *Ganga Retreat & Towers Ltd.* v *State of Rajasthan* (2003)12 SCC 91.
7 *Kalyanpur Lime Works Ltd.* v *State of Bihar* 1954 SCR 958; AIR 1954 SC 165.
8 *Ganga Retreat & Towers Ltd.* v *State of Rajasthan* (2003)12 SCC 91.
9 *Harendra Nath Ghose* v *Union of India* (2007)3 CHN 34.
10 *Rabindranath Sahu* v *Maya Devi* AIR 1991 Pat 192.

(*b*) is of such nature that if permitted it would defeat the provisions of any law; or

(*c*) is fraudulent; or

(*d*) involves or implies injury to the person or property of another; or

(*e*) the court regards it as immoral or opposed to public policy.

FORBIDDEN BY LAW Article 299 of the Constitution lays down that all contracts made in the exercise of the executive power of the Union or of a State shall be expressed to be made by the President or by the Governor of the State, as the case may be, and all such contracts and all assurances of property made in the exercise of that power shall be executed on behalf of the President or the Governor by such persons and in such manner as he may direct or authorize. A contract not in compliance with Art. 299 is not specifically enforceable.[11] In *U.P. Rajkya Nirman Nigam Ltd.* v *Indure Pvt. Ltd.*,[12] it was held that a contract between a public undertaking and third parties should be approved and signed on behalf of the undertaking or the Government with its seal by an authorised or competent officer and the doctrine of "indoor management"cannot be extended to such a contract.

CALCULATED TO DEFEAT THE PROVISIONS OF ANY LAW In *B.P. Samiyapan* v *Arunthavaselvan,*[13] it was held that an agreement for sale in violation of the provisions of s. 23 of the Tamil Nadu Land Reforms (Fixation of Ceiling on Land) Act 1961 was void in law. In *Shoba Viswanatha* v *D.P. Kingsley,*[14] the agreement for sale was executed by the defendant who was not a citizen of India and the sale had therefore to be approved by the Reserve Bank of India under the Foreign Exchange Regulation Act 1973 (now the Foreign Exchange Management Act). It was held that if specific performance was permitted it would defeat the provisions of the law and was not enforceable. In *P. Gopirathnam* v *Feerodous Estate Pvt. Ltd.*[15] the Full Bench of the High Court of Madras had to deal with an agreement for sale which was in violation of s. 6 of the Tamil Nadu Urban Land (Ceiling and Regulation) Act 1978 which prohibits not only a completed transfer but also a proposed transfer. The suit for specific performance was therefore dismissed. It may however be pointed out that the Tamil Nadu Urban Land (Ceiling and Regulation) Act 1978 has since been repealed. However, in *Neminath Appayya Hanamananavar* v *Jamboo Rao Satappa Kocheri,*[16] the suit for

11 *Sohan Lal* v *Union of India* AIR 1991 SC 955; (1991)1 SCC 438; JT 1991(5) SC 102; *State of Haryana* v *Lal Chand* AIR 1984 SC 1326; (1984)3 SCR 715; (1984)3 SCC 634; *State of Punjab* v *Om Prakash* AIR 1988 SC 2149; 1988 (Supp) SCC 722; JT 1988(3) SC 616.

12 AIR 1996 SC 1373; (1996)2 SCC 667; JT 1996(2) SC 322.

13 (1994)1 LW 399; (1994)1 MLJ 146.

14 (1996)1 LW 721; (1996)1 CTC 620.

15 (1999)3 LW 249 (FB).

16 AIR 1966 Mys 154.

specific performance was resisted by the defendant on the ground that if the contract was enforced it would result in the plaintiff holding land in excess of the ceiling prescribed under the Bombay Tenancy and Agricultural Lands Act 1948 and so void. The contention was rejected by the High Court and on appeal, the Supreme Court confirmed the judgment of the High Court holding that s. 5 of the Bombay Tenancy and Agricultural Lands Act did not prohibit transfer of land from one agriculturist to another.

In *Nahar Singh* v *Harnak Singh*,[17] the trial court decreed the suit for specific performance of an agreement for sale of immovable property. The first Appellate Court found that the agreement was entered into to save stamp duty and registration fee and was therefore opposed to public policy and the relief of specific performance could not be claimed. In the Second Appeal, the High Court concurred with the view of the first Appellate Court and dismissed the Second Appeal. In the SLP moved before the Supreme Court, the learned Judges refused to interfere with the decision of the lower Appellate Court which has been confirmed by the High Court in Second Appeal in exercise of the power under Art. 136 of the Constitution.

A decree for specific performance cannot be refused on the ground that low value of the property was shown in the document to avoid stamp duty and income tax and it was for the authorities under the relevant Acts to take action if there was any violation of the relevant provisions.[18] This view is in conflict with the view expressed by the Supreme Court.[19]

The land in dispute belonged to the Government and was assigned to the first defendant. Section 3 of the Kerala Government Land Assignment Act 1960 authorised the Government to prescribe conditions and limitations when assignments were made. Under r. 8(1) of the Land Assignment Rules, the assigned lands are hereditary and alienable. But r. 8(1A) provides that unoccupied lands assigned on registry shall not be alienable for a period of three years from the date of registry. The agreement to sell in this case was within the period of three years and it was contended that the agreement was one forbidden by law and was void. Repelling the contention, the Kerala High Court held that when the assignment was made the land was not unoccupied and hence the bar did not apply. The contract for sale was held valid and enforceable.[20]

When the legal bar to transfer on the date of decree of specific performance is lifted statutorily the contract does not suffer from vice of hitting s. 23 of the Contract Act and such a contract becomes enforceable.

17 (1996)6 SCC 699; JT 1996(9) SC 701; (1996)8 Supreme 17.

18 *John Thomas* v *Joseph Thomas* AIR 2000 Ker 408; *Anup Krishna Kaul* v *Jagdish Swaroop Agarwal* AIR 2004 Raj 185.

19 *Nahar Singh* v *Harnak Singh* (1996)6 SCC 699; JT 1996(9) SC 701; (1996)8 Supreme 17.

20 *Krishnan Kesavan* v *Kochukunju Karunakaran* AIR 1988 Ker 107.

In a Supreme Court case the disputed house was mortgaged by the predecessors of the debtor. The debtor filed an application under s. 4 of the UP Encumbered Estates Act 1934 to the Collector who transmitted the same to the special judge under s. 6 of the said Act. Subsequently the debtor submitted an application to the Collector that the disputed house may not be sold in the proceedings under the Act and may be exempted as provided in s. 24 of the said Act. The Collector in exercise of powers under s. 24 of the Act exempted the disputed house from sale in the proceedings under the Act and thereafter the agreement for sale of the house in dispute, was entered into. Subsequently the debtor again wanted the house to be included in the property for sale in the proceedings under the Act to which the purchaser objected and this objection was disposed of by the Collector by his order dated 23.6.1961 reiterating the position that by order dated 26.3.1943 this house has been exempted from the proceedings under this Act and therefore that order cannot be reopened. The order dated 23.6.1961 also refers to an order dated 14.6.1945 wherein permission to sell his house which was sought by the debtor under s. 7 of the said Act, was rejected by the Deputy Commissioner. The mortgage which was executed by predecessors of the debtor was also considered as a claim under s. 14 of the Act and ultimately a decree was passed in favour of the mortgage by the special judge under the Act. The purchaser pressed the debtor for execution of the sale deed in pursuance of the contract and ultimately filed a suit for specific performance of the contract for sale. It was held by the apex court that with the passing of the order under s. 24 of the U.P. Encumbered Estates Act 1934 the mortgage in existence before the proceedings ceased to be effective and this entails the property being sold in pursuance of the suit for specific performance of the contract.[1] Where the contract for sale stood frustrated on account of refusal of permission by the Ceiling Authority, the subsequent repeal of the Urban Land (Ceiling and Regulation) Act 1976 pending appeal removed the hurdle and specific performance could be ordered. However, it was held that in view of the sharp escalation of prices, the plaintiff was not entitled to specific performance and the earnest money of ₹41,670 was ordered to be refunded to the plaintiff with interest at 12% and damages in the sum of ₹20,000.[2]

FRAUDULENT Section 19 of the Indian Contract Act 1872 relates to voidability of agreements without free consent. Exception to s. 19 provides that if consent was caused by misrepresentation or by silence, fraudulent within the meaning of s. 17, the contract, nevertheless, is not voidable, if the party whose consent was so caused had the means discovering the truth with ordinary diligence. Section 17 of the said Act defines fraud which includes

1 *Gaya Prasad* v *Surendra Bahadur Singh* AIR 1987 SC 925; (1987)2 SCC 383; (1987)2 UJ (SC) 89.

2 *Raghuvir Singh Bhatty* v *Ram Chandra Waman Subhedar* AIR 2002 All 13.

commission of acts by a party to a contract or with his conivance or by his agent with intent to deceive another party. The act of fraudulence is to be found in the transactions which are not all dishonest in the nature, but only such as the law will not allow.[3] Where *A* agrees to pay ₹1,000 to *B* on condition to taking ostensible transfer of *A*'s entire immovable property with a view to delaying or defeating *A*'s creditors the consideration was held to be fraudulent and the contract is void. See also *illustrations* (*e*) and (*g*) under s. 23 of the Indian Contract Act.

INJURY TO THE PERSON OR PROPERTY OF ANOTHER An agreement to pay a sum to another in consideration of the latter causing hurt to a third person is not valid in law as it will involve injury to the person or property of another.

IMMORAL OR OPPOSED TO PUBLIC POLICY Where *A* agrees to let her daughter to *B* on hire for concubinage, the agreement is void because it is immoral [*Illustration* (*k*) to s. 23 of the Contract Act]. There is a difference of opinion as to whether it is immoral to remunerate a woman for her past services as a concubine.

An agreement opposed to public policy is void in law. The expression "public policy" is incapable of precise definition and no court has attempted to indulge in this futile exercise. Public policy never remains static in any community and it may vary from time to time. It is "a principle of judicial legislation or interpretation founded on the current needs of the community".[4] Public policy or policy of the law is an illusive concept; it has been prescribed as "untrustworthy guide", "variable quality", "uncertain one", or "unruly horse".[5] An agreement in restraint of marriage is void as opposed public policy. Any agreement for sale in violation of the provisions of the statutes such as the Foreign Exchange Regulation Act 1973 (now the Foreign Exchange Management Act 1999), the Tamil Nadu Land Reforms (Fixation of Ceiling on Land) Act 1961 and the Tamil Nadu Urban Land (Ceiling and Regulation) Act 1978, has been held to be against public policy.[6]

PUBLIC POLICY The term 'public policy'[7] is not capable of a precise definition and whatever tends to injustice of operation, restraint of liberty, commerce

3 *Dr. Vimila* v *Delhi Administration* AIR 1963 SC 1572; *Haycraft* v *Creasy* [1801]2 East 92.

4 *Muralidhar Aggarwal* v *State of U.P.* AIR 1974 SC 1924; (1975)1 SCR 575; (1974)2 SCC 472.

5 *Gherulal Parakh* v *Mahadeodas Maiya* AIR 1959 SC 781; 1959 Supp (2) SCR 406.

6 *B.P. Samiappan (died)* v *Arunthavaselvam* (1994)1 LW 399; *Shoba Viswanathan* v *Kingley* (1996)1 LW 721; *P. Gopiratnam* v *Feerodous Estate (P) Ltd.* (1999)3 LW 249 (FB).

7 The words "public policy" or "opposed to public policy", *inter alia*, find reference in s. 23 of the Contract Act, s. 7(1)(*b*)(*ii*) of the Foreign Awards (Recognition and Enforcement) Act 1961, s. 3(1) of the U.P. (Temporary) Control of Rent and Evictions Act 1947 and s. 34(2)(*b*)(*ii*) of the Arbitration and Conciliation Act 1996.

and natural or legal rights; whatever tends to the obstruction of justice or to the violation of a statute and whatever is against good morals can be said to be against public policy.[8] It does not remain static in any given community and varies from generation to generation. Judges, as trusted interpreters of the law, have to interpret it. While doing so, precedents will also guide them to a substantial extent.[9] Variability lies at the heart of the concept. According to Professor Winfield,[10]

> Public policy is necessarily variable. It may be variable not only from one century to another, not only from one generation to another but even in the same generation..... This variability of public policy is a stone in the edifice of the doctrine and not a missile to be flung at it. Public policy would be almost useless without it.

It has been described as "untrustworthy guide", "unruly horse" etc. This "unruly horse" of public policy has influenced English law.[11] The history of the concept shows that there were some judges who managed this "unruly or unmanageable judges". Lord Denning was one such judge. He observed:[12]

> "With a good man in the saddle, the unruly horse can be kept in control. It can take jump over obstacles."

But, the question remains as to what is 'public policy' or part of it and what is not. The bird's eye view of 'public policy', its magnitude and complexity is narrated in *Words and Phrases*.[13] It is stated as under:

> "'Public policy' imports something that is uncertain and fluctuating, varying with the changing economic needs, social customs, and moral aspirations, of the people.[14]
>
> 'Public policy' is in its nature so uncertain and fluctuating, varying with the habits and fashions of the day, with the growth of commerce and the usages of trade, that it is difficult to determine its limits with any degree of exactness. It has never been defined by the courts, but has been let loose and free from definition in the same manner as fraud.[15]
>
> 'Public policy' is a term that is not always easy to define and it may vary as the habits, opinions and welfare of a people may vary, and what

8 *P. Rathinam* v *Union of India* (1994)3 SCC 394; AIR 1994 SC 1844.

9 *Indian Financial Assocn. of Seventh Day Adventists* v *M.A. Unneerikutty* (2006)6 SCC 351.

10 P.H. Winfield, *Public Policy in the English Common Law*, 42 Harvard Law Review 76 (November 1928).

11 For details as to how the concept of "public policy" has influenced English law, see, W. Friedman, *Legal Theory*, 5th Ed., p. 479.

12 *Enderby Town Football Club Ltd.* v *Football Association Ltd.* [1971] Ch 591, 606.

13 Permanent Ed., vol. 35, 1963, pp. 455 and 456.

14 *Barwin* v *Reidy* 307 P 2d 175 (181); 62 NM 183.

15 *Pendeleton* v *Greever* 17 ALR 317.

may be the public policy of one State or country may not be so in another."[16]

Thus, according to Chitty,[17] objects which on grounds of public policy invalidate contract may, for convenience, be generally classified into five groups:

first, objects which are illegal by common law or by legislation;

secondly, objects injurious to good government either in the field of domestic or foreign affairs;

thirdly, objects which interfere with the proper working of the machinery of justice;

fourthly, objects injurious to marriage and morality; and,

fifthly, objects economically against the public interest.

This classification is adopted primarily for ease of exposition. Certain cases do not fit clearly into any of these five categories.

Commenting upon "public policy", Cheshire, Fifoot & Furmston have made the following observation in their *Law of Contract*:[18]

> Assuming, then, that contracts vitiated by some improper element must be divided into two classes, how are the more serious examples of 'illegality' at common law to be distinguished from the less serious? Which of the contracts that have been frowned upon by the courts are so patently reprehensible — so obviously contrary to public policy — that they must be peremptorily styled illegal? Judicial authority is lacking, but it is submitted that the epithet 'illegal' may aptly and correctly be applied to the following six types of contract:
>
> - A contract to commit a crime, a tort or a fraud on a third party.
> - A contract that is sexually immoral.
> - A contract to the prejudice of the public safety.
> - A contract prejudicial to the administration of justice.
> - A contract that tends to corruption in public life.
> - A contract to defraud the revenue.
>
> There remain three types of contract which offend 'public policy', but which are inexpedient rather than unprincipled:
>
> - A contract to oust the jurisdiction of the court.
> - A contract that tends to prejudice the status of marriage.
> - A contract in restraint of trade.

16 *Franklin Fire Ins. Co.* v *Moll* 58 NE 2nd 947, 950, 951; 115 Ind App 289.
17 Chitty on *Contracts*, 28th Ed., vol. 1, p. 838.
18 14th Ed., p. 407.

In India, s. 23 of the Contract Act uses the term 'public policy'. Though the expression 'public policy' has not been defined by the Indian Contract Act, it connotes some matter which concerns the public good and the public interest.[19] A contract being "opposed to public policy" is a defence under s. 23 of the Contract Act and the courts while deciding the validity of a contract have to consider:

(*a*) Pleadings in terms of Or. 6, CPC.

(*b*) Statute governing the case.

(*c*) Provisions of Parts III and IV of the Constitution of India.

(*d*) Expert evidence, if any.

(*e*) The materials brought on record of the case.

(*f*) Other relevant factors, if any.[20]

However, a contract may be unlawful or partly lawful or partly unlawful. If it is lawful, it will be given effect to whereas in case it is wholly unlawful being opposed to the public policy, it would not be. In case a transaction is partly lawful and partly unlawful, if they are severable, the lawful part shall be given effect to.[1]

NO SPECIFIC PERFORMANCE, IF AGREEMENT OPPOSED TO PUBLIC POLICY Parties cannot contract out of a statute, that is against public policy, but this principle will not apply unless the case was clearly brought within the principle of decisions as to the contract against public policy.[2] If a contract is made contrary to public policy, performance cannot be enforced either at law or in equity. A promise to pay a reward for services rendered in performing certain rites is not contrary to public policy.[3] Thus, where a person residing in the U.S.A made an agreement for selling property in India without obtaining permission of the Reserve Bank of India under the FEMA, it was held that such agreement, if enforced by court, would amount to enforcing illegal contract being violative of the provisions of FEMA. It is settled law that grant of specific performance is a discretionary relief. In a suit for specific performance, if the court finds that the suit is filed with an ulterior motive, that conduct also will have to be taken into consideration while exercising the discretion.[4]

19 *Indian Oil Corporation Ltd.* v *Raaj Unocal Lubricants Ltd.* (1997)2 Mah LJ 281; (1997)1 Bom CR 292.

20 *State of Rajasthan* v *Basant Nahata* (2005)12 SCC 77; AIR 2005 SC 3401.

1 *Canbank Financial Services Ltd.* v *Custodian* (2004)8 SCC 355; *BOI Finance Ltd.* v *Custodian* (1997)10 SCC 488.

2 See Halsbury's *Laws of England*, 4th Ed., vol. 9, paras 392, 393.

3 *Bapuji* v *Natranjan* AIR 1935 Nag 119.

4 *Shoba Viswanathan* v *D.P. Kingsley* (1996)1 LW 721.

SPECIFIC PERFORMANCE BY ARBITRATOR, IF OPPOSED TO PUBLIC POLICY In *Sulochana Uppal* v *Surinder Sheel Bhakri,*[5] the High Court of Delhi held that in view of the provisions of ss. 10 and 20 of the Specific Relief Act read with ss. 23 and 24 of the Indian Contract Act it is not permissible to any arbitrator to give an award, directing specific performance of an agreement to sell. Such an award would go contrary to the terms and spirit of the Specific Relief Act. In *Olympus Superstructures (P) Ltd.* v *Meena Vijay Khetan*[6] a question was raised as to whether an arbitrator has the power and jurisdiction to grant specific performance of contracts relating to immovable property. Answering the question in the affirmative, the Supreme Court observed as under:

> We are of the view that the right to specific performance of an agreement of sale deals with contractual rights and it is certainly open to the parties to agree—with a view to shorten litigation in regular courts—to refer the issues relating to specific performance to arbitration. There is no prohibition in the Specific Relief Act, 1963 that issues relating to specific performance of contract relating to immovable property cannot be referred to arbitration. Nor is there such a prohibition contained in the Arbitration and Conciliation Act, 1996 as contrasted with Section 15 of the English Arbitration Act, 1950 or Section 48(5)(*b*) of the English Arbitration Act, 1996 which contained a prohibition relating to specific performance of contracts concerning immovable property.

It is, therefore, submitted that in view of the decision of the Supreme Court in *Olympus Superstructures* (supra), the law laid down by Delhi High Court is no longer good law and consequently an arbitrator has jurisdiction to give an award, directing specific performance of an agreement to sell, if the parties give their consent to get their dispute resolved through an arbitrator.

MEANING OF 'LAW' UNDER SECTION 23 OF THE INDIAN CONTRACT ACT The term 'law' has not been defined under s. 23 of the Contract Act. It is defined under Art. 13 of the Constitution to include any Ordinance, order, bye-law, rule, regulation, notification, custom or usage having in the territory of India the force of law. But, this definition of 'law' as provided by Art. 13 of the Constitution has no relevance in deciding a question whether an agreement is void and is not enforceable in law. The word "law" in the expression "defeat the provisions of any law" in s. 23 of the Contract Act is limited to the expressed terms of an Act of the legislature.[7]

MEANING OF 'OBJECT' UNDER SECTION 23 OF THE INDIAN CONTRACT ACT The word "object" in s. 23 means "purpose" or "design" of the contract.[8] If the

5 AIR 1991 Del 138.
6 (1999)5 SCC 651.
7 *Union of India* v *Col. L.S.N. Murthy* (2012)1 SCC 718.
8 *Sreenivasa Rao* v *Korrapati Raja Rama Mohana Rao* AIR 1952 Mad 579.

purpose is unlawful being opposed to public policy, the contract is void and consequently not enforceable. Thus, an agreement between *A* and *B* to purchase property at an auction sale jointly and not to bid against each other at the auction is perfectly lawful, though the object may be to avoid competition between the two. But if there is an agreement between all the competing bidders at the auction sale, be it of the court sale or revenue sale, or sale by the government of its property or privilege and formed a ring to peg down the price and to purchase the property at knock out price, the purpose or design of the agreement is to defraud the third party, namely the debtor or government whose property is sold out at the court auction or revenue sale, or public welfare. The object or consideration of the contract, oral or written, to share such property is unlawful. There is also implied "injury to the debtor" within the meaning of s. 23. Therefore, the contract was fraudulent. The contract thus is also opposed to public policy and is void.[9]

TESTS OF 'PUBLIC POLICY' Section 23 of the Contract Act is concerned with only the object or consideration of the transaction and not the reasons or motive which prompted it. Public policy imposes certain limitations upon freedom of contract. Certain objects of contract are forbidden or discouraged by law; though all other requisites for the formation of a contract are complied with, yet if these objects are in contemplation of the parties when they entered into the agreement, the law will not permit them to enforce any rights under it. Whenever a plea of illegality or against public policy is raised as a defence to a contractual claim, the test to be applied is: Does public policy require that the claimant, in the circumstances which have occurred, should be refused relief of which he would otherwise have been entitled with respect to all or part of his claim? In addition, once the court finds that the contract is illegal and unenforceable, a second question should be posed which would also lead to greater clarity: Do the facts justify the granting of some consequential relief (other than enforcement of the contract) to either of the parties to the contract?[10]

POLICY OF LAW FOR CLASSIFICATION OF AGREEMENTS The recognized heads in the classification of agreements to do that which is the policy of law to prevent are: (*i*) agreements which injure the State in its relation with other States; (*ii*) agreements tending to injure the public service; (*iii*) agreements which tend to pervert abuse of legal process; (*iv*) agreements which tend to prevent the course of justice; (*v*) agreement which are contrary to good morals; and (*vi*) agreements which affect the freedom of trade.[11]

9 *Gurmukh Singh* v *Amar Singh* (1991)3 SCC 79.
10 *Gurmukh Singh* v *Amar Singh* (supra).
11 *Musammat Bhagwan Dei* v *Pt. Murari Lal* ILR (1917)39 All 51 (FB); 36 Ind Cas 259.

Recognized public policy Certain heads contrary to or opposed to public policy are well known and recognized. These are: (*a*) a contract for marriage brokerage, (*b*) creating of a perpetuity, (*c*) contract in restraint of trade, (*d*) gaming or wagering contract, (*e*) assisting of the King's enemies. These are all unlawful.[12]

Five classes of contracts invalidated on ground of public policy Contracts can be invalidated on the ground of public policy under five heads: (*i*) objects are illegal by common law or by legislation; (*ii*) objects injurious to good Government either in domestic field or in foreign affairs; (*iii*) objects interfere with the proper working of the machinery of justice; (*iv*) objects injurious to marriage and morality; (*v*) objects economically against the public interest.[13]

(4) *Certainty in contract* The specific performance of a contract is the actual execution of the contract according to its stipulations and terms, and the courts direct the party in default to do the very thing which he contracted to do. The stipulations and terms of the contract have, therefore, to be certain and the parties must have been *consensus ad idem*. The burden of showing the stipulations and terms of the contract and that the minds were *ad idem* is, of course, on the plaintiff. If the stipulations and terms are uncertain, and the parties are not *ad idem*, there can be no specific performance, for there was no contract at all.[14] Section 29 of the Indian Contract Act embodies the above-said principle. Thus, in respect of an agreement for sale, it must conform to the following requirements:

(1) it must be certain with regard to parties to the agreement;

(2) it must be certain in respect of the subject matter;

(3) it must be certain with regard to consideration;

(4) it must be certain in respect of the terms of the agreement; and

(5) it must be certain in respect of the time for specific performance.

When these ingredients are lacking either in a written agreement or an oral agreement, the obligation contemplated under s. 16 of the Specific Relief Act to convey the immovable property would not arise.[15] Merely because the agreement itself does not contain the survey number or the area, the document cannot be branded as void when the name of the land by which it can be identified is mentioned in the agreement.[16] But the stipulation in an agreement to pay the prevailing market rate is void for

12 *Janson* v *Drienfontein Consolidated Mines Ltd.* [1902] AC 484 at pp. 491-492.
13 Chitty on *Contracts*, 30th Ed., vol. 1, para 16-005.
14 *Mayawanti* v *Kaushalya Devi* (1990)3 SCC 1.
15 *Sivaji Saravanan* v *V.L. Thiagarajan* AIR 1988 NOC 40 (Kant).
16 *Mithukhan* v *Pipariyawali* AIR 1986 MP 39.

uncertainty.[17] A contract to grant renewal of a lease on such conditions as shall be reasonable and proper at the time of such a renewal is not void for uncertainty and the court treats it as valid, for, the court specifically enforces the agreement to execute the deeds with "usual clauses and with usual covenants."[18] It is important that law ought to uphold rather than destroy the apparent contracts.[19] Solemn contracts entered into between the parties are not to be readily declared invalid for uncertainty as to certain terms, at any rate in those cases where the parties have acted upon the contracts which have been fully executed. In construing a contract, the object of the court is to do justice between the parties and the court will do its best, if satisfied that there was an ascertainable and determinate intention to contract, to give effect to that intention, looking at substance, and not mere form. It will not be deterred by mere difficulties of interpretation. Difficulty is not synonymous with ambiguity so long as any definite meaning can be extracted.[20] Lord Denning has expressed the view that it is open to the court to impute or impose a term whenever it is reasonable to do so in order to do what is fair and just between the parties.[1] In appeal, however, the House of Lords though agreeing with the conclusion of Lord Denning did not accept the broad proposition that the Court is entitled to read in by implication all reasonable terms. The House of Lords observed that terms may be implied on the basis of established usage or for giving business efficacy to the contracts or on the ground of necessity.[2] Under Indian law, however, a contract can become void under s. 29 of the Indian Contract Act only when its terms cannot be made certain. Mere vagueness or uncertainty which can be removed by proper interpretation cannot make a contract void. In dealing with commercial and business contracts which have been acted upon by the parties, the court should be very slow in finding defects and to reject them as meaningless. This should be done only in extreme cases.[3]

In *Phuljhari Devi* v *Mithai Lal*,[4] it was held that specific performance is an equitable relief and the contract of sale of which specific performance is sought must be definite and precise. If it is uncertain no oral evidence is admissible to add to its terms and the contract would be void under s. 29 of the Indian Contract Act. In a suit for specific performance, the contract

17 *Remington Rand of India* v *Shoganlal Rajgharia* AIR 1984 Cal 153.
18 *Secretary of State for India* v *Volkart Bros.* AIR 1927 Mad 513.
19 *Kandomath Cine Enterprises P. Ltd.* v *John Pillipose* AIR 1990 Ker 198.
20 *Seemsall* v *Guston* [1941]1 All ER 14 (HL) 25; *Uttam Singh Dugal & Co. Pvt. Ltd., New Delhi* v *Hindustan Steel Ltd., Bhilai Steel Project* AIR 1982 MP 206.
1 *Liverpool City Council* v *Irwin* [1975]3 All ER 658; [1977] AC 239.
2 *Liverpool City Council* v *Irwin* [1976]2 All ER 39 at pp. 43-44 (HL).
3 *Uttam Singh Dugal & Co. Pvt. Ltd., New Delhi* v *Hindustan Steel Ltd., Bhilai Steel Project* AIR 1982 MP 206.
4 *Phuljhari Devi* v *Mithai Lal* AIR 1971 All 494.

must be specific and precise. If it is uncertain, it is void under s. 29 of the Indian Contract Act. The contract must be correct and precise. No oral evidence is admissible to add to the terms of the agreement.[5]

Vagueness is a misleading term. A contract may be so vague that it cannot be understood, in such a case it is of no effect. There is another kind of vagueness which arises from the property not being ascertained at the date of the contract, but if at the time when the contract is sought to be enforced the property has come into existence and is capable of being identified, the contract cannot be so vague as to be incapable of being enforced. Thus, a mortgage of property to which a person may become entitled during its pendency, or of property which is to come into existence in future, is valid.[6] But, the *"force majeure"* clause mentioned in an agreement cannot be said to be the reason or ground of contract being vague or uncertain. It needs mention that where reference is made to *"force majeure"*, the intention is to save the performing party from the consequences of anything over which he has no control.[7] Where the land for sale in a contract was neither ascertainable nor identifiable, it was held that such contract was not certain and hence not enforceable.[8] The court prefers a construction of an ambiguous contract which will make it valid and not void.[9] A statement may be said to be ambiguous when it has two or more primary meanings, each of which may be adopted without distortion of the language.[10] Evidence is admissible only to resolve latent ambiguity.[11] Patent ambiguity is ambiguity which appears from the language of the instrument, whereas latent ambiguity only becomes apparent when the language is applied to a factual situation.[12] In order to resolve a latent ambiguity, any relevent evidence is admissible including direct evidence of the intention of the parties. Where the ambiguity in a contract consists of an expression of defined alternatives, the law will sometimes permit the ambiguity to be resolved by the election of one of the parties to it.[13]

5 *Phuljhari Devi* v *Mithai Lal* (supra).
6 *Baldeo Parshad Sahu* v *A.B. Miller* ILR (1904)31 Cal 667; *Sree Sankarachari Swamier* v *Varada Pillai* ILR (1904)27 Mad 332; *New Beerbhoom Coal Co.* v *Bularam* ILR (1880)5 Cal 932 (PC).
7 *Dhanrajamal Gobindram* v *Shamji Kalidas & Co.* (1961)3 SCR 1020; AIR 1961 SC 1285.
8 *Pawan Kumar Dutt* v *Shakuntala Devi* (2010)15 SCC 601.
9 *Raneegunge Coal Assocn. Ltd.* v *Tata Iron & Steel Co.* ILR (1929)53 Bom 271; 117 Ind Cas 417.
10 *Sechuler (L) AG* v *Wickman Machine Tool Sales Ltd.* [1973]2 All ER 39.
11 *Mannai Investment Co. Ltd.* v *Eagle Star Life Assurance Co. Ltd.* [1997] AC 749; [1997]3 All ER 352.
12 *British Gas Corporation* v *Universities Superannuation Scheme* [1986]1 All ER 978.
13 *Bushwall Properties* v *Vortex Properties* [1976]2 All ER 283.

However, the court cannot undertake to supply the defects or remove ambiguities according to its own notion of what is reasonable. If the court does so, then it would not be an enforcement of the contract made by the parties. The court would then make a new contract for them.[14] A court cannot supply lacunae to perfect an imperfect agreement wherein the language used is not clear and meaningful or is ambiguous.[15]

CONTINUANCE OF CONTRACT—BASIS The whole edifice of specific performance of contract stands on existence of the contract. So, once the plaintiff terminates the contract he is not entitled to sue for specific performance of contract. So, in respect of contract for building a housing complex when the plaintiff wrote to defendant to the effect "since you committed breach of agreement by not executing a deed of conveyance I am left with no alternative other than to terminate the contract", a suit for specific performance of contract thereafter is not tenable.[16]

The suit claiming damages or for refund of earnest money, however stems out of the plaintiff's election to treat the contract as broken. In a suit for specific performance the plaintiff proceeds on the footing that the contract still subsists. So, once the plaintiff claims the only relief of damages or refund of earnest money he cannot amend the plaint to claim specific performance as first relief and the relief of damages or refund of earnest money as alternative relief.[17] As pointed out by Their Lordships of the Judicial Committee in *Ardeshir H. Mama* v *Flora Sassoon*,[18] where a party to a contract for sale made a claim for damages on the footing of its breach by the other party it would amount to a definite election on his part to treat the contract as at an end and thereafter no suit for specific performance could be maintained by him, for, by such election, he had disabled himself from making the averment that he had always been ready and willing to perform his part of the contract.

A party laying his claim before arbitrator for only damages for breach of contract, impliedly accepts the contract as broken. By subsequent amendment he cannot convert his claim to specific performance of contract because then he must have to treat the contract as subsisting.[19]

The reason of the rule as succinctly stated in a Madras case is that "it will not be open to a party to a contract, who has once elected to accept

14 *Scammeli* v *Ouston* [1941]1 AC 251; [1941]1 All ER 14.

15 *Teamco (P) Ltd.* v *T.M.S. Mani* AIR 1967 Cal 168.

16 *Andheri Bridge View Co-op. Housing Society Ltd.* v *Krishnakant Anandrao Deo* AIR 1991 Bom 129.

17 *Roop Chand Chaudhari* v *Ranjit Kumari* AIR 1991 P&H 212 overruling *Tarsem Singh* v *Daljit Kaur* 1985 PLJ 534 affirming *Jai Bhagwan* v *Raja Ram* (1989)2 Raj LR 214.

18 AIR 1928 PC 208.

19 *Indian Iron & Steel* v *C.G. Engineering Pvt. Ltd.* AIR 1983 Cal 6; (1982)1 Cal LJ 291; 87 CWN 61.

the breach assuming there was a breach on the part of the otherside to cancel that election and treat the contract as if it were subsisting."[20]

To claim specific performance plaintiff must be ready and willing to perform his part of the contract and secondly, he must treat the contract as subsisting. When the plaintiff once has repudiated the contract and elected to sue for damages, he cannot thereafter claim specific performance of contract.[1]

Contracts concluded & completed and contracts incomplete or inchoate A contract, oral or written, gets legal validity only if it is completed and concluded. Unless there is a concluded contract, the suit for specific performance would not arise.[2] The onus to prove that the contract is concluded is on the plaintiff. An incomplete or inchoate contract is no contract in the eye of law and cannot be enforced. A plaint in a suit for specific performance should allege a concluded contract. Reference may be made to 1st Schedule, Appendix A, Form No. 48 of the Civil Procedure Code 1908.[3]

The question whether a concluded contract has come into existence or not depends upon the intention of the parties and it has to be gathered from the writing, if any, the conduct of the parties, and the special facts and circumstances of the particular case.[4] Where parties start their negotiations under the umbrella of the "special contract" formula or some similar expression of intention, it is really hopeless for one side or the other to say that a contract has come into existence because the parties have become of one mind, notwithstanding that no formal contracts have been exchanged. Parties can get rid of the qualification "subject to contract" only if both parties agree that it should be expunged or if such an agreement was necessarily to be implied.[5]

Contracts concluded In *Motilal* v *Nanhelal,*[6] the sanction of certain revenue authorities was necessary for the sale of cultivating rights in the suit land and in a suit for specific performance of an agreement for sale of such rights, it was held by Their Lordships of the Judicial Committee of the Privy Council that the vendor having agreed to transfer the cultivating rights in

20 *K.S. Sundaramayyar* v *K. Jagadeesan* AIR 1965 Mad 85 (86-87).
1 *Ayissabi* v *Gopala Konar* AIR 1989 Ker 134; (1988)2 Cur Civ Cas 635 (Ker).
2 *Trimurthy Constructions* v *Vijay Lakshmi* AIR 1993 AP 95.
3 *Viswesardas Gokuldas* v *B.K. Narayan Singh* AIR 1969 SC 1157; (1969)1 SCC 547.
4 *Ridgway* v *Wharton* [1857]6 HLC 238 at p. 263; *Von Hatzfeldt Wildenburg* v *Alexander* [1921]1 Ch 284 at p. 288; *Rossiter* v *Miller* [1878]3 AC 1124; *Currimbhoy & Co. Ltd.* v *Creet* AIR 1933 PC 29.
5 *Tevanam* v *Noman Brett Builders Ltd.* [1972]223 Eg 1945; see also *Cohen* v *Nessdale Ltd.* [1982]2 All ER 97 affirming [1981]3 All ER 118 and applying *Sherbrooke* v *Dipple* [1980] 41 P & CR 173.
6 AIR 1930 PC 287.

the land, there was an implied covenant on his part to do all things necessary to effect such transaction, which would include an application to the revenue officer to sanction the transfer according to the C.P. Tenancy Act. In other words, the fact that such an application has not been made and the sanction of the appropriate authorities obtained was not a bar to the grant of a decree for specific performance of the agreement to sell. A similar view was taken by the High Court of Calcutta in *Gokulchandra Lal* v *Haji Md. Din.*[7] In *Dr. C.L. Katial* v *Mrs. C.W.V. Madden,*[8] the agreement for sale of a house situated in New Delhi contained a clause to the effect that the vendor has to obtain the sanction of the Chief Commissioner for transfer of the site on which the house was constructed within two months (special sanction became necessary on account of the condition in the ground lease) does not remain incohate unless and until the sanction is obtained when there is nothing to suggest that the application for sanction is likely to be rejected. So far as the parties are concerned, the agreement is a completed one. The mere fact that sanction of the Chief Commissioner is to be obtained before the sale, it was held, that did not make the agreement incomplete and there was no bar to grant a decree for specific performance. This decision went up on appeal to the Supreme Court in *Chandnee Widya Vati Madden* v *C.L. Katial*[9] and the Apex Court held that the contract was not a contingent contract and can be specifically performed.

In *Kollipara Sriramulu* v *T. Aswathanarayana,*[10] the Respondent and all the partners of the firm except the appellant entered into an oral agreement for sale of their shares and a written agreement was to be drawn in two or three days and the mode of payment of the purchase money was to be settled later. It was further agreed that the sale deed would be executed in three months. It was contended that the contract was not completed and the sale was conditional upon the execution of the regular agreement. Rejecting the contention, Ramaswamy, J observed: "It is well established that a mere reference to a future formal contract will not prevent the binding bargain between the parties. The fact that the parties refer to the preparation of an agreement by which the terms agreed upon are to be put in a more formal shape does not prevent the existence of a binding contract." It was held on the facts that the evidence adduced did not show that the drawing up of a written agreement was a prerequisite to the coming into effect of the oral agreement. The court also held that the mere omission to settle the mode of payment did not affect the completeness of the contract when the vital terms of the contract like the price and the area of the land and the time for completion of the sale had all been fixed.

7 AIR 1938 Cal 136.
8 AIR 1963 Punj 136.
9 AIR 1964 SC 978; (1964)2 SCR 495; (1964)2 SCJ 824.
10 AIR 1968 SC 1028; (1968)3 SCR 387.

In *Amrit Lal Suri* v *C.P. Gupta*,[11] the appellant purchased a plot in a colony which was owned by a cooperative society. The appellant started construction but could not complete it because of paucity of funds. He approached the respondent and offered to sell the property for a consideration of ₹50,000 and the respondent agreed to the proposal. The bye-laws of the society did not prohibit the sale of the plots to non-members, but it was necessary that they should become members thereafter. The appellant wrote letters expressing his intention to the concerned authorities. Subsequently, the appellant turned round and took the stand that he received the amount as interest free loan and not by way of a sale and tried to rescind the agreement on various grounds. Meanwhile, the application of the respondent to become a member of the society had been accepted by the society. It was held that there was a completed contract and the Respondent was eligible to purchase the property and the decree passed for specific performance.

When an agreement for sale is brought into existence by exchange of letters and the defendant seller acknowledges the receipt of earnest money and gives time to pay the balance, the contract is concluded and may be specifically performed.[12] Vendee alleged to have parted with an amount as part consideration of an agreement to sell an immovable property but balance consideration was neither paid nor possession of property was taken by him. Such document purporting to be an agreement to sale and it cannot be treated as sale. Such document is loan agreement.[13]

The document embodying a concluded contract may not be apparently so. In a case the document was titled as a receipt acknowledging the receipt of earnest money for sale of a plot of land and the essential and basic ingredients were embodied in the said document. It was held that the document is a contract for sale and the vendee can seek specific performance.[14]

Where the approval of the society was necessary for transfer of the flat and the vendee had already applied for such approval and had also applied for the membership of the society and the society had not refused permission, specific performance of the contract could be granted and the owner of the flat could be directed to execute the deed of sale in respect of the flat and direct the society to consider the application of the vendee for membership and prayer for transfer of flat in accordance with law in terms of the bye-laws.[15]

Where the essential terms of a sale are all settled and it is stipulated that a document is to be executed and approved by the parties or their pleaders, the condition of such approval is simply to be regarded as one of the terms

11 AIR 1990 Del 224.
12 *P.G. Sinha* v *Commodore K.C. Chatterjee* AIR 1991 Cal 327.
13 *Ram Bahadur* v *Brij Mohan* AIR 2018 All 295.
14 *Nanak Builders & Investors Pvt. Ltd.* v *Vinod Kumar Alag* AIR 1991 Del 315.
15 *Anjali Das* v *Bidyut Sarkar* AIR 1992 Cal 47.

of the contract and it cannot be held that there was no concluded contract until such execution or approval took place.[16]

Agreement to sell—whether a concluded contract In *Jiwan Lal* v *Brij Mohan*,[17] it was observed by the Supreme Court that agreement to sell is a concluded contract as seller becomes liable to sell and the buyer becomes liable to buy from the very inception of the contract. The question may be raised that a contract could not be said to be concluded until the price is in fact paid because it would then be open to an offeree to hold the offeror to ransom. But, such argument is not legally acceptable. The legal consequence of a concluded contract will remain irrespective of how a particular party in a given situation might abuse the rights flowing from it. It is platitudinous that the possibility of abuse of a right cannot determine whether the right exists as a matter of law. Such arguments are normally met by the aphorism "*hard cases make bad law*".[18] But, when an agreement is entered into subject to ratification by others, a concluded contract is not arrived at. Whenever ratification by some other persons, who are not parties to the agreement is required, such a clause must be held to be a condition precedent for coming into force of a concluded contract.[19]

The letter of intent cannot be said to be an agreement to sell for the simple reason that according to the contents of the letter of intent, only upon payment of the entire purchase price, the parties to the contract were to enter into an agreement with regard to sale of a particular property.[20]

Agreement to sell and power of attorney holder A power of attorney is not an instrument of transfer in regard to any right, title or interest in an immovable property. The power of attorney is creation of an agency whereby the grantor authorizes the grantee to do the acts specified therein, on behalf of grantor, which when executed will be binding on the grantor as if done by him.[21] It is revocable or terminable at any time unless it is made irrevocable in a manner known to law. Even an irrevocable attorney does not have the effect of transferring title to the grantee.[1] A grant of power of attorney is essentially governed by Chapter X of the Contract Act. By reason of a deed of power of attorney, an agent is formally appointed to act for the principal in one transaction or a series of transactions or to manage the affairs of the principal generally conferring necessary authority upon another person. A deed of power of attorney is executed by the principal in favour of the agent. The

16 *Harichand* v *Govind* [1924]50 IA 25; AIR 1923 PC 47.
17 (1972)2 SCC 757.
18 *Claude-Lila Parulekar* v *Sakal Papers (P) Ltd.* (2005)11 SCC 73.
19 *M.V. Shankar Bhat* v *Claude Pinto* (2003)4 SCC 86.
20 *Hansa V. Gandhi* v *Deep Shankar Roy* (2013)12 SCC 776.
21 Section 1A and s. 2 of the Powers of Attorney Act 1882.
1 *Suraj Lamp and Industries (P) Ltd. (2)* v *State of Haryana* (2012)1 SCC 656; (2012)1 SCC (Civ) 351.

agent derives a right to use his name and all acts, deeds and things done by him and subject to the limitations contained in the said deed, the same shall be read as if done by the donor. A power of attorney is, as is well known, a document of convenience.[2] It is settled that a power of attorney has to be strictly construed. In order to agree to sell or effect a sale by a power of attorney, the power should also expressly authorize the power to agent to execute the sale agreement/sale deed, i.e. (*a*) to present the document before the Registrar; and (*b*) to admit execution of the document before the Registrar.[3]

Cancellation of agreement and specific performance of agreement Section 31 of the Specific Relief Act deals with 'cancellation of instruments' and s. 31 refers to both void and voidable document.[4] Two suits were filed, one for cancellation of agreement on the ground of allegation of fraud and the other for specific performance thereof. Suit for cancellation was dismissed and that of the respondents was decreed. The appellants failed to point out any error in findings recorded by courts below. Only contention they made was that the agreement was unconscionable as price of land at the time of the agreement was more than twenty lakhs. In absence of any plea having been raised or an issue framed or evidence led on the point in the written statement, it cannot be held that the agreement to sell was unconscionable. Thus, there was no interference with the judgment of the court below.[5]

If a suit for cancellation of a sale deed is filed on the ground of fraud and misrepresentation, burden of proof lies on plaintiff. If he fails to do so, defendant cannot be asked to discharge negative burden.[6]

Inadequacy of consideration Mere inadequacy of consideration is not a criterion to reject specific performance.[7]

Section 10 of the Indian Contract Act 1872 relates to agreements which are contracts. This section sets out various elements which may affect the validity of a contract and thus prevent it from being legally binding or enforceable. This section has to be read along with s. 2. There must be a proposal and acceptance of proposal in order to constitute an agreement. Such an agreement is legally binding and enforceable provided the following conditions are satisfied: (1) There must be free consent of the parties (ss. 11-23). (2) The parties must be competent to contract (ss. 11, 12). (3) The consideration must be lawful (s. 23). (4) The object must be lawful

2 *State of Rajasthan* v *Basant Nahata* (2005)12 SCC 77.
3 *Church of Christ Charitable Trust & Educational Charitable Society* v *Ponniamman Educational Trust* (2012)8 SCC 706.
4 *Prem Singh* v *Birbal* AIR 2006 SC 3608.
5 *Akbar Ali* v *Vinod Khanna* AIR 2004 SC 3940.
6 *Daya Ram* v *Lakshmina* AIR 2008 All 123.
7 *T. Krishna Murthy* v *Gangadharaiah* AIR 2011 NOC 51 (Kar).

(ss. 23-25). (5) The agreement must not be expressly declared to be void (ss. 26-30). (6) The agreement must comply with the provision of any law requiring it to be in writing or attested or registered. Thus, when the deceased took out a policy on his life, he was examined by authorized doctor who found that most of his teeth were removed and consequently the rate of premium was increased, there was a concluded contract.[8] In another case[9] the tender of the petitioner was accepted by Fax message subject to finalization of terms as to schedule of stage payments. The tenderer participated in negotiations about schedule of payments held after the Fax message, but submitted a revised schedule of payments. It was held that there was no concluded contract between the parties. Under a construction contract claim was made by the contractor for certain extra items of work. If the rates are not specified in the contract, the same are to be ascertained from the evidence produced before the court.[10]

Contracts incomplete and inchoate Where in a suit for specific performance of a contract for sale, it was found that the alleged letter of acceptance of the offer of the price on behalf of the purchaser by the seller referred to future negotiation for finalization of more terms of contract, it was held by the High Court that it could not be said that there was a concluded contract between the parties on the basis of which a decree for specific performance could be granted.[11]

If the way of ascertainment of the price is specified, the contract becomes absolute only when the price has been determined in the manner agreed upon.[12] So also, where the parties stipulate that the contract would not be complete until a formal deed was executed.[13] In a contract of letting, the terms were followed by the words "subject to the conditions and entering into a regular lease", it was held that the entering into of a regular lease was a condition precedent and the agreement could not be enforced till then.[14]

Where a contract has not been concluded as where the plaintiff upto the conclusion of the negotiations has been trying to obtain more favourable terms, a suit for specific performance is not maintainable.[15] Where sanction was not obtained under a certain law which prohibited the exchange of lands without previous sanction of the Darbar, it was held that the agreement was inchoate and specific performance could not be granted.[16]

8 *Babooram Jain* v *LIC of India* AIR 1990 MP 351; 1991 ACJ 521.
9 *Gammon India Ltd.* v *Punjab State Electricity Board* AIR 1997 P&H 43.
10 *S.A. Jaish & Co.* v *Gujarat Electricity Board* AIR 1988 SC 254.
11 *Sathya Prakash Goel* v *Ramakrishna Mission* AIR 1991 All 343.
12 *Nair Service Society* v *R.M. Palat* AIR 1966 Ker 311.
13 *Subodh Chandra Nandy* v *Himanshu Bala Bose* 60 CWN 423.
14 *Simon* v *Haji* 24 Bom LR 466.
15 *Gulab Rani Chowdhury* v *Jagannath Chowdhury* 1969 Pat LJR 156.
16 *Ramditta* v *Dhani Ram* AIR 1955 HP 23.

The highest bidder at the Municipal auction cannot ask for injunction restraining the Municipality from holding re-auction. This is because there is no concluded contract in his favour until the auction is approved by the resolution of the Municipal Council.[17]

An agreement is incomplete when parties reach agreement on certain matters of principle leaving some important points unsettled. For example, there may be an agreement for lease, but it fails to specify the subject matter or the date of commencement of the terms of the lease; in such a case, the agreement is incomplete. In the following situations an agreement may be termed as incomplete:[18]

(1) Agreements "subject to contract". These include (*a*) requirement of exchange of contracts, (*b*) mitigations of the requirement, (*c*) exceptions to the requirement, (*d*) collateral contract.

(2) Execution of formal documents required.

(3) Terms left open. These include (*a*) terms "to be agreed", (*b*) options and rights of pre-emption, (*c*) criteria or machinery specified in the agreement.

(4) Facts to be ascertained.

(5) Contract to make a contract. This includes (*a*) agreement to execute formal document, (*b*) express agreement to negotiate, (*c*) implied agreement to negotiate.

Recession of agreement to sell Agreement did not specify period of outer limit within which payment of balance purchase money is to be paid, obligation to ensure performance of agreement to sell on the vendor. Purchaser was required to deposit balance consideration and some amount towards unearned increase in land price. Dismissal of application to rescind contract was held to be proper.[19]

Contracts contingent and non-contingent A "contingent contract" is a contract to do or not to do something, if some event, collateral to such contract, does or does not happen [*vide* s. 31 of the Indian Contract Act]. In English law, it is called conditional contract.[20] Whether a contract is an absolute or contingent one depends upon the facts and circumstances of each case. The essential features of a contingent contract are:

(1) the uncertainty and futurity of the event to which the contract is related; it is this dependence on a future event which distinguishes a contingent contract from other contracts; and

(2) the event to be collateral to the contract.

17 *Doshi Mohanlal Durlabhji* v *Savarakundla Municipality* AIR 1982 Guj 6.
18 Treitel, *The Law of Contract*, 13th Ed., pp. 52-62.
19 *S.K. Gupta* v *S. Kuldip Singh* AIR 2011 Del 54.
20 Pollock's *Principles of Contracts*, 13th Ed., p. 222.

A contingent or a conditional promise is distinguished from an absolute promise by the fact that the performance of the contract becomes due on the happening of a condition or contingency, so it is not due immediately on the making of the contract.[1] For instance, a contract of insurance is a contingent contract.[2] Life insurance in a broader sense comprises any contract in which one party agrees to pay a given sum upon the happening of a particular event contingent upon the duration of human life, in consideration of the immediate payment of a smaller sum or certain equivalent periodical payments by another party.[3] In *Commissioner of Wealth Tax, Mysore* v *Vijayaba, Dowger Maharani Saheb*,[4] it was held that a letter having the effect of family arrangement between the parties might contain element of contingent contract within the meaning of s. 31 of the Indian Contract Act 1872, but under s. 32 of the Act it is enforceable by law on the failure of the elder son to pay the part of the specified sum. A contingent contract is a contract after all and has to be distinguished from a case where there is no concluded contract but only an offer has been made by one party which has not been accepted by the other. Thus, where a house was put up for sale, the first defendant was the highest bidder, but the sale was subjected to a stipulation that it would be confirmed on receipt of the Collector's order and after a long delay the Collector refused to confirm the sale. It was held that there was no contract.[5]

In *R. Velappan* v *R. Deivasigamani*[6] an agreement for sale provided that the "B" scheduled properties would have to be conveyed to the purchaser, if the purchaser came to the conclusion that the "A" scheduled properties could not be sold on account of some unforeseen result of the suit filed by a third person by name Mahabub Bibi and the purchaser did not exercise the option but agreed to purchase the "A" scheduled properties, it was held that the vendor was bound to sell the "A" schedule properties. A contingent contract is never complete until the uncertain future event happens and cannot be enforced unless and until that event happens. In *Narain Pattro* v *Aukhoy Narain Manna*,[7] a certified guardian of certain minors contracted to sell certain land belonging to the minors contingent upon the leave of the court. The court sanctioned the sale at a higher price than that was agreed upon between the plaintiff and the guardian. It was held that the contract as it stood never became a complete contract at any time as it was

1 Chitty on *Contracts*, 30th Ed., vol. 1, para 2-144.
2 *CEPT* v *Ruby General Insurance Co. Ltd.* 1957 SCR 1002; AIR 1957 SC 669.
3 Halsbury's *Laws of England*, 3rd Ed., vol. 22, p. 273; *Chandulal Harjivandas* v CIT (1967)1 SCR 921; AIR 1967 SC 816.
4 AIR 1979 SC 982.
5 *Muthu Pillai* v *Secretary of State for India* 45 MLJ 67. See Cheshire, Fifoot & Furmston *on Contract*, 14th Ed., pp. 137, 163.
6 AIR 1933 Mad 100.
7 ILR (1885)12 Cal 152.

contingent upon the permission of the court and the permission of the court did not extend to the terms of the contract agreed upon between the parties.

A suit for specific performance is premature if it is instituted before the conditions are fulfilled, on the fulfillment of which alone a contract will become absolute.[8] In a case, the plaintiff booked a flat to be constructed by the defendant, but the booking was provisional, *i.e.* depending on the availability of additional F.A.R. (Floor Area Ratio). At no point of time the additional F.A.R. was sanctioned, so, the defendant was unable to offer the flat. The contract was contingent one and so was held to be not specifically enforceable.[9] The contract for sale of a factory which was then subject to existing laws contemplated the surrender of possession by the lessee as a condition precedent to the contract taking effect. When the lessee had refused to give up his rights prematurely and surrender possession, the question arose whether the vendee was entitled to specific performance subject to the lease. It was held that when the condition precedent was not fulfilled, there can be no subsisting contract at all and no question of specific performance could arise. In *Dalsukh M. Pancholi* v *Guarantee Life & Employment Insurance Company,*[10] the properties of one *R* were under attachment and in order to avoid court sale "R" entered into an agreement for sale of the property with the plaintiff. One of the conditions of the contract was that the E.M.D. should be paid at the time of the attaching court giving approval to the transaction. *R* applied to the court under Or. 21, r. 23, CPC praying that the price offered by the plaintiff may be accepted but the application was rejected by the court. In a suit filed by the plaintiff for specific performance Sir Madhavan Nair, J speaking for the Board observed that "In Their Lordships' opinion, the contract was contingent one and as the contingency failed there was no contract which could be made the basis for specific performance." In *Harbans Atma Singh* v *Ramesh Kumar,*[11] the defendant agreed to sell a plot of land allotted to her out of the defence quota which was liable to resumption if the construction was not started within a year from the date of allotment. The agreement for sale provided that "No Objection Certificate" was to be obtained from the concerned authorities, i.e. Estate Officer. The 'No Objection Certificate' was not granted and it was held that the suit for specific performance by the buyer would fail and that his only remedy was for damages.

8 *Harihar Prasad* v *Udaibir Singh* 1978 AWC 79.
9 *Baij Nath* v *Ansal & Saigal Properties P. Ltd.* AIR 1993 Del 285; *T.V. Kochuvareed* v *P. Mariappa Gounder* AIR 1954 Trav Co 10.
10 AIR 1947 PC 182.
11 AIR 1986 P&H 14.

In a Full Bench decision of the High Court of Gujarat in *Shah Jitendra Nanalal* v *Patel Lallubhai Ishverbhai*,[12] the question was whether a conditional decree for specific performance subject to the condition of the plaintiff obtaining exemption from the State Government under cl. (*b*) of sub-sec. (1) of s. 20 of the Urban Land (Ceiling and Regulation) Act 1976 can or cannot be passed. The Full Bench held that the passing of conditional decree for specific performance of the obligation of the holder to transfer the vacant land in excess of the ceiling limit held by him subject to exemption being obtained under s. 20 was permissible.

Contract of transfer needs registration and specific performance of oral agreement The words "any contract" in s. 10, Specific Relief Act are eloquent enough to show that the contract that can be specifically performable may also be oral. An oral agreement of sale is also specifically performable.[13]

But the burden of proof is very heavy upon a person who intends to get an oral agreement specifically enforced through a court of law.[14] Absence of signature of the purchaser on the agreement to sell the property would not disentitle him to file a suit if the document is executed by owner of property.[15] As to the need of registration of a written contract, the answer is that it is not compulsorily registrable. In view of s. 17(2)(*v*), Registration Act 1908 a document which merely creates a right to obtain another document is not compulsorily registrable. Therefore an unregistered agreement of transfer is admissible in a suit for specific performance of contract of sale by virtue of proviso to s. 49, Registration Act 1908.[16] Since the agreement of reconveyance limited the right in the prior conveyance it was void for non-registration under s. 17(1)(*b*) of the Registration Act 1908.

Rejecting the argument, the court held the agreement fell within the exemption under s. 17(2)(*v*) and in any case a suit for specific performance could be founded under proviso to s. 49 of the Registration Act. For this view the court relied on the following observation of Shah, J in *Harkishandas Bhagvandas* v *Bai Dhanu*,[17] where the learned judge said—

> "The real test, in my opinion, is not whether the transaction is the same, but whether the intention of the parties in a given case is to create or limit the right to immovable property worth ₹100 and over by an agreement not registered or to keep strictly within the limits contemplated by cl. (*v*) of

12 AIR 1984 Guj 145 (FB).

13 *Krishnan Kesavan* v *Kochukunju Karunakaran* AIR 1988 Ker 107; 1987 Ker LJ 1085.

14 *Ouseph Verghese* v *Joseph Aley* (1970)1 SCR 921; (1969)2 SCC 539; *Ranganath Sharma* v *Tetari Bibi* AIR 1991 Pat 198.

15 *A. Sankariah* v *V. Ravichandran* AIR 2017 Mad 77.

16 *Narayanaswami* v *Muniamma* AIR 1974 Mys 13.

17 AIR 1926 Bom 497 (FB).

s. 17, sub-sec. (2). Where there is nothing in the terms of the agreement to show that by itself it creates or limits any right in immovable property, but merely gives a right to obtain another document and where the intention of the parties *ex hypothesi* as contemplated by the question, is to treat the document as strictly limited by the terms, I do not see any reason why the exemption allowed under the said clause of the section should not take effect with reference to it ......

"The question whether a particular agreement satisfies the requirements of cl. (*v*) of s. 17(2) must depend upon the terms of the document. For instance, if the agreement purports to create some right in immovable property, and also gives a right to obtain another document in future, it would not satisfy the requirements of that clause. But in the instant case (the agreement of reconveyance was executed contemporaneously) the terms of the document do not go beyond the requirement of the clause and where the intention of the parties as found or assumed in the question is to keep it strictly within the limits of its terms, the mere fact that it is a part of the same transaction and is not an independent transaction is not sufficient to render the document as anything more than what it purports to be *viz.*, an agreement by the vendee to recovery the property to the vendor on payment of money by him."[18]

In *Dave Ramshankar Jivatram* v *Bai Kailasgauri*,[19] the appellant had purchased the property from the respondent on 25.6.1959. The sale deed was executed on the same day but was registered on 26.6.1959. However, on the same day the appellant had agreed to reconvey the property to the vendor within a period of seven years from the date of the agreement of reconveyance.

It was held that reading the two documents together, it was clear that they were not part of the one and the same transaction. Thus the agreement did not require registration. The question of variation did not arise in this situation if the document which has not been registered is really a part and parcel of the transaction, which is only partly evidenced by the registered document, then it is clear that the other document also requires to be registered. But, if the document to reconvey can be treated as a separate transaction, then under s. 54 of the Transfer of Property Act 1882, it vests no interest in the property and need not be registered.

Agreement to transfer immovable property need not be registered and can form basis for specific performance even though not registered by virtue of s. 17(2)(*v*) and proviso to s. 49, Registration Act.[20]

18 *Harkishandas Bhagvandas* v *Bai Dhanu* AIR 1926 Bom 497 (FB).
19 AIR 1974 Guj 69.
20 *Bhaskaran* v *George Joseph* AIR 1988 Ker 255; 1987 Ker LJ 1396; (1988)1 Ker LT 107; *Senmoonchi Gounder* v *Naina Gounder* AIR 1988 Mad 345.

In view of last para of s. 54, Transfer of Property Act 1882, an agreement of sale does not of itself create any interest in or charge on such property. It is merely a document embodying right to obtain another document.[1]

As to the need of registrability of agreement of sale s. 17 of the Registration Act enumerates the list of documents which require registration. Section 17(1)(*b*) of the Act provides for the registration of non-testamentary instruments which purport or operate to create, declare, assign, limit or extinguish, whether in present or in future, any right, title or interest, whether vested or contingent, of the value of one hundred rupees and upwards, to or in immovable property.

An agreement of sale does not come under s. 17(1)(*b*), Registration Act 1908 and is not compulsorily registrable.[2]

The enforceability of oral agreements for sale of immovable properties and unregistered written agreements for sale of immovable properties have given rise to a plethora of wasteful litigations. False and fictitious verbal agreements and collusive ante-dated written agreements for sale of immovable properties are flooding the courts causing irreparable damages and strain to the legal process and to the public. It is high time that the Parliament wakes up to this deplorable state of affairs and amends the law rendering agreements for sale of immovable properties of the value of ₹100 and upwards to be made only by registered instruments. It may be pointed out that in Uttar Pradesh, under the Uttar Pradesh Civil Laws (Reforms & Amendments) Act 1976, the provisions of s. 54 of the Transfer of Property Act 1882 and s. 49 of the Registration Act 1908 have been amended and an agreement to sell immovable properties can be made only by registered instruments and as such no unregistered document or oral evidence is admissible to prove any contract to sell immovable properties.

An intending purchaser, who enters into an agreement for sale with the owner of the property and got delivery of possession of the property, cannot claim the benefits under s. 53A of the Transfer of Property Act 1882 unless the deed of agreement for sale which contemplates such delivery of possession is registered. But the said provision shall not affect the right of a transferee for consideration who has no notice of the contract or of the part performance thereof. It is not as if all the agreements for sale referring to instance of delivery of possession shall be compulsorily registered under s. 17(1A) of the Registration Act. Only when the agreement for sale which speaks about delivery of possession is filed to claim benefit of part performance as contemplated under s. 53A of the Transfer of Property Act, court will have to find out whether the document was registered or not. If such document

1 *Dave Ramshankar Jivatram* v *Bai Kailasgauri* AIR 1974 Guj 69.
2 *Bhaskaran* v *George Joseph* AIR 1988 Ker 255 at p. 256; 1987 Ker LJ 1396; (1988)1 Ker LT 107.

was not registered, then the benefit of s. 53A of the Transfer of Property Act cannot be claimed by the prospective purchaser of the property.[3]

It is pertinent to point out here and now that s. 17 of the Registration Act 1908 has been amended by the Registration and Other Related Laws (Amendment) Act 2001 and s. 3 of the said Amendment Act has introduced sub-sec. (1A) in s. 17 to the following effect:

> "17(1A). The documents containing contracts to transfer for consideration, any immovable property for the purpose of section 53A of the Transfer of Property Act, 1882, shall be registered if they have been executed on or after the commencement of the Registration and Other Related Laws (Amendment) Act, 2001 and if such documents are not registered on or after such commencement then they, shall have no effect for the purposes of the said section 53A."

It is thus clear that in order to avail the benefit of the doctrine of part-performance under s. 53A, an agreement for sale of any immovable property entered into after the commencement of the aforesaid Amendment Act of 2001 has to be registered. Why should not such a provision be introduced in respect of all agreements for sale?

Agreement of sale/sale by power of attorney/living will transfer Irrespective of intention, the consequences of SA/GPA/Will transactions are disturbing and far-reaching, adversely affecting the economy, civil society and law and order. First, it enables large-scale evasion of income tax, wealth tax, stamp duty and registration fees thereby denying the benefit of such revenue to the Government and the public. Secondly, such transactions enable persons with undisclosed wealth/income to invest their black money and also earn profit/income, thereby encouraging circulation of black money and corruption. These kinds of transactions have disastrous collateral effects also. For example, when the market value increases, many vendors (who effected power of attorney sales without registration) are tempted to resell the property taking advantage of the fact that there is no registered instrument or record in any public office thereby cheating the purchaser. When the purchaser under such "power of attorney sales" comes to know about the vendor's action, he invariably tries to take the help of musclemen to "sort out" the issue and protect his rights. On the other hand, real estate mafia many a time purchase properties which are already subject to power of attorney sale and then threaten the previous "power of attorney sale" purchasers from asserting their rights. Either way, such power of attorney sales indirectly lead to growth of real estate mafia and criminalization of real estate transactions. Some States have made some efforts to control such "power of attorney sales" by subjecting agreements of sale involving delivery of possession and irrevocable powers of attorney for consideration

3 *Palaniammal* v *K.R.C. Anbalagan* (2013)3 CTC 477; (2013)127 AIC (Sum 17) 11.

to the same stamp duty as deeds of conveyance or by making such documents compulsorily registrable. But the steps taken are neither adequate nor properly implemented resulting in multiple transactions in regard to the same property by greedy and unscrupulous vendors and/or purchasers giving nightmares to *bona fide* purchasers intending to buy a property with certainty regarding title. It also makes it difficult for lawyers in tracing and certifying title. The Registration Act 1908 was enacted with the intention of providing orderliness, discipline and public notice in regard to transactions relating to immovable property and protection from fraud and forgery of documents of transfer. This is achieved by requiring compulsory registration of certain types of documents and providing for consequences of non-registration.[4]

Section 17 of the Registration Act clearly provides that any document (other than testamentary instruments) which purports or operates to create, declare, assign, limit or extinguish whether in present or in future "any right, title or interest" whether vested or contingent of the value of ₹100 and upwards to or in immovable property. Section 49 of the said Act provides that no document required by s. 17 to be registered shall, affect any immovable property comprised therein or received as evidence of any transaction affecting such property, unless it has been registered. Registration of a document gives notice to the world that such a document has been executed.[5] It is submitted that a transfer of immovable property by way of sale can only be by a deed of conveyance (sale deed). In the absence of a deed of conveyance (duly stamped and registered as required by law), no right, title or interest in an immovable property can be transferred. Therefore, an SA/GPA/Will transaction does not convey any title nor creates any interest in an immovable property. Such transactions cannot be relied upon or made the basis for mutations in municipal or revenue records. What is stated above will apply not only to deeds of conveyance in regard to freehold property but also to transfer of leasehold property. A lease can be validly transferred only under a registered assignment of lease. It is time that an end is put to the pernicious practice of SA/GPA/Will transactions known as GPA sales.[6]

Oral contract partly performed An oral contract may be specifically enforced where there has been partial performance thereof so that it can be considered as fair and equitable. The theory on the basis of which a court will decree specific performance of an oral contract which has been partially performed is not primarily the enforcement of the contract, but rather the prevention of the use of the statute of frauds as an instrument of, or cloak for, fraud, so that the defendant will be required to do the things he contracted to do

4 *Suraj Lamp & Industries (P) Ltd.* v *State of Haryana* (2009)7 SCC 363.
5 *Ibid.*
6 *Suraj Lamp & Industries (P) Ltd.* (2) v *State of Haryana* (2012)1 SCC 656.

where he has led the other party to change his position in reliance on the agreement.[7]

Refund of consideration when contract is void or impossible When *B* contracts for sale of land to *A*, but to which *B* had no title, and when *B* had already received some consideration as advance, at the suit filed by *A*, for refund of consideration *B* is bound to refund the advantage (here part of the consideration he received), no matter that *A* was given possession of the land by *B*. It is not that the cause of action would arise only when *A* is dispossessed. Cause of action arises when *B* fails to register proper title deed and to convey title to *A*. This principle emanates from s. 65, Indian Contract Act which embodies a well-known rule of equity. It provides for restitution of or compensation for any advantage received under an agreement which becomes void.

Section 56 of the Contract Act also would apply to the facts of the case, the contract having become impossible by reason of the fact the defendant had no title and the State did not grant lease in favour of the defendant and the principle of paying back the advantage received under s. 65 applies also to a case which falls within the ambit of s. 56.[8] Section 65 of the Indian Contract Act says that when a contract becomes void any person who has received any advantage under such contract is bound to restore it to the person from whom he received it.[9] Section 65 which is based on equitable doctrine, provides for the restitution of any benefit received under a void agreement or contract and, therefore, mandates that any "person" which obviously would include a party to the agreement, who has received any advantage under an agreement which is discovered to be void or under a contract which becomes void, has to restore such advantage or to pay compensation for it, to the person from whom he received that advantage or benefit.[10]

Contracts specifically performable—statutory provisions A party aggrieved by the failure on the part of the other party to the agreement to perform his part of the agreement, shall have two kinds of remedies: (1) by accepting the breach as termination of the contract and seeking re-payment of the benefit derived by the party who committed the breach and also reasonable damages for such breach of obligation under the agreement; and (2) not to recognise the breach as a termination of the contract and insist upon performance of the obligations, as per the terms of the contract and in case of refusal, to approach the court for the necessary relief of specific performance and or damages. In neither case, he shall be required to seek

7 *Corpus Juris Secundum*, vol. 81, p. 856.
8 *Orissa State Electricity Board* v *Indian Metals and Ferro Alloys* AIR 1991 Ori 59.
9 *National Insurance Co. Ltd.* v *Seema Malhotra* (2001)3 SCC 151.
10 *Tarsem Singh* v *Sukhminder Singh* (1998)3 SCC 471.

a declaration that the cancellation of the agreement would amount to breach of the contract giving rise to the above said remedies. Seeking a prayer for declaration that a particular act on the part of a party to the contract is not against law shall not be a condition precedent for seeking the remedy based on such breach, namely refund of the advance amount and payment of damages or specific enforcement of the contract and damages.[11] The relevant statutory provisions are contained in ss. 10 to 13, Specific Relief Act 1963.

Section 10 of the Specific Relief Act 1963 deals with cases in which specific performance of contracts is enforceable. But the Specific Performance (Amendment) Act 2018 has substituted s. 10 which deals with specific performance in respect of contracts. It reads as "the specific performance of a contract shall be enforced by the court subject to the provisions contained in sub-sec. (2) of s. 11, s. 14 and s. 16".

After passing of the Amendment Act of 2018, s. 20 deals with substituted performance of contract. Prior to amendment in 2018, the specific performance of any contract may, in the discretion of the court, be enforced—(*a*) when there exists no standard for ascertaining actual damage caused by the non-performance of the act agreed to be done or (*b*) when the act agreed to be done is such that compensation in money for its non-performance would not afford adequate relief. Explanation (*i*) added to s. 10 of the Specific Relief Act provides for the court to presume the breach of a contract to transfer immovable property cannot be adequately relieved by compensation in money.[12] Further, there was nothing in s. 10 of the Specific Relief Act 1963 prior to amendment in 2018 to suggest that when a breach was committed by a party to the agreement by unilaterally cancelling the agreement, the contract could not be specifically enforced without seeking a declaration that the cancellation was bad. Similarly, no provision in the Indian Contract Act says that the remedy of specific enforcement of a contract cannot be sought for without seeking a declaration that the act of non-performance or cancellation on the part of the other party to the agreement is a bad in law and illegal.[13]

However, prior to amendment in 2018, s. 10 of the Act provided that the specific performance of contract may be enforced where (*i*) there was no standard of ascertaining actual damage and (*ii*) where the relief by way of compensation in money for non-performance was inadequate. The law relating to these two conditions prior to amendment is discussed below. The law has, however, undergone complete change. The conditions and explanations given in s. 10 have been removed and the discretion of the court has also been done away with so far as the enforcement of the specific

11 *R. Karuppusamy* v *P. Sivaraj* (2014)6 Mad LJ 654; 2015 AIR CC 2391.
12 *Mohinder Singh* v *Guljit Singh* PLR (2000)126 P&H 115; (2000)3 ICC 460.
13 *R. Karuppusamy* v *P. Sivaraj* (2014)6 Mad LJ 654; 2015 AIR CC 2391.

performance of contract is concerned in the new scheme of s. 10 of the Act by way of the Specific Relief (Amendment) Act 2018.

Clause (a)—no standard of ascertaining actual damage The basis of this rule is uncertainty of any calculation of damages as they must in such a case, be in a great measure conjectural. This clause covers cases where the subject matter is so unique that it would be impossible to say what it would fetch in the market.[14] This includes matters mingled with nostalgic affection, breach of contract in respect of which cannot have any standard of ascertaining the value. The value of affection is seldom appreciated by third persons. It needs a very enlightened benevolence and philosophy very uncommon to sympathize with tastes different from our own. All contracts concerning unique and precious articles, heirlooms or paintings, old furniture and the like for which there is no market price to furnish any criterion nor any other means of estimating the *pretium affectionis* which constitutes the real value to the owner, also contracts for delivery of deeds or other instruments of title and instruments in writing whose value to the owner might be priceless and be beyond the competency of a court to decide by application of certain legal rules, may be specifically enforced.[15]

The leading English case is *Pusey* v *Pusey*[16] where the heir sued, with success and sued, to recover a horn which bore an inscription and which had from time out of mind, been the token by which the family estate had, from time out of mind been held. An article may not have much intrinsic value, but by reason of peculiar association or some special considerations, it may have obtained in the eyes of its holders a value that cannot be estimated in any ordinary medium of exchange.

Specific performance may be granted in case of chattels which though not unique, possessed a special and peculiar value and importance to the plaintiff.[17] A stipulation in a contract to be liable to repay the amount paid[18] or to pay double the amount of earnest money,[19] to pay compensation if the promisor sold the property to another person,[20] does not detract from the right to specific performance.

Clause (b)—inadequacy of reliefs by way of compensation in money for non-performance and legal presumptions In view of the Explanation to s. 10, Specific Relief Act in cases of contracts relating to the transfer of immovable property, the law presumes that compensation in money will not afford

14 Story, *Commentaries on Equity Jurisprudence*, s. 722A.
15 *Montgomery Enterprises* v *Empire Theatre Co.* 204 Ala 566 [1920].
16 23 Eng Rep 465 [1684].
17 Fry on *A Treatise on the Specific Performance of Contracts*, 6th Ed., p. 36.
18 *Laxman Ram* v *Kishana Ram* AIR 2007 Raj 84.
19 *Gopal Dass* v *Sonu* AIR 2010 P&H 126.
20 *Sobharam Jivan* v *Tolaram Sitaram* AIR 1952 Nag 244.

adequate relief.[1] Therefore, to put it differently, according to s. 10 of the Specific Relief Act, the specific performance of any contract may, in the discretion of the court, be enforced when there exists no standard for ascertaining the actual damage caused by the non-performance of the act agreed to be done or when the act agreed to be done is such that compensation in money for its non-performance could not afford adequate relief. It also provides, unless and until the contrary is proved, the court shall presume that the breach of a contract to transfer immovable property cannot be adequately relieved by compensation in money.[2] The locality, character, vicinage, soil, easements or accommodations of the land or other immovable properties, generally, may give a peculiar and special value in the eyes of the purchaser which cannot be replaced by other properties of the same precise value, having the same precise legal conveniences or accommodations. Damages can hardly pay satisfactory relief in the case of contract for sale of immovable property and therefore ordinarily specific performance of the contract should be decreed.[3] The same is the position in regard to contracts for the transfer of movable property where the property is not an ordinary article of commerce, or is of special value or interest to the plaintiff, or consists of goods which are not obtainable in the market.

Presumption also applies where the property is held by the defendant as an agent or a trustee of the plaintiff, the idea being that persons who stand in fiduciary position to the plaintiff should not be allowed to retain the property even if the plaintiff may be fully compensated by the payment of damages. This seems to be based on the rule laid down in *Wood* v *Rowcliffe*.[4]

Obviously, as a result of this presumptive proof, the burden of proof lies on the defendant that damages would provide adequate relief.

As to this presumption emanating from Explanation to s. 10, since substituted, the words "shall presume" need careful notice. The presumption is not a discretionary one. It is one of the laws which the court must raise in every case.[5] The general rule is that burden lies on the party asserting a particular fact to be true. But that party can take advantage of presumptions which may be available to him to lighten the burden. These are (*a*) permissive presumptions or presumptions of fact; (*b*) rebuttable presumption of law and (*c*) irrebuttable presumption of law. Presumptions of fact are inferences from certain facts and patterns drawn from the experience and observations of common course of nature, the constitution of the human mind, the springs of human action, the usages and habits of the society and ordinary

1 This is perhaps based on the view that immovable property has a unique value for the buyer. But it is not understood how this applies in the case of vendor.
2 *R. Karuppusamy* v *P. Sivaraj* (2014)6 Mad LJ 654; 2015 AIR CC 2391.
3 *Beharilal* v *Swan Singh* (1975)77 PLR 478.
4 [1874]2 Ph 383.
5 Saharay & Saharay, *Law of Evidence*, p. 88.

course of human affairs. Section 114 of the Evidence Act 1872 is a general section dealing with such presumptions. The court has discretion in each case to draw such presumption of fact. There is no such discretion in case of presumption of law. While the presumption of fact merely affects the burden of going forward with the evidence, presumption of law goes so far as to shift the legal burden of proof so that, in the absence of evidence sufficient to rebut it on a balance of probability a verdict must be directed.[6] A presumption in itself is not evidence but only makes a *prima facie* case for the party in whose favour it exists. It is a rule concerning evidence. It indicates the person on whom the burden of proof lies. When the presumption is conclusive, it obviates the production of any other evidence to dislodge the conclusion to be drawn on proof of certain facts. But when it is rebuttable it only points out the party on whom lies the duty of going forward with evidence. When the party against whom the presumption is to be drawn has produced evidence fairly and reasonably tending to show that the real fact is not as presumed the purpose of presumption is over.[7]

The words "shall presume" and "may presume" mean in respect of the former "legal presumption" and in the latter "factual presumption." Whenever the legislature uses the word "shall presume" it shall regard the matter as proved unless and until it is disproved. In respect of legal presumption court is bound to raise the presumption; when in respect of factual presumption it is discretionary.[8]

Presumptions of law differ from presumptions of fact in the following respects: (1) Presumptions of law derive their force from law, while presumptions of fact derive their force from logic. And though many of the former have intrinsic logical weight, being indeed derived from the latter, yet there are others which have none. Thus, after a person has been absent for 6 years 364 days there can be no presumption of death, yet the addition of one more day's absence will enable the presumption to be applied. (2) A presumption of law applies to a class the conditions of which are fixed and uniform; a presumption of fact applies to individual cases, the condition of which are inconstant and fluctuating. Thus, the presumption of death arises whenever seven years' unexplained absence is proved; but when it is necessary to establish the time of death more precisely the question must be decided on the evidence adduced in each specific case. (3) Presumptions of law are drawn by the court, and in the absence of opposing evidence are conclusive for the party in whose favour they operate; presumptions of fact

6 *Syad Akbar* v *State of Karnataka* AIR 1979 SC 1848; 1979 CrLJ 1374.

7 *Sodhi Transport* v *State of U.P.* AIR 1986 SC 1099 at pp. 1105-1106; (1986)1 SCR 939; (1986)2 SCC 486.

8 *State of Madras* v *A. Vaidyanatha* AIR 1958 SC 61 at p. 65; 1958 SCR 580; 1958 CrLJ 232; *R.K. Mullick* v *State of W.B.* (1975)2 Cal LJ 154 at p. 165; *Shyam Sundar* v *Dharanidhar Padhi* (1971)1 Cut WR 784.

are drawn by the jury, who may disregard them, however cogent. In practice, however, these distinctions are by no means easy to apply; and the line of demarcation, even when visible, is often overlooked. A presumption which is regarded by some judges and textwriters as one of law is treated by others as one of fact, or of mixed law and fact; indeed, the same judges have not infrequently placed the same presumption in different categories at different times.[9]

In view of the words "unless and until the contrary is proved" the presumption is, a rebutable presumption and in a given case the court may find that the breach of the contract can be adequately relieved by payment of compensation in money.[10]

Specific performance for delivery of goods Section 58 of the Sale of Goods Act 1930 [corresponding to s. 52 of the (English) Sale of Goods Act 1979] dealing with specific performance for delivery of the goods provides that in an action for breach of contract the court may, on an application of the plaintiff by its judgment or decree, direct the contract shall be performed specifically, without giving the defendant any option of relating the goods on payment of damages. For such decree of judgment of specific performance the goods to be delivered by the defaulting seller are "specific or ascertained" goods. The Privy Council held that an order for specific performance could not be made where the seller agreed to supply all the coal that might required for the buyers' steel work.[11] In *Bahnke* v *Bede Shipping Co. Ltd.*[12] it was held that a ship was a specific chattel in respect of which an order for specific performance could be made. Section 58 of the Sale of Goods Act is supplementary to the provisions of Chapter-II of the Specific Relief Act as regards specific performance of contract relating to movable property which is an exception to the general rule of grant of damages, but in exceptional cases there is no bar for specific performance.[13] Section 58 empowers the court to decree specific performance of a contract for sale of movable goods, provided the suit is for breach of contract to deliver specific or ascertained goods. "Specific goods" has been defined in s. 2(14) of the Sale of Goods Act to mean goods identified and agreed upon at the time a contract of sale is made. Where the contract was to deliver specific and ascertained goods as contemplated by s. 58 of the Sale of Goods Act, the court would be entitled to grant a decree for specific performance even in case of sale of movable goods. Further, even if the plaintiff in such a case is entitled to a decree for specific performance, being a case covered by

9 Phipson on *Evidence*, 13th Ed, pp. 1047-1048.

10 *Dave Ramshankar Jivatram* v *Bai Kaliasgauri* AIR 1974 Guj 69 at p. 73.

11 *Dominion Coal Co. Ltd.* v *Dominion Iron & Steel Co. Ltd.* [1909] AC 293.

12 [1927]1 KB 649.

13 *A.P. Tobacco Growers Co-op. Union Ltd., Ongole* v *Sri Anjaneya Tobacco Co., Tangutur* (1998)2 AP LJ 471; (1998)5 ALD 188; (1998)5 ALT 331.

s. 58 of the Sale of Goods Act breach of an implied negative covenant can also be restrained by an order of injunction.[14] In an English case,[15] Lord Cairns, LC. observed:

> My Lords, if there had been a negative covenant, I apprehend, according to well settled practice, a Court of Equity would have had no discretion to exercise. If parties, for valuable consideration, with their eyes open, contract that particular thing shall not be done, all that a Court of Equity has to do is to say, by way of injunction, that which the parties have already said by way of covenant, that the thing shall not be done; and in such case the injunction does nothing more than give the sanction of the process of the court to that which already is the contract between the parties. It is not then a question of the balance of convenience or inconvenience, or of the amount of damage or of injury — it is specific performance, by the court, of that negative bargain which the parties have made, with their eyes open, between themselves.

The principle laid down above in *Richard Wheeler Doherty* (supra) has been relied by the Supreme Court with approval in *Dalpat Kumar* v *Prahlad Singh.*[16]

Specific enforcement of buyer's duty to take delivery Where the buyer wrongfully refuses to perform his duty to take delivery, that duty is specifically enforceable. In *P.&O. Nedloyd BV* v *Arab Metals Co.*[17] a CIF buyer to whom the bill of lading had been endorsed, wrongfully refused to take delivery of the goods from the carrier. On a claim for specific performance by the carrier against the buyer, the issue was whether this remedy was barred by lapse of time. The assumption underlying, seems to be that the remedy was, in principle, available to the carrier; and if it were so available, it should, in appropriate circumstances, also be available to a CIF seller against the buyer.[18]

Immovable property The definition of immovable property in s. 3 of the Transfer of Property Act 1882 is couched in negative form in that it does not include standing timber, growing crops or grass. The statute avoids positively defining 'immovable property', but merely excludes certain types of property from being treated as immovable property.[19] There is no definition of immovable property in the Act or in the Contract Act to which reference has to be made in respect of words or expressions not defined in the Act

14 *Jairam Valjee* v *Indian Iron & Steel Co. Ltd.* AIR 1940 Cal 466.
15 *Richard Wheeler Doherty* v *James Clagston Allman and W.C. Dowden* [1878]3 AC 709.
16 (1992)1 SCC 719; AIR 1993 SC 276.
17 [2007] EWCA Civ 1717; [2007]2 All ER (Comm) 401.
18 Benjamin's *Sale of Goods,* 9th Ed., para 19-246.
19 *Ram Rattan* v *Bajrang Lal* AIR 1978 SC 1393.

but defined in that Act [s. 2(*e*)]. Section 3(26) of the General Clauses Act gives the following definition of "immovable property":

> "Immovable property" shall include land, benefits to arise out of land, and things attached to the earth or permanently fastened to anything attached to the earth.

Benefits arising from land include right to extract mines and minerals, right to receive rent, right to transfer of leasehold rights, rights of a mortgagee with possession, right to collect market dues, right of way, right to produce of land and water (not merely right to tame water for it is not a *profit a prendre,* water not being a product of the soil), right to catch or carry away fish, right to tap trees, right to take out soil. The latter part of the definition embraces buildings, permanent structures erected on the land, pumping station installations, power houses etc.

But where a right is given to pluck leaves of trees, or to cut and carry away bamboo or timber and the process is to be completed in a short time, it is not a benefit arising out of land. So also, where the lessee fixes machinery for the use of his business. It is not clear whether goodwill attaching to a particular premises is movable or immovable property. In any case, unless the goodwill is annexed to the premises and the contract is for the sale of both premises and goodwill, it will not be specifically enforced.[20]

Broadly speaking, the degree, manner, extent and strength of attachment of the chattel to the earth or building are the main features to be considered. The attachment should be such as to partake of the character of the attachment of the trees or shrubs rooted to the earth or walls or building embedded in that sense; the further test is whether such an attachment is for the permanent beneficial enjoyment of the immovable property to which it is attached. An oil engine attached to the earth but removable is not immovable property.[1]

The real test for determining whether a tree is movable or immovable property is not the nature of the tree, but the way in which it is intended to be dealt with. If the intention of the parties in respect of a particular transaction is that the tree if to be cut by the purchaser and removed, it will be timber and movable property. But if the intention is that it should after the purchase continue to grow, it may not be timber and it is immovable property.[2]

Apex court in *Suresh* v *Kundan,*[3] standing timber on the land are part of the immovable property.

20 *Darbey* v *Whitaker* [1857]4 Drew 134 at p. 140.
1 *Perumal Naicker* v *T. Ramaswami Kone* AIR 1969 Mad 346.
2 *District Board, Benaras* v *Churu Rai* AIR 1956 All 680.
3 *Suresh Chand* v *Kundan* (2001)10 SCC 221.

Movable property Every property which is not immovable property is movable property and includes, water, electricity, copyright, patents, trade marks, designs, interest of a partner in the firm, share of a company, choses in action. Since a contract for the sale of immovable property does not create any interest in the property, it is also an instance of movable property.[4]

Movables are only if intended to be severed and sold separately. But if anything is to pass along with land, it is not movable.[5]

Black's *Law Dictionary*[6] defines movable property as "property that can be moved or displaced, such as personal goods; a tangible or intangible thing in which an interest constitutes personal property; specific, anything that is not so attached to land as to be regarded as a part of it as determined by local law".

In cases of contracts relating to the transfer of movable property, the presumption is otherwise, *viz.* that the breach can be relieved by payment of compensation in money, unless and until the case is proved to the contrary and the property is not an ordinary article of commerce, or is of special value or interest to the plaintiff, or consists of goods which are not easily obtainable in the market. Even so, there is no presumption that breach of such contracts cannot be relieved by payment of compensation in money.

Ordinary article of commerce Explanation to s. 10, Specific Relief Act provides that directing specific performance of contract is permissible when the act agreed to be done is such that compensation in money is not adequate relief. And unless and until the contrary is proved, the court shall presume that breach of contract in respect of movable property can be adequately compensated by money except when the property is not an ordinary article of commerce or is of special value or interest to the plaintiff.

In this context the meaning and implication of the words "an ordinary article of commerce" become apposite.

The Calcutta High Court has held that while it is difficult to say that it did not contemplate an article manufactured or prepared at the instance or specification of the buyer, it really means and speaks of certain rare things which cannot be produced or manufactured even at the specification or at the behest of the buyer[7] (large industrial machine built to order). The court held that even though the machinery was not an ordinary article of commerce

4 *Satyabrata Ghose* v *Mugneeram Bangur & Co.* AIR 1954 SC 44; 1954 SCR 310; 1954 SCJ 1; *Radhakishan Laxminarayan Toshniwal* v *Shridhar Ramchandra Alshi* AIR 1960 SC 1368; (1961)1 SCR 248; (1961)1 SCJ 215.

5 *CIT* v *Bhurangya Coal Co.* AIR 1959 SC 254.

6 10th Ed. 2014.

7 *Maheswari & Co Pvt. Ltd.* v *Corporation of Calcutta* AIR 1975 Cal 165 at p. 169; but see and compare *Societe des Industries Matallugiques SA* v *Bronx Engineering Co. Ltd.* [1975]1 Lloyds Rep 465 (CA).

and substantial delay and loss of profit would be involved in obtaining a substitute, yet damages would be adequate remedy.

In a case Corporation granted permission to the plaintiff to display advertisement board on electric poles, but Electricity Board objected. Injunction to restrain the Board from obstructing the fixing of advertisement board failed. It was held that the agreement is not jointly enforceable against the Corporation and the Board and specific performance of the contract, even if that can be decreed against the Corporation, would not entitle the appellant to pray for permanent or temporary injunction against the Board. Secondly, the "property" envisaged in Explanation (*ii*)(*a*) to s. 10 would be the right to put up the advertisement boards and that right would not be "movable property" within the meaning of the term employed in cl. (*ii*). If the advertisement boards, are considered to be "movable property" envisaged under cl. (*ii*), still the position will not be different because an advertisement board cannot be said to be "not an ordinary article of commerce." Obviously, the agreement did not create any "property" in the electric poles of the appellant.[8]

Property of special value or interest to the plaintiff Where the property is of special value or interest to the plaintiff on account of its unusual beauty or rarity or unique value, the contract will usually be specifically enforced, e.g. a jewel[9] the China vases,[10] stone from old Westminister Bridge,[11] an ornamental door designed by the famous architect Adam,[12] a ship,[13] (Contrast, however, *Societe des Industries Metallurgique SA* v *Bronx Engineering Co. Ltd. ante*).

Right to be acknowledged about plaintiff's service rendered to the defendant is one of special value which cannot be adequately expressed in terms of money. In a case the appellant, a film producer who claimed that the respondent an Italian film producer entered into an agreement with the appellant for the production and exhibition of a television serial based on an Italian novel. According to the appellant, the respondents were unable to make any headway in their project and they were not even able to obtain the permission of the Government of India for shooting the film in India which was a prerequisite before they could start their project. The appellant helped the respondent to get the permission from Government of India. The Supreme Court held that it was just and necessary that the appellant should be granted interim relief by injuncting the respondents from exhibiting

8 *Sagar Art Service, New Delhi* v *Municipal Corpn. Gwalior* AIR 1988 MP 46; 1988 MPLJ 392.

9 *Pearne* v *Lisle* [1749] Amb 75 at p. 77.

10 *Falcke* v *Gray* [1859]4 Drew 651; [1859]62 ER 250.

11 *Thorn* v *Commissioners of Public Works* [1863]32 Beav 490.

12 *Philips* v *Lamdin* [1949]1 All ER 770; [1949]2 KB 33.

13 *Behnke* v *Bede Shipping Co.* [1972]1 KB 649 at p. 661.

the film except after displaying an acknowledgment of the appellant's services, because in a matter of such type the award of damages is not a complete and adequate remedy or relief. Moreover, the appellant made clear, that he was not interested so much in the monetary aspect of the deal he claimed to have entered into with the respondents. The gain by way of reputation as well as goodwill which the appellant would secure if his services is acknowledged in the title shots of the film was not one which could be adequately expressed in terms of money.[14]

Delivery of defective goods supplied to consumers The concept of specific performance as a remedy of non-delivery of goods, but there is the further possibility that specific relief may be sought in respect of delivery which is defective in the sense that the goods delivered are not in conformity with the contract. This principle is particularly applied to a buyer who deals as a consumer.[15]

Where goods not easily obtainable in the market Specific performance of contract is enforceable when the goods contracted to be transferred is not easily obtainable in market. "Goods" means every kind of movable property other than actionable claims and money; and includes stock and shares, growing crops, grass, and things attached to or forming part of the land which are agreed to be served before sale or under the contract of sale [Sale of Goods Act 1930, s. 2(7)]. As far as Explanation to s. 10 of thc Specific Relief Act which has been omitted by the Amendment Act of 2018 is concerned, a breach of contract to transfer immovable property can be adequately relieved except if the property is not an ordinary article of commerce or is of special value or interest or consists of goods which are not easily obtainable in the market.[16] That apart, s. 58 applies only to the claim of purchaser or buyer of certain goods and of the seller.[17]

Where goods are easily obtainable in the market, damages would provide adequate relief in the event of the breach of the contract.

Section 58 of the Sale of Goods Act provides that where the contract relates to the delivery of specific or ascertained goods, the court may order specific performance of the contract without giving the defendant the option of retaining the goods on payment of damages. "Specific goods" are defined by s. 2(14) of the Sale of Goods Act to mean goods identified and agreed upon at the time a contract of sale is made. The goods must be identified

14 *Suresh Jindal* v *Rizsoli Corriere Della Sera Prodzioni* AIR 1991 SC 2092 at p. 2093; 1991 Supp (2) SCC 3; JT 1992(1) SC 33.

15 Benjamin's *Sale of Goods,* 9th Ed., para 19-232.

16 *Britannia Industries Limited* v *Sulochana Cotton Spinning Mills Private Limited* (2011)3 MWN (Civil) 433; (2011)5 LW 492; (2012)1 Mad LJ 86.

17 *Maheswari and Co. Pvt. Ltd.* v *Corporation of Calcutta* AIR 1975 Cal 165.

at the time of the contract and not merely be "identifiable".[18] Sale of forest timber of a certain height, to be cut by buyer was given 15 years' time. It was held that the timber was not an identified goods, though it is not a condition that the goods would presently exist. There is no definition of "ascertained goods", but they mean "goods ordinarily ascertained which are identified in accordance with the parties' agreement after the contract of sale is made."[19] And if the court makes the order, the buyer will receive goods themselves in the same way as the seller's right of stoppage in transit entitles the seller to recover possession of the goods, In re, *Wait (ante)*. So specific performance was refused where the seller had agreed to sell all the coal that might be required for the buyer's steel works.[20] Likewise, where there was a sub-contract to sell 500 tons out of a consignment of 1,000 tons of wheat bought by the seller, the order was refused on the ground that the 500 tons were neither specific nor ascertained goods, since an unappropriated part of a larger ascertained bulk did not constitute an ascertained part, *In re, Wait (ante)*.

Even so, the provision is subject to the equitable principles contained in the Specific Relief Act and if the court finds that the breach can be relieved by payment of damages it would not order specific enforcement of the contract. It is also to be noted that this provision is for the benefit of the buyer and the seller cannot force the buyer to take the goods.[1]

On the same principle, the court refused to order specific performance of the contract for the purchase of waste coal ash from a power station on the ground that the plaintiff had not led any evidence to show that the ash was required by the plaintiff for his own purpose or was of special value or interest to him and further that the ash was easily available in the market.[2]

From every contract, there immediately and directly results an obligation on each of the contracting parties to the other of them to perform such of the terms of the contract as he has undertaken to perform and if the person on whom this obligation rests fails to discharge it, there results to the other party a right, at his election, either to insist on the actual performance of the contract or to obtain compensation for the non-performance of it.[3] In *Chandrakant Shankar Pradhan* v *Verma Investment Corporation*,[4] cl. (16) of the agreement provided the plaintiff with an alternative remedy to insist on obtaining similar accommodation elsewhere or monetary compensation. The defendant contended that this clause operated as a bar to the suit for

18 *Kursell* v *Timber Operators & Contractors Ltd.* [1927]1 KB 298.
19 Re *Wait* [1927]1 Ch 606 at p. 630 (CA).
20 *Dominion Coal Co. Ltd* v *Dominion Iron & Steel Co. Ltd.* [1909] AC 293 at p. 311.
1 *Maheswari & Co. Private Ltd.* v *Corporation of Calcutta* AIR 1975 Cal 165 at p. 169.
2 *Tej Singh* v *State of U.P.* AIR 1981 All 103.
3 *Nilkanta Roy Chowdhury* v *Lalit Mohan Banerjee* AIR 1916 Cal 774.
4 AIR 1992 Bom 257.

specific performance. Rejecting the contention, the High Court of Bombay held that the plaintiff's legal right to such specific performance of the suit agreement was not barred by cl. (16) of the agreement which conferred an additional right on the plaintiff and it did not deprive him of his normal remedies. In *N.L. Devender Singh* v *Syed Khaja*,[5] Their Lordships of the Supreme Court held that the mere insertion of a clause in the contract for sale of immovable property providing for liquidated damages or a penalty for a breach is not sufficient to show that damages are an adequate remedy.

Specific performance of a part of a contract (s. 12 of the Act) Section 12 of the Specific Relief Act 1963 combines ss. 14 to 17 of the Act of 1877. The consolidation has been made on the following recommendation of the Law Commission:

> "While s. 17 enunciates the general rule that the court will not enforce specific performance of a part of a contract, ss. 14, 15 & 16 provide exceptions to this general rule and the Privy Council has held[6] that ss. 14 to 17 taken together constituted a complete Code and that any claim for specific relief of part of a contract must be brought within the terms of these sections. In these circumstances, it is desirable to amalgamate ss. 14 to 17 into one section."

Sub-section (3) to s. 12 of the Specific Relief Act 1963 corresponds to s. 15 of the Specific Relief Act 1877. But there is one difference between the two provisions, whereas under s. 15 of the old Act, the party seeking specific performance of a part of a contract was required to pay the entire sale consideration stipulated under the contract, under s. 12 of the present Act, the specific performance of a part of the contract can be granted on payment of proportionate consideration, provided the plaintiff relinquishes all claims to the performance of the remaining part of the contract and all right to compensation either for the deficiency or for the loss or damage sustained by him in the default of the defendant.[7]

The general rule as embodied in s. 12 of the Act is that the Court must not direct specific performance of a part of a contract.[8] But, it is possible where a share of a contracting party is identifiable, severable and separate from the share of the one against whom specific performance of the agreement cannot be enforced.[9] Sub-section (1) of s. 12 has an overriding effect and unless the conditions of sub-secs. (2) to (4) are fulfilled, the courts will not direct specific performance of a part of a contract.[10] The

5 AIR 1973 SC 2457; (1974)1 SCR 312; (1973)2 SCC 515.
6 *Graham* v *Krishna Chandra* 52 Cal 335 (PC).
7 *S. Nagulal Rao* v *Medam Jayaramaiah* (1996)4 ICC 699.
8 *Gopal Dass* v *Khan Chand* AIR 2006 P&H 136.
9 *Kartar Singh* v *Harjinder Singh* (1990)3 SCC 517; AIR 1990 SC 854.
10 *Subramani* v *Kannappa Reddiar* AIR 1973 Mad 393.

court should abstain from remodeling of a contract and the section cannot be used to override an express agreement of the parties.[11] Another requirement for specific performance of a part of a contract is that the part performed bears a substantial portion in value and the unperformed portion admits of compensation in money.[12] Where the performance of a whole of a contract is not possible, there can be a direction given by the court for specific performance of the contract that can be performed in case the part that cannot be performed is a small portion of the entire contract.[13]

As to specific performance of a part of a contract, the Madras High Court has quoted Pomeroy on *A Treatise on Specific Performance of Contracts* as under: "When the vendor's title proves to be defective in some particulars, or his estate is different from that which he agreed to convey, or is subject to encumbrances or outstanding rights to third persons, or the subject matter generally the land is deficient in quantity, quality or value, it is plain that the contract cannot be specifically performed, according to its exact terms, at the suit of either party. In such a case there are only three possible alternatives for a court of equity to pursue, either to refuse this remedy entirely; or to enforce the contract without any regard to the partial failure, compelling the purchaser to take what there is to give and to pay the full price as agreed; or to decree the conveyance of the vendor's actual interest and allow to the vendee pecuniary compensation or abatement from the price, proportional to the amount and value of the defect in title or deficiency in the subject matter."[14]

The principles applicable to different kinds of circumstances in English law have been summed up by the Privy Council in *Duncan Rutherford* v *William Acton Adams.*[15]

If a vendor sues and is in a position to convey substantially what the purchaser has contracted to get, the court will decree specific performance with compensation for any small and immaterial deficiency, provided that the vendor has not, by misrepresentation or otherwise, disentitled himself to his remedy. Another possible case arises where a vendor claims specific performance and where the court refuses it unless the purchaser is willing to consent to a decree on terms that the vendor will make compensation to the purchaser, who agrees to such a decree on condition that he is compensated. If it is the purchaser who is suing the court holds him to have an even larger right. Subject to considerations of hardship he may elect to take all he can get, and to have a proportionate abatement from the purchase

11 *Secretary of State* v *Volkart Bros.* AIR 1928 PC 258.
12 *Baij Nath* v *Ansal & Saigal Properties P. Ltd.* AIR 1993 Del 285.
13 *Krishnaswamy* v *Munian* 1988(2) CCC 417.
14 *A.L. Partha Sarathi Mudaliar* v *Venkata Kondiah Chettair* AIR 1965 Mad 188 at p. 189.
15 AIR 1915 PC 113; [1915] AC 866.

money. But this right applies only to a deficiency in the subject matter described in the contract.

Even where the suit property is un-partitioned and unspecified, it was held that the suit for specific performance of contract by a third person who has entered into the agreement of sale with respect to the said property is maintainable inasmuch as whenever a share in the property is sold the vendee has a right to apply for the partition of the property and get the share demarcated.[16]

The above stated principles were embodied in ss. 14 to 17 of the Specific Relief Act 1877 and it was held in the Madras case.[17] Sections 14 to 17 of the old Act provided the remedies for partial specific performance of the contract with compensation. Section 14 is applied to a case where a party to contract is unable to perform the whole or part of it. On account of some incurable defect in title or deficiency in quantity of the subject matter or of some legal impediment, when the court may at the suit of either party direct the performance of so much of the contract as can be performed and award compensation in money for the deficiency by proportionate abatement of the purchase money. But two conditions are necessary before s. 14 can be applied, namely, the part which must be left unperformed bears only a small proportion to the whole in value, that is, so small that it is inconsiderable, such as small mistake or inaccuracy and it may be compensated in money by allowing an abatement of the purchase money by calculating the difference between what was contracted to be done and what can actually be done or sold. In other words, where a substantial part of the contract is capable of performance, then equity will enforce specific performance of that part. The above formulation of law applies even in the present s. 15 of the Specific Relief Act 1963.[18]

Normally, it is not permissible to seek specific performance of a part of a contract. This is on the view that in a limited sense when a court decrees specific performance of a part of a contract, it virtually amounts to the court making a new bargain for the contracting parties which they never would have made for themselves, and it is for this reason that it is only in special cases, subject to certain conditions, that a party can claim specific performance of a part of a contract.[19]

But where the part stands on a separate and independent footing from another part which cannot be specifically performed, remedy can be sought in respect of that part which can be specifically enforced [s. 12(4)]. A brother in a case entered into contract to sell to the plaintiff on his own

16 *Namrita Kalra* v *Ram Swaroop* (2001)58 DRJ 338; (2001)91 DLT 145.
17 *A.L. Partha Sarathi* v *Venkata Kondiah Chettiar* AIR 1965 Mad 188 at p. 189.
18 *Ibid.*
19 *Subramani* v *Kannappa Reddiar* AIR 1973 Mad 393 at p. 394.

behalf and on behalf of his sister to sell his share in entirety in the property and the share of the sister in entirety. The sister later refused to execute the part of the contract so far as her share was concerned. The Supreme Court held it was not a case attracting the bar of s. 12, Specific Relief Act, which relates to specific performance of part of contract. The agreement is that the brother contracted to sell whole of his property. The contracts, *viz.* for the sale of his share and of his sister were separate and severable from each other although they were incorporated in one agreement. In fact there was no contract between the appellant and the sister of the respondent and the only valid contract was with respect to the share of the brother.[20]

In *Sri Krishna Keshar Kulkarni* v. *Balaji Ganesh Kulkarni,*[1] two brothers entered into an agreement to sell two houses to the plaintiff and the language of the agreement showed that the houses were jointly owned by the two brothers. The plaintiff at first filed a separate suit against the first brother for specific performance with respect to one house and obtained a decree and subsequently he filed another suit against the other brother in respect of the other house. It was held that specific performance for a part of the contract could not be granted, that in view of ss. 91 and 92 of the Evidence Act, oral evidence to show that the agreement in fact consisted of two separate agreements and that each brother owned one of the houses separately, that each brother was to receive half of the consideration separately, was barred. In *Sardar Singh* v *Krishna Devi,*[2] Their Lordships of the Supreme Court observed that "any suit for specific performance of a contract for sale of property in regard to the entire property by the purchaser, partial enforcement of the contract can be allowed when the property is capable of division instead of refusing it in its entirety.

In *Kartar Singh* v *Harjinder Singh,*[3] the respondent entered into an agreement with the appellant for himself and on behalf of his sister for sale of properties belonging to both. The sister refused to sell her share. Their Lordships of the Supreme Court decreed the suit for specific performance in respect of the respondent's share and held that the vendee had a right to apply for partition and get his share demarcated. The High Court of Madras relying on the above decision of the Supreme Court held that s. 12(1) of the Specific Relief Act did apply to a case where the party who is unable to perform the whole or part of the contract sues for specific performance. It was held on the facts of the case that the party to the suit for specific performance would not be said to be one so unable to perform and granted specific performance in respect of the share of the property

20 *Kartar Singh* v *Harjinder Singh* AIR 1990 SC 854; (1990)3 SCC 517; JT 1990(1) SC 253.

1 AIR 1976 Bom 342.

2 AIR 1995 SC 491; JT 1994(3) SC 465.

3 AIR 1990 SC 854; JT 1990(1) SC 253.

held by the promisor excluding the share of the co-sharer who did not join in the contract, on payment of proportionate price to the promisee.[4]

In *K.S. Krishan* v *Krishnan,*[5] where three co-owners entered into an agreement for sale of property, it was held that such an agreement can be specifically enforced against one of the co-owners. Where the agreement for sale was entered into by a brother in respect of his share and also in respect of the share of his sister, having no authority from her, the share of two being identifiable and separate from each other, the vendee was held entitled for specific performance of the share of the brother only when the sister did not agree to the sale.[6]

Where the agreement is a composite one so that the part which cannot be specifically enforced cannot be separated from the part which can be, specific performance will not be ordered,[7] (agreement of lease coupled with a covenant that lessee will be employed throughout the tenancy on commission). Likewise, piecemeal performance will not be decreed.[8] A lady entered into contract of sale in respect of $^1/_3$rd share but she had only $^1/_9$th share. The contract being indivisible and her share having no independent existence, s. 12(4) was held inapplicable and specific performance was refused.[9] When the agreement of sale was entered into, the seller had no right to alienate his undivided share in the Hindu joint family property in respect of specific portions of the property, the purchaser would not be entitled to any decree for specific performance of contract. Though subsequently, a suit for partition had been instituted the seller was given $^1/_5$th share in the joint family property, it was held other coparceners would not be bound by the agreement for sale. The purchaser was held not entitled to specific performance of contract. However, court on consideration of facts awarded interest at the rate of 12% p.a. on amount received by seller from purchaser and also exemplary cost of ₹5,000.[10] Where, however, the part which it is impossible to enforce has already been performed, a decree will be passed.[11] Likewise, if a contract is severable into a series of independent contracts, an assignee or sub-purchaser of a severable part of the original contract may require completion of that part without having to procure completion of the original contract in its entirety.[12]

4 *Taka Shahul Hameed* v *K. Abdul Rasheed Khan* (1992)2 Civ LJ 588 (Mad).
5 AIR 1993 Ker 134.
6 *Kapar Singh* v *Surinder Singh* 1993(1) Simla LJ 826 (P&H).
7 *Ogden* v *Fassick* 32 LJ Ch 73; 45 ER 1240.
8 *Odessa Tramways Co.* v *Mendel* [1878]8 Ch D 235.
9 *T.K. Santha* v *A.G. Rathnam* AIR 1990 Ker 69 relying on *A.L. Partha Sarathi* v *Venkata Kondiah Chettiar* AIR 1965 Mad 188.
10 *Triloki Vishwakarma* v *Zaitun Nisa* AIR 1992 Pat 40.
11 *Hope* v *Hope* [1856]52 ER 1143; *Re Caborne, Hodge & Nabarro* v *Smith* [1943] Ch 224.
12 *Wilkinson* v *Clements* [1872]8 Ch App 96.

In a case the defendant got a decree in respect of a plot of land in entirety. Dispute cropped up in respect of purchase of the said plot from the defendant by the plaintiff. An arbitrator was appointed who made and published an award directing the defendant to convey only 5,172 square yards of land. It was contended that the arbitrator could not split up the package deal. Repelling the contention it was held that the arbitrator had ample discretion to mould the relief or grant specific performance in part, *i.e.* restricted to the conveyance of the land depending upon the equities of the case and assessment of the case and assessment of the situation and overall view of the facts and conduct of the parties. In this view of the matter the High Court refused to set aside the arbitration award.[13]

It is open to the parties to arrive at any agreement convenient to them, unless, of course, such an agreement is rendered void by some provisions like those enacted in s. 23 of the Indian Contract Act. There is no provision either in the Specific Relief Act or in any other Act which forbids the parties concluding an agreement not conforming to the provisions of s. 12(1). This would come into play only if there is no agreement to the contrary between the parties or if its benefits are not waived by the party entitled to avail of the same.[14] (Provisions of s. 12 of the Specific Relief Act do not involve any questions of public policy).

It was also observed that "the court will have regard to the substance rather than to the form of the contract and will not allow the impossibility of a literal fulfillment to prevail as a defence, and that if the agreement can be carried out substantially, it will do so as to effectuate the intention of the parties and do entire justice between them."[15]

Where an agent was authorised by power of attorney to sell half right over property and on basis of that power he entered into an agreement with purchaser plaintiff to sell the entire property, the authorized portion was separable from the unauthorized portion in a claim by plaintiff under s. 22 of the Specific Relief Act for enforcement of agreement for sale only that extent of agreement was enforceable over which alone the agent had the authority.[16]

Where the plaintiff had made an agreement to purchase two houses from two brothers under one contract of sale, it was not permissible to sue for the specific performance of the contract for a single house, nor was it open to the plaintiff to lead evidence to the effect that the two brothers were separate and the houses were owned by them separately.[17] But where

13 *Farohar and Co.* v *Hemant Monohar Nabar* AIR 1992 Bom 8.
14 *Nirmala Sundari Dutta Chowdhary* v *Kumode Bandhu Deb* AIR 1976 Gau 58 at p. 60 (DB) relying on *T.V. Kochuvarsad* v *P. Mariappa* AIR 1954 Trav-Co 10.
15 *Ibid.*
16 *Ahammad* v *Mammad Kunhi* AIR 1987 Ker 228.
17 *Shrikrishna Keshav Kulkarni* v *Balaji Ganesh Kulkarni* AIR 1976 Bom 342.

a part of the contract has already been carried out outside the court, it would mean real hardship to non-suit the plaintiff on the principle that he is claiming specific performance of a part of the contract only.

Land was jointly inherited by two brothers and three sisters. Agreement to sell was executed by two brothers but sisters were not made parties. Section 12 of the Specific Relief Act 1963 cannot be invoked by the vendee to obtain sale of individual share of two brothers with a right to force partition on sisters.[18]

Agreement to sell property nowhere contains that in the event the permission to sell minor's share was not obtained within the period specified therein, the same shall become invalid or otherwise unenforceable in law. Application for grant of permission to sell minor's share was rejected only during pendency of the suit. Contract thus was not contingent contract. Vendors having definite shares in the property excluding minor's share did not enter into composite contract. Decree for specific performance of contract regarding vendors excluding share of minor can be passed. More so, purchaser relinquished his claim in respect of property belonging to minor by way of amendment. Alternative plea for refund of earnest amount and damage cannot itself be bar to claim decree for specific performance of contract. Decree for partition and separate possession of property can be granted in addition to decree for specific performance of contract.[19]

Vendor agreed to sell property in its entirety, but later it transpired that the vendor had only half share in the property and his wife held remaining half share. Agreement would be binding on the vendor as it is without being fractured. Thus, there would be no impediment for enforcement of agreement against vendor to the extent of his half share in the property.[20]

In a suit for specific performance of contract plaint was amended to change description of suit property. Despite amendment substantial portion of suit land remained the same. Decree for specific performance can be granted as regards part of the suit property. Additional averment or proof of readiness and willingness is not necessary since substantial parts of suit property remained the same. Plaintiff paid part of sale consideration on execution of the agreement. Averment in plaint that he had gone to Registration Office for getting sale deed executed and registered, but vendor did not turn up. Balance consideration was deposited on the date of filing of suit. Readiness and willingness of plaintiff stood proved.[1]

Pleading with regard to performance of a small portion of the contract has to be made by the plaintiff as an alternative plea to enforce the whole

18 *Shanmughasundaram* v *Diravia Nadar* AIR 2005 SC 1836.
19 *P.C. Varghese* v *Devaki Amma Balambika Devi* AIR 2006 SC 145.
20 *Kammana Sambamurthy* v *Kalipatnapu Atchutamma* AIR 2011 SC 103.
1 *Gurdial Kaur* v *Piara Singh* AIR 2008 SC 2019; (2008)14 SCC 735.

of the contract. Dealing with the similar issue Bombay High Court observed that when the court finds that only a small portion of the contract could be performed, whether the relief of specific performance is to be granted or not cannot be determined automatically in a suit where the plaintiffs plead only for the specific performance of the whole contract. If the plaintiff seeks performance, in the alternative of that part of the contract that could still be performed, however small that may be, he must plead appropriately, for, it is only on such pleadings that questions calling for decision within the scope of s. 12(3) can be decided by the court. On appropriate pleading by plaintiff, they will have to be answered by defendant. Where there is no such pleading, relief with regard to enforcement of a portion only will not be granted.[2] This view also finds support from the decisions of Kerala High Court[3] and Andhra Pradesh High Court.[4]

A court dealing with a suit for specific performance of contract is entitled to grant lesser relief than the one claimed in the suit; but the law is equally clear that in such a situation, the plaintiff must come up with the prayer for amendment of plaint disclosing his intention of being satisfied with the lesser relief than the one claimed in the suit and indicating his intention of relinquishing his original claim. Such amendment of plaint can also be filed before the Appellate Court.[5]

Specific performance of part of a contract can be claimed even at the belated stage of the proceeding. It is open to the plaintiff to relinquish a part of the contract even at the belated stage of the proceedings.[6]

Relief after lapse of long time Fifteen years of inactivity of plaintiff and eight years delay after sanctioning of mutation of inheritance are sufficiently long time in passing any decree of possession by way of specific performance. Suit is also barred in absence of any valuable evidence explaining the reasons of delay. Thus, execution of agreement and readiness and willingness on the part of the plaintiff to perform his part of contract have little value. Refusal of relief of specific performance is held to be proper.[7] In respect of property in urban areas, it was held by the Supreme Court that the value of property escalates in urban areas very fast and it would not be equitable to grant specific performance after the lapse of a long period of time.[8]

2 *Bhaurao Shamrao Bhalme* v *Mahadeo Raghu Yelekar* AIR 1979 Bom 208.
3 *Sanku Balakrishnan* v *Raman Kunjikrishnan* AIR 1982 NOC 18 (Ker).
4 *Doma Varalakshmi* v *Momidisetti Malleswara Rao* (1999)4 ICC 643; 2000 AIHC 896.
5 *Shyam Sundar Sharma (Gour)* v *Suresh Sharma* (2009)2 CHN 368; (2009)3 ICC 194; (2009)1 Cal LT 521; *Surinder Singh* v *Kapoor Singh* (2005)5 SCC 142.
6 *Bhajan Singh* v *Jaswant Singh* AIR 2006 P&H 145; *Rachakonda Narayana* v *Ponthala Parvathamma* (2001)8 SCC 173.
7 *Gurdev Singh* v *Jora Singh* AIR 2016 P&H 14.
8 *Vimaleshwar Nagappa Shet* v *Noor Ahmed Shariff* (2011)12 SCC 658; AIR 2011 SC 2057.

Similar view was reiterated in *Nanjappan* v *Ramasamy*[9] and *Saradamani Kandappan* v *S. Rajalakshmi*.[10] Thus, merely because the court has discretionary power to grant decree of specific performance, it cannot grant such relief. In such cases, the *doctrine of comparative hardship* plays an important role. The doctrine has been statutorily recognized in India under s. 20 of the Specific Relief Act 1963. Therefore, performance of the contract involving some hardship on the defendant which he did not foresee while non-performance involving no such hardship on the plaintiff, is one of the circumstances in which the court may properly exercise discretion not to decree specific performance.[11] Thus, severe hardship may be a ground for refusing specific performance even though it results from circumstances which arise after the conclusion of the contract, which affect the person of the defendant rather than the subject matter of the contract, and for which the plaintiff is in no way responsible.[12]

Specific performance and refund of earnest money One cannot dispute the legal position that once the bargain to sale/purchase of any land fails, the unsuccessful buyer becomes entitled in law to claim refund of earnest money from the seller under s. 22 of the Specific Relief Act 1963.[13] Thus, where the suit was for specific performance in respect of agreement to sell with alternative relief for refund of earnest money with interest thereon @15% per annum, the defence was that the time was the essence of the contract and plaintiffs failed to pay within time. Stipulation for forfeiture of earnest money in the event of failure to execute sale deed was also made. This indicates that time was never intended by parties to be the essence of the contract. Defendant could not substantiate the plea that time was essence of the contract and that plaintiff avoided to perform their part of the contract. Plaintiffs were, therefore, entitled to decree. Plaintiffs were entitled to seek alternative relief of refund of earnest money in the event decree for specific performance cannot be granted for any reason.[14]

Other exceptions—specific performance of a part There are other exceptions to the rule. Where a party to the contract is unable to perform the whole of his part of it, but the part which cannot be performed bears only a small proportion to whole in value and admits of compensation in money, the court has power to order the specific performance of the performable part and award compensation for the other part [s. 12(2) of the Specific Performance Act]. While it is true to say that to grant a decree for property

9 (2015)14 SCC 341.

10 (2011)12 SCC 18.

11 *K. Narendra* v *Riviera Apartments (P) Ltd.* (1999)5 SCC 77.

12 Chitty on *Contracts*, 27th Ed., vol. 1. p. 1296.

13 *Revanasiddayya* v *Gangamma* (2018)1 SCC 610.

14 *Balasaheb Dayandeo Naik* v *Appasaheb Dattatraya Pawar* AIR 2008 SC 1205.

other than the one contracted for is contrary to the very notion of specific performance, it all depends on the circumstances of the individual case.[15]

In *Mahendra Nath* v *Baikunthi Devi*[16] the trial court decreed the suit, but on appeal the court took the view that since the agreement of sale was hit by s. 5(*c*)(*ii*) of the U.P. Consolidation of Holdings Act 1953, the agreement could not be enforced. It also held that since the plaintiff wanted the enforcement of the entire agreement, it could not be enforced even in respect of the house. On further appeal, the question was whether the agreement to sell could be specifically enforced in respect of chak No. 10 which included some new plots not included in the deed of agreement.

Answering the question in the affirmative, the High Court held that since all the plots which were the subject matter of the contract were included in the joint chak [with the exception of plot No. 172 (.06 acre) and in lieu of which also another plot No. 164 (.03 acre) was allotted] and the plaintiff was ready to forgo his claim for the balance, the decree would be passed. The decision was affirmed by the Supreme Court.[17]

When the defendant had lost the contract property as a result of a scheme of consolidation and his right, title and interest ceased in that property by virtue of cl. (*a*) of s. 30 of the U.P. Consolidation of Holdings Act 1953, the agreement of sale became void within the meaning of s. 56 of the Contract Act and it was futile to urge that the agreement was saved by cl. (*a*) or cl. (*b*) of s. 30 of that Act.[18]

In cases falling under sub-sec. (2) of s. 12, the question to be determined is whether the part left unperformed is small or considerable; if the proportion is small and admits of compensation in money, then the court may in the suit of either party, direct specific performance of so much of contract as can be performed and award compensation in money for the deficiency. The principle on which sub-sec. (2) is based, is that equity looks to the substance rather than to the mere letter of the contract. Where the defect of title is not substantial or the defect in quantity of the subject matter is small, the court will decree specific performance at the instance of either party with abatement or compensation for the defect or deficiency. Thus, when the vendor sued for specific performance and was in a position to convey substantially what the purchaser had contracted to get, the court decreed the specific performance with compensation to the purchaser for any small or immaterial deficiency, provided the vendor had not by misrepresentation or otherwise disentitled himself to this remedy.[19]

15 *Narain Singh* v *Dalip Singh* AIR 1973 Raj 45.

16 AIR 1976 All 150 (FB).

17 *Baikunthi Devi* v *Mahendra Nath* AIR 1977 SC 1514; (1977)2 SCC 496. But see *Piarey Lal* v *Harilal* AIR 1977 SC 1226; (1977)2 SCC 221; (1977)2 SCR 915.

18 *Chandrika Chaubey* v *Mst. Pyari* 1983 All LJ 230.

19 *Duncan Rutherford* v *William Acton Adams* [1915] AC 866; *Arun Prokash Boral* v *Tulsi Charan Bose* AIR 1949 Cal 510.

Thus, if there is a misdescription of the property as regards its character, quality or title, but the misdescription is light and admits fairly of compensation, equity will enforce the contract at the instance of either party, but only with compensation for the misdescription. Cases of this kind occur normally where deficiency in acreage appears on measurement after the contract is made. Here if the purchaser will get substantially what he bargained for, the vendor can compel him to take it with compensation for the difference at an abated price and the purchaser can also compel the vendor to convey for a lower price. Where according to the contract the vendor promised to give vacant possession to the purchaser but was unable to give such possession owning to his own default, the purchaser in a suit for specific performance has the option to take the house without vacant possession with compensation. If the purchaser so elects, the defendant cannot be allowed to say that the contract was to deliver vacant possession and not the delivery of the property with tenant, for, a party cannot rely on his own default and excuse himself from performance of his contract.[20]

In *Baikunthi Devi* v *Mahendra Nath,*[1] it was held that the plaintiff was entitled to a decree of specific performance of a contract to sell agricultural land entered into pending consolidation proceedings, after the close of the proceedings, where the land allotted to the owner was substantially the same less a tiny bit. In a case, the natural guardian of Hindu minors contracted for sale of his own property and that of the minors without obtaining the requisite permission from the court, the contract was unenforceable against the minor's property in view of s. 8 of the Hindu Minority and Guardianship Act 1956. But the minor's property bore only a small portion to the whole property, as out of the total extent of 94 cents only 18 cents belonged to the minors, and the small portion admitted compensation in money, the plaintiff, in view of s. 12(2) of the Specific Relief Act, was granted the decree of specific performance so far as the property of the guardian was concerned.[2] In *Mohamed Asgar Mohamed Mazhar* v *Arvind Raghunath Sawant,*[3] the property belonged to a Hindu undivided family in which minors had share. The minors were not parties to the agreement for sale. There was no evidence to show any legal necessity for the sale. The Supreme Court held that the courts below were justified in refusing relief for specific performance.

Under s. 12(3) of the Specific Relief Act, where the part constitutes a considerable part of the whole though admitting of compensation in money, the court may compel the specific performance of the remaining part,

20 *Arun Prokash Boral* v *Tulsi Charan Bose* AIR 1949 Cal 510; see also *Ramani Ammal* v *Susilammal* AIR 1991 Mad 163; (1991)2 LW 43.

1 AIR 1977 SC 1514; (1977)2 SCC 496.

2 *Santhos Kumar* v *Varghese George* AIR 1988 Ker 277.

3 (2001)5 Supreme 396.

provided that the plaintiff has paid the full consideration for the part which can be performed reduced by the consideration for the part left unperformed and also relinquishes all of his claims to the performance of the remaining part of the contract as well as his rights to compensation either for the deficiency or for the loss or damage sustained by him owing to defendant's default.

But where the party does not admit of any compensation in money, the plaintiff has not only to pay the entire consideration without any abatement, but also to relinquish all his claims to the performance of the balance part and to compensation as in the former case [s. 12(3)]. It is made clear that the defendant shall be deemed to be unable to perform the entire contract, if a portion of its subject matter existing at the date of the contract has ceased to exist at the time of the performance (*Expl.* to s. 12).

The party in default refers to the party who is unable to perform the whole of his part of the contract and not to the party by whose default the inability was caused.[4]

Where the plaintiff brings a suit for the entire contract, it is not permissible to him to tell the court that he may be granted decree for only a part, for the frame of a suit for specific performance of the whole contract is distinct from that for specific performance of a part of it, as different considerations arise in the two suits.[5]

Inability to perform a part emanating from one's own default or self-created disability The words "unable to perform" suggest that the sub-sec. (2) of s. 12 of the Act is applicable only when the party cannot for any reason perform the whole of what he has promised. The inability may arise from several causes including statutory limitations, misdescription, defect in title, legal prohibition.

But this inability to perform must not arise from plaintiff's own wrong or self-created disability. On the general principle of avoiding injustice and absurdity, any construction will, if possible, be rejected (unless the policy of the Act requires it) if it would enable a person by his own act to impair an obligation which he has undertaken, or otherwise to profit by his own wrong. A man may not take advantage of his own wrong. He may not plead in his own interest a self-created necessity.[6] Thus whereas per contract of sale the vendor has agreed to give vacant possession of a portion in possession of tenants at the time of the sale deed but had not taken any step to evict the tenant the vendee was entitled to ask for executing the sale deed without vacant possession with the tenant in view of s. 12(3).[7] In *P. Jagadeesan &*

4 *Venkiteswara Pai Rama Pai* v *Luis* AIR 1964 Ker 125 (FB).
5 *Bhaurao Shamrao Bhalme* v *Mahadeo Raghu Yelekar* AIR 1979 Bom 208 at 213 [cf. *Ram Niwas* v *Omkari* AIR 1983 All 310 (DB) post].
6 Maxwell on *Interpretation of Statutes*, 12th Ed., p. 212.
7 *Ramani Ammal* v *Susilammal* AIR 1991 Mad 163; (1991)2 LW 43.

Co. v *A. Krishnan,*[8] the plaintiff which was a partnership firm was carrying on business as a lessee in Door No. 12, Sambanda Moorthy Street, Madurai Town, belonging to the defendant. The defendant wanted to demolish and reconstruct the entire building and agreed that the plaintiff would continue as tenant as before and wanted the plaintiff to vacate a portion of the building and continue to occupy rest of the portion and the plaintiff agreed to the same. But the defendant did not complete the construction in full in two months' time as agreed to, and consequently the plaintiff filed the suit for specific performance. The trial court decree the action, but the Appellate Court reversed the decree. In the second appeal, the High Court pointed out that under s. 12 of the Specific Relief Act, if either party to the contract is unable to perform the whole of his part and the part which must be left unperformed is only a small proportion to the whole in value, the court may direct specific performance of so much of a contract as can be performed and directed the defendant to handover the constructed portion to the plaintiff.

The factual matrix of this Madras case is similar to that of a Calcutta case where the defendant having agreed to sell on evicting the defendant, but this condition was defaulted Calcutta High Court Division Bench decreed the suit for specific performance, nevertheless.[9]

If the plaintiffs induce the other party to enter into an agreement of sale by making false promises and then backout, this conduct cannot be said to be fair and above board. In a case two contemporaneous agreements to sell were executed, one between plaintiff and defendant and other between defendant and third party and the plaintiffs had first taken full responsibility for the successful performance of the agreement between third party and the defendant but at the relevant time they quietly slipped away from the scene. Having first led the defendant to the garden path by making false promise and inducing the defendant to enter into agreement of sale in their favour on the promise that they would be fully responsible for the performance of another contemporaneous agreement, the plaintiff cannot now turn around to say that their responsibility was not absolute. This conduct of the plaintiff does not speak favourably as to their *bona fide* and shows that they did not make even a reluctant effort to persuade third party to execute the sale deed in favour of defendant as agreed. Since the plaintiffs have failed to prove their readiness and willingness to perform all the essential terms of the agreement which were to be performed by them, the plaintiffs would not be entitled to the relief of specific performance, as the enforcement of one agreement only against the defendant is bound to work serious prejudice and will be inequitable.[10]

8 (2002)1 LW 526.

9 *Purnima Rani Dutta* v *Lakshmi Bala Dasi* AIR 1988 Cal 148; (1987)2 CHN 224.

10 *Tribhuwan Dutta Tripathi* v *Ramji Tiwari* AIR 1991 All 268.

In *Prithi Sansi* v *Jatiram*,[11] after the execution of an agreement for sale and after the vendee filed the suit for specific performance, the vendor inducted respondents into possession of the suit land under an agreement for sale. It was contended by him that the court should grant the vendee the alternative relief instead of granting a decree for specific performance in view of the fact that third parties were in possession and taking possession from them would involve further litigation. This contention was rejected by the High Court and the decision of the High Court was upheld by the Supreme Court. It was observed "having regard to the fact that the respondents 2 and 3 are not *bona fide* purchasers and admittedly came into possession after the suit was instituted and the agreement was entered into, the High Court has rightly rejected their contention and if their contention is to be accepted no contract for specific performance can be enforced and the party will seek to avoid the contract by inducting third persons into possession."

A contract contains certain stipulations and specific performance is the actual execution of the contract. When a party to the contract does not perform its obligations thereunder the party seeking performance of the contract approaches the court to compel the other to perform his/her obligations the court in his discretion would refuse relief. The law on the subject is, however, the same in India as in England. The growth of law in England was as an equitable remedy. Therefore, all the requirements which a plaintiff seeking relief in equity had to be satisfied before such a relief could be granted and these are relevant to find out whether the plaintiff is entitled to the discretionary relief to specific performance.[12]

Alternative relief When a person files a suit for specific performance of a contract for the transfer of immovable property, in appropriate case, he may also ask for possession or partition and separate possession, in addition to such performance or any other relief to which he may be entitled including the refund of the earnest money or deposit paid by him, in case of refusal of specific performance, but none of these reliefs could be granted to him until and unless it is specifically claimed in his plaint and if, by chance the plaintiff has omitted to make a prayer for such a relief in the plaint originally, the court has got the jurisdiction to allow him to amend the plaint on such terms as may be just, at any stage of proceeding, to include any of the aforesaid alternative prayers. Thus, the *sine qua non* is the pleading in respect of any of the claims mentioned in cls. (*a*) and (*b*) of sub-sec. (1) of s. 22 of the Specific Relief Act 1963.[13] Section 21 of the Specific Relief Act 1963 provides that compensation or damages may be claimed in a suit for specific performance as an alternative relief.[14]

11 AIR 1997 SC 1598; (1996)5 SCC 457; JT 1996(9) SC 11.
12 *Nanak Builders & Investors* v *Vinod Kumar Alag* AIR 1991 Del 315.
13 *Lavinder Kumar Sharma* v *Pramod Kumar* AIR 2011 P&H 30.
14 *Motilal Jain* v *Ramdasi Devi* (2000)6 SCC 420.

Inability to perform considerable part The expression "considerable part" implies that the part which is left unperformed is either large as regard to quantity or quality. In other words, it must be material and not insignificant, so that a reasonable objection can be taken by the promisee to refuse to accept performance.

The phrase "does not admit of compensation" implies that there are no data for ascertaining a fair and reasonable amount as the money value of the difference between what can be performed and the express subject matter of the contract. The amount need not be mathematically accurate. If a reasonable estimate of the amount as the money value can be made, it will not be a case where the compensation is unascertainable.

There is nothing in s. 12 or any other provision of the Specific Relief Act which requires that the facts relevant to the applicability of these provisions should be pleaded in the plaint or be set out in an application otherwise it would be rendering this beneficial provision too narrow and technical.

Relinquishment of part of claim The issue is covered by s. 12(3)(*b*)(*ii*) of the Specific Relief Act. The relinquishment of claim to further performance of the remaining part of the contract and of right to compensate can be made at any stage of the litigation.[15] So, where a plaintiff wants performance of a part of a contract, he can relinquish all his claims to the performance of the remaining part of the contract at any stage of the litigation including the appellate stage. The claim of the plaintiff for grant of benefit under s. 12(3) cannot therefore be rejected on the simple ground that it was not made at the trial stage but has been made for the first time at the appellate stage. The claim also cannot be rejected on the ground that it was not incorporated in the plaint or was not set forth in writing before the trial court. In many cases, it may be doubtful and may require an enquiry and trial to come to a conclusion as to whether a person will be entitled to perform a contract only in part and to refuse relief to a plaintiff on the sole ground that relinquishment was not made at an earlier stage will highly prejudice his right.[16] In *Rachakonda Narayana* v *Ponthala Parvathamma*,[17] The Supreme Court has pointed out that an appeal is a continuation of the suit and it was open to the plaintiff to move for amendment of the plaint pleading therein the ingredients for part performance of the contract as provided under sub-sec. (3) of s. 12 of the Act.

In respect of a joint Hindu family property if one of the coparceners does not join the contract, then the intending vendee may relinquish the claim in respect of the unwilling coparcener and enforce specific performance

15 *Kalyanpur Lime Works* v *State of Bihar* AIR 1954 SC 165; 1954 SCR 958; 1954 SCJ 99; *Partha Sarathi* v *Venkata Kondiah* AIR 1965 Mad 188.

16 *T.K. Santha* v *A.G. Rathnam* AIR 1990 Ker 69 at 70.

17 (2002)1 LW 487 (SC); (2001)6 Supreme 321.

in respect of the rest.[18] Relinquishment of the claim can however be made at any stage including the appellate stage.[19]

Where part of the property is not in possession of the defendant,[20] or where it is found that the defendant did not own a part of the land agreed to be sold,[1] the plaintiff may relinquish that part, and specific performance can be granted for the remaining land.

Plea of part performance vis-a-vis specific performance Section 53A, Transfer of Property Act 1882 dealing with part performance which reads as follows—

> 53A. *Part performance.* Where any person contracts to transfer for consideration any immovable property by writing signed by him or on his behalf from which the terms necessary to constitute the transfer can be ascertained with reasonable certainty,
>
> and the transferee has, in part performance of the contract, taken possession of the property or any part thereof, or the transferee, being already in possession, continues in possession in part performance of the contract and has done some act in furtherance of the contract,
>
> and the transferee has performed or is willing to perform his part of the contract,
>
> then, notwithstanding that where there is an instrument of transfer, that the transfer has not been completed in the manner prescribed therefor by the law for the time being in force, the transferor or any person claiming under him shall be debarred from enforcing against the transferee and persons claiming under him any right in respect of the property of which the transferee has taken or continued in possession, other than a right expressly provided by the terms of the contract:
>
> Provided that nothing in this section shall affect the rights of a transferee for consideration who has no notice of the contract or of the part performance thereof.

It may be pointed out that the Registration and Other Related Laws (Amendment) Act 2001 [Act 48 of 2001] has amended the Registration Act and the Transfer of Property Act introducing a radical change in the application of the doctrine of part performance. Section 3 of the Registration and Other Related Laws (Amendment) Act 2001 has introduced sub-sec. (1A) in s. 17 of the Registration Act 1908 which deals with documents of which registration is compulsory to the following effect:

18 *Ram Kishan Das* v *Bhavi Chand* AIR 1988 Del 20; (1988)1 Arb LR 133.

19 *Ram Niwas* v *Omkari* AIR 1983 All 310 (DB); *Kalyanpur Lime Works* v *State of Bihar* AIR 1954 SC 165; 1954 SCR 958; 1954 SCJ 99; approving *Waryam Singh* v *Gopi Chand* AIR 1930 Lah 34; *Harnam Kaur* v *Jagtar Singh* AIR 1992 Punj 138.

20 *Poorna Nand* v *Prakashwati* AIR 2006 Uttranchal 76; *Ambikaderi* v *M. Easwasi* AIR 2004 Ker 349.

1 *Bhajan Singh* v *Jaswant Singh* AIR 2006 P&H 145.

(1A). The documents containing contracts to transfer for consideration, any immovable property for the purpose of section 53A of the Transfer of Property Act, 1882 (4 of 1882), shall be registered if they have been executed on or after the commencement of the Registration and Other Related Laws (Amendment) Act, 2001, and if such documents are not registered on or after such commencement, then they shall have no effect for the purposes of the said section 53A.

Section 6 of the Registration and Other Related Laws (Amendment) Act 2001 has amended s. 49 of the Registration Act dealing with the effect of non-registration of documents required to be registered, deleting the words "or as evidence of part performance of a contract for the purposes of s. 53A of the Transfer of Property Act 1882 (4 of 1882)" in the proviso and s. 10 of the above Amendment Act 2001 has amended s. 53A of the Transfer of Property Act deleting the words "the contract, though required to be registered has not been registered, or" in paragraph 4 of s. 53A. The result of these amendments is that a contract for sale of immovable property entered into after the commencement of the Amendment Act, i.e. 24.9.2001 must be in writing registered in order to invoke the provisions of s. 53A of the Transfer of Property Act. It may be pertinent to ask why such a provision for compulsory registration should not be extended to all agreements for sale of immovable property which will have the effect of putting an end to unfair practices of setting up oral agreements and collusive ante-dated written agreements and saving considerable judicial time.

After the coming into force of the Registration and Other Related Laws (Amendment) Act 2001, the agreement for sale of immovable property entered into said Amendment Act shall be registered and if such documents are not registered on or after such commencement, then, those shall have no effect for the purposes of s. 53A.

Thus, the amended provision sub-sec. (1A) of s. 17 of the Registration Act 1908 makes it clear that, if the benefit of s. 53A of the Transfer of Property Act is to be available then the contract for sale shall be registered. If it is not registered then it will have no effect for the purpose of the said s. 53A. However, this provision is made prospective and it applies to a contract for sale executed on or after the commencement of the Registration and Other Related Laws (Amendment) Act 2001.[2]

A transferee, who has come in possession of the property in part performance of a written agreement, can continue in its possession if he is ready and willing to perform his part of the agreement, no matter whether the defendant has sued for specific performance of contract or not.[3]

2 *A.N. Nagarajaiah* v *B. Aravind* AIR 2014 Kar 140; 2015 AIR Civil Cases 58.
3 *Chaman Lal* v *Surinder Kumari* AIR 1983 P&H 323.

The doctrine of part performance would apply even where the vendee's suit for specific performance has become barred or has become otherwise unenforceable.[4]

Section 53A of the Transfer of Property Act imports in India only partially the equitable doctrine of part performance as explained in *Madison* v *Alderson*[5] and applied by the Privy Council in *Mohamed Musa* v *Aghore Kumar Ganguly*.[6] The essentials of the section are (*a*) there must be a contract to transfer immovable property; (*b*) the contract must be for consideration; (*c*) it must be in writing signed by or on behalf of the transferor [the contracts executed on or after the commencement of the Registration and Other Related Laws (Amendment) Act 2001 must be registered]; (*d*) the terms can be ascertained from the writing; (*e*) the transferee has taken possession or is already in possession of the property; (*f*) he has done some act in furtherance of the contract, and (*g*) the transferee has performed or is willing to perform his part of the contract.[7]

If the aforesaid conditions co-exist the transferor or any person claiming under him is precluded from enforcing against the transferee or persons claiming under him any right in respect of the property.[8]

Thus, the doctrine of part performance is not applicable when the contract is not in writing.[9] Further the agreement in writing must incorporate the terms and conditions of transfer so as to enable the court to ascertain thereabout with reasonable certainty.[10] Where a party is put in possession of any immovable property in part performance of the agreement to sell under s. 53A of the Transfer of Property Act, it was held by the Supreme Court that he cannot be dispossessed except according to law.[11] Such person can defend his possession in a suit for recovery of possession even if suit for specific performance appears to be barred by limitation.[12] But, the conditions precedent, as enumerated, in s. 53A of the Transfer of Property Act, must be complied with.[13] In explaining the position of law, the Supreme Court observed:

> The Special Committee's report which is reflected in the aims and objects of the amending Act 1929 shows that one of the purposes of enacting

4 *Maruti Gurappa* v *Krishna Bala* AIR 1967 Bom 34.
5 [1883]8 AC 467.
6 AIR 1914 PC 27.
7 *Sardar Govindrao Mahadik* v *Devi Sahai* AIR 1982 SC 989; (1982)1 SCC 237; (1982)2 SCR 186.
8 *Nathulal* v *Phoolchand* AIR 1970 SC 546; (1969)3 SCC 120; (1970)1 SCWR 175; 1970 All LJ 742.
9 *Vasundhra Bhalla* v *Haridas Bhagat & Co.* AIR 1995 Mad 172 (DB).
10 *Ranganath Sharma* v *Tetari Bibi* AIR 1991 Pat 198 at p. 201.
11 *Sunkara Venkata Rao* v *K. Venkata Rao* (2005)11 SCC 436.
12 *Huvappa Irappa Ballari* v *Basava* (2005)12 SCC 164.
13 *Vasanthi* v *Venugopal* (2017)4 SCC 723.

s. 53A was to provide protection to a transferee who in part performance of the contract had taken possession of the property even if the limitation to bring a suit for specific performance has expired.[14]

But, it was propounded that the right to claim protection under s. 53A of the T.P. Act would not be available, if the transferee remains passive without taking effective steps and abstains from performing his part of the contract or conveying his readiness and willingness to that effect.[15]

However, if a person has entered into possession over immovable property under a contract for sale and is in peaceful and settled possession of the property with the consent of the person in whom the title vests, he is entitled to protect his possession against the whole world, excepting a person having a title better than what he or his vendor possesses. If he is in possession of the property in part performance of contract for sale and the requirements of s. 53A of the Transfer of Property Act are satisfied, he may protect his possession even against the true owner. Section 6 of the Specific Relief Act 1963, provides for any person dispossessed without his consent of immovable property otherwise than in due course of law being entitled to claim and successfully sue for recovery of possession thereof, notwithstanding any other title that may be set up in such suit if the suit is brought before the expiry of six months from the date of dispossession except against the Government. Article 64 of the Limitation Act 1963 contemplates a suit for possession of immovable property based on previous possession, and not on title, being brought within twelve years from the date of dispossession. Such a suit is known in law as a suit based on possessory title as distinguished from proprietary title. The law discourages people from taking the law into their own hands, howsoever good and sound their title may be. Possession is nine points in law and law respects peaceful and settled possession.[16] However, where the prospective buyer's case for specific performance is dismissed, the protection available under s. 53A of the T.P. Act is no longer available to him and his possession upon the immovable property becomes unauthorized and illegal. In such eventuality, he can only claim refund of earnest money from the seller under s. 22 of the Specific Relief Act 1963.[17]

Absolute and unconditional willingness essential The doctrine of readiness and willingness is an emphatic way of expression to establish that the transferee always abides by the terms of the agreement and is willing to perform his part of the contract. Part performance, as statutory right, is

14 *Shrimant Shamrao Suryavanshi* v *Pralhad Bhairoba Suryavanshi* (2002)3 SCC 676.
15 *A. Lewis* v *M.T. Ramamurthy* (2007)14 SCC 87; AIR 2008 SC 493.
16 *Ramesh Chand Ardawatiya* v *Anil Panjwani* (2003)7 SCC 350; *Shrimant Shamrao Suryavanshi* v *Pralhad Bhairoba Suryavanshi* (2002)3 SCC 676.
17 *Revanasiddayya* v *Gangamma* (2018)1 SCC 610.

conditioned upon the transferee's continuous willingness to perform his part of the contract in terms covenanted thereunder.[18] Willingness to perform the terms of the contract ascribed to a party in a contract, is primarily a mental disposition. Such willingness in the context of s. 53A of the T.P. Act must be absolute and unconditional. If willingness is studded with a condition, it is in fact no more than an offer and cannot be termed as willingness. When transferee expressed willingness to pay, provided the vendor cleared the Income Tax arrears and it was held that such willingness was conditional and the transferee was not entitled to the benefit of s. 53A.[19]

The provisions of s. 12, Specific Relief Act are, quite distinct from those of s. 53A of the Transfer of Property Act.[20]

The doctrine of part performance embodied in s. 53A is an equitable doctrine. The object of this section is to prevent a transferor or his successor-in-interest from taking any advantage on account of non-registration of the document, provided that the transferee has performed his part of the contract and in pursuance thereof has taken possession of some immovable property. This right is available to the transferee as a defence in order to protect his possession. The defendant may therefore in an action of ejectment in certain circumstances effectively plead possession under an unregistered contract of sale in defence to the action.[1]

When a suit for specific performance of agreement of sale is instituted but the agreement of sale in reality is found to be a completed sale deed but unregistered namely that entire consideration was paid and simultaneously possession too was delivered then the suit for specific performance must fail, but plaintiff cannot be non-suited, he may be granted a decree of permanent injunction restraining the defendant-vendor from interfering with plaintiff's possession basing on doctrine of part performance.[2] But if the deed of sale is executed in respect of land without prior permission of the competent authority as required by law, the transaction is void and the benefit of s. 53A cannot be claimed.[3]

It is not correct to say that s. 53A, Transfer of Property Act can be invoked only by a defendant. It can also be invoked by a plaintiff so long he uses it as a shield. So, a plaintiff may sue for injunction for restraining the defendant on the plea of part performance provided, the requisite

18 *Mohan Lal* v *Mirza Abdul Gaffar* (1996)1 SCC 639.
19 *Jacobs Pvt. Ltd.* v *Thomas Jacob* AIR 1995 Ker 249 (DB).
20 *Bharat Chandra Das* v *Md. Ramjan Chowdhury* (1941)45 CWN 489 and *Jahangir Begum* v *Gulam Ali Ahmed* AIR 1955 Hyd 101.
1 *Durga Prasad* v *Kanhiyalal* AIR 1979 Raj 200 at pp. 202-203.
2 *Madan Mohan* v *Gauri Shankar* AIR 1988 MP 152.
3 *Sadhu Meher* v *Rajkumar Patel* AIR 1994 Ori 26.

Redefined with versatility

ADR

Alternative Dispute Resolution

Along with the Gram Nyayalayas Act 2008

The Arbitration and Conciliation (Amd.) Act 2019 **Highlighted**

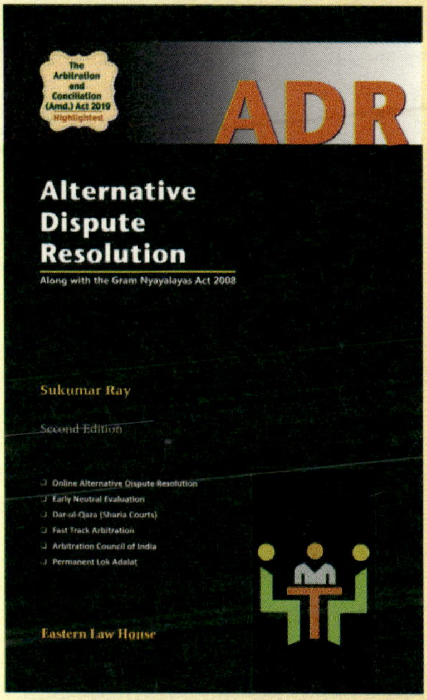

by **Sukumar Ray** LLM
District and Sessions Judge

Key areas covered

- Online Alternative Dispute Resolution
- Early Neutral Evaluation
- Dar-ul-Qaza (Sharia Courts)
- Fast Track Arbitration
- Arbitration Council of India
- Permanent Lok Adalat

This outstanding work covers and aptly analyses all the topics of the subject, such as Arbitration, Mediation, Lok Adalat, Plea Bargaining, Minitrial, Lokpal, Fast Track Court, Nyaya Panchayat, etc. The Arbitration and Conciliation (Amendment) Act 2019 has received due treatment. The Gram Nyayalayas Act 2008 is discussed in the light of the verdicts of the apex court and different High Courts. To complete the circle of this subject, new chapters on 'Online Alternative Dispute Resolution', 'Dar-ul-Qaza' and 'Early Neutral Evaluation' are incorporated.

Second Edition 2020 ISBN 978-81-7177-352-7 **Hardcover ₹1095**

Eastern Law House

www.elh.co.in

Also of interest

Fifth Edition 2019

ISBN 978-81-7177-349-7

Hardcover ₹1290

Majumder's
Plaints

by **Purnendu Bhattacharyya** MA, LLM
Former District & Sessions Judge and
Director, West Bengal Judicial Academy

The instant edition of this utility oriented work, as the true successor of its earlier one, has taken adequate care to maintain its traditional standard and reputation. Divided in two parts, the first one deals with the substantive laws while the other part catalogues the specimen of plaints and petitions. In the present edition certain additions and alterations have been made to keep pace with the changed situations in law from the practical point of view and to assist the young lawyers to locate their area of interest. By covering all the important subjects, the work caters more than 600 specimen of plaints, petitions and the written statements to meet instantly the need of the young and busy lawyers.

Fifth Edition 2019

ISBN 978-81-7177-345-9

Hardcover ₹2850

Mitra's
Civil Reference

A Virtual ENCYCLOPAEDIA on CIVIL LAWS

by **Sukumar Ray** LLM
District and Sessions Judge

An outstanding work covering almost all the civil laws of the land appears into its Fifth Edition. The instant edition made room for a number of Acts and legal principles for the present need of the legal fraternity. The Acts which are recently appeared are also incorporated in this edition. All the leading civil subjects *inter alia* Marriage & Divorce, Succession, Property laws, Family laws, Clinical Establishment, Consumer Protection, Environment Protection, Electricity, Maintenance & Welfare of Parents and Senior Citizens, etc. have received appropriate discussion. The completely updated edition may be treated as an indispensable companion to legal fraternity.

Eastern Law House Private Ltd

- 54 Ganesh Chunder Avenue, Kolkata 700 013
  Tel: (033) 2215-1989 **Email:** mail@elh.co.in
- 36 Netaji Subhash Marg, Daryaganj, New Delhi 110 002
  Tel: (011) 2327-9982 **Email:** delhi@elh.co.in

Find us on www.facebook.com/easternlawhouse

Visit us on www.elh.co.in
Also available at amazon.in & flipkart.com

conditions for calling in aid the section are fulfilled.[4] The right conferred by s. 53A, Transfer of Property Act is a right available to the defendant to protect his possession. It imposes a statutory bar to the transferor. It confers no active title to the transferee.[5] Plaintiff's right to invoke the doctrine of part performance was emphasised in *Babu Ram* v *Basdeo,*[6] which held the equitable doctrine of part performance is available to the plaintiff not only where he is physically in possession of the property on the date of the suit but also where he physically has been found to have been illegally dispossessed by some person claiming under the transferor. The contention that unless the transferee is in possession he cannot invoke s. 53A, Transfer of Property Act if accepted would reduce the utility of the provision to a naught, because a powerful transferor or a person claiming under him would be able to defeat the provisions by forcibly dispossessing the transferee and leading him to a court as plaintiff. Such a course and the result would not be conducive to the interest of an orderly social order. The transferee is entitled to resist any attempt on the part of the transferor to disturb the transferee's lawful possession under the contract for sale and his possession either as the plaintiff or as the defendant could make no difference.[7]

In *Sardar Govindrao Mahadik* v *Devi Sahai*[8] the plaintiff sued for specific performance of an oral agreement of sale. The plaintiff asserted that in part performance of the contract, he had entered into possession of the property in part and that the defendant applied for permission to transfer the disputed land to the plaintiff from Deputy Commissioner in terms of s. 46, Chotanagpur Tenancy Act 1908. The plea of part performance did not stand as the agreement was oral. As to permission from Deputy Commissioner it was pointed out that the stated object of sale was the marriage of defendant's daughters but the said daughters had been married long ago, secondly, it did not stand to reason that after paying earnest money for sale the plaintiff would not keep track with the application for permission. But here the plaintiff sued only after coming to know from reliable source that such permission had been granted. The suit failed.[9]

A suit for eviction of tenant under a rent control statute cannot be sought to be stayed under s. 10, CPC, on the ground that tenant has earlier filed a suit for specific performance against the landlord on basis of agreement

4 *Akram Mea* v *Secunderabad Municipal Corporation* AIR 1957 AP 859; *Chaitan Das* v *Murli Dalai* AIR 1971 Ori 41; *S.F. Munuswami* v *Erusa Goundar* AIR 1975 Mad 25; (1974)1 Mad LJ 497; 57 Mad LW 291 contra *Amrao Singh* v *Sanatan Dharma Sabha* AIR 1985 P&H 195; 1984 Punj LJ 542.

5 *Garaj Narain Singh* v *Babulal Khemka* AIR 1975 Pat 58; 1974 BLJR 757; *Conceicoa Antonio Fernandez* v *Dr. Artano* AIR 1975 Goa 27.

6 AIR 1982 All 414.

7 *Dharmaji* alias *Baban Bajirao Shinde* v *Jagannath Shankar Jadhav* AIR 1994 Bom 254.

8 (1982)1 SCC 237.

9 *Ranganath Sharma* v *Tetari Bibi* AIR 1991 Pat 198.

of sale of demised premises in favour of the tenant. He cannot resort to s. 53A of the Transfer of Property Act as a weapon of offence of claiming adversary title alleging that by virtue of agreement of sale he continued in possession not as a tenant but as a transferee. It is well settled that s. 53A, Transfer of Property Act can be used as a shield and not as a sword.[10]

Doctrine of part performance The essential features of the equitable doctrine of part performance as statutorily modified and incorporated in s. 53A of the Transfer of Property Act 1882 are—[11]

(1) a contract to transfer immovable property;

(2) the transfer should be for consideration;

(3) the contract must be in writing;

(4) it should be signed by or on behalf of the transferor;

(5) the terms of the contract can be ascertained with reasonable certainty from the writing;

(6) the transferee takes possession of the whole or part of the property or if already in possession continues in possession;

(7) such taking of or continuance in possession should be in part performance of the contract;

(8) the transferee should do some act in furtherance of the contract; and

(9) he should have performed, or be willing to perform, his part of the contract.

The effect of an act of part performance is to enable evidence to be given of all the terms of the contract.[12] The act or action relied upon as "evidencing part performance" must be of such nature and character that its existence would establish the contract and its implementation. Again, merely because the suit for specific performance at the instance of the vendee has become barred by limitation that by itself is not enough to deny the benefit of the plea of part performance of agreement of sale to the person in possession.[13] Moreover, the equitable doctrine of part performance is not available against a subsequent purchaser when after the time to enforce the agreement of sale lapsed.[14] Where the plaintiff was given possession of the suit land prior to the execution of the sale-deed and consequently has constructed his building on the said land, it was held that the plaintiff will get the protection of s. 53A of the Transfer of Property Act.[15] In fact, the longer the possession

10 *N.P. Tripathi* v *Dayamanti Devi* AIR 1988 Pat 123 at p. 124.
11 *FGP Ltd.* v *Saleh Hooseini Doctor* (2009)10 SCC 223.
12 *Brough* v *Nettleton* [1921]2 Ch 25.
13 *Mahadeva* v *Tanabai* (2004)5 SCC 88; AIR 2004 SC 3854.
14 *Raj Kumar Baghel Singh* v *Devinder Kaur* (1999)1 ICC 369.
15 *Bhajan Lal* v *Bal Govind* AIR 2007 All 199.

in part performance, the higher will be the equities.[16] Though s. 53A confers no active title on the transferee, it gives him a right to protect his possession.[17] Even if the suit for specific performance is dismissed for being barred by limitation, injunction may be granted.[18] It is available as an independent right and a person in part performance of the agreement, if shown that he is always ready and willing to perform his part of agreement and has been delivered the possession in performance of the agreement, is entitled to the protection of permanent injunction. It is not required that he should file a suit for specific performance within limitation.[19]

Part performance—invocation by transferee qua plaintiff On the strength of an agreement of sale when vendor receives consideration or part thereof and vendee enters into possession, this possession is in part performance of the contract. If the vendee sues for specific performance of contract, the vendee is entitled to protect his possession till the decree is passed.[20] A person is entitled to retain possession of the property under s. 53A of the T.P. Act 1882 despite the fact that he cannot file a suit for specific performance on account of the expiry of the period of limitation. What s. 53A of the T.P. Act 1882 seeks to do is to protect the possession of the defendant even where the defendant's right to obtain specific performance of the agreement has been barred by time.

Pleadings and proof It is for the vendee to plead and prove his claim to the benefit of s. 53A of the Transfer of Property Act. Unless the plea is specifically raised, it cannot be allowed to be flung as a surprise on the transferor for the first time in the appeal.[1] If there is no such pleading of any agreement in his favour or assignment of the agreement, the transferee or any person claiming under him cannot claim the benefit of s. 53A.[2] In *Illikkal Devaswom* v *Pottakkatt Narayanan Raghavan*[3] it is indicated that in the absence of foundation laid in the pleadings, the plea of s. 53A cannot be invoked. However, the absence of a specific averment in his pleadings by the defendant of the defence under s. 53A cannot be a ground to refuse the benefit of this section when the question of applicability of s. 53A has been gone into at the hearing by the trial court as well as by the first Appellate Court and both of them have found that the defendant was entitled to avail himself of the provisions of s. 53A.[4] Similarly, where the defendant makes a prayer for

16 *Mahadeva* v *Rangamma* AIR 2013 Kar 56.
17 *Mahalingam* v *Ayyathurai* (1972)85 LW 869.
18 *Balasaheb Manikrao Deshmukh* v *Rama Lingoji Warthi* AIR 2000 Bom 337.
19 *Rani Sambhi* v *Lt. Col. (Retd). R.L. Vashisht* (2004)1 ICC 490.
20 *Anjali Das* v *Bidyut Sarkar* AIR 1992 Cal 47.
1 *Baruna Giri* v *Rajakishore Giri* AIR 1983 Ori 107.
2 *A.M.A. Sultan* v *Seydu Zohra Beevi* AIR 1990 Ker 186.
3 AIR 1966 Ker 96 (FB).
4 *Nanjedevaru* v *H.P. Rama Rao* AIR 1959 Mys 173.

amendment of his written statement for incorporating the specific plea of s. 53A, it was held that where the clear foundation for plea under s. 53 is laid in the written statement, though no averment is made therein, the prayer for incorporation of the defence of s. 53A should be allowed, since such defence is not unconnected with the claim of the plaint. The proposed amendment cannot be said to be immaterial or useless.[5]

Part performance vis-a-vis adverse possession Plea of part performance cannot be taken in a suit where the plea of adverse possession has already been taken as defence and *vice versa*. Pithily stated, both cannot go together. In *Mohan Lal* v *Mirza Abdul Gaffar*[6] it was held that the plea of adverse possession in a case where the defence already taken is under s. 53A of the Transfer of Property Act is inconsistent. It was held that where 'A' having come into possession under the agreement, must disclaim his right thereunder and plead and prove assertion of his independent hostile adverse possession to the knowledge of the transferor or his successor in title or interest and that the latter had acquiesced to his illegal possession during the entire period of 12 years, i.e. up to completing the period of his title by prescription *nec vi, nec clam, nec precario*. Since his claim is founded on s. 53A, it goes without saying that he admits by implication that he came into possession of the land lawfully under the agreement and continued to remain in possession till date of the suit. Thereby the plea of adverse possession is not available to him. Similarily, in *Roop Singh* v *Ram Singh*[7] it was held that the pleas of adverse possession and retaining the possession by operation of s. 53A of the Act are inconsistent with each other. Such a plea is not available to a proposed vendee.

Part performance—invocation by an obstructor Where an obstructor resisted the execution of decree on the ground that his possession in the decreetal property is on the basis of an oral and undated agreement of sale and the protection of s. 53A of the Transfer of Property Act is thus available to him, it was held that such plea cannot be taken by an obstructor when he fails to fulfil the requirements of s. 53A of the Act. The rights of an obstructor are provided in Or. 21, r. 97 of the CPC. His only right is a right to protect his possession by showing a legitimate, legal and better right to possession than the decree-holder. Secondly, the only objection such an opponent can raise or which would be permissible would be such as would enable him to protect his possession, and such objection must have a direct nexus with the possession sought to be protected. Such a right would not extend to challenging the decree under execution, on any ground whatsoever, at least in proceedings under Or. 21, r. 97. In other words, the obstructionist is confined to his locus and status of the opponent in the application under

5 *Jacob Cherian* v *Himanshu Kumar Mukherjee* (1993)1 CHN 21.
6 (1996)1 SCC 639.
7 (2000)3 SCC 708.

Or. 21, r. 97 and to take a view that he could raise any and all objections (including an objection which goes beyond the decree or an objection which hits the decree on merits), would extend the locus and status of the obstructionist to that of a judgment-debtor. Clearly, this is not permissible, inasmuch as the entire scheme of Or. 21, when seen as a whole, and the scheme of rr. 97 to 101, when read collectively, clearly demarcate and keep apart the locus and status of the obstructionist as against the judgment-debtor. To permit such contentions to be raised would merge the interest of the obstructionist with that of the judgment-debtor. The requirements of s. 53A of the TP Act have to be fulfilled in order to claim the benefit of the doctrine of part performance and where the obstructor fails to prove the same, his claim for protection of his possession in the decreetal property must fail.[8]

Contracts in respect of trusts—specific performance—enforceability Section 11(1) of the Specific Relief Act provides that the specific performance of a contract shall be enforced when the act agreed to be done is in performance wholly or partly of a trust. The word "trust" carries the same meaning as in s. 3 of the Indian Trusts Act 1882 and includes an obligation in the nature of a trust within the meaning of Chapter IX of that Act [s. 2(*c*) of the Specific Relief Act].

Section 3 of the Indian Trusts Act 1882 provides that a 'trust' is an obligation annexed to the ownership of property, and arising out of a confidence reposed in and accepted by the owner, or declared and accepted by him, for the benefit of another, or of another and the owner. The person who reposes or declares the confidence is called the 'author of the trust'; the person who accepts the confidence is called the 'trustee', the person for whose benefit the confidence is accepted is called the 'beneficiary'; the subject matter of the trust is called trust property or trust-money; the 'beneficial interest' or 'interest' of the beneficiary is his right against the trustee as owner of the trust-property; and the instrument by which the trust is declared is called the 'instrument of trust'. The word 'trust' therefore includes all kinds of trusts, such as implied trusts, constructive trusts. When a person has property or rights which he holds or is bound to exercise for or on behalf of another or others or for the accomplishment of some particular purpose or particular purposes, he is said to hold the property or rights in trust for that other or those others or for that purpose or those purposes and he is called a trustee.[9]

An express trust is expressed either by words in writing or by words of mouth; it does not include a trust which arises from the acts of the parties or to a resulting trust or to an implied trust or to a constructive trust.[10]

8 *G.G. Bharathidasan* v *Malini Mai* (2014)8 Mad LJ 525; AIR 2015 NOC 701 (Mad).
9 Halsbury's *Laws of England*, 4th Ed., vol. 48, para 501, p. 272.
10 *Sands* v *Thompson* [1883]48 LT 210.

The facts and dealings between persons may be such that in equity a fiduciary character is imposed on one of them towards the other in relation to property held by the former, who then may be said to hold it on a constructive trust, the extent and obligations of the trust depending on the relationship between the parties.[11]

Section 11(1) of the Specific Relief Act enacts that in absence of a contrary provisions in the Act specific performance of a contract shall be enforced when the act agreed to be done is in the performance wholly or partly of a trust, be it an express, implied or constructive trust.

Sub-section (2) of s. 11, Specific Relief Act provides that, first, a contract made by trustee cannot be specifically enforced when it is in excess of his powers, it then being beyond his competence; secondly, it cannot be specifically enforced when it entails a breach of trust, it then being unlawful.

The phrase "in excess of his powers" postulates a situation when the trustee in his capacity as such is not competent to make the particular contract, or in other words it is beyond his powers and it is *ultra vires.*[12]

Where a contract is made by a trustee in excess of his powers or in breach of trust it cannot be specifically enforced. Section 36 of the Indian Trusts Act 1882 defines the general authority of the trustee. It says that in addition to the powers expressly conferred by the Trusts Act (ss. 37 to 44 subject to s. 45) and by the instrument of trust and subject to the restrictions, if any, contained in such instrument, and to the provisions of s. 17 of the Indian Trusts Act, a trustee may do all acts which are reasonable and proper for the realisation, protection or benefit of the trust-property, and for the protection or support of a beneficiary who is not competent to contract. But this is subject to the provision that no trustee shall, except with the permission of the principal civil court of original jurisdiction, lease trust-property for a term exceeding twenty-one years from the date of executing the lease, nor without reserving the best yearly rent that can be reasonably obtained.

Breach of trust means a breach of any duty imposed on a trustee as such, by any law for the time being in force (s. 3, Indian Trusts Act). Duties of the trustee are defined in ss. 11 to 22 of the Indian Trusts Act.

There will, however, be no specific performance of an agreement to execute a voluntary deed of trust in respect of property voluntarily assigned.[13]

Contracts not specifically enforceable The relevant statutory provision is contained in ss. 14 and 11 of the Specific Relief Act. After the amendment

11 Halsbury's *Laws of England,* 4th Ed., vol. 48, para 586, p. 323.
12 *Mahomed Esmat* v *Nunda Dulal* (1912)16 IC 390.
13 *Lister* v *Hodgson* [1867] LR 4 Eq 30.

of s. 14 of the Act in 2018 by the Specific Relief (Amendment) Act 2018, in the following cases, the contracts cannot be specifically enforced:

(*a*) where a party to the contract has obtained substituted performance of contract in accordance with the provisions of s. 20;

(*b*) a contract, the performance of which involves the performance of a continuous duty which the court cannot supervise;

(*c*) a contract which is so dependent on the personal qualifications of the parties that the court cannot enforce specific performance of its material terms;

(*d*) a contract which is in its nature determinable.

(*e*) In addition, s. 11(2) of the Act also provides for non-enforcement of contract specifically; and

(*f*) where the contract is made by a trustee in excess of his powers or in breach of trust [s. 11(2)].

Specific performance when property agreed to be transferred later acquired and compensation awarded A contract for the sale of immovable property is a contract that sale of such property shall take place on terms settled between the parties but such a contract, does not of itself, create any interest in or charge on such property. Hence where property agreed to be sold is compulsorily acquired, the vendee suing for specific performance is not even entitled to the compensation awarded by the Collector in respect of such property. The vendee has at best, only an agreement for sale in his favour. Such an agreement has not the effect of transferring any legal or equitable estate in his favour. The question of payment of compensation to the vendee would have arisen only if, by an agreement of sale, any charge was created on the suit property. The plaintiff's right in the suit property, if any, will arise only after the execution of the sale deed in his favour. If, on account of certain eventualities, the agreement as such could not be legally enforced as having become impossible of its performance, then the question of allowing any compensation awarded with respect to the suit property, does not arise on that basis.[14]

Where compensation is adequate Equity intervenes to supply the deficiency of law in the matter of damages; but where the law itself awards adequate compensation there is nothing more to do for equity. Whether the compensation is adequate or not will depend on the circumstances of the case. It should, however, be remembered that the court will presume that contracts relating to immovable property and movable property where the property is of special value or interest or is not an ordinary article of

14 *Sujan Singh Sadhana v Mohkam Chand Jain* AIR 1983 Punj 180; ILR (1983)2 P&H 24.

commerce or consists of goods which are not easily obtainable in the market, or where the property is held by the defendant as an agent or trustee cannot be adequately relieved by compensation in money.

The test is whether the plaintiff can get the equivalent of what he contracted for from another source. The compensation has to be determined in accordance with the principles set out in ss. 73 and 74 of the Indian Contract Act. It is, however, not open to the subsequent purchaser to take up cudgels on behalf of the original vendor and urge that compensation would provide adequate relief. The provision is for the benefit of the vendor only.[15]

The expression "adequate relief" which was in s. 14(1)(*a*), Specific Relief Act (prior to its Amendment in 2018), presupposes that it must be adequate for some reason found, as a fact, for holding it to be adequate relief, in spite of the opinion of the plaintiff that it is inadequate. But where the plaintiff considers that damages would be adequately compensated, e.g. in case of sale of immovable property, and by his conduct indicates that he is willing to accept damages for the breach of contract, the court may be justified in decreeing compensation as adequate relief instead of decreeing specific performance.[16] Specific performance, being an equitable relief, is allowed only in cases where damages in money do not afford an adequate remedy. So, the court will not allow specific performance when compensation in money is a sufficient remedy. For the bar to apply there must be proof that compensation is adequate.[17] In determining the question of adequacy of compensation the court is guided by considerations which have respect to classes of contracts having the same or similar qualities and incidents connected with their subject matter, terms of parties, and rules are established with greater or less certainty, precision, and comprehensiveness for each class separately. The court may, however, decide that, though it has jurisdiction to enforce the specific performance of a contract, yet the justice of the case will be better met by awarding damages instead. But there may be cases, where the award of damages will not be an adequate remedy; in those cases, specific performance would be the rule. And in cases where no definite evidence is available to show to what extent the prices of the property have gone up, specific performance is the proper remedy and not the compensation.[18] Where the notice issued by the plaintiff indicated that the plaintiff was interested more in refund of earnest money and damages, specific performance would be refused.[19]

Contract for loan—money As a rule, a contract to lead or borrow money is not specifically enforceable on the view that damages would provide adequate

15 *Abdul Kayum Ahmed* v *Damodhar Paikaji Kinhekar* AIR 1964 Bom 46 at p. 47.
16 *Hari Krishna Agarwala* v *K.C. Gupta* AIR 1949 All 440; 1949 All WR (HC) 2.
17 *M.L. Devender Singh* v *Syed Khaja* AIR 1973 SC 2457.
18 *Ramchander* v *Ramappa* AIR 1954 Hyd 158 (FB); ILR (1954) Hyd 115.
19 *E. Bhagwan Das* v *Dilip Kumar* AIR 1998 AP 374.

relief.[20] It is immaterial whether the loan is to be with security or without security or whether the loan is to be for a fixed period and it makes no difference whether the loan is to be paid in one sum or by instalments. But where money has been advanced either wholly or in part and the borrower refuses to execute the agreed mortgage, specific performance is enforced, provided that in the latter case the lender has been ready and willing to advance the remaining sum according to the agreement. Similarly where a creditor has already advanced money on condition that the debtor shall execute a mortgage deed of the specified property owned by the debtor, such agreement to execute a mortgage deed can be specifically got enforced under this section.[1] But if the loan is liable to be repaid at once and the borrower is willing to pay it off, specific performance is not granted.[2] In *Makharia Brothers* v *State of Nagaland,*[3] specific performance was refused for enforcing a promise to extend a bank guarantee given for securing performance of a contract because compensation was found to be an adequate relief. Where an apparent agreement for transfer of property is really a financial arrangement made as security for repayment of the debt or outstanding amount, specific performance of such agreement cannot be granted. The court may rather grant return of the debt or the amount outstanding.[4]

The principle that a contract of loan is not specifically enforceable has suffered a jolt in the limited area of cases where the lender is the State or an instrumentality of the State under Art. 12 of the Constitution. That is the epoch-making judgment of the Supreme Court in *Gujarat State Financial Corporation* v *Lotus Hotels Ltd.*[5] where the promisee altered his position by spending large sums of money in constructing a hotel on the promise made by the Gujarat State Financial Corporation. Applying the principle of promissory estoppel, D.A. Desai, J speaking for the Bench observed:

> "It is too late in the day to contend that the instrumentality of the state which would be 'other authority' under Article 12 of the Constitution can commit breach of a solemn undertaking on which other side has acted, and

20 *Sichel* v *Mosenthal* [1862]30 Beav 371; 31 LJ Ch 386; *Larios* v *Bonany* (1873) LR 5 PC 346; *Phul Chand* v *Chand Mal* (1908)30 All 252; *Meenakshi Sundara Mudaliar* v *Ratnasami Pillai* ILR (1918)41 Mad 959; *Rajagopal* v *Sheik* 34 MLJ 342; *Rogers* v *Challis* [1859]27 Beav 175.

1 *State Bank* v *Kushan Vallabh Dhas* (1994)1 Guj LR 655.

2 *Meenakshi Sundara Mudaliar* v *Rathnasami Pillai* (1918)8 LW 438; AIR 1919 Mad 322.

3 AIR 1999 SC 3466; (2000)10 SCC 503; 2000(3) Raj 151.

4 *Firm Srinivasa Ram Kumar* v *Mahavir Prasad* AIR 1951 SC 177; 1951 SCR 277; 1951 SCJ 261; *Rangaraja Naidu* v *Thirunavukkarasu* AIR 1995 SC 1769; 1995 Supp (2) SCC 680; *Tejram* v *Patirambhau* AIR 1997 SC 2702; (1997)9 SCC 634; JT 1997(4) SC 677; *Sitaramlal* v *Jamsewar Das* AIR 1995 Ori 260; *Kamarunissa Widow of Mirza Beg* v *Pramod Kumar Gupta* AIR 1997 MP 106.

5 AIR 1983 SC 848; (1983)3 SCC 379.

then contend that the party suffering by the breach of contract may sue for damages but cannot compel specific performance of the contract ..... By its letter of offer dated July 24, 1978 and the subsequent agreement dated February 1, 1979 the appellant entered into a solemn agreement in the performance of its statutory duty to advance the loan of ₹30 lakhs to the respondent. Acting on the solemn undertaking, the respondent proceeded to undertake and execute the project of setting up a 4-star hotel at Baroda. The agreement to advance the loan was entered into in performance of the statutory duty cast on the Corporation by the statute under which it was created and set up. On its solemn promise evidenced by the aforementioned two documents, the respondent incurred expenses, suffered liabilities to set up a hotel. Presumably, if the loan was not forthcoming, the respondent may not have undertaken such a huge project. Acting on the promise of the appellant evidenced by documents, the respondent proceeded to suffer further liabilities to implement and execute the project. In the backdrop of this incontrovertible fact-situation, the principle of promissory estoppel would come into play."

"If appellant entered into solemn contract in discharge of its statutory duty and the respondent acted upon it, the statutory corporation cannot be allowed to act arbitrarily so as to cause harm and injury, following from its unreasonable conduct, to the respondent. In such a situation, the Court is not powerless from holding the appellant to its promise and it can be enforced by a writ of *mandamus* directing it to perform its statutory duty...."[6]

Explaining the scope of promissory estoppel which pins down the promisor to the promise and obligates to honour his promise— specific performance compellable by statute. Indeed in the leading case *Motilal Padampat Sugar Mills* v *State of U.P.*[7] the Apex Court held it is a principle evolved by equity to avoid injustice and though commonly named 'promissory estoppel', it is neither in the realm of contract nor in the realm of estoppel. The true principle of promissory estoppel seems to be that where one party has by his words or conduct made to the other a clear and unequivocal promise which is intended to create legal relations or effect a legal relationship to arise in the future, knowing or intending that it would be acted upon by the other party to whom the promise is made and it is in fact so acted upon by the other party, the promise would be binding on the party making it and he would not be entitled to go back upon it, if it would be inequitable to allow him to do so having regard to the dealings which have taken place between the parties, and this would be so irrespective of whether there is any pre-existing relationship between the parties or not.[8]

6 *Gujarat State Financial Corporation* v *Lotus Hotels Ltd.* AIR 1983 SC 848; (1983)3 SCC 379.
7 AIR 1979 SC 621; (1979)2 SCR 641; (1979)2 SCC 409.
8 *M.P. Sugar Mills* v *State of U.P.* AIR 1979 SC 621; 1979 All LJ 386.

The ratio of *Motilal Padampat Sugar Mills* case (*ibid*) was followed by the Supreme Court in *Pournami Oil Mills* v *State of Kerala.*[9] There the State Government under s. 10, Kerala General Sales Tax Act 1963 granted concession to new Small Scale Industries to boost industrialization in the State. Exemption from sales tax and purchase tax was granted and in response to the concession the promoters of Small Scale Industries set up their industries in the State. But, by a subsequent order the concession was curtailed with retrospective effect. It was held that the doctrine of promissory estoppel stands in the implementation of the second notification and the State Government is obliged to continue concession to industries set up on the assurance of concession.

In a Supreme Court case the company was invited to set up industries by ensuring it the supply of raw materials. The factories of the company became ready and were in a position to utilise the raw materials. The State Government subsequently by legislative enactment tried to get out of the commitments. It was held the fact situation gives rise to a situation of estoppel and the principle of promissory estoppel obligates the State Government to honour the commitment.[10]

In a Gujarat case the original land acquisition proceeding was stopped for technical reason. At no point of time the Government made a promise that the land would not be acquired in future. When the Government issues fresh notification, there is no scope for promissory estoppel over the Government.[11]

The principles of promissory estoppel apply with full force to the administrative action of State which does not give rise to contractual obligations between the parties and that if a citizen has acted upon an administrative assurance to his disadvantages the State can be pinned down to its promise.[12]

Doctrine of promissory estoppel The doctrine of promissory estoppel is now well recognized in India. It is an evolving doctrine the contours of which are not yet fully and finally demarcated. The rule of promissory estoppel being an equitable doctrine, has to be moulded to suit the particular situation. It is not a hard and fast rule but an elastic one, the objective of which is to do justice between the parties and to extend equitable treatment to them. Though the doctrine has been variously described as "equitable estoppel", "quasi-estoppel" and "new estoppel", it is a doctrine evolved by equity in order to prevent injustice.[13] In order to invoke the doctrine of promissory

9 AIR 1987 SC 590; (1987)1 SCR 654; 1986 (Supp) SCC 728.
10 *Vij Resins* v *State of J&K* AIR 1989 SC 1629; (1989)3 SCC 115.
11 *Promodebhai Bhulabhai Desai* v *Officer on Special Duty L.A., Ahmedabad* AIR 1989 Guj 187; (1989)30 Guj LR 194.
12 *Ashutosh Biswas* v *State of Orissa* AIR 1989 Ori 120.
13 *Intrans Systems Pvt. Ltd.* v *State of Kerala* AIR 1996 Ker 161.

estoppel it is not necessary for the promisee to show that he suffered detriment as a result of acting in reliance on the promise. The detriment in such a case is not some prejudice suffered by the promisee by acting on the promise, but the prejudice which would be caused to the promisee, if the promisor were allowed to go back on the promise.[14] Before the doctrine of promissory estoppel can be clamped on an authority of public body, it must be shown that there was an unambiguous promise.[15]

The principle of promissory estoppel is applicable to administrative law and not between private parties.[16] The doctrine of promissory estoppel has been applied against Government and the defence based on executive necessity has been categorically rejected. Where the Government makes a promise knowing or intending that it would be acted upon by the promisee and in fact the promisee acting in reliance on it alters his position, the Government would be held bound by the promise and the promise would be enforceable against the Government at the instance of the promisee notwithstanding that there is no consideration for the promise and the promise is not recorded in the form of a formal contract as required by Art. 299 of the Constitution. Since the doctrine of promissory estoppel is an equitable doctrine, it must yield when equity so requires.[17] Thus, non-execution of the contract in terms of Art. 299 of the Constitution does not militate against the applicability of the doctrine of promissory estoppel against the Government.[18] The doctrine of promissory estoppel is applicable to the Government in the exercise of its executive functions. Government cannot invoke the defence of executive necessity or freedom of future executive action.[19]

The doctrine of promissory estoppel may be applied against the Government where the interest of justice, morality and common fairness dictate such a course. The doctrine is applicable against the State even in its governmental, public or sovereign capacity where it is necessary to prevent fraud or manifest injustice. However, the Government or even a private party under the doctrine of promissory estoppel cannot be asked to do an act prohibited by law. The nature and function which the Government discharges is not very relevant. The Government is subject to the rule of promissory estoppel and if the essential ingredients of this doctrine are

14 *Motilal Padampat Sugar Mills* v *State of U.P.* AIR 1979 SC 621.
15 *Ude Ram* v *State of Haryana* AIR 1994 P&H 175.
16 *Hamir Ram* v *Varisng Raimal* AIR 1998 Guj 165.
17 *Intrans Systems Pvt. Ltd.* v *State of Kerala* AIR 1996 Ker 161.
18 *Food Corpn. of India* v *Babulal Agrawal* (2004)2 SCC 712.
19 *Jeet Ram Shiv Kumar* v *State of Haryana* AIR 1980 SC 1285; (1980)3 SCR 689; (1981)1 SCC 11; *Union of India* v *Godfrey Philips India Ltd.* AIR 1986 SC 806; 1985 Supp (3) SCR 123; (1985)4 SCC 369; *Motilal Padampat Sugar Mills* v *State of Uttar Pradesh* AIR 1979 SC 621; (1979)2 SCR 641; (1979)2 SCC 409; *K.M.L. Narasimhan Larsen & Toubro Ltd.* v *Union of India* AIR 1994 Mad 83.

satisfied, the Government can be compelled to carry out the promise made by it. But, in no case, the doctrine of promissory estoppel can be pressed into aid to compel the Government or a public authority to carry out a representation or promise which is contrary to law or which was outside the authority or power of the officer of the Government or of the public authority to make. No promise can be enforced which is statutorily prohibited or is against public policy.[20] However, it has been held by the Supreme Court that if public interest is considered as *superior equity* which can override individual equity, the principle would be applicable. If there is a supervening public equity, the Government would be allowed to change its stand and has the power to withdraw from representation made by it which induced persons to take certain steps which may have gone adverse to the interest of such persons on account of such withdrawal.[1]

The last provision is in addition to that in s. 71(12) of the Companies Act 2013 (corresponds to s. 122 of the Companies Act 1956) which provides that "A contract with a company to take up and pay for any debentures of the company may be enforced by a decree for specific performance." 'Debenture' is defined as it includes debenture stock, bonds or any other instrument of a company evidencing a debt, whether constituting a charge on the assets of the company or not s. 2(30) of the Companies Act 2013 (corresponds to s. 2(12) of the Companies Act 1956).

A contract to pay a debt out of specific property is also specifically enforceable on the view that in such a case an equitable assignment is created in favour of the creditor. In the words of Lord Truro in *Rodick* v *Gandell*,[2] "The extent of the principle to be deducted is that an agreement between a debtor and creditor that the debt owing shall be paid out of a specific fund coming to the debtor, or an order given by a debtor upon a person owing money or holding funds belonging to the giver of the order, directing such person to pay such funds to the creditor, will create a valid equitable charge upon such fund, in other words, will operate as an equitable assignment of the debts or fund to which the order refers."

Lord Wrenbury, however, added "An agreement for valuable consideration that a fund shall be applied in a particular way may found an injunction to restrain its application in another way. But if there be nothing more, such a stipulation will not amount to an equitable assignment. It is necessary to find further that an obligation has been imposed in favour of the creditor to pay the debt out of the fund. This is but an instance of a familiar doctrine of equity that a contract for valuable consideration to transfer or charge a subject matter passes a beneficial interest by way of property in the subject

20 *Monnet Ispat & Energy Ltd.* v *Union of India* (2012)11 SCC 1.

1 *M.P. Mathur* v *DTC* (2006)13 SCC 706; *Rishi Kiran Logistics (P) Ltd.* v *Kandla Port Trust* (2015)13 SCC 233.

2 42 ER 749 at p. 754.

matter if the contract is one of which a court of equity will decree specific performance."[3]

Doctrine of promissory estoppel or equitable estoppel is a rule of equity. It represents a principle of equity to avoid injustice. The basis of the doctrine is that where a party by his word or conduct made an unequivocal promise or representation by words or in writing to the other party which is intended to create legal relations knowing fully well that the other party would act upon such promise, assurance or representation, it would be binding on the party making it and that party should not be permitted to go back upon it, because it would be inequitable to allow him to do so, having regard to the dealings which have taken place or are intended to take place between the parties.[4] There are several factors which are to be taken into considerations by the court to attract the doctrine of promissory estoppel and these are as follows:[5] (*i*) A party must make an unequivocal promise or representation by word or conduct to the other party. (*ii*) The representation is intended to create legal relations or affect the legal relationship to arise in future. (*iii*) A clear foundation has to be laid in the petition with supporting documents. (*iv*) It is to be shown that the party invoking the doctrine has altered its position relying on the promise. (*v*) It is possible for the Government to resile from the promise when public interest would be prejudiced if the Government is required to carry out the promise. (*vi*) The court will not apply the doctrine in abstract. The doctrine is applicable when a representation is made by State in exercise of its power to exempt or abolish a commodity as taxable commodity. Such promise must be made by persons having power to implement the representation.[6] In order to invoke the doctrine, clear, sound and positive foundation must be laid in the petition itself by the party invoking the doctrine.[7]

The Government can resile from a promise even if there is no public interest involved provided that no one is put in any adverse situation which cannot be rectified.[8] In a leading case[9] the Privy Council has held that the Indian Evidence Act has not enacted any law in India which is different from the law of England on the subject of estoppel. The English decisions are, therefore, relevant for determination of question arising for decision under the Indian Evidence Act.[10]

3 *Palmer* v *Carey* [1926] AC 703 applied in *Swiss Bank Corpn.* v *Lloyds Bank* [1981]2 All ER 449 (CA); [1982] AC 584.
4 *Kasinka Trading* v *Union of India* AIR 1995 SC 874.
5 *State of Bihar* v *Kalyanpur Cement Ltd.* (2010)3 SCC 274.
6 *Tata Iron & Steel Co. Ltd.* v *State of Jharkhand* AIR 2005 SC 2871; (2005)4 SCC 272.
7 *State of Arunachal Pradesh* v *Nezone Law House, Assam* AIR 2008 SC 2045.
8 *Dai-Ichi Karkaria Ltd.* v *Union of India* (2000)4 SCC 57; AIR 2000 SC 1741.
9 *Sarat Chandra Dey* v *Gopal Chunder Laha* (1892)19 IA 203 (PC); see *Mercantile Bank of India* v *Central Bank of India* AIR 1938 PC 52.
10 *Khan Gul* v *Lakha Singh* ILR (1928)9 Lah 701; AIR 1928 Lah 609.

English law and American law—a comparison In England, where the Judges apprehending that if a cause of action is allowed to be founded on promissory estoppel it would considerably erode, if not completely overthrow, the doctrine of consideration, have been fearful to allow promissory estoppel to be used as a weapon of offence, it is interesting to find that promissory estoppel has not been confined to a purely defensive role. Lord Denning himself said in *Combe* v *Combe*[11] that promissory estoppel "may be a part of a cause of action", though "not a cause of action itself". In fact, there have been several cases where promissory estoppel has been successfully invoked by a party to support his cause of action, without actually founding his cause of action exclusively upon it. Two such cases are: *Robertson* v *Minister of Pensions*[12] and *Evenden* v *Guildford City Association Football Club Ltd.*[13] The English courts have thus gone a step forward from the original position when promissory estoppel was regarded merely as a passive equity and allowed it to be used as a weapon of offence to a limited extent as a part of the cause of action, but still the doctrine of consideration continues to inhibit the judicial mind and that has thwarted the full development of this new equitable principle and the realization of its vast potential as a juristic technique for doing justice. It is true that to allow promissory estoppel to find a cause of action would seriously dilute the principle which requires consideration to support a contractual obligation, but that is no reason why this new principle, which is a child of equity brought into the world with a view to promoting honesty and good faith and bringing law closer to justice, should be held in fetters and not allowed to operate in all its activist magnitude, so that it may fulfil the purpose for which it was conceived and born. It must be remembered that law is not a mausoleum. It is not an antique to be taken down, dusted, admired and put back on the shelf. It is rather like an old but vigorous tree, having its roots in history, yet continuously taking new grafts and putting out new sprouts and occasionally dropping dead wood. It is essentially a social process, the end product of which is justice and hence it must keep on growing and developing with changing social concepts and values. Otherwise, there will be estrangement between law and justice and law will cease to have legitimacy. It is true, as pointed out by Mr. Justice Holmes, that continuity with the past is a historical necessity but it must also be remembered at the same time, as pointed out by Mr. Justice Cardozo that "conformity is not to be turned into a fetish".[14]

It is well-known that in the United States the law has always shown a greater capacity for adjustment and growth than elsewhere. The doctrine of

11 [1951]1 All ER 767.
12 [1949]1 KB 227; [1948]2 All ER 767.
13 [1975]3 All ER 269.
14 *Motilal Padampat Sugar Mills Co. Ltd.* v *State of U.P.* (1979)2 SCC 409.

promissory estoppel has displayed remarkable vigour and vitality in the hands of American Judges and it is still rapidly developing and expanding in the United States. It may be pointed out that this development does not derive its origin in any way from the decision of Lord Denning in the *High Trees'* case[15] but antedates this decision by a number of years; perhaps it is possible that it may have helped to inspire that decision. It was long before the decision in the *High Trees'* case that the "Restatement of the Law of Contracts of the American Law Institute" came out with the following proposition in s. 90:

> Section 90. ***Promise reasonably inducing definite and substantial action is binding.*** A promise which the promisor should reasonably expect to induce action or forbearance of a definite and substantial character on the part of the promisee, and which does induce such action or forbearance is binding if injustice can be avoided only by enforcement of the promise.[16]

This proposition was explained and elucidated by several illustrations given in the article and one of such illustrations was as follows:

> *A* promises *B* to pay him an annuity during *B*'s life. *B* thereupon resigns a profitable employment, as *A* expected that he might. *B* receives the annuity for some years, in the meantime becoming disqualified from again obtaining good employment. *A*'s promise is binding.

It is true that the Restatement has not the same weight as a source of law, as actual decisions of courts of high standing, yet the principle set out in s. 90 of the Restatement of the Law of Contracts has in fact formed the basis of a number of decisions in various States and it is now becoming increasingly clear that a promise may in the United States derive contractual enforceability if it has been made by the promisor intending that it would be acted on and the promisee has altered his position in reliance on it, notwithstanding that there is no consideration in the sense in which that word is used in English and Commonwealth jurisprudence. However, in *Orennan* v *Star Paving Company*[17] Traynor, J explicitly adopted as good law the text of s. 90 of the Restatement of the Law of Contracts as delineated above and stated in so many words that "*the absence of consideration is not fatal to the enforcement of such a promise*". This is also the view expressed in *American Jurisprudence*:[18]

> A number of courts have upheld the validity of charitable subscriptions on the theory of promissory estoppel holding that while a mere promise to

15 *Central London Property Trust Ltd.* v *High Trees House Ltd.* [1956]1 All ER 256; 1947 KB 130.

16 *Restatement of the Law of Contracts of the American Law Institute*, ss. 85-94, with Missouri Annotations, vol. 18(1), Washington University Law Review (January 1932).

17 (1958)31 Cal 2d 409.

18 Vol. 19, p. 657.

contribute is unenforceable for want of consideration, if money has been expended or liabilities have been incurred in reliance on the promise so that non-fulfilment will cause injury to the payee the donor is estopped to assert the lack of consideration, and the promise will be enforced.

Suffice it to state for the present that the doctrine of promissory estoppel has been taken much further in the United States than in English and Commonwealth jurisdictions and in some States at least, it has been used to reduce, if not to destroy, the prestige of consideration as an essential of valid contract.[19]

Proprietary[20] and promissory estoppels—contrast[1] Though there are some points in common between the doctrine of proprietary estoppel and the doctrine of promissory estoppel, yet there are also important differences between the said two doctrines. The scope of the doctrine of proprietary estoppel is narrower than the doctrine of promissory estoppel in two respects. First, proprietary estoppel is restricted to promises relating to property. Promissory estoppel may arise out of any promise that strict legal rights will not be enforced. Secondly, proprietary estoppel requires the promisee to have acted to his detriment, while promissory estoppel may operate even though the promisee merely performs a pre-existing duty and so suffers no detriment in doing something that he was not previously bound to do. This difference between the two doctrines follows from the fact that promissory estoppel is concerned only with the variation or abandonment of rights arising out of a pre-existing legal relationship between promisor and promisee.[2] On the other hand, the scope of proprietary estoppel is in two respects wider than that of promissory estoppel. First, promissory estoppel arises only out of a representation or promise. But proprietary estoppel arises where there is no actual promise. Secondly, while promissory estoppel is essentially defensive in nature, proprietary estoppel can give rise to a cause of action.[3] The promisee is not simply entitled to raise the estoppel as a defence to an action of trespass or to a claim for possession, the court can make an order for the land to be conveyed to him, or for compensation,[4] or for such other remedy as appropriate. There are two aspects of proprietary

19 Spencer Bower and Turner, *Estoppel by Representation*, 2nd Ed., p. 358. quoted and relied upon in *Motilal Padampat Sugar Mills Co. Ltd.* v *State of U.P.* (1979)2 SCC 409.

20 The concept of 'proprietary estoppel' may be taced back to the decision of Lord Cranworth in *Ramesden* v *Dyson* [1866] LR 1 HL 129. It is also known as 'estoppel by acquiescence'.

1 *See* also Prof. LC Saxena, *The Twilight of Promissory Estoppel in India: A Constrast with English Law* (1974)16 JILI and Salman Khurshid, *Estoppel Advent* (1981)3 SCC 33-51.

2 Treitel, *The Law of Contract*, 13th Ed., pp. 155-157.

3 *Crabb* v *Arun DC* [1976] Ch 179.

4 *Eves* v *Eves* [1975]1 WLR 1338.

estoppel. These are that the acts done by the promisee are not ones which he was under any previous legal obligation to perform; and that generally their effect would be unjustly to enrich the promisor if he were allowed to go back on his promise. In these respects the facts on which proprietary estoppel is based provide more compelling grounds for relief than those commonly found in cases of promissory estoppel.

Contract for share If the shares are easily available in the market, damages will be the usual remedy in the event of breach, but where the shares are not easily available in the market, the contract may be specifically enforced, as, for example, in the case of shares of a private company.[5] Further, where the agreement is to take and pay for shares or to allot shares, it may also be specifically enforced.[6] But if, in the meantime, before the suit is filed, all the shares have been allotted to other persons, the only remedy of the plaintiff claiming allotment is in damages.[7] Specific performance may also be ordered where the contract relates to transfer of shares on which nothing has been paid,[8] or even though pending litigation the company has gone into liquidation.[9] However, it is stated that in order to institute a suit for enforcement of a contractual obligation of the right of pre-emption, as regards purchase of share, it is not necessary to make a company a party to the suit, but the shareholder, against whom the pre-emptive right is sought to be exercised, is a necessary party.[10]

Where, the contract to sell shares has been made before the commencement of the winding-up, specific performance will not be decreed if the contract is sought to be enforced after the winding-up order has been made, for, in such a case, it would amount to forcing upon the buyer who had agreed to take a fully effective transfer of the shares, a transfer that, although valid as between him and the vendor, would be void against the company.[11] Likewise, where the contract to take shares is disclaimed by a trustee in bankruptcy, the contract is at an end, and the company's remedy is a claim for damages against the estate of the bankrupt.[12]

5 *Jainarain* v *Surajmal* AIR 1949 FC 211; *Bank of India Ltd.* v *Jamsedji A.H. Chinoy and Chinoy & Co.* AIR 1950 PC 90 and *Transport Co. Ltd.* v *Tirunvali Motor Bus Service Co.* [1955]2 MLJ 141.

6 *Odessa Tramways Co.* v *Mendel* [1878]8 Ch D 235 (CA) and *Sri Lanka Omnibus Co. Ltd* v *Parera* [1952] AC 76.

7 *Farguson* v *Wilson* [1866] LR 2 Ch 77.

8 *Cheale* v *Kenward* [1858]3 De G&J 27.

9 *Paine* v *Hutchinson* [1868]3 LR Ch App 388.

10 Halsbury's *Laws of England*, 4th Ed., vol. 7(1), p. 221 at para 378; *Radhabari Tea Company (P.) Ltd.* v *Mridul Kumar Bhattacharjee* (2010)2 Gau LR 231: (2010)153 Comp Cas 579.

11 *Sullivan* v *Henderson* [1973]1 All ER 48 at p. 50.

12 *Hooley ex parte United Ordance & Engineering Co., re* [1899]2 QB 579.

Specific performance may be decreed where the contract is for the purchase of Government stock and prayer is made for the delivery of certificates which give legal title to the stock.[13]

Contract for goodwill The goodwill of a business is an intangible asset being the whole advantage of the reputation and connection formed with the customers together with the circumstances which make the connection durable. It is that component of the total value of the undertaking which is attributable to the ability of the concern to earn profits over a course, of years because of its reputation, location and other features.[14]

In its legal sense the word 'goodwill' means every affirmative advantage as contrasted with negative advantage that has been acquired in carrying on the business, whether connected with the premises or its name or style and everything connected with or carrying with it, the benefit of the business. It includes the whole advantage of the reputation and connections of the firm or the owner which may have been built up by years of hard work, or gained by lavish expenditure, beyond the mere value of the capital stock and property embarked in the business, in consequence of the general public patronage and encouragement, which is received from specie of connections in trade.[15] A simple contract for the sale of goodwill will not be specifically enforced.[16]

Contract for sale of debt It has been held that such contracts are also an exception to the rule and will be specifically enforced.[17]

Contract for patent As defined in s. 2(*m*) of the Patents Act 1970 "patent" means a patent for any invention granted under the Patents Act 1970 and "patentee" means the person for the time being entered on the register as the grantee or proprietor of the patent.[18]

The effect of the grant of patent is *quid pro quo, quid* is the knowledge disclosed to the public and *quo* is the monopoly granted for the term of the patent. Section 48 of the Patents Act 1970 provides that a patent once granted confers upon the patentee the exclusive right to prevent third parties from the act of making, using, offering for sale, selling or importing for those purposes that product in India and of authorizing others to do so. This is *quo*. The *quid* is compliance with the various provisions resulting in the grant of patent.[19]

13 *Doloret* v *Rothschild* 57 ER 233; [1824]1 Sim & St. 590.

14 *Khushal Khemgar Shah* v *Khorshed Banu Dadiba Bratwala* AIR 1970 SC 1147; 1971 Mah LJ 1.

15 *State of Rajasthan* v *Bundi Electric Supply Co.* AIR 1970 Raj 36; *Dulaldas* v *Ganeshdas* AIR 1957 Cal 280.

16 *Baxter* v *Conolly* [1820]37 ER 487.

17 *Wright* v *Bell* [1918]5 Price 325; 146 ER 622.

18 Section 2(*p*) of the Patents Act 1970.

19 *Raj Prakash* v *Mangat Ram Chowdhry* AIR 1978 Del 1; ILR (1977)2 Del 412; 1977 Rajdhani LR 440.

Agreement for the sale of patent is specifically enforceable.[20] In *Printing & Numerical Registering Co.* v *Sampson,*[1] it has been held that a vendor may agree to assign to the purchaser his all future patent rights.[2]

Agreement deed materially altered—bar of specific performance 'Material alteration' in its ordinary meaning would mean important alterations, such as those which materially or substantially change the front or structure of the premises.[3] A material alteration is one which varies the rights, liabilities or legal position of the parties as ascertained by the deed in its original state or otherwise varies the legal effect of the instrument as originally expressed or reduces to certainty some provision which was originally unascertained and as such void, or may otherwise prejudice the party bound by the deed as originally executed.[4] The effect of making such an alteration without the consent of the party bound is exactly the same as that of cancelling the deed.[5] However, it should be distinguished from a forgery.[6]

In a case the deed of agreement was interpolated so much so that in the gap between the last line of contents and signatures etc., a line was introduced to show that possessory right was conveyed to the plaintiff so as to enable him to acquire part performance of the contract. Such a contract was held not enforceable at all.[7] Contract for expectant interests is void and will not be specifically enforced.[8]

Where court cannot enforce material terms of the contract

(a) ***Contract running into minute or numerous details*** A court of equity does not deem it expedient to make a decree for specific performance of a contract which runs into minute or numerous details, and leaves a party to seek his remedy in damages. In such cases, the court refuses to interfere, not because the court cannot formulate a decree which shall order everything necessary for a complete performance or which shall not be absolutely incapable of compulsory execution but because the enforcement of the decree would unreasonably tax the time, attention and resources of the court, and thereby interfere too much with its public duties to other suitors, and in the general administration of justice. Upon the same principle, a court often abstains from enforcing in specie a contract to execute works which the court cannot superintend. This clause does not supply any test

20 *Cognet* v *Gibson* [1864]55 ER 485.
1 [1874-75] LR 19 Eq 462.
2 *Macdonald* v *Eyles* [1921]1 Ch 631.
3 *Babu Monmohan Das* v *Bishun Das* AIR 1967 SC 643; (1967)1 SCR 836.
4 *Nathulal* v *Gomti Kaur* AIR 1940 PC 160; *Anirudhan* v *Thomco's Bank* AIR 1963 SC 746; 1963 Supp (1) SCR 63; (1964)1 SCJ 495.
5 Halsbury's *Laws of England*, 4th Ed., vol. 12, at pp. 552-53, para 1378.
6 Halsbury's *Laws of England*, 4th Ed., Reissue, vol. 9(1), at pp. 552-53, para 1058.
7 *Janab M.H.M. Yakoob* v *M. Krishnan* AIR 1992 Mad 80.
8 *K.L. Jagannada Raju Garu* v *Sri Rajah Prasad Rao Garu* ILR (1916)39 Mad 554.

whereby the limit of the court's capacity for superintendence may be determined. It is vague. The court may also sometimes find it not in the public interest to decree specific performance in a particular case.[9]

This is based on the principle that is the court were to decree specific performance of such contracts, it will unduly tax its time, attention and resources at the cost of other suitors. For illustration please see the case of *Nagar Mahapalika, Kanpur* v *Punjab Association.*[10]

(b) *Contracts depending on personal volition or qualification of the defendant*
Section 14(*c*) of the Specific Relief Act provides that a contract cannot be specifically enforced which was so dependent on the personal qualifications or volition of the parties, or otherwise from its nature was such, that the court cannot enforce specific performance of its material terms.

Volition is no more than status of mind, the will to do or not to do. Such contracts are usually referable to contracts of personal service where a particular quality possessed by a person for which the contract is entered into, depends upon his willingness or the state of mind like singing, dancing, teaching, etc. which if specifically enforced, may lead to result not contemplated in the original contract.[11]

The performance of the contract is not dependent on personal volition and hence can be enforced. The delay in obtaining permits from the forest department may entail postponement of payment but that would not bring the contract within the ambit of s. 14(*b*) of the Specific Relief Act.[12]

If a person enters into a contract, the performance of a part of which depends upon his volition and he performs his part and then refuses to perform the remaining part which does not depend upon his volition, he cannot resist the suit for specific performance of the remaining part on the ground that the agreement on the date, when it was made, depended partly on his volition. If he has already performed that part of the contract which depended upon his volition, he can be compelled to perform the remaining part which he did not perform.

When the matter has got to be decided by arbitrators on a reference, it cannot be said that the matter being dependent on the volition of the arbitrators, specific performance cannot be ordered; there is a clear distinction between decision and volition. Arbitrators act as judges and their decision is not a matter of volition with them.[13]

9 Banerjee on *Law of Specific Relief*, 13th Ed., p 269.
10 1980 All LJ 869.
11 *Robert D'Silva* v *Roshini Enterprises* AIR 1987 Kant 57; (1986)1 Kant LJ 120; (1986)1 Civ LJ 523.
12 *Robert D'Silva* v *Roshini Enterprises* (supra).
13 *Bai Mangu* v *Bai Vijli* AIR 1967 Guj 81 at p. 86.

(i) Contract of personal service Under the common law the court will not ordinarily force an employer to retain the services of an employee whom he no longer wishes to employ. But this rule is subject to certain well-recognized exceptions. It is open to the courts in an appropriate case to declare that a public servant who is dismissed from service in contravention of Art. 311 of the Constitution continues to remain in service, even though by so doing the State is in effect forced to continue to employ the servant whom it does not desire to employ. Similarly under the industrial law, jurisdiction of the labour and industrial tribunals to compel the employer to employ a worker, whom he does not desire to employ, is recognized. The courts are also invested with the power to declare invalid the act of a statutory body, if by doing the act the body has acted in breach of a mandatory obligation imposed by statute, even if by making the declaration the body is compelled to do something which it does not desire to do.[14]

A contract of service exists if the following three conditions are fulfilled; (*i*) The servant agrees that in consideration of a wage or other remuneration he will provide his own work and skill in the performance of some service for his master. (*ii*) He agrees, expressly or impliedly, that in the performance of that service he will be subject to the other's control in a sufficient degree to make that other master. (*iii*) The other provisions of the contract are consistent with its being a contract of service.[15] A contract for personal service includes all matters relating to the service of the employee, e.g. confirmation, suspension, transfer, termination, etc.[16]

As to contract of personal service involving the relationship of master and servant, Halsbury lays down "A judgment for specific performance of a contract for personal work or services is not pronounced, either at the suit of the employer or the employee. The court does not seek to compel persons against their will to maintain continuous personal and confidential relations. However, this rule is not absolute and without exception. It has been held that an employer may be restrained from dismissing an employee in breach of contract if there is no loss of confidence between employer and employee or if (at least in a contract of employment to carry out a public duty) the employee has been dismissed in a manner which does not comply with statutory or contractual regulations governing dismissal.

No court may, whether by way of an order of specific performance of a contract of employment or an injunction restraining a breach or threatened breach of such a contract, compel an employee to do any work or attend at any place for the doing of any work.

14 *S.R. Tewari* v *District Board* (1964)3 SCR 55; AIR 1964 SC 1680.

15 *Ready Mixed Concrete (South East) Ltd.* v *Minister of Pensions and National Insurance* [1968]1 All ER 433.

16 *Apollo Tyres Ltd.* v *C.P. Sebastian* (2009)14 SCC 360.

This principle applies not merely to contracts of employment, but to all contracts which involve the rendering of continuous services by one person to another, such as a contract to work a railway line.[17]

It is a well-settled principle of law that a contract of personal service cannot be specifically enforced and a court will not give a declaration that the contract subsists and the employee continues to be in service against the will and consent of the employer.[18] Section 14, read with s. 41(*e*) of the Specific Relief Act 1963, specifically bars the enforcement of such a contract.[19] When there is a purported termination of a contract of service, a declaration that the contract of service still subsisted would not be made in the absence of special circumstances, because of the principle that courts do not ordinarily enforce specific performance of contracts of service.[20] The remedy is to sue for damages. However, there are certain exceptions to the rule, such as in the case of a public servant dismissed from service in contravention of Art. 311 of the Constitution; reinstatement of a dismissed worker under the Industrial law; a statutory body acting in breach of statutory obligations and the like.[1]

The court refuses to enforce such contracts. The rule is partly based on difficulty of supervision and partly on grounds of public policy that no person shall be made to work against his will. Lord Justice Fry said, "The courts are bound to be jealous, lest they should turn contracts of services into contracts of slavery."[2]

When the relationship is one of master and servant, a suit for declaration that an employee is still in service, the employment having been terminated is hit by s. 14(1)(*b*), Specific Relief Act (since substituted) and is not tenable.[3]

In *C.H. Giles & Co. Ltd.* v *Morris*[4] Megarry, J has observed that the matter was one of balance of advantage and disadvantage in relation to the particular obligations in question and the fact the balance would usually lie

17 Halsbury's *Laws of England*, 4th Ed., vol. 44, p. 407 quoted in *Nandganj Sihori Sugar Co. Ltd.* v *Badri Nath Dixit* AIR 1991 SC 1525; (1991)2 SCR 468; (1991)3 SCC 54.
18 *Pearlite Liners (P) Ltd.* v *Manorama Sirsi* (2004)3 SCC 172; 2004 SCC (L&S) 453.
19 *Maharashtra State Coop. Housing Finance Corpn. Ltd.* v *Prabhakar Sitaram Bhadange* (2017)5 SCC 623.
20 *Executive Committee of U.P. State Warehousing Corporation Ltd.* v *Chandra Kiran Tyagi* AIR 1970 SC 1244; (1970)2 SCR 250; (1970)1 SCJ 790; *Indian Airlines Corporation* v *Sukhdeo Rai* AIR 1971 SC 1828.
1 *Nandganj Sihori Sugar Co. Ltd., Rai Bareli* v *Badri Nath Dixit* AIR 1991 SC 1525 following *Executive Committee of Vaish Degree College* v *Lakshmi Narain* AIR 1976 SC 888 (897); (1976)2 SCR 1006 at p. 1020.
2 *De Francesco* v *Barnum* [1890]45 Ch D 430 at p. 438.
3 *S.R. Tiwari* v *District Board, Agra* AIR 1964 SC 1680; (1964)3 SCR 55; *Executive Committee of U.P. State* v *Chandra Kiran Tyagi* AIR 1970 SC 1244; (1970)2 SCR 250; (1969)2 SCC 838; *Subh Narayan Sinha* v *Hari Singh* (1975)1 Cal LJ 390.
4 [1972]1 All ER 960.

on one side did not turn the probability into a rule. "If a singer contracts to sing, there could no doubt be proceedings for committal, if ordered to sing, the singer remained obstinately dumb. But if instead the singer sang flat, or sharp, or too fast, or too slowly, or too loudly, or too quietly, or resorted to a dozen of the manifestations of temperament traditionally associated with some singers, the threat of committal would reveal itself as a most unsatisfactory weapon, for who could say whether the imperfections of performance were natural or self-induced? To make an order with such possibilities of evasion would be vain, and so the order will not be made."

In such cases a court may not even declare that the contract subsists, or that the employee, even after having been removed from service, is deemed to be in service against the will and consent of the employer.

INDUSTRIAL DISPUTES When the employee is governed by the Industrial Disputes Act 1947, suit for reinstatement in civil court is barred and the remedy lies in an appropriate proceeding under the Industrial Disputes Act.[5]

Civil court's jurisdiction is ousted if the dispute is an industrial dispute arising out of a right or liability under the general common law and not under the Act, the jurisdiction of the civil court is alternative, leaving it to the election of the suitor concerned to choose his remedy for the relief which is competent to be granted in a particular dispute.

If the industrial dispute relates to the enforcement of a right or an obligation created under the Act, then the only remedy available to the suitor is to get an adjudication under the Act.[6] But, if a right is claimed under the Industrial Disputes Act or the sister laws, the jurisdiction of the civil court would be barred, but if no such right is claimed, civil court will have jurisdiction.[7] It is, however, interesting to note that both in *Premier Automobiles* case (supra) and *Rajasthan SRTC* case (supra), the Supreme Court extensively relied upon the law laid down in *Wolverhampton New Waterworks Co.* v *Hawkesford*[8] where the following observation was made:

> There are three classes of cases in which a liability may be established by statute. There is that class where there is a liability existing at common law, and which is only re-enacted by the statute with a special form of remedy; there, unless the statute contains words necessarily excluding the common law remedy, the plaintiff has his election of proceeding either under the statute or at common law. Then there is a second class, which consists of those cases in which a statute has created a liability, but has given no

5 *Jitendra Nath Biswas* v *Empire of India and Ceylone Tea Co.* AIR 1990 SC 255; (1989)3 SCR 640; (1989)3 SCC 582.

6 *Premier Automobiles* v *K.S. Wadke* AIR 1975 SC 2238; (1976)1 SCR 427; (1976)1 SCC 496.

7 *Rajasthan SRTC* v *Mohar Singh* (2008)5 SCC 542.

8 (1859)6 CBNS 336; 141 ER 486.

special remedy for it; there the party may adopt an action of debt or other remedy at common law to enforce it. The third class is where the statute creates a liability not existing at common law, and gives also a particular remedy for enforcing it.... With respect to that class it has always been held, that the party must adopt the form of remedy given by the statute.

Thus, in India, the Supreme Court[9] has succinctly laid down the following propositions of law applicable to the jurisdiction of the civil court in relation to an industrial dispute:

(1) If the dispute is not an industrial dispute, nor does it relate to enforcement of any other right under the Act and the remedy lies only in the civil court.

(2) If the dispute is an industrial dispute arising out of a right or liability under the general or common law and not under the Act, the jurisdiction of the civil court is alternative leaving it to the election of the suitor concerned to choose his remedy for the relief which is competent to be granted in a particular remedy.

(3) If the industrial dispute relates to the enforcement of a right or an obligation created under the Act, then the only remedy available to the suitor is to get an adjudication under the Act.

(4) If the right which is sought to be enforced is a right created under the Act such as Chapter VA then the remedy for its enforcement is either s. 33C or the raising of an industrial dispute, as the case may be.

A suit by an employee of a cooperative society challenging his retrenchment is tenable in a civil court, the dispute not touching the business of the society.[10] In *Yashvir Singh* v *Modern Food Industry (India) Ltd.*,[11] the order of termination of service of an industrial employee was challenged on the ground of violation of natural justice, *viz.* the principle of *nemo debet esse judex in propria sua causa* [no one can be a judge of his own cause]. The appellant employee was found guilty of stopping the car of and misbehaving with Respondent who himself was the authority to pass order for termination. He himself issued the charge sheet to the employee and eventually passed the order of termination of his service. It was contended that having regard to the fact that respondent who was a witness since it was his car which it is alleged the petitioner had stopped and it was with him that the petitioner misbehaved, he ought not to have issued the charge

9 *Premier Automobiles* v *K.S. Wadke* AIR 1975 SC 2238; (1976)1 SCR 427; (1976)1 SCC 496.

10 *Allahabad Dist. Co-op. Ltd.* v *Hanuman Dutt Tewari* AIR 1982 SC 120; (1981)4 SCC 431.

11 AIR 1993 SC 961; JT 1992(1) SC 109; 1992(1) SLR 420.

sheet and he ought not to have passed the impugned order, because to do so would be to allow him to appreciate the worth of his own evidence and that merely because the appellate authority had confirmed the order would not remove the taint which attaches to the order of termination. The other side pointed out that as Respondent was the authority under the standing orders to pass the impugned order, he did so out of necessity. Their Lordships of the Supreme Court disposed of the matter by awarding a compensation of the employee and rejected his prayer for reinstatement.

It is respectfully submitted that this decision of the Supreme Court is not in accordance with the time-old concept of natural justice that a person cannot be a judge of his own cause. In *Syndicate Bank* v *General Secretary, Syndicate Bank Staff Association,*[12] Their Lordships of the Supreme Court pointed out that—

> "There are two essential elements of natural justice which are (*a*) no man shall be judge in his own cause; and (*b*) no man shall be condemned, either civilly or criminally, without being afforded an opportunity of being heard in answer to the charge made against him,"

The doctrine of necessity cannot be stretched to the extent of making the complainant a judge in the enquiry in his own complaint. In fact, the learned Judges of the Supreme Court in *Yashvir Singh's* case[13] did not go into the question whether the principle of natural justice was violated or whether the doctrine of necessity applied in the instant case and disposed of the matter in a short judgment with brief statement as follows:

> "After hearing these rival contentions, we thought it proper to put an end to the matter by directing payment of adequate compensation to the workmen but not granting him reinstatement with back wages. We, therefore, do not interfere with the order on condition that ₹75,000 will be paid by way of compensation to the petitioner within a period of one month."

If the order of termination of the services of the petitioner was legally sustainable, where is the question of awarding compensation to the petitioner? It is also submitted, as has been held by the Supreme Court after the decision of *Yashvir Singh* (supra), that the ordinary rule is that a worker, when retrenched in violation of principles of natural justice, is entitled to reinstatement with back wages.[14] However, there cannot be any precise formula as to whether the full back wages should be allowed or not. It all depends upon the facts and circumstances of each and every case.[15]

12 AIR 2000 SC 2198; (2000)5 SCC 65; JT 2000(5) SC 243.

13 *Yashvir Singh* v *Modern Food Industry (India) Ltd.* AIR 1993 SC 961; JT 1992(1) SC 109.

14 *Deepali Gundu Surwase* v *Kranti Junior Adhyapak Mahavidyalaya* (2013)10 SCC 324.

15 *U.P. State Brassware Corpn. Ltd.* v *Uday Narain Pandey* (2006)1 SCC 479.

Similarly, rules of natural justice do not apply in respect of termination of service which was given in violation of relevant standing orders or rules.[16]

In *Bangalore Water Supply and Sewerage Board* v *A. Rajappa*,[17] the Supreme Court has given a new orientation to the concept of "industry". Overruling a catena of judicial decisions such as *Management of Safdarjang Hospital* v *Kuldip Singh*,[18] the Supreme Court laid down that "if the activities are productive of either service or goods and employees are involved, an enterprise can be treated as an "industry". Thus, clubs, educational institutions, research institutes and charitable projects would all come within the purview of "industry". The scope for declaratory relief and specific enforcement is correspondingly enlarged.

(II) Contract of service under the State or Instrumentality of State In view of s. 14(*b*), Specific Relief Act, when the relationship is governed by master and servant relationship neither the master can compel the servant to continue his service nor the servant can compel the master to keep him in employment.

But whenever one is appointed *qua* public servant under the State or as an employee under the Instrumentality of State, his relationship *vis-a-vis* his master is elevated to status because then he is in the matter of service governed by either service conditions framed under Art. 309, Constitution or by Standing Orders. Then in the matter of service the rule of hire and fire does not apply. Where there is a breach of requirement of a statute, the court will give a declaration that the dismissal is ineffective and the servant continues to be in service.[19]

The courts are also invested with power to declare invalid the act of a statutory body, if by doing the act, the body has acted in breach of a mandatory obligation imposed by statute, even if by making a declaration the body is compelled to do something against his volition. But it is not every breach of statutory provision that entitles an employee to ask for a declaration that he is in service despite order of dismissal. It is only when a statutory status is given to an employee and that status has been affected in violation of a statutory provision, the employee can ask for a declaration that order is nullity and he be deemed to be still in service.[20] So far as the Government servants are concerned the origin is contractual. There is an

16 *Calcutta Jute Manufacturing Co. Ltd.* v *First Industrial Tribunal* (2007)1 CHN 422.
17 AIR 1978 SC 969; (1978)3 SCR 207; (1978)2 SCC 213.
18 AIR 1970 SC 1407; (1971)1 SCR 177; (1970)1 SCC 735; *Madras Gymkhana Club Employees' Union* v *Gymkhana Club* AIR 1968 SC 554; (1968)1 SCR 742; *University of Delhi* v *Ramanath* AIR 1963 SC 1873; (1964)2 SCR 703.
19 *High Commissioner for India* v *I.M. Lal* AIR 1948 PC 121; *Ashok Kumar Srivasthava* v *National Insurance Company* AIR 1998 SC 2046; (1998)4 SCC 361; JT 1998(3) SC 519.
20 *Biswanath Das* v *Ramesh* ILR (1978)2 Cut 500; (1980)1 Lab 35; 46 Cut LT 593; (1979)54 FJR 108; 1979 Lab IC 319; 37 Fac LR 344.

offer and acceptance in every case. But once appointed to his post or office the Government servant acquires a status, his rights and obligations are governed by statutory rules, the hallmark of status being the attachment to a legal relationship of rights and duties imposed by the public law and not by mere agreement by the parties.[1] Not only to the Government servants similar protection is also available to the employees of a government-corporation who can be called the instrumentality of the Government under Art. 12 of the Constitution.[2]

In such case the embargo on specific performance of contract of service is subject to three well-recognized exceptions—

(1) where a public servant is sought to be removed from service in contravention of the provisions of Art. 311 of the Constitution,

(2) where a worker is sought to be reinstated on being dismissed under the industrial law; and

(3) where a statutory body acts in breach of violation of the mandatory provisions of the statute.[3]

Even when court finds the statutory invalidity of act of employer in suspending or dismissing an employee is covered by statutory trappings, court may in appropriate case refuse specific performance. In a Supreme Court case an employee, a teacher in Educational Institution governed by the U.P. High School and Intermediate College (Payment of Salaries of Teachers and other Employees) Act 1971 was out of teaching employment for long 25 years. He was in teaching job only for 1 or 2 years. The Supreme Court held that his reinstatement as a teacher was not justified because he lost the quality of a teacher. In educational institutions, the court cannot focus only on the individual forgetting all else. The court must have regard to varying circumstances in the academic atmosphere and radically changed position of the individual sought to be reinstated. The court must have regard to interests of students as well as the institution.[4]

1 *Roshanlal Tandon* v *Union of India* AIR 1967 SC 1889 at p. 1894; (1968)1 SCR 185.

2 *A.L. Kalra* v *Project and Equipment Corporation* AIR 1984 SC 1361; 1984 Lab IC 961; 1984 UJ (SC) 733; (1984)3 SCC 316; *Hindusthan Steel* v *R.N. Banerjee* 88 CWN 1049; *W.B. State Electricity Board* v *Gour Chandra Sarkar* (1985)1 Cal LJ 1.

3 *Nandganj Sihori Sugar* v *Badri Nath Dixit* AIR 1991 SC 1525; (1991)2 SCR 468; (1991)3 SCC 54; *Executive Committee of Vaish Degree College, Shamli* v *Lakshmi Narain* AIR 1976 SC 888 at 897; (1976)2 SCR 1006; (1976)2 SCC 58; *Sirsi Municipality* v *Cecelia Kom Francis* AIR 1973 SC 855; (1973)3 SCR 348; (1973)1 SCC 409; *Executive Committee of U.P. State Warehousing Corpn* v *Chandra Kiran Tyagi* AIR 1970 SC 1244 at pp. 1251, 1254; (1970)2 SCR 250; (1969)2 SCC 838 relying on *Barbar* v *Manchester Hospital Board* [1958]11 All ER 322; *Francis* v *Municipal Councillors* [1962]3 All ER 633 and *Vine* v *National Dock Labour Board* [1956]3 All ER 939.

4 *Kayastha Pathsala* v *Rajendra Prasad* AIR 1990 SC 415; 1989 All LJ 1401; 1989 Supp (2) SCC 732.

It has been said when the relationship between the employer and employee is covered by statutory trappings, the ordinary rule of hire and fire is not applicable. Section 14(*b*), Specific Relief Act provides no bar to declaration of statutory status of employee. In this connection it is apposite to refer that Art. 14, Constitution stands as a bar to executive Government acting arbitrarily. The following extracts from the Supreme Court case[5] is material.

Today the Government in a welfare state is the regulator and dispenser of special services and provider of a large number of benefits, including jobs contracts, licences, quotas, mineral rights etc. The Government pours forth wealth, money, benefits, services, contracts, quotas and licences. The valuables dispensed by Government take many forms but they all share one characteristic. They are steadily taking the place of traditional forms of wealth. These valuables which derive from relationships to Government are of many kinds. They comprise social security benefits, cash grants for political suffers and the whole scheme of State and local welfare. Then again, thousands of people are employed in the State and the Central Government and local authorities.

Article 14 of the Constitution strikes at arbitrariness in State action and ensures fairness and equality of treatment. It requires that State action must not be arbitrary but must be based on some rational and relevant principle which is non-discriminatory; it must not be guided by any extraneous or irrelevant consideration, because that would be denial of equality. The principle of reasonables and rationality which is legally as well as philosophically an essential element of equality or non-arbitrariness is projected by Art. 14 and it must characterise every State of action, whether it be under authority of law or in exercise of executive power without making of law. The State cannot, therefore act arbitrarily in entering into relationship, contractual or otherwise with a third party, but its action must conform to some standard or norm which is rational and non-discriminatory.[6]

(III) CONTRACT OF SERVICE WITH NEGATIVE STIPULATION Under the common law in England a man is entitled to exercise any lawful trade or calling as and where he wills. The law has always regarded zealously any interference with trade, even at the risk of interference with freedom of contract, as it is public policy to oppose all restraints upon liberty of individual action which are injurious to the interests of the State. A person may be restrained from carrying on his trade by reason of an agreement voluntarily entered into by him with that object and in such a case the general principle of freedom of trade must be applied with due regard to the principles that public policy requires for persons

5 *Kayastha Pathsala* v *Rajendra Prasad* AIR 1990 SC 415; 1989 All LJ 1401; 1989 Supp (2) SCC 732.

6 *Ramana Dayaram Shetty* v *International Airport Authority of India* AIR 1979 SC 1628; (1979)3 SCR 1014; (1979)3 SCC 489.

of full age and understanding the utmost freedom to contract. Traditionally the doctrine of restraint of trade applied to covenants whereby an employee undertakes not to compete with his employer after leaving the employer's service and covenants by which a trader who has sold his business agrees not thereafter to compete with the purchaser of the business.[7]

A contract of service may often contain negative stipulations, the enforcement of which will result in specific performance. In such cases also the court is reluctant to grant any relief.[8] Even though it is well settled that restrictions that are to operate only while the employee is contractually bound to serve his employer are never regarded as in restraint of trade at law.[9] However, the court takes a far stricter and less favourable view of covenants entered into between employer and employee than it does of similar covenants between vendor and purchaser or in partnership agreements, and accordingly a restraint may be unreasonable as between employer and employee which would be reasonable as between the vendor and purchaser of a business.[10]

As regards granting of injunction in such cases, it was held that an injunction to enforce an obligation, so far obligations, other than contractual ones, are concerned, is mostly perennial in nature. As an illustration, a neighbour is under a legal obligation to respect his neighbour's possession of land or house. This obligation never ceases in the similar capacity. The obligation is, thus, perennial in nature. Therefore, while granting injunction under s. 42 of the Specific Relief Act, it will have to be borne in mind that the injunction, to be granted to enforce a negative covenant, cannot be such as would be perennial in nature, the reasons being, broadly speaking, two. One reason is that a contractual obligation, which is the obligation contemplated in s. 42, ceases, once the obligation is discharged. Hence, injunction has to be granted only till the discharge of the obligation. The other reason is that if such an injunction is granted, which operates in perpetuity, it will amount to specific performance of the contract, which a court would not, and cannot, under the limitations cast on it under s. 41(*e*) of the Act, do. Consequently, enforcement of a negative stipulation, if amounts to specific performance of the positive stipulation, would not be granted.[11]

7 *Gujarat Bottling Co. Ltd.* v *Coca Cola Co.* AIR 1995 SC 2372; (1995)5 SCC 545.

8 *Lalbhai Dalpatbhai & Co.* v *Chittaranjan Chandulal Pandya* AIR 1966 Guj 189.

9 *Gaumont British Picture Corpn. Ltd.* v *Alexander* [1936]2 All ER 1686; *Warner Bros. Pictures* v *Nelson* [1936]3 All ER 160; *Marco Productions Ltd.* v *Pagola* [1945]1 All ER 155; *Charlesworth* v *MacDonald* ILR (1898)23 Bom 103; *V.S. Deshpande* v *Arvind Mills Ltd.* AIR 1946 Bom 423.

10 Halsbury's *Laws of England*, 4th Ed., vol. 47, paras 9 to 26; *Niranjan Shankar Golikari* v *Century Spg. and Mfg. Co. Ltd.* (1967)2 SCR 378; AIR 1967 SC 1098.

11 *Sati Oil Udyog Ltd.* v *Avanti Projects and Infrastructure Ltd.* (2010)2 Gau LR 512.

But this has also been held that a case for declaration of a statutory invalidity of an act of dismissal of an employee is wholly different from the enforcement of a contract of personal service.[12]

In *People's Union for Democratic Rights* v *Union of India*[13] Bhagwati, J said:

> "It is therefore clear that even if a person has contracted with another to perform service and there is consideration for such service in the shape of liquidation of debt or even remuneration, he cannot be forced, by compulsion of law or otherwise, to continue to perform such service, as that would be forced labour within the inhibition of Article 23. This article strikes at every form of forced labour even if it has its origin in a contract voluntarily entered into by the person obligated to provide labour or service.[14] The reason is that it offends against human dignity to compel a person to provide labour or service to another if he does not wish to do so, even though it be in breach of the contract entered into by him. There should be no serfdom or involuntary servitude in a free democratic India which respects the dignity of the individual and the worth of the human person. Moreover in a country like India where there is so much poverty and unemployment and there is no equality of bargaining power, a contract of service may appear on its face voluntary but it may, in reality, be involuntary, because while entering into the contract, the employee, by reason of his economically helpless condition, may have been faced with Hobson's choice, either to strave or to submit to the exploitative terms dictated by the powerful employer. It would be travesty of justice to hold the employee in such a case to the terms of the contract and to compel him to serve the employer even though he may not wish to do so. That would aggravate the inequality and injustice from which the employee even otherwise suffers on account of his economically disadvantaged position and lend the authority of law to the exploitation of the poor helpless employee by the economically powerful employer. Article 23 therefore says that no one shall be forced to provide labour or service against his will, even though it be under a contract of sevice."

The learned judge was giving this ruling in the case of contract labour who had to part with a sum out of their wages to *jamadars* (supervisors) (though they also belonged to the labour class) thereby reducing their wages below the minima fixed under the Minimum Wages Act 1948.

It was also observed, "Of course, if there is a breach of the contract of service, the employee would be liable to pay damages to the employer, but

12 *Calcutta Electric Supply Corpn. Ltd.* v *Ramratan Mahato* AIR 1973 Cal 258.
13 AIR 1982 SC 1473; (1983)1 SCR 456; (1982)3 SCC 235.
14 *Pollock* v *Williams* [1943]322 US 4; 88 L Ed 1095.

he cannot be forced to continue to serve the employer without breaching the injunction of Article 23."[15]

(IV) CONTRACT FOR SERVICE Such contracts are also not specifically enforceable, examples are: contract for agency,[16] contract to compose and write reports of court cases,[17] contract to furnish drawings to enable plaintiffs to engrave and publish a series of maps from those drawings,[18] contract to revise book for republication,[19] contract to appoint plaintiff as a broker,[20] contract for forming a joint stock company for the purpose of working plaintiff's patent and plaintiff to devote his whole time to the interests of the company and the improvement of the patent.[1] However, there is well-recognized difference between '*contract for services*' and '*contract of service*'. A "contract for services" implies a contract whereby one party undertakes to render services e.g. professional or technical services, to or for another in the performance of which he is not subject to detailed direction and control but exercises professional or technical skill and uses his own knowledge and discretion. A "contract of service" implies relationship of master and servant and involves an obligation to obey orders in the work to be performed and as to its mode and manner of performance.[2]

In *Rigby* v *Connol*,[3] it has been held that agreements which are strictly personal in their nature will not be specifically enforced, whether they be for the purpose of pleasure, as for scientific pursuits, or of charity.[4] It was pointed out by the Judicial Committee of the Privy Council[5] that when there has been purported termination of a contract of service, a declaration that the contract of service still subsisted would rarely be made and would not be made in the absence of special circumstances, because of the principle

15 It is not understood how this is going to help the poor worker, who is first made to sign a contract for a term, and if he later on finds a better job and has to leave the old job, he has to pay damages for breach of contract. If the judgment is taken to its logical conclusion, it will have to be held either that the contract of service is void or voidable at the will of the worker, or that the contract is binding on the employer only. It is submitted that the observations are *per incuriam* and every case will have to be decided on its own facts. *People's Union for Democratic Rights* v *Union of India* AIR 1982 SC 1473; see also *Baily* v *Alabama* 219 US 219; 55 L Ed 191.

16 *Chinnock* v *Sainsbury* [1860]30 LJ Ch 409; *Morris* v *Delobbel-Flipo* [1892]2 Ch 352.

17 *Clarke* v *Price* 37 ER 270.

18 *Boldwin* v *Society for Diffusion of Useful Knowledge* 9 Simons, R. 393; 59 ER 409.

19 *Stevens* v *Benning* 24 LJ Ch 153.

20 *Brett* v *East India & London Shipping Co. Ltd.* 71 ER 520.

1 *Stocker* v *Wedderburn* 69 ER 1162; *Douglas* v *Baynes* [1908] AC 477, cf. however *London Corpn.* v *Southgate* 38 LJ Ch 141.

2 Halsbury's *Laws of England*, 4th Ed., vol. 16, para 501; *Dharangadhara Chemical Works Ltd.* v *State of Saurashtra* 1957 SCR 152; AIR 1957 SC 264; Stroud's *Judicial Dictionary*, 5th Ed., p. 540; *Simmons* v *Heath Laundry Co.* [1910]1 KB 543.

3 [1880]4 Ch D 482.

4 *Millican* v *Sulivan* [1888]4 TLR 203.

5 *A. Francis* v *Municipal Councillors of Kuala Lumpur* [1962]3 All ER 633.

that the courts do not grant specific performance of contracts of service. It must be iterated that similar view was also expressed by the Supreme Court.[6] However, contract of personal service may be enforced by some tribunal or quasi-judicial bodies like the Labour Court or Industrial Tribunal. A contract for personal service includes all matters relating to the service of the employee, e.g. confirmation, suspension, transfer, termination, etc.[7]

(c) *Contract of such a nature that it cannot be specifically enforced* The following examples illustrate the rule:

(*a*) where *A* lets land to *B* and *B* contracts to cultivate it in a particular manner for, say, three years next after the date of the lease;

(*b*) where *A* and *B* contract that, in consideration of annual advance to be made by *A, B*, will, say, for three years next after the date of the contract grow particular crops on the land in his possession and deliver them to *A* when cut and ready for delivery;

(*c*) where *A* contracts with *B* that, in consideration of ₹1,000 to be paid to him by *B*, he will paint a picture for *B*;

(*d*) where *A* contracts with *B* to execute certain works which the court cannot superintend;

(*e*) where a contract to supply *B* with all the goods of certain class which *B* may require;

(*f*) where *A* contracts with *B* to take from *B* a lease of a certain house for a specified term at a specified rent.

"If the drawing-room is handsomely decorated" even if it is held to have so much certainty that compensation can be recovered for its breach;

(*g*) where *A* contracts to marry *B*; and

(*h*) where by a charterparty entered into in Calcutta between *A*, the owner of the ship, *B*, the charterer, it is agreed that the ship shall proceed to Rangoon and there load a cargo of rice, and thence proceed to London, freight to be paid, one-third on arrival at Rangoon, and two-thirds on delivery of the cargo in London.

Contracts not specifically enforceable (English law) There are certain contracts which are not enforceable whether or not damages are an inadequate remedy.[8] These types of contracts are dealt with below:

(1) *Contracts involving personal service* It has long been settled that a contract of personal service or employment will not as a general rule be specifically

6 *Bool Chand (Dr.)* v *Chancellor, Kurukshetra University* (1968)1 SCR 434; AIR 1968 SC 292.

7 *Apollo Tyres Ltd.* v *C.P. Sebastian* (2009)14 SCC 360.

8 Chitty on *Contracts,* 32nd Ed., vol. 1, para 27-023.

enforced at the suit of either party.[9] In the case of contract of employment this principle is now embodied in legislation which provides that an employee shall not be compelled to perform a contract of employment.[10]

(2) ***Adequacy of damages*** Specific performance will not be granted where damages would provide adequate relief.[11] The reason why damages are considered inadequate is because no substitute for the failed performance can be brought. Damages may be inadequate where the contract provided for a series of regular payments but damages could only be sought as each payment fell due or where the loss is suffered by a person who is not a party to the contract.

(3) ***Constant supervision*** The court will not enforce specific performance of a contract under which one party is bound to continuous duties, the due performance of which might require constant supervision by the court. In *Ryan* v *Mutual Tontine Westminster Chambers' Association*,[12] the lease of a service flat gave the tenant the right to the services of a porter who was to be "constantly in attendance". Specific enforcement of this right was refused on the ground that it would have required that constant superintendence by the court. But in *Posner* v *Scott-Lewis*[13] a covenant to employ a resident porter was specifically enforced.

(4) ***Conduct and hardship*** Since specific performance is a discretionary remedy, the court relies on the maxim that "He who comes to equity must come with clean hands." Thus, the court can take into account the fact that the claimant's conduct has been tricky or unfair or that the claimant has tried to take advantage of a mistake on the part of the defendant.[14] The court takes into account of the conduct of the defendant. The court can refuse specific performance if it finds that to grant this relief would cause great hardship to the defendant.[15]

(5) ***Inadequacy or lack of consideration*** It is a settled law that mere inadequacy of consideration is not a ground for refusing to grant the remedy of specific performance.[16] But inadequacy of consideration may be a ground for refusing specific performance if it is "such as shocks the conscience and amounts in itself to conclusive and decisive evidence of fraud."[17] In case of lack of consideration equity will not aid a volunteer. Specific performance is not

9 *Wilson* v *St. Helen's BC* [1999]2 AC 52.
10 Trade Union and Labour Relations (Consolidation) Act 1992, s. 236.
11 *Harnett* v *Yielding* [1805]2 Sch & Lef 549; *South African Territories Ltd.* v *Wallington* [1898] AC 309.
12 [1893]1 Ch 116.
13 [1987] Ch 25; [1987]3 All ER 513.
14 Anson's *Law of Contract*, 30th Ed., p. 614.
15 *Malins* v *Freeman* [1837]2 Keen 25.
16 *Collier* v *Brown* [1788]1 Cox CC 428.
17 *Coles* v *Trecothick* [1804]9 Ves 234.

ordered of a gratuitous promise even though it is binding at law because it is made by deed or supported by a nominal consideration and an action at law for the agreed sum or the damages can be brought upon it.[18]

(6) *Contract expressed to be terminable* Where it is specifically provided in the contract that it is revocable by a party against whom an order of specific performance is sought, the order will be refused, because the defendant can render it nugatory by exercising the power to terminate.[19] On this ground a contract to enter into a partnership at will is not specifically enforceable.[20] Similarly, a contract for a lease which by virtue of a contract itself is determinable by the defendant as soon as the lease is executed. But a tenancy from year to year determinable by either party by half a year's notice to quit is specifically enforceable.[21]

(7) *Impossibility* Specific performance is not ordered against a person who has agreed to sell land which he does not own. Impossibility of enforcing an order of specific performance on the ground that the defendant is not and has no assets within the jurisdiction may also be the reason for refusing to make such an order.[1]

(8) *Vagueness* An agreement may be so vague that it cannot be enforced even by an action for damages. The specific performance has been refused of a contract to publish an article because the parties have disagreed as to the exact text.[2]

(9) *Mistake, misrepresentation and delay* Specific performance may be refused on the ground of mistake, misrepresentation and delay even where these factors do not justify rescission or bar a common law remedy, such as damages or the action for the agreed sum.[3]

Contracts not specifically enforceable (American law) Generally, where the damages are recoverable at law which will constitute adequate compensation for the breach of a contract, equity will not decree specific performance. In determining whether adequate damages may be recovered in an action at law so as to bar specific performance, the court will enquire as to whether the award of damages will put the injured party in a situation beneficial to him. The grant of specific performance of a contract is not a matter of absolute right in the parties demanding it. It is said to be a matter of grace and application for such relief is addressed to the sound discretion of the court. The right to specific performance depends on the mutuality of

18 Chitty on *Contracts*, 32nd Ed., vol. 1, paras 27-038, 27-039.
19 *R (Supportways Community Services Ltd.)* v *Hampshire* CC [2006] EWCA Civ 1035.
20 *Sheffield Gas Co.* v *Harrison* [1853]17 Beav 294.
21 Chitty on *Contracts*, 32nd Ed., vol. 1, para 27-045.
1 *Ibid*, para 27-035.
2 *Joseph* v *National Magazine Co.* [1959] Ch 14.
3 Chitty on *Contracts*, 30th Ed., vol. 1, para 27-043.

obligations and of remedy. A decree for specific performance of contract will not be granted if it would be or could be made, nugatory and useless or if it would be ineffectual or not beneficial to the plaintiff.[4]

Generally, equity will not decree the specific performance of contract which may be terminated or abandoned by either of the parties at any time. Similarly, where the performance of the contract is impossible and the decree of specific performance cannot be enforced, the court will deny the remedy. Where the defendant's performance depends on the consent or approval by a person who is not a party to the contract and who is likely to withhold his consent, specific performance of the contract will not be decreed. No specific performance will be granted where title to the property by the defendant is wanting or defective. Specific performance is generally refused where enforcement of the contract would be difficult. No specific performance will be decreed where enforcement of the contract would be inequitable or inflict hardship. Subsequent events or change in circumstances furnish sufficient reasons to refuse specific performance. Specific performance may also be denied where enforcement of contract would be inequitable or unjust as to innocent third persons.[5]

Specific performance of master-servant contract If the master rightfully ends the contract, there can be no complaint. If the master wrongfully ends the contract, then the servant can pursue a claim for damages. The significant aspect, however, is that there should not be specific performance of a master-servant contract of service, and damages should be the appropriate remedy.[6]

Master and servant relationship—tests In law the time honoured expression 'master' and 'servant' indicates the relationship which exists when one person employs another to do certain work and exercises right to control over the performance of work to the extent of prescribing manner under which it is to be executed. The identifying mark of an employee is that he should be under the control or supervision of the employer in respect of the details of working. When the factors essential for establishing right to control the employee's manner and method of working are absent, there is no relationship of 'employer' and 'employee' between them.[7] Covenants in contracts of employment limiting the freedom of the employee to trade etc., after the termination of his employment are viewed by the courts with great jealousy. The employer who seeks to enforce such agreement, must show that it is reasonable in the interest of the parties. That is, it must afford adequate protection and no more than adequate protection to the covenantee

4 *Corpus Juris Secundum*, vol. 81, p. 731.
5 *Corpus Juris Secundum*, vol. 81, p. 742.
6 *Kailash Singh* v *Mayo College* (2018)18 SCC 216.
7 *Triloki Nath Pandey* v *State of U.P.* AIR 1990 All 143 at p. 144.

irrespective of the sufficiency or otherwise of the consideration. In order that restraint may not be hit by s. 27 of the Indian Contract Act, it must not be unreasonable either in the interest of the parties or in the interest of the public which require that a man should not be prevented from supporting himself and that public should not be deprived of the services as a useful member of the society.[8]

Where contract in its nature determinable Such contracts are those which can be determined by the defendant at will, for example, a tenancy at will or a partnership at will. But simply because the contractual right is of a short duration and is revocable is no ground for refusing specific performance,[9] where the Council had granted a licence for its hall for two days only and wanted to revoke it for fear of the breach of the peace. The court restrained the Council from revoking the licence. This was, of course, a case of injunction, but the result was the specific performance. *A fortiori*, a tenancy for a year or from year to year determined by either party by six months' notice to quit would be specifically enforceable.[10]

When termination of a mining lease prematurely relying on a clause of the deed of lease, without giving to the lessee any opportunity to be heard has been held illegal, there is no scope for the argument that the lessee cannot continue *qua* lessee because the contract in its nature is terminable and s. 14(1)(*c*), Specific Relief Act applies [now s. 14(*d*)]. For it is a breach of statutory duty, it is not a case where because of its nature the lease is terminable.[11]

Under s. 14(1)(*c*), Specific Relief Act [now s. 14(*d*)], a contract which is in its nature determinable cannot be specifically enforced.[12] In a case the plaintiff was appointed as exclusive stockist of the defendant for sale of watches for a period of six months only and in view of the agreement the defendant reserved the right to terminate the contract within the period of six months with or without notice at any time and without assigning any reason. There was no negative covenant in the agreement in the sense that no condition had been imposed on the petitioner that it will not be authorized stockist or dealer for any other watch company. The respondent started sale of its watches through other dealers in the area and the plaintiff brought a suit for injunction against the defendant. It was held that temporary injunction could not be granted.[13]

8 *Herbet Morris Ltd.* v *Saxelby* [1916]1 AC 688.
9 *Verrall* v *Great Yarmouth Borough Council* [1980]1 All ER 839.
10 *Gray* v *Spyer* [1922]2 Ch 22; *Lever* v *Koffler* [1901]1 Ch 543.
11 *Dharam Veer* v *Union of India* AIR 1989 Del 227.
12 *Indian Oil Corporation Ltd.* v *Amritsar Gas Service* (1991)1 SCC 533; 1990 Supp (3) SCR 196; JT 1990(4) SC 601.
13 *S.K. Gupta* v *Hyderabad Allwyn Ltd* AIR 1988 Del 324; (1987)2 Arb LR 265.

Where a contract allows the defendant to terminate the contract without notice and without assigning any reason, the contract is not specifically enforceable.[14] Where a distributorship contract could be terminated by the Indian Oil Corporation in accordance with the terms of the agreement and the arbitrator had found that the termination was not valid and ordered the breach of contract to be remedied by restoration of distributorship, it was held that the relief of restoration of distributorship, even in the event that the breach was committed by the Corporation, was held contrary to the mandate under s. 14(1)(*c*) of the Specific Relief Act [now s. 14(*d*)], the contract being by nature of determinable.[15] Nor can an injunction be granted in such cases to restrain the determination of the contract.[16] Granting of injunction in such cases would not be permissible in view of s. 14(1)(*c*) [now s. 14(*d*)] read with s. 41 of the Specific Relief Act.[17] If a party is not entitled to any relief under s. 14(1)(*c*) [now s. 14(*d*)] and 41 of the Specific Relief Act, he cannot also be entitled to any relief under s. 9 of the Arbitration and Conciliation Act.[18] The word 'determinable' as used in s. 14(1)(*c*) of the Act [now s. 14(*d*)] means that which can be put an end to.[19]

Contract of partnership Although, as a rule, an agreement to enter into a partnership is not specifically enforceable for the reason that it will be forcing unwilling persons to work together,[20] where the suit is for the execution of a formal deed of partnership, the parties having commenced to carry on the business of the partnership, or in respect of an agreement to purchase the share of a partner of the firm, it will be decreed [s. 14(3) of the Specific Relief Act, is omitted by the Amendment Act of 2018]. A contract for a fixed term may also be specifically enforced if there has been part performance.[21] It may be that where an agreement of partnership has not at all been acted upon, the court may in a proper case refuse to decree specific performance thereof because it may not be considered just or equitable to force partnership on an unwilling partner. However, the position is different where a partnership agreement has been acted upon for several

14 *Dharam Veer* v *Union of India* AIR 1989 Del 227; *Airport Authority of India* v *Dilbagh Singh* AIR 1997 Del 340; *Rajasthan Breweries Ltd.* v *Stroh Brewery Co.* AIR 2000 Del 450.

15 *Indian Oil Corporation Ltd.* v *Amitsar Gas Service* (1991)1 SCC 533; 1990 Supp (3) SCR 196.

16 *Ramachandra Thanwar* v *Ram Rakhmal Amichand* AIR 1971 Raj 292; see also *Orissa Manganese & Minerals Pvt. Ltd.* v *Adhunik Steel Limited* AIR 2006 Ori 113.

17 *Oil and Natural Gas Corporation Ltd.* v *Streamline Shipping Co. Pvt. Ltd.* AIR 2002 Bom 420.

18 *Divyanshi Saxena* v *Shri Ram School* ILR (2006)1 Del 447.

19 *Jaipir Metals and Electricals Ltd* v *Jain Industries* ILR (1994)2 P&H 253.

20 *Hercy* v *Birch* 32 ER 640; *New Brunswick & Canada Ry and Land Co. Ltd* v *Muggeridge* 62 ER 263 and *Scott* v *Rayment* [1868] LR 7 Eq 112.

21 *England* v *Curling* [1844]8 Beav 129; see also *Suresh Kumar Sanghi* v *Amit Kumar Sanghi* AIR 1982 Del 131.

years and the partnership is still subsisting. Certainly after the commencement and during the continuation of a partnership, it will be equitable for the court in many a case to interpose to decree specific performance of articles/terms of the partnership. The necessity for such an action arises when the conduct of a partner virtually imperils the success of partnership enterprise—*per* J.D. Jain, J.

In *Homfray* v *Fothergill*[1] articles of partnership provided, if any partner wanted to sell his share he had to offer it to the co-partners collectively and if they declined, then to some of them desirous of purchasing collectively, but if they also declined, then to the individual partners, and if they too declined, then to any buyer of his choice. One of the four partners offered his share to the remaining three. He, however, knew that one of them would not purchase. The remaining two, however, declared their willingness to buy. On his refusal to complete, *held* the offer to the three enured for the benefit of the two and specific performance would be decreed.

In *Byrne* v *Reid*[2] a partner was entitled to nominate and introduce into the firm his son or any other male person. He did so, but the other partners refused to accept him. On action, held that the nomination was valid, but since the son could not sue for specific performance, he would be entitled to the equitable relief of being a partner in equity.

In *Lingen* v *Simpson,*[3] the court decreed that as per articles of partnership upon the dissolution of the partnership, a particular book used in the trade should become the exclusive property of one of the partners and that a copy of it should be delivered to the other.

Power of attorney A power of attorney is not an instrument of transfer in regard to any right, title or interest in an immovable property. The power of attorney is creation of agency whereby the grantor authorizes the grantee to do the acts specified therein, on behalf of the grantor, which when executed will be binding on the grantor as if done by him.[4] A promise contained in a power of attorney that it will not be revoked except on certain grounds, is not specifically enforceable.[5] To the general law that an agency evidenced by a power of attorney is revocable at the pleasure of the principal, s. 201 of the Indian Contract Act carves an exception in laying down that it is irrevocable only when it is coupled with interest. What is meant by authority coupled with interest being irrevocable is that when an agreement is entered into for sufficient consideration, whereby an authority

1 [1866] LR 1 Eq 567.
2 [1902]2 Ch 735.
3 57 ER 236.
4 *Suraj Lamp & Industries (P) (Ltd.) (2)* v *State of Haryana* (2012)1 SCC 656. See ss. 1A and 2, Powers of Attorney Act 1882.
5 *Govindoss Krishnadoss* v *Gopeshwar Lalji Maharaj* AIR 1930 Mad 231.

is given for the parties to secure some benefit to the donee of the authority, such an authority is irrevocable.

In civil dispute the conduct of the parties is material. Therefore, where a party to the suit does not appear in the witness box and states his own case on oath and does not offer himself to be cross-examined by the other side, a presumption would arise that the case set up by him is not correct.[6] Further, a power of attorney holder cannot depose on behalf of the principal except the facts relating to the acts he has done. Order 3, rr. 1 and 2 of the CPC is relevant for the purpose. In other words, if the power of attorney holder has rendered some "acts" in pursuance of power of attorney, he may depose for the principal in respect of such acts, but he cannot depose for the principal for the acts done by the principal and not by him. Similarly, he cannot depose for the principal in respect of the matter of which only the principal can have a personal knowledge and in respect of which the principal is entitled to be cross-examined.[7]

Power of attorney holder to depose in a suit for specific performance The propositions of law as to who should give evidence in regard to matter involving personal knowledge such as readiness and willingness of a party in specific performance of a contract:

(*a*) An attorney holder who has signed the plaint and instituted the suit, but has no personal knowledge of the transaction can only give formal evidence about the validity of the power of attorney and the filing of the suit.

(*b*) If the attorney holder has done any act or handled any transactions, in pursuance of the power of attorney granted by the principal, he may be examined as a witness to prove those acts or transactions. If the attorney holder alone has personal knowledge of such acts and transactions and not the principal, the attorney holder shall be examined, if those acts and transactions have to be proved.

(*c*) The attorney holder cannot depose or give evidence in place of his principal for the acts done by the principal or transactions or dealings of the principal, of which the principal alone has personal knowledge.

(*d*) Where the principal at no point of time had personally handled or dealt with or participated in the transactions and has no personal knowledge of the transaction, and where the entire transaction has been handled by an attorney holder, necessarily the attorney holder alone can give evidence in regard to the transaction. This happens very often in case of principals carrying on business through attorney

6 *Vidhyadhar* v *Manikrao* AIR 1999 SC 1441; (1999)3 SCC 573.

7 *Janki Vashdeo Bhojwani* v *Indusind Bank Ltd.* (2005)2 SCC 217.

holders or persons residing abroad managing their affairs though their attorney holders.

(*e*) Where the entire transaction has been conducted through a particular attorney holder, the principal has to examine that attorney holder to prove the transaction, and not a different subsequent attorney holder.

(*f*) Where different attorney holders had dealt with the matter at different stages of the transaction, if evidence has to be led as to what transpired at those stages, all the attorney holders will have to be examined.

(*g*) Where the law requires or contemplates the plaintiff or other party to a proceeding, to establish or prove something with reference to his "state of mind" or "conduct", normally the person concerned alone has to give evidence and not an attorney holder. A landlord who seeks eviction of tenant on the ground of his "*bona fide*" need and a purchaser seeking specific performance who has to show his "readiness and willingness".[8]

Again, in terms of Or. 3, rr. 1 and 2 of the CPC, the power of attorney holder can depose as a witness to that extent which he knows about the case and not for the acts personally done by the principal of which he alone can have personal knowledge.[9]

In a suit for specific performance, a power of attorney holder, who has acted in pursuance of the said power, may depose on behalf of the principal in respect of such acts but cannot depose for the principal for the acts done by the principal and not by the power of attorney holder. Likewise, the power of attorney holder cannot depose for the principal in respect of matters of which the principal alone can have personal knowledge and in respect of which the principal is entitled to be cross-examined.[10]

Where specific performance involves continuous duty Illustrative of such type of contracts are the ones relating to supply of engine-power and keeping the whole railway in good repair to enable the other party to run its carriages on the line,[11] supply of coal from a particular mine,[12] contracts to provide a house-keeper,[13] to work in a mine in a particular manner for the benefit of the lessor,[14] to maintain wire and telephonic apparatus,[15] to publish an

8 *Mankaur* v *Hartar Singh Sangha* (2010)10 SCC 512.
9 *Punjabrao* v *Himmatrao* (2014)5 AIR Bom R 194; (2015)1 ICC 139.
10 *Mohinder Kaur* v *Sant Paul Singh* (2019)9 SCC 358.
11 *Blackett* v *Bates* [1865] LRI Ch App 117.
12 *Pollard* v *Clayton* [1855]1 K&J 462.
13 *Barnes* v *City of London Real Property Co.* [1918]2 Ch 18.
14 *Wheatly* v *Westminister Brymbo Coal Co.* [1869] LR 9 Eq 538.
15 *Keith Prowse & Co.* v *National Telephone Co.* [1894]2 Ch 147; cf. however *Cochrane* v *Exchange Telegraph Co.* [1896]65 LJ Ch 334.

article without agreement as to the terms of the article,[16] agreement by an electric railway company to run its cars on certain streets at certain hours etc.,[17] to preserve secret of invention.[18] In this case, Lord Eldon observed, the difficulty in such a case is, how to decree the specific performance. Either it is a secret, or it is none. If a secret, what means does the court have to enforce its order.[19]

Section 14(1)(*d*) [now s. 14(*b*)] of the Specific Relief Act 1963 provides that performance should not be ordered when it involves performance of a continuous duty which the court cannot supervise. This restriction should be kept in view by courts while issuing high prerogative writ.[20]

As pointed out in Halsbury's *Laws of England*, 4th Ed., Re-issue, vol. 44(1), para 806:

> "The court does not enforce the performance of contract which involves continuous act and requires the watching and supervision of the court and that, in particular, the court does not normally order specific performance of the contract to build or repair."

The courts are now more ready to enforce contracts requiring supervision. The question is whether the contract sufficiently defines the work to be done, expressly or by implication, to permit the court to make an order which enables the defendant to know what he has to do to comply with it. But in *Co-operative Insurance Society Ltd.* v *Argyll Stores Holdings Ltd.*,[1] a lease having 19 years to run contained a negative covenant that the lessee shall not use the premises other than as a retail store and a positive covenant to keep the premises open for retail trade during the usual hours of business. The Court of Appeal granted specific performance compelling the defendant to carry on business during the remainder of the term of the lease or until an earlier sub-let or assignment, if possible. The House of Lords, on appeal, reversed the judgment and reiterated the "settled practice" that orders cannot be made requiring a party to run a business. After referring to various decisions, the Law Lords concluded:

> "The cumulative effect of these various decisions, none of which will necessarily be sufficient on its own, seems to me to show that the settled practice is based upon sound sense."

The implementation of the agreement to construct buildings for the weaker sections of the community as per the scheme to be prepared and sanctioned under s. 21 of the Urban Land (Ceiling and Regulation) Act

16 *Joseph* v *National Magazine Co. Ltd.* [1958]3 All ER 52.
17 *City of Kingston* v *Singston Portsmouth & Catarqui Electric Ry. Co.* 25 AR 462 (Can).
18 *Newbery* v *James* 35 ER 1011.
19 Cf. *Amber, Size & Chemical Co.* v *Mansel* [1913]2 Ch 239.
20 *Parag Engineering* v *Union of India* AIR 1989 Gau 77.
1 [1998]1 AC 1.

1976 would require continuous supervision of the court and specific performance cannot be granted.[2]

So far as interim injunction in such cases is concerned, it should not be granted by the court or the arbitrator.[3]

Arbitration agreements Arbitration agreements are specifically enforceable only in the manner laid down in the Arbitration and Conciliation Act 1996 but if an agreement is made which is not covered by the Arbitration and Conciliation Act 1996 and the plaintiff refuses to perform his part, the existence of such an agreement shall bar him from instituting any suit in respect of any subject which is referable under the agreement [s. 14(2) of the Specific Relief Act, though omitted by the Amendment Act of 2018].

As far as s. 14(2) (omitted by the Amendment Act of 2018) of the Specific Relief Act 1963 is concerned, no doubt it states that "Save as provided by the Arbitration Act, 1940, no contract to refer present or future differences to arbitration shall be specifically enforced; but if any person who has made such a contract (other than an arbitration agreement to which provisions of the said Act apply) and has refused to perform it, sues in respect of any subject which he has contracted to refer, the existence of such contract shall bar the suit." Opening words of sub-sec. (2) of s. 14 of the Specific Relief Act are very material which clearly say that "Save as provided by the Arbitration Act 1940."[4] Therefore, if a party to the arbitration clause files a suit whether such a suit is to be maintained or not depends upon conduct of the other side, and the provisions contained to the Arbitration Act. In such a situation, parties setting up an arbitration agreement are required to raise objections based upon the arbitration agreement before they take steps in the suit. Section 34 of the Arbitration Act 1940 provides that, if a party raises objections based upon the arbitration agreement before taking any steps, in such an event, a suit relating to the subject matter of which can form the arbitration proceedings shall have to be stayed by the court.[5] The expression "before taking any other steps" must not receive a narrow meaning. The step must be taken in the main proceeding of the suit and it should be such a step as would clearly and unambiguously manifest the intention to waive the benefit of the arbitration agreement and to acquiesce in the proceeding. Taking step in an interlocutory proceeding, e.g. taking time for reply to plaintiff's prayer for interim injunction is not taking step.[6]

2 *Her Highness Maharani Shantidevi Gaikwad* v *Savjibhai Haribhai Patel* AIR 2001 SC 1462; (2001)5 SCC 101.

3 *Spice Digital Ltd.* v *Vistaas Digital Media Pvt. Ltd.* (2012)114 (6) Bom LR 3696.

4 This Act is now replaced by the Arbitration and Conciliation Act 1996.

5 *Nayar Ahmed Sheriff* v *Zahoor Ahmed Sheriff* AIR 1990 Kant 348 at p. 351.

6 *Food Corporation of India* v *Yadab Engineers* AIR 1982 SC 1302; 1982 UJ (SC) 605; (1982)21 Del LT 396 (SC); *Indian Oil Corporation* v *Indian Carbon* AIR 1984 Bom 138; 1984 Mah LJ 297.

Further, unworkability is not a ground afforded by law makers to thwart obligations as "indefeasible" rights to arbitral proceedings. Nor can the court, through an interpretive mechanism create exceptions (from the obligation to relegate parties to arbitration) when no explicit ground exists. Doing so would not only distort the statute, but eventually undermine obligations accepted by parties to international agreements, with open eyes.[7]

But s. 14(2) (prior to Amendment of 2018) did not bar a suit where the contract provided that the decision of a named officer should be binding.[8] On facts, *held*, the clause was distinct from the arbitration clause; nor does it in any way come in the way of a suit challenging the award on the ground of fraud.[9] So also, where the other party is able to establish its apprehension that the named arbitrator or his nominee may not act fairly and justly, the court may release him from the bargain.[10]

If the arbitrators make an award directing specific performance of a contract for the transfer of movable property without holding that the goods come within the exception mentioned in s. 10 of the Specific Relief Act (prior to substitution by the Specific Relief (Amendment) Act 2018) it involved a legal proposition which in the face of *Expln. (ii)* to s. 10 was clearly erroneous and the error being apparent from the record, the award was liable to be set aside.[11]

The Arbitration Act 1940 has been repealed by and re-enacted as the Arbitration and Conciliation Act 1996 [Act 26 of 1996] and 'arbitration agreement' has been defined in s. 7(*i*) and power to refer parties to arbitration where there is an arbitration agreement is stated under s. 8 of the Arbitration and Conciliation Act 1996.

The reference to the Arbitration Act 1940 in sub-sec. (2) of s. 14 [since substituted by the Specific Relief (Amendment) Act 2018] of the Specific Relief Act 1963 has to be read as reference to the Arbitration and Conciliation Act 1996 by virtue of s. 8 of the General Clauses Act 1897. Hence, if any person has made a contract to refer present or future differences to arbitration other than arbitration agreement to which the provisions of the Arbitration and Conciliation Act 1996 apply and has refused to perform it, in a suit in respect of any subject which he has contracted to refer, the existence of such contract shall bar the suit.

7 *W.P.I.L.* v *NTPC Ltd.* (2009)108 DRJ 404; (2009)1 Arb LR 378.

8 *State of Bihar* v *Rama Bhushan Basu* AIR 1964 Pat 326 (DB).

9 *Vineet Kumar* v *Bhagwan Dei* AIR 1978 All 312.

10 *Fertiliser Corporation of India Ltd.* v *Domestic Engineering Installation* AIR 1970 All 31 at p. 42 (DB) relying on *U.P. Co-operative Federation Ltd.* v *Sunder Brothers* AIR 1967 SC 249; 1966 (Supp) SCR 215.

11 *Indian Iron & Steel Co. Ltd.* v *C.G. Engineering Private Ltd.* AIR 1983 Cal 6.

Arbitrator's power to award specific performance of contract An award does not operate as a conveyance, but an arbitrator may normally award specific performance of any contract other than a contract relating to land or an interest in land. Unless contrary intention is expressed in the agreement arbitrator or umpire has some power as the court to order specific performance of a contract other than a contract relating to land.[12]

Specific performance in building contract Where the suit is for enforcement of a contract for the construction of any building or the execution of any work, the courts are not obliged to grant specific performance of contract. The situation becomes flexible if the plaintiff has a substantial interest in the performance of the contract and the interest is of such a nature that compensation for money for non-performance of the contract is not an adequate relief.[13]

12 Halsbury's *Laws of England*, 4th Ed., vol. 2, para 611.
13 *Sabh Infrastructures Ltd.* v *Jay Shree Bagley* 2010(114) DRJ 493 (DB).

CHAPTER 2

By and Against Whom Contracts Enforceable

Statutory provision The question by or against whom a contract is specifically enforceable is dealt with by ss. 15 to 19 of the Specific Relief Act.

Plaintiff Even if the contract is specifically enforceable, it is not enough: the plaintiff must also be capable of obtaining the specific performance and should not suffer from any personal bar.

Section 15 enumerates the nine categories of persons who may obtain specific performance of the contract *qua* plaintiff, namely,

(*a*) any party thereto [s. 15(*a*)];

(*b*) the representative in interest or the principal, of any party thereto:

Provided that where the learning, skill, solvency or any personal quality of such party is a material ingredient in the contract, or where the contract provides that his interest shall not be assigned, his representative in interest or his principal shall not be entitled to specific performance of the contract, unless such party has already performed his part of the contract, or the performance thereof by his representative in interest, or his principal, has been accepted by the other party [s. 15(*b*)];

(*c*) where the contract is a settlement on marriage, or a compromise of doubtful rights between members of the same family, any person beneficially entitled thereunder [s. 15(*c*)];

(*d*) where the contract has been entered into by a tenant for life in due exercise of a power, the remainderman [s. 15(*d*)];

(*e*) a reversioner in possession, where the agreement is a covenant entered into with his predecessor in title and the reversioner is entitled to the benefit of such covenant [s. 15(*e*)];

(*f*) a reversioner in remainder, where the agreement is such a covenant and the reversioner is entitled to the benefit thereof and will sustain material injury by reason of its breach [s. 15(*f*)];

(*fa*) when a limited liability partnership has entered into a contract and subsequently becomes amalgamated with another limited liability partnership, the new limited liability partnership which arises out of the amalgamation [s. 15(*fa*)].[1]

(*g*) when a company has entered into a contract and subsequently becomes amalgamated with another company, the new company which arises out of the amalgamation [s. 15(*g*)];

(*h*) when the promoters of a company have, before its incorporation, entered into a contract for the purposes of the company, and such contract is warranted by the terms of the incorporation, the company:

Provided that the company has accepted the contract and has communicated such acceptance to the other party to the contract [s. 15(*h*)].

Principles summarised Following principles may be summarized in respect of ss. 15 to 19 of the Act. They are as under:[2]

(*i*) Under ss. 15(*b*) and 19(*b*) of the Specific Relief Act 1963, the representative in interest of a contracting party can maintain a suit for specific performance of a contract, where learning, skill, solvency or personal quality of such party is not material ingredient in the contract. In an agreement to sell personal quality of a party thereto is not a material ingredient. Such a contract therefore can be enforced at the instance of a representative in interest, including his heirs and legal representatives except a *bona fide* transferee who had paid money in good faith and without notice.

(*ii*) Normally a contract can be enforced by or against the parties and their legal heirs unless a contrary intention express or implied, appears from it.

(*iii*) Where the estate of a deceased devolves upon his legal representatives they would be liable for the liabilities incurred by him including the liability created under a contract to which the deceased was a party. But this will be to the extent of the estate coming in the hands of the legal representatives. In case of a contract other than whose performance depends upon the personal qualities of the deceased, the same would be binding on its heirs, assignees and successors-in-interest to the extent of his estate.

1 Section 15(*fa*) of the Specific Relief Act is inserted by the Specific Relief (Amendment) Act 2018.

2 *Sarala Devi v Daya Ram* ILR (1996)2 Del 860; (1995)60 DLT 3; (1995)35 DRJ 36; 1996 AIHC 3152.

"Parties to the agreement" Section 15(*a*) of the Specific Relief Act entitles any party to the contract to seek specific performance of such contract. Therefore, any third party or stranger to the agreement does not fall within the meaning of "*parties to the agreement*".[3] Thus, the stranger to the contract would not come either under s. 15 or s. 19 of the Act.[4]

Any party to the contract As is to be seen from the provisions of s. 15(*b*) of the Specific Relief Act 1963, specific performance of the contract may be obtained by "any party thereto" or "their representative-in-interest". This expression clearly includes the transferees and assignees from the contracting party in whose favour the right exists. Such right of seeking specific performance would, however, be not available in terms of the proviso below cl. (*b*) where "the contract provides that his interest shall not be assigned".[5]

Any party to the contract—suit by benamdar In terms of s. 15(*a*) of the Specific Relief Act 1963, the suit for specific performance of contract can be filed by "any party" to the contract.[6] Any party included a *benamdar* (ostensible owner) who had the property standing in his name,[7] but the real owner of such a property could not sue if the property did not stand in his name unless he had complied with the provisions of s. 281A of the Income Tax Act 1961. The position of law that stood earlier suffered a sea-change by s. 4 of the Prohibition of Benami Property Transactions Act 1988, s. 4(1) of the Act stands as follows:

> 4(1). No suit, claim or action to enforce any right in respect of any property held *benami* against the person in whose name the property is held or against any other person shall lie by or on behalf of a person claiming to be the real owner of such property.

In view of the words "no suit, claim" "shall lie" in s. 4(1) it has been consistently held that the bar is retrospective so much so that it affects also pending appeal.[8] It also affects execution of decree based on the plea of *benami*.[9] The bar to taking the plea of *benami* also extends to the plea that the transaction was sham and no effective title did pass despite the deed of transfer.[10]

3 *Bharat Karsondas Thakkar* v *Kiran Construction Co.* (2008)13 SCC 658.
4 *Anjana Vij* v *Krishan Dev* (2011)122 DRJ 620
5 *Shyam Singh* v *Daryao Singh* (2003)12 SCC 160; AIR 2004 SC 348
6 *DDA* v *Gaurav Kukreja* (2015)14 SCC 254
7 *Gur Narayan* v *Sheolal Singh* AIR 1918 PC 140.
8 *Mithilesh Kumari* v *Prem Behari Khare* AIR 1989 SC 1247; (1989)2 SCJ 98; (1989)2 Cur Civ Cas 33; *Velayudhan Rama Krishnan* v *Rajeev* AIR 1989 Ker 12.
9 *Urmila Bala Dasi* v *Probodh Chandra Ghosh* AIR 1989 Cal 283; (1989)1 Cal LJ 1; (1989)1 CHN 179; 93 CWN 306; *C. Narayanan* v *Gangadharan* AIR 1989 Ker 256.
10 *Mohonan* v *Yesoda* AIR 1989 Ker 286; (1989)2 Cur Civ Cas 645 (Ker); but see *Bethula Anasuya* v *Bethula Rayudu* AIR 1989 AP 290 holding that Benami Ordinance (Ordinance 2 of 1988) did not apply to nominal transactions.

There was an exception to the bar had been engrafted in s. 4(3), Benami Transactions (Prohibition) Act 1988 (since deleted) reads as follows:

> 4(3). Nothing in this section shall apply—
>
> (*a*) where the person in whose name the property is held is a coparcener in a Hindu undivided family and the property is held for the benefit of the coparceners in the family; or
>
> (*b*) where the person in whose name the property is held is a trustee or other person standing in a fiduciary capacity, and the property is held for the benefit of another person for whom he is a trustee or towards, whom he stands in such capacity.

In a case the defendants purchased the property in court auction and had entered into an agreement with the plaintiff at the time of the court sale that they would convey it to the plaintiff for debit of a sum different from the price paid at the court sale. In a suit for specific performance, s. 66, CPC (since deleted) was pleaded as a bar. It was held, that the plea, in such a situation, could not be sustained. It further held that a suit at the instance of a nominee of the promisee cannot be maintained.[11]

Vague contract The contract should not be vague since specific performance of a vague contract is not permissible.[12]

J&K Specific Relief Act 1920 Section 15 of the J&K Specific Relief Act makes it abundantly clear that where a party to a contract is unable to perform the whole of his part of it, the court may at the suit of the other party, direct the party in default to perform specifically so much of his part of the contract as he can perform.[13]

Death of the agreement holder When once the agreement holder dies, naturally, his rights would pass on to his legal representatives. Section 15 of the Specific Relief Act is specific that the rights of the agreement holder will automatically pass on to the successor in interest, in case of death of the agreement holder. Therefore, where after the death of the agreement holder, the suit for specific performance was filed by the father of the deceased, it was held that in the absence of any specific plea in the written statement with regard to the maintainability of the suit by the father as the legal representative of the deceased agreement holder, the relationship being undisputed, it is not open to raise the issue of want of privity of contract between the parties. The suit was held to be maintainable.[14]

11 *Gorakhram Sadhuram* v *Laxmibai* AIR 1953 SC 443.
12 *Thirumeni* v *Amirthalingam* (1998)1 ICC 341 (Mad).
13 *Manzoor Ahmed Magray* v *Ghulam Hassan Aram* (1999)7 SCC 703
14 *V. Udayakumar* v *Navaneethammal* (2002)1 CTC 334; (2002)2 LW 287; (2002)1 Mad LJ 519; (2002)2 ICC 561 (Mad).

Nominee of a party—specific performance at the behest of nominee Except in very special circumstances, a person agreeing to purchase a property is not bound to purchase it by himself and he may arrange for the purchase of the property by some other person as his nominee on the terms of the agreement entered into by him.[15]

Reiterating this view Calcutta High Court held that ordinarily the benefits and obligations under a contract are claimable by and enforceable against not only the parties to the contract but also by or against the representative-in-interest of such parties, unless there is anything contrary expressly made in the contract itself. The representative-in-interest may be (*a*) an assignee of contract from the original promisor, or (*b*) his legal representative after his death.[16] But in that case the plaintiff who was a nominee of the person who entered into a contract for the purchase of a property, sued for specific performance of the contract for sale. The plaintiff was a mere nominee for getting the deed of sale executed in his name. It was held that where under the agreement for sale, the plaintiff was a mere nominee without any obligation and not an assignee of any benefit or obligation under the said agreement, a suit at the instance of such a nominee for enforcement of the contract for sale is not maintainable.[17]

Co-contractees Specific performance of a contract can be enforced by any party to the contract. If there are more parties than one, specific performance of a contract cannot be decreed in the absence of some of the parties to the contract. If some of the parties entitled to the benefit of the contract are not willing to be arrayed as plaintiffs they should be impleaded as defendants. Section 23(*a*) of the Specific Relief Act 1877 (now s. 22) covers such a case.[18] In *Nirmala Bala Dasi* v *Sudarsan Jana*[19] it is held that one of the co-promisees may sue for specific performance making the other co-promisees as defendants. Judgment can be given in favour of the persons interested whether they are joined as plaintiffs or as defendants.[20] In a case where property was agreed to be transferred to three co-promisees and all the three filed a suit for specific performance of the contract but only one of them came to the witness box in support of the claim, it has been held that the other two co-promisees would also be entitled to a decree of specific performance. In the case of co-contractees it is not necessary that all of them should be ranged on the same side for obtaining specific performance. It is sufficient if all of them are before the court.[1]

15 *Umar Noor Mohammad* v *Dayal Saran Darbari* AIR 1967 All 253.
16 *B.B. Goswami* v *T.K. Chakravarty* 90 CWN 849.
17 *B.B. Goswami* v *T.K. Chakravarty* (supra).
18 *Mukesh Kumar* v *Col. Harbans Waraich* (1999)9 SCC 380; AIR 2000 SC 172.
19 AIR 1980 Cal 258; (1980)2 Cal LJ 11.
20 *Monghibai* v *Cooverji Umersey* AIR 1939 PC 170; 66 IA 210.
1 *Jagdeo Singh* v *Bisambhar* AIR 1937 Nag 186; ILR (1938) Nag 41

Representative in interest or principal The words 'representative in interest' are not used in the context of property rights, but only in the context of the specific performance of a contract, and, therefore, do not exclude a person who become entitled to the benefit of the contract. A contract is ordinarily assignable, unless the personal quality of a party is a material ingredient in the contract or where the contract shows an intention that the interest shall not be assigned. Where the benefit of a contract has been assigned, the assignee may, as a general rule, enforce specific performance, provided that the assignee can himself perform or procure the performance of the assignor's obligations under the contract. The words "representative in interest" include an assignee of an interest, who can also seek specific performance, unless the contract itself prohibits assignment, either expressly of by implication, when there is a prohibition to assign a contract, representative in interest of a deceased party to the contract cannot enforce the contract, unless there was performance by the deceased of his part of the contract or performance by the legal representative which has also been accepted by the other party.[2] It is now well established that in the absence of a contrary intention, express or implied, the contract will be enforceable by and against the parties and their legal heirs and legal representatives including assignees and transferees.[3]

Purchasers—priority inter se Where there is a competition between the parties, the party entering into a contract with notice of a prior contract will not be entitled to the specific performance.[4]

Where a vendor sold his property by an agreement on 30th May 1947, the sale-deed in respect of which was executed on 28th November 1947 and subsequently sold the same property to another purchaser on 12th September 1947 sale-deed in respect of which was executed on 24th August 1948 it was held that the first purchaser will have priority over the second purchaser.[5]

Likewise where an agreement was executed in favour of *A* on 1st of July and two months was given to him for the execution of the deed, and the other agreement in respect of the same property was executed in favour of *B* on 15th of July but one month was given to him for the execution of the deed, it was held that equity was in favour of *A*.[6] Prior vendee is not entitled when his agreement had become unenforceable.[7]

2 *Palaniammal* v *K.R.C. Anbalagan* (2013)3 CTC 477; (2013)1 LW 998; (2013)127 AIC (Sum 17) 11.

3 *Khardah & Co. Ltd.* v *Raymon & Co.* AIR 1962 SC 1810; (1963)3 SCR 183; *Ram Baran Prasad* v *Ram Mohit Hazra* AIR 1967 SC 744 at p. 745; *Golam Mohit Mondal* v *Abdul Jalil Sepal* AIR 1978 Cal 443; *T.M. Balakrishna Mudaliar* v *Sathyanarayana Rao* AIR 1993 SC 2449; (1993)2 SCR 888; (1993)2 SCC 740; *Habiba Khatoon* v *Ubaidul Huq* AIR 1997 SC 3236; (1997)7 SCC 452; JT 1997(7) SC 298.

4 *Gobinddas* v *Shantibai* AIR 1972 SC 1520; (1973)3 SCC 418.

5 *Bala Prasad Asaram* v *Asmabi* AIR 1954 Nag 328.

6 *Sampat Ram* v *Baboo Lal* AIR 1955 All 24.

7 *Raminder Singh* v *Sham Lal* AIR 1984 P&H 145.

Joint promisees It is not necessary that all the joint promisees should file the suit.

There is nothing in s. 15 which forbids one of the joint promisees to institute a suit for enforcing a contract and on the contrary the words "any party thereto" clearly envisage that one or some of the joint promisees can institute such a suit. If the intention of the legislature was that the joint promisees should have to be clubbed together as plaintiffs it could have used "either party thereto" instead of "any party thereto". It is, however, necessary that all the joint promisees must be before the court whether as plaintiffs or as defendants.[8]

Even so, there is nothing in law to prevent parties to a suit stating before the court that even though they are, in law, entitled to a decree being passed in their favour, still, in view of some arrangement or agreement between them, the decree should be passed in favour of one of them. Of course, the real point is that the contesting defendant should not be worse off on account of the adoption of such a course ...... When a third party assignee can enforce the agreement against the promisor why cannot there be an *inter se* arrangement amongst the legal representatives of the deceased promisee that the benefit of the agreement should be had by one of them with the consent and concurrence of the rest of the legal representatives.[9]

Hindu guardian—contract of sale or purchase on behalf of minor On the question whether natural guardian of a Hindu minor is competent to enforce the contract on behalf of minor there was a cleavage of opinion in Privy Council itself. The Privy Council in a case,[10] reversed the view of Calcutta High Court,[11] which held that there was no want of mutuality in the case and that the agreement is enforceable against the minors and that acts of the guardian in this country bind the minor though there is no difference between his position and powers and those of a manager. The Privy Council held that they were unable to accept the view of the Division Bench that there was no difference between the position and powers of the manager and those of a guardian. Holding that it is not within the competence of a manager of a minor's estate by a contract for the purchase of immovable property and that the minor was not bound by the contract for want of mutuality, the Privy Council held that a decree for specific performance cannot be granted.

A guardian of a minor is competent to enter into a contract on behalf of the minor so as to bind him if it is for the benefit of the minor. Though

8 *Nirmala Bala Dasi* v *Sudarsan Jana* AIR 1980 Cal 258.
9 *Sheomurat Ram* v *Savitri* AIR 1977 All 322 at p. 327.
10 *Kakulam Subrahmanyam* v *Kurra Subba Rao* AIR 1948 PC 95; 75 Ind App 115.
11 *Mir Sarwarjan* v *Fakhruddin Mahomed* ILR (1912)39 Cal 232.

the decision of *Mir Sarwarjan* v *Fakhruddin Mahomed Chowdhury* (supra) was brought to its notice, the Privy Council did not refer to it but referred to its earlier decision in *Hannumenpersad Pandey* v *Mussumat Babooee Munraj Koonwaree*,[12] where it was stated that "the act of the mother and guardian in entering into a contract of sale was an act done on behalf of the minor appellant."

Setting at rest the controversy and overruling *Sarwarjan's* case *(ibid)* the Supreme Court held that after passing of the Hindu Minority and Guardianship Act 1956, the guardian of a Hindu minor has power to do all acts which are necessary or reasonable and proper for the benefit of the minor or for realisation, protection or benefit of the minor's estate. This provision makes it clear that the guardian is entitled to act so as to bind the minor if it is necessary or reasonable and proper for the benefit of the minor. The power thus conferred by s. 8 of the Hindu Minority and Guardianship Act is in no way restricted than that was recognised under Hindu law. This applies even to a contract for purchase of immovable property. As it is within the competence of the guardian the contract is entered into effectively on behalf of the minor and the liability to pay the money is the liability of the minor under the Transfer of Property Act. It cannot be said that in a contract for purchase of property, the guardian would be binding the minor by this personal covenant. Thus the contract entered into by the guardian on behalf of the minor is enforceable.[13]

A contract entered into by a guardian of a Hindu minor for purchase or sale of immovable property is specifically enforceable by or against the minor. Under the Hindu law the natural guardian is empowered to enter into a contract on behalf of the minor and the contract would be binding and enforceable if the contract is for the benefit of the minor.[14]

The true test for the validity and enforceability of a contract by a minor's guardian is not the existence of mutuality but the competence of the guardian and legal necessity or benefit to the minor or his estate.[15]

In respect of the claim of minor through the guardian (here mother) for specific performance of contract of sale in favour of minor, in view of s. 20(4), Specific Relief Act 1963 there is no scope for contending that the doctrine of mutuality will defeat a contract of specific performance. For purchase of a property of the minor, no permission of court is necessary and there seems to be no restrictions in the power of guardian, except about transfers as provided in sub-sec. (2) of s. 8 of the Hindu Minority and Guardianship Act, if such acts of the guardian are necessary, reasonable

12 (1856)6 Moo Ind App 393.
13 *Manik Chand* v *Ramchandra* AIR 1981 SC 519; (1980)4 SCC 22.
14 *Roomal* v *Siri Niwas* AIR 1985 Del 153; (1985)27 DLT 188.
15 *Bhupal* v *Mam Chand* AIR 1973 All 543; 1973 All LJ 639.

or proper for his benefit unless such acts bind the minor personally or impose a personal liability on him.[16]

A mother on behalf of minor despite the father of the minor being alive can enter into a contract for purchase of land and such contract is enforceable.[17]

Where the agreement for sale was entered into by the vendor and the money was utilised for averting the sale of the property and the minor son was also benefited thereby the vendee was held entitled to insist that the deed of sale should be executed on behalf of the minor son also.[18]

Suit for specific performance against third party Section 19 catalogues the persons against whom specific performance of a contract may be enforced. It is clear from s. 19 that apart from subsequent transferee and apart from any person coming under the purview of cls. (*c*), (*ca*), (*d*) and (*e*) of s. 19 the contract cannot be enforced against a third party. In a Patna case defendants having accepted earnest money entered into a contract for sale of a building. Later they defaulted the promise. In the suit for specific performance they took the plea that subsequent to the agreement there was an amicable partition and the disputed property fell to the allotment of a third party namely *B*. It was held that *B* being stranger to the contract was not a necessary party. It was further held that the contract, if any, can be enforced only against a person who is a party to it and not against a person who is not a party to it; but the person who is a party to the contract for sale is bound to execute the sale deed if other terms are fulfilled by the purchaser, even though the property in question might not be belonging to him, as in that case the purchaser would take the risk or purchasing from him with his open eyes. It is obvious that the person to whom the property might be legally belonging cannot be bound by that sale, but all the same the parties to the contract would be bound by the contract to sell and the purchaser under the contract can enforce the vendor under the contract to perform his part of the contract. The question of title to property cannot be decided in such a suit.[19] Thus a stranger has no right to be a party.[20] It was held in an Allahabad case after the filing of the suit the plaintiff claimed himself to be the *benamidar* of *R* who was the real purchaser and prayed that the decree may be passed in favour of either of them. *Held R* was a stranger. It is settled law that a person not a party to a contract

16 *Radheshyam Kamila* v *Kiran Bala Dasi* AIR 1971 Cal 341; 75 CWN 391.
17 *Mukesh* v *Deonarayan* AIR 1987 MP 85.
18 *V.X. Joseph* v *D. Pasupathi* AIR 1994 Mad 193.
19 *Diwali Lal* v *Baldev Singh* AIR 1985 Pat 344.
20 *Mool Chand* v *Ram Phool* AIR 1979 All 189 at p. 191. See also *Prem Sukh Gulgulia* v *Habib Ullah* AIR 1945 Cal 355; *M.C. Chacko* v *State Bank of Travancore* AIR 1970 SC 504 at p. 507; (1970)1 SCR 658; (1969)2 SCC 343.

cannot, subject to certain well recognised exceptions, enforce the terms of the contract; the recognised exceptions are that beneficiaries, under the terms of the contract or where the contract is a part of the family arrangement, may enforce the covenant. In case *A* entered into a contract to sell the property to *B* and *A* also executed a power of attorney in favour of *B*. The plaintiff had an agreement with *B* and the plaintiff sued for specific performance of contract against *B*, impleading also *A* as there was then no formal deed of conveyance by *A* to *B*. The plaintiff has no privity of contract with *A*. Nevertheless *A* could be held as a proper party and the suit was not bad for misjoinder of parties.[1]

The general rule is that the obligation to perform cannot be assigned by the promisee to third persons except by novation of the contract with the consent of the promisee.[2] There is no equitable principle in favour of a stranger either.[3]

Seller of goods Section 58 of the Sale of Goods Act does not cover the case of a seller, since the provision is for the benefit of a buyer.[4]

Decree-holder A decree for specific performance passed on the basis of a contract of sale of immovable property does not create any interest in the property in favour of the decree-holder. It only super-adds the sanction of the court to enforce it through the medium of courts. As such, the decree-holder can enforce the said contract and get it enforced through court, subject to whatever interest the judgment-debtor had at the time of execution.[5]

Beneficiary Specific performance may be decreed at the instance of a person entitled to the benefit of the contract though not a party to it.[6]

Assignment A contract of resale of land is assignable in the absence of contract to the contrary in respect of such assignments. Mere absence of the phrase "heir", "assignees", "administrator" is not sufficient to raise any such contrary intention. Benefit of such contract is assignable.[7] Assignment is a transfer of interest or title usually expressed in writing whereby contracting parties covenant for themselves and their assigns so that upon the happening of certain events the assigns may stand in the shoes of

1 *Andheri Bridge View Co-op. Society Ltd.* v *Krishnakant Anandrao Deo* AIR 1991 Bom 129.

2 *Tolhurst* v *Associated Portland Cement Manfgs* [1902]2 KB 660 affd. on other grounds in [1903] AC 414.

3 *Howard* v *Miller* [1915] AC 318; *Scruttons* v *Midland Silicones* [1962]1 All ER 1 (HL).

4 *Maheshwari & Co. Pvt. Ltd.* v *Corporation of Calcutta* AIR 1975 Cal 165 at p. 168.

5 *Hiralal* v *Bhagirathi* AIR 1975 Cal 445 at p. 447.

6 *Hook* v *Kinnear* 36 ER 931 LC; *Beswick* v *Beswick* [1967]2 All ER 1197; *Avadh* v *Sita* 1 ALJ 329.

7 *Ali Mistri* v *Kayem Ali Sk.* AIR 1955 Cal 621.

original covenantees. Thus, no one can sue upon a contract unless he be either an original party or the lawful transferee or assignee of an original party. If a contract of resale or reconveyance of immovable property is capable of being enforced by or at the instance of a person who is a party to it, there appears to be no reason why a person who obtains the right under it should be deprived of its benefits. The right to have a property carries with it the right to transfer. A transfer without conferring upon the transferee the rights which the transferor had would be meaningless and useless. Therefore, a contract in the absence of a contrary intention, express or implied, will be enforceable by or against the parties and their heirs and legal representatives, including their assigns and transferees.[8]

An agreement to sell or buy of a movable property and both assignable and saleable, and unless the agreement contains prohibition against assignment, attachable also.[9] The court also in the case of *Swami Motor Transports Ltd.* v *Sankaraswamigal Mutt*[10] did not cast any doubt on this proposition of law. Further, it is immaterial that the assignee is a minor.[11]

Even when there are no express words in the contract itself to the effect that it was enforceable by the assignee, if there is no restrictive clause, an assignee of the vendor as his representative in interest, is entitled to seek specific performance.[12] A stranger having an assignment of right of reconveyance from one of the heirs of the party to the sale deed designated in the deed as beneficiary to the exclusion of the other heirs, can claim specific performance.[13] So also can an assignee of an option for repurchase, where the option has been exercised by the party assignor in due conformity with the terms of the contract[14] or the assignee and successor in interest of parties to a partition deed containing a pre-emption clause[15] or a co-purchaser who has got assigned the rights of the other co-purchasers.[16]

8 *Munawwar Hasen* v *Jakir Husen* 1984 All LJ 139 (FB); see also *Chinna Munnuswami Nayudu* v *Sagalguna Nayudu* AIR 1926 Mad 699 affd. in AIR 1928 PC 174 *sub nom Sakalaguna Nayudu* v *Chinna Munnuswami Nayudu* AIR 1940 Bom 339; *Ali Mistri* v *Kayam Ali* AIR 1955 Cal 621; *Rashid Ali* v *Darparam Namasundra* AIR 1954 Assam 95; *Bipin Behari* v *Marab Ali* AIR 1961 Assam 173; *Umar Noor Mohammad* v *Dayal Saran Darbari* AIR 1967 All 253; *P.N. Kapoor* v *S.N. Anand* 1970 LJ 721; *Sinnakaruppa Gounder* v *M. Karuppuswami Gounder* AIR 1965 Mad 506; *Sayad Abdulla* v *Ahmad* AIR 1929 All 817; *S.V. Gobardhan* v *Raghubir Singh* AIR 1930 All 101 (DB).

9 *Bhairon Prasad Chaurasiya* v *Tara Devi* 1979 All LJ 1324; AIR 1980 All 36 (FB).

10 AIR 1963 SC 864; 1963 Supp (1) SCR 282; (1964)1 SCJ 530.

11 *Ramchandra Sarma* v *Ayeesha Begum* AIR 1969 Mad 470.

12 *T.M. Balakrishna Mudaliar* v *M.S. Rao* AIR 1993 SC 2449; (1993)2 SCR 888; (1993)2 SCC 740.

13 *Habiba Khatoon* v *Ubaid Ul Huq* AIR 1997 SC 3236; (1997)7 SCC 452; JT 1997(7) SC 298.

14 *Sinnakaruppa Gounder* v *M. Karuppuswami Gounder* AIR 1965 Mad 506.

15 *Ram Baran Prosad* v *Ram Mohit Hazra* AIR 1967 SC 744; (1967)1 SCR 293.

16 *K.M. Madhava Krishnan* v *S.R. Swami* AIR 1995 Mad 318.

Where the plaintiff who filed a suit for specific performance assigned his rights for personal reasons and the assignee filed an application to implead himself as a party, the assignee can be regarded as representative in interest and the relief can be granted in his favour.[17]

It has already been stated that the benefit of a contract is assignable. But there may be contracts which in their nature cannot be enforced against the assignee or legal representative of the promisee. Thus when a painter undertakes to paint a picture or a dancer undertakes to dance or an author undertakes to write a book, such a contract is not assignable at all by the promisee who undertakes to paint, or dance, or write.

Thus, the legal proposition is that in the absence of prohibition against assignment, the vendee under an agreement to sell is entitled in law to assign his rights, title and interest under the agreement to any person of his choice. Once he assigns his rights under the agreement, the assignee steps into his shoes and being his representative in interest, he can seek specific performance of the contract, in view of the statutory right conferred upon him by s. 15(b) of the Specific Relief Act.[18]

Assignees—priority inter se The normal rule is that the assignees prior in time shall have the first right to seek enforcement.

In *Dahyabhui Chimanlal* v *Ambalal Himatlal*,[19] *J*, *T* and *P* were trustees as well as beneficiaries under a trust. They individually raised loans of ₹1 lakh each and assigned the benefit of the trust income from dividends to the lender. Notice of assignment was given to the trust. Later on, *J*, *T* and *P* raised further loans and assigned the same income to the second lender. The second lender, however, did not know of the earlier assignment. There was no notice to the companies from which dividend was received.

On there arising disputes between the two assignees, the second assignee contended that since the first assignee had failed to give notice of the assignment to the companies or to take a power of attorney to collect the dividend directly and had instead given extension of time for repayment of debt on a mere representation of the debtors that they had not received the income, which was of course false, the first assignee was postponed to the second assignee.

Rejecting the contention, the Supreme Court held that the priority of the first assignee would be maintained. The court also observed that in any case notice to the companies would have been ineffective since companies do not recognize any trust.

17 *SVR Mudaliar* v *Rajabu F. Buhari* AIR 1995 SC 1607; (1995)4 SCC 15; JT 1995(3) SC 614.
18 *Rajeev Gupta* v *J.K. Kashyap* (2011)122 DRJ 671; (2011)178 DLT 40.
19 AIR 1981 SC 1556; (1981)3 SCC 644.

In short, a 'mere right to sue' is a right, which arises out of contract, which is not specifically enforceable, or a right, whose specific performance of contract cannot be obtained. Since a contract for sale of immovable property creates an obligation annexed to the ownership of the land and the obligation arising thereunder is specifically enforceable, such a right cannot be regarded as a mere right to sue, within the meaning of s. 6(*e*) of the TP Act, and such a right, in the light of the provisions of s. 15(*b*) of the Specific Relief Act, is transferable and/or assignable. Logically, therefore, a person, who was not a party to a contract for sale of an immovable property, can demand specific performance of the contract if he is an assignee of the promisee provided that the contract does not prohibit assignment or the contract does not involve learning, skill, solvency or any personal quality of the promisee a necessary ingredient of the contract.[20]

Contract of repurchase Section 15(*b*) of the Specific Relief Act 1963 lays down that except as otherwise provided the specific performance of a contract may be obtained by the representative-in-interest or the principal, of any party thereto. Thus normally any interest in a contract could be assigned to any representative-in-interest who also can enforce the specific performance of the contract against the contracting party. However if the terms of the contract, expressly or by necessary implication, prohibited the beneficiary from transferring his contractual interest to third parties, then only such an assignee cannot sue for specific performance.[1] Similar view was expressed earlier also by the Supreme Court.[2]

Heirs—joint promisees In *Katip Bibi* v *Fakir Chandra*,[3] it was held that unless there were several joint promisees from the inception of the contract (although in the instant case there was only one promisee) one or more of the several heirs of the original promisee, a single individual, could not by himself or themselves institute a suit for specific performance of the contract of reconveyance by making the remaining heirs as parties-defendants to suit. On the death of the original promisee, his heirs do not themselves become several joint promisees.

However, dissenting from this view, the Allahabad High Court in *Sheomurat Ram* v *Savitri*[4] has taken the view that "while it is necessary that all the parties should be before the court so that it may be in a position to grant the necessary relief, it is not necessary that the parties should be arrayed on the side of the plaintiff. Some of them can be put in the array of the defendants if they refuse to join as co-plaintiffs. If this was not the correct

20 *Prabir Kumar Das* v *Amulya Bhushan Pal* (2006)1 Gau LR 618; AIR 2005 Gau 128.
1 *Habiba Khatoon* v *Ubaidul Huq* (1997)7 SCC 452.
2 *T.M. Balakrishna Mudaliar* v *M. Satyanarayana Rao* (1993)2 SCC 740.
3 AIR 1960 Cal 187.
4 AIR 1977 All 322.

position, it would be open to one or the other of several legal representatives to defeat the claims of the remaining legal representatives to seek relief against the promisor. Under Or. 1, r. 10, CPC the court can always transpose the parties".

The learned Judge also observed that the court should not therefore insist on evidence being produced to substantiate that those who have been joined as co-defendants had categorically refused to join as co-plaintiffs. Further, joint interest can arise in various circumstances. For example, there can be joint promisees at the inception of the contract. Joint interest can also arise on account of the death of a sole promisee who leaves behind several legal representatives to survive him and they can be described as jointly interested in the claim to which their predecessor-in-interest as the sole promisee was entitled. "The view of the Calcutta High Court is, therefore, directly opposed to *Amina Bibi* v *Abdul Kader Saheb*;[5] *Abdul Shaker Sahib* v *Abdul Rahiman Sahib*,[6] *Jagdeo Singh* v *Bishambhar*[7] and *Monghibai* v *Cooverji Umersey*".[8]

Sub-purchaser The rights of a sub-purchaser to enforce a contract against the original vendor are substantially the same as those of an assignee of the benefit of a contract.[9] The vendor, however, owes no fiduciary duty to the sub-purchaser. His right is to have the purchaser enforce the contract against the vendors.[10]

Even so, if the performance of the contract is dependent on the personal quality, learning, skill or solvency of the party to the contract or where the assignment is prohibited, it will not be competent to the representative in interest or the principal, as the case may be, to claim specific performance himself. But if such party has already performed his part of the contract, or the performance of the contract by a representative-in-interest or the principal has been accepted by the other party, the right will ensue.

Beneficiaries under settlement or compromise Clause (*c*) of s. 15 provides that where the contract is a settlement on marriage, or a compromise of doubtful rights between members of the same family, any person beneficially entitled thereunder may obtain specific performance of the contract.

"Settlement" is defined in s. 2(*b*) of the Specific Relief Act, as meaning an instrument (other than a will or codicil as defined by the Indian Succession Act 1925), whereby the destination or devolution of successive interests in movable or immovable property is disposed of or is agreed to be disposed

5 ILR (1902)25 Mad 26.
6 AIR 1923 Mad 284.
7 AIR 1937 Nag 186.
8 AIR 1939 PC 170.
9 *Shaw* v *Foster* [1872] LR 5 HL 321 at pp. 338, 339.
10 *Berkley* v *Earl Poulett* [1977]242 EG 39.

of. This is the general definition, but the settlement contemplated by this clause is the settlement on marriage.

Settlement on marriage and a family compromise form exceptions to the rule that none but parties and privies may enforce the contract.[11] Any person who is beneficially entitled to under such agreement, may sue for specific performance even though he himself is not a party to the agreement. In *Nawab Khawaja Mohamed* v *Nawab Hussaini Begum*[12] the plaintiff's father-in-law entered into an agreement with the plaintiff's father to pay to the plaintiff a sum of ₹500 p.m. as *Karachi-I-pandan* in consideration of marriage of the plaintiff with the defendant's son. It was held by Their Lordships of the Judicial Committee that though the wife was not a party to the agreement, she was entitled to enforce her claim she being the only person beneficially entitled thereto. A Burmese Buddhist was also held entitled to sue for specific performance of an ante-nuptial contract entered into by the parents of both sides.[13]

In the same way, compromise refers to the compromise of doubtful rights between the members of the same family.

A family arrangement is an agreement between the members of the family intended to be generally and reasonably for the benefit of the family either by compromise of rival disputed rights for preserving the family property, peace and security of the family by avoiding litigation and for saving the honour of the family.[14] It may merely recognise pre-existing rights or it may create fresh rights in persons who do not possess or it may amount to abatement of rights by persons who possessed them. Though conflict of legal claims in present or future, is generally a condition for the validity of the family arrangement, it is not necessarily so. Even *bona fide* disputes present or possible which may not involve legal claims will suffice.[15]

Remainderman The remainderman is entitled to sue where the contract has been entered into by the tenant for life in due exercise of his powers.

A "remainder" is an interest which is limited to take effect in possession upon the natural termination of a prior particular estate. A future interest is not a remainder if it is designed so as to spring up in the future.

The tenant for life means a person who is for the time being beneficially entitled under a settlement to possession of settled land for his life. A tenant for life has power to sell or exchange the settled land or any part thereof, or any easement, right or privilege of any kind over or in relation

11 *S.K. Khadimal Haque* v *Marai Dubey* AIR 1965 Pat 262.
12 14 CWN 865 (PC).
13 *Mae Tin* v *Ma Byaw* AIR 1930 Rangoon 172.
14 *Gulam Abbas* v *Haji Kayyum Ali* AIR 1973 SC 554; (1973)2 SCR 300; (1973)1 SCC 1.
15 *Maturi Pullaiah* v *Maturi Narasimhan* AIR 1966 SC 1836.

to the land, to grant leases, to raise money by the grant of a legal mortgage of the settled land, to effect improvements, to accept leases of other land, to contract to grant options, to accept surrender of leases etc. Moreover, his powers are indestructible in the sense that they are not capable of assignment or release, but remain exercisable by him notwithstanding any assignment by operation of law or otherwise of his beneficial interest under the settlement. Nevertheless he must so act, as an upright, independent and righteous man would act in dealing with the affairs of others.[16]

Reversioners A reversioner may obtain the specific performance of the contract, if in possession, if he is entitled to the benefit of the covenant entered into with his predecessor-in-title, or if in remainder, if he is entitled to the benefit of the covenant entered into with his predecessor-in-title and will sustain material injury by reason of its breach.

A "reversion" is the undisposed of interest in land which reverts to the grantor after the exhaustion of the particular estate, e.g. for years, for life, which he may have created.

"Remainder", on the other hand, is that residue of an estate in land, depending upon a particular estate and created together with the same; and in law Latin it is called "*remanere*". If *A* grants estate for life to *B* and subject thereto to *C* in fee, the estate of *C* is a remainder.

Promoters A promoter is one who undertakes to form a company with reference to a given project and to set it going and who takes the necessary steps to accomplish that purpose.[17] The provision of s.15(*h*) of the Specific Relief Act is in this regard very clear. For any reason whatsoever, the incorporation of a company could not be completed and it is being incorporated and there is urgency in executing a contract the promoters of the company named in the prospectus of the company for and on behalf of the company as promoters can execute a contract, when ultimately the said company after incorporation has got a scope to accept and thereby to ratify the stand of the promoters.[18]

Amalgamating company A company is a distinct juristic person. But it may be desirable to amalgamate it with another company. On amalgamation, it loses its identity and gets merged in the new company, and so its assets and liabilities. Naturally, therefore, the new company has been given a right to sue for specific performance in respect of the contracts entered into by the

16 Re, *Marquis of Ailesbury's Settlement Estates* [1892]1 Ch 506, 546, per Fry, J.

17 Cockburn, C.J. in *Twycross* v *Grant* (1877)2 CPD 469; Palmer's *Company Law*, 19th Ed., p. 322.

18 *Murari Ganguly* v *Kanailal Garai* AIR 2003 Cal 105; (2002)4 ICC 287; (2002)2 Cal LJ 629.

amalgamated company. It should, however, be noted that mere contract to amalgamate will not confer any rights on the amalgamating company. Amalgamation must have been actually carried out by s. 15(*g*) of the Specific Relief Act 1963.

Pre-incorporation contracts Section 15(*h*) of the said Act provides that when the promoters of a company have, before its incorporation, entered into a contract for the purposes of the company, and such contract is warranted by the terms of the incorporation, the company will be entitled to sue, provided that the company has accepted the contract and has communicated such acceptance to the other party to the contract.

It is well-known that a company comes into being only after its incorporation under the law. Prior to that, it has no capacity to enter into any contract; but it may be necessary to enter into contracts before the formal incorporation. This is done by the promoters. But such contracts become binding on the company only if the objects of the company warrant such contracts and the company accepts the contracts after its incorporation, and also communicates its acceptance to the other party to the contract.

Under the English Common Law, an unincorporated corporation could not have become an owner of the property. The law in India, however, is different. Section 5 of the Transfer of Property Act provides for transfer in favour of the company which was unincorporated. The effect of the Transfer of Property Act, therefore, postulates transfer in favour of the unincorporated company. It does not create any bar. Moreover, s. 19(*e*) of the Act provides for grant of a decree of specific performance of a contract against a company when the promoters of a company before incorporation entered into a contract for the purpose of the company and such contract is warranted by the terms of incorporation. Under the old Act,[19] not only ratification and adoption of the contract was mandatory, such contract was to be warranted by the terms of the incorporation. The words "ratified and adopted" have been dropped from the main section and in s. 19 of the Specific Relief 1963, a proviso has been added that the company has accepted the contract and communicated such acceptance to the other party of the contract. An express ratification of the contract, therefore, is no longer warranted.[20]

As to *locus standi* of a cooperative society it is the registration of the society on which it becomes a legal person and it is after its registration that it acquires the capacity to enter into contracts. The promoters of a society cannot act on behalf of the society before it has been registered and has come into existence. Therefore an agreement of lease entered into by a non-existent

19 Section 27 of the Specific Relief Act 1877.
20 *Jai Narain Parasrampuria* v *Pushpa Devi Saraf* (2006)7 SCC 756.

cooperative society is a nullity and does not give rise to cause of action for the plaintiff-society and cannot be specifically enforced.[1]

Specific performance for enforcement of agreement to issue debentures A contract with a company to take up and pay for debentures or debenture stock of the company may be enforced by an order for specific performance, but where debentures have been issued payable by instalments and have been forfeited, the company cannot enforce payment.[2]

Enforcement of contract by specific performance to take shares Specific performance of an agreement to take and pay for shares or to allot shares may be obtained.[3] In addition to a decree for the specific performance of the contract to allot share, the aggrieved party may also obtain damages equal to the dividend at the rates declared by the company between the date when the shares should have been allotted and the date of actual allotment.

Hypothecation of bills of lading, specifically enforceable An agreement to transfer bills of lading as security may be specifically enforceable,[4] but this rule does not seem ever to have been applied to a simple undertaking to deliver bills of lading under a contract of sale.[5]

Contract to sell shares A contract for sale of shares may be made orally. Specific performance may be ordered of a contract to sell shares even though the company, pending the litigation, has gone into liquidation.[6]

Suit for specific performance Tenant claimed specific performance of contract of sale against landlord only regarding tenanted premises. Agreement contained only boundaries of property. Plan which could make description of subject matter of sale was not attached. Sketch of map annexed to plaint did not confirm to plan which was to be made a part of agreement for sale. Finding by High Court that agreement of sale being vague, no decree for specific performance could be granted was proper.[7]

There was an agreement for sale between plaintiff and defendants. Defendants subsequently sold suit property in favour of appellants. There was impleadment of appellants who are subsequent purchasers. Restriction placed on appellant is that they cannot raise plea of readiness and willingness. Such restriction is proper. Only issue that can be adjudicated in suit is whether appellants were *bona fide* purchasers for value without notice.[8]

1 *Shri Ramji Mandir Narsinji* v *Narsinh Nagar Co-operative Housing Society Ltd., Navsari* AIR 1979 Guj 134.
2 Halsbury's *Laws of England*, 4th Ed., vol. 7, para 831.
3 *Sri Lanka Omnibus Co. Ltd.* v *Perara* [1952] AC 76 (PC).
4 *Lutscher* v *Comptoir d' Escompte de Paris* [1876]1 QBP 709.
5 Benjamin's *Sale of Goods*, 9th Ed., para 19-231.
6 Halsbury's *Laws of England*, 4th Ed., vol. 7, para 391.
7 *Vimlesh Kumari Kulshrestha* v *Sambhajirao* AIR 2009 SC 806.
8 *M.M.S. Investments, Madurai* v *V. Veerappan* AIR 2007 SC 2663.

Two suits for specific performance Two suits for specific performance were filed in respect of same property by two purchasers one of them was appellant before the Supreme Court. A consent decree was passed. Appellant not being party in such compromise was not bound by consent decree. Compromise was hit by s. 52 of the T.P. Act 1882 and s. 19 of the Specific Relief Act 1963. Court can pass discretionary order under s. 20 of the 1963 Act in the suit filed by the appellant.[9]

Suit by one of joint promisees One joint purchaser filed a suit for damages against owners on the ground of breach of contract. Parties entered into compromise. Consent decree was passed. Part of contract thus stood rescinded. Suit for specific performance of agreement in same form by other joint purchaser is not tenable, because other joint purchaser neither opposed recording of compromise nor filed a suit for specific performance immediately thereafter.[10]

Suit for specific performance of contract of sale Finding of fact was recorded by the first appellate court that the vendees had not established payment of ₹17,000 as initial sale consideration. The said finding, after consideration of entire evidence was affirmed by the High Court in the second appeal. It cannot be interfered with on appeal under Art. 136 of the Constitution of India. Sale deed in favour of vendees would not convey any title to them and hence after lawful repudiation, they would not be entitled to claim performance.[11]

Specific performance and injunction In the case of overseas sale by a foreign seller, practical difficulty of enforcement may be a ground for refusing specific performance to the buyer. Thus where goods are manufactured by the seller in a foreign country having no presence in the country of the buyer, and the seller was required to do his performance of the contract in his country, a claim by the buyer for mandatory injunction to secure the delivery of goods in the country of the buyer was refused. One reason for the refusal was that such an injunction would "require an unacceptable degree of supervision [of the seller's performance] in a foreign land".[12] Another reason was that it was "not apparent .... how such an order could be enforced if it were broken" since "none of the traditional methods of enforcement would work."[13]

Specific performance and injunction (English law as to Sale of Goods) Under s. 52 of the Sale of Goods Act 1979 (corresponding to s. 58 of the Indian

9 *Arjan Singh* v *Punit Ahluwalia* AIR 2008 SC 2718.
10 *G. Jayashree* v *Bhagwandas S. Patel* AIR 2009 SC 1749; (2009)3 SCC 144.
11 *Janak Dulari Devi* v *Kapildeo Rai* AIR 2011 SC 2521; see *Chadi Mahalakshmi* v *Koppada Sathiraju* AIR 2011 AP 125 (vendee having made false plea of payment of sale consideraiton was not entitled for equitable relief of specific performance).
12 *SSL International Ple* v *TTK LIG Ltd.* [2011] EW HC 1695 (Ch).
13 *Ibid.*

Sale of Goods Act 1930) the court is empowered to pass an order for specific performance of contract on a claim by the buyer and not by the seller. Normally, the seller's action for the price will have the similar effect to that of an order for specific performance if the buyer is compelled to pay the price, he will be induced to take delivery of goods, and if he delays in taking delivery, the seller may claim for storage and other expenses. In appropriate cases, the seller may claim an injunction to prevent the buyer from breaking his contractual obligation, e.g. under an exclusive purchasing agreement.[14] In *Behuke* v *Bede Shipping Co. Ltd.*[15] in addition for an order of specific performance, the court also granted injunction restraining the seller from parting with the ship.

Parties to specific performance of contract The expression "any party thereto" or "the representative in interest" used in s. 15(*b*) of the Specific Relief Act 1963 clearly includes the transferees and assignees of the contracting party in whose favour the right exists. Such right of seeking specific performance would, however, be not available in terms of proviso to cl. (*b*) where the contract provides that the interest shall not be assigned. In the absence of any words or expressions in the documents indicating prohibition on assignment or transfer of right of repurchase and in the face of clear provisions of s. 15(*b*) an implied prohibition cannot be read into the terms of the documents. Merely because in the documents, there is mention of "heirs" of contracting parties but not their "assignees" or "transferees", the legal right of assignment available to the benefit of original contracting party under s. 15(*b*) of the Act cannot be denied to it. Unless the contents of the document in question and evidence in relation thereto are so clear to infer a prohibition against assignment or transfer, the right of repurchase has to be held to be assignable or transferable and cannot be treated as personal to the contracting parties.[16]

"Necessary party" and "proper party" in a suit for specific performance A "necessary party" is a person who ought to have been joined as a party and in whose absence no effective decree could be passed by court. If a "necessary party" is not impleaded, the suit itself is liable to be dismissed. A "proper party" is a party who, though not necessary party is a person whose presence would enable the court to completed, effectively and adequately adjudicate upon all matters in disputed in the suit, though he need not be a person in favour or against whom the decree is to be made. The fact that a person is likely to secure a right/interest in a suit property after the suit is decided against the plaintiff, will not make such person a necessary or a proper party

14 Benjamin's *Sale of Goods*, 9th Ed., para 16-093.
15 [1927]1 KB 649.
16 *Shyam Singh* v *Daryao Singh* AIR 2004 SC 348.

to a suit for specific performance of contract.[17] Therefore, a combined reading of ss. 15 and 19 of the Act makes it clear that the parties to the contract and their representatives in interest can claim enforcement of the contract and the contract can be enforced against either party or any other person claiming under him by a title arising subsequently to the contract. Thus, the subsequent purchaser, who purchased the subject matter of the suit from one of the parties is a necessary party to have a binding decree against other parties.[18] However, it was also held that the subsequent purchaser is not a necessary party after the filing of the suit.[19]

As to the test to ascertain who is a necessary and proper party in a suit, it may be stated that against a necessary party there must be a right to some relief in respect of the matters involved in the proceeding in question; it must not be possible to pass an effective decree in the absence of such party. The test for determining the effectiveness of decree is whether the decree can be executed without the presence of the party in question as regards the property sought to be decreed in favour of the plaintiff.[20] Only such persons are necessary parties who have interests in the subject matter of the suit and who are likely to be affected.[1] A necessary party is one without whom no order can be made effectively and proper party is one in whose absence an effective order can be made but whose presence is necessary for a complete and final decision on the question involved in the proceeding.[2]

In a suit for specific performance of a contract for sale a third party or a stranger claiming independent title and possession over the contracted property is neither necessary nor proper party and is not, therefore, entitled to join as party defendant in the suit. Two tests by which a person who is seeking addition in a pending suit for specific performance of contract for

17 *Mumbai International Airport Pvt. Ltd.* v *R.C. Centre & Hotels Pvt. Ltd.* AIR 2010 SC 3109.

18 *K.P. Rajendran* v *N.R. Nachimuthu* (2011)1 CTC 331; (2010)5 LW 905; (2011)3 Mad LJ 251; (2011)99 AIC 557; *Kasturi* v *Iyyamperumal* 2005(2) CTC 676 (SC); (2005)6 SCC 733.

19 *S.G. Kannappan* v *S. Murugesan* (2002)1 MLJ 90.

20 *Benaras Bank* v *Bhagwan Das* AIR 1974 All 18; *Deputy Commissioner, Hardoi* v *Rama Krishna* AIR 1953 SC 521; 1954 SCR 506; 1953 SCJ 664; ILR (1954)1 All 168; *Jivandas* v *Narbada Bai* AIR 1959 Cal 519; *Badshah* v *Board of Revenue* AIR 1962 MP 12; *Hardeva* v *Ismail* AIR 1970 Raj 167; *S.C. Law* v *K.S. Roy* AIR 1974 Cal 274; *Panna Khushali* v *Jeewanlal* AIR 1976 MP 148; *Hitkarini Sabha* v *D. Mangal Wadi* (1988)1 Cur Civ Cas 469 (MP).

1 *Ram Sharan* v *Mahipatrao* AIR 1987 MP 29; 1987 Jab LJ 115; 1987 Cur Civ Cas LJ 34 (MP).

2 *Udit Narain Singh* v *Addl. Member, Board of Revenue* AIR 1963 SC 786; 1963 Supp (1) SCR 676; (1964)1 SCJ 151; *Bhagawanti* v *Custodian General* AIR 1976 J&K 29; *Academy of General Education* v *S. Venkataraj* (1977)2 Kant LJ 491.

sale must be satisfied: Two tests are—(1) There must be a right to some relief against such party in respect of the controversies involved in the proceedings, (2) no effective decree can be passed in absence of such party.[3]

Strangers who claim adverse to the title of the defendant-vendor alleging that they are co-owners of the property sought to be sold are not necessary parties nor proper parties.[4] In a suit for specific performance of contract by *A* against *B*, *A* claiming that whatever interest *B* had must pass to *A*, *B*'s sister claimed herself to have a share in the property, held *B*'s sister is not a necessary party.[5] When *X* files a suit for specific performance against *Y*, *Y*'s coparcener who claims that *Y* cannot transfer the property as it is not beneficial to the family can be impleaded as a party, for then it cannot be said the coparcener by his joinder seeks a decision on his or his vendor's title only.[6] A suit by one joint promisee for specific performance of contract is tenable on impleading other promisee as co-defendant on their refusal to sue as plaintiff.[7] When *A* has sued *B* for specific performance of contract of sale, *C* who claims to have entered into another contract with *B* during the pendency of suit cannot be impleaded, he being not a necessary party.[8] When *A* enters into a contract of sale with *B*, in suit by *B* for specific performance *C* claiming that the property is joint property of *A* and *C* cannot be impleaded.[9] In a case *A* filed a suit for specific performance of contract of sale against *B* (the promisor) and *C*, the subsequent transferee. But meanwhile *D* pre-empted the property from *C*. It was held in the suit for specific performance *D* is not a necessary party, nor *D* can claim himself to be added as a defendant.[10] But person claiming under earlier agreement of sale and in possession is a necessary party even when neither possession nor injunction is prayed for.[11]

Personal restrictions and bars to specific relief (ss. 16, 17 and 18) Even if the plaintiff belongs to category of persons who can obtain specific performance of a contract, it would not be enforced in the following cases:

(*a*) if he has obtained substituted performance of contract under s. 20 [s. 16(*a*)];

3 *Kasturi* v *Iyyamperumal* AIR 2005 SC 2813.
4 *Panna Khushali* v *Jeewanlal Mathoo Khatik* AIR 1976 MP 148; 1976 Jab LJ 84.
5 *Rasiklal Shankerlal Soni* v *Natverlal Shankerlal Upadhyaya* AIR 1975 Guj 178; (1975)16 Guj LR 533. See also *Jugraj Singh* v *Jaswant Singh* AIR 1970 SC 1039; (1970)3 SCR 266; (1971)1 SCJ 41; (1971)1 SCWR 79.
6 *Atul Sharma* v *Gurinder Sinha* AIR 1984 Punj 365; 1984 Rev LR 283.
7 *Ponnuswami* v *Rama Boyan* AIR 1979 Mad 130; *Nirmala Bala Dasi* v *Sudarsan Jana* AIR 1980 Cal 258; (1980)2 Cal LJ 11.
8 *Mohammadbhai* v *Trustees, Cal. Improvement* AIR 1984 Cal 219.
9 *Ram Bilash Pandey* v *Jai Narayan* AIR 1984 Pat 218.
10 *Gourhari* v *Bimal Kumar* 88 CWN 1067.
11 *Bala Narasimha* v *Ganga Putra Co-op. Housing* AIR 1984 AP 166 contra *Rasiklal* v *Natverlal* AIR 1975 Guj 178.

(*b*) if he has become incapable of performing his part of the contract, or violates any essential term of the contract that on his part remains to be performed, or acts in fraud of the contract, or wilfully acts at variance with or in subversion of the relation intended to be established by the contract [s. 16(*b*)];

(*c*) if he fails to prove that he has performed or has always been ready and willing to perform the essential terms of the contract which are to be performed by him, other than the terms the performance of which has been prevented or waived by the defendant.

However, this bar will not apply if plaintiff avers performance of, or readiness and willingness to perform, the contract according to its true construction. Even if the contract involves the payment of money, it is not essential for him actually to tender to the defendant or to deposit in court any money except when so directed by the court [s. 16(*c*)];

(*d*) if he as a vendor or lessor of property (movable or immovable) has contracted to sell or let the property knowing that he has no title to the property or even if believing that he had a good title to the property cannot at the time fixed by the parties or by the court for the completion of the sale or letting, give the purchaser or lessee a title free from reasonable doubt [s. 17];

(*e*) likewise, where the contract is in writing, and the defendant sets up a variation thereto, the plaintiff cannot obtain the specific performance except with the variation so set up in the following cases, namely: (*a*) where by fraud, mistake of fact or misrepresentation, the written contract is in its terms or effect different from what the parties agreed to, or does not contain all the terms agreed to between the parties on the basis of which the defendant entered into the contract; (*b*) where the object of the parties was to produce a certain legal result which the contract as framed is not calculated to produce; (*c*) where the parties have subsequently to the execution of the contract, varied its terms [s. 18].

Where plaintiff not entitled to recover damages Section 16(*a*) contemplates a situation where the plaintiff is not entitled to recover compensation. It contemplates not a case when the plaintiff despite being so entitled has not asked for it. As stated by Banerjee;[12] "The principle involved in this clause is of general application. The plaintiff may be guilty of some wrongful acts as against the defendant, or against the public. The court would refuse specific performance if the plaintiff has been guilty of some wrong or wrongful conduct, if in its opinion, it is such as to disentitle him to recover

12 Banerjee on *Law of Specific Relief* (Tagore Law Lectures), 13th Ed., p. 255.

compensation for its breach. The maxim is he who comes in to equity must come in clean hands."

The words "would not be entitled" postulate therefore contingencies where it is inequitable to allow to recover compensation for breach of the contract and secondly a legal bar to the recovery of compensation. As stated in Broom the rule (allowing relief of specific performance as equitable relief) is subject to limitation, and does not apply where the express provisions of any law are violated by the contract, nor, in general, where the interest of the public, or of third parties, would be injuriously affected by its fulfilment. *Pacta, quae contra leges constitutionesque vel contra bonos mores fiunt nullam vim habre, indubitati juris est;* and *privatorum conventio juri publico non derogat*. The first legal maxim means 'it is a matter of unquestionable law that contracts against the laws and statutes, or against moral standards, have no force'.[13] The second legal maxim means "on agreement of private persons does not derogate from public law".[14] "If the thing stipulated for is in itself contrary to law, the paction by which the execution of the illegal act is stipulated must be held as intrinsically *null; pactis privstorum juri publico non derogatur.*"[15]

Such types of contracts namely, where the plaintiff is not entitled to recover damages, may be illustrated by the following example.

A, in the character of agent for *B*, enters into an agreement with *C* to buy *C*'s house. *A* is in reality acting not as agent for *B*, but of his own account, *A* cannot enforce specific performance of his contract.

Where plaintiff incapable of performance etc. This covers contracts where the plaintiff has become incapable of performing the contract that on his part remains to be performed, or violates any essential term of that contract, or acts in fraud of the contract, or wilfully acts at variance with or in subversion of the relation intended to be established by the contract. Such incapacity may be physical or mental or legal.[16]

The question whether the plaintiff is or is not entitled to recovery of compensation for breach of contract will have to be decided in accordance with the provisions of s. 73 of the Indian Contract Act. A plaintiff who is guilty of forgery and fraud is not entitled to the decree of specific performance.[17] In *Athar Jamath Majith* v *T. Krishnaswamy Naidu*[18] a religious society sued for specific performance of a contract for sale of property in its favour. The President and Secretary who sued on behalf of the religious

13 Black's *Law Dictionary*, 10th Ed.
14 *Ibid*.
15 Broom's *Legal Maxims*, 12th Ed., p. 506; Black's *Law Dictionary*, 9th Ed., p. 1858.
16 *Umar Noor Mohammad* v *Dayal Saran Darbari* AIR 1967 All 253.
17 *Rabindra Nath Sahu* v *Maya Devi* AIR 1991 Pat 192.
18 AIR 1955 Mad 591.

society mutilated the document evidencing the contract by scissoring off at the top and at the bottom some clauses which were prejudicial to the suit claim for specific performance and this misconduct was sufficient to disentitle the plaintiff for the claim of specific performance. Clause (*a*) of s. 16 must be read with s. 236 of the Indian Contract Act which provides that a person with whom a contract has been entered into in the character of agent, is not entitled to require specific performance of it, if he was in reality acting, not as agent, but on his own account. Where the plaintiff repudiates the contract and claims damage, he cannot turn around and claim relief of specific performance.[1] The court is not entitled to invoke the power under Or. 7, r. 7, CPC to override the statutory limitation contained in s. 16 of the Specific Relief Act and Art. 54 of the Limitation Act which preclude the grant of relief of specific performance of a contract except within the period prescribed therein.[2] In a suit for specific performance of a contract, a transferee can take the defence that the transferor has no title but the transferor against whom such a suit is filed by the transferee no such plea in defence can be raised by the transferor.[3]

A contracts to sell *B* a house, and to become a tenant thereof for a term of, say, 14 years from the date of the sale at specified yearly rent. *A* becomes insolvent. Neither he nor his assignee can enforce specific performance of the contract.

A person who is incapable of performing the essential term of a contract to be performed by him cannot be said to be ready or willing to perform it however much he may say that he is ready and willing to perform it.[4] *Held* on facts plaintiff had no means of performing the contract. Later, the Supreme Court approved the view of the High Court.[5]

For want of independent means of livelihood a beneficiary of a contract may be held to be unable to perform his or her part of the contract. But in a particular fact or situation specific performance can be allowed. When the plaintiff in a suit for specific performance of contract of transfer of land in lieu of maintenance entered into by her husband failed to aver and prove her willingness as required in the statute namely the liability to discharge certain debts of her husband, the suit for specific performance was resisted, *inter alia* on the ground that she failed to discharge her obligation under the contract. The court held that she was a lady having no independent means of livelihood and as such she was disabled to discharge her obligation. Nevertheless the court held that in view of the long lapse of time, she may

1 *Ayissabi* v *Gopal Konar* (1988)2 CCC 635.
2 *Thakamma Mathew* v *M. Azmathulla Khan* AIR 1993 SC 1120; JT 1993(1) SC 5.
3 *N. Venkataramanna* v *Mahakali* (1994)1 CCC 941.
4 *Har Pratap Singh* v *Satya Narain Misra* AIR 1980 All 52.
5 *Satya Narain Misra* v *Har Pratap Singh* (2007)15 SCC 585.

not be mulcted at this distance of time to pay the funeral expenses which would not be possible to be ascertained and the debt, due to defendant as well. Accordingly it was held that the lower court committed grievous error of law and fact in not considering the case from the above perspective and arbitrarily refusing to decree the suit. In such a situation despite the omission to aver and prove her continuous readiness and willingness, relief of specific performance should be granted to her.[6]

Where vendee committed breach of agreement for sale of immovable property by not paying the instalments of sale consideration within the time period stipulated in the sale deed, it was held that he is not entitled to decree of specific performance of agreement.[7] Similarly, where the plaintiff failed to perform his part of the contract regarding the balance consideration within the period stipulated in the agreement, he cannot obtain decree of specific performance.[8]

Relief under the Bengal Money Lenders Act in suit for specific performance under Or. 7, r. 7, CPC Order 7, r. 7, CPC provides that it is not necessary for the plaintiff to ask for general or other relief which may always be given as the court may think just to the same extent as if it had been asked for. Plaintiff may claim relief on a particular provision of law erroneously but court can grant relief on correct provision of law if the party is entitled to the relief under the law.

The plaintiff's case in a decision of Calcutta High Court was that his predecessor-in-interest had transferred the suit property and on the date of transfer the defendant had executed an unregistered agreement to reconvey the suit property on receipt of the consideration money within three years. The plaintiff had offered the requisite consideration money to the defendant but on latter's refusal to accept the same and reconvey the property, he had filed the suit for specific performance of the contract. The courts below concurrently found that the unregistered agreement was fraudulent and void and the appellate court below found that the suit was not maintainable against the minor defendant and was liable to be dismissed. The appellant urged that the transaction was a loan in substance, that the minority of one of the defendants did not merit the dismissal of the suit and that the plaintiff's suit ought to have succeeded in view of Or. 7, r. 7 of the Code of Civil Procedure. Repelling the contention it was held that where the plaintiff did not make a case in the alternative and no alternative prayer was made, and the defendant did not admit it to be a loan in the written statement but contended that the agreement for reconveyance was fraudulent which was proved in the courts below, any alternative relief under the

6 *Syed Sultan Pai* v *Syed Bikhu Sahed* AIR 1986 AP 342.
7 *Pemmada Prabhakar* v *Youngmen's Vysya Assn.* (2015)5 SCC 355.
8 *Padmakumari* v *Dasayyan* (2015)8 SCC 695.

provisions of Or. 7, r. 7 of the Code of Civil Procedure could not be granted to the plaintiff.[9]

Averment by minor or pauper Clause (*b*) of s. 16 of the Specific Relief Act specifically forbids enforcement of specific performance of a contract in favour of a person "who has become incapable of performing any essential term of the contract that on his part remains to be performed" the readiness and willingness to perform the essential term of a contract to be performed by him and which is required to be averred and proved under cl. (*c*) of s. 16, has to be a real readiness and willingness, backed by the capacity to do so. A person who is incapable of performing the essential term of a contract to be performed by him cannot be said to be ready or willing to perform it how-so-ever much he may say that he is ready and willing to perform it.[10]

Essential terms Essential terms are those which are absolutely vital to the bargain, a violation whereof will alter the mutual relationship of the parties in such a manner that it would no longer be equitable to decree the specific performance of the contract on the principle of continuation of the mutual relationship as existed at the time when the contract was made. Whether a particular term in an agreement is essential or not depends upon the construction of the term.[11]

Violation of essential part of contract Section 16(*b*), Specific Relief Act 1963 also contemplates a situation where the plaintiff violates an essential term of the contract that on his part remaining to be performed such a plaintiff is not entitled to the relief of specific performance.

The words "violates the essential term" refer to a term which is absolutely vital to the bargain of the parties in such a material manner that it would be no longer equitable to decree of specific performance as if their mutual relationship continued to be the same as it was at the time when the bargain was entered into. This will not, however, apply where the violation relates only to the manner of payment of the consideration for an agreement to sell immovable property and for which liabilities in the nature of a penalty by forgoing part of the consideration were provided.[12] When a particular mode of payment has been provided in the contract, the plaintiff must comply with that mode. If he does not, he cannot be deemed to be ready and willing to perform his part of the contract. It is because it is not open to the plaintiff to chalk out his own manner of performing his part of the contract.[13]

9 *J.N. Banerjee* v *A.B. Kayal* 90 CWN 528.

10 *Satya Narain Misra* v *Mahabir Prasad* (1979)5 ALR 529.

11 *Ceean International Private Limited* v *Ashok Surana* AIR 2003 Cal 263; (2002)4 ICC 597; Cal LT 2003(2) HC 322.

12 *Sellappa Chetty* v *Marappa Gounder* AIR 1965 Mad 37 at p. 41 (DB).

13 *Bishambhar Nath Agarwal* v *Kishan Chand* AIR 1990 All 65; (1989)3 Cur Civ Cas 518.

The following examples illustrate the rule:

A, holding land under a contract with *B* for a lease, commits waste, or treats the land in an unhusbandlike manner. *A* cannot enforce specific performance of the contract.

A contracts to let, and *B* contracts to take, an unfinished house. *B* contracting to finish the house, and the lease to contain covenants on the part of *A* to keep the house in repair. *B* finishes the house in a very defective manner, he cannot enforce the contract specifically, though *A* and *B* may sue each other for compensation for breach of it.

When two agreements are entered into for mutual benefit and they are to be performed simultaneously, enforcement of one agreement only against the defendant is bound to work serious prejudice and will be inequitable.[14] Under the terms of the agreement notice was given stating that the buyer can take possession of the premises on paying the full consideration. The buyer did not act and so the agreement stood cancelled. It was held that there was no question of enforcing the agreement.[15] The plaintiff took an unfair advantage and kept the rental amount with himself for nearly 20 years running to several thousands, the High Court denied to the plaintiff the relief of specific performance.[16] On appeal, the Supreme Court while dismissing the claim for specific performance, granted the plaintiff a decree for the mortgage amount with interest.[17] Where the plaintiff has been found guilty of acts in fraud or contravention of or at variance with the essential terms of a contract or acts tending to the rescission of the contracts and the subversion of the relationship established by it he is no longer entitled to the intervention of the court in specific performance.[18] *A* contracts to sell *B* a house and garden in which there are ornamental trees, which were material elements in the value of the property as a residence. *A* without *B*'s consent fells the trees. *A* cannot therefore enforce specific performance of the contract. [Illustration of cl. (*b*) of s. 24 of the repealed Specific Relief Act 1877]. Where *M* contracts to let and *N* contracts to take an unfinished house and *M* contracts to finish the house and the lease to contain covenants on the part of *N* to keep the house in repair but finishes the house in a defective manner, he cannot enforce the contract specifically, though *M* and *N* may sue each other for compensation and its breach.[19] In *Sahida Bibi* v *Sk. Golam Muhammad*,[20] the purchaser falsely claimed that he had

14 *Tribhuwan Dutt Tripathi* v *Ramji Tiwari* AIR 1991 All 268.
15 *Manicklal Mukherjee* v *Commissioner of Sanchaita Investment* AIR 1993 SC 1571; 1992 Supp (1) SCR 967; (1993)1 SCC 505.
16 *B.R. Mulani* v *Dr. A.B. Aswathanarayana* AIR 1993 Kant 257.
17 *B.R. Mulani* v *Dr. A.B. Aswathanarayana* AIR 1993 SC 1318.
18 *Fry on* Specific Performance 6th Ed., p. 450.
19 *Tildesley* v *Clarkson* [1862]30 Beav 419.
20 AIR 1983 Cal 216.

paid the vendor a certain sum and offered to pay the balance. He was held to have violated the essential term of the contract and was disentitled to specific performance. In a case which came up before the Judicial Committee of the Privy Council in *Sri Chandra Rai* v *Rai Banomali Rai*,[21] the parties had made a compromise, comprising an agreement, the chief consideration for which was the execution of an *ekrar* by plaintiff acknowledging the title of the defendant as the adopted son of the last owner of the property. The plaintiff then brought a suit to impeach the adoption alleging that the *ekrar* had been obtained from him by fraud. His suit for specific performance in terms of the compromise was therefore dismissed as the conduct of the plaintiff was at variance and amounted to subversion of relationship intended to be established by the compromise.

Time is the essence of the contract Whether time is essence of the contract of sale is question of fact and can be addressed by the trial court after parties lead evidence. Such question cannot be dealt with on an application under Or. 7, r. 11(*d*), CPC.[1] Where time is the essence of the contract, failure to stick to the time disentitles the defaulter to seek specific performance. The question whether time is the essence of the contract has to be decided not only with reference to the terms of the contract but also with reference to the conduct of the parties and the facts and circumstances of the case. Thus, where time is the essence of the contract is an inference from proved facts and is therefore a question of law.[2] Where a contract relates to sale of an immovable property, it will normally be presumed that time is not the essence of the contract. As held by the Supreme Court that the fixation of period within which the contract has to be performed does not make a stipulation as to time as the essence of the contract.[3] But the parties may expressly provide that time shall be of the essence of the contract and where there is a power to determine the contract on a failure to complete by a specified date, the stipulation as to time will be treated as fundamental. Where there is evidence to show that the vendor required the purchase for an urgent purpose (money was needed to meet specific commitment and 10 days time was fixed), time was treated as of essence of the contract.[4] The intention to treat time as of the essence of the contract may be evidenced by the circumstances which should be essentially strong to displace the normal presumption that in a contract for sale of land stipulation as to time is not of essence of the contract[5] unless

21 31 IA 107 (PC).
1 *Himmatlal* v *Rajratan Concept* (2018)3 MP LJ 235; AIR 2018 MP 197.
2 *Sriram Cotton Pressing Factory* v *K.E. Narayanasami* AIR 1965 Mad 352.
3 *Gomathinayagam Pillai* v *Palanisami Nadar* AIR 1967 SC 868; (1967)1 SCR 227; *Govind Prasad Chaturvedi* v *Hari Dutt Shastri* AIR 1977 SC 1005; (1977)2 SCR 877; (1977)2 SCC 539.
4 *Kamal Rani* v *Chand Rani* AIR 1980 Del 188.
5 *Govind Prasad Chaturvedi* v *Hari Dutt Shastri* AIR 1977 SC 1005.

specifically provided to that effect.[6] When an agreement for sale provides that the vendor shall have the right to refund the amount received if the vendee omits to pay the balance amount within a specified period after issuance of notice by the vendor, the agreement of sale stands cancelled.[7] Where a property is sold by auction and it is agreed that if the price is not paid by a stated hour on a specific date, the contract shall be liable to be cancelled, in such case time must be deemed to be of the essence of the contract.[8] A stipulation in the agreement for sale of immovable property that the sum of ₹98,000 shall be paid by the 2nd party to the 1st party within a period of 10 days only, and the balance of ₹50,000 at the time of registration of the deed of sale before the Sub-Registrar shows that the parties intended to make time as the essence of the contract.[9] In a contract for reconveyance of the immovable property, it is settled law that time shall be deemed to be of the essence of the contract and the failure on the part of the plaintiff to perform his part within the stipulated time is fatal.[10] The grant of extension of time by the vendor at the vendee's request can be considered as a waiver of the original condition in respect of the completion of the sale only to the extent of substituting the extended time in the original time.[11]

Time for performance of contract In a suit for specific performance unless time is affirmatively stipulated in the contract as essential for performance, the failure of the plaintiff to perform on the very day fixed in the contract for performance does not necessarily defeat the suit for specific performance. The remedy may be available provided that a *bona fide* excuse exists for non-performance and that the delay does not make enforcement inequitable. Where parties make performance at the stipulated time essential, any default which is not waived or executed, will defeat the right to specific performance of the contract.

Specific plea to be made in averments Forms 47 and 48 of the Appendix A of the First Schedule of the Code of Civil Procedure prescribe the manner in which averments are required to be made by the plaintiff in a suit for specific performance of contract. The plaintiff must raise a plea that he had

6 *K.S. Vidyanandam* v *Vairavan* (1997)3 SCC 1; *Ranjana Nagpal* v *Devi Ram* AIR 2002 HP 166.

7 *Manicklal Mukherjee* v *Commissioner of Sanchaita Investment* AIR 1993 SC 1571; 1992 Supp (1) SCR 967; (1993)1 SCC 505.

8 *Pichai Mohideen* v *C.K.D. Das* AIR 1933 Mad 736; *Duraikannu* v *Savanna Chettiar* AIR 1969 Mad 468.

9 *Chand Rani* v *Kamal Rani* AIR 1993 SC 1742; (1993)1 SCC 519; JT 1993(1) SC 74.

10 *Sheik Far John Mian* v *Tajusahu* (1998)3 ELJR 1863 (Pat); *Bismillah Begam* v *Rahmatullah Khan* (1998)2 SLJ 866 (SC); (1998)1 LW 825; *Sri Baburam* alias *Durga Prasad* v *Sri Indra Pal Singh (died) by LRs* (1999)1 LW 72 (SC); *Jananath Pedayani* v *Elumalai* (2002)1 LW 92.

11 *Barkley* v *Messenger* 43 LJ Ch 449; *Shaji Fakir* v *Sheik Abdullah* 12 Bom 658.

all along been and even on the date of filing of suit was ready and willing to perform his part of contract and he would also prove the same. Only in certain exceptional situation where although in letter and spirit, the exact words had not been used, but readiness and willingness can be culled out from reading all the averments made in the plaint as a whole coupled with the materials brought on record at the trial of the suit, to the said affect, the statutory requirement of s. 16(*c*) of the Specific Relief Act 1963 may be held to have been complied with. The plaintiff cannot be said to have substantially complied with the requirements of the law. Thus, it was one of the reasons for which the impugned judgment of the High Court was set aside.[12]

Oral agreement A suit for specific performance can be filed on oral agreement also. However, the burden is on the plaintiff to prove the existence of the oral agreement between the parties.[13] The proviso 2 of s. 92 of the Evidence Act also lays down that the existence of any separate oral agreement as to any matter on which a document is silent, and which is not inconsistent with its terms, may be proved.[14]

Suit based on unregistered document A suit for specific performance of contract based on unregistered document is permissible as the proviso[15] to s. 49 of the Registration Act 1908 carves out an execption in respect of the suit for specific performance.[16] The Supreme Court in *S. Kaladevi* v *V.R. Somasundaram*,[17] has considered the scope of proviso to s. 49 in a case of specific performance and held that as per the proviso to s. 49 unregistered documents affecting the immovable property can be admitted in the evidence in a suit for specific performance. Such unregistered sale deed can also be admitted in evidence for collateral transactions.

Readiness and willingness There can be no strait jacket formula with regard to readiness and willingness. It will have to be construed in the facts and circumstances of each case in the light of all attending facts and circumstances. Readiness has been interpreted as capacity for discharge of obligations with regard to payment. The grant of relief for specific performance under s. 16(1)(*c*) of the Act is a discretionary and equitable

12 *Manjunath Anandappa* v *Tammanasa* AIR 2003 SC 1391.

13 *Ajay Avinash Solanki* v *Asha Umesh Yadav* (2018)3 Mah LJ 231; (2018)2 AIR Bom R 53; 2018 AIR CC 1019; (2018)5 Bom CR 302.

14 *Padma Rani Sikdar* v *Karupur Shaw* (1988)1 CHN 258.

15 "Provided that an unregistered document affecting immovable property and required by this Act, or the Transfer of Property Act 1882, to be registered may be received as evidence of a contract in a suit for specific performance under Chapter II of the Specific Relief Act 1877, or as evidence of any collateral transaction not required to be effected by registered instrument."

16 *Sham Pundalik Dhumatkar* v *Pushpa Mohanlal Talreja* (2016)6 Mah LJ 736; (2016)5 AIR Bom R 552; (2017)170 AIC 287; (2017)3 Bom CR 248.

17 2010(3) MPLJ (SC) 500.

relief. Under s. 16(1)(*c*), the plaintiff has to demonstrate readiness and willingness throughout to perform his obligations under the contract.[18]

Only self-serving statements without any proof of financial resources cannot be relied upon to return a finding that the plaintiff is ready and willing to perform his part of the contract.[19]

Merely delay in filing the suit after the accrual of cause of action, inference cannot be made against the plaintiff that he was not ready and willing to perform, if the suit is files within the period of limitation. The reason is that in India, it is well settled that the rule of equity that exists in England, does not apply, and so long as a suit for specific performance is filed within the period of limitation, delay cannot be put against the plaintiff.[20]

A finding on the issue of readiness and willingness is one of the important and relevant findings in a suit for specific performance of an agreement. It is a finding based on facts and once it is recorded, it becomes a finding of fact. Unless such finding is found to be against the pleadings or contrary to the evidence or the law governing the issue, it is binding on all courts.[21]

A finding on readiness and willingness of the plaintiff is necessarily a finding of fact, which has to be rendered by the court on the basis of the nature of agreement, evidence and the material on record in the context of readiness of the parties.[22] A plea of readiness and willingness has to be raised in the trial court, since such plea cannot be raised in appeal.[23]

Failure to aver and prove performance or readiness and willingness to perform

Section 16(*c*) places another bar on the plaintiff to claim specific performance, where he fails to aver and prove that he has performed the essential terms of the contract excepting those the performance of which has been prevented or waived by the defendant, or that he has always been ready and willing to perform them.

Explanation, to some extent, relaxes the rigour of the provision by providing that where the contract involves the payment of money, it is not essential for the plaintiff actually to tender to the defendant or to deposit in court any money except when so directed by the court, and, further, that the plaintiff need only aver performance of, or readiness and willingness to perform, the contract according to its true construction, but not according to the wishes of the defendant.

18 *Ravi Setia* v *Madan Lal* (2019)9 SCC 381.
19 *Ritu Saxena* v *J.S. Grover* (2019)9 SCC 132.
20 *R. Lakshmikantham* v *Devaraji* (2019)8 SCC 62.
21 *Vijay A. Mittal* v *Kulwant Rai* (2019)3 SCC 520.
22 *Tousif Ahmed* v *Ferozkhan* (2019)1 Mah LJ 914; (2018)4 AIR Bom R 71; (2018)5 Bom CR 233.
23 *Jai Prakash Agarwal* v *Brahma Kumar Jutsi* (2018)3 MP LJ 462.

Plaint of a suit for specific performance must conform to s. 16(c) of the Specific Relief Act and Form Nos. 47 and 48 of the Appendix A of the First Schedule of the Code of Civil Procedure, i.e. it must allege plaintiff's continuous readiness and willingness to perform his part of the contract, else the suit is liable to be dismissed no matter whether the defendant has taken the objection or not.[24] No matter whether an issue is raised or not—not even remand is permissible.[25]

In an agreement to sell a mere plea in the plaint that plaintiff/vendee was always ready and willing is not sufficient. The vendee must prove with satisfactory evidence that he was always ready and willing to perform his part of contract at all material times. Conduct of plaintiff in issuing notice after a period of three years was held to disentitle him to discretionary relief of specific performance.[26]

An agreement of sale was cancelled by the vendor by receiving part consideration. Vendee stated that he was present at Sub-Registrar's office but due to absence of vendor, sale deed could not be executed. No written statement was filed by the vendor but the vendor filed a caveat petition and executed a sale deed in favour of a third party. This third party cannot be considered as *bona fide* purchaser. Readiness and willingness on the part of the vendee was proved and the vendee is entitled to decree of specific performance of contract.[27]

Plaintiff has not pleaded his willingness and readiness to pay the balance consideration money in the plaint. There is also no description of property, even place where it is situated in the agreement. Thus, no relief of specific performance was granted.[1]

Pleading and proof In a suit for specific performance plaintiff has to show that his conduct has been blemishless throughout. Provision imposes personal bar in the event plaintiff fails to do so. Dismissal of suit on the

24 *Gomathi Nayagam Pillai* v *Palaniswami Nadar* AIR 1967 SC 868; (1967)1 SCR 227; *Premraj* v *D.L.F. Housing* AIR 1968 SC 1355; (1968)3 SCR 648; *Ouseph Varghese* v *Joseph Alley* (1969)2 SCC 539; (1970)2 SCJ 703; (1970)1 SCR 921; *Surendra* v *Baikuntha* AIR 1973 Gau 21; *Idris Ali* v *Abdul Samad* AIR 1973 Gau 132; *Rajinder Raj* v *Rajdevi Rai* AIR 1974 All 294; 1974 All LJ 378; *Prabhakaran* v *Bhavani* AIR 1974 Ker 153; ILR (1974)2 Ker 82; 1974 Ker LT 115; *G. Shivayya* v *Shivappa Basappa* AIR 1978 Kant 98; ILR (1978)1 Kant 748; *Bhaurao* v *Mahadeo* AIR 1979 Bom 208; *Suraj* v *Sohan* AIR 1981 All 331; *Jagar Nath Mishra* v *Umar Mishra* 1981 All LJ 1; *Bijai Bahadur* v *Shri Shiv Kumar* AIR 1985 All 223; *Bhaskaran* v *George Joseph* AIR 1988 Ker 255; (1988)1 Ker LT 107; *Ayissabi* v *Gopala Konar* (1988)2 Cur Civ Cas 635 (Ker).

25 *H.G. Krishna Reddy* v *M.M. Thimmiah* AIR 1983 Mad 169; 96 Mad LW 88.

26 *Ayithi Appalanaidu* v *Petla Papamma* AIR 2011 AP 172.

27 *V. Krishnappa* v *J.C. Gangalakshmaiah* AIR 2018 Kant 113.

1 *Manohar Lal* v *Ramnihore* AIR 2011 Chh 111.

ground that requirements of s. 16(*c*) of the Specific Relief Act 1963 were not met was proper.[2]

Obligation upon the court The obligation imposed by s. 16 is upon the court not to grant specific performance to a plaintiff who has not met the requirements of cls. (*a*), (*b*) and (*c*) thereof. A court may not, therefore, grant to a plaintiff who has failed to aver and to prove that he has performed or has always been ready and willing to perform his part of the agreement the specific performance whereof he seeks. There is, therefore, no question of the plea being available to one defendant and not to another. It is open to any defendant to contend and establish that the mandatory requirement of s. 16(*c*) has not been complied with and it is for the court to determine whether it has or has not been complied with and, depending upon its conclusion, decree or decline to decree the suit.[3]

Suit for specific performance of contract—proof of readiness and willingness to perform The plaintiff in a suit of specific performance cannot succeed unless he proves that he is ready and willing to performs the contract.[4] Agreement was executed between parties stipulating terms of reconveyance on payment of loan amount by plaintiff to defendant. Notices were sent in time and again for execution of sale deed. Plaintiff deposited money before date fixed in judgment for specific performance. It could be referred that plaintiff was always ready and willing to discharge his obligation and perform his part of agreement. Plaintiff was entitled to decree for specific performance. For compliance of s. 16(*c*) of the Specific Relief Act 1963 it is not necessary for the plaintiff to over in the some words used in the section, i.e. ready and willing to perform the contract. Absence of the specific words in the plaint would not result in dismissal of the suit if sufficient facts and evidence are brought on record to satisfy the court the readiness and willingness to perform his part of the contract. The readiness and willingness of person seeking performance means that the person claiming performance has kept the contract subsisting with preparedness to fulfil his obligation and accept the performance when the time for performance arrives.[5] At the same time, the court should meticulously consider all facts and circumstances before granting specific performance. The court should take care to see that it is not used as an instrument of oppression to have an unfair advantage.[6]

2 *Sita Ram* v *Radhey Shyam* AIR 2008 SC 143.

3 *Ram Awadh* v *Achhaibar Dubey* (2000)2 SCC 428; *B. Vijaya Bharathi* v *P. Savitri* (2018)11 SCC 761.

4 *Pramod Building & Developers (P) Ltd.* v *Shanta Chopra* AIR 2011 SC 1424; (2011)4 SCC 741.

5 *Biswanath Ghosh* v *Gobinda Ghosh* AIR 2014 SC 1582; *Sugani* v *Rameshwar Das* AIR 2006 SC 2172.

6 *R. Deb and Associates* v *Sunanda Roy* (1996)4 SCC 423.

Ready and willing to perform The words "ready" and "willing" imply that the person was prepared to carry out the terms of the contract.[7] Concurrent findings of fact on record after consideration of evidence that the appellants-buyers were not ready and willing to perform terms and conditions of agreement for sale cannot be interfered with by the Supreme Court. Besides, buyers failed to pay balance consideration before agitating the matter before the Supreme Court.[8]

The basic principles behind s. 16(*c*) read with *Explanation* (*ii*) is that any person seeking benefit of the specific performance of contract must manifest that his conduct has been blemishless throughout entitling him to the specific relief. The provision imposes a personal bar. The court is to grant relief on the basis of the conduct of the person seeking relief. Where there is a clear averment in the plaint that the plaintiff purchaser was always ready to get the sale deed prepared after paying necessary consideration, order decreeing the suit for specific performance of contract in favour of the plaintiff is proper.[9]

A vendee sent a legal notice rescinding a contract and thereafter filed a suit claiming refund of advance paid by him. The suit was decreed by the trial court in his favour, but he himself being dissatisfied with the decree filed a revisional application against it. It can be said in such a case that he was not ready and willing to perform his part of the contract. Thus, no decree for specific performance could be passed in his favour. Suit filed by him would not be maintainable.[10]

For readiness and willingness to perform contract it is not necessary that entire amount of consideration should be kept ready by the plaintiff. The plaintiff failed to establish that he had been all along ready and willing to perform his part of contract. It would not be necessary to enter into question as to whether defendants were *bona fide* subsequent purchasers for value without notice or not. Defendants had been living in property in question for more than 30 years in their own right. Defendants cannot, therefore, be forced to vacate said property at this juncture. In the interest of justice court directed defendants to pay a sum of ₹60,000 to plaintiff which sum would include amount of advance paid by him.[11]

Ready and willing to perform—how to determine It is now well settled that the conduct of the parties, with a view to arrive at a finding as to whether the

7 *J.P. Builders* v *A. Ramadas Rao* (2011)1 SCC 429.
8 *A.K. Lakshmipathy* v *Rai Saheb Pannalal H. Lahoti Charitable Trust* AIR 2010 SC 577.
9 *Aniglase Yohannan* v *Ramlatha* AIR 2005 SC 3503; *Sugani* v *Rameshwar Das* AIR 2006 SC 2172.
10 *Pukhraj D. Jain* v *G. Gopalakrishna* AIR 2004 SC 3504; *Nanjachary* v *P. Chennaveerachasi* AIR 2015 Mad 73.
11 *Azhar Sultana* v *B. Rajamani* AIR 2009 SC 2157.

parties to the suit are all along and still are ready and willing to perform their part of contract as is mandatorily required under s. 16(*c*) of the Specific Relief Act must be determined having regard to the entire attending circumstances. A bare averment in the plaint or a statement made in the examination-in-chief would not suffice. The conduct of the parties must be judged having regard to the entirety of the pleadings as also the evidences brought on records.[12] In *Parasharam Sakharam Dhumal* v *Shamrao Mahadeo Dhumal,*[13] it was held that plaintiff neither tendered consideration amount nor he deposited said amount in court at the time of presentation of suit it showed that he was never ready to perform his part of contract.

'Readiness and willingness' is one of the criterion to grant specific performance. It is not necessary that vendee must have money in hand but atleast capacity to pay the balance consideration has to be proved. If vendee is unable to prove that he had money to make payment of the balance amount, he is not entitle to a decree of specific performance.[14]

Conduct of the parties The conduct of the parties is relevant and cannot be ignored while weighing the question of exercise of discretion for decreeing or denying a decree for specific performance.[15] The conduct must be blemishless throughout entitling him to the specific relief.[16]

Form of pleading—'readiness and willingness' The language in s. 16(*c*) does not require any specific phraseology but only that the plaintiff must aver that he has performed or has always been and is willing to perform his part of the contract. So the compliance of "readiness and willingness" has to be in spirit and substance and not in letter and form. So to insist for a mechanical production of the exact words of a statute is to insist for the form rather than the essence. So the absence of form cannot dissolve an essence if already pleaded.[17] In addition, not only should there be such an averment in the plaint but the surrounding circumstances must also indicate that the readiness and willingness continue from the date of the contract till the hearing of the suit.[18]

Compliance with s. 16(c) of the Act For the compliance with s. 16(*c*) of the Act it is not necessary for the plaintiff to aver in the same words used in the section, i.e. ready and willing to perform the contract. Absence of the specific words in the plaint would not result in dismissal of the suit if sufficient fact and evidence are brought on record to satisfy the court the readiness and willingness to perform his part of the contract.[19]

12 *Umabai* v *Nilkanth Dhondiba Chavan* (2005)6 SCC 243.
13 AIR 2018 Bom 202.
14 *Most. Mini Sinha* v *Smt. Reena Devi* AIR 2018 Pat 172.
15 *Silvey* v *Arun Varghese* (2008)11 SCC 45; AIR 2008 SC 1568.
16 *Aniglase Yohannan* v *Ramlatha* (2005)7 SCC 534; AIR 2005 SC 3503.
17 *Syed Dastagir* v *T.R. Gopalakrishna Setty* (1999)6 SCC 337.
18 *Pukhraj D. Jain* v *G. Gopalakrishna* (2004)7 SCC 251; AIR 2004 SC 3504.
19 *Biswanath Ghosh* v *Gobinda Ghosh* (2014)11 SCC 605; AIR 2014 SC 1582.

Averment to be made in plaint In a suit for specific performance averments are to be made as to readiness and willingness of the plaintiff. Suit was dismissed for want of pleadings and evidence. Finding was factually incorrect. Finding that plaintiff has not proved his capacity to perform as he has not deposited sale consideration within time granted by trial court was factually incorrect. Thus, the dismissal of suit was liable to set aside.[20]

Averment made in the plaint that plaintiff is and was ready to pay balance consideration and to comply with the terms of sale agreement was sufficient. Refusing decree on the ground that willingness to pay interest is not averred is improper. It is contrary to facts and materials on record.[21]

Respondent-purchaser pleading was that consideration offered was refused by the appellant seller on the ground that the agreement was fabricated. The appellant, however, adduced no evidence to substantiate his assertion. Concurrent finding about readiness and willingness was recorded in favour of the respondent. Mere absence of specific pleading about continued readiness and willingness to perform his part of agreement and availability of fund necessary for payment cannot be a ground to upset concurrent finding in second appeal.[22]

As far back as 1928, the Privy Council held—plaintiff must establish that he was since the date of the contract continuously ready and willing to perform his part of the contract. If he fails to do so, his claim for specific performance must fail ...... The plaintiff must plead and prove that he was ready and willing to perform his part of the contract continuously between the date of the contract and the date of hearing of the suit.[1]

But in *Bank of India* v *Jamsetji,*[2] Lord Macdermott said: "Even if plaintiff states that he had not sufficient ready money to meet the price and that no definite arrangements had been made for finding it at the time of repudiation, it was not relevant. To prove himself ready and willing a purchaser has not necessarily to produce the money or to vouch a concluded scheme for financing the transaction." Strangely enough, in this case no reference was made to *Ardeshir H. Mama* (supra).

In *Gomathinayagam Pillai* v *Palaniswami Nadar,*[3] the Supreme Court followed the proposition of *Ardeshir Mama*[4] but the majority did not even refer to the case of *Bank of India*. No specific case when is put forward by the

20 *Most. Etwart Devi* v *Most. Parvati Devi* AIR 2006 SC 970. See *H.P. Pyarejan* v *Dassappa* AIR 2006 SC 1144 (plaintiff shall aver and prove that he has performed his part of contract).

21 *Rameshwar Prasad* v *Basanti Lal* AIR 2008 SC 2050.

22 *Narinderjit Singh* v *North Star Estate Promoters Ltd.* AIR 2012 SC 2035.

1 *Ardeshir H. Mama* v *Flora Sassoon* AIR 1928 PC 208 at p. 216.

2 AIR 1950 PC 90.

3 AIR 1967 SC 868; (1967)1 SCR 227.

4 AIR 1928 PC 208.

plaintiff as to his willingness to purchase the property, the equitable relief of specific performance of contract of sale cannot be granted to the plaintiff.[5]

The Supreme Court in a later case reaffirmed the view that absence of pleading as to continuous readiness and willingness to perform his (plaintiff's) part of the contract entails dismissal of the suit.[6] As a matter of fact, continuous readiness and willingness on the part of the plaintiff is a condition precedent for obtaining a relief of grant of specific performance of contract.[7]

In a case for specific performance of contract plaintiff agreed to purchase shops from prospective purchasers who had agreed to purchase it from real owner. The plaintiff paid an advance to the said perspective purchaser. Rest of the balance price sent by the plaintiff to prospective purchaser by draft was returned unserved. The plaintiff sent no notice demanding conveyance to the prospective purchaser. He only lodged protest with the vendors. It was held that such a conduct of the plaintiff did not constitute any expression of readiness and willingness to perform his part of the contract and the plaintiff suit for specific performance was liable to be dismissed.[8]

In a particular fact/situation the averment about plaintiff's continuous readiness and willingness to perform his part of the contract may be unnecessary. It may be unnecessary to tender the consideration money or balance thereof to the promisor.

When in a suit for specific performance of contract of transfer or reconveyance the plaintiff is put into possession of the disputed property and entire consideration is already paid the averment about the continuous readiness and willingness to perform his part of the contract is not needed.[9]

In a Bombay case there was an agreement of reconveyance and entire consideration was already paid and nothing further was required to be done. It was held that the averment about continuous readiness and willingness is unnecessary.[10]

As to tendering the consideration or balance of consideration there is no strait-jacket rule on the point. Agreement was executed which contained a specific provision that immediately on receipt of intimation from the Rehabilitation Department for depositing $^{4}/_{5}$th of the amount of the price,

5 *Shanmugha Sundaram* v *A.S. Narayanaswami* AIR 1988 Mad 330; (1988)1 Mad LJ 56.

6 *Abdul Khader Rowther* v *P.K. Sarabai* AIR 1990 SC 682; (1989)4 SCC 313; JT 1989(3) SC 527.

7 *Azhar Sultana* v *B. Rajamani* (2009)17 SCC 27; AIR 2009 SC 2157.

8 *P. Saravanam* v *V.L. Thiyagraj* AIR 1988 NOC 40 (Kant).

9 *Trimbak Shankar* v *Nivratti Shankar* AIR 1985 Bom 128.

10 *Dagadu Bapu Shinde* v *Vasant Shankar Nimbalkar* AIR 1988 Bom 22; (1987)1 Bom CR 543.

the defendant should inform the plaintiff; but the defendant tried to keep the plaintiff in dark and did not give him opportunity to perform his part of the contract by making payment of balance amount of the price of the plot and instead himself deposited the balance amount and secured the sale certificate from the Department and the plaintiff, when he came to know about, promptly filed the suit for specific performance without losing any time. It is held that the contention of the defendant that the plaintiff had neither pleaded nor proved that he had sufficient financial resources with him or that he had tendered the amount of consideration to the defendant was without substance.[11]

In a case the vendee made an agreement to sell after obtaining partition and separation of his half share in the property in question. The sale deed was to be executed within one month of the decision of the suit for partition. The day that suit was dismissed for non-prosecution, the vendee filed the suit for an injunction restraining the vendor from transferring the property to anyone else. Soon thereafter the vendor transferred the property and, thus, prevented the vendee from performing his part of the contract. In these circumstances, the averment of the vendee that he was willing and ready to perform his part of the agreement and was still prepared to do so, was held to be sufficient compliance with the provisions of s. 16(*c*) and it was not incumbent upon him to further aver that he had made a demand upon the vendor to execute the sale deed on a particular date and to show that he had the money to offer to him on that particular date.[12]

The view that the averment "plaintiff is and has been ready and willing to perform his part of the contract" stems out of the principle that the plaint must show the plaintiff's intention to treat the contract as subsisting. This the plaintiff can do otherwise. Thus the view that the plaintiff must reproduce the very words used in s. 16(*c*), Specific Relief Act was mollified to a great extent when in a case,[13] it has been laid down that failure on the part of the plaintiff to reproduce in the plaint the exact words of the statute would not be fatal. All that is required is that the facts pleaded in the plaint and the other averments made therein should disclose substantial compliance with the requirements of the law. To insist on a mechanical reproduction of the exact words of the statute would be to insist on form rather than substance. If on an analysis of the facts averred in the plaint the court finds that even though the exact words of the statute are not reproduced, but the facts reveal that the plaintiff has performed all the essential terms and conditions of the contract up to the date of the institution of the suit and

11 *Surjeet Singh* v *Kartar Singh* AIR 1988 P&H 53; 1987 Punj LJ 184.
12 *Harbaksh Singh Gill* v *Ram Rattan* AIR 1988 Punj 60; (1987)91 Punj LR 185.
13 *Prem Raj* v *DLF Housing and Construction P. Ltd.* AIR 1968 SC 1355; (1968)3 SCR 648.

has shown his willingness to perform the remaining terms of the contract, the requirement of law, would stand satisfied.[14]

Readiness and willingness has to be adjudged in a broad perspective. The substantive provision in s. 16(*c*) of the Specific Relief Act does not insist upon a particular set of words to be used; the averment must in substance indicate the continuous readiness and willingness on the part of the person suing to perform his part of the contract.[15] Thus, in suitable cases it can be culled out from the totality of circumstances and the allegations made in the plaint. If the totality of circumstances and the allegations in the plaint disclose that the requirements of the statute are satisfied, the omission on the part of the plaintiff to adhere to the language or phraseology of the forms of the statute will be of no consequence.[16]

The provisions of s. 16(*c*) of the Specific Relief Act should be used only as a step in aid of justice and not as a road-block to justice.[17] When a defendant, who participated in the trial without any objection regarding absence of plea of readiness and willingness and suffered a decree, raises such a plea in appeal the court should not throw out the plaint but should give him a reasonable opportunity to make good the defect.[18] That means the defect even if it is there is only curable and not fatal. In this case there was no such defect also to be cured.[19]

In a suit for specific performance of a contract of sale of land it need not be stated in so many words that the plaintiff was continuously ready and willing to perform his part of the contract. It is enough if it is made clear in the recitals of the plaint that he was so.[20] But when a plaintiff seeks relief of specific performance it is incumbent on him affirmatively to establish that all through he was willing to perform his part of the contract and failure to do so may in an appropriate case disentitle him to relief. On facts

14 *Rajya Tulsibhai* v *Benar Enterprise* AIR 1988 Guj 42; (1987)2 28 Guj LR 1082.

15 *Krishnan Kesavan* v *Kochukunju Karunakaran* AIR 1988 Ker 107; see also *Anwarul Haq* v *Nizam Uddin* AIR 1984 All 136; *Mani Amma* v *Kololichalil Choyi* 1983 Ker LJ 246. Relying on *Ramesh Chandra* v *Chunilal* AIR 1971 SC 1238; (1971)2 SCR 573; (1970)3 SCC 140.

16 *Rajya Tulsibhai* v *Benar Enterprise* AIR 1988 Guj 42; *Dhian Singh* v *Tara Chand* AIR 1984 All 4; *Anwarul Haq* v *Nizam Uddin* AIR 1984 All 136; *Krishnan Kesavan* v *Kochukunju Karunakaran* AIR 1988 Ker 107; see also *Anwarul Haq* v *Nizam Uddin* AIR 1984 All 136; *Mani Amma* v *Kololichalil Choyi* 1983 Ker LJ 246. Relying on *Ramesh Chandra* v *Chunilal* AIR 1971 SC 1238; (1971)2 SCR 573; (1970)3 SCC 140.

17 *Kalipada Das* v *Bimal Krishna Sen Gupta* AIR 1983 SC 876; (1983)1 SCC 14; 1982 UJ (SC) 866.

18 *Byomkesh* v *Nani Gopal Banik* AIR 1987 Cal 92.

19 *Krishnan Kesavan* v *Kochukunju Karunakaran* AIR 1988 Ker 107 (111); 1987 Ker LJ 1085.

20 *Prag Dutt* v *Saraswati Devi* AIR 1982 All 37; *Devaram* v *Lajya Wanti* (1985)2 Cur Civ Cas 125 (Del).

held that the plaintiff was not ready and willing to perform his part of the contract.[1]

Commenting upon *Ramesh Chandra Chandiok*, the Madras High Court has observed that the observations related to the mode of proof only and did not in any way detract from the ratio.[2]

It is settled law that pleadings cannot be interpreted in a pedantic manner. The court should be slow to throw out a claim on a mere technicality of pleading when the substance of the thing is there and no prejudice is caused to the other side, however, clumsily or inartistically the plaint may be worded.[3]

Pleadings are loosely drafted in courts and the courts should not scrutinise it with such meticulous care so as to result in genuine claims being defeated on trivial grounds.[4] Pleadings are not statutes and legalism is not verbalism, common sense should not be kept in cold storage when pleadings are construed. Parties win or lose on substantial questions not 'technical-tortures' and court cannot be abettors.[5] Pleadings have to be interpreted not with formalistic rigour but with latitude or awareness or low legal literacy of poor people.[6] In order to have a fair trial essential material facts should be stated. But, pleadings should receive a liberal construction.[7]

In *Rathnasabapathi Pillai* v *Ramasami*,[8] a Bench of the High Court of Madras observed as follows:

> "In our view, the court need not insist that the very language of the section should be repeated in the plaint. After all, the intendment behind the statutory provision is to find out as to whether the plaintiff treated and treats the contract at all relevant points of time as subsisting on the basis of which alone he can ask for specific performance of the contract. Pleadings need not be thrown out on the simple ground that the plaintiff has not borrowed the language of the statutory provisions. If, on a comprehensive

1 *Sandhya Rani* v *Sudha Rani* AIR 1978 SC 537; (1978)2 SCR 839; (1978)2 SCC 116.

2 *Ardeshir* v *Flora Sassoon* AIR 1928 PC 208; *Gomathi Nayagam Pillai* v *Palaniswami Nadar* AIR 1967 SC 868; (1967)1 SCR 227; *Premraj* v *DLF* AIR 1968 SC 1355; (1968)3 SCR 648. See also *Krishna Reddy* v *Thimmiah* AIR 1983 Mad 169.

3 *Kedar Lal* v *Hari Lal* AIR 1952 SC 47; 1952 SCJ 37; 1952 SCR 179; (1952)1 Mad LJ 431.

4 *Madan Gopal* v *Mamraj* AIR 1976 SC 461; (1977)1 SCC 669; *Ganesh Trading* v *Moji Ram* AIR 1978 SC 484; (1978)2 SCC 91; (1978)2 SCR 614; (1978)2 SCJ 98; *Kishori* v *Tincori* AIR 1980 Cal 204.

5 *S.B. Noranah* v *Prem Kumari* AIR 1980 SC 193; (1980)1 SCR 281; (1980)1 SCC 52.

6 *Manjushree Raha* v *B.L. Gupta* AIR 1977 SC 1158; (1977)2 SCR 944; (1977)2 SCC 174.

7 *Ram Sarup Gupta* v *Bishun Narain Inter College* AIR 1987 SC 1242; (1987)2 SCJ 279; (1987)2 UJ (SC) 162; (1987)2 SCC 555.

8 (1910) ILR 33 Mad 452; 20 MLJ 301.

reading of the plaint allegations the plaintiff has clearly made out that he has always been ready and willing to perform the essential terms of the contract, that would suffice the requirement of making averments under s. 16(c) of the Act. In our opinion, the averments in the plaint are adequate and unambiguous to the effect required by s. 16(c) of the Act."

In considering the plea in any pleadings, the court must keep in mind that the plea is not an expression of art and science, but an expression through words to place fact and law of one's case for a relief. Such an expression may be pointed, precise, sometimes vague, but still can be gathered what he wants to convey from the pleadings read as a whole.[9] The averment of readiness and willingness in a plaint is not a mathematical formula. If the averments read as a whole clearly indicate the readiness and willingness, the fact that they are differently worded will not militate against readiness and willingness and will not disentitle the plaintiff to the relief of specific performance.[10] It will be the height of injustice to throw out the plaint for technical non-compliance with s. 16(*c*) of the Specific Relief Act for not reproducing the exact words thereof when all the essential facts are already in the plaint.[11] Even though the expression "willing" is not used in the pleadings, if in special sense the plaintiff has averred that he has been and is being willing and ready to perform his part of the contract, it is sufficient.[12]

Readiness and willingness—views of different High Courts The views of the different High Courts are set out below:

Allahabad Section 16(*c*) is mandatory,[13] but in *Prag Dutt* v *Saraswati Devi.*[14] S.J. Hyder, J observed:

"......The requirements of s. 16(c) and of Form 47 of Appendix A to Civil Procedure Code are not to be interpreted narrowly and in a hypertechnical manner. It is the substance of the matter which is of importance. If from the averments made in the plaint and the surrounding circumstances, it is established in substance that the plaintiff was ready and willing to perform his part of the contract and had remained ready and willing to perform the

9 *Syed Dastagir* v *T.R. Gopalakrishna Setty* AIR 1999 SC 3029; (1999)6 SCC 337; JT 1999(5) SC 642.

10 *Motilal Jain* v *Smt. Ramdasi Devi* (2000)1 LW 388 (SC); AIR 2000 SC 2408.

11 *Unni Madhavan Nair* v *Kamalakshy* AIR 1993 Ker 357.

12 *Nambarukanda Marakkar* v *Nallithodi Thavalaparambil Appu* AIR 1991 Ker 1.

13 *Rajendra Prasad Rai* v *Rajdeva Rai* AIR 1974 All 294; *Manohar Lal* v *Rajeshwari Devi* AIR 1977 All 36; *Mahmood Khan* v *Ayub Khan* AIR 1978 All 463 (DB); *Suraj Singh* v *Sohanlal* AIR 1981 All 330; *Narendra Bahadur Singh* v *Baij Nath Singh* AIR 1981 All 410; *Oudh Behari Lal* v *Radha Kishan* 1981 All LJ 62; *Ganesh Prasad* v *Saraswati Devi* AIR 1982 All 47; *Bhorey Nirottam Das* v *Mool Chand* 1982 All LJ 1049; *Shamsher Bahadur Sinha* v *Raghu Nath Prasad Saxena* 1982 All LJ 948; *Rahat Jan* v *Hafiz Mohd. Usman* AIR 1983 All 343.

14 AIR 1982 All 37; *Devaram* v *Lajya Wanti* (1985)2 Cur Civ Cas 125 (Del).

same throughout, it would not be proper to non-suit him on a verbal omission here or there. It has to be remembered that s. 16(c) or Form 47 of Appendix A of Civil Procedure Code does not provide for booby trap of which an unscrupulous litigant should be allowed to take advantage."

In *Dhian Singh* v *Tara Chand*,[15] it is admitted that the plaintiff did not make any averment regarding his being ready and willing to perform his part of the contract, although it was averred that he had been ready and willing to perform his part of the contract prior to the institution of the suit and had also furnished proof that he was and continued to be ready and willing to perform his part under the contract. The defendant contended that this failure to aver was fatal to the plaintiff's suit.

Rejecting the contention, B.D. Agrawal, J held: Section 16(*c*) does not insist upon a particular set of words being employed; the averment according to s. 16(*c*) must in substance indicate the continuous readiness and willingness on the part of the person suing. The Form prescribed under Or. 6, r. 3, CPC is procedural; it is a rule of pleading; this has for its object the advance of the cause of justice and is not intended to short-circuit decision on merits. It is procedure, something designed to facilitate justice and further its end, not a penal enactment.[16] The proper approach to matters of this kind is laid by the Supreme Court in *Ramesh Chandra Chandiok* v *Chuni Lal*[17] 'Readiness and willingness cannot be treated as a strait-jacket formula. These have to be determined from the entirety of facts and circumstances relevant to the intention and conduct of the party concerned.' ......To my mind the dictum of the Supreme Court quoted above clearly points the broad perspective in the light whereof the issue covering the averments as well as the proof has to be adjudged. It would be much too artificial and highly technical to draw a dichotomy in construing the pleading on the one hand and in appreciating the evidence on the other. The strait-jacket formula discarded for purposes of appreciation of evidence cannot be adopted as good to construe the pleadings which, as is well known, seldom conform strictly to the exemplars contained in various Forms incorporated in Appendix A of the First Schedule of the Code of Civil Procedure.[18] In common sense the meaning of such an averment of readiness and willingness must be that the non-compliance of the contract was not the fault of the plaintiffs and that they were disposed and able to complete it if it had not been renounced by the defendant ...... If that is the true test,

15 AIR 1984 All 4.

16 *Smt. Dipo* v *Wassan Singh* AIR 1983 SC 846; (1983)3 SCR 20; (1983)3 SCC 376; *Kalipada Das* v *B.K. Sen Gupta* AIR 1983 SC 876; (1983)1 SCC 14; *Sangram Singh* v *Election Tribunal* AIR 1955 SC 425; (1955)2 SCR 1; 1955 SCJ 431.

17 AIR 1971 SC 1238; (1971)2 SCR 573; (1970)3 SCC 140.

18 *Sharda Prasad Singh* v *Sheo Shanker Lal* 1982 All CJ 80; *Prag Dutt* v *Saraswati Devi* AIR 1982 All 37; *Kamdev Nath Choudhury* v *Devendra Kumar Nath* AIR 1979 Gau 65; *Cort* v *Ambergate etc. Rly. Co.* [1851]117 ER 1229.

it is enough compliance of s. 16, if it is asserted in a plaint that the plaintiff was not responsible for non-completion of the contract and he was disposed and able to complete it had it not been renounced by the defendant.[19]

Where the plaintiff neither made any averment as to his readiness and willingness, nor stated anything about this in his evidence but merely stating that he was ready to pay the money and get the sale deed executed on the date the statement was recorded, *held* the statement was not sufficient to meet the requirements of law.[20]

Where under a compromise decree, the defendant was obliged to offer the property to the plaintiff first before offering the same to a third person and did offer the same to the plaintiff; but the plaintiff instead of accepting the offer challenged the power of the defendant to sell any portion of the disputed property and set up himself as sole owner of the property to the exclusion of the defendant, *held*, plaintiff was not ready and willing to perform his part of the contract.[1]

Where the plaint alleged—

> "That when the plaintiffs asked the defendant several times to execute the sale deed but he continued to prevaricate. At last the plaintiffs gave a registered notice ...... with acknowledgment due in which they made it clear that the defendant should execute the sale deed in their favour within a week and that the said notice was refused by him....."

Held, the averment did not comply with the provisions of s. 16(*c*) and rendered the plaint without a cause of action for a suit for specific performance.[2]

Andhra Pradesh Where from the evidence and the nature of the defence, it cannot be inferred that the defendant had waived any of the essential terms of the contract, and the plaintiff's positive case that he has already performed his part of the contract of payment of the entire consideration was found to be false, in absence of the plea by the plaintiff that he is still ready and willing to pay consideration and has necessary capacity to raise the funds, the court cannot reconstruct the terms of contract and direct payment of amount of consideration.[3]

19 *Premraj* v *D.L.F. Housing & Construction P. Ltd.* AIR 1968 SC 1355; (1968)3 SCR 648; *Ouseph Varghese* v *Joseph Alley* (1970)1 SCR 921; *Narendra Bahadur Singh* v *Baij Nath Singh* AIR 1981 All 410 and *Mahmood Khan* v *Ayub Khan* AIR 1978 All 463 rest upon the particular state of pleadings in individual cases. It is submitted that the distinction is without a difference. If the learned Judge wanted to dissent from the Bench decisions, comity required the matter to be referred to a larger bench.

20 *Mukhtiar Singh* v *Dharmpal Singh* 1981 All LJ 119 (DB).

1 *Bhagwan Ram* v *Parbhu Ram* 1983 All LJ 637.

2 *Jagarnath Misra* v *Umar Misra* 1981 All LJ 1 (DB).

3 *G. Rosaiah* v *C. Balarami Reddy* AIR 1989 AP 179.

Calcutta If the plaintiff can show that he was in a position to raise the money required at or about the time when the contract was to be performed he discharges the obligation of proving readiness and willingness so far as the financial aspect is concerned.[4] The plaintiff must prove his continuous readiness and willingness to perform his part of contract till the date of hearing.[5]

Even though it is not necessary actually to tender the money, the plaintiff must be ready and willing to perform his part of the contract. Where plaintiff alleges that he paid some money which is however denied by the defendant and it is proved that he did not pay the money he cannot be said to be ready and willing to perform his part of the contract.[6]

Gauhati Where the plaintiff fails to aver and prove his readiness and willingness to perform his part of the contract, the suit will fail.[7]

If the plaint does not contain the specific words as set out in the forms and/or specific words "readiness and willingness" on the part of the plaintiff but read as a whole it appears to the court that it complies with the provisions of law in substance, the plaint should not be thrown out. It is enough compliance of s. 16 if it is asserted in a plaint that the plaintiff was not responsible for non-compliance of the contract and he was disposed and able to complete it, had it not been renounced by the defendant,[8] (the act of deposit of the consideration money into court is full and complete compliance of the provisions of s. 16, even though no specific averment regarding readiness and willingness made) relying on *Cort* v *Ambergate etc. Railway Co.*,[9] *Kedar Lal Seal* v *Hari Lal Seal*[10] and *Ganesh Trading Co.* v *Moji Ram.*[11]

Gujarat Absence of averment as to continuous readiness and willingness to perform his part of the contract in the plaint tentamounts to absence of disclosure of the cause of action entailing rejection of plaint. However if the totality of the averments spell out the continuous readiness and willingness to perform his part of the contract, it is enough.[12]

4 *Jitendra Nath Roy* v *Maheshwari Bose* AIR 1965 Cal 45 at p. 50 (DB). (*Held* on facts plaintiff was not ready and willing) following *Ardeshir Mama* v *Flora Sassoon* AIR 1928 PC 208; *Bank of India Ltd.* v *Jamsetji A.H. Chinoy* AIR 1950 PC 90 and *Subeyya Chowdary* v *Veeraya* AIR 1957 AP 307.
5 *P.G. Sinha* v *Commodore K.C. Chatterjee* AIR 1991 Cal 327.
6 *Sahida Bibi* v *Sk. Golam Muhammad* AIR 1983 Cal 216 (DB); *Manik Chandra Bhowmik* v *Abhoy Charan Gope* AIR 1917 Cal 283 (DB); *Srish* v *Banomali* 31 Cal 584 at p. 596 (PC).
7 *Surendra Chandra Roy* v *Baikuntha Chandra Roy* AIR 1973 Gau 21.
8 *Kamdev Nath Choudhury* v *Devendra Kumar Nath* AIR 1979 Gau 65 at pp. 66-67.
9 [1851]117 ER 1229 at p. 1236.
10 AIR 1952 SC 47; 1952 SCR 179; 1952 SCJ 37.
11 AIR 1978 SC 484; (1978)2 SCR 614; (1978)2 SCC 91.
12 *Rajya Tulsi Bai* v *Benar Enterprise* AIR 1988 Guj 42.

Himachal Pradesh It is incumbent upon the buyer to satisfy the court that he was ready and willing with the money or had the capacity to pay for the property and that he had at all events made proper and reasonable preparations and arrangement for securing the purchase money.[13]

Karnataka Simply because the plaintiff had deposited the balance consideration for the sale of property during the pendency of the suit without there being any averment regarding the readiness and willingness in the plaint or because the plaintiff had shown his readiness and willingness in his notice to the defendant is not sufficient compliance with s. 16(*c*).[14]

If the plaintiff had deposited the balance money after 4$^1/_2$ years though the agreement provided for payment within one year it could not be said that the plaintiff was willing or ready to perform his part of the contract and accordingly such suit for specific performance could not be decreed.[14]

Kerala Section 16(*c*) is not an empty formality and the averment with regard to the willingness and readiness of the plaintiff to perform his part of the contract is indeed essential to sustain an action for specific performance.[15]

Madhya Pradesh In a suit for specific performance, it need not be stated in so many words that the plaintiff was continuously ready and willing to perform the contract: it is enough if it was made clear in the recitals in the plaint that he was so willing.[16]

Madras Section 16(*c*) is prohibitory in that a duty is cast on courts by a public statute that specific performance of a contract cannot be granted in favour of a person unless he avers and proves his readiness and willingness to perform his part of the contract. That being the nature of the statute, it would be the duty of the court to see whether the person who seeks to enforce the contract satisfied the mandatory provisions of s. 16 of the Specific Relief Act 1963. The Privy Council and the Supreme Court have interpreted the section to mean that if the conditions are not satisfied the court is bound to dismiss the suit.[17]

Failure to plead the statutory requirement in accordance with s. 16(*c*) of the Specific Relief Act will result in declining the benefit of s. 53A of the

13 *Rakha Singh* v *Santokha* AIR 1976 HP 66 at pp. 67-68.

14 *Gurupadayya Shivayya Hiremath* v *Shivappa Basappa Guramanvar* AIR 1978 Kant 98.

15 *Prabhakaran* v *Bhavani* AIR 1974 Ker 153 at p. 154; *Govindan Vishnu Namboodiri* v *Ulahannan Mathan* AIR 1988 NOC 42 (Ker); 1987 Ker LJ 1102.

16 *Badruddin* v *Tufail Ahmad* AIR 1963 MP 31 following *Subeyya* v *Veeraya* AIR 1957 AP 307.

17 *H.G. Krishna Reddy & Co.* v *M.M. Thimmiah* AIR 1983 Mad 169 (DB) at p. 181 applying *Shiba Prasad Singh* v *Srish Chandra* AIR 1949 PC 297 (s. 72 of the Contract Act) and *Surajmull Nagoremull* v *Triton Insurance Co. Ltd.* AIR 1925 PC 83 (contract of sea insurance without expressing it in the policy of insurance as provided in s. 7 of the Stamp Act 1899).

Transfer of Property Act.[18] The pleading under s. 53A of the Transfer of Property Act must be in accordance with s. 16(*c*) of the Specific Relief Act. The averments in the written statement was that the defendant intended to file the suit for specific performance to enforce the covenant for renewal of the lease but failed to file the suit and this conduct showed that their readiness and willingness had fallen to ground.[18]

Orissa Where the plaintiff does not assert that he was ready and willing to perform his part continuously between the date of the contract and the date of hearing of the suit and the only averment is that he is ready and willing to pay the consideration money, it is not necessary for the contesting defendant to make any assertion to traverse such facts in his written statement and the absence of any averment to that effect in the written statement is of no consequence.[19]

However, mere non-mention of the fact that the plaintiff has always been ready and willing to perform his part of the contract in the notice would not deprive him of the relief.[20]

Patna Even if the plaintiff has led evidence to prove that he was ready and willing to perform the contract, but does not make averment to that effect in the plaint, he will not be allowed to amend the plaint if in the meantime time prescribed for filing the suit has expired,[1] court held that even if the plaintiff brings in his evidence the ingredients of s. 16(*c*), it only satisfies a part of the section, leaving the other part, that is, averment in the plaint unfulfilled.

Rajasthan Section 16(*c*) lays down a condition precedent to the enforcement of a contract. It is based on the maxim "who seeks equity, must do equity", and more so in the case of specific performance. The law is well settled that the plaintiff must aver and prove that he was ready and willing to perform the essential terms of the contract which he was required to perform. However, it depends upon the facts and circumstances of each case whether this has been done or not. But while doing so one cannot lose sight of the provisions of Or. 8, rr. 3 and 5 of the CPC.[2]

Some more examples Where the plaintiff stated that he was ready and willing to pay the amount as the court may deem payable, it cannot be held that he was not ready or willing to pay.[3]

18 *S. Sivakumar* v *Bharat Petroleum Corporation Ltd.* (1997)3 LW 520 (Mad).
19 *Durjyodhan Palei* v *Padana Charan Dass* AIR 1978 Ori 5 at p. 7.
20 *Hadupani Sabato* v *Ganta Ratnam* AIR 1981 Ori 42 (DB).
1 *Ram Singhasan Choubey* v *Sudama Prasad Sah* AIR 1982 Pat 200 following *Mahmood Khan* v *Ayub Khan* AIR 1978 All 463.
2 *Kirpal Singh* v *Kartaro* AIR 1980 Raj 212 (DB).
3 *Chandrabali Shah* v *Pritam Singh* AIR 1965 Pat 211.

In *Sankatha Prasad* v *Abdul Aziz Khan*[4] the plaint contained this allegation: "The defendant neither showed the title deeds nor executed the sale deed in favour of the plaintiff. Therefore on 13th November 1962 the plaintiff sent notice to the defendant requiring him to execute the sale deed in favour of the plaintiff within a week after showing the title deeds etc." *Held*, it did not comply with s. 16(*c*).

In *Biswanath Mahto* v *Janki Devi*[5] plaintiff falsely alleged that out of the total consideration of ₹7,200, he had paid ₹200 to the defendant and that a sum of ₹2,400 was payable to a prior mortgagee. *Held* plaintiff was not ready and willing.

Where the plaintiff alleges that the consideration payable by him is different from the real amount, but that he has no objection to paying the defendant any sum that the court may fix, readiness will be inferred.[6]

Likewise, if the defendant is unwilling to carry out his part of the commitment, it would be highly inequitable to call upon the plaintiff to take the hazard of making payment to the defendant in the full belief that the latter would not recover the property to him and he will have to knock at the door of the court for specific performance. Contracts based on such clauses as "At any time within five years from today if you return the consideration money, I shall be bound to execute a reconveyance in your favour. Otherwise, you will have the right to get the deed of reconveyance through court" fall under s. 51 rather than under s. 55 of the Contract Act.[7]

Where the plaintiff fails to appear in the witness box and depose that he has always been ready and willing to perform his part of the contract, it was held that the plaintiff failed to prove his readiness and willingness.[8] The plaint mentioned that the plaintiff convened the panchayat thrice and the defendant agreed to execute the conveyance, but sold the property to someone else, it was held that there was sufficient compliance on the part of the plaintiff for making the necessary averments.[9]

Where there was averment in the plaint that the plaintiff had been and was ready to perform his part of the contract, the absence of an expression "willing" could not be said to be fatal on the basis of the pleadings read as a whole.[10]

When vendor did not execute sale deed, vendee had sent notice to him for execution of sale deed and remained present in Sub-Registrar office on

4 AIR 1976 All 95.
5 AIR 1978 Pat 190.
6 *Arjuna* v *Lakshmi* AIR 1949 Mad 265.
7 *Benode Behari Das Gupta* v *Benoy Bhusan Choudhury* AIR 1973 Gau 66 (DB).
8 *SKM Mohamed Amanullah* v *TCS Rama Sangama Pandian* (1994)2 SCC 289.
9 *Nallaya Gounder* v *P. Ramasami Gounder* AIR 1993 Mad 275.
10 *N. Marakkar* v *N.T. Appu* AIR 1991 Ker 1.

date as per notice. Facts were proved properly and sufficiently by vendee by evidences which were not controverted by vendor. Readiness and willingness of vendee to perform his part of contract were also proved.[11]

As per condition of contract vendors agreed to sell property free from all encumbrances. Vendee demanded income tax clearance certificate and vacant and peaceful possession of property after eviction of tenants. Delay was caused in obtaining sale deed for reason of non-fulfilment of the said condition. Vendee cannot be blamed for the said delay. It cannot be said that vendee was not ready and willing to perform his part of contract. Thus, vendee was entitled to relief.[12]

Relief was claimed on the basis of acknowledgment receipt of earnest money in connection with an oral agreement to sale. Interpolations/ overwritings were made in acknowledgment receipt. These raised suspicion as to the validity of the contract. Thus, vendee was not entitled to any relief claimed. There was also lack of pleading of readiness and willingness on the part of the vendee to perform his part of contract.[13]

Plaintiffs stated in plaint that they were always ready with fund and are still ready and willing to complete the sale transaction are payment of balance consideration money. But they failed to aver and prove that they have recovered possession of suit premises from unauthorised occupier thereof. Defendant had no notice of earlier sale agreement between plaintiff and his vendors. Defendant was a *bona fide* purchaser for value without notice of earlier agreement for sale. This comes within exception clause mentioned in s. 19(*b*) of the Specific Relief Act 1963 and as such suit for specific performance of contract was not maintainable against defendant. Plaintiffs made deliberate wrong statement in plaint that they got possession of suit premises from vendor and also sought for relief to protect their possession therein. Plaintiffs did approach the court seeking equitable relief of specific performance with clean hands. Thus, refusal to grant relief was held to be proper.[14]

Some more decisions of the Apex Court

Specific performance decreed The plaintiff had paid ₹3,000 as earnest money and averred that he was ready to deposit the balance of sale consideration of ₹9,000 and to get the sale deed executed and registered in his favour. Plaintiff had also deposited the said sum of ₹9,000 in the court within the time allowed by the trial court which decreed the suit for specific performance. The High Court reversed the judgment and decree on the

11 *Dharmveer* v *Suresh Chandra Bhardwaj* AIR 2016 All 48.
12 *Mohammed Abdul Azeem* v *South India Prime Tannery Pvt. Ltd.* AIR 2016 Hyd 170.
13 *Diwakar Mullick* v *Ganga Khandelwal* AIR 2016 Chh 53; see *Daya Ram Soni* v *Gyarsi Bai Khandelwal* AIR 2016 Chh 73.
14 *Palay Dutta* v *Md. Ali Afsar* AIR 2016 Cal 199.

ground that the plaintiff did not pay sufficient court fee on the date of presenting the plaint and the deficit was made good sometime thereafter. This was not a proper ground for refusing specific performance. However, taking in view the long lapse of time, the Supreme Court directed the plaintiff to pay an additional sum of ₹12,000 to the credit of the suit.[15]

The plaintiff was present at the Sub-Registrar's office on the date agreed upon to execute and register the deed of sale. But the vendor did not appear. At the request of the buyer, the Sub-Registrar had entered his attendance in the office register. It was held that the buyer was ready and willing to perform his part of the contract and has necessary funds for payment. The suit was decreed for specific performance.[16]

The plaint averred that the purchaser sent registered notices to the seller to execute the deed of sale, that he was willing to pay the fees required to pay the cost of registration and the balance of amount of sale consideration. He also deposed to that effect before the court. It was held that the buyer had not only averred but also proved that he was ready and willing to perform his part of the contract as required under s. 16(*c*) of the Specific Relief Act.[17]

The compliance of readiness and willingness has to be in spirit and substance and not in letter and form. Plaintiff recited that all the balance amount of consideration under the contract were paid to the vendor except ₹120 which he tendered in court. It was held that the provisions of s. 16(*c*) of the Specific Relief Act cannot be said to be not complied with. The order of the High Court was set aside and the suit was decreed.[18]

Agreement for reconveyance The suit was for specific performance of an agreement for reconveyance filed within three years from the stipulated period or from the date of refusal to perform the contract, by a person who was subsequently declared insolvent. The adjudication was annulled unconditionally and it was held that the suit was maintainable and a decree for reconveyance and specific performance was passed.[19]

The plaint clearly indicated the plaintiff's readiness and willingness to perform his part of the contract. The only obligation was complying with the payment of the balance of ₹8,000 which, according to the plaintiff, he

15 *Suriya Narayan Upadhyaya* v *Ram Rup Pandey* AIR 1994 SC 105; 1995 Supp (4) SCC 542.

16 *Sukhbir Singh* v *Brij Pal Singh* AIR 1996 SC 2510; (1997)2 SCC 200; JT 1996(6) SC 389.

17 *Pandurang Ganpat Tanawade* v *Ganpat Bhairu Kadam* AIR 1997 SC 463; (1996)10 SCC 51; JT 1996(9) SC 18.

18 *Syed Dastagir* v *T.R. Gopalakrishna Setti* AIR 1999 SC 3029; (1999)6 SCC 337; JT 1999(5) SC 642.

19 *Sri Babu Ram* v *Sri Indra Pal Singh (died by LRs)* (1999)1 LW 729 (SC).

called upon the defendant to receive and execute the deed of sale. The plaintiff had parted with two-thirds of the consideration at that time and Their Lordships held that there was no reason why he would not pay the balance of $^1/_3$rd consideration to have the property conveyed to him. In the circumstances the suit filed nine months after the last notice was held not belated as to deny the relief for specific performance.[20]

There was a concurrent finding by the trial court and the first appellate court that the plaintiffs were ready and willing to perform their part of the contract. The fact that he had not offered the amount of consideration to the defendant nor deposited the amount before the court was held inconsequential in view of Explanation (*i*) of s. 16(*c*) of the Specific Relief Act and the decree for specific performance was confirmed.[1]

Where the agreement for sale specified that the sale was to be finalised within 60 days after the vendor obtained and handed over to the vendee their documents of title, it was held that the obligation to execute the deed would arise only after the documents were delivered to the plaintiff by the defendants and it could not be said that the plaintiff was not ready and willing and had delayed execution of the deed of sale.[2]

This is an interesting case where the agreement was for reconveyance. The trial court as well as the High Court dismissed the suit on the ground that time was the essence of the contract and the plaintiff was not ready and willing to perform his part of the contract. The Supreme Court held that in an agreement for reconveyance time is not always the essence of the agreement unless there are special facts and circumstances which must be pleaded and the issue raised. There in that case, there was no express plea in the written statement nor any issue raised in that behalf. The Supreme Court therefore held that the plaintiff was ready and willing to perform his part of the contract. The amount payable for reconveyance was a sum of ₹4,000. The learned Judges asked the counsel for the appellant as to what amount his client was willing to pay and the learned counsel in fairness stated that the appellant was willing to pay a sum of ₹40,000 in lump sum. Their Lordships considered the offer very fair and held that ends of justice and equity would require and be met by directing the appellant to deposit the sum of ₹40,000 in the trial court within a period of six months and on the appellant so depositing, the respondent was directed to produce his title deeds and reconvey the property, and in case he refused to do so, the trial court shall execute the deed of reconveyance.[3] Time stipulated for

20 *Motilal Jain* v *Smt. Ramdassi Devi* AIR 2000 SC 2408; (2000)6 SCC 420; JT 2000(8) SC 59.

1 *Boramma* v *Krishna Gowda* (2000)9 SCC 214; JT 2000(8) SC 13.

2 *A. Abdul Rasheed Khan* v *P.A.K.A. Shahul Hamid* (2000)10 SCC 636; JT 2000(7) SC 483.

3 *B.B. Jaibunisha* v *Jagdish Pandit* (1997)2 LW 257 (SC).

reconveyance is the essence of the contract.[4] The law on the subject is fairly well settled.[5]

Substantial question of law The suit was for specific performance of an agreement of sale. The trial court as well as the appellate court found that time was not of the essence of the contract and the plaintiff was always ready and willing to preform his part of the contract. In the second appeal, the High Court framed the following "substantial question of law":[6]

> Whether in the circumstances of the case, the plaintiff has established that he has been ready and willing to perform her part of the contract?

The High Court answered the question in the negative. Consequently the appeal was allowed. The Supreme Court came down heavily on the High Court and observed, "we have noted with distress that despite amendment, the provisions of s. 100 of the CPC have been liberally construed and generously applied by some Judges of the High Court with the result that the objective intended to be achieved by the amendment of s. 100 appears to have been frustrated." Their Lordships pointed out that the question of law formulated in this case as "substantial question of law" cannot in any way be termed to be a question of law much less as "substantial question of law". Their Lordships concluded that the High Court was not justified in disturbing the finding of fact arrived at on appreciation of evidence while disposing of the second appeal and held that the impugned judgment of the High Court being against the settled provisions of law, was not sustainable.

Thus, the question as to whether the plaintiff was ready and willing to perform its part of contract by itself may not give rise to a substantial question of law. Substantial question of law should be formulated relying on findings of fact arrived at by trial court and the First Appellate Court.[7]

Both the trial court and the First Appellate Court, on consideration of all the evidence, came to the conclusion that the appellant was ready and willing to perform his obligation under the agreement and was entitled to specific performance of it. The error committed by the High Court in second appeal was in disturbing the concurrent finding of fact merely on a construction of the plaint on a point not raised by the respondent at any stage of the proceedings. The Supreme Court pointed out that it was not the respondent's responsibility to state either in the written statement or in the trial court or in the First Appellate Court that the appellant was not

4 *Raj Kishore* v *Prem Singh* (2011)1 SCC 657.

5 *Chunchun Jha* v *Ebadat Ali* AIR 1954 SC 345; *Bismillah Begum* v *Rahmatullah Khan* (1998)2 SCC 226; *Gauri Shankar Prasad* v *Brahma Nand Singh* (2008)8 SCC 287.

6 *Veerayee Ammal* v *Seeni Ammal* (2002)1 LW 594 (SC); AIR 2001 SC 2920.

7 *Abdul Rahem* v *Karnataka Electricity Board* AIR 2008 SC 956.

entitled to specific performance only because he has allegedly claimed the variation in the consideration price. On the other hand, it was the respondent, who had all along claimed such a variation. The appellant expressed his readiness and willingness to perform the agreement by paying the consideration, fixed not once but repeatedly in several paragraphs of the plaint. The High Court erred in overlooking the fact that the appellant had never said that the consideration for reconveyance under the agreement was less than what was stated. Conceding that the appellant had merely claimed credit for certain amount, that could not mean that he was seeking variation in the agreement itself, consequently, the Supreme Court allowed the appeal and decreed the suit for specific performance.[8]

Specific performance denied In the agreement for sale of immovable property, it was stipulated that the amount in part was to be paid within 10 days of the agreement and the balance at the time of registration of the deed and it was agreed that the vendor should redeem the property which was mortgaged and also obtain Income Tax clearance certificate. The vendee failed to pay the amount within 10 days of the agreement as stipulated and insisted on the delivery of possession and Income Tax clearance certificate and redemption of the property before making any payment which was contrary to the terms of the agreement. It was held that the purchaser was not ready and willing and was disentitled to specific performance.[9]

Where the plaintiff neither deposited the amount of sale consideration nor furnished a bank guarantee as per the directions of the trial court and he was never ready either with money or the source to fulfil his part of the contract, the dismissal of the suit on the finding that the plaintiff was not ready and willing to perform his part of the contract, is justified.[10] A plaintiff, who repudiates the contract and sues for damages, cannot subsequently claim specific performance of that contract.[11]

The question of readiness and willingness to perform his part of the contract has to be inferred from the conduct of the parties and attending circumstances. The vendor was in dire need of cash to celebrate his daughter's marriage and in the agreement for sale it was stipulated that the plaintiff must give the draft sale deed within seven days of the execution of the agreement. It was held that time was of the essence of the contract and the plaintiff was not ready and willing to perform his part.[12]

8 *V. Pechimuthu* v *Gowrammal* AIR 2001 SC 2446.
9 *Chand Rani (died) by LRs* v *Kamal Rani (died) by LRs* AIR 1993 SC 1742; (1993)1 SCC 519; JT 1993(1) SC 74.
10 *N.P. Thirugnanam (deceased)* by LRs v *Dr. Jagan Mohan Rao* AIR 1996 SC 116; (1995)3 SCJ 386; (1995)5 SCC 115.
11 *Ayissabi* v *Gopala Konar* AIR 1989 Ker 134.
12 *H.H. Acharya Swamy Dassiji* v *Sri Sitaram Rapar* AIR 1996 SC 2095; (1996)4 SCC 526; JT 1996(5) SC 460.

One of the conditions of the agreement for sale of immovable property was that the purchaser should make part payment of ₹4 lakhs within the stipulated time. This payment was an essential term of the contract as any late payment may affect the vendor's right to obtain suitable alternative residential accommodation. The purchaser failed to comply with the terms of the agreement and the Supreme Court held that a decree for specific performance cannot be granted as it would be unfair and unreasonable to do so.[13]

The agreement for sale contained certain time-limits for taking steps by one or the other party. It was held that there must be some significance in fixing this time-limit. The total inaction on the part of the purchaser for $2^1/_2$ years in violation of the terms of the agreement coupled with substantial rise in price disentitled the plaintiff to the equitable relief of specific performance.[14] The Supreme Court reversed the decision of the High Court in *Vairavan* v *K.S. Vidyanandam*[15] and overruled the decision of the High Court in *S.V. Sankara Linga Nadar* v *Rathnasamy Nadar.*[16]

Holding that time is the essence of the contract in contracts relating to reconveyance, the Supreme Court held that the plaintiff made no efforts to pay the sale consideration within the time fixed and held that the plaintiff was not entitled to specific performance for reconveyance.[17] But where the plaintiff paid ₹62,700 out of consideration money of ₹87,000 and was ready and willing to pay the balance amount towards registration and execution of sale deed and the owner did not do the same though the time was not the essence of the contract, decree of specific performance of contract should be granted in favour of the plaintiff.[18]

The purchaser falsely alleged to have paid a sum amount of money to the vendor and abandoned the plea at or before the trial. The trial court as well as the first appellate court found that the purchaser was not ready and willing to perform his part of the contract and dismissed the suit. The High Court allowed the appeal and decreed the suit for specific performance as the purchaser was ready to pay the entire amount. The Supreme Court held that the interference by the High Court with the concurrent finding of the courts below was unwarranted and suffered from the vice of exercise of such jurisdiction as did not vest in the High Court in law. Holding that the judgment of the High Court was wholly unsustainable. Their Lordships of

13 *P.R. Deb & Associates* v *Sunanda Rao* AIR 1996 SC 1504; (1996)4 SCC 423; JT 1996(2) SC 684.
14 *K.S. Vaidyanathan* v *Vairavan* AIR 1997 SC 1751; (1997)3 SCC 1; JT 1997(2) SC 375.
15 AIR 1996 Mad 353.
16 AIR 1952 Mad 389.
17 *Bismillah Begam* v *Rahamathulla Khan* (1998)1 LW 825 (SC).
18 *Kanak Majumdar* v *Indrani Roy* AIR 2013 Cal 81.

the Supreme Court allowed the appeal setting aside the judgment of the High Court and restored those of the trial court and the first appellate court dismissing the suit for specific performance.[19]

The vendor who was a displaced person was allotted some blocks of buildings by the Government. The plaintiff entered into an agreement with the defendant for advancement of loans to the defendant and agreeing to pay to the Government on behalf of the defendant allottee the cost of the blocks, interest and arrears and the defendant agreed to transfer one block to the plaintiff. The vendee plaintiff failed to pay the amount to the Government. It was held that he was not ready and willing to perform his part of the contract. The suit for specific performance was therefore dismissed.[20]

Contract for supply of printed booklets Time was essence of contract and there was requirement of booklets to be supplied on time bound basis. But supplies were not made within stipulated time even within one month after extension of time. Communication was made to printer that work order stands cancelled. Printing of booklets thereafter was wholly unauthorised. Communication issued subsequently that certain specified number of booklets may be accepted was not enforceable. High Court enforcing the said illegal communication was held to be not justified.[21] It is to be noted that the time is of the essence of contract if the parties have expressly stipulated that it should be so. The intention may also be implied from the interrlelationship of various clauses of the contract or otherwise from the surrounding circumstances.[1]

Readiness and willingness—meaning and implications There is a distinction between readiness to perform the contract and willingness to perform the contract. "Readiness" means the capacity of the plaintiff to perform the contract; this includes his financial ability to pay the purchase price. But "willingness" postulates an enquiry into the conduct of the plaintiff.[2]

Kerala Full Bench did not agree with this view in view of the totality of the pleadings reflecting both readiness and willingness of the plaintiff to perform his part of the contract.

In the Kerala Full Bench case the averment was that the plaintiff has been and always ready to perform his part of the contract. The word "willing" was absent. This absence was not held fatal. It was pointed out that the

19 *Ram Kumar Aggarwal* v *Thawa Dass (died) by LRs* AIR 1999 SC 3248; (1999)7 SCC 303; JT 1999(6) SC 179.

20 *Ajaib Singh* v *Smt. Tulsi Devi* AIR 2000 SC 2493; (2000)6 SCC 566; JT 2000(8) SC 403.

21 *State of Madhya Pradesh v Ruchi Printers* AIR 2016 SC 2841.

1 Halsbury's *Laws of England*, 4th Ed., p. 525, para 900.

2 *Raj Rani* v *Kartar Singh* AIR 1975 Del 137 at p. 141 (DB).

averments in a plaint should be read as an indivisible whole to understand the correct meaning and scope of the averments, and the pleadings should not be dissected and accepted in part and rejected in the remainder, but they must be taken as a whole. The pleadings should not be constructed in a pedantic manner and have to be interpreted not with formalistic rigour but with softness.[3]

Readiness and willingness means that person claiming performance has kept the contract subsisting with preparedness to fulfil his obligations and accept performance when the time for performance arrives. When such readiness and willingness is not spelt out of the plaint, the suit fails.[4]

The words "ready" and "willing" in the Specific Relief Act 1963 imply that the person was prepared to carry out the terms of the contract. The distinction between "readiness" and "willingness" is that the former refers to financial capacity and the latter to the conduct of the plaintiff wanting performance. Generally, readiness is backed by willingness.[5]

As held by an Allahabad case so far as the question of readiness and willingness is concerned while 'willingness' is merely a mental process, 'readiness' is something to do with translating that will into action and is preceded by a necessary preparation for being in a position to be ready. As to the averments about this continuous readiness and willingness the law never insists on any particular form and the necessary averment may be made in any language the plaintiff may choose to employ. The language is not important. The crucial thing is that the totality of the averments made in the plaint must indicate the readiness and willingness of the plaintiff, even though by necessary inference.[6]

As held in an AP case the objection that the plaintiff in his plaint stated "he was willing" instead of that "he is ready and willing" to perform his part of the contract is too technical to be accepted particularly when the plaintiff in his "examination-in-chief" stated that "he is ready and willing" to perform the contract.[7]

A sale agreement stipulated that the vendor required to measure land, clear loan and produce original documents of property to ascertain remaining sale consideration. There was no proof of measurement of land by vendor. Vendee repeatedly requested vendor to measure the land for depositing

3 *Nambarukandi Marakkar* v *Nallithodi Thavalaparambil Appu* AIR 1991 Ker 1.

4 *Bhaskaran* v *George Joseph* AIR 1988 Ker 255; 1987 Ker LJ 1396; (1988)1 Ker LT 107.

5 *J.P. Builders* v *A. Ramadas Rao* (2011)1 SCC 429.

6 *Bijai Bahadur* v *Shri Shiv Kumar* AIR 1985 All 223; *Bishambhar Nath Agarwal* v *Kishan Chand* AIR 1998 All 195.

7 *K. Sambasiva Rao* v *P. Bangaru Raju* AIR 1985 AP 393; (1985)2 Cur Civ Cas 666; (1985)1 Andh LT 441; (1985)1 APLJ (HC) 241.

balance consideration. Readiness and willingness on the part of the vendee was proved. Non-deposit of balance consideration in court is not fatal. Vendee is entitled to decree of specific performance.[8]

Financial readiness The expression "readiness and willingness" has been the subject-matter of interpretation in many cases even prior to its insertion in s. 16(c) of the Specific Relief Act 1963. While examining the question as to how and in what manner, the plaintiff is required to prove his financial readiness so as to enable him to claim specific performance of the contract/ agreement, the Privy Council in a leading case[9] observed as under:

> "it is not necessary for the plaintiff to produce the money or vouch a concluded scheme for financing the transaction to prove his readiness and willingness."

It is submitted that the question is one of fact and it all depends upon facts and circumstances of each case. It is sufficient for the party to establish that he had the capacity to pay the sale consideration. It is not necessary that he should always carry the money with him from the date of the suit till the date of the decree.[10] After conclusion of an agreement vendee issuing various notices reminding vendor for registering sale deed. Defendant never applying for survey of land. Vendee was ready with ₹20,00,000 for execution of sale deed. Vendee's willingness cannot be doubted.[11]

Plea of the defendant was that agreement of sale was loan transaction but there was no record to show that defendant was advanced loan by plaintiff. Financial capacity of plaintiff was proved and the plaintiff was ready and willing to perform his part of contract. Plaintiff is entitled to relief of specific performance.[12] But when vendee is not in a fit financial condition to pay balance amount to vendor, he is not entitled to a decree of specific performance.[13]

When it is proved that the purchaser have sufficient amount in his account to pay the balance consideration and he gave legal notice to the seller for getting sale deed executed, it is held the purchaser is ready and willing to perform his part of contract.[14]

Burden of proof If a plaintiff has to prove that he was always ready and willing to perform his part of the contract, that is, to perform his obligations in terms of the contract, necessarily he should step into the witness box

8 *S. Deivanai* v *V.M. Kothandaraman* AIR 2018 Mad 14.
9 *Bank of India Ltd.* v *Jamsetji A.H. Chinoy* (1949-50)77 IA 76; AIR 1950 PC 90.
10 *A. Kanthamani* v *Nasreen Ahmed* (2017)4 SCC 654; *Sukhbir Singh* v *Brij Pal Singh* (1997)2 SCC 200; AIR 1996 SC 2510.
11 *V. Kalavathi* v *T.R. Srinivasan* AIR 2018 Hyd 84.
12 *Mohanlal Patle* v *Surjeet Singh Saluja* AIR 2019 Chh 32.
13 *Kalawati (D) through L.Rs.* v *Rakesh Kumar* AIR 2018 SC 960.
14 *Kiran Mehta* v *Lila Devi Ram Lakhan Prasad* AIR 2018 Pat 157.

and give evidence that he was all along been ready and willing to perform his part of the contract and subject himself to cross-examination on that issue.[15] A plaintiff cannot obviously examine in his place, his attorney-holder who did not have personal knowledge either of the transaction or of his readiness and willingness. Readiness and willingness refer to the state of mind and conduct of the purchaser, as also his capacity and preparedness on the other. One without the other is not sufficient. Therefore a third party who has no personal knowledge cannot give evidence about such readiness and willingness, even if he is an attorney-holder of the person concerned.[16]

Proof of readiness and willingness to perform contract Not only to aver but also it is needed for the plaintiff to prove his continuous readiness and willingness and financial capacity to perform his part of the contract. In a Supreme Court case the plaintiff, a seller of earthen pots with a meagre income of ₹100 to ₹150 per month, to meet the expenditure of the treatment of his ailing son sold his house to the defendant for a sum of ₹7,000 and he remained in the house as a tenant at a monthly rental. Contemporaneously the defendant executed a contract for reconveyance for ₹7,000 and the times stipulated was ten years.

Limitation In view of Article 54 of the Limitation Act 1963, a suit for specific performance of contract has to be filed within three years of the date fixed for the performance or if no such date is fixed where plaintiff has notice that performance is refused.[17]

Order under Or. 8, r. 10, CPC When the defendant in a suit fails to file the written statement within time, the Court may pass order under Or. 8, r. 10 of the CPC. In a suit for specific performance it is mandatorily required by s. 16 of the Specific Relief Act to plead readiness and willingness of the plaintiff to perform his part of the contract. The court, before acting under Or. 8, r. 10 has to scrutinize the facts set out in the plaint to find out whether all the requirements, specially those indicated in s. 16 of the Specific Relief Act, have been complied with or not.[18]

Ability, readiness and willingness to perform It is the general principle of law that a person seeking specific performance must show that he has performed or offered to perform or is ready, able and willing to perform, all the essential acts required by the contract and he must not remain quiet or hold himself aloof so as to enforce or abandon the contract as events may prove advantageous. The plaintiff is entitled to specific performance where he

15 *Vijay Kumar* v *Om Parkash* AIR 2018 SC 5098.
16 *Man Kaur* v *Hartar Singh Sangha* (2010)10 SCC 512.
17 *Thakamma Mathew* v *M. Azamathulla Khan* 1993 Supp (4) SCC 492.
18 *Balraj Taneja* v *Sunil Madan* (1999)8 SCC 396; AIR 1999 SC 3381.

alleges and proves that he has complied substantially with the conditions of the contract or is able, ready and willing to perform the contract.[19]

Lack of pleading of continuous readiness and willingness—plea in execution Well settled is the rule that an executing court cannot go behind the decree. It however does not mean that it has no duty to find out the true effect of the decree. It can and in appropriate cases it ought to take into consideration the pleadings as well as the proceeding leading up to the decree. In order to find out the meaning of the words employed in a decree the court often has to ascertain the circumstances under which those words came to be used. The jurisdiction of the execution court does not begin and end with merely looking at the decree as it is finally drafted.[20] In appropriate case executing court when the decree is ambiguous can look into the pleadings and the proceedings leading to the decree.[21]

Lack of averment as to continuous readiness and willingness in plaint in suit for specific performance of sale does not render the decree a nullity and in execution stage the lack of pleading aforesaid cannot be canvassed.[22]

Specific pleading in plaint The High Court found that no plea as to readiness and willingness was raised and as such no specific performance was granted. It was held by the Supreme Court that the finding of the High Court was factually incorrect and as such the decree was set aside. The plaintiff was entitled to decree for specific performance.[23]

Continuous readiness and willingness—issue and proof As to the averment of continuous readiness and willingness to perform plaintiff's part of contract, when the parties are aware of the need of proof thereof, non-framing of issue on the point does not vitiate the trial.[24] Where the issues upon which the parties went to trial fully and adequately covered all the material points in the case and the parties were fully conscious of the same, even if the plaint suffered from omission of necessary averments or lack of particulars, appellant cannot be permitted to raise objection to a finding on such a

19 *Corpus Juris Secundum*, vol. 81, pp. 950-951. See also *Satya Jain* v *Anis Ahmed Rushdie* AIR 2013 SC 434; (2013)8 SCC 131. (Purchaser's refusal to pay certain amount to seller for payment to I.T. authorities cannot be construed by invoking principle of business efficacy as purchaser's default of agreement. Purchaser is entitled to decree for specific performance).

20 *Bhagwan Vaja* v *Solanki* AIR 1972 SC 1371; (1973)2 SCC 40; *Chandra Mall* v *Abdul Gani* AIR 1976 Gau 54; *Omarali* v *Aibi* AIR 1980 Cal 361.

21 *Bhagwan Vaja* v *Solanki Hanuj* AIR 1972 SC 1371; (1972)1 SCWR 453; *Sarat Chandra* v *Narasinha Rao* AIR 1976 Ori 12; (1975)2 Cut WR 724; *Raj Kumar* v *Harbanslal* AIR 1978 Punj 186.

22 *Hira Devi* v *Harinath* AIR 1989 All 11.

23 *Ramakrishna Pillai* v *Muhammed Kunju* AIR 2008 SC 1601.

24 *K. Venkaji Rao* v *M. Abdul Khuddur Kureshi* AIR 1991 Kant 119.

question.[25] When the parties went to trial fully knowing the rival cases and led all the evidence not only in support of their case but also in refutation of the case of other side, it cannot be said that absence of a specific issue is fatal to the case to that there occurred a mistrial vitiating the proceedings. The suit cannot be dismissed on this narrow ground.[1]

The burden lies on the plaintiff to prove his continuous readiness from the date of the contract till the date of hearing of the suit to perform his part of the contract.[2] The plaintiff must in such a suit aver in the plaint and prove in evidence that he was continuously ready and willing to perform his part of the contract right from the date of agreement till the date of decree or hearing of the suit; but he is not required to do so that on each and every date of hearing he had money ready with him.[3] Even if there is no evidence on the side of the defendant, the plaintiff cannot take advantage of it as he has not himself stated in his evidence that he was ready and willing to perform his part of the contract and he is not entitled to decree of specific performance.[4]

To prove the continuous readiness and willingness, it is not always necessary that the plaintiff must examine himself or herself as a witness. In a case she appointed her husband to look after the matter as attorney by a power of attorney. Requests to vendor to specifically perform the contract used to be made by the lady through her husband. It was held the lady need not examine herself. Her husband's testimony about continuous readiness and willingness is enough.[5]

Notice sent by the plaintiff demanding specific performance sometimes may afford clinching evidence of continuous readiness and willingness of the plaintiff. The notice when sent by post goes out of sender's power once it is put in transmission and whatever is written or mentioned there is incapable of being altered. Where the closed undelivered envelopes containing notices sent by plaintiffs are opened in court when plaintiff's oral evidence is tendered, the contents of these notices become the best index of plaintiff's intention or state of his mind which is supremely relevant to determine whether he was or was not ready and willing to perform his

25 *Krishna Singh* v *Mathura Ahir* AIR 1972 All 273; 1972 All LJ 155.

1 *Kameswaramma* v *Subbarao* AIR 1963 SC 884; (1963)2 SCR 208; *Kunju Kesavan* v *M.M. Philip* AIR 1964 SC 164; (1964)3 SCR 634; *Bhagawati Prasad* v *Chandramaul* AIR 1966 SC 735; (1966)2 SCR 286; *Badridas Goenka* v *Gopal Jew Thakur* AIR 1967 Ori 99; 33 Cut LT 995; *Hirabhai Chouhan* v *Bhagirathibai* AIR 1969 MP 241; *Budha* v *Bedariya* AIR 1981 MP 76; *Abdul Razak* v *Abdul Rahaman* 83 CWN 821; *Banka Behari* v *Gour Mohon* AIR 1981 Cal 185; *Vijay Ram* v *Janak Raj* 1982 Sri LJ 189; *Katya Bala Dasi* v *Nilmoni Pakhira* AIR 1987 Cal 248; (1986)2 Cal LJ 1.

2 *N. Venkatappa* v *Lingappa Reddy* AIR 1998 Kant 372.

3 *Sadharam* v *Jagmal Singh* (1998)3 CCC 17 (All).

4 *Mathew* v *Scaria* AIR 1998 Ker 253.

5 *Triloki Vishwakarma* v *Zaitun Nisa* AIR 1992 Pat 40.

part of the contract notwithstanding the fact that the notices had not been delivered. Merely because the notices were not actually delivered it cannot be inferred that the notices are irrelevant. These notices are certainly relevant for the purpose of indicating the state of plaintiff's mind and his offer to have the sale deed executed within the stipulated period.[6]

Continuous readiness and willingness and financial capacity to launch litigation A person may be fully equipped for performing the contract but if, for any reason circumstances compel him to seek recourse by way of suit, he may find himself in a situation that he may be unable to manage the extra expenses required for litigation. The capacity to perform the contract and the capacity, to finance litigation are two distinct aspects. Mere incapability to fend for the litigation cannot necessary lead to the conclusion that he lacks money for performing his part of the contract. It is not always justifiable to draw an inference against plaintiff's capacity when the plaint in a suit for specific performance is filed with deficient court-fee. This approach may sometimes be dangerous and misplaced. There may be several reasons of not filing the plaint with full court-fee. This is not invariably for the reason that plaintiff has no arrangement for meeting his obligation under the contract. Therefore, in all such cases the court would be advised to approach with caution and where a plausible explanation is forthcoming due weight should be given to it.[7]

Amendment of plaint There was a mistake in description of suit property in plaint. Amendment was sought to rectify mistake in plaint as well as in contract. It can be amended in view of s. 26 of the Specific Relief Act. Nature of suit is not changed by amendment.[8]

Amendment in suit for specific performance—introduction of plea of continuous readiness The model form of plaint given in Form Nos. 47 and 48 in Appendix A of First Schedule of CPC indicates how this averment of continuous readiness and willingness to perform his part of the contract may be averred. In a suit for specific performance of contract the plaintiff cannot be allowed to amend his plaint;[9] at any rate after the case being closed to introduce the averment about his readiness and willingness to perform his part of the contract;[10] nor when on the date of amendment the

6 *Nathu Singh* v *Jagdish Singh* AIR 1992 All 174.
7 *Nathu Singh* v *Jagdish Singh* (supra).
8 *Puran Ram* v *Bhaguram* AIR 2008 SC 1960.
9 *Thimmegowda* v *Kalegowda* (1986)2 Cur Civ Cas 11 (Kant); *Paltur Honnur Saheb* v *Propanna Annapurna* AIR 1986 Kant 109; ILR (1985) Kant 3243. In this Karnataka case the view of Bombay High Court in *Trimbak Shankar Tidke* v *Nivratti Shankar* AIR 1985 Bom 128 was held to be obiter.
10 *Manick Lal* v *K.P. Chowdhury* AIR 1976 Cal 115; *Ram Singhasan* v *Sudama Prosad* AIR 1982 Pat 200; *Ramswaroop Singh* v *Bijoy Kumar Singh* AIR 1986 Pat 60.

suit is barred by limitation,[11] nor after an unduly long time after institution of the suit (about two years);[12] nor after dismissal in appellate stage.[13]

In an Allahabad case the court held that in a suit for specific performance of contract the plaintiff shall not be allowed to amend the plaint and incorporate in the plaint the averment that the plaintiff has been willing to perform his part of the contract because such an amendment would help the plaintiff to bring out a cause of action in the plaint which was conspicuous by its absence in the plaint originally filed.[14]

But if the averment regarding readiness and willingness is not made, the plaintiff can be allowed to amend his plaint to incorporate the averment subsequently (even at the appellate stage) if the application has been made within limitation period.[15]

The ratio of this decision[16] was not accepted in Kerala case,[17] holding that an amendment to the plaint can be incorporated to the effect that the plaintiff has performed or has been willing to perform his part of the contract which was not specifically averred in the plaint. It was pointed out that the very fact that the suit is for specific performance is more than sufficient to presume that the plaintiff has pleaded some of the essential facts bringing out the cause of action and if that be so, the proposed amendment cannot be said to be an attempt to bring out a new cause of action.[18]

In a case amendment was made to include the averment about the plaintiff's continuous readiness and willingness to perform his part of the contract at the argument stage but within the period of limitation. The amendment was held proper.[19]

When the plaintiff pleads that he is ready and willing, he can amend his pleading to incorporate that the plaintiff has been and is still ready and willing to perform his part of the contract.[20] Where in a suit for specific performance of contract there were averments to the effect that the plaintiff is all along ready to pay the balance consideration money and to get the sale deed executed the intention of the plaintiff to perform his part of the

11 *United Pioneer Society* v *Chand Bibi* (1986)1 Andh LT 372.
12 *Ahammed* v *Mammad Kanhi* AIR 1987 Ker 228.
13 *Daryodhan Patel* v *P.C. Das* AIR 1978 Ori 5; *Mahammad Khan* v *Ayub Khan* AIR 1978 All 463 contra *Rama Nand Chaudhry* v *Bhonri* AIR 1978 P&H 291; *B. Roy* v *W.B. Housing Board* 88 CWN 1024.
14 *Mahmood Khan* v *Ayub Khan* AIR 1978 All 463.
15 *Kandhai* v *Cobrey* 1982 All LJ 569 applying *Ouseph Verghese* v *Joseph Alley* (1970)1 SCR 921.
16 *Mahmood Khan* v *Ayub Khan* AIR 1978 All 463.
17 *Oskar Louis* v *K.V. Saradha* AIR 1991 Ker 137.
18 *Oskar Louis* v *K.V. Saradha* (supra).
19 *Joga Singh* v *Pakhar Ram* AIR 1990 P&H 314.
20 *Ram Avtar Sharma* v *Jagadish Ram* AIR 1985 Pat 1.

contract is eloquent. Belated amendment seeking to add the averment about plaintiff's continuous readiness and willingness to perform his part of the contract is to be allowed.[21]

When the plaintiff avers about his repeated request to purchase stamp and the suit is instituted shortly after the promised date, the plaint indicates in substance his willingness. In such case the categorical averment about continuous readiness and willingness may be supplied by an amendment because the law in a defective pleading may be cured by amendment when the cause of action is not ab initio completely absent.[1]

In a Bombay case the trial court allowed the amendment to cure the absence of averment of readiness and willingness to perform his part of the contract because the defendant's advocate conceded to the amendment on payment of cost. The first appellate court however dismissed the suit setting aside the amendment at the belated stage. High Court decreed the suit for specific performance on the grounds, namely that the averment in that case was entirely of format and academic character because all that the plaintiff was to perform was to pay ₹800 which he had deposited on the date of institution of the suit and nothing remained on his part to perform as his part of the contract, secondly, when defendant's advocate had given his consent to the amendment proposed, there was no point in disturbing the amendment.[2]

Waiver of plea of readiness and willingness in lower court—opportunity to amend When a suit in the trial court proceeds despite absence of averment in the plaint as to readiness and willingness to perform the contract because of no objection raised in the trial court but the plea is pressed in the appellate court, and the appellate court finds that there is enough evidence to show that the plaintiff was and has been ready and willing to perform his part of the contract, the appellate court should give him an opportunity to make good the defect by amendment of the plaint.[3]

In a case the plaint was amended by consent of parties to incorporate the averment about the continuous readiness and willingness to perform plaintiff's part of the contract. No objection was raised in the memo of appeal that the defendants advocate did not so consent. It was held that setting aside the amendment in appeal is improper.[4]

21 *Cudise Trinath Rao* v *Sudhangshu Prosad Padni* AIR 1992 Ori 168.

1 *Diwali Lal* v *Sardar Baldev Singh* AIR 1985 Pat 344 at p. 349; *B. Roy* v *W.B. Housing Board* AIR 1985 Cal 362; 88 CWN 1024; *United Pioneer Society* v *Chand Bibi* (1986)1 Andh LT 372 at p. 383 relying on *Ganesh Trading* v *Moji Ram* AIR 1978 SC 484; (1978)2 SCR 614; (1978)2 SCC 91.

2 *Dagadu Bapu Shinde* v *Vasant Shankar* AIR 1988 Bom 22.

3 *Byomkesh* v *Nani Gopal Banik* AIR 1987 Cal 92; (1987)91 CWN 272.

4 *Dagadu Bapu Shinda* v *Vasant Shankar* AIR 1988 Bom 22; (1987)3 Bom CR 543.

The plaintiff's ailing son died. It was not known how much out of the sum of ₹7,000 was spent in the treatment. On the point of time when the date of reconveyance reached, the plaintiff left no stone unturned to get a reconveyance and after sending to the defendant a telegram requesting him to be present at the office of the sub-registrar and he waited the whole day at sub-registrar's office but the defendant did not turn up there. Eventually the plaintiff filed a suit for specific performance of contract of reconveyance with usual averment of his continuous readiness and willingness to perform his part of the contract of reconveyance and he further stated in the plaint that he had deposited ₹7,000 in the bank. All the three subordinate courts in view of the non-production of the bank pass book held against plaintiff's continuous readiness and willingness. The Supreme Court reversed the decision of the High Court and observed: "The High Court committed the same error of drawing an adverse inference against the plaintiff for not producing the pass book in disregard of the fact that neither the defendant had called upon him to do so at his instance nor on its own."

"The second serious error which has crept into the judgment of the courts below is shutting their eyes to the question whether the defendant was ready and willing to perform his part of the contract and whether he had remained present at the sub-registrar's office on the appointed day. On the other hand the court's have been obsessed by the issue as regards the income of the plaintiff and the question as to whether and how the plaintiff could have effected a saving as stated by him on oath. Not one question was put in order to elicit this information from the plaintiff. Even so the trial court came to the conclusion that the plaintiff could not have saved the amount as he was selling earthen pots and his income was of the order of ₹100 to ₹150 per month. It was overlooked that a sum of ₹7,000 was obtained by the plaintiff when he entered into the transaction with the defendant in 1967 and the son for whose treatment the said amount had been raised by recourse to this transaction had died. No question was put to him whether the entire amount had been spent for the treatment and in payment of other debts etc. No question was put to him as to the amount of his expenses. Notwithstanding these salient circumstances, the trial court came to the conclusion that the plaintiff could not have saved the amount.[5]

When the continuous readiness and willingness to perform his part of the contract is averred in the plaint is neither specifically denied in the written statement, nor defendant deposes to the effect that no such readiness or willingness existed, the readiness and willingness must be deemed to have been proved.[6]

5 *Indira Kaur* v *Sheo Lal Kapoor* AIR 1988 SC 1074 at pp. 1082-1083; JT 1988(1) SC 652(2).

6 *P. Lakshmi Ammal* v *S. Ammal* AIR 1991 Mad 137.

Defendant willing to perform contract When the defendant in his written statement comes with the case that he is ready and willing to perform his part of contract, the plaintiff may be directed to deposit the entire or balance of consideration in court that it may earn interest and both parties' interest is safeguarded.[7]

Plaintiff must prove even if defendant refused to perform It is not sufficient for the plaintiff to show that the defendant has refused to perform. Even if the plaintiff has proof that the defendant has refused to perform, he is not obviated to aver and prove his readiness and willingness to perform. For example, take a case where there is a contract for sale for a consideration of ₹10 lakhs and earnest money of ₹1 lakh was paid and the vendor wrongly refuses to execute the sale deed unless the purchaser is ready to pay ₹15 lakhs. In such a case there is a clear breach by the defendant. But in that case, if the plaintiff did not have the balance ₹9 lakhs (and the money required for stamp duty and registration) or the capacity to arrange and pay such money, when the contract had to be performed, the plaintiff will not be entitled to specific performance, even if he proves breach by the defendant, as he was not "ready and willing" to perform his obligations.[8]

Continuous readiness and willingness admitted when in defence evidence The question whether plaintiff requires to prove any further his continuous readiness and willingness when the defendant admits in evidence plaintiff's such readiness cropped up in an Orissa case. Where the lower appellate court ignoring the admission of the defendant about the plaintiff's continuous readiness and willingness to perform his part of the contract, reversing the decree of specific performance passed by the trial court, dismissed the suit on the ground that plaintiff did not prove his post-suit readiness and willingness to perform his part of the contract. Orissa High Court pointed out that the admission in witness box which was to the effect "At present I am not prepared to carry out my part of the contract though plaintiff is ready to perform his part of the contract", held that on such admission the plaintiff need not prove any further his continuous readiness and willingness to perform his part of the contract.[9]

It is however to be mentioned that in a suit for specific performance the plaintiff is to prove his continuous readiness and willingness to perform his part of the contract till the date of hearing.[10] If no evidence was placed on record by the plaintiff to prove that he had sufficient fund to pay the

7 *C.L. Jain* v *Gopi Chand* AIR 1990 Del 280.
8 *Man Kaur* v *Hartar Singh Sangha* (2010)10 SCC 512.
9 *Jagannath Sahu* v *Harihar Pradhan* AIR 1992 Ori 180.
10 *Kumar & Kumar* v *Union of India* AIR 1978 Pat 192; *P.G. Sinha* v *Commodore K.C. Chatterjee* AIR 1991 Cal 327.

balance consideration. Readiness and willingness not proved and accordingly relief of specific performance cannot be granted.[11]

Readiness and willingness—interpretation of contract to accord with plea
Performance or readiness and willingness to perform must be according to the true construction of the contract. Section 16(c) of the Specific Relief Act 1963 is based on the recommendations of the Law Commission which preferred the Madras view in *Arjuna* v *Lakshmi*[12] and is not intended to deprive a plaintiff of pleading alternative constructions of a contract which he seeks to enforce. A contract may be open to more than one construction and a plaintiff may allege the alternative constructions to which the contract may be open and claim relief on that basis. The true construction of the contract would be that construction which is finally accepted by the court. The plaintiff for entitling him to the relief of specific performance will have to satisfy that he alleged and proved his readiness and willingness to perform the contract in accordance with that construction which is ultimately accepted by the court, and if he succeeds in establishing that, he would not fail merely because other alternative constructions which are not accepted by the court were also alleged and relief was claimed on that basis. Alternative constructions, if persisted throughout the trial, may, in some cases, create difficulty in proving readiness and willingness from the date of contract according to true construction, for if the alternative constructions are inconsistent, proof of readiness and willingness according to one construction may be destructive of readiness and willingness according to other construction.[13] The readiness and willingness has to be according to the true construction of the contract and not according to what the plaintiff wishes to or wants to fashion it at the trial: for the question of readiness and willingness would assume different aspects in relation to the real agreement.[14]

When a particular mode of payment is provided in a contract for transfer of property but the plaintiff does not make the payment according to the term provided, he must be deemed to be not ready to get the conveyance executed.[15]

Where the plaintiff fails to aver and prove his readiness and willingness to perform his part of the contract, this renders the plaint without a cause of action, and if, by the time the application for amendment is made, a fresh suit would be barred by time, plaintiff cannot be allowed to deprive the

11 *Mukkani Fathima* v *Kundu Valappi Fathima* AIR 2019 Ker 38.
12 AIR 1949 Mad 265.
13 *Bajranglal* v *Purushottamdas Puranlal Narele* AIR 1972 MP 137 (DB).
14 *Md. Ziaul Haque* v *Calcutta Vyaper Pratisthan* AIR 1966 Cal 605 at p. 614 relying on *Nil Kanta Rai Chowdhury* v *Lalit Mohan Banerjee* AIR 1916 Cal 774; *Rustom Ali* v *Sheikh Ahidey Rahman Mia* (1941)45 CWN 837; *Narinjan* v *Md. Yunus* AIR 1932 Lah 265.
15 *Bishambhar Nath Agarwal* v *Kishan Chand* AIR 1990 All 65; (1989)3 Cur Civ Cas 518.

defendant of the valuable right that has accrued to him by efflux of time.[16] But, where there was no delay on the part of the plaintiff and the stage for recording evidence had not arrived, amendment of the plaint was allowed even though a new action would have been barred by statute.[17] In *L.J. Leach & Co. v Jardine Skinner Co.*,[18] the Supreme Court pointed out that even if limitation was one of the matters to be taken into account in the exercise of the judicial discretion under Or. 6, r. 17 of CPC, it was not necessary to dismiss an application for amendment merely because it would bring within time a suit which would have been barred by time by then. See also the observations of Bhattacharya, J in *Manick Lal Seal* v *K.P. Chowdhury*.[19]

As held by the Supreme Court in *Jai Jai Ram* v *National Buildings*,[20] "A party cannot be refused just relief merely because of some mistake, negligence, inadvertence or even infraction of the rules of procedure. The court always gives leave to amend the pleading of the party, unless it is satisfied that the party applying was acting mala fide or that by his blunder, he had caused injury to his opponent which may not be compensated for by an order of costs. However, negligent or careless may have been the first omission, and, however, late the proposed amendment, the amendment may be allowed if it can be made without injustice to the other side."

An application for amendment of the plaint, in order to make the pleadings conform to the requirement of law, should be allowed by the court if the amendment merely seeks to repel the technical objections based on omission of phraseology of the statute provided the bundle of facts constituting the cause of action has otherwise disclosed compliance.[1] In *Lakhi Ram (dead) through LRs* v *Trikha Ram*,[2] Their Lordships have pointed out that amendment inserting the relevant averments regarding the plaintiff's readiness and willingness to perform his part of the contract as per s. 16(*c*) of the Specific Relief Act did not amount to change in the cause of action and is legally permissible. In *S.K. Rowshan Ali* v *Kezi Abdul Jalil*,[3] the High Court of Calcutta has held that by incorporating the amendment as required by s. 16(*c*) of the Specific Relief Act by applying for amendment of the plaint no fresh cause of action arises.

16 *Narendra Bahadur Singh* v *Baijnath Singh* AIR 1981 All 410; see *Rajendra Prasad Rai* v *Rajdeva Rai* AIR 1974 All 294; *Mahmood Khan* v *Ayub Khan* AIR 1978 All 463; *Mukhtar Singh* v *Dharma Pal* 1981 All LJ 119; *Prem Raj* v *DLF* AIR 1968 SC 1355; (1968)3 SCR 648.

17 *Rama Nand Chaudhary* v *Bhonri* AIR 1978 P&H 291 relying on *L.J. Leach & Co.* v *Jardine Skinner Co.* AIR 1957 SC 357; 1957 SCR 438; 1957 SCJ 313.

18 AIR 1957 SC 357.

19 AIR 1976 Cal 115 at p. 121.

20 AIR 1969 SC 1267; (1970)1 SCR 22; (1969)1 SCC 869.

1 *Rajya Tulsi Bai Patel* v *Benar Enterprises* AIR 1988 Guj 42.

2 AIR 1998 SC 1230; (1998)2 SCC 720; JT 1998(1) SC 665.

3 Cal LT 1998(1) HC 455.

Sufficiency of tender by vendor (Amendment law)[4] Whether a deed should be tendered by the vendor before filing a suit for specific performance is a question on which there appears to be divergent views. According to some decisions a tender of the deed before the suit is necessary. In such case the rule that it is sufficient for the vendor to perfect his title at the rendition of the decree, does not apply to excuse a tender of the deed made a condition precedent to sue. According to other decisions, a tender of the deed by the vendor before suit is unnecessary, and the failure to make a tender effects only the question of costs. A tender in the pleading is held to be sufficient. Where the subject matter of the contract includes personal property, it has been held that the plaintiff need not tender an assignment personally before bringing suit for specific performance. Where the payment of the purchase money or a part thereof by the vendee and the conveyance by the vendor are concurrent and dependent acts, the vendor must tender to the vendee the appropriate conveyance. A tender by vendor is excused where the vendee expressly repudiates the contract or takes such a position that the tender would be a useless and idle ceremony.

Absence of averment of readiness and willingness—agitated in appeal Averment relating to continuous readiness and willingness to perform his part of contract, in suit for specific performance of contract is obligatory in view of Explanation (*ii*) to s. 16(*c*) of the Specific Relief Act 1963. The question of absence of such pleading is one of law and can be agitated in second appeal.[5]

Who can raise the plea of want of readiness and willingness The plea about want of readiness and willingness of the plaintiff is specifically available to the vendor or his legal representatives and it was personal to him. The subsequent purchasers have got only the right to defend the purchase on the premise that they had no prior knowledge of the agreement for sale with the plaintiff and they are *bona fide* purchasers for valuable consideration.[6] This decision in *Jugraj Singh's* case was doubted by the Supreme Court in *Lakhiram* v *Trikharam.*[7] But the appeal therein was decided on another point. The question came up directly before a three-Judge Bench of the Supreme Court in *Ram Awadh (dead) by LRs* v *Achaibar Dubey.*[8] Their Lordships held that the defence was available not only to the defendant vendor but also to the subsequent purchasers and even to the legal representatives of the subsequent purchasers and held that the decision in

4 *Corpus Juris Secundum*, vol. 81, p. 966.

5 *Manicklal Seal* v *K.P. Chowdhury* AIR 1976 Cal 115; *Malkhan Singh* v *Raghuvir* AIR 1981 All 96; *Byomkesh* v *Nani Gopal Banik* AIR 1987 Cal 92.

6 *Jugraj Singh* v *Labh Singh* AIR 1995 SC 945; (1995)2 SCC 31.

7 AIR 1998 SC 1230; (1998)2 SCC 720; JT 1998(1) SC 665.

8 AIR 2000 SC 860; (2000)2 SCC 428; JT 2000(1) SC 535.

Jugraj Singh's case was erroneous.[9] The same view was reiterated by the Supreme Court.[10]

Amendment of pleadings

General The Supreme Court said: Procedural law is intended to facilitate and not to obstruct the course of substantive justice. Provisions relating to pleadings in civil cases are meant to give to each side intimation of the case of the other so that it may be met, to enable courts to determine what is really at issue between parties, and to prevent deviations from the course which litigation on particular causes of action must take.

It is true that if a plaintiff seeks to alter the cause of action itself and to introduce indirectly through an amendment of his pleadings an entirely new or inconsistent cause of action, amounting virtually to the substitution of a new plaint or a new cause of action in place of what was originally there, the court will refuse to permit it if it amounts to depriving the party, against which a suit is pending of any right which may have accrued in its favour due to lapse of time. But, mere failure to set out even an essential fact does not by itself constitute a new cause of action. A cause of action is constituted by the whole bundle of essential facts which the plaintiff must prove before he can succeed in his suit. It must be antecedent to the institution of the suit. If any essential fact is lacking from averments in the plaint, the cause of action will be defective. In that case, an attempt to supply the omission has been and could sometime be viewed as equivalent to an introduction of new cause of action which, cured of its shortcomings, has really become a good cause of action.

This, however, is not the only possible interpretation to be put on every defective state of pleadings. Defective pleadings are generally curable if the cause of action sought to be brought out was not ab initio completely absent. Even very defective pleadings may be permitted to be cured, so as to constitute a cause of action where there was none, provided necessary conditions, such as payment of either any additional court fees, which may be payable, or of costs of the other side are complied with.

It is only if lapse of time has barred the remedy on a newly constituted cause of action that the courts should ordinarily refuse prayers for amendment of pleadings.[11]

In a suit for specific performance of agreement to sell, the plaintiff vendee sought incorporation of legal plea of readiness and willingness to perform its

9 AIR 1995 SC 945; (1995)2 SCC 31.

10 *Azhar Sultana* v *B. Rajamani* (2009)17 SCC 27; (2011)1 SCC (Civ) 761; AIR 2009 SC 2157.

11 *Ganesh Trading Co.* v *Moji Ram* AIR 1978 SC 484; (1978)2 SCR 614; (1978)2 SCC 91; *Oskar Louis* v *K.V. Saradha* AIR 1991 Ker 137.

part of contract by way of amendment. Since there was no change in cause of action or introduction of any new case, the amendment was allowed.[12]

As laid down in a Calcutta case: The principles as established by judicial decisions in respect of the amendment of plaint are as follows:

(1) All amendments will be generally permissible when they are necessary for determination of real controversy in the suit.

(2) All the same, substitution of one cause of action or nature of the claim for another in the original plaint or change of the subject matter of or controversy in the suit is not permissible;

(3) Introduction by amendment of inconsistent or contradictory allegations in negation of the admitted position on facts or mutually destructive allegations of facts are also impermissible though inconsistent pleas on the admitted position can be introduced by amendments;

(4) Generally the amendments should not cause prejudice to the other side which cannot be compensated in costs;

(5) Amendment of a claim or relief which is barred by limitation should not be allowed to defeat a legal right accrued except when such consideration is outweighed by the special circumstances of the case.[13]

Amendment seeking alternative claim of damages In a suit for specific performance of contract amendment is sought to include alternatively the claim of damages, the amendment must be allowed in view of the proviso to s. 21(5), the Specific Relief Act. This proviso would govern the prayer for such amendment notwithstanding Or. 2, r. 2, CPC.[14] On plaintiff's failure in suit for specific performance when he did sue for specific performance simpliciter, he cannot be allowed the refund of consideration because of bar of s. 22, Specific Relief Act. But court may direct the plaintiff to amend the plaint—the court can so permit at any stage—to incorporate the relief of refund of consideration. And on plaintiff's so doing court can grant a decree of refund of consideration.[15]

The new provision contained in the proviso to sub-sec. (5) of s. 21 of the Specific Relief Act 1963, makes it obligatory on the court to grant amendment of the plaint to include the relief for compensation or refund of earnest money, even if the claim was barred by limitation at the time the amendment

12 *Jagath Swapna & Co. Jagtial* v *Church of South India Trust Assocn.* AIR 2011 AP 81.

13 *Kanailal Das* v *Jiban Kanai Das* (1977)1 Cal LJ 285; AIR 1977 Cal 189; see also *J. Hiralal* v *Gulabchand* AIR 1983 Kant 30.

14 *Andheri Bridge View Co-op. Housing Society Ltd.* v *Krishnakant Anandrao Deo* AIR 1991 Bom 129 at p. 144.

15 *Sahida Bibi* v *Golam Mohammad* AIR 1983 Cal 216; 86 CWN 727; (1982)1 Cal LJ 475.

was sought, the discretion being confined only to assess the terms on which the amendment is to be allowed.[16] The Supreme Court[17] has also held that the court should allow amendment at any stage of the proceedings and the plaintiff should not be prevented from adding a plea for compensation in lieu of or in addition to that of specific performance of the contract. Compensation must be claimed in a suit for specific performance; if the plaintiff has no right to amend the plaint at any stage of the proceedings.[18] It is necessary for the plaintiff to make a claim for compensation, even if it be in the alternative, and the court is bound to grant the amendment under the purview of sub-sec. (5) of s. 21 of the Specific Relief Act 1963. Authorities under the repealed Act to the effect that compensation could be awarded without a specific prayer in the plaint are no longer good law. The object of the provisions contained in sub-sec. (5) of s. 21 of the Specific Relief Act 1963 is to prevent multiplicity of proceedings.[19]

But when the suit is for damages for breach of contract or refund of earnest money simpliciter, by amendment it cannot be converted to a suit for specific performance, because suit for damages etc. postulates breach of contract, plaintiff later cannot turn to say that the contract is still subsisting and he wants specific performance.[20]

Amendment to include claim for possession In view of the proviso to s. 22(2), Specific Relief Act at any stage of the proceeding the plaint may be amended to include claim for recovery of possession of the property contracted to be transferred. Where the reliefs laid down in cls. (*a*) and (*b*) of s. 22(1) of the Specific Relief Act 1963, were not claimed in the plaint as originally filed. But the plaintiff has a right to amend the plaint at any stage of the proceedings. While under the Code of Civil Procedure the court has discretion to allow amendment, under this provision which overrides the Code of Civil Procedure, the court has no option but to allow the amendment. Section 22 enacts a rule of pleading that in order to avoid multiplicity of proceedings the plaintiff may claim a decree for possession in a suit for specific performance, even though strictly speaking, the right to possession accrues only when suit for specific performance is decreed. The expression "in appropriate case" in s. 22(1) only indicates that it is not always incumbent on the plaintiff to claim possession or partition or separate possession in a suit for specific performance of a contract for the transfer

16 *Manohar Thunthi Raj Joshi* v *Jhunnu Lal Hariram Yadav* 1983 Mah LT 369.

17 *Jagdish Singh* v *Natthu Singh* AIR 1992 SC 1604; (1992)1 SCC 647; JT 1991(5) SC 400.

18 *Andheri Bridge View Co-op. Housing Society Ltd.* v *Krishnakant Anandrao Deo* AIR 1991 Bom 129.

19 See also under the heading "Amendment to incorporte claims for compensation and possession at any stage" at p. 387 of this book.

20 *Roop Chand Chaudhari* v *Smt. Ranjit Kumari* AIR 1991 P&H 212.

of immovable property because the relief for specific performance of the contract of sale embraces within its ambit not only the execution of the sale deed but also possession over the property agreed to be conveyed. Therefore, s. 22(2), Specific Relief Act provides for amendment of plaint at any stage of the proceeding. The word 'proceeding' is a comprehensive term and generally speaking means a prescribed course of action for enforcing a legal right. It includes a prescribed mode in which a judicial business is conducted. It includes even an execution proceeding. So, amendment is permissible even in execution stage.[1]

In a Delhi case a suit without prayer for recovery of possession was decreed on compromise and when the decree-holder put the decree in execution and asked for possession, objection was raised, so the High Court allowed to amend the plaint by adding a prayer for recovery of possession and thereon allowed the plaintiff to recover possession.[2] No amendment to include recovery of possession, however, is permissible after disposal of execution case on full satisfaction.[3]

When the property in respect of which relief for possession is sought for and the said relief is sought to be amended by incorporating another property situated outside the jurisdiction of the court, amendment cannot be allowed.[4]

A suit for specific performance was decreed against the vendor but not against the subsequent transferee although Supreme Court lays down the proper form of decree is to direct the subsequent transferee to join the execution,[5] in execution stage when decree was sought to be amended, it was held such amendment is not permissible.[6]

This view of the Patna High Court that the amendment cannot be allowed in the execution stage is no longer good law in view of the decision of the Supreme Court in *Babulal* v *Hazarilal*,[7] where it has been held that the expression "at any stage of the proceedings" would include an execution proceedings as well. The expression is comprehensive enough to include execution proceedings as well as proceedings at the appellate stage.[8]

Amendment of plaint seeking recovery of possession of property beyond jurisdiction of the court Section 22 empowers the plaintiff in a suit for specific performance to amend the plaint to include relief for possession 'in

1 *Babu Lal* v *Hazari Lal Kishori Lal* AIR 1982 SC 818; (1982)1 SCC 525.
2 *Ex-Servicemen Enterprises* v *Sumey Singh* AIR 1976 Del 181.
3 *Swarnalatika Sarkar* v *Prativa Rani Sarker* AIR 1981 Cal 79.
4 *Raj Kumar Singhania* v *Benoy Kumar Mazumdar* AIR 1985 Cal 328.
5 *Durga Prasad* v *Deep Chand* AIR 1954 SC 75; 1954 SCR 360.
6 *Rukmini Devi* v *Pawan Kumar Gupta* AIR 1979 Pat 88.
7 AIR 1982 SC 818; (1982)3 SCR 94; (1982)1 SCC 525.
8 *Raj Kumar Singhania* v *Benoy Kumar Mazumdar* AIR 1985 Cal 328; *Sahida Bibi* v *Golam Md.* AIR 1983 Cal 216; *Ex-Servicemen Enterprises* v *Sumey Singh* AIR 1976 Del 181; *Lotu Bandu Sonavane* v *Pundalik Nimba Koli* AIR 1985 Bom 412.

an appropriate case'. But s. 22 does not seek to interfere with the jurisdiction of a court and it provides that "in an appropriate case" a claim for possession and ancillary reliefs can be sought by way of amendment in order to avoid multiplicity of proceedings. When the decree for possession could not have been asked for in the original plaint as the court would be incompetent to entertain and try a suit for land and the legislature in enacting s. 22 did not override cl. (12) of the Letters Patent. As such, the expression "in an appropriate case" must necessarily mean and refer to a case where the plaintiff was competent to make a claim for possession and/or seek other ancillary reliefs, to avoid multiplicity of proceedings. It was not the intention of the legislature to give jurisdiction to a court which had none, and it would be travesty of justice to allow a prayer for possession to be brought into the pleadings in this circuitous manner, when admittedly the original court lacked jurisdiction to do so, and the plaintiff well knew his limitations.[9]

Suit for specific performance—amendment to base it on part performance Failure of party to bring forward his claim for specific performance within time is no ground to deny a claim founded on part performance.[10] Even if the suit for specific performance by the defendant is barred by lapse of time, the defendant is nevertheless entitled to his own possession on the strength of s. 53A of the Transfer of Property Act.[11]

But when a plaintiff sues for specific performance of contract and realising that he may fail, seeks to introduce the story of his getting possession in pursuance of contract to avail himself of the benefit of s. 53A of the Transfer of Property Act, the amendment is to be refused.[12]

Vendor warranting title erroneously or free from doubt Section 17 places a bar on the right of a vendor or a lessor of property (be it movable or immovable) to claim specific performance of his contract if he knowing himself not to have any title to the property has contracted to sell or let the property [sub-sec. (1)(*a*)]; or if he, though when he entered into the contract he believed that he had a good title to the property, cannot, at the time fixed by the parties or by the court for the completion of the sale or letting, give the purchaser or lessee a title free from reasonable doubt [sub-sec. (1)(*b*)].

Illustration of the first type of cases is a contract where *A* without *C*'s authority contracts to sell to *B* an estate which A knows to belong to *C*. A cannot enforce specific performance of this contract even though *C* is willing to confirm it.

9 *Raj Kumar* v *Benoy Kumar* AIR 1985 Cal 328.

10 *Sobharam Jiwan* v *Totaram Sitaram* AIR 1952 Nag 244.

11 *Nanasaheb Gajaba Banker* v *Appu Ganu Banker* AIR 1957 Bom 138; *Maruti Gurappa* v *Krishna Bala* AIR 1967 Bom 34.

12 *Gayatri Devi* v *Om Prakash Gautam* AIR 1985 All 356.

There is a distinction between good title and marketable title.[13] Held on facts that the agreement was for marketable title and not for good and marketable title.

"Marketable" title is one which both in the strict and reasonable sense means that the vendor would be in a position to force the property concerned on an unwilling purchaser under all circumstances. The title should be shown to be free from and not afflicted by doubts. Such doubts, no doubt, ought not to be capricious or frivolous doubts, but which a court of law would be disposed to accept as serious or sufficient. If the vendor has no title, or in any event, has no marketable title free from reasonable doubt, it follows that the vendee is not entitled to specific performance as a matter of right.[14]

The party who professes to have marketable title during agreement of sale or lease must prove his title. The onus lies on him. A trust claimed title and possession over the suit property which is offered for sale. It was held that onus to prove title lies upon the trust.[15]

Under s. 2(4) of the City Tenants Protection Act, the tenant does not acquire any interest in the land. It is merely a privilege or personal right which is only heritable, but not transferable and is not a subject of sale.[16]

The rule is further illustrated by the following examples:

A, being in possession of certain land, contracts to sell it to Z. On enquiry it turns out that *A* claims the land as heir of B, who left the country several years before, and is generally believed to be dead, but of whose death there is no sufficient proof. *A* cannot compel Z specifically to perform the contract.

A bequeaths his land to trustees declaring that they may sell it with the consent in writing of *B*. *B* gives a general prospective assent to any sale which the trustees may make. The trustees then enter into a contract with C to sell him the land. *C* refuses to carry out the contract. The trustees cannot specifically enforce this contract, as in the absence of *B*'s consent to the particular sale to C, the title which they can give to C is, as the law stands, not free from reasonable doubt.

The time for making an enquiry into the title of the vendor is the time of performance. He may in the meantime lose his right[16] (surrender of leasehold rights pursuant to lessee's inherent right to surrender the leasehold right) Likewise he may acquire the title later. This is covered by s. 13(1)(*a*).

Vendor having no marketable title A vendor cannot, in a suit for specific performance by the vendee, take a defence that since he has no title to the

13 *Md. Ziaul Haque* v *Calcutta Vyaper Pratisthan* AIR 1966 Cal 605 at p. 611.
14 *Rajendrakumar Bhandari* v *Poosammal* AIR 1975 Mad 379 at p. 382 (DB).
15 *Bishwanath Prasad Verma* v *Bhagwat Pandey* AIR 1982 Pat 219 at p. 224.
16 *Rajendrakumar Bhandari* v *Poosammal* AIR 1975 Mad 379 at p. 383 (DB).

property agreed to be sold by him, the promisee cannot seek specific performance of the agreement executed by him. But if really the vendor has no marketable title to the property agreed to be sold by him, and the purchaser files a suit for specific performance of that agreement, making the real owner of the property also a party to the suit, and seeks a decree for specific performance against the real owner also along with the promisor, the real owner can defend the suit on the ground that the promisor has no title to the property agreed to be sold by him, and no decree can be passed against him.[17]

Permission under Urban Land (Ceiling and Regulation) Act 1976 The permission for sale under the Urban Land (Ceiling and Regulation) Act 1976 is not a condition precedent to grant of decree of specific performance. If after getting the decree such permission is refused the decree-holder shall not be able to enforce the decree, but it cannot be said that such permission is condition precedent to grant of decree of specific performance.[18]

Rule laid down in s. 17 The section enacts that contracts to sell or let or hire properties cannot specifically be enforced in favour of sellers or lessors or persons letting for hire, if they have no title to the property. But that does not mean that in a suit filed by the purchaser or lessee, for specific performance the defendant can be allowed to take benefit of the plea that his title was defective. If the purchaser is unwilling to complete an agreement he may resist specific performance on the ground that the vendor has a defective title, but the vendor cannot take this as a defence for non-performance.[19]

Vendee's remedy Where the vendor sells the property to which he has no title, the vendee is entitled to damages and also to refund of the earnest money.[20] The vendee's right to recover the deposited amount depends upon the question whether the vendor is entitled to successfully maintain an action for specific performance brought by him. This is the test to apply in such cases.[1]

Non-enforcement except with variation Section 18 also provides a contingency when the plaintiff is debarred from getting the relief of specific performance. It provides that where the contract is in writing, and the defendant sets up a variation thereto, the plaintiff cannot obtain the specific performance except with the variation so set up in the following cases, namely (*a*) where

17 *Ramanivas Gupta* v *Maliram* 2002(5) ALD 362, 2003(3) ALT 787
18 *Ajit Prashad Jain* v *N.K. Widhani* AIR 1990 Del 42.
19 *Netyam Venkataramanna* v *Mahankali Narasimhan* AIR 1994 AP 244.
20 *Dwarka Prasad* v *Kathlen Florence* AIR 1955 Nag 58.
1 *Meenakshi Ammal* v *Munusamy* ILR (1966)1 Mad 114.

by fraud, mistake of fact or misrepresentation, the written contract is in its terms of effect different from what the parties agreed to, or does not contain all the terms agreed to between the parties on the basis of which the defendant entered into the contract; (*b*) where the object of the parties was to produce a certain legal result which the contract as framed is not calculated to produce; or (c) where the parties have subsequently to the execution of the contract, varied its terms.[2]

The ingredients for application of s. 18, as laid down in Banerjee on *Law of Specific Relief (Tagore Law Lectures)*,[3] are as follows:

(1) the plaintiff must seek the specific performance of a contract;

(2) the contract must be in writing;

(3) to the claim for specific performance, the defendant must set up a variation;

(4) that variation must be based on the plea, that—

by fraud, or mistake of fact, or misrepresentation—

(*a*) the contract—

(*i*) is in terms, or

(*ii*) in effect,

different from that which the parties agreed to; or

(*b*) the contract does not contain all the terms agreed to between the parties.

If the variation set forth as above is established, the plaintiff cannot obtain the specific performance sought, except with the variation so set up.

The provision is obviously curative and remedial. It is meant to serve as a panacea for human frailties at legal parlance. It recognises the universal truth that what is apparent may not always be real. When any action is founded on any written contract, the provision envisages, court's duty to find the true nature of the transaction arises from forensic sanctity attached to the execution *per se* of a written instrument. An endeavour has to be made to enforce the written contract and in that sense the provision is complementary to s. 20 under which general guidelines are laid down for the exercise of discretion in actions for specific performance of contract of any type. Courts are required to make earnest effort, unless the very execution of the document is denied, to give effect to the written agreement and enforce the contract with such terms as may be pleaded and proved by the defendant even if those are at a variance with the terms stated in the

2 *K. Narendra* v *Riviera Apartments (P) Ltd.* AIR 1999 SC 2309; (1999)5 SCC 77.

3 13th Ed., p. 400.

4 *Uttam Chand* v *Radha Bai* AIR 1991 MP 296 at pp. 301-302.

instrument in question. That is the total effect of the enumeration of the triune circumstances ("cases") stated in cls. (*a*), (*b*) and (*c*) of s. 18 and that reflects positively the object of the provision. A voidable contract such as tainted by fraud, mistake of fact or misrepresentation is even made specifically enforceable if the defendant himself washed off the taints and sets up a different contract with terms other than those embodied in the instrument in question. Cases of novation even are embraced by cl. (*c*); and in terms of cl. (*b*), the frame of the instrument is made amenable to change in the object sought to be achieved thereunder and a different "legal result" is allowed to be achieved in the course of enforcement of the written contract with necessary modification made therein by court upon determination of legally and truly enforceable rights and obligations of parties.[4]

Section 18 of the Specific Relief Act 1963, permits to a certain extent the defendant to prove an oral variation of a written contract contrary to the provisions of s. 92 of the Evidence Act. In *Uttam Chand* v *Radha Bai*,[5] the plaintiff filed a suit for specific performance of an agreement for sale and the defendant contended that the real nature of the transaction was that of security for a loan and that the document was executed as collateral security. While upholding the variation set up by the defendant and ordering specific performance in terms as found upon the variation, the court ordered the plaintiff to repay the loan for which the document was a security. But the defendant who has once admitted due execution of the agreement set up by the plaintiff in his suit for specific performance, he cannot be allowed to amend the written statement to allege that the agreement stood cancelled and superseded by a subsequent agreement.[6]

Further liabilities On the other hand, the vendor or the lessor, as the case may be, will be subject to the following liabilities at the instance of the purchaser or the lessee, as the case may be, that is, (1) if he has subsequently to the contract acquired any interest in the property, he may be compelled to make good the contract out of such interest [s. 13(1)(*a*)], (2) where the concurrence of other persons is necessary for validating the title and those other persons are bound to concur at his request, he may be compelled to procure such concurrence; likewise when the conveyance by other persons is necessary to validate that title and they are bound to convey it at his request, he may be compelled to procure such conveyance [s. 13(1)(*b*)], (3) where he as a vendor professes to sell his property as unencumbered property, though the property is mortgaged for an amount not exceeding the purchase money and he has in fact only a right to redeem it, he may be compelled to redeem the mortgage and to obtain a valid discharge and also a conveyance from the mortgagee, where necessary [s. 13(1)(*c*)], (4) if he has filed a suit

5 AIR 1991 MP 296.

6 *Shri Krishan Swarup Bhatnagar* v *Shri Chander Mohan Rewal* AIR 2000 HP 53.

for specific performance of the contract and his suit fails on the ground of want of title or imperfect title, he is liable to the purchaser or the lessee as the case may be for the return of his deposit, if any, with interest thereon, as well as the costs of the suit and the purchaser or the lessee shall also have a lien on the vendor's or the *lessor's* interest, if any, in the property which is the subject matter of the contract, for such deposit, interest and costs [s. 13(1)(*d*)].

The provisions of s. 13 of the Specific Relief Act 1963 are analogous to s. 43 of the Transfer of Property Act which runs thus:

> "43. Transfer by unauthorised person who subsequently acquires interest in property transferred. Where a person fraudulently or erroneously represents that he is authorised to transfer certain immovable property and professes to transfer such property for consideration, such transfer shall, at the option of the transferee, operate on any interest which the transferor may acquire in such property at any time during which the contract of transfer subsists.
>
> Nothing in this section shall impair the right of transferees in good faith for consideration without notice of the existence of the said option.

The fundamental distinction between s. 13 of the Specific Relief Act and s. 43 of the Transfer of Property Act is that while s. 13 of the Specific Relief Act applies only where the matter is still in the stage of a contract and has no application to cases where the actual transfer has taken place in respect of the property to which the vendor or lessor has no title or has only an imperfect title, s. 43 of the Transfer of Property Act applies to cases after the transfer of immovable property over which the transferor has no title. In *Silla Chandrasekaran* v *Lalita Shahuasi*,[7] it has been held in the light of s. 18 of the old Act (corresponding to s. 13 of the Specific Relief Act 1963) that there must first be a sale of the property by a person having an imperfect title thereto before applicability of the section can be considered. If after such a sale that person acquires an interest in the property, the vendor may compel him to make good the contract out of such interest and that if there was no sale at all but merely a contract for sale, this section would not apply. This decision has been reversed in appeal by the Supreme Court and it is no longer good law.[8] Their Lordships of the Supreme Court pointed out that the expression "subsequently" in s. 13 must be construed to mean "subsequent to the execution of the contract" and not subsequent to the execution of the sale deed.

In *Ehsanul Haq* v *Mohd. Umar*,[9] defendant agreed to sell a house property on 12.4.1958. As the house property was an evacuee property, it was sold by auction. The defendant being the highest bidder, the property was knocked

7 AIR 1959 Ori 169.

8 *Sille Chandrasekaram* v *Ramchandran Sahu* AIR 1964 SC 1789; (1964)7 SCR 858.

9 AIR 1973 All 425.

down to him on 14.4.1958. A sale certificate was also issued to him, by which he became the owner of the property with effect from 1st February 1959. However, instead of conveying the property to the plaintiff, he sold the property to another on 24.6.1959, who knew about the prior sale to the plaintiff. On suit by the plaintiff, the suit was decreed. On appeal, it was contended that the agreement was hit by s. 6(*a*) of the Transfer of Property Act.

Rejecting the contention, Malik, J held that the possibility of acquiring the property was neither so remote nor of the same category as enumerated in s. 6(*a*) of the Transfer of Property Act. Though the execution of the sale deed might have depended upon the ultimate sanction of the Custodian-General, since the defendant had paid a portion of the sale price, the sanction did not depend on a mere chance or whim of the Custodian-General. The Custodian-General having sanctioned the auction sale, the inchoate right of the defendant to the property had matured into a perfect right to execute the sale deed in favour of the plaintiff. The words 'any interest' in the sub-section make it clear that at the time of agreement the vendor may not have any interest to the property at all. The agreement is, therefore, enforceable.[10]

Where a sale is prohibited without the sanction of the Government, but an agreement for sale without previous sanction of the Government is entered into, such an agreement is not invalid in law. After the vendor subsequently obtains the sanction of the Government, the agreement may be enforced under cl. (*a*) of s. 13(1) against the vendor and even against the subsequent purchaser from him by the person in whose favour the agreement for sale was originally executed.[11] One *R* entered into an agreement with *RM* to purchase some agricultural land of which he was a tenant stipulating that the said *RM* was to apply for permission from the Collector to convert the agricultural land into a village site, that is non-agricultural, and the deed of sale was to be executed after the requisite permission had been obtained. Within a month of such agreement *R* entered into another agreement with one *J* to sell the same land at a higher price after getting the deed of sale from *RM*. But the right, title and interest of *RM* ceased under the Saurashtra Land Reforms Act 1951 and *R* was recognised by the Government as the occupant of the land and obtained the occupancy certificate and also permission to convert the land into a village site. *J* called upon *R* to execute the conveyance and on his failure to do so, *J* sued for specific performance and it was held that he was entitled to enforce a

10 *Prem Sukh Gulgulia* v *Habib Ullah* AIR 1945 Cal 355.

11 *Dr. C.L. Katial* v *Mrs. Chandnee Widya Vati Madden* AIR 1963 Punj 136 affirmed by the Supreme Court in *Chandnee Widya Vati Madden* v *Dr. C.L. Katial* AIR 1964 SC 978; (1964)2 SCR 495; (1964)2 SCJ 824.

contract specifically.[12] In *Motilal* v *Nanhelal*[13] S agreed to transfer to the plaintiff his cultivating rights in ser lands and according to the CP Tenancy Act, the sanction of the revenue authorities was a prerequisite for the transfer. The plaintiff's suit for specific performance was resisted on the ground that the court had no jurisdiction to require the defendant to make such an application to the revenue officer. It was held that S having agreed to transfer the cultivating rights of ser lands, there was an implied covenant on his part to do all things necessary to effect such a transfer and this would include an application to the revenue officer and that the court can direct the defendant to apply for the requisite sanction and convey the property to the plaintiff after the sanction was obtained.

Where a suit is filed only against the vendor who has executed the agreement and in whose name the patta of the lands stands, the court will not go into the question whether his title is defective or whether the property belongs to the partnership of which he is only a partner.[14]

Defendant Once it is established that plaintiff does not suffer from any disability and is otherwise competent to obtain specific performance, he may enforce it against:

(*a*) either party to the contract [s. 19(*a*)];

(*b*) any other person claiming under him by a title arising subsequently to the contract, except a transferee for value who has paid his money in good faith and without notice of the original contract [s. 19(*b*)];

(*c*) any person claiming under a title which, though prior to the contract and known to the plaintiff, might have been displaced by the defendant [s. 19(*c*)];

(*ca*) when a limited liability partnership has entered into a contract and subsequently becomes amalgamated with another limited liability partnership, the new limited liability partnership which arises out of the amalgamation [s. 19(*ca*)];[15]

(*d*) the amalgamating company [s. 19(*d*)]; and

(*e*) the company on its incorporation in respect of pre-incorporation contracts made by its promoters for the purpose of the company, provided that the contract is warranted by the terms of its incorporation and the company has accepted the contract and communicated the acceptance to the other party to the contract [s. 19(*e*)].

12 *Rajasara Ramjibhai Dahyabhai* v *Jain Narottam Das* AIR 1986 SC 1912; (1986)2 SCR 447; (1986)3 SCC 300.

13 AIR 1930 PC 287.

14 *Mir Abdul Hakeem* v *Abdul Mannan Khadri* AIR 1972 AP 178 relying on *Baluswami Aiyar* v *Lakshmana Aiyar* AIR 1921 Mad 172 (FB).

15 *Inserted* by the Specific Relief (Amendment) Act 2018 vide s. 8 (w.e.f. 1-10-2018).

A contract of sale between the parties to the contract does not create any interest or charge on the land but creates an obligation between the contracting parties. As a general rule a contract cannot be enforced except by a party to it. This rule is, however, subject to some exceptions contained in s. 15 of the Specific Relief Act 1963 which lays down that specific performance of a contract for sale of immovable property, viz. land, may be obtained by any party thereto or by the representative-in-interest or the principal of any part thereto. Ordinarily the benefits and obligations under a contract are claimable by and enforceable against not only the parties to the contract but also by or against the representative-in-interest of such parties, unless there is anything contrary expressly made in the contract itself. The representative-in-interest may be (*a*) an assignee of the contract from the original promise, or (*b*) his legal representative after his death.[16]

Party Specific performance of contract may be enforced against either party to the contract. A legal representative of either party to the contract answers the first part of cl. (*b*) of s. 19, Specific Relief Act and specific performance may be enforced against such legal representative too. The expression "party" as stated in Banerjee on *Law of Specific Relief* (Tagore Law Lectures),[17] includes both an actual contracting party and all of whom the contracting party represents while making the contract; that is, for whose benefit the contract is made. Thus, a Hindu son may be sued to fulfil the obligation of his deceased father, so that his liability under the contract may be determined. When the son steps into the shoes of his deceased father, e.g. Dayabhaga succession the son obviously answers the first part of cl. (*b*) of s. 19, Specific Relief Act. But when a decree has been made against the karta of joint Hindu family, it can be enforced against his son, a member of the coparcenary.[18]

A minor may be sued when the contract is made by his guardian for a necessary and beneficial purpose.[19] A contract entered into by the guardian of a minor, for purchase or sale of immovable property, is specifically enforceable by or against the minor if it was within the competency of the guardian to enter into on his behalf so as to bind him by it and if it is for the benefit of the minor.[20] But in *Nivarti Govind Ingale* v *Revanagouda Bhimanagouda Patil*,[1] the question of agreement being for the benefit of the minor was held not to arise in an agreement for reconveyance made in terms of deed of sale executed by the vendor.

16 *B.B. Goswami* v *T.K. Chakravarty* 90 CWN 849.

17 Banerjee on *Law of Specific Relief* (Tagore Law Lectures), 13th Ed., pp. 405-406.

18 *Tiruvenkatachariar* v *Venkatachariar* 23 IC 621; 26 Mad LJ 218; *Kosuri Ramaraju* v *Ivalury Ramalingan* ILR (1903)26 Mad 74; 12 Mad LJ 400.

19 *Krishnaswamy* v *Sundarappaayyar* ILR (1875)18 Mad 415.

20 *Roomal* v *Siri Niwas* AIR 1985 Del 153; *Kallathil Sridharan* v *Komath Pandyala Prasanna* (1996)6 SCC 218; JT 1996(8) SC 40; *Kokulam Subramanian* v *Kurra Subba Rao* AIR 1948 PC 95.

1 (1997)1 SCC 475; (1996)8 Supreme 794.

It may be apposite in this connection that a Hindu son in Hindu Law has a pious obligation towards his father to liquidate the debt of his father and to do the act promised by his father.

A party cannot escape such liability by adopting a devious device.

In *Jones* v *Lipman*[2] the defendant made a binding contract for the sale of land. But latter on he changed his mind and transferred the land to a company acquired by him solely for this purpose with a view to avoiding the performance. In an action by the plaintiff for specific performance against the defendant, the court held that the decree would be made since the company was the creature of the vendor, a device and a sham, a mask which he held before his face in an attempt to avoid recognition by the eye of Equity.

This type of action is popularly known as "piercing the veil".

However, strangers to the contract making a claim adverse to the title of the vendor contending that they are the co-owners of the contracted property are neither necessary nor proper parties and are, therefore, not entitled to be joined as parties to the suit.[3] As held in a Delhi case in suit for specific performance of contract of sale of property strangers cannot claim to be impleaded alleging they are co-owners as this would change the nature of the suit.[4] There is no jurisdiction to add a party in any other case merely because that would save a third person from the botheration of a separate suit.[5] A person to be added must be necessary to effectively and completely adjudicate upon and settle all points in the suit. A party cannot be added merely to avoid multiplicity of suits.[6]

A contract made with the Municipal Commissioner for displaying advertisement boards on electric poles was held to be not enforceable against the Electricity Board which objected to the display.[7] Where the purchaser of a flat had entered into an agreement for purchase of the flat with a builder, the owner of the land on which the building would be constructed was held to be not a necessary party in a suit for specific performance of such an agreement for sale.[8] Similarly in a suit filed by a purchaser for specific performance of a flat in a Co-operative Society, the Society was

2 [1962]1 All ER 442.

3 *Panne Khushali* v *Jeewanlal Mathoo Khatik* AIR 1976 MP 148 at p. 152 (FB) relying on *Prem Sukh Gulgulia* v *Habib Ullah* AIR 1945 Cal 355; *Banaras Bank* v *Bhagwandas* AIR 1947 All 18 (FB); *Nagi* v *Damodhar Jagobaji* AIR 1948 Nag 181; *Razia Begum* v *Anwar Begum* AIR 1958 SC 886; 1959 SCR 1111; 1958 SCJ 1214 and *Kshetra Mohan* v *Mohd. Sadir* AIR 1964 Tri 16 and overruling *Roopkishore* v *Tarabai* 1970 MPWR (SN) 132; *Raj K. Mehra* v *Anjali Bhaduri* AIR 1981 Del 237.

4 *Raj K. Mehra* v *Anjali Bhaduri* AIR 1981 Del 237.

5 *Rasiklal* v *Natverlal* AIR 1975 Guj 178; (1975)16 Guj LR 533.

6 *Arjan Singh* v *Kartar Singh* AIR 1975 Punj 184.

7 *Sagar Art Signs* v *Municipal Corporation* AIR 1988 MP 46.

8 *Chandrakant Bhojilal Gohil* v *Purshottam Mohanlal Makhwana* AIR 2000 Bom 18.

held not to be a necessary party; it will be bound to recognise and admit the plaintiff as its member if a decree is passed in his favour.[9]

As to third party's (not a party to contract of transfer) right to be joined in the suit under Or. 1, r. 10(2), CPC, the following guidelines may be borne in mind, namely (*i*) that such person has a direct interest in the subject matter of litigation, whether it reaches questions relating to movable or immovable property, as distinguished from indirect or commercial interest; (*ii*) that the facts constituting the interest claimed in the subject matter of the litigation should be such that in the absence of such third party court cannot effectually and completely adjudicate upon and settle all the issues involved in the suit.[10]

Where one of the co-owners had agreed to sell the entire property and the purchaser filed a suit for specific performance against him, the other co-owners are not necessary parties to the suit, nor can they seek to be impleaded in that suit.[11] Where "C" acquired as a co-owner title to the property under a decree of the court, and sought to be impleaded as a party to a pending suit in respect of the same property between *A* & *B*, it was held by the Supreme Court that having acquired title under a decree of the court, it was not a matter arising out of or in respect of the same act or transaction or series of acts or transactions in relation to the claim made in the suit and hence "C" was neither a necessary nor a proper party to the suit.

The rule that third party to the contract, i.e. strangers to contract should not be joined in a suit for specific performance, is based on the principle that the scope of a suit for specific performance of a contract for sale ought not to be enlarged and the suit turned also into a title suit between one or either of the parties to the contract and stranger to the contract.[12]

In a Kerala case the plaintiff sued for specific performance against defendant in respect of sale of a building and land underneath. Defendant in his written statement raised the plea that he had executed a ground rent lease in favour of his wife in respect of the land where the theatre building in dispute and other structures were constructed. In this factual, situation impleading the wife and defendant is unexceptionable, although she was not a party to the agreement.[13]

The scope of suit for specific performance should not be enlarged but where a stranger is a person in actual possession of the property and might

9 *Haren Krishna Kumar Metha* v *Kerala Pridudas Nebhanani* AIR 2001 Bom 187.

10 *Narayana Rao* v *Bheema Rao* AIR 1979 Kant 33; *Surjit Kaur* v *Chand Singh* AIR 1984 Punj 207; 1984 Rev LR 158.

11 *E. Ajaykumar* v *Tulsi Bai* AIR 1973 Bom 330; *H.G. Tej Kar* v *Jeet Singh* AIR 1998 Raj 201.

12 *Prem Sukh Gulgulia* v *Habib Ullah* AIR 1945 Cal 355.

13 *K.S. Abraham* v *Chandy Rosamma* AIR 1989 Ker 167.

be affected by the relief claimed, he may be joined as a party to the suit.[14] See also Fry on *A Treatise on the Specific Performance of Contracts.*[15]

> "A stranger to the contract may so mix himself up with it by setting up a claim to some benefit resulting from it, as to render himself liable to be made a party to proceedings for the enforcement of the contract .... In some cases where a portion of the relief claimed might affect the person in actual possession of the property, that person may properly be made a party to an action for the specific performance of the contract ......"[16]

Protection to bona fide purchaser Section 19(*b*) protects the *bona fide* purchaser in good faith for value without notice of the original contract. This protection is in the nature of exception to the general rule. Hence the onus of proof of good faith is on the purchaser who takes the plea that he is an innocent purchaser. Good faith is a question of fact to be considered and decided on the facts of each case. Section 52 of the Indian Penal Code emphasises due care and attention in relation to good faith. In the General Clauses Act emphasis is laid on honesty.[17] However, the person claiming protection has to prove that he had no notice of prior agreement.[18]

Person having adverse possession Section 19 is exhaustive on the question as to who are the parties against whom a contract for specific performance may be enforced. Therefore, the persons seeking addition in the suit for specific performance of the contract for sale who were not claiming under the vendor but they were claiming adverse to the title of the vendor do not fall in any of the categories enumerated in cls. (*a*) to (*e*) of s. 19 of the Specific Relief Act.[19]

Specific performance and third party What is the legal position when a promisee seeks specific performance in favour of a third party? In *Beswick* v *Beswick*,[20] *A* promised *B* (in return for *B*'s transfer of his business to *A*) to pay an annuity to *B*'s widow, *C* after *B*'s death. The House of Lords held that this promise could be specifically enforced by B's personal representative, C against *A*. Thus, *A* was ordered to pay the annuity to C who in this way obtained the benefit of the contract to which she was not a party even though the case did not fall within the exception to the common law doctrine of privity of contract. In deciding the case the House of Lords stressed three points: (1) that *B*'s remedy at law was inadequate, because, the damages

14 *Bai Devkabai* v *Shah Shamji Mulji* AIR 1971 Guj 256 at p. 258 relying on *Mahadevappa Parakanhatti* v *Shivappa Parappa Kupati* AIR 1943 Bom 27.
15 6th Ed., p. 90.
16 Halsbury's *Laws of England*, 4th Ed., vol. 44, para 512.
17 *R.K. Mohd. Ubaidullah* v *Hajee C. Abdul Wahab* (2000)6 SCC 402; AIR 2001 SC 1658.
18 *Meena Bibi* v *Hilda Glady Sylus* (2006)2 CHN 24.
19 *Kasturi* v *Iyyamperumal* (2005)6 SCC 733.
20 [1968] AC 58.

would be nominal; (2) that the promisor A had received the entire consideration for his promise; and (3) that the contract could be specifically enforced by *A*, had *B* refused to perform his promise to transfer the business. But *Beswick* v *Beswick*,[1] is not a direct authority for availability of such a remedy in any of the following cases:[2] (1) where the promisee has a remedy at law other than for a nominal damages; (2) where the promisor has not received the whole or any part of consideration for his promise; (3) where the contract is wholly executory and cannot be specifically enforced by the promisor; and (4) where the promise sued upon would not have been specifically enforceable by the promisee, if it had been made to him for his own benefit. As a general principle the promisee should be able to obtain specific performance in favour of the third party whenever that is the most appropriate method of enforcing the contract which is actually made.

Bona fide purchaser for value without notice According to s.19 of the Act, a transferee for value, who has paid his money in good faith and without notice of the original contract, is excluded from the purview of cl. (*b*) of s.19. To fall within the excluded class, a transferee must show that:

(*a*) he has purchased for value the property (which is the subject-matter of the suit for specific performance of the contract);

(*b*) he has paid his money to the vendor in good faith; and

(*c*) he had no notice of the earlier contract for sale (specific performance of which is sought to be enforced against him).

The provision is based on the principle of English law which fixes priority between a legal right and an equitable right. If '*A*' purchases any property from '*B*' and thereafter '*B*' sells the same property to '*C*', the sale in favour of '*A*', being prior in time, prevails over the sale in favour of '*C*' as both '*A*' and '*C*' acquired legal rights. But, where one is a legal right and the other is an equitable right"a *bona fide* purchaser for valuable consideration who obtains a legal estate at the time of his purchase without notice of a prior equitable right is entitled to priority in equity as well as at law".[3] Thus, a transferee for value who has paid his money in good faith and without notice of the original contract cannot be made a defendant for specific performance of that original contract. In England, a contract of specific performance gives rise to an equitable estate, but not so in India. Although there is no equitable estate created by agreement for sale of real property in India yet the third party doctrine prevails here. It is a doctrine of justice;

1 [1968] AC 58.
2 Chitty on *Contracts*, 30th Ed., vol. 1, para 27-051.
3 *Ram Niwas* v *Bano* (2000)6 SCC 685; AIR 2000 SC 2921; see also Snell's *Equity*, 13th Ed., p. 48.

it prevails by the force of justice, and has forced its way into the Indian status law.[4]

Good faith Section 19(*b*) uses the phrase transferee for value who has paid his money in good faith. The terms 'good faith' and '*bona fide*' are understood to be synonymous. Section 3(22) of the General Clauses Act 1897, states that "a thing shall be deemed to be done in good faith, where it is in fact done honestly, whether it is done negligently or not". Similarly, s. 52 of the Indian Penal Code 1860 defines good faith. It states that "Nothing is said to be done or believed in good faith which is done or believed without due care and attention". The distinction between the definition of the word "good faith" in s. 3(22) of the General Clauses Act 1897 and in s. 52 of the Indian Penal Code 1860 was pointed out by the Supreme Court in *Harbhajan Singh* v *State of Punjab*,[5] in the following words:

> "The element of honesty, which is introduced by the definition prescribed by the General Clauses Act, is not introduced by the definition of the Code".

Thus, honest, though negligent, conduct will satisfy the test of good faith under the General Clauses Act, while negligence will negative good faith for the purpose of the Penal Code. However, the definition of 'good faith' in s. 2(*h*) of the Limitation Act 1963 is almost in pari materia with the definition appearing in Indian Penal Code, except that the Penal Code also takes within its fold "belief". But, it must be noted that the word "good faith" is not defined in the Specific Relief Act 1963, though the word appears in s. 19(*b*) of the Act. Section 2(*e*) of the Specific Relief Act 1963, states that all other words and expressions not defined therein, but defined under the Indian Contract Act 1872, shall have the same meaning assigned to them under that Act. But the Indian Contract Act 1872 also does not define the expression good faith. Therefore, the expression "good faith" appearing in s. 19(*b*) of the Specific Relief Act 1963, should be understood in the light of the definition of the expression under s. 3(22) of the General Clauses Act 1897, since s. 3 of the General Clauses Act, declares that the definitions provided therein apply to all Central Acts and Regulations, made after the commencement of that Act, unless there is anything repugnant in the subject or context.[6]

Persons claiming title under the party subsequent to contract Such persons include heirs, administrators, executors, assignees and other transferees of the party. But a sharer on partition of joint Hindu family does not derive title to his share from any one else and, therefore, it cannot be said that he is claiming under somebody for the purpose of this section. Therefore, even

4 *Archit Banijya & Biniyog Pvt. Ltd.* v *Asha Lata Ghosh* (2000)2 CHN 640.
5 AIR 1966 SC 97.
6 *B. Nemi Chand Jain* v *G. Ravindran* (2010)2 CTC 751.

assuming that a compromise decree which is put in defence is fraudulent or collusive, it is not possible to apply s. 19(*b*) to the case. The concept of joint Hindu family property is that each of the coparceners is entitled to the same right as the other and they all hold together the coparcenary property, and that when a partition is effected all that happens is not a transfer of interest from one to the other, but only release of the interest of one coparcener in favour of the other in specific immovable property allotted to the latter as and for his share.[7] The Apex Court has approved the broad proposition that partition is not a transfer of property but would only signify the surrender of a portion of joint right in exchange of similar right from the other co-sharer or co-sharers.[8] A Calcutta case held that partition is a severance of joint status and all that is necessary to constitute partition is a definite and unequivocal indication of intention of a member of joint family to enjoy his share in severalty, although such intention is required to be communicated to the other members of the family.[9]

A suit for specific performance of a contract to grant lease of agricultural lands can be enforced by lessor's legal heirs. Where the daughters of the vendor-defendant acquire pending a suit for specific performance right as coparceners by virtue of the Andhra Pradesh Hindu Succession (Amendment) Act 1986, their rights will be subject to the agreement for sale and the result of such a suit.[10]

In *Vasantha Viswanathan* v *V.K. Elayalwar*,[11] the High Court recorded a categorical finding that some of the defendants were not *bona fide* purchasers without notice of the agreement for sale between the plaintiff and the first defendant. Under s. 19(*b*) of the Specific Relief Act, specific performance of a contract can be enforced not only against either party thereto but also against any other person claiming under him by a title arising subsequent to the contract, except a transferee for value who has paid his money in good faith and without notice of the original contract. In view of the aforesaid provision, the Supreme Court held that the High Court was quite justified in passing a decree against them as well.

But where partition is proved to be fraudulent designed to defeat the rights of the plaintiff under his contract of sale by the vendor giving up the chance of the suit properties or a share in them being allotted to him in a fair division, in such a case the allottees may be treated as subsequent

7 *K. Appa Rao* v *P. Balasubramania Gramani* AIR 1976 Mad 70 at p. 73 (DB) relying on *Rangayya Reddi* v *Subramania Iyer* AIR 1918 Mad 681 (FB).

8 *Mohar Singh* v *Devi Charan* AIR 1988 SC 1365 at p. 1368; 1988 Supp (1) SCR 255; JT 1988(2) SC 492.

9 *Fatechand Maheshri* v *State of West Bengal* AIR 1972 Cal 177; 76 CWN 137.

10 *Vanimisatti Anil Kumar* v *Jayavarapu Krishnamurthy* AIR 1995 AP 105.

11 (2001)6 Supreme 442; AIR 2001 SC 3367.

transferees with notice.[12] So also where an undivided coparcener of a joint Hindu family consisting of himself and his brother entered into a contract for the sale of his share in the joint family properties which consisted of only two items of land and subsequently effected a settlement conveying his share to his brother who took the settlement with knowledge of the contract, the promisee under the contract was held entitled to specific performance as against the brother who took the settlement as a transferee within the meaning of s. 19(*b*).[13]

Some of several legal representatives of promisee declining to get the contract performed In view of s. 15(*a*) & (*b*), Specific Relief Act, contract of transfer may be enforced at the instance of any party to the contract as also by any of his legal representatives. On the death of the promisee or on the transfer of right under the agreement of transfer which is an actionable claim the heirs of the promisee or the promisee's transferee may enforce the contract against the promissor by virtue of s. 15(*b*) of the Act. If some of such heirs or legal representatives of promisee declines to join in the suit for specific performance, one only may sue impleading the other heirs or legal representatives as pro forma defendants. Then the plaintiff may be treated to be representative-in-interest because their interest in the suit property is the same and the plaintiff can represent their interest.[14]

Exception to the rule—subsequent transferee—specific performance against As to specific performance against a subsequent transferee s. 19(*b*) of the Specific Relief Act 1963 also provides that specific performance of a contract may be enforced against any person claiming under any party to the contract by a title arising subsequent to the contract, except a transferee for value who has paid his money in good faith and without notice of the original contract. Where a person has purchased a property subsequent to the agreement of which the plaintiff seeks specific performance, such a person is protected where he had acquired it acting *bona fide*, for value and without notice of the plaintiff's prior agreement in which case the plaintiff will not be entitled to claim specific performance of contract against him.[15] After referring to this provision, Madras Division Bench points out that the plain language of the cl. (*b*) shows that the subsequent transferee can retain the benefit of his transfer by purchase which, *prima facie*, he had no right to get, only after satisfying two conditions concurrently viz., (1) he must have paid the full value for which he purchased the property, and (2) he must have paid it in good faith and without notice of the prior contract. The payment need not be in money, it may be in money's worth or adjustment

12 *Rangayya Reddi* v *Subramania Iyer* AIR 1918 Mad 681 (FB).
13 *J. Venkataramayya* v *J. Raghavalu* AIR 1925 Mad 492.
14 *Jagdish Singh* v *Ram Lal* AIR 1988 All 12.
15 *Jagan Nath* v *Jagdish Rai* AIR 1998 SC 2028; (1998)5 SCC 537; JT 1998(3) SC 551.

of some kind, but that must be actual and not promised and nothing should remain to be paid or adjusted.[16] Further, it was also observed therein that the burden of proof is upon the subsequent purchaser to establish these conditions in order that his rights might prevail over the prior agreement of sale.[17] Generally speaking if a person as the owner of the property, has entered into an agreement to sell the property, he cannot thereafter convey the same property to any other person, as after the prior agreement of sale, he cannot be said to be a free owner of the property. If he subsequently alienates the property he can alienate it only subject to the rights created under the prior agreement of sale.[18]

Merely because the subsequent purchaser is owner of the adjacent land, it cannot be said that he is not a *bona fide* purchaser for value.[19] When the subsequent purchasers did not enquire about the property in question, from the office of Sub-Registrar, as to whether any sale deed or agreement to sell was executed, they could not be termed as *bona fide* purchasers.[20]

Subsequent purchaser must be a *bona fide* purchaser. The fact that he has paid a larger amount does not give him greater equity.[1] But "*bona fide*" or "good faith" does not postulate a fishing enquiry. All that it requires is that the purchaser should take reasonable care to ascertain that the transferor had power to make the transfer.[2]

In *Abdul Mazid* v *Burhanuddin Ahmed*[3] the court held that unless there be an overt act on the part of the contractee or the tenant to be conspicuous to the subsequent purchaser, who makes an honest and reasonable enquiry suited to the facts and circumstances, his claim should not be negatived, and that the concept of notice as envisaged in s. 3, *Expln.* II of the Transfer of Property Act was the same as in s. 19(*b*).

Subsequent purchaser when had full knowledge of earlier agreement of sale, decree for specific performance of earlier agreement is justified.[4] On the other hand as an agreement of sale does not create a charge on the property nor any interest subsequent transferee for consideration without notice of prior agreement of sale is not bound by the disputed agreement of sale.[5]

16 *Mrs. Futnani Dairy* v *T. Rangasamy* (1994)II CCC 107 (Mad).
17 *Veeramalai* v *Thadikara* AIR 1968 Mad 383 followed in *Vimala Ammal* v *C. Suseela* AIR 1991 Mad 209 (210-211); *Muralidhar* v *Yellappa Lalu* AIR 1994 Bom 358.
18 *Veeramalai* v *Thadikara* AIR 1968 Mad 383 at p. 385.
19 *P. Laxmi Ammal* v *S. Laxmi Ammal* AIR 1991 Mad 137.
20 *Ram Swarup Singh* v *Karan Singh* AIR 2010 Utt 122.
1 *Abdul Kayum Ahmad* v *Damodhar Kinhekar* AIR 1964 Bom 46.
2 *Ram Lakhan* v *Ram Govind* AIR 1977 All 328 at p. 330; but see *Basruddin Khan* v *Gurudarshan Das* AIR 1970 Pat 304 at p. 309 (DB) (*bona fide* means proper enquiry).
3 AIR 1980 Gau 44 (DB).
4 *Jagdish Singh* v *Ram Lal* AIR 1988 All 12.
5 *Narayana Pillai* v *Kunju Amma* AIR 1990 Kar 177.

The relevant time for notice is the time of the completion of the transfer and not the time at which the contract was entered into.[6]

Where the prior contractee transferee is in possession of the property by a registered deed of usufructuary mortgage, it cannot be said that the buyer of the property had no notice.[7] On facts held that the appellants were not *bona fide* purchasers without notice. In this case the new plea that even if the appellants had notice of the possession, it would only mean that they were in possession in pursuance of a usufructuary mortgage and not in pursuance of an agreement of sale was not allowed to be raised. The court, however, observed that this defence would have had some substance if it had been taken in the pleadings and spoken to in the evidence.[8]

But where the subsequent purchaser was aware of the plaintiff being in possession of the suit property as tenant and did not make any enquiry at the time of his purchase, the Supreme Court has held that the subsequent purchaser was not a *bona fide* purchaser for value without notice and the decree for specific performance in favour of the tenant against third parties has been upheld.[9]

There is no constructive notice of an agreement of sale of a property, since it does not require any registration under the Registration Act.[10]

The words "who has paid this money" are not equivalent to "who has agreed to pay his money".[11]

Even so relief may be denied even against a transferee with notice if the plaintiff just stands by and neither objects nor gives notice.[12]

But in *Bai Dosabai* v *Mathuradas Govinddas*,[13] the Supreme Court has said—

> "The concept and creation of duality of ownership, legal and equitable, on the execution of an agreement to convey immovable property, as understood in England, is alien to Indian Law which recognises one owner, i.e. the legal

6 *Mumford* v *Stohwasser* [1874] LR 18 Eq 556.

7 *Ram Bilas Ojha* v *Bishwa Muni* AIR 1978 SC 1094; (1979)1 SCC 21.

8 *Damacharia Venkata Seshaiah* v *Damacharla Venkayya* AIR 1974 AP 193 (DB); *Bannobi* v *Afrozzia* AIR 1979 All 124; *H.N. Narayanaswamy Naidu* v *Deveeramma* AIR 1981 Kant 93; *Veeramalai Vanniar* v *Thadikara Vanniar* AIR 1968 Mad 383 at p. 386 (DB); *Parvathathammal* v *Sivasankara Bhattar* AIR 1952 Mad 265; In re, *M.R.P. Yella Reddi* AIR 1954 Andh 20.

9 *R.K. Mohamed Ubaidullah* v *Haji C. Abdul Wahab* AIR 2001 SC 1658.

10 *Hiralal* v *Bhagirathi* AIR 1975 Cal 445 at p. 448 (DB).

11 *Veeramalai Vanniar* v *Thadikara Vanniar* AIR 1968 Mad 383; *Himatla Motilal* v *Vasudev Ganesh Mhaskar* 36 Bom 446 (giving a promissory note for the balance); *Simanchal Mahapatro* v *Budhiram Padhi* AIR 1976 Ori 113 at p. 115 (DB).

12 *Jhandoo* v *Ramesh Chandra* AIR 1971 All 189 at p. 191.

13 AIR 1980 SC 1334.

owner.[14] The ultimate paragraph of s. 54 of the Transfer of Property Act expressly enunciates that a contract for the sale of immovable property does not, of itself create any interest in or charge on such property. But the ultimate and penultimate paragraphs of s. 40 of the Transfer of Property Act make it clear that such a contract creates an obligation annexed to the ownership of immovable property, not amounting to an interest in the property, but which obligation may be enforced against a transferee with notice of the contract or a gratuitous transferee of the property. Thus, the equitable ownership in property recognised by Equity in England is translated into Indian Law as an obligation annexed to the ownership of property, not amounting to an interest in the property but an obligation which may be enforced against a transferee with notice or a gratuitous transferee."

Conditions under s. 19(b) The purchase contemplated under cl. (*b*) of s. 19 must satisfy four conditions: (1) that the transfer is for value; (2) that the payment of full value has been made; (3) that the purchase was done in good faith; and (4) that the purchase, including payment of money was without the notice of the original contract.[15]

Subsequent transferee and vendor—need of joining and remaining as parties In suit for specific performance subsequent transferee is a necessary party.[16] Expressing similar view a Madras case held in suit for specific performance of agreement of sale the subsequent purchaser of the property is a necessary party and unless he is impleaded, the decree is nullity and cannot be executed against him. Thus valid title to the suit property would remain with the subsequent purchaser and he cannot be dispossessed pursuant to the said decree.[17]

In a decree for specific performance of contract of sale when the contracted property had been transferred to subsequent transferee, the decree must direct the vendor to execute the deed and in that deed the subsequent transferee must join.[18]

It follows therefore in such suits not only subsequent transferee but also their vendor is a necessary party.[19] A suit against a subsequent transferee transferee is subject to a limitation period of three years.[20]

14 *Rambaran Prasad* v *Ram Mohit Hazra* AIR 1967 SC 744; (1967)1 SCR 293 and *Narandas Karsondas* v *S.A. Kamtam* AIR 1977 SC 774; (1977)2 SCR 341.

15 *Sujata Sanzgiry* v *Ankush R. Naik* (2006)1 Mah LJ 639; (2006)2 Bom CR 179: AIR 2005 Bom 404.

16 *Narayana Pillai* v *Kunju Amma* AIR 1990 Ker 177.

17 *Vimala Ammal* v *C. Suseela* AIR 1991 Mad 209.

18 *Dwarka Prasad Singh* v *Harikant Singh* AIR 1973 SC 655; (1973)2 SCR 1064; (1973)1 SCC 179.

19 *Khadir Saheb* v *Amin Saheb* AIR 1981 Kant 89.

20 *Kali Narayan Roy* v *Dilip Kumar Roy Choudhury* AIR 2013 Cal 16.

In suit for specific performance of contract of sale, possession too should be prayed for. If not so prayed, the plaint may be amended to include the prayer at any stage. So, if one co-sharer contracts to sell a property, the other co-sharer in possession is at least a proper party. Such a co-sharer may get himself impleaded in the suit for specific performance.[1]

In a suit for specific performance when the plaintiff has been put into possession of the property regarding which agreement of sale had been entered into and he had already paid the entire sale price to the karta of the coparcenary family, the coparceners are not necessary parties.[2]

In a Patna case an interesting question as to the effect of absence of a transferee cropped up. In that case defendant No. 1, the widow of one Sukhlal on 21st April 1969 executed an agreement of sale to transfer $^1/_6$th share in suit property having received a substantial sum as earnest money. Subsequently defendants No. 1 to 4, who were the widow and daughters of Sukhlal sold to defendants No. 5 and 6 under a registered sale deed. Defendants No. 5 and 6 sold the property purchased by them to defendants No. 7 to 13 under registered sale deed. So far as defendant No. 7 is concerned, he purchased the suit property in the name of his father who was none else than defendant No. 14. Defendant No. 7 died during the pendency of the suit without being substituted. The plaintiffs to wriggle out of the difficulty from the situation that the suit had abated urged that the whole appeal would not become incompetent because respondent No. 7 was not a necessary party, but was a pro forma defendant as he is purchaser from the purchaser and the specific performance decree could have been enforced only against the vendor of this respondent who alone could have taken defence that he was a purchaser for value without notice. He further contended that respondent No. 7 is not a necessary party for another reason namely according to the defendants themselves defendant No. 7 had purchased the property in the name of the defendant No. 14 (respondent No. 7) which shows that defendant No. 14 was a benamdar for defendant No. 7 and defendant No. 7 was really the owner of the property who was made a party in the suit and who is alive. Repelling the contention and holding that defendant No. 7 was a necessary party and his death without being substituted entails the suit being rendered incompetent, the Patna High Court held that in absence of a *benamdar* the matter can be decided if the real owner has been impleaded as party in the suit.[3]

The logic behind making subsequent transferee a necessary party is that he is required to pass on the title which resides in him to the proper transferee.[4] Further, the subsequent transferee is the person within whose

1 *B. Mahboob Ali* v *B. Subhan Saheb* (1986)1 Andh LT 67 (NRC).
2 *Aman Behal* v *Arun Kansal* AIR 1987 P&H 52.
3 *Pradip Narain Singh* v *Brij Nandan Prasad* AIR 1988 Pat 147.
4 *Dilip Bastimal Jain* v *Baban B Kamble* (2012)1 ICC 652 (Bom).

knowledge the facts as to whether he has paid and whether he had notice of the original contract lie, and the provisions of ss. 103 and 106 of the Indian Evidence Act 1872, have a bearing on the question. The plaintiff does not necessarily have knowledge of either matter.[5]

Other illustrations *A* contracts to convey certain land to *B* by a particular day. *A* dies intestate before that day without having conveyed the land. *B* may compel *A*'s heir or other representative-in-interest to perform the contract specifically.

A contracts to sell certain land to *B* for ₹5,000. *A* afterwards conveys the land for ₹6,000 to *C* who has notice of the original contract. *B* may enforce specific performance of the contract as against *C*.

A contracts to sell land to *B* for ₹5,000. *B* takes possession of the land. Afterwards *A* sells it to *C* for ₹6,000. *C* makes no enquiry of *B* relating to his interest in land. *B*'s possession is sufficient to affect *C* with notice of his interest and he may enforce specific performance of the contract against *C*.

A contracts in consideration of ₹1,000 to bequeath certain of his lands to *B*. Immediately after the contract *A* dies intestate, and *C* takes out administration to his estate. *B* may enforce specific performance of the contract against *C*.

A contracts to sell land to *B*. Before the completion of the contract *A* becomes a lunatic and *C* is appointed his committee. *B* may specifically enforce the contract against *C*.

Subsequent transfer—burden of proof of exception In view of s. 19, Specific Relief Act 1963 except as otherwise provided by Chapter II of the Specific Relief Act specific performance of a contract may be enforced *inter alia*, against either party thereto or any other person claiming under the defendant by a title arising subsequent to the contract. Clause (*b*) to s. 19 provides an exception to the rule by laying down if any person claiming under the defendant be a transferee for value paying his money in good faith and without notice of the original contract, then specific performance cannot be enforced against him. Thus, where a transferee establishes that he has purchased the land in good faith for valuable consideration without notice of the original contract, the specific performance can be refused.[6]

It is true that the initial burden is always on the vendee to show that he had no knowledge of the agreement. But the vendee has only to discharge this burden by leading a negative evidence. The negative evidence can only consist of his own statement denying that he had knowledge of the same.

5 *Padmini Raghavan v H.A. Sonnappa* ILR (2014) Kar 233; (2014)1 KCCR 1; (2014)1 AIR Kant R 706; 2014 AIR CC 1079; (2014)2 ICC 735.

6 *Pandurang Bayaji Pisal v Dagadu Arjuna Jadhav* (2015)5 Mah LJ 228; (2015)4 Bom CR 710; (2015)155 AIC 513; (2016)2 CCC 457.

As soon as the vendee denies knowledge of the notice, the burden shifts on to the vendor (prior buyer) that the vendee had the notice of the earlier agreement.[7]

Where sale deed is registered after the filing of the suit, the subsequent purchaser would not be entitled to the benefit of s. 19(*b*).[8] Notice of prior contract cannot be assumed only because the transferee is an adjacent owner.[9]

Where consideration is paid in full and vendees are ignorant of the original contract, good faith must be presumed in the absence of evidence to the contrary.[10] Honesty of intention is the essence of good faith. If after honest investigation nothing comes to his knowledge about the pre-existing right, title or contract and nothing is found to put him to further inquiry and consequently an honest purchase is made and value paid, law will protect such purchaser.[11]

As held in *Veeramalai Vanniar* v *Thadikara Vanniar*[12] the burden of the proof is upon the subsequent purchaser to establish that his rights prevail over the prior purchaser.

The onus is on the defendant who has taken a registered sale deed executed after the contract for sale in favour of the plaintiff to prove that he is a *bona fide* purchaser for value without notice of the earlier contract.[13]

In view of s. 19, Specific Relief Act 1963 except as otherwise provided by Chapter II of the Specific Relief Act specific performance of a contract may be enforced *inter alia*, against either party thereto or any other person claiming under the defendant by a title arising subsequent to the contract. Clause (*b*) to s. 19 provides an exception to the rule by laying down if any person claiming under the defendant be a transferee for value paying his money in good faith and without notice of the original contract, then specific performance cannot be enforced against him.

In view of the principle that one who likes to take advantage of an exception is to bring his case under the penumbra of the exception once the

7 *Dhadi Dalal* v *Basudeb Satpathy* AIR 1961 Ori 129; *Ramchander Singh* v *Bibi Asghari Begum* AIR 1957 Pat 224; *Kirtarath Rai* v *Sripat Rai* AIR 1928 All 307; *Aunachala Thevar* v *Govinda Rajan Chettiar* ILR (1977)2 Mad LJ 431; *P. Laxmi Ammal* v *S. Laxmi Ammal* AIR 1991 Mad 137.

8 *Har Narain* v *Mam Chand* (2010)13 SCC 128.

9 *P. Laxmi Ammal* v *S. Laxmi Ammal* AIR 1991 Mad 137.

10 *Kanshi Ram* v *Iswhardas* AIR 1923 Lah 108.

11 *Abdul Mazid* v *Burnahuddin Ahmed* AIR 1980 Gau 44 at pp. 52 and 55 (DB).

12 AIR 1968 Mad 383 at p. 385 (DB).

13 *Basruddin Khan* v *Gurudarshan Das* AIR 1970 Pat 304 at p. 308 (DB) relying on *Harendra Chandra Dass* v *Nanda Lal Roy* AIR 1933 Cal 98; *Saukhi Sah* v *Mahamaya Prasad Singh* AIR 1934 Pat 518; *Bhupnarain Singh* v *Gokulchand Mahton* AIR 1934 PC 68; *Shankarlal Narayandas Mundade* v *New Mofussil Co. Ltd.* AIR 1946 PC 97; *Brajabala* v *Radhakamal* AIR 1969 Ori 63.

plaintiff proves his agreement and that such agreement is otherwise enforceable it is for the defendant, subsequent transferee to prove (1) the transfer he claims protection under, was for value, (2) the money had been paid, (3) the purchase was *bona fide* and (4) the purchase including payment of money was without notice of prior contract. The first two elements are positive while the last two are negative and inferential.[14]

In suit for specific performance of contract of sale if the plaintiff proves his prior contract and the defendant is found to have transferred the property to a subsequent transferee, the onus is upon the subsequent transferee to prove the first, the subsequent transfer is for value and secondly he is a purchaser with no notice of prior agreement.

A purchaser under an agreement for sale of property can enforce his contract against a subsequent purchaser who has notice of the earlier agreement.[15] Notice under this clause may be expressed or implied upon the subsequent transferee. The term has a meaning wider than the word "knowledge".[16] It would include notice given to one of the partners of the firm.[17] A person who purchases the property without enquiries, is not entitled to the protection under this provision.[18] In *Akilandathammal* v *Ramasamy Udayar*,[19] a third party depended entirely on the vendor and made no independent enquiry and therefore was held not entitled to the benefit of the provision. Similarly, the purchaser who relied on the assertion of the vendor and abstained from making any enquiry into the real nature of the possession, is deemed to have notice of the earlier agreement for sale.[20] Where the vendor is not in possession of the property under the agreement for sale and the purchaser wilfully abstained from making any enquiry into the nature of interest held by the person in possession, he is not a person without notice of the rights of the person in possession, even though he has registered his own document as against an unregistered deed of sale in favour of the person in possession.[1]

In *Mummich Reddi Papanagiri Yella Reddi* v *Sulla Subhi Reddi*,[2] it was observed that where a person purchases property from the owner knowing that it is in possession of another, he is under a duty to enquire into the nature of that possession and in the absence of such enquiry, knowledge of title under which possession is held should be attributed to the purchaser.

14 *Dinesh Chandra Guha* v *Satchidananda Mukherjee* AIR 1972 Ori 235 at p. 238.
15 *Govinda* v *Shanti Bai* AIR 1972 SC 1520; (1973)3 SCC 418.
16 *Ram Nivas* v *Bano* AIR 2000 SC 2921; (2000)6 SCC 685; JT 2000(8) SC 340.
17 *Kanhiyalal* v *Devidas Jaganath* AIR 1931 Lah 227.
18 *Babu Ram Bak* v *Madhab Chandra Pallay* AIR 1914 Cal 333.
19 (1966)2 Mad 117.
20 *Ram Nivas* v *Bano* AIR 2000 SC 2921; (2000)6 SCC 685; JT 2000(8) SC 340.
1 *Sastha Kumarasamy* v *Joseph Alasius* AIR 1950 Travancore & Cochin 61 (FB); *Muralidhar* v *Yellappa Lalu* AIR 1994 Bom 358.
2 AIR 1994 AP 20.

The question whether registration of the original contract for sale is sufficient notice of the contract within the meaning of this clause, there has been a difference of judicial opinion. The High Courts of Calcutta and Madras have held that it is not a notice.[3] The Bombay and Allahabad High Courts have taken a different view.[4] In view of the amendment of s. 3 of the Transfer of Property Act 1882, registration is not notice unless the conditions contained in the Explanation are complied with viz., that registration is made according to the provisions of the Registration Act and Rules made thereunder and entered in the books prescribed. In any case, a purchaser who did not make necessary enquiry about the existence of an earlier registered agreement by inspecting the registration record is deemed to have notice of such an agreement.[5]

The onus of proof of absence of any notice of prior agreement upon the subsequent transferee but very little evidence sometimes mere denial discharges the burden.[6]

Test to implead subsequent purchaser In a suit for specific performance, when a subsequent purchaser is sought to be impleaded, the true test that has to be applied by the court is to determine whether the purchaser claims title under the vendor of the plaintiff or whether, contrariwise, he claims a title independent of or adverse to the title of the vendor.[7] However, there is no requirement of producing any material or evidence for establishing that the subsequent purchaser is not a *bona fide* purchaser, at the stage when leave for impleadment/consequential amendments is being applied for.[8]

Proof of notice sent by registered post The question of receipt of notice is relevant in two circumstances. First, to an intending subsequent purchaser a notice by registered post may be sent communicating the factum of existence of formal agreement of sale. If such notice is proved to have been received, the subsequent purchaser should be treated to be a purchaser having notice of prior agreement and if despite notice he purchases the property which had been agreed to be sold there is no bar to passing a decree for specific performance against him.

3 *Preonath Chatopadhya* v *Ashutosh Ghosh* 27 Cal 358; *Shan Maun Mull* v *Madras Building Co.* 15 Mad 268.

4 *Lakshman Das Sarupchand* v *Dasrat* 6 Bom 168; *Janki Prasad* v *Kishan Dutti* 16 All 478.

5 *Godhan Pola* v *Ram Biyas* AIR 1995 All 357.

6 *Durga Prosad* v *Lilawati* AIR 1972 All 396; *Rameshwar* v *Hari Narayan* AIR 1984 Pat 277; 1984 Pat LJR 827.

7 *Shri Swastik Developers* v *Saket Kumar Jain,* (2014)2 Mah LJ 968; (2014)2 ICC 896; (2015)1 Bom CR 741; (2014)4 CCC 59

8 *Nitin Gandhi* v *Dinyar Pheroz Dubash* (2015)2 Mah LJ 850; (2014)6 AIR Bom R 558; (2015)1 Bom CR 750; 2015 AIR CC 292; (2015)2 ICC 951; (2015)3 CCC 330.

Secondly, sending a notice by a contractee to the contractor who has agreed to transfer may show the continuous readiness and willingness of the contractee to perform his part of the contract.

In a case the plaintiff to whom the defendant had agreed to transfer, sent a notice to the defendant by registered post two days prior to the stipulated date of execution of sale deed requesting the defendant to attend the office of the sub-registrar. The notice came back with the endorsement "the addressee has gone out of station". The plaintiff by drawing a presumption of proper service, filed a suit for specific performance of contract subsequently. The defendant denied on oath the receipt of the notice and the defence case was that he was not a defaulter in not coming to the sub-registrar's office on the appointed date. The further defence case was that the plaintiff before the appointed date was never ready to get the sale deed executed in terms of the contract for sale and further that the plaintiff was not ready to pay the entire consideration to the defendant before the stipulated date. The question hinged around the answer whether or not the defendant received the notice. The Allahabad High Court held that in view of the denial of the defendant on oath about the receipt of the notice the presumption emanating from Illustration (*e*) of s. 114, Evidence Act stands rebutted. When the plaintiff had not accompanied the postman and he had not produced any other evidence to show the receipt of notice, plaintiff's readiness to perform his part of the contract has not been proved.[9]

A popular and convenient mode of service of notice is transmission by registered post. When the notice is sent by registered post in correct address and it is prepaid there arises a presumption of due service by reason of s. 114(*e*), Evidence Act.

Section 27, General Clauses Act 1897 also states that when a statute authorises or requires any document to be served by post, whether the expression "service" or either of the expression "give" or "send" or any other expression is used, then, unless a different intention appears, the service shall be deemed to be effected by properly addressing, pre-paying and posting by registered post, a letter containing the document, and unless the contrary is proved, to have been effected at the time at which the letter would be delivered in the ordinary course of post.

Section 27 of the General Clauses Act is in pari materia with s. 28 of the Bengal General Clauses Act. Since the Specific Relief Act no where mandates the service of a notice by registered post, s. 27 of the General Clauses Act or s. 28 of the Bengal General Clauses Act has no scope to operate.[10]

9 *Ram Rati* v *Fakira* AIR 1988 All 75.

10 *Monaranjan Dasgupta* v *Suchitra Ganguly* AIR 1989 Cal 14; 92 CWN 929; (1988)1 Cal LJ 250; (1988)1 CHN 219.

As to presumption under s. 114(*e*), Evidence Act, to invoke the presumption examination of postal peon is not necessary.[11] Such presumption can be raised irrespective of whether any acknowledgment due is received or not from the addressee. Non-production of the register by defendant company alleged to be served with notice where such registers are duly maintained gives rise to an adverse inference against the defendant.[12] Such presumption is raised irrespective of whether any acknowledgment due is received or not. Presumption relates to everything that is contained in the notice. The presumption is rebuttable.[13] In *Saibalini's*[14] case, however, the endorsement "refused" was proved although not by the serving peon. It lent some support to the theory that before invoking the presumption the formal proof of the endorsement was necessary. The point was clarified in *Munni* v *Puspalata*[15] which laid down that for invoking the presumption the formal proof of the endorsement was not necessary. The decisions of the other High Courts too are in the same line.[16] Further presumption is permissible that date of tender written by postal peon is correct.[17]

In *Kedarnath* v *Kewala*[18] the facts were interesting. There the postman made two endorsements on two different dates. The postman made several efforts to serve the envelope on the addressee. As the addressee could not be met the postman did not return the same to the office but retained the same. His efforts to serve the notice continued from 24th December 1967 to 2nd January 1968 when he ultimately made the endorsement "refused". The question arose if the court was entitled to presume that it was refused on 24th December 1967. The court held in the negative for the reason namely that as the postman retained the envelope with him such presumption could not be drawn. The court held that it may be presumed that the envelope was tendered to the addressee on 2nd January 1968.

When a notice sent by post has not been returned to the sender then it is a case where the presumption under s. 114(*e*), Evidence Act operates. Whether such a presumption has been rebutted or not depends on the acceptability of the evidence denying the tender or delivery offered by the defendant. Mere denial will not lead invariably to rebuttal of presumption

11 *Sushil* v *Ganesh* AIR 1958 Cal 251; 62 CWN 193; *Saibalini Saha* v *Snehalata Bose* 65 CWN 690; *Chhaya Devi* v *Lahoriram* 67 CWN 819.

12 *Tide Water Oil* v *K.D. Banerjee* 86 CWN 456; AIR 1982 Cal 127.

13 *Harcharan Singh* v *Shivrani* AIR 1981 SC 1284; (1981)2 SCR 962; (1981)2 SCC 535.

14 65 CWN 690.

15 *Munni* v *Puspalata* 71 CWN 282.

16 *Sayed Ahmed* v *Sayed Qaman* AIR 1973 All 24; *Gangaram* v *Phulwati* AIR 1970 All 446; 1970 All LJ 336; 1970 Ren CJ 485; *Memon Adambhai* v *Bhaiya Ramdas* (1974)15 Guj LR 655; 1975 Ren CJ 59; *Budha* v *Bedariya* AIR 1981 MP 76.

17 *Shyam Narayan Shah* v *Raghunath Prasad* AIR 1977 Pat 155.

18 *Kedarnath* v *Kewala* 1976 Ren CJ 216.

properly raised.[19] Mere denial of notice served by post will not be sufficient to rebut the presumption arising under s. 114(*e*), Evidence Act when there is an endorsement of refusal by the postal authorities.[20] A somewhat different note has been struck by a large number of decisions. They lay down that when a notice has been returned with endorsement "refused" it is undoubtedly for the defendant to satisfy the court that the letter was not tendered on him. But the defendant can only do so by making a statement on oath. This must usually remain uncontroverted unless the postman who tendered the letter to him is summoned and makes a statement that he tendered the cover containing the summons to the defendant and on cross-examination his evidence may be believed. If the postman is not summoned by the plaintiff on the face of the denial by the defendant the statement on oath by the defendant remains uncontroverted and in such a case there is sufficient ground for holding that notice was not tendered.[1] When the defendant denies the service of summons, the prima facie presumption of service disappears and then it is for the plaintiff to prove the service by examining the postal peon.[2]

This view was endorsed by the Supreme Court in *Puwada Venkatasewara Rao* v *C.V. Ramana*.[3] It held for raising the presumption examination of serving peon is not necessary. Denial of service may be found incorrect from the party's own admission or conduct. But when such finding is not possible, onus springs back upon the plaintiff to prove service by some further evidence. Relying upon this Supreme Court case it has been held in a Calcutta case that when a notice sent by registered post returns with the endorsement refused and the defendant denies on oath the service, the presumption of service stands rebutted. The plaintiff then cannot succeed without further proof and service.[4]

Puwada Venkatasewara Rao's case was followed in an Allahabad case[5] holding the Evidence Act nowhere prescribes that the testimony of a witness cannot be believed unless corroborated. In the said case the defendant had stated on oath that no notice was delivered to him nor he had refused to

19 *Sukumar* v *Naresh Chandra* AIR 1968 Cal 49 relying on *Chhaya Devi* v *Lahoriram* 67 CWN 819.

20 *Asa Ram* v *Ravi Prakash* AIR 1966 All 519; 1966 All LJ 421; *Mushiat Wala* v *Abdul Wahab* AIR 1972 All 539; 1972 Ren CJ 783; *Chuttan* v *Sheodhar* (1979)1 Ren Cl 41.

1 *Meghji Kanji Patel* v *Kundanman Chamanlal Mehtani* AIR 1968 Bom 387.

2 *Ambaj Rao Subba Rao* v *Shakula Ram Hastimal* (1963)2 Mys LJ 482; *Somanna* v *Hiraji* (1938)16 Mys LJ 485; *Padmabathi Rai* v *Parvathiamma* AIR 1976 Kant 97; (1976)1 Kant LJ 35.

3 *Puwada Venkatasewara Rao* v *C.V. Ramana* AIR 1976 SC 869; (1976)3 SCR 551; (1976)2 SCC 409.

4 *Amal Kumar Banerjee* v *Santi Devi* 83 CWN 753; *Khagendra Nath Paul* v *Achal Pada De* (1986)1 Cal LJ 259 at p. 274.

5 *Amarnath* v *Champa Devi* (1978)4 All LR 90; (1978) All WC 84.

take any notice. If a witness makes a statement on oath the presumption is that it is correct unless proved otherwise. In that case when the defendant was not at all cross-examined nor there existed any such circumstances on the record on the basis of which his statement could be discredited there is no reason why the court should hold that his statement was not enough to rebut the presumption of service. In the said case neither the plaintiff came forward to depose that he had accompanied the postman and it was in his presence the defendant had refused to take the notice nor the postman was examined. No other person in whose presence the defendant may have refused to take the notice was produced. Therefore, there was no reason why the statement on oath of the defendant, which could not be shaken in cross-examination, should not have been believed to rebut the presumption of service.

Similar view was taken by the Delhi High Court in *Jagat Ram Khullar* v *Battumal.*[6] It was held that when the postal cover has been correctly addressed and prepaid and has been sent by registered post the evidence of actual tender and refusal is not necessary to bring about the presumption of valid service. Such evidence would be redundant, because if such evidence is necessary, such evidence by itself would be sufficient to prove the service. But this presumption stands rebutted by bare denial of the tender and refusal—if such denial is accepted by court to be true, and then the burden is thrown back upon the party alleging service to prove by other evidence the fact of tender and refusal of the postal cover. Similarly in *Kameswar Singh* v *Sahadeb Singh*,[7] the notice sent to defendant's normal address was redirected to another address wherefrom it came back with the endorsement "refused". The postal cover itself was not clear if the letter was redirected. It was found that presumption of service was rebutted by the oral evidence of the defendant denying the tender, absence of any other evidence of tender would bring the conclusion that the notice was not properly served.

In a Madras case according to the endorsement of postal peon either the tenant was not found in the premises or the premises were found locked whenever the postman called. Differing from the view of the trial court, the appellate court held on the strength of presumption under s. 114, Evidence Act and s. 27, General Clauses Act there was valid service of notice. Setting aside this view the High Court laid down, in view of the endorsement above the presumption is not justified. It further observed there is no presumption in law that because an addressee was absent from his premises or because his front door was shut during the brief moments of the postman's visit, the addressee-tenant was seeking to evade service of legal notice addressed to him.[8]

6 *Jagat Ram Khullar* v *Battumal* AIR 1976 Del 111.
7 *Kameswar Singh* v *Sahadeb Singh* 86 CWN 438.
8 *C.M.K. Ramu Mudaliar* v *Kanthamani Natarajan* (1979)1 Mad LJ 346; 92 Mad LW 5.

Suit for specific performance of contract In *Dheeraj Developers Pvt. Ltd.* v *Om Prakash Gupta*[9] the Supreme Court has held after referring to the factual matrix that the High Court has apparently gone wrong in decreeing the suit on the basis of the finding on genuineness of a document. It should have been borne in mind that suit was for specific performance and obviously there were also several other aspects of the matter including the aspect of readiness and willingness which required consideration by the High Court. Thus, the appeal was allowed, impugned judgment was set aside and the First Appeal was remitted to the High Court for fresh hearing.

Agreement was entered into between parties on alleged ground of need of money for marriage of daughter of vendor and it was mentioned in the agreement that when the vendee would ask vendor, then the vendor would receive the balance amount of sale consideration and execute the sale deed. Thus, time was not the essence of the contract out of total consideration $^{2}/_{3}$ of the amount was already paid by vendee and vendee had proved his readiness and willingness to perform his part of duty. Cause of action in the suit arose after one year from the date of agreement between parties and the suit was instituted within three years of date of entering into agreement to sell after giving legal notice. Thus, vendee was entitled to specific performance of contract.[10]

Meaning of 'title' under s. 19(*b*) The expression 'title' used in cl. (*b*) of s.19 is referable to the complete legal title. An agreement for sale subsequent to the original contract shall be out of purview of the expression 'title' in s. 19(*b*). The context in which the word 'title' has been used in s. 19(*b*) is entirely different from the context in which the word 'title' has been used in *Explanation* II to s. 3 of the Transfer of Property Act.[11]

Subsequent transfer during pendency of suit for specific performance In view of s. 19(*b*), Specific Relief Act a contract may be enforced *inter alia*, against any person claiming under the person agreeing to transfer by a title arising subsequently to the contract except a transferee for a value who has paid his money in good faith and without notice of the original contract.

It may so happen that subsequent transfer has been effected during the suit for specific performance of original contract. The question whether the sale to the subsequent transferee is hit by doctrine of *lis pendens* arises in this perspective. And the question is to be answered in the affirmative. Subsequent transfer of immovable property during pendency of suit in respect of the immovable property is hit by doctrine of *lis pendens* enacted in s. 52, Transfer of Property Act. It reads as follows:

9 AIR 2016 SC 1438.
10 *Gopal Ji* v *Naseeran Bibi* AIR 2016 All 142.
11 *Sujata Sanzgiry* v *Ankush R. Naik* (2006)1 Mah LJ 639; (2006)2 Bom CR 179; AIR 2005 Bom 404.

52. *Transfer of property pending suit relating thereto.* During the pendency in any court having authority within the limits of India excluding the State of Jammu and Kashmir or established beyond such limits by the Central Government of any suit or proceedings which is not collusive and in which any right to immovable property is directly and specifically in question, the property cannot be transferred or otherwise dealt with by any party to the suit or proceedings so as to affect the rights of any other party thereto under any decree or order which may be made therein, except under the authority of the court and on such terms as it may impose.

The rule of *lis pendens* as embodied in s. 52 of TP Act are:

(*i*) the right to immovable property directly and specifically in question in any suit or proceeding;

(*ii*) there should be transfer made of such immovable property or the same be otherwise dealt with without the authority of the court;

(*iii*) the transfer impugned be made during the pendency of any such suit or proceeding;

(*iv*) the suit or proceeding concerned be not collusive.

The effect of s. 52 of the Transfer of Property Act is not to wipe off a sale *pendente lite* altogether, but to subordinate it to the rights based on the decree in the suit. As between the parties to the transaction it is perfectly valid and operates to vest the title of the transferor to the transferee.[12]

Section 52 of the Transfer of Property Act which embodies the *maxim pendente lite nihil innovetur* does not avoid subsequent conveyance, but only makes it subject to the rights of the parties to the pending litigation even though the subsequent transferee was ignorant of the previous transaction of the pending litigation.[13] The burden is on the party invoking s. 52 relying on the effect of s. 52 and pleading *lis pendens* to prove that his suit was instituted before the execution of deed of transfer which he is impeaching.[14]

The doctrine of *lis pendens* applies also to a suit for specific performance of contract of sale and the transfer during the pendency of a suit is affected by the doctrine of *lis pendens*.[15]

The words 'and in which any right to immovable property is directly and specifically in question' in s. 52 are broad enough to include a suit for specific performance of contract to sell immovable property inasmuch as, in such suits the right to immovable property is directly and specifically in question.

12 *Nagubai* v *Shama Rao* AIR 1956 SC 593; 1956 SCR 451; 1956 SCJ 655.

13 *Nivarti Govind Ingale* v *Ramanagouda Beemanagouda Patil* (1997)1 SCC 475; (1996)8 Supreme 794.

14 *Narayana Pillai Chandrasekara Nair* v *Kunju Amma Thankamma* AIR 1990 Ker 177.

15 *Vraj Kuwar Bai* v *Kunjbiharilal Krishna Chandra* AIR 1971 MP 109; (1971) MP LJ 44.

The transferee cannot rely upon s. 27(*b*) of the Specific Relief Act 1877 or s. 19(*b*) of the Specific Relief Act 1963 for avoiding the applicability of s. 52 of the TP Act. Nor is there any necessity for the courts to go into the question whether the transfer *pendente lite* was *bona fide* and for value.[16]

In other words, neither *bona fides* nor notice is relevant to the application of the principle of *lis pendens* which is based on the principle of public policy that neither party to a litigation can alienate the property in dispute pendente lite so as to affect his opponent.[17]

Section 52, TP Act has an overriding effect on s. 19(*b*), Specific Relief Act when during the pendency of suit for specific performance, the defendant transfers the property to a third party, the doctrine of *lis pendens* applies. The subsequent transferee cannot defeat the claim of the plaintiff if he succeeds.[18]

Therefore a transfer of immovable property pending a suit relating to that property does not affect the decree passed in that suit even if the transferee took the property *bona fide* and for value totally oblivious of the pendency of the litigation. A person who has purchased a suit property pending suit need not be impleaded as a defendant.[19] It has been held in *Vairavan* v *K.S. Vidyanandam*[20] that a subsequent purchase would be hit by the doctrine even where the transaction was made after the dismissal of the suit and appeal is filed later and allowed. But this decision of the Madras High Court has been reversed by the Supreme Court in *K.S. Vidyanandam* v *Vairavan*[1] on another point, viz. that the plaintiff was not ready and willing to perform his part of the contract.

Meaning of bona fide purchaser The expression '*bona fide* purchaser' means and implies a purchaser who purchases a property without notice, actual or constructive of any adverse rights, claims, interest or equities of other in and to the property sold.[2] Therefore, the person, who wishes to take advantage of the doctrine of the *bona fide* purchaser, must show that he comes squarely under the doctrine. The plea of the *bona fide* purchaser is in the nature of an excuse. The *bona fide* purchaser does not, and cannot dispute the existence of the rights, title or estate which he is seeking to defeat. It is not for others to show that he has got notice, that he must have got notice. It is he himself who has to establish his status of a *bona fide* taker for value without notice.

16 *Ganga Charan* v *Bans Bahadur Singh* AIR 1975 All 25.
17 *Chanda Sahib* v *Jamshedkari* AIR 1993 Kant 338.
18 *Joginder Singh* v *Sardar Singh* AIR 1984 NOC 319 (Del); (1984)36 Del LT 162.
19 *Abdul Azeiz* v *District Judge* AIR 1994 All 167.
20 AIR 1996 Mad 353.
1 AIR 1997 SC 1751; (1997)3 SCC 1; JT 1997(2) SC 375.
2 *Nitin Gandhi* v *Dinyar Pheroz Dubash* (2015)2 Mah LJ 850; (2014)6 AIR Bom R 558; (2015)1 Bom CR 750; 2015 AIR CC 292; (2015)2 ICC 951; (2015)3 CCC 330.

It is a special situation where even the defendant might be faced with the burden of proving the case on the basis of which he wishes to succeed. If for example, in a situation of a specific performance suit, a subsequent taker seeks to defeat the original contract, he has to prove his *bona fide* status and his dealings, in ignorance, which have taken place for honest consideration, at least honest from his side.[3]

Parties to the suit In the absence of the subsequent purchaser as a party the court will not grant a decree for specific performance to enforce a prior contract for sale.[4] The cause of action, viz. to obtain a deed of sale and possession of the property purchased, concerns both the vendor and the subsequent transferee and entitles the plaintiff to relief against both the defendants. Where the defendant alleges that he has sold the property to other persons, they are necessary parties and amendment for their impleading cannot be refused on the ground of delay.[5]

Parties to suit were aware of subsequent purchasers of properties with knowledge of earlier agreement. Thus, subsequent purchaser during the pendency of the suit can be added as a party under Or. 1, r. 10 and Or. 22, r. 10 of Code of Civil Procedure 1908.[6]

Effect of lis pendens There was subsequent sale of same property by owner to second purchaser. Second sale was effected after filing of suit for specific performance by first vendee. Principle of *lis pendens* will apply notwithstanding the fact that right of subsequent purchaser could be protected under s. 19(*b*) of the Specific Relief Act.[7]

The rule of *lis pendens* is applicable also to suits for specific performance of contract to transfer immovable property.[8] Where pending a suit seeking specific enforcement of agreement for sale of property, the vendor sold the property to his close relatives at a price much less than the market price, held, the provisions of s. 52 of the Transfer of Property Act applied and sale was not binding on the plaintiff.[9]

The transferee *pendente lite* is treated in the eye of law as a representative-in-interest of the judgment debtor though neither has the defendant chosen to bring the transferee on record by apprising his opponent and the court of the transfer made by him nor has the transferee chosen to come or record

3 *Archit Banijya & Biniyog Pvt. Ltd.* v *Asha Lata Ghosh* (2000)2 CHN 640.
4 *Vimala Ammal* v *C. Suseela* AIR 1991 Mad 209.
5 *Birbal Yadhav* v *Suchan Thakur* AIR 1999 Pat 6.
6 *Thomson Press (India) Ltd.* v *Nanak Builders & Investors (P.) Ltd.* AIR 2013 SC 2389.
7 *Guruswamy Nadar* v *P. Lakshmi Ammal* AIR 2008 SC 2560.
8 *Gouri Dutt Maharaj* v *Sheikh Sukur Mohammed* (1948)2 Mad LJ 79 (PC); *Vedachari* v *Narasinha Mudali* AIR 1924 Mad 307; *G. Rukmani Bai* v *Saraswati Ammal* 1989 TLNJ 40; *P. Laxmi Ammal* v *S. Laxmi Ammal* AIR 1991 Mad 137.
9 *Harbaksh Singh Gill* v *Ram Rattan* AIR 1988 P&H 60.

by taking recourse to Or. 22, r. 10, CPC and it does not make any difference whether such transfer or assignment has taken place after passing the decree or before the passing of the decree without notice or leave of the court.[10]

The Supreme Court has laid down in several decisions the proper form of a decree in a suit by a purchaser for specific performance against the vendor and the subsequent transferees.[11] The direction is that both the vendor and the subsequent transferee should join in the conveyance, but the subsequent transferee merely passes on his title and does not participate in any special covenants made between the vendor the plaintiff. In a decree for specific performance against a vendor and a subsequent purchaser, there should be a direction to the latter to join in the execution of the deed or to execute the conveyance to the plaintiff. The view that the court can order the original promisor to carry out his contract by executing the sale in favour of the plaintiff, after declaring as null and void the transaction of the subsequent purchaser and cancelling it, is no longer good law, nor is a decree in proper form, where it directs only the vendor to execute the deed of sale.

Where the relief of specific performance was refused holding that the subsequent purchasers were *bona fide* purchasers for value without notice and the refund of the amount paid by the plaintiff under the earlier agreement was ordered, it was improper for the court to allow the plaintiff to retain possession of the property until the amount was refunded and keep the subsequent purchasers out of possession.[12] In a suit for specific performance against the original contracting party and his transferees with notice of previous contract, a decree for compensation in substitution of specific performance can be passed against both the defendants.[13] But, in *Jagan Nath* v *Jagdish Rai*[14] while a suit for specific performance was rejected, as the subsequent purchaser was found to be a *bona fide* purchaser for a value without notice of the plaintiff's agreement, Their Lordships awarded damages to the plaintiff from the subsequent purchaser on a proposal from the subsequent purchaser himself.

The doctrine of *lis pendens* as already pointed out, is based on public policy and upon expediency and it is immaterial that the purchaser pendente lite had or had no notice of the suit. The rule may no doubt operate so as to work hardship in the case of a real and fair purchase without notice of the pending lis, but it is founded upon public policy, as otherwise alienations

10 *Raj Kumar* v *Sardari Lal* (2004)2 SCC 601.

11 *Durga Prasad* v *Deep Chand* AIR 1954 SC 75; 1954 SCR 360; 1954 SCJ 17; *Ramesh Chandra* v *Chunni Lal* AIR 1971 SC 1238; (1971)2 SCR 573; (1970)3 SCC 140; *Dwarka Prasad Singh* v *Harikant Singh* AIR 1973 SC 655; (1973)2 SCR 1064; (1973)1 SCC 179.

12 *Balaram Barikh* v *Banam Bara Maharana* AIR 1982 Ori 271.

13 *Dalmia Jain & Co. Ltd.* v *Kalyanpur Line Worms Ltd.* AIR 1963 Pat 298.

14 AIR 1998 SC 2028; (1998)5 SCC 537; JT 1998(3) SC 551.

made during a pending action may defeat its own purpose and there would be no end to litigations. The hardship attending upon the application of the rule to transferees without notice of the pending proceedings was removed in England by the Judgment Act 1838. This Act provided for registration of every *lis pendens* and enacted that no *lis pendens* should bind the purchase or mortgage without express notice thereof unless and until it was duly registered. The Land Charges Act 1925 has consolidated the law relating to *lis pendens* and provides that a Register of pending actions should be kept in the Land Registry. Any action, information or proceedings pending in court relating to land or any interest or charge on land may be registered in the Register of Pending Actions. A purchaser is not bound by an unregistered pending action unless he has express notice. The registration of *lis pendens* ceases to have effect at the expiration of five years of registration unless it is renewed in which case it would be in effect for five years from the date of renewal. The court is empowered to vacate a lis on the determination of the proceedings and even during the pendency of the case if it is satisfied that the proceedings are not proceedings in good faith. The States of Maharashtra and Gujarat have amended s. 52 of the Transfer of Property Act providing for the registration of the lis with particulars mentioned therein. It is high time that the Parliament takes note of this unsatisfactory state of law and introduces a suitable amendment to s. 52 of the Transfer of Property Act.

Addition of transferee pendente lite party in suit for specific performance
Under Or. 22, r. 10 of the Code of Civil Procedure 1908, Legislature has intended that proceedings would continue by or against the original party, although he ceased to have any interest in the subject of dispute despite the failure to apply for leave to continue by or against the person upon whom the interest has devolved for bringing him on record. Thus a subsequent transferee can be impleaded as party in the suit where purchaser is seeking enforcement of an agreement for sale and has come up for specific performance though it is wholly unnecessary for him to challenge conveyance/sale deed executed by vendor during pendency of suit in favour of the party proposed to be brought on record in the suit.[15]

Agreement to sell was executed by one of the defendant in favour of the plaintiff. Hardly one week left for expiry of time stipulated for execution of sale deed the defendant executed and registered settled deed in respect of the said property in favour of his wife. Defendants suppressed the fact of execution of settlement deed in respect of the said property in their counter statement to injunction petition and thereafter deviated their stand in written statement. Trial court found no *bona fides* in their version. Thus, decree

15 *Ram Naresh* v *Additional District Judge* AIR 2016 All 15 relying on *Thomson Press (India) Ltd.* v *Nanak Builders Pvt. Ltd.* AIR 2013 SC 2389; (2013)5 SCC 597; *Amit Kumar Shaw* v *Farida Khatoon* AIR 2005 SC 2209.

was granted in favour of the plaintiff. The appellate court confirmed the decree in the facts and circumstances of the case.[16]

Common grounds for refusing specific performance

Lack of consideration The equity will not aid a volunteer, specific performance will not be ordered of a gratuitous promise.[17]

Contract expressed to be terminable If a contract is expressed to be revocable by the party against whom an order of specific performance is sought for, the order will be refused as the defendant could render it nugatory by exercising his power to terminate.[18]

Goodwill The court's order to prevent the specific enforcement of contract for sale of goodwill alone without business premises was difficult to pass.[19] In *Beswick* v *Beswick*,[20] the common law rule of privity of contract and its exceptions have been dealt with.

Mistake, misrepresentation and delay Specific performance may be refused on the ground of mistake, misrepresentation and delay.[1]

Refusal of relief There was an agreement to sell between the commission agent of fertilisers, the purchaser and the farmer, the seller. The purchaser proved the agreement to sell an immovable property which is an agricultural land. The defence raised by the farmer that the purchaser had obtained his thumb impression on plain paper, but no evidence was led on this aspect. The plea could not be outrightly rejected. Only a paltry sum was paid by the purchaser as earnest money. It was held by the Supreme Court that the refusal of relief of specific performance of agreement was proper. The plaintiff-purchaser was entitled to refund of earnest money and costs up to High Court to the extent of his success.[2]

Moulding of relief Agreement to sell joint family property for necessity was made. Litigation was pending for years. In the mean time property price was soaring. To settle equities court directed purchaser to pay higher price to seller for executing decree. But property in question was in possession of third party. Third party was claiming title by adverse possession which third party failed to prove. Court to prevent another round of litigation directed third party to handover possession to seller.[3]

16 *Sachidanandham* v *Vijesh* AIR 2016 Ker 149.
17 *Jeffreys* v *Jeffreys* [1841] Cr & Ph 138.
18 *R. (Supportways Community Services Ltd.)* v *Hamshire* CC [2006] EWCA Civ 1035.
19 *Bozon* v *Farlow* [1816]1 Mer 459.
20 [1968] AC 58.
1 Chitty on *Contracts*, 30th Ed., vol. 1, para 27-045.
2 *Manohar Lal* v *Maya* AIR 2003 SC 2362.
3 *Pratap Lakshman Muchandi* v *Shamlal Uddavadas Wadhwa* AIR 2008 SC 1378.

Omission to claim relief of specific performance Omission to claim relief of specific performance of agreement to sell would amount to relinquishment of that part of claim. Subsequent inclusion of plea of specific performance by way of amendment after 11 years of filing of the suit cannot be allowed being barred by limitation under Art. 54 of the Limitation Act 1963.[4]

Discretion of court Agreement to sell between the plaintiff and the defendant No. 1 was finalised, but the sale deed was not executed by the defendant No. 1 even after receipt of consideration money and he executed another agreement in favour of the defendant No. 2 who was aware of the earlier agreement. Plaintiff was a *bona fide* purchaser and was ready and willing to perform his part of obligations. The plaintiff purchased stamp paper, went along with the defendant No. 1 to Sub-Registrar's office for registration. The defendant No. 1 sneaked away last moment. The defendants filed a collusive suit and obtained a compromise decree. Conduct of the defendants showed that there was preconceived agreement between them to defraud and cheat the plaintiff. Refusal to grant relief of specific performance was not, therefore, proper. The plaintiff was entitled to take appropriate proceedings for eviction of the defendant No. 2.[5]

Specific performance of contract and minor The contract with a minor is void, so no question of specific performance can arise. But if the contract is entered into on behalf of an infant by one who is competent to act, e.g. a certified guardian and the contract is for the benefit of the minor specific performance would be allowed.[6] In *Mir Sarwarjan* v *Fakhuruddin*[7] the Privy Council has held that a suit does not lie for specific performance of an arrangement made by the natural guardian of an infant for the sale of immovable property to the infant during his minority. It is not within the competence of the guardian to bind the minor by a contract for the purchase of immovable property and the minor cannot obtain specific performance of the contract unless perhaps the contract is for the minor's benefit.[8]

Subsequent transfer and register on the date of suit—burden of proof When the suit for specific performance is instituted on the very date of execution and registration of transfer, the transfer does not attract the doctrine of *lis pendens*.[9]

In this case document transferring the immovable property was registered at 2-30 p.m. on the same day suit for specific performance was filed.

4 *Van Vibhag Karamchari Griha Nirman Sahakari Sanstha Maryadit* v *R. Chander* AIR 2011 SC 41.
5 *Devalsab* v *Ibrahimsab F. Karajagi* AIR 2005 SC 1940.
6 *Etwarnia* v *Chandra* 10 CWN 763; *Baburam* v *Saidunnissa* ILR (1913) 35 All 499.
7 ILR 39 Cal 232 (PC); *Rambilas* v *Lokenath* AIR 1949 Pat 405.
8 *Dhapo* v *Rao* AIR 1934 All 1019.
9 *Narayana Pillai* v *Kunju Amma* AIR 1990 Ker 177; (1989)3 Cur Civ Cas 123.

Although institution of the suit was made earlier than 2-30 p.m. Kerala Single Judge has pointed out that it does not mean that the execution and presentation for registration were at that time. It must have been executed and presented much earlier. Only after the formalities and in the usual course it could come up before the Sub-Registrar at 2-30 p.m. It further held that burden lies upon the party relying on the effect of s. 52, TP Act and pleading *lis pendens* to prove that his suit was instituted before the execution of the deed of transfer which he is impeaching.[10]

Agreement of sale—specific performance Though it is true that relief of specific performance of agreement of sale is discretionary, ordinary rule is that specific performance should be granted. It is well settled that the discretion should not be exercised arbitrarily but on sound principles of law. Unless there are compelling circumstances, the relief of specific performance is not to be ordinarily refused. The courts cannot wriggle a contract between the parties and deny the relief of specific performance on some minor flaws or on inequitable grounds.[11]

Attachment of agreement of sale An agreement to sell or an agreement to purchase is a property and is a saleable property and there is no bar to its attachment and sale.[12] Allahabad Full Bench did not subscribe to the view that the Supreme Court in *Swami Motor* v *Shankarbal*,[13] expressed a contrary view and pointed out that there was only concerned with the constitutional validity of an enactment wholly different in content and scope from s. 60, CPC.

In a Supreme Court case[13] the court was concerned with an amendment effected by Madras Act 13 of 1960 in respect of the Madras City Tenants' Protection Act 1921 (Principal Act) as amended by an Act of 1955. The Government made an order notifying the town of Tanjore to have come within the purview of the Principal Act. The rights which the tenants had, inter alia, acquired under the Amending Act of 1955 was, *inter alia* that the tenant, other rights apart, had the right at his option, to apply within the prescribed time to the court for an order directing the landlord to sell the land to him for a price fixed by the court, whether a decree for ejectment had or had not been passed. Subsequently, by Madras Act 13 of 1960 the Principal Act was again amended. The effect of the amendment was to withdraw the protection given to tenants of non-residential building in the municipal town of Tanjore and certain other towns. A further result of this

10 *Narayana Pillai* v *Kunju Amma* AIR 1990 Ker 177; (1989)3 Cur Civ Cas 123 relying on *Refenddin* v *Brij Mohon* 21 IC 602 followed in *Mathew Philip* v *Ithak* 1959 Ker LT 301.

11 *Mathurabai* v *Suresh* (2019)1 Mah LJ 439.

12 *Bhairon Prosad* v *Tara Devi* AIR 1980 All 36 (FB); 1979 All LJ 1324 (FB).

13 AIR 1963 SC 864.

amending Act in respect of non-residential buildings, in places other than the city of Madras and the other specified municipal towns, was that all proceedings pending in courts in respect of those buildings abated and the rights acquired by tenants under the 1955 Act in respect of the said buildings were extinguished. In the Supreme Court case,[14] it was contended that this withdrawal of the right of tenant to purchase the tenanted premises with retrospective effect infringed Art. 19(1)(*f*) [as it then stood] under the Constitution. In this context the Supreme Court observed that the right conferred by the Principal Act was the right to purchase land. Such a right when conferred under a contract is not a right of property. The fact that such a right stems from a statute cannot expand its content or make it any less a non-proprietary right. A statutory right to apply for the purchase of land is not a right of property. It is settled law that a contract to purchase a property does not create an interest in immovable property.

Attachment—subsequent to contract of sale When contract of sale is made prior to attachment of the property by the court, that attachment does not affect the contract of sale. The question fell for consideration in the cases,[15] and it was held that an attachment made after a contract for specific performance does not affect a prior agreement to sell and attachment could only fasten the debtor's right to the unpaid purchase money.[16] When property is attached and then sold but the property is subject matter of prior agreement of sale or mortgage, then it can be sold subject to the agreement or mortgage, for, an attaching decree-holder attaches not the physical property but only the right of the judgment-debtor in the property, but if this right on the date of attachment is qualified, by an obligation, such obligation cannot be ignored by the auction purchaser, an attaching decree-holder.[17] In the same line AP High Court held that an agreement of sale does not create any right, title or interest in the property under s. 54, Transfer of Property Act, it creates some interest in the property by operation of second paragraph of s. 40, Transfer of Property Act and this right prevails over s. 64, CPC, so, on the face of attachment before judgment, a prior agreement of sale is not void. An attachment before judgment does not prevail over a contract of sale.[18]

Prior to the contract Section 19(*c*) provided that relief may also be claimed against any person who claims title to the property prior to the contract and

14 *Swami Motor* v *Shankarbal* AIR 1963 SC 864; 1963 Supp (1) SCR 282; (1964)1 SCJ 530.

15 *Kochu Ponchi Varughese* v *Ouseph Lonan* AIR 1952 TC 467; *Veerappa Thevar* v *G.S. Venkatarama Aiyar* AIR 1935 Mad 872; *Purna Chandra Basak* v *Daulat Ali Mollah* AIR 1973 Cal 432; *Narayanan Nair* v *Zacharia Kuriakose* AIR 1991 Ker 152.

16 *Narayanan Nair* v *Zacharia Kuriakose* AIR 1991 Ker 152 at p. 154.

17 *Angu Pillai* v *M.S.M.K. Chottiar* AIR 1974 Mad 16; (1973)1 Mad LJ 334; 86 Mad LW 94 contra *S.U.S. Davey* v *P.N. Narayanaswami* AIR 1983 Mad 217; 96 Mad LW 1.

18 *Devarpalli Venkata Narasimharao* v *P. Ramayyamma* (1987)1 Andh LT 718.

of which the plaintiff is aware, provided that title has been displaced by the defendant. Defendant here means the contractor.

Banerjee in his *Law of Specific Relief* (Tagore Law Lectures) expounding the scope of s. 19(*c*), Specific Relief Act lays down:

> "The clause lays down that specific performance of a contract may be enforced against any person claiming under a title, which, though prior to the contract and known to the plaintiff, might have been displaced by the defendant. It embraces cases, where the suit is not brought against the contracting party, but against another whose title has been displaced by the former. Where a title is liable to be so displaced, it is immaterial that the title is antecedent to the contract and the plaintiff had notice of it. The contractual title prevails over prior title *ex lege*. The case, therefore, strictly speaking, is not of specific performance."[19]

Clause (*d*) of s. 19 is converse to s. 15(*g*). It has been held in *Indian Bank* v *K. Usha*[20] that a settlement entered into between the employee and the transferor bank and its management will be binding on the transferee bank in view of s. 19(*d*) of the Specific Relief Act and s. 2 of the Banking Regulations Act. The employee was therefore held entitled to enforce the terms of the settlement against the bank which took over the transferor bank under a scheme of amalgamation.

Clause (*e*) of s. 19 contains a converse to cl. (*h*) of s. 15.

Suit for specific performance—cause of action Plaintiff's land was acquired for construction of office of Industrial Development Corporation. Suit was filed challenging acquisition. Compromise was reached between parties. Corporation agreed to reconvey part of land and use, the remaining part for its office. Remaining part of land was allotted to industrial unit. Plaintiff filed suit for specific performance of compromise and for reconveyance of remaining land. Facts showed that even before filing of suit corporation had initiated proceedings to cancel allotment. Cause of action for filing suit cannot be said to have arisen. Moreover, no notification to withdraw land from acquisition was issued. Government was, therefore, in continuous possession and owner of land. Merely for delay to construct administrative building, decree for specific performance cannot be granted.[21]

Suit for specific performance—duty of the plaintiff Specific performance of a contract for sale can be enforced both against the party to the contract as well as the subsequent transferee. The first thing that a plaintiff in such a suit has to prove, therefore, is that there was a valid contract for sale between him and the owner of the immovable property and that despite

19 Banerjee on *Law of Specific Relief*, 13th Ed., p. 430.
20 AIR 1998 SC 866; (1998)2 SCC 663; JT 1998(1) SC 265.
21 *Tarabai* v *Govt. of Karnataka* AIR 2013 SC 2881.

fulfilment of the terms and conditions of the said contract by the plaintiff, the owner has failed to execute a deed of sale. In other words, the plaintiff has to prove the existence of a valid contract for sale and performance of his part of the contract. Once that is done and it is shown that despite that the other party failed to execute the contract, the Court can order specific performance of the contract and direct the owner to execute the sale deed in terms of the contract. In a case where subsequent to the contract the property has been transferred to some other person, the contract can be enforced against the transferee also unless such transferee claims to be a *bona fide* transferee without notice as provided in the exception to s. 19(*b*) of the Act. In that case the burden will be on such transferee to prove the same.[1]

Unregistered sale agreement in suit for specific performance Unregistered sale agreement was tendered in evidence in a suit for specific performance. The said document was tendered not as evidence of complete sale, but as proof of agreement of sale. It is admissible in evidence as evidence of oral agreement of sale purchaser is entitled to relief of specific performance.[2]

Specific performance claimed on conditional letter of intent Plaintiff was intending to purchase a flat. Conditional letter was issued by the builder. Mere letter of intent does not give right to plaintiff to purchase a flat. Moreso, when letter of intent specifically provided that after full payment agreement of sale would be executed. In absence of registered agreement for sale suit filed by plaintiff was not maintainable. In absence of registered agreement subsequent purchaser of flat cannot be said to be purchaser with knowledge of earlier agreement. Plaintiff was not entitled to relief of specific performance and the builder was directed to refund purchase price with interest.[3]

Suit for specific performance of agreement—ex parte decree—valid Defendant vendor did not file written statement. Decree as prayed for was passed under Or. 7, r. 10, CPC. Decree though *ex parte* is valid for all purposes. Parties allowed the decree to become final, and thereafter, they cannot turn round and challenge it as unexecutable. Purchaser sought execution of decrees only 6½ years after its passing. In the meantime prices of land shoot up. Obligation of vendor to pay unearned increase grew four times the balance of sale consideration. The said unconscionable liability arose only on account of delay in execution. There was an application by vendor for rescission of contract. Court dealt with such application to balance equity. Purchaser also delayed in payment of balance consideration on

1 *Nepal Chandra Das* v *Astalal Das* (1992)1 Gau LR 283.
2 *Akshay Doogad* v *State of MP* AIR 2016 MP 83 relying on *S. Kaladevi* v *V.R. Somasundaram* AIR 2010 SC 1654.
3 *Hansa V. Gandhi* v *Deep Shankar Roy* AIR 2013 SC 2873.

ground that vendor did not fulfil his obligation. Neither party approached court for appropriate directions to come out of this situation. Both parties were of fault. Court to balance equities directed purchaser to pay land value at increased rate and also pay unearned increase. In case purchaser failed to pay, vendor was directed to compensate purchaser by paying the increased land value. Suit for specific performance of contract to sell does not end with passing of decree. Court retains control over decree.[4]

Company Section 19(e) of the Act provides for grant of a decree of specific performance of a contract against a company when the promoters of a company before incorporation entered into a contract for the purpose of the company and such contract is warranted by the terms of incorporation.[5]

4 *Rajendra Kumar* v *Kuldeep Singh* AIR 2014 SC 1155.

5 *Jai Narain Parasrampuria* v *Pushpa Devi Saraf* (2006)7 SCC 756.

CHAPTER 3

Defences under Law of Contracts

The provision Section 9 of the Specific Relief Act provides for the defence respecting suits for relief based on contract which states that except as otherwise provided in the Act, where any relief is claimed under Chapter II (ss. 9 to 25) in respect of a contract, the person against whom the relief is claimed may plead by way of defence any ground which is available to him under any law relating to contracts.[1]

The essentials of s. 9 are first, the relief must be claimed under Chapter II of the Specific Relief Act, secondly, the relief must be claimed in respect of a contract as defined in the Contract Act.

The expression "Except as otherwise provided herein" means except as otherwise provided in Chapter II that is, in ss. 9 to 25 both inclusive.

The words "in respect of a contract" in s. 9 of the Specific Relief Act go to suggest that the section is applicable only where a relief is claimed under this chapter (i.e. Chapter II) in respect of a contract, and therefore, it will not have any application to cases falling under s. 25, but that section itself provides that this section (which is included in Chapter II) shall apply to awards and testamentary directions to execute settlements.[1]

Contractual capacity Incapacity of either party to enter into an agreement for sale is a valid defence to an action for specific performance.[2]

Contract vitiated by coercion, undue influence, fraud, misrepresentation or mistake—defence in suit for specific performance In order to bring about a contract, the consent must be "free", that is, it must not have been caused

1 Banerjee, *Law of Specific Relief*, 13th Ed., p. 128.

2 See under the heading 'Competency of Parties' in Part 2, Chapter 1, *supra* for a detailed discussion.

by coercion, undue influence, fraud, misrepresentation or mistake. Consequently therefore the pleas that the contract is vitiated by coercion, undue influence, fraud, misrepresentation, mistake can operate as good defence in a suit for specific performance.

Coercion "Coercion" is the committing, or threatening to commit, any act forbidden by the Indian Penal Code, or the unlawful detaining, or threatening to detain, any property to the prejudice of any person whatever, with the intention of causing any person to enter into an agreement. It is immaterial whether the Indian Penal Code is or is not in force in the place where the coercion is employed (s. 15 of the Contract Act).

The threat to commit suicide is coercion.[3] No coercion is found in a consent decree.[4] Coercion in s. 72 of the Contract Act must be understood in the ordinary sense. It includes every kind of compulsion even if it does not measure up to definition under s. 15 of the Contract Act.[5] It is submitted that coercion also includes cases of economic duress.[6]

Coercion under the Contract Act is much wider than what is duress under the English Law. It includes unlawful retention of property, may be committed by any person not necessarily a party to the contract, and may be directed against any person, even a stranger, and unlike duress, causing of immediate violence or unnerving a person of ordinary firmness of mind are not necessary under the Indian Law.[7]

Fixation of sugar prices in the exercise of statutory power is not coercion.[8] In a claim of damages under supplemental work, contention that the supplemental agreement was the result of coercion, the award of damages without considering the fact of coercion is improper.[9]

Undue influence "Undue influence" refers to a situation where the relations subsisting between the parties are such that one of the parties is in a position to dominate the will of the other and uses that position to obtain an unfair advantage over the other. And a person is deemed to be in a position to dominate the will of another where he holds a real or apparent authority over the other or where he stands in a fiduciary relation to the other, or where he makes a contract with a person whose mental capacity is temporarily

3 *Purabi Banerjee* v *Basudev Mukherjee* AIR 1969 Cal 293.
4 *Gangadeep Pratisthan (P) Ltd.* v *Maharo* AIR 2005 SC 1958; (2005)11 SCC 273.
5 *T.G.M. Aside & Sons.* v *Coffee Board* AIR 1969 Mys 230.
6 *Paon On* v *Lau Yiu Long* [1979]3 All ER 65; *North Ocean Shipping Co. Ltd.* v *Hyundai Construction Co. Ltd.* [1978]3 All ER 1170; *Dai-Ichi Karkaria Rita* v ONGC AIR 1992 Bom 309.
7 *Karuppayi Ammal* v *Karuppiah Pillai* (1987)2 MLJ 138 at p. 148.
8 *U.P. Coop. Care Unions Federations* v *West U.P. Sugar Mills Assn.* AIR 2004 SC 3697; (2004)5 SCC 430.
9 *State of Kerala* v *M.A. Mathai* (2007)10 SCC 195; AIR 2007 SC 1537.

or permanently affected by reason of age, illness or mental or bodily distress (s. 16 of the Contract Act).

A close reading of s. 16 of the Contract Act would go to show that sub-sec. (2) creates a fiction of domination on the part of certain persons on the will of others. Clause (*a*) of sub-sec. (2) of s. 16 states that where a person holds a real or apparent authority over the other, or where he stands in a fiduciary relation to the other, it shall be deemed that such person is in a position to dominate the will of the other. However, it needs to be underlined that it is not required in all cases that in order to presume domination the authority should be proved to be real.[10]

"Undue influence" is said to be a subtle species of fraud whereby mastery is obtained over the mind of the victim, by insidious approaches and seductive artifices. Sometimes the result is brought about by fear, coercion, importunity or other domination, calculated to prevent expression of the victim's true mind. It is a constraint undermining free agency overcoming the powers of resistance, bringing about a submission to an overmastering and unfair persuasion to the detriment of the other.[11] In *Someshwar Dutt* v *Tribhawan*[12] the Privy Council said, "Acts of undue influence *must* range themselves under one or other of these heads—coercion or fraud."

A person standing in a fiduciary relation to another has a duty to protect the interest given to his care and the court watches zealously all transactions between such persons so that the protector may not use his influence or the confidence to his advantage. When the party complaining shows such relation, the law presumes everything against the transaction and the onus is cast upon the person holding the position of confidence or trust to show that the transaction is perfectly fair and reasonable, that no advantage has been taken of his position. This principle has been ingrained in s. 111 of the Indian Evidence Act.[13] The principle is discussed in Ashburner's *Principles of Equity*[14] as under;

> When the relation between the donor and donee at or shortly before the execution of the gift has been such as to raise a presumption that the donee had influence over the donor, the court sets aside the gift unless the donee can prove that the gift was the result of a free exercise of the donor's will.

The corollary to that principle is contained in s. 16(3) of the Indian Contract Act.[15]

10 *Lakshmi* v *Muthusamy* 2012(3) ICC 344.
11 *Karnal Distillery Co. Ltd.* v *Ladli Prasad* AIR 1958 Punj 190.
12 AIR 1934 PC 130.
13 *Krishna Mohan Kul* v *Pratima Maity* (2004)9 SCC 468.
14 2nd Ed., p. 229.
15 *Krishna Mohan Kul* v *Pratima Maity* (2004)9 SCC 468.

When an illiterate woman put her thumb impression on two deeds, honestly believing that the thumb impressions taken from her were in respect of a single document namely the gift deed in favour of her daughter in respect of her properties as per her desire, but in fact two documents were got executed from her only one of which was gift deed but the other was a sale deed of her properties in favour of persons who perpetrated the fraud, the fraud/misrepresentation practised on the woman was not limited to contents or legal effect to the documents but extended to fraudulent misrepresentation as to character of the document itself. The sale deed so executed was therefore totally void and not voidable.[16] Specific performance in respect of such contracts is out of question, such deeds are liable to be set aside.

Where the relationship subsisting between parties is such that one of the parties is in a position to dominate the will of the other and uses that position to obtain an unfair advantage over the other, it is said as undue influence.[17] If a deed of sale had been procured by undue influence and coercion, it can be cancelled.[18] When a deed of sale was executed by a tribal woman, who was old, illiterate and blind, in favour of her relative with whom she was living till her death and was totally dependent on him and when no consideration passed on at the time of the sale, the onus lies on him to prove that the deed of sale was not executed under undue influence.[19]

The pleading with respect to 'undue influence'[20] must be there before it can be set up as a defence in a suit for specific performance. A plea of undue influence, where set up, is a special plea. Section 103 of the Evidence Act places the burden of substantiating such a plea on the party which sets it up.[1] At the same time, unlike English law,[2] Indian law does not envisage raising of a presumption in favour of undue influence. A party alleging the same must prove the same subject of course to just exceptions.[3] Merely because the parties are nearly related to each other or merely because the donor was old or of weak character, no presumption of undue influence can arise.[4]

16 *Dularia Devi* v *Janardan Singh* AIR 1990 SC 1173; (1990)1 SCR 799; 1990 (Supp) SCC 216.

17 *Marci Celine D'Souza* v *Renie Fernandez* AIR 1998 Ker 280; *Bellachi* v *Pakeeran* (2009)12 SCC 95; AIR 2009 SC 3293.

18 *Karthik Prasad Gorai* v *Neami Prasad Gorai* AIR 1998 Cal 728.

19 *Mst. Sethani* v *Bhana* AIR 1993 SC 956; JT 1992(2) SC 427; see also *Krishna Mohan Kul* v *Pratima Maity* AIR 2003 SC 4351.

20 *Subhas Chandra Das Mushib* v *Ganga Prasad Das Mushib* (1967)1 SCR 331; AIR 1967 SC 878.

1 *Surendra Pal* v *Saraswati Arora (Dr.)* (1974)2 SCC 600.

2 Halsbury's *Laws of England*, 3rd Ed., vol. 17, p. 681; see also *Surendra Pal* v *Saraswati Arora (Dr.)* (1974)2 SCC 600.

3 *Bellachi* v *Pakeeran* (2009)12 SCC 95; AIR 2009 SC 3293.

4 *M. Rangaswamy* v *Rangammal* AIR 2003 SC 3120; see Dutt, *Contract*, 11th Ed., p. 220.

Fraud Fraud, as is well known, vitiates all solemn acts[5]and it is axiomatic to say that "fraud and justice never dwell together".[6] "Fraud" means and includes any of the following acts committed by a party to a contract, or with his connivance, or by his agent, with intent to deceive another party thereto or his agent, or to induce him to enter the contract: (1) the suggestion, as a fact, of that which is not true, by one who does not believe it to be true; (2) the active concealment of a fact by one having knowledge or belief of the fact; (3) a promise made without any intention of performing it; (4) any such act fitted to deceive; and (5) any such act or omission as the law specially declares to be fraudulent. Mere silence as to facts likely to affect the willingness of a person to enter into a contract is not fraud, unless the circumstances of the case are such that, regard being had to them, it is the duty of the person keeping silence to speak, or unless his silence is, in itself, equivalent to speech, (e.g. a guarantee obtained by a creditor by keeping silence as to a material circumstances is invalid) (s. 17, the Contract Act). However, it is not fraud, where a person on whom fraud is committed is in a position to discover the truth by due diligence.[7]

Thus, where a deed of sale was executed admittedly with a fraudulent design to defeat the creditors and the vendee later started asserting title in a suit filed by the vendor for cancellation of the deed of sale, it was held that the vendor could not be permitted to take advantage of his own fraud. If both the parties are in *pari delicto*, the court should decline to help either party and let things remain as they are and let both parties reap the consequences of their own fraud and dishonesty.[8] Where a property is detained by playing fraud, it must be restored to those deprived of the property.[9] Fraud, like any other charge of criminal offence, whether made in a civil or criminal proceedings, must be established beyond reasonable doubt and a finding of fraud cannot be based on suspicion, surmise or conjecture.[10]

Fraud, which vitiates the contract, must have a nexus with the acts of the parties prior to entering into the contract.[11]

5 *Ram Chandra Singh* v *Savitri Devi* (2003)8 SCC 319; *Tanna & Modi* v *CIT* (2007)7 SCC 434 and *Rani Aloka Dudhoria* v *Goutam Dudhoria* (2009)13 SCC 569; JT 2009(3) SC 616.

6 *Meghmala* v *G. Narasimha Reddy* (2010)8 SCC 383; *Chandradhoja Sahoo* v *State of Orissa* (2012)13 SCC 419; AIR 2013 SC 367.

7 *Shri Krishnan* v *Kurukshetra University* (1976)1 SCC 311.

8 *Sultan Ahmad* v *Rasheed Ahamad* AIR 1990 All 47.

9 *Delhi Development Authority* v *Skipper Construction Compamy Pvt. Ltd.* (1996)4 SCC 622; AIR 1996 SC 2005; JT 1996(4) SC 679.

10 *Narayana Chettiar* v *Official Assignee* AIR 1939 PC 93. Followed in *Unique Alliance Industries* v *Anupama Agencies* (1994)2 KLT 831. See also *Savithriammal* v *H. Gurappa Reddi* AIR 1996 Kant 99.

11 *Reliance Salt Ltd.* v *Cosmos Enterprises* (2006)13 SCC 599.

Fraud is a conduct either by letter or words which includes the other person or authority to take a definite determinative stand as a response to the conduct of the former either by words or letters. Misrepresentation itself amounts to fraud. Fraud and collusion vitiates even the most solemn proceedings in any civilized system of jurisprudence. Suppression of material document would also amount to fraud on the court.[12]

Misrepresentation It means and includes (1) the positive assertion, in a manner not warranted by the information of the person making it, of that which is not true, though he believes it to be true; (2) any breach of duty which, without an intent to deceive, gains an advantage to the person committing it, or any one claiming under him, by misleading another to his prejudice, or to the prejudice of any one claiming under him; and (3) causing, however innocently, a party to an agreement to make a mistake as to the substance of the thing which is the subject of the agreement.[13]

Normally, misrepresentation should be of such type that it will give a right to rescind the contract; but even if it is not of that type, specific performance may be refused if the purchaser can show that but for the misrepresentation he would not have entered into the contract.[14]

Where *A* entered into a contract for the sale of his house to *B* and before signing the agreement he asked *B* whether he was purchasing the property for *C* or his nominee and *C* replied "No", when in fact he was buying for the nominee of *C*, it was held that the contract could not be specifically enforced,[15] where the contract was held to be specifically enforceable. In this case the vendor refused to sell the property to one *C*, on the ground that he had wanted to buy the property for Roman Catholic Committee for use as a Roman Catholic place of worship. Plaintiff who was a manager of *E*, a Mineral Water Co. offered to buy the property and succeeded in his bargain. Defendants knew that the plaintiff was buying the property for the company. Later on, the defendants refused to complete the sale on the ground that the plaintiff was buying the property as agent for the Roman Catholic Committee to whom they would not sell the property. *Held*, that on evidence plaintiff was not buying the property as agent for the Roman Catholic Committee but in fact in his own right to resell the property to them. And as to misrepresentation as to the company, it was immaterial because the vendors did not care whether they sold the property to the company or to the plaintiff and as between them no consideration entered as an element into the contract.

12 Dutt, *Contract*, 11th Ed., p. 244. See *State of A.P.* v *T. Suryachandra Rao* (2005)6 SCC 149.
13 Section 18, Contract Act.
14 *Holliday* v *Lockwood* [1917]2 Ch 47 at pp. 56, 57.
15 *Archer* v *Stone* [1878]78 LT 34 *cf.* however, *Nash* v *Dix* [1897]78 LT 445.

In *Dyster* v *Randall & Sons*,[16] it has been held that if personal quality is not an ingredient of the contract, the mere non-disclosure of the person actually entitled to the benefit of the contract is no defence to an action for specific performance even though the plaintiff knew that if the disclosure had been made the defendant would not have entered into it. This decision was not, however, followed *in re Pascoe*.[17]

Order 6, r. 4 of the Code of Civil Procedure requires that complete particulars of fraud, misrepresentation or undue influence shall be stated in the pleadings. The particulars of alleged fraud, misrepresentation or undue influence which are required to be stated in the plaint, will depend upon the facts of each particular case and no abstract principle can be laid down in this regard.[18]

The common law defence of *non est factum* to actions on specialties in its origin was available where an illiterate person, to whom the contents of a deed had been wrongly read, executed it under a mistake as to its nature and contents, he could say that it was not his deed at all. In its modern application, the doctrine has been extended to cases other than those of illiteracy and to other contracts in writing. In most of the cases in which this defence was pleaded the mistake was induced by fraud; but that was not, perhaps, a necessary factor, as the transaction is "invalid not merely on the ground of fraud, where fraud exists, but on the ground that the mind of the signor did not accompany the signature; in other words, that he never intended to sign, and therefore, in contemplation of law never did sign, the contract to which his name is appended.[19]

INSTANCES OF MISREPRESENTATION An execution of a deed of sale was set aside on the ground of mere misrepresentation when it appeared that there was a difference in substance between the thing bargained for and obtained.[20] A seller of land professing to be the owner though he was merely a leaseholder, was guilty of misrepresentation.[1] So also a Hindu father who sold the property without necessity alleging that he was the sole owner thereof.[2] Where the vendor whether on enquiry or otherwise, gave false information about the income or rental of the property sold, he was liable for misrepresentation.[3] It is misrepresentation where an endorsement contained on acknowledgment of full satisfaction of a mortgage, when it was not so satisfied,[4] or where the

16 [1926] Ch 932.
17 [1944] Ch 219.
18 *Ramesh B. Desai* v *Bipin Vadilal Mehta* (2006)5 SCC 638.
19 *Bismillah* v *Janeshwar Prasad* (1990)1 SCC 207; Chitty, *Contracts*, 25th Ed., p. 341
20 *Ratan Singh Gulab Singh* v *Nanikram Chatomali* AIR 1927 Sind 219.
1 *J.W. Thomas* v *Hanuman Prasad* AIR 1929 All 837.
2 *Ratan Singh Gulab Singh* v *Nanikram Chatomali* AIR 1927 Sind 219.
3 *Prem Chand* v *Ram Sahai* AIR 1932 Nag 148.
4 *Rangappa Gangappa Lingayat Wani* v *Sayed Imamuddin* AIR 1934 Nag 29.

landlord falsely informed a prospective tenant that the house had specific number of bedrooms as required by the tenants.[5] Where misrepresentation is merely about the contents of the document, the transaction becomes voidable, but where it relates also to the nature or character of the transaction, the entire transaction is void.[6] In the aforesaid decision, in *Dularia Devi's* case,[7] there was fraudulent misrepresentation as to the character of the document executed by an illiterate woman and not merely as to its contents or as to its legal effect; her mind in such a case did not accompany her thumb impression and hence the document was held totally void.

When the illiterate lady signed a document which she was given to believe by trusted agents that she was creating a licence but it was in fact a settlement. This amounted to breach of duty. She had the right to cancel the licence.[8]

EFFECTS OF MISDESCRIPTION Problem as to the effectiveness of a condition against error or misdescription can arise where the misdescription did not form part of the contract, but it was a misrepresentation for inducement. In such case the representee can rescind the contract for misrepresentation. If the matter misrepresented was not substantial, it is likely that the court would, in absence of a condition, reject a claim to rescind the contract for misrepresentation, it would declare the contract as subsisting and award damages in lieu of rescission. A condition is regarded as unreasonable in so far as it excluded the purchaser's right to compensation or his right to rescind for a misrepresentation relating to a matter that was of substantial importance.[9]

When the applicant made a misdeclaration about his income in the application form for dealership of petroleum products, it was held that cancellation of the letter of intent issued to him was proper. The contention that the fact wrongly declared had no bearing as the eligibility criterion was not accepted.[10]

However, rectification of such misdescription in contract is permissible in view of s. 26 of the Specific Relief Act 1963. A defendant in any such suit, may, in addition to any other defence open to him, ask for rectification of the instrument. The court has discretion in such cases to allow such rectification in the pleadings or in the instrument itself.[11]

Mistake It may be a mistake of fact or of law. It may relate to the person or to the subject matter. If both the parties are under a mistake regarding

5 *Alla Baksh Khan* v *RE Bayron* AIR 1917 Lah 173.
6 *Ningawara* v *Byrappa Shiddappa* AIR 1968 SC 956; (1968)2 SCR 797; *Dularia Devi* v *Janardan Singh* AIR 1990 SC 1173; (1990)1 SCR 799; 1990 (Supp) SCC 216.
7 *Dularia Devi* v *Janardhan Singh* AIR 1990 SC 1173; 1990 (Supp) SCC 216.
8 *Khandu Charan Polley* v *Chanchala Bhuniya* AIR 2003 Cal 213.
9 *Walker* v *Boyle* [1982]1 WLR 495.
10 *Shiv Kant Yadav* v *Indian Oil Corp.* AIR 2007 SC 1534; (2007)4 SCC 410.
11 *Puran Ram* v *Bhaguram* (2008)4 SCC 102.

a matter of fact essential to the agreement, which includes a mistake as to law not in force in India, the agreement itself is void. But if it is mistake of law, or the mistake involves an erroneous opinion as to the value of the thing which forms the subject matter of the agreement, or if only one party is under a mistake as to the fact, the consent is not vitiated thereby.

Mistakes of fact are of three kinds *viz.*, unilateral, common and mutual. *Anson*[12] would, however, treat a common mistake as synonymous with mutual mistake. But there is a vital difference between the two.

The Supreme Court[13] has held that a mistake may be unilateral or mutual, but it is always unintentional. If it is intentional, it ceases to be a mistake.

UNILATERAL MISTAKE A mistake on the part of only one of the parties to the contract is what is known as unilateral mistake and it is generally no ground to avoid a contract. However, a mistake of fact, even though unilateral, sometimes brings about want of consensus so as to make the contract void. This can be illustrated with reference to the defence of *non est factum*. Where a person who has executed a written document was mistaken not merely as regards the contents thereof but also as to the essential nature of the contract, he can plead *non est factum*. (It is not my deed; *scriptum predictum non est factum*; that is, writing is not my deed).[14] The doctrine of *non est factum* in its modern application has been extended to cases other than those of illiteracy and to other contracts in writing. In most of the cases in which this defence is pleaded, the mistake is induced by fraud; but that is not perhaps a necessary factor, as the transaction is invalid not merely due to fraud but because the mind of the signor did not accompany the signature and therefore, in the contemplation of law, he never did sign the contract to which his name is appended.[15]

COMMON MISTAKE Section 20 of the Contract Act deals with common mistake. In the case of common mistake both parties to the contract make the same mistake, in other words, both parties are labouring under the same mistake of fact and in such a case, the contract is devoid of force and efficacy as both are mistaken about the same fact which is vital to the agreement.[16] In *Cooper* v *Phibbs*,[17] A agreed to take a lease of a fishery

12 Anson's *Law of Contract*, 30th Ed., p. 271.

13 *W.B. SEB* v *Patel Engg. Co. Ltd.* (2001)2 SCC 451; AIR 2001 SC 682.

14 *Thoroughgood's* case [1584]2 Co Rep 9a; *Foster* v *Mackinnon* [1869]4 CP 704; *Mitibowa* v *Dordan Naik* AIR 1983 Ori 174; *Abhimanya Biswas* v *Abdul Sk.* AIR 1981 Cal 144; *Amar Krisha Mukherjee* v *Asha Rani Ghosh* AIR 1985 Cal 398.

15 *Bismillah* v *Janeshwar Prasad* AIR 1990 SC 540; (1990)1 SCC 207; JT 1989 (Supp) SC 407.

16 *UP Government* v *Lalananhoo Mal Gupta* AIR 1960 All 420. See *illustration* to s. 20 for proper appreciation of common mistakes.

17 LR (1867)2 HL 149; 16 LT 678; 15 WR 1049 (HL).

from *B*, though contrary to the belief of both parties at the time, *A* was tenant for life of the fishery and *B* had no title at all. Lord Westbury applied the principle that if parties contract under a mutual mistake and misapprehension as to their relative and respective rights, the result is that the agreement is liable to be set aside as having proceeded upon a common mistake. The transfer of ownership being impossible, the stipulation was *naturali ratione inunitilis*.

The rule laid down in *Cooper's* case was followed in other cases also.[18] But, a somewhat different opinion was expressed by Lord Atkin in *Bell* v *Lever Bros. Ltd.*[19] In *Bell* v *Lever Bros. Ltd.*, an agreement of service between the company and two of the directors of its subsidiary company was terminated on payment of compensation. The parties proceeded on the assumption that the service agreement was not liable to immediate termination by reason of misconduct of the directors which assumption proved to be mistaken. Fraud was however negatived. In an action by the company for rescission of contract and repayment of moneys paid the agreement was set aside on the ground of mutual mistake as to the quality of the service contract. The accepted proposition was that whenever it is to be inferred from the terms of the contract or its surrounding circumstances that the consensus has been reached upon the basis of a particular contractual assumption, and that assumption is not true, the contract is avoided; *i.e.* it is void *ab initio* if the assumption is of present fact and it ceases to bind if the assumption is of future fact.

The assumption must have been fundamental to the continued validity of the contract or a foundation essential to its existence. Lord Atkins observed that the common standard for mutual mistake and implied conditions as to the existing or as to future fact is: Does the state of new facts destroy the identity of the subject-matter as it was in the original state of facts? It is submitted that in such cases the court has to ascertain "the sense of the promises.[20]

Thus, if *B* were to offer to sell his Ford Sierra car to *A* and *A* were to accept in the belief that the offer related to a Ford Granada. In such a case, no doubt, if the minds of the parties could be probed, genuine consent would be found wanting. But the question is not what the parties had in their minds, but what reasonable third parties would infer from their words or conduct.[1] The net result is that if, from the entire evidence, a reasonable man would infer the existence of a contract in a given sense, the court,

18 *Earl Beauchamp* v *Winn* [1873]6 HL 223; 22 WR 193; *Huddersfield Banking Co.* v *Lister (Henry) & Sons* [1895]2 Ch 273; 64 LJ Ch 523; 72 LT 703.

19 [1932] AC 161; [1931] All ER 1, 27 (Rep).

20 Austin, *Lectures on Jurisprudence*, Lecture-21, note 89.

1 Cheshire, Fifoot and Furmston, *Law of Contract*, 15th Ed., p. 306.

notwithstanding a material mistake, will hold that a contract in that sense is binding upon both parties. The apparent contract will stand.[2]

MUTUAL MISTAKE Mutual mistake occurs where the parties misunderstand each other and are at cross purposes. There is no real corresponding offer and acceptance. The parties are not really *consensus ad idem*. There is thus no agreement at all and the contract is void. For example, *A* intends to offer 8 HP motor but *B* believes it to be 10 HP. Here there is a misunderstanding in the communication between the parties which prevents there being an effective agreement. In *Raffles* v *Nichelhaus*,[3] the defendant contracted to buy a cargo of cotton to arrive in "Ex. Peerless" from Bombay. There were two ships of that name and both sailed from Bombay. But one left in October and the other in December. Here, both parties were behaving reasonably, but had different things in mind. There was no contract. The court, considering the matter objectively, was unable to determine which ship was the contracted ship. Similarly there is no consent when the parties intended to contract at different terms, for example, when *A* intends to buy for £30 and *B* intends to sell for 30 Guineas.[4] In *Tarsem Singh* v *Sukhminder Singh*,[5] there was a contract for sale of land in which one party thought the area in terms of *bighas* and the other in *karnals*. The agreement was held void. In such cases, genuine consensus would be lacking and no contract really comes into existence. There is no agreement upon the same thing in the same sense.

The application of the doctrine of mutual mistake depends upon the true construction of the contract made between the parties.[6] A written document can be varied by leading oral evidence in view of Proviso 1 to s. 92 of the Evidence Act 1872.[7] Further, a written document can be rectified under s. 26 of the Specific Relief Act, if it suffers from mutual mistake.[8]

Mistake of law generally does not render a contract void. Mistake with regard to the law of registration of assignment deed is a mistake of law and under s. 21, the Contract Act such contract is not rendered void.[9] However, ignorance of law is not mistake of law. Deliberate disregard of law is not mistake of law.[10]

2 Cheshire, Fifoot and Furmston, *Law of Contract*, 15th Ed., p. 307; *Wood* v *Scarth* [1858]1F&F 293.
3 [1864]2 H&C 906.
4 G.R. Treitel, *The Law of Contract*, 13th Ed., pp. 324-327.
5 AIR 1998 SC 1400; (1998)3 SCC 471; JT 1998(2) SC 149.
6 *I.T.C. Ltd.* v *George Joseph Fernandes* (1989)2 SCC 1.
7 *Tulsiram Rajaram Brahman* v *Durgaprasad Ramprasad Brahman* 2002 AIHC 317.
8 *Beni Mahto* v *Hulas Mahto* (2004)21 AIC 788; (2004)3 JLJR 336.
9 *Kalyanpure Lime Works* v *State of Bihar* AIR 1954 SC 165; 1954 SCR 958; 1954 SCJ 99; (1954)1 Mad LJ 305.
10 *Anath Bandhu Deb* v *Dominion of India* AIR 1955 Cal 626.

Even if the mistake is not a mistake at law, if it is a mistake in equity, specific performance may be refused.[11] Landlord under the impression that the 1939 letting had no application to the re-constructed flat and therefore not serving notice of increase,[12] defendant believing that the property agreed to be sold was in the occupation of a statutory tenant, which was however not true,[13] lease of premises for 15 years while planning permission only for two years.[14]

It may be observed, as laid down in Broom's *Legal Maxims*, 12th Ed., p. 201 a purchaser seeks to avoid specific performance of a contract of purchase, on the ground of a mistake of fact, he can only do so provided he shows that the mistake was mutual to both parties; or that he entered into the bargain under a mistake of fact which, although not contributed to by the other party, would inflict a hardship amounting to injustice if the court held him to his bargain,[15] or where the mistake was one to which the other party contributed, in other words if the party seeking relief was misled by any act of the vendor into making the bargain.[16]

In criminal cases the maxim as to *ignorantia facti* applies, except in cases where mens rea in the ordinary sense is not requisite—see the *maxim actus non facit reum nisi mens sit rea*, when a man intending to do a lawful act, does that which is unlawful. In this case there is not that conjunction between the deed and the will which is necessary to form a criminal act; but in order that he may stand executed, there must be a reasonable mistake of fact, and not an error in point of law. If a man, intending to kill a burger under circumstances which would justify him in so doing, by mistake kills one of his own family, this is no criminal act; but if a man thinks he has a right to kill an excommunicated person wherever he meets him, and does so, this is murder. For a mistake in point of law, which every person of discretion not only may, but is bound and presumed to know is in criminal cases, no sort of defence.[17]

Specific performance may also be refused if the mistake is unilateral, but the plaintiff has contributed to the defendant's mistake however unintentionally.[18] In *Stewart* v *Kennedy*,[19] even though the mistake was

11 *Webster* v *Cecil* [1861]30 Beav 62 (mistake in writing correct price).
12 *Solle* v *Butcher* [1949]2 All ER 1107.
13 *Grist* v *Bailey* [1966]2 All ER 875.
14 *Laurence* v *Lexcourt Holdings* [1978]2 All ER 810.
15 *Tamplin* v *James* 15 Ch D 215 at p. 221.
16 *Goddard* v *Jeffreys* 51 LJ Ch 57.
17 Blackstone's *Commentaries*, (IV, 27); Doctor and Student, Dial. 2, C. 46; Wharton, *The Law Lexicon*, 1847, p. 307. See also Re, Barronet I.E. & B.I. *Ignorantia corum quod quise score tincture non excusat*.
18 *Wilding* v *Sanderson* [1897]2 Ch 534.
19 [1890]15 Ch App 75.

that of the defendant alone, the court refused the decree on the view that it would be highly unreasonable to pass the decree.[20] Decree would cause hardship amounting to injustice.

Mistake apparent on record A mistake apparent on record is a patent mistake which does not require to be established by a long drawn process of reasoning. The power of court to rectify a mistake should be patent one and quite obvious.[21]

Coercion, fraud, misrepresentation and undue influence—pleading Contract vitiated by fraud, coercion etc. is not specifically performable. In suit for specific performance of contract of transfer defence plea namely that the contract is vitiated by fraud, undue influence, coercion, misrepresentation can be taken and such plea is tenable. But pleading as to fraud etc. is governed by Or. 6, r. 4, CPC.

Under Or. 6, r. 4 in case of fraud, undue influence and coercion the parties pleading it must set forth full particulars and the case can only be decided on the particulars as laid. There can be no departure from them in the evidence. General allegations are insufficient even to amount to an averment of fraud of which any court, ought to take notice, however strong the language in which they are couched may be. Such categories must be separately pleaded.[1] This practice must be insisted on even if no objection is taken by the party on this score.[2] If there is a general allegation of fraud, the party alleging it cannot lead evidence in excess of the plea.[3] Plaintiff must give particulars of fraud when he sues to set aside an *ex parte* decree on the ground of fraud in service of summons.[4] When pleading is never interpreted as containing allegation of fraud in trial court, and no opportunity of tendering evidence in support or in denial of fraud has been made available, the plea of fraud cannot be taken for the first time in appeal.[5]

20 *Tamplin* v *James* [1880]15 Ch D 215.
21 *Commission of Central Excise* v *RDC Concrete (India) Pvt. Ltd.* (2011)12 SCC 166 following *T.S. Balaram* v *Volkart Bros.* AIR 1961 SC 699.
1 *Bishnudeo* v *Seogeni Rai* AIR 1951 SC 280; 1951 SCJ 413; ILR 30 Pat 947; *Indian Airlines Corpn.* v *Ramniwas Ladu* ILR (1969)19 Raj 67; *Fatima Bi Ammal* v *A. Mohammad* (1971)2 Mad LJ 451; *Bakshi Lochan Singh* v *Jathedar Santokh Singh* AIR 1971 Del 277; *Harekrishna* v *Bhagirathi* AIR 1975 Ori 97; 40 Cut LT 597; *Madan Panda* v *H. Panda* AIR 1974 Ori 110; ILR (1973) Cut 647; *T. Ibeltombi* v *M.R. Singh* AIR 1974 Gau 65; *Swarnalata Devi* v *K.L.F. & Works* AIR 1974 Cal 393 (this Calcutta decision laying down that a decree cannot be set aside on the ground of prejured evidence); *Bishnu Priya* v *Brishbhanu* (1976)1 Cut WR 73; *Talfiquor* v *Sital Prasad* AIR 1977 Gau 25; *Asghar Ali* v *Chidda* AIR 1982 All 186.
2 *Bharat D.S. Ltd.* v *Harish* 41 CWN 746; *Chiranjilal* v *Jaihind Investment* AIR 1978 Cal 177.
3 *Union of India* v *Motilal Kamalia* AIR 1962 Pat 384; *Swarna Lata Devi* v *K.I.F. Metal Works (P) Ltd.* AIR 1974 Cal 393.
4 *Dasarath* v *Bhagirathi* AIR 1977 NOC 344 (Ori).
5 *Mohanlal* v *Anandibai* (1971)1 SCC 813; AIR 1971 SC 2177; (1971)3 SCR 929.

The court must scrutinize the pleadings to find out that such a case has been made out and that full particulars of undue influence have been given as in the case of fraud.[6] A vague or general plea can never serve this purpose; the party pleading must therefore be required to plead the precise nature of the influence exercised, the manner of use of the influence, and the unfair advantage obtained by the other.[7] If a particular fraud is pleaded and another fraud is sought to be proved at the time of the trial through the evidence, the entire story of fraud is liable to be rejected.[8] A bald allegation of fraud is not sufficient.[9] Fraud is a conduct either by letters or words which induces the other person or authority to take a definite determinative stand as a response to the conduct of the former either by words or letters. Although negligence is not fraud, but it can be evidence on fraud.[10] The particulars of alleged fraud, which are required to be stated in the plaint, will depend upon the facts of each particular case and no abstract principle can be laid down in this regard. Where some transaction of money takes place to which 'A', 'B' and 'C' are parties and payment is made by cheques, in normal circumstances a third party 'X' may not get knowledge of the said transaction unless he is informed about it by someone who has knowledge of the transaction or he gets an opportunity to see the accounts of the parties concerned in the Bank. In such a case an assertion by 'X' that he got no knowledge of the transaction when it took place and that he came to know about it subsequently through some proceedings in court cannot be said to be insufficient pleading for the purpose of Or. 6, r. 4, CPC. In such a case 'X' can only plead that he got no knowledge of the transaction and nothing more.[11] But, the pleading with regard to fraud is not necessary if the fraud is apparent from the face of the record.[12]

As to undue influence if the relationship between the donor and donee is such that donee can dominate the will of the donor and the transaction appears to be unconscionable, then the burden of proving that the contract was not induced by undue influence lies upon the person who is in the position to dominate the will of donor. But, merely because the parties were nearly related to each other or merely because the donor was old or of weak

6 *Subhas Chandra Das Mushib* v *Ganga Prasad Das Mushib* (1967)1 SCR 331; AIR 1967 SC 878.

7 *Ladli Parshad Jaiswal* v *Karnal Distillery Co. Ltd.* (1964)1 SCR 270; AIR 1963 SC 1279.

8 *Bama Charan Naskar* v *Ayen Ali Molla* 64 CWN xli (Notes); *Keshavrao* v *Chandrabhan* AIR 1980 Bom 380.

9 *Saheb Khan* v *Mohd. Yousufuddin* (2006)4 SCC 476.

10 *R.P. Yadav* v *U.P. Board of H.S. and Intermediate Education* AIR 2003 SC 4268 relying on *Derry* v *Peek* [1889]14 AC 337.

11 *Ramesh B. Desai* v *Bipin Vadilal Mehta* (2006)5 SCC 638.

12 *Lachhman Dass* v *Jagat Ram* (2007)10 SCC 448.

character, no presumption of undue influence arises.[13] Though pleading with respect to 'undue influence'is required, however, lack of details in the pleadings cannot be a ground to reject a case for the reason that it can be supplemented through evidence by the parties.[14] If there are facts on the record to justify the inference of undue influence, the omission to make an allegation of undue influence specifically, is not fatal to the plaintiff being entitled to relief on that ground; all that the court has to see is that there is no surprise to the defendant.[15]

If misrepresentations are alleged, the party then should state as to each misrepresentation, its date and whether it was made in writing or it was verbal; and if it is verbal, to each occasion thereof.[16]

The same is the position of law in respect of pleading of undue influence.[17]

While it is true that 'undue influence', 'fraud' and 'misrepresentation' are cognate vices and may in part overlap in some cases, they are in law distinct categories and are required to be separately pleaded with specificity, particularity and precision. A general allegation in the plaint that the plaintiff was an old man who reposed great confidence in the defendant is too insufficient to amount to an averment of undue influence.[18]

In case of allegation of collusion implying some kind of fraud it is not enough to state in general terms that there was collusion. Particulars must be furnished.[19]

Plea of fraud for the first time in appellate court is not permissible.[20] Details of improper conduct must be pleaded;[1] details of negligence similarly are to be pleaded.[2]

13 *Subhas Chandra Das* v *Ganga Prosad* AIR 1967 SC 878; (1967)1 SCR 331; *Dharam Kaur* v *Gurdev Singh* (1988)2 Cur Civ Cas 654 (Punj).

14 *Hari Singh* v *Kanhaiya Lal* (1999)7 SCC 288; AIR 1999 SC 3325.

15 *Joseph John Peter Sandy* v *Veronica Thomas Rajkumar* (2013)3 SCC 801; AIR 2013 SC 2028.

16 *Padma Bewa* v *Krupasindu Biswal* AIR 1986 Ori 97; (1986)1 Cur Civ Cas 3; (1985)2 Ori LR 391; (1985)60 Cut LT 531.

17 *Subhas Chandra Das* v *Ganga Prosad* AIR 1967 SC 878; (1967)1 SCR 331; *Madan Panda* v *H. Panda* AIR 1974 Ori 110; ILR (1973) Cut 647; *K.P. Abdur Rahim* v *Kunchi* AIR 1975 Ker 150; *P. Saraswathi* v *Lakshmi* AIR 1978 Mad 361; *Goodu Saheb* v *Rakiabi* (1978)2 Mad LJ 426; *Syed Sultan Pai* v *Syed Bhiku Saheb* AIR 1986 AP 342.

18 *Afsar Seikh* v *Soleman Bibi* AIR 1976 SC 163; (1976)2 SCC 142; *Kunhamina Umma* v *Special Tehshildar* AIR 1977 Ker 41; *Padma Bewa* v *Krupasindhu Biswal* AIR 1986 Ori 97; *Bishnudeo Narain* v *Seogini Rai* AIR 1951 SC 280.

19 *V.S. Viswavidyalaya* v *Raj Krishna Tripathi* AIR 1977 SC 615; (1977)2 SCR 213; (1977)1 SCC 279.

20 *T. Ibeltombi* v *Mutum Rohini Singh* AIR 1974 Gau 65.

1 *Union of India* v *P.K. More* AIR 1962 SC 630; (1961)2 LLJ 427.

2 *Punjab National Bank* v *Firm Ishwarbhai Lalubhai Patel* AIR 1971 Bom 348; 1971 Mah LJ 9.

Want of consideration as defence in specific performance The third element in a contract is the lawful consideration and the object of the promise. Consideration refers to such act, abstinence or promise as the promisee or any other person has, at the desire of the promisor, done or abstained from doing, or does or abstains from doing, or promises to do or to abstain from doing something [s. 2(*d*) of the Contract Act]. Detriment suffered by the promisor for the benefit of another person, not a party to the consideration, was held as good consideration.[3]

Not only should there be a consideration for every contract, but the consideration should also be lawful. Section 23, Contract Act provides that consideration of an agreement is lawful unless it is forbidden by law, or is of such a nature that, if permitted, it would defeat the provisions of any law; or is fraudulent; or involves or implies injury to the person or property of another, or the court regards it as immoral, or opposed to public policy. Thus in suit for specific performance of contract, illegality of consideration or the fact that the consideration is hit by s. 23, Contract Act is a good defence. The same is the position with regard to the object of the agreement. However, it needs mention that the legal term "consideration" does not mean payment of money only, but it means a reasonable equivalent or other valuable benefit passed on by the promisor to the promisee or by a transferor to a transferee.[4]

In *Neminath Appayya Hanamannanavar* v *Jamboorao Satappa Kocheri*,[5] defendants resisted the suit on the ground that if the contract were enforced, it would result in plaintiff holding land in excess of ceiling prescribed under the Bombay Tenancy and Agricultural Lands (Vidarbha Region) Act 1958 and so void under 3rd para of s. 23 of the Contract Act.

In *Nutan Kumar* v *Addl. District Judge,*[6] an agreement of lease of land in violation of the Rent Control Act was held to be void. The lessee had no status and was ejectable. He was like a trespasser. Suit for his ejectment was not barred by s. 23 of the Contract Act.

If the agreement is without consideration or the consideration is unlawful, the agreement is void. Section 25 of the Contract Act, however, enumerated three types of agreements which may be made without consideration. Contract of agency also does not require any consideration [s. 185 of the Contract Act].

Likewise, an agreement to sell land to a person holding more than 12½ acres of land is not hit by s. 154 of the U.P. Zamindari Abolition and Land Reforms Act 1950 for the reason that the prohibition takes effect from the

3 *Prakashwati Jain* v *Punjab State Industrial Devpt. Corpn.* AIR 2012 P&H 13.
4 *P. Jagadeesan & Co.* v *A. Krishnan* (2001)4 CTC 356; (2002)1 LW 526.
5 AIR 1966 Mys 154 (DB).
6 AIR 2002 SC 3456; (2002)8 SCC 31.

date of sale and not from the date of agreement to sell and such an agreement is also not violative of s. 23 of the Contract Act.[7]

A compromise is valid even if plaintiff's claim was bogus.[8] Order 23, r. 3A, CPC applies to any compromise which is unlawful and not only a compromise which is unlawful within the contemplation of s. 23 of the Contract Act 1872.[9]

An overdraft arrangement between a banker and its customer constitutes a contract and cannot be unilaterally terminated by the bank without notice. It is immaterial that the facility is temporary and the bank did not have any security.[10]

Consideration—bargain requirement The consideration or the bargain requirement is the basis of a promise. In essence it means that something is to be given in return for a promise. Thus, gratuitous promise or a promise to give gift will not be enforced by law, for example, *A* says to his nephew that *A* will give him a certain sum of money when he will attain 21 years of age and *A* does not ask anything in return. This is a gratuitous promise and is not enforceable. Similarly, *A* gives *B* certain money without anything in return. *A* cannot take it back on the ground that there was no consideration. Law of contract is not concerned with promise with executed or already performed contract but is concerned with executory promise.

Consideration and object In a suit for specific performance, it is open to the defendant to contend that there was no consideration for the agreement for sale or that the consideration or object was unlawful.

Money was paid by way of illegal gratification for purposes of arranging the job for complainant's son pursuant to agreement between the petitioner and the complainant. The agreement is void, consideration therein being unlawful.[11] Where land jointly owned by five brothers is sold by one of them alone for single consideration by holding out that he is the sole owner of the land, it implies injury to the property of the other brothers. The object of the agreement being unlawful is void as per s. 23 of the Contract Act.[12]

Contract—executed consideration and executory consideration—contrast An executed consideration consists of an act from a promise. It is the act which

7 *Pahunchi Lal* v *Man Singh* AIR 1971 All 444 distinguishing *Sita Ram* v *Kunj Lal* AIR 1963 All 206.

8 *Indubala Devi* v *Jitendra Nath Ghose* AIR 1971 Cal 411 following *Jayawickreme* v *Amarasuriya* AIR 1918 PC 287.

9 *Palden Bhutia* v *Januka Chettri* AIR 2007 Sikkim 15. See also *Banwari Lal* v *Chando Devi* (1993)1 SCC 581; AIR 1993 SC 1139.

10 *Indian Overseas Bank* v *Naranprasad Govindlal Patel* AIR 1980 Guj 158 at p. 159.

11 *Virender Singh* v *Laxmi Narain* 2007 CrLJ 2262 (Del).

12 *Udho Rai* v *Ambika* Tiwari AIR 2007 Pat 136.

forms the consideration. No contract is formed unless and until the act is performed, *e.g.* the payment for a railway ticket, but the act stipulated for exhausts the consideration, so that any subsequent promise without further consideration is merely a *nudum pactum*. In an executed consideration the liability is outstanding on one side only; it is present as opposed to a future consideration.

In an executory consideration the liability is outstanding on both sides. It is in fact a promise for a promise, one promise is bought by the other. The contract is concluded as soon as the promises are exchanged. In mercantile contracts this is by far the most common variety. In other words, a contract becomes binding on the exchange of valid promises, one being the consideration for the other.[13]

It is clear therefore that there is nothing to prevent one of the parties from carrying out his promise at once, *i.e.* performing his part of the contract, whereas the other party who provides the consideration for the act of or detriment to the first may not carry out his part of the bargain simultaneously with the first party. If the contract has been fully and completely performed on both sides no question of any further rights and liabilities under the contract is likely to arise. If, however, the contract is one for which the consideration is executed on one side, there will be a right on one side and an outstanding liability on the other. If the consideration is executory on both sides, there will be outstanding rights and liabilities on both sides.[14]

Certainty Section 29, Contract Act, declares that an agreement, the meaning of which is not certain, or capable of being made certain, is void. The uncertainty may relate to the parties or to the terms or the subject matter of the agreement. Thus want of certainty is a good defence in specific performance of contract of sale.

Uncertainty as to parties Where the vendee is not sure whether the agreement executed by the vendor was on his own behalf or on behalf of his wife, the agreement is invalid.[15] In the same way, where the plaintiff asserted that the deed was to be executed in the name of the co-operative society of which he was a member, while defendant maintained that the deed was to be executed in the name of the plaintiff himself, the agreement merely saying "plaintiff through the co-operative society", it was held that the agreement was indefinite and unenforceable.[16]

13 *P. Jagadeesan & Co.* v *A. Krishnan* (2001)4 CTC 356.

14 *Union of India* v *Chamman Lal Loona* AIR 1957 SC 652; 1957 SCJ 719; 1957 SCA 825.

15 *Phuljhari Devi* v *Mithai Lal* AIR 1971 All 494 at p. 498.

16 *Umar Noor Mohd.* v *Dayal Saran Darbari* AIR 1967 All 253 at p. 258.

Uncertainty due to lack of consideration If there is no agreement as to consideration then the agreement is void for lack of consideration and also for uncertainty in view of ss. 23 and 29 of the Indian Contract Act.[17] Thus, where the agreement was in the nature of a receipt for advance against sale without having any details about the consideration for the transaction, it was held that such agreement is void for want of consideration and also uncertainty.[18]

Uncertainty as to terms If the terms are such that they do not yield any meaning, the agreement would be void, but if it is possible to spell out a meaning, the agreement will be valid. Illustrations of the first type of contracts are, "to pay a certain sum after deductions as would be agreed upon",[19] "on such terms and conditions as may be agreed upon."[20] "Purchaser to pay price based upon agreed estimates of the net cost of works and general overheads with margin for profit of 5%" holding that the agreement was only an agreement to negotiate.[1]

In *Nair Service Society* v *R.M. Palat*[2] the plaintiff filed a suit on the basis of a compromise, which *inter alia*, provided that the value of the trees was to be fixed by the two advocates appearing for the parties or their nominees and in the event of any difference between them by an umpire. The advocates appointed the valuers but one of the parties withdrew his valuer so that no valuation could be made. The court held that the agreement was void, observing that if there is no statement in the contract regarding the price to be paid, the law allows a standard of reasonableness; but when the terms of a contract exclude the intention of a fair or reasonable market price, it is not possible to imply such a term.[3]

In a Delhi case,[4] a partnership firm for long years was acting as distributor of Indian Oil Corporation. Subsequent to a change of policy this dealership was not given to the said firm. A writ-petition was filed by the partnership firm to compel the IOC, an Instrumentality of State within the meaning of Art. 12, Constitution to give dealership to the firm. It was held that the partnership firm substantially sought for the specific performance of the alleged contract. It is neither precise, definite nor certain. How much goods are required and how long at what consideration are all vague. Such a contract cannot be specifically enforced.

17 *Ranbaxy Laboratories Ltd.* v *Doon Apartments (P) Ltd.* ILR (1979)1 Del 84.
18 *S.K. Gupta* v *Ashok Malhotra* (1995)33 DRJ 594; (1995)2 Arb LR 95.
19 *Kovuru Delappa Devara* v *Kumar Krishna Mitter* AIR 1945 Mad 10.
20 *Hitkarini Sabha* v *Jabalpur Corpn.* AIR 1961 MP 324.
1 *Courtney and Fairbairn* v *Tolaini Bros (Hotels) Ltd.* [1975]1 All ER 716.
2 AIR 1966 Ker 311 at p. 313 (DB).
3 *Milness* v *Gery* [1807]4 Ves Jun 400.
4 *Mahabir Auto Stores* v *Indian Oil Corporation* AIR 1989 Del 315.

When consideration left to be determined at a later date during transfer of shares, such transfer was not void for uncertainty. Section 9 of the Sale of Goods Act allows such transfers.[5]

In *Sudbrook Trading Estate Ltd.* v *Eggleton,*[6] plaintiffs had an option to buy the reversion in at a price to be determined by two valuers to be nominated by the parties and, in the event of their disagreement by an umpire to be appointed by the valuers. Defendants refused to nominate their valuer. Plaintiffs, thereupon, issued a writ. The Court of Appeal dismissed the writ on the ground that the agreement was incomplete and could not be enforced.

On further appeal, reversing the decision of the Court of Appeal, the House of Lords held that the agreement would be given effect to and bargain completed at a fair value.

Lord Fraser said:

"I recognise the logic of the reasoning which has led to the courts refusing to substitute their own machinery for the machinery which has been agreed on by the parties. But the result to which it leads is so remote from that which parties normally intend and expect, and is so inconvenient in practice, that there must, in my opinion, be some effect in the reasoning. I think the defect lies in construing the provisions for the mode of ascertaining the value as an essential part of the agreement. That may have been perfectly true early in the nineteenth century, when the valuer's profession and the rules of valuation were less well established than they are now. But at the present day these provisions are only subsidiary to the main purpose of the agreement, which is for sale and purchase of the property at a fair or reasonable value. In the ordinary case the parties do not make any substantial distinction between an agreement to sell at a fair value, without specifying the mode of ascertaining the value, and an agreement to sell at a value to be ascertained by valuers appointed in the way provided in these leases. The true distinction is between those cases where the mode of ascertaining the price is an essential term of the contract and those cases where the mode of ascertainment, though indicated in the contract, is subsidiary and non-essential.[7]

"The present case falls, in my opinion, into the latter category. Accordingly when the option was exercised, there was constituted a complete contract for sale, and the clause should be construed as meaning that the price was to be a fair price.

"On the other hand, where an agreement is made to sell at a price to be fixed by a valuer who is named, or who, by reason of holding some

5 *M.S. Madhusoodharan* v *Kerala Kaumudi P. Ltd.* (2004)9 SCC 204; AIR 2004 SC 909.

6 [1982]3 All ER 1 (HL).

7 Fry on *Specific Performance*, 6th Ed., 1921, paras 360, 364.

office such as auditor of a company whose shares are to be valued, will have special knowledge relevant to the question of value, the prescribed mode may well be regarded as essential. Where, as here, the machinery consists of valuers and an umpire, none of whom is named or identified, it is, in my opinion, unrealistic to regard it as an essential term. If it breaks down there is no reason why the court should not substitute other machinery to carry out the main purpose of ascertaining the price in order that the agreement may be carried out.

"In the present case the machinery provided for in the clause has broken down because the lessors have declined to appoint their valuer. In that sense the breakdown has been caused by their fault, in failing to implement an implied obligation to co-operate in making the machinery work. The case might be distinguishable in that respect from cases where the breakdown has occurred for some cause outside the control of either party, such as the death of an umpire or his failure to complete the valuation by a stipulated date. But I do not rely on any such distinction. I prefer to rest my decision on the general principle, that where the machinery is not essential, if it breaks down for any reason the court will substitute its own machinery ......

"The appropriate means for the court to enforce the agreements is in my opinion, by ordering an inquiry into the fair value of the reversions. That was the method used in *Talbot* v *Talbot*.[8] The alternative or ordering the lessors to appoint a valuer would not be suitable because, in the event of the order not being obeyed, the only sanction would be imprisonment for contempt of court, which would clearly be inappropriate."[9]

It is well settled that a definite price is an essential element of a binding agreement. Although a definite price need not be stated in the contract, but assertion thereof either expressly or impliedly is imperative. A contract cannot be uncertain. It must not be vague.[10] Thus, in an Assam case,[11] a lease deed stipulated sale of land if the lessor was ever required to sell and if the lessee agreed to purchase at a reasonable price. The High Court pointed out that the time at which the option was to be exercised was not a fixed period. The price was also not fixed and there was also no provision as to how the reasonable price would be determined in case of a dispute and as such a contract was not specifically performable.

But where the agreement provided that "the landlord will ...... grant lease of the demised premises for a further term of ten years from the expiration of the said term containing like covenants and provisos as are

8 [1967]2 All ER 920.

9 *Agar* v *Macklew* [1825]2 Sm & St 418; 57 ER 405; *Vickers* v *Vickers* [1967] LR 4 Eq 529 overruled.

10 *DDA* v *Joint Action Committee, Allottee of SFS Flats* (2008)2 SCC 672.

11 *Hem Chandra Choudhury* v *Ajadhya Bala Choudhury* AIR 1969 Gau 43.

herein contained and at a rent to be mutually agreed between the parties hereto due regard being paid to rents then prevailing in the same locality" it was held that the agreement was not hit by s. 29 of the Contract Act. The court observed: "It cannot be said that the rents prevailing in the locality for similar properties cannot be found or deciphered. It cannot equally be said that after such an enquiry into the reasonable rent, it would be impossible for the parties to agree upon that just resultant of that enquiry as the rent payable by one to the other."[12] Likewise, where the contracts provided "If you take possession, according to your requirements of extra land over and above this *patta*, we shall settle such land with you at a proper rate,"[13] "the tenant should pay increased rent according to the rent of the neighbouring wet lands",[14] "upon such terms and conditions as shall be judged reasonable."[15] "subject to such fair and equitable enhancement as lessor shall determine",[16] "at a figure to be agreed upon between the vendor and the purchaser of a right of pre-emption",[17] "at a rent to be fixed having regard to the market value of the premises at the time of exercising this option taking into account to the advantage of the tenant any increased value of such premises attributable to structural improvements made by the tenant during the currency of this present lease",[18] it was held that the contracts did not suffer from uncertainty.

Where the compromise contained the following clause, *viz.*,

> "Each party has to sell to the other respective portions of the properties which have come to their share as above at a price fixed by two members of the Panchas when either party wants to sell its share,"

it was held that it embodied an arbitration agreement between the parties and that having regard to the provisions of the Arbitration Act 1940, there was no distinction between the present case and illustration (*e*) to s. 29 of the Contract Act. (*A* agrees to sell to *B* "one thousand maunds of rice at a price to be fixed by C". As the price is capable of being made certain, there is no uncertainty here to make the agreement void).

In *Puspabala Ray* v *Life Insurance Corpn. of India*[19] the original plaintiff was the Managing Director of Peerless Life Insurance Co. Ltd. but on account of paucity of funds did not draw any remuneration from January 1943 to December 1947. Consequently on 2nd July 1948 the company passed the following resolution:

12 *Khivraj Chordia* v *Esso Standard Eastern Inc.* AIR 1975 Mad 374 at p. 376 (DB).
13 *New Beerbhom Coal Co.* v *Bularam Mahata* 7 IA 107.
14 *Sankarachariswamiar* v *Varada Pillai* 27 Mad 332.
15 *Secretary of State for India* v *Volkart Bros.* AIR 1927 Mad 513.
16 *D.I. Mangalmurti* v *State of Bombay* AIR 1959 SC 639; 1959 Supp (2) SCR 180.
17 *Smith* v *Morgan* [1971]2 All ER 1500.
18 *Brown* v *Gould* [1971]2 All ER 1505.
19 AIR 1978 Cal 221.

"Resolved unanimously that the sum of ₹26,000 being the amount of remuneration forgone by the Managing Director Mr. R. Roy up to December 1947, be paid to him in a lump sum in one or more instalments in one or more years as and when the company is in a position to do so."

The company was taken over by the defendant. Plaintiff then filed a suit for the recovery of the amount. *Held*, the resolution was uncertain and vague and without consideration and any agreement recorded thereby was void and unenforceable.[20]

In *Shaharyar Bano* v *Sanwal Das*[1] Mrs. Bano entered into a contract for the sale of her house. The agreement read—

"Today, *i.e.* on 17.9.1958, one house in which I am living situate at Gojarpura, I agree to sell the entire house apart from the side portion of the door which has been given to be maternal uncle according to the religious law of Mohammedanism for a consideration of ₹31,375 to Seth Sanwaldas son of Motilal Sarraf Chouk with the consent of my sister. The entire door is included in the said house, I have realised a sum of ₹2,000 as an earnest money. No other (person) has a right (in that house) and there is no necessity of any advice. Tomorrow morning you consult your pleader and get *pacci* receipt executed and I shall have no objection."

The house actually consisted of three portions and a passage. In one portion the defendants were living, in the other, the tenants and in the third, the maternal uncle. The passage was common. Respondent-plaintiff contended that the appellant had sold the entire portion and the passage excepting that in the occupation of the maternal uncle. *Held*, plaintiff was entitled only to the portion in which the defendants were living and not the portion in the occupation of the tenants or the passage.

There is no uncertainty as to the subject matter where the agreement describes the subject matter, as for instance, "all his estate and interest",[2] "so much of a thing as may be necessary",[3] "sale of business lock, stock and barrel."[4]

Where the defendant purchased land and agreed that he would cede a part thereof to the plaintiff, but it not being certain as to what part to cede, *held* that the court will not allow the defendant to take shelter behind uncertainty and he may be compelled to give the whole estate at a price which he paid.[5]

20 *Keshavlal Lallubhai Patel* v *Lalbhai Trikumalal Mills Ltd.* AIR 1958 SC 512; 1959 SCR 213; 1958 SCJ 866.
1 AIR 1976 SC 2073; (1976)1 SCC 95.
2 *Priddle* v *Wood* [1864]4 New Rep 320.
3 *Rumble* v *Heygate* [1870]18 WR 749.
4 *Elliot* v *Pierson* [1948]1 All ER 939.
5 *Chattock* v *Muller* [1978]8 Ch D 177; *Pallant* v *Morgan* [1952]2 All ER 951.

Where the agreement was for the purchase of lease but without mentioning the length of the lease, it was held that the agreement was uncertain.[6]

In a case where the identity of the property was in question, it was held if the property itself cannot be identified, the relief of specific performance cannot be granted.[7]

For seeking specific performance, the contract in question must be correct and precise. When the plaintiff had failed to identify the property by giving its *Khasra* number or boundary number, such agreement of sale being void for uncertainty, it could not be specifically enforced.[8]

An agreement which is vague as to price, time and person purchasing it cannot be specifically enforced. Unless there is a contract for sale of land at an ascertained or ascertainable price, specific performance cannot be ordered. There is an agreement to sell evacuee property to which the Government of India was not a party and which provided the price to be fixed by an expert appointed by the Government and the price was to be paid in compensation of the claims of the vendee, who could also join another evacuee to make up the claims, sufficient to make up the price, was held not to be specifically enforceable.[9] Nor can specific performance be granted where the agreement did not mention the *khasra* number or the exact area of the land sold, its boundaries, length and breadth or the point from which the property would be measured.[10]

Thus, ordinarily an endeavour should be made by the court to give effect to the terms of the agreement but it is also a well-settled principle of law that an agreement is to be read as a whole so as to enable the court to ascertain the true intention of the parties.[11] The rule was laid down long back by the House of Lords in *Hillas & Co. Ltd.* v *Arcos Ltd*[12] in the following words:

> "It is the duty of the court to construe agreements made by businessmen—which often appear to those unfamiliar with the business far from complete or precise—fairly and broadly, without being astute or subtle in finding defects; on the contrary, the court should seek to apply the maxim *verba ita sunt intelligenda ut res magis valeat quam pereat*. That maxim, however, does not mean that the court is to make a contract for the parties, or to go outside the words they have used, except insofar as there are appropriate implications of law, as, for instance, the implication of what is just and reasonable to be ascertained by the court as matter of machinery where the

6 *Southern* v *Harriman* [1866]14 WR 487.
7 *Nahar Singh* v *Harnak Singh* (1996)6 SCC 699.
8 *Surendra Kumar Gupta* v *Narayan Ram* AIR 2011 Chh 138.
9 *Sri Amarnath Mills Corporation* v *D.B. Godbole* AIR 1957 Bom 119.
10 *Nahar Singh* v *Harnak Singh* (1996)6 SCC 699; JT 1996(9) SC 701.
11 *Vimlesh Kumari Kulshrestha* v *Sambhajirao* (2008)5 SCC 58.
12 1932 All ER Rep 494 (HL).

contractual intention is clear but the contract is silent on some detail. Thus in contracts for future performance over a period the parties may not be able nor may they desire to specify many matters of detail, but leave them to be adjusted in the working out of the contract."

Further, it must be noted that throughout the law of contract there is respect for the sanctity of contract and the need to give effect to the reasonable expectation of an honest man. It is important that law ought to uphold rather than destroy apparent contracts. Solemn contracts entered into between parties are not to be readily declared invalid for uncertainty or vagueness.[13]

However, where the agreement provides for the acceptance of the opinion of third party on a particular matter, it cannot be said that the contract is void for vagueness or uncertainty. Thus, a contract can become void under s. 29, Contract Act only when its terms cannot be made certain. Mere vagueness or uncertainty which can be removed by proper interpretation cannot make a contract void. In dealing with commercial and business contracts which have been acted upon by the parties, the court should be very slow in finding defects and to reject them as meaningless.[14]

Subject matters of specific performance Specific performance is not limited to any particular class of contract, but it is confined to specific property, usually immovable property or personal property of peculiar nature or value. Sections 10 to 13 of the Specific Relief Act 1963 describe the classes of contract in respect of which the court may grant decree for specific performance of contract.

Representation when gives rise to contract There were some disputes between the stepmother and the stepsons regarding a property. The stepmother filed a suit; but the same was compromised under which stepsons accepted that the mother was entitled to the property and that the entries in settlement record of rights were wrong. On her part, the stepmother promised that in case she sold the property, she shall offer the property first to the sons.

It was contended that since the sons were not obligated to purchase the property, this was not a concluded contract.

Negativing the plea, the court held that the contract was a concluded contract. Even otherwise since the mother had made a representation that in future she shall sell the property first to the sons, and the sons had acted on it by accepting the title of the mother to the property in suit, the representation amounted to an agreement enforceable by law.

13 *Kandamath Cine Enterprises (P) Ltd.* v *John Philipose* AIR 1990 Ker 198 quoted with approval in *Pawan Kumar Dutt* v *Shakuntala Devi* (2010)15 SCC 601.

14 *Uttam Singh Dugal & Co. Pvt. Ltd., New Delhi* v *Hindustan Steel Ltd., Bhilai Steel Project* AIR 1982 MP 206.

"There is undoubtedly a clear distinction between a representation of an existing fact and representation that something shall be done in future. The former may, if it amounts to a representation as to some fact alleged to be actually in existence, raise an estoppel, if another person alters his position relying upon that representation. A representation that something will be done in the future may result in a contract, if another person to whom it is addressed acts upon it. A representation that something will be done in future is not a representation that it is true when made. But between a representation of a fact which is untrue and a representation—express or implied—to do something in future, there is no clear antithesis. A representation that something will be done in future may involve an existing intention to act in future in the manner represented. If the representation is acted upon by another person it may, unless the statute governing the person making the representation provides otherwise, result in an agreement enforceable at law; if the statute requires that the agreement shall be in a certain form, no contract may result from the representation and acting therefor, but the law is not powerless to raise in appropriate cases an equity against him to compel performance of the obligation arising out of his representation."[15]

Contracts containing option clause The option clause cannot be classified as a mere "agreement to make an agreement." In modern terminology, it is to be classified as a unilateral or "if" contract. Although it creates from the outset a right on the part of contractee, which he will be entitled, but not bound, to exercise against the contractor at a future date, it does not give rise to any legal obligation on the part of either party, unless and until the contractee gives requisite notice to the contractor, within the stipulated period, of his desire to purchase. The giving of such notice, however, converts the "if" contract into a synallagmatic or bilateral contract, which creates mutual legal rights and obligations on the part of both the parties.[16] Moreover, whether an agreement is an option to purchase or an "ordinary" agreement would depend on the interpretation of its provisions. Sometimes the option is expressly and in terms granted. In others, the right may be implicit. Thus when an agreement provides that the right to obtain a sale is subject to the fulfilment of certain conditions by the purchaser, the agreement would in effect be an option to purchase, as the right to purchase would only accrue upon the voluntary performance of the conditions specified by the owner. The vendor cannot compel the performance of the conditions by the purchaser and then ask for the contract to be specifically performed.[17]

15 *Nirmala Bala Dasi* v *Sudarsan Jana* AIR 1980 Cal 258; see also *Gujarat State Financial Corporation* v *Lotus Hotels Ltd.* AIR 1983 SC 848; (1983)3 SCC 379.

16 *Sudbrook Trading Estate Ltd.* v *Eggleton* [1982]3 All ER 1 at p. 5 (*per* Lord Diplock).

17 *V. Pechimuthu* v *Gowrammal* (2001)7 SCC 617; AIR 2001 SC 2446.

Rescission of contract If a party rescinds from contract, the other party has no obligation to perform his part of the contract. Rescission of contract when is justified the other party cannot claim specific performance of contract.

The wilful refusal by the plaintiff to make the deposit would be a relevant stand to rescind the contract under s. 28(1) of the Specific Relief Act. As per s. 28(1) of the Act the court can extend time for the payment of purchase money. In such case, it is not something to be done under the Code of Civil Procedure. Therefore, s. 148, CPC has no application in such case.[18] Under s. 28 of the Specific Relief Act 1963, a vendor is free to apply to the court which made decree to have the contract rescinded in case the purchaser has not paid the purchase money or other sum which the court has ordered him to pay within the period allowed by the decree or such other period as the court may allow. On such an application, the court may, by order, rescind the contract "*as the justice of the case may require*". It is now settled law that a suit for specific performance does not come to an end on passing of a decree and the Court which passed the decree retains control over the decree even after the decree has been passed and the decree is sometimes described as the preliminary decree.[19]

The effect of s. 28 is to empower the court which passed the decree for specific performance to rescind the contract and set aside the decree which it has passed earlier if the successful plaintiff failed to comply with the terms of the decree by making payment of the purchase money or other sums which the court ordered him to pay.[20]

In a Calcutta case respondent, the landlord of a premises agreed to transfer the premises to his tenant appellant within a particular period of time. There was a clause in the agreement that the respondent would deliver to the appellant the title deeds etc. to enable the appellant to cause searches and investigation etc. The appellant claimed that he was always willing to perform his part of the contract but the respondent unnecessarily delayed in getting the title deed available to the appellant. The High Court disbelieved this case and held that the appellant took no initiative in getting the copy of sale deed 30th June 1975 was the date for completion of sale, on 29th March 1975 the respondent called upon the appellant to complete the purchase within seven days and gave notice that if the appellants failed to do so, the agreement would stand rescinded with effect from 6th April 1975. As the appellant did not reply the respondent sold the property to other respondents. The court held the story that respondent intentionally refused to give inspection of the document of title is not true. The conduct

18 *Kaniyahil Ummakulsumma* v *P.T. Vijaya Kumar* AIR 2015 Ker 289.
19 *Rajinder Kumar* v *Kuldeep Singh* (2014)15 SCC 529; AIR 2014 SC 1155.
20 *Narayan Gangadhar Deshpande* v *Rago Krishna Dixit* AIR 2003 Mad 248. See Pollock & Mulla, *The Indian Contract and Specific Relief Acts*, 14th Ed., p. 2064.

of the appellant spelt out the absence of their readiness and willingness and to cancel the contract. The respondent was justified in rescinding the contract. The suit for specific performance by the appellant against the respondents must fail.[1]

It is not necessary in all cases where a person who has got option to avoid the contract should issue a notice under s. 64 terminating the contract. If no notice is issued the contract may be treated as alive. But however, a person who committed default of non-compliance cannot seek the relief of specific performance when there is undue delay on his part once time is made the essence of the contract. Therefore, irrespective of the validity of the rescission of the contract the court can examine the question whether the plaintiff is entitled to the relief of specific performance while he committed default when the time is made the essence of the contract.[2]

Limitation on rescission of contract Application for rescission of contract is to be filed within three years from the date of decree for specific performance.[3]

Exercise of discretion Power under s. 28 is discretionary and the court cannot ordinarily annul the decree once passed by it. Where decree is made conditional upon depositing amount and the amount is not deposited, nor is extension sought, recession can be ordered.[4] Section 28 of the Specific Relief Act does not enable the decree holder to seek extension of time but it is the discretion to be exercised by the court in an application by the judgment debtor to rescind the contract having regard to the facts and circumstances of the case.[5] Decree for specific performance must be executed by making separate application, and not under s. 28(3) of the Specific Relief Act.[6]

Bars to rescission (English Law) A voidable contract cannot be rescinded for certain bars which are as follows: (*i*) Rescission of a contract will be barred if it is not possible to restore the defendant to his former position before the contract was made. The doctrine of restitutio in integrum operates as a bar to rescission when the defendant cannot be restored to his original position.[7] (*ii*) The right to rescission is waived if the person entitled to rescind elects to waive the right and affirms the contract. When the contract is affirmed, it becomes effective, but the claimant, can still sue the defendant

1 *Laxmi Prosad* v *Amulya Chandra Guin* AIR 1989 Cal 71.
2 *K. Suryanarayana Reddy* v *C. Chellayyamma* AIR 1989 AP 276 at p. 282.
3 *B.V. Gururaj* v *M.R. Rathindran* AIR 2010 Mad 129.
4 *Chanda* v *Rattni* AIR 2007 SC 1514; (2007)14 SCC 26.
5 *L. Venkata Krishna Reddy* v *M. Arjappa* AIR 2009 AP 179.
6 *Balasa Sarada* v *Talluni Anasuyamma* AIR 2007 AP 130. See Pollock & Mulla, *The Specific Relief Act 1963*, 14th Ed., p. 234.
7 *Spence* v *Crawford* [1939]3 All ER 271; see *Halpern* v *Halpern* [2007] EWCA Civ 291.

for breach of contract.[8] (*iii*) It is a settled principle that the claimant may be barred from rescinding a contract if a substantial period of time has elapsed before he sought to rescind it.[9] What constitutes a substantial period of time is a question of fact which depends on the particular circumstances of the case. (*iv*) Rescission is traditionally barred where the effect of rescission of the contract made by the parties thereto would impair the rights of third parties.[10] (*v*) Where a contract has been induced by non-fraudulent misrepresentation. This is a discretionary bar to rescission where the court considers it to be equitable to award damages instead of rescinding the contract.[11]

No man can avoid a contract, so as to resume the property which he pasted with under it, and at the same time retain the money or other advantage he has obtained under it.[12] The right to recission is destroyed, when restitution integrim becomes impossible; it must be exercised within a reasonable time.[13]

Agreements of reconveyance An agreement of reconveyance is in fact an option agreement, since under this agreement the vendee gives an option to the vendor to ask for reconveyance of the property to him on his fulfilling certain conditions as to time and payment etc. If the agreement does not specify any time, the vendor must exercise the option within a reasonable time. In contracts for sale or lease of immovable property time is not of the essence of the contract. In this matter equity does not help the vendor and instead arrays itself with common law and enforces such agreements in accordance with their tenor and strict conditions.

The Madras High Court *held*—

> "An option to repurchase reserved to a vendor under a conveyance can be regarded as an irrevocable offer by the vendee to reconvey the property on the terms and conditions specified therein. The consideration for such an offer is the benefit received by the vendee under the original conveyance. This offer will lapse after the time stipulated expires or on the failure to perform any of the conditions contained in the document or contract. Thus an option to purchase may not by itself constitute a contract. But when the option is exercised in due conformity with the terms of the contract that

8 *Car and Universal Finance Co. Ltd.* v *Caddwell* [1965]1 QB 525.

9 *Leaf* v *International Galleries* [1950]2 KB 86.

10 *Tement* v *The City of Glasgow Bank and Liquidators* [1879]4 App Cas 615; *Society of Lloyds* v *Leighs* [1997] EWCA Civ 2283.

11 See *Contractual Duties: Performance, Breach, Termination and Remedies* by Prof. Neil Andrews, Prof. Malcolm Clarke, Prof. Andrew Tettenborn, Prof. Graham Virgo, 2011 Ed., para 3-044.

12 *Clough* v *London & NY Rly Co.* [1871] LR 7 Exch 26; *Tejpal* v *Ganga* ILR (1902) 25 All 59.

13 *Western Bank of Scotland* v *Addie* [1867]1 LR Scotch Appeals 145; *Seddon* v *North Eastern Salt Co. Ltd.* [1905]1 Ch 326. See also Banerjee, *Law of Specific Relief*, 13th Ed., p. 646.

will amount to an acceptance of the offer with the result that a binding contract for reconveyance of the property results."[14]

Explaining the reasons for strict compliance of the conditions of the agreement for reconveyance, the same High Court said: "The right to repurchase is equitable to an option or a privilege granted to the vendor in the primary sale to seek for such reconveyance. As privileges cannot be gained at the whim and fancy of the grantee, he should be alert and seek for its performance. A prescription as to time in an agreement of reconveyance cannot be made elastic as by the end of the definite time fixed for its performance, there is an automatic lapsing of that privilege and the loss of the option in the grantee of the same. By reason of such a stipulation sale is kept in abeyance till the expiry of the period within which time the grantee of the privilege can obtain reconveyance of the property by seeking of specific performance of the agreement for reconveyance. This nebulous state of affairs in the title of the purchaser under the primary sale cannot be kept in abeyance for a length of time beyond the prescribed period of time agreed upon between the parties. This would result in the purchaser being asked to wait without justification and look to the convenience of the grantee of the privilege to seek for specific performance of the agreement of reconveyance."[15]

An agreement of reconveyance contained the following clause:

> "If it is purchased for your own use, a reconveyance deed shall be executed; if it has to be sold to some other person, a reconveyance deed shall not be executed. It is also not valid."

The suit was resisted by the defendant on the ground that the right being personal, the legal representatives of the deceased vendor were not entitled to the relief.

Rejecting the contention, V. Ramaswami, J (then of the High Court of Madras) held that the legal representatives were neither assignees nor third parties to the contract. They were the legal representatives of the person in whose favour the agreement had been executed and as such they were the

14 *Sinnakaruppa Gounder* v *M. Karuppuswami Gounder* AIR 1965 Mad 506 at p. 507 (DB). See also *Du Sautoy* v *Symes* [1967]1 All ER 25; *Murray* v *Two Strokes Ltd.* [1973]3 All ER 357; *Mountford* v *Scott* [1975]1 All ER 198 (CA); *First National Securities* v *Chiltern District Council* [1975]2 All ER 766; *Pritchard* v *Briggs* [1980]1 All ER 294; [cf. *Shree Ram* v *Ratanlal* AIR 1965 All 83 at p. 85 (DB)].

15 *Mangalam Pillai* v *C.S.A. Udayar* AIR 1976 Mad 360 at pp. 364-5 (DB). See also *Bahadur* v *Motiram* AIR 1972 Raj 250; *H.N. Narayanswamy Naidu* v *Deveeramma* AIR 1981 Kant 93 at p. 95 [Purchaser of the vendor's rights not entitled to protection under s. 19(*b*)]; *Samarpuri Chettiar* v *Sudarshana Chariar* AIR 1919 Mad 544; *Balasundara Mudaliar* v *Muthur Venkatachala* AIR 1954 Mad 799; *Shanmugham Pillai* v *Annalakshmi Ammal* AIR 1950 PC 38; *Caltex India Ltd.* v *Bhagwan Devi* AIR 1969 SC 405; (1969)2 SCR 238; *Simrathmul* v *Nanhalingaih* AIR 1963 SC 1182; 1962 Supp (3) SCR 476; *M. Sakuntala Devi* v *Sakuntala* AIR 1978 AP 337 (DB).

representatives in interest within the meaning of s. 15(*b*) of the Specific Relief Act.[16]

The right to obtain specific performance of a contract is a heritable right and legal representatives of any party to such a contract can avail themselves of that right. The right is, therefore, not a personal right.[17] (Sale of shares subject to permission of RBI. Sanction given but vendor dying thereafter. Objection by heirs that the permission was personal rejected). An agreement was made between vendor and vendee providing for reconveyance of plot sold. Reconveyance deed not stipulating that right reconveyed to vendor is in any manner. No condition in deed showing that said right can be exercised by vendor or his heirs alone. Reconveyance in favour of vendor can easily be assigned to stranger.[18]

However, the mere fact that an agreement for sale is described as a reconveyance does not by itself mean that it is an option to repurchase nor does it in any way alter the substance of the deed. It merely records a historical fact—that the property which is to be sold was being purchased by the person who used to be the owner. No logical distinction can be drawn between an agreement to repurchase and an ordinary agreement of purchase just because the vendor happens to be the original purchaser and the purchaser happens to be the original vendor. The agreement remains an agreement for sale of immovable property and must be governed by the same provisions of law.[19]

In *Umar Noor Mohammed* v *Dayal Saran Darbari*[20] the court held—"Except in some special circumstances a contract to sell property is not dependent upon any personal qualification of the individual who agrees to purchase and it is a matter of no consequence to the vendor that the person who is going to be the vendee is not the same person with whom he had entered into a contract for sale. Such a contract is therefore enforceable not only by the person to whom the property was agreed to be sold but also by his representatives in interest and assignees ...... it is open to the person who has agreed to purchase the property to employ a competent person to purchase it. Certainly, before he can be deemed to have discharged his liability under the contract, he has to ensure and see that the promise is performed inaccordance with the stipulated terms, but if he does so, the person who has agreed to sell the property cannot, after declining to accept

16 *T.M. Doraiswami* v *Kannippa Reddi* AIR 1972 Mad 460 relying on *Hazari* v *Neiki* AIR 1968 SC 1205; (1968)2 SCR 833 and *Ram Baran* v *Ram Mohit* AIR 1967 SC 744; (1967)1 SCR 293.

17 *Ramanand Agarwalla* v *Richardson Hooghly Holding Ltd.* AIR 1979 Cal 335 at p. 337 (DB).

18 *Shanti Devi* v *Jagdish Lal* AIR 2018 All 216.

19 *V. Pechimuthu* v *Gowrammal* (2001)7 SCC 617.

20 AIR 1967 All 253.

performance of the contract by the nominee of the person, who had agreed to purchase, charge the latter with not having carried out his promise."

Plaintiff stated that transfer of property was only by way of security for repayment of loan. But plaintiff failed to prove that he tendered the amount of loan to purchaser within the date stipulated in the agreement for reconveyance. In a contract for reconveyance time is always the essence of the contract. Thus, in claim by plaintiff for reconveyance made in default of the said stipulation must fail, for, right of reconveyance cannot be saved in case of default for forfeiture. Decree for specific performance cannot be granted.[21] When time is not the essence of contract, the buyer is ready and willing, bank balance is irrelevant factor and the suit is within limitation, in such case specific relief is allowed.[1]

Suit is based on agreement for resale for lesser consideration than for sale. Plaint contains allegation that by a second agreement for resale terms of the first agreement were made complete. The second agreement made no reference to the first agreement. Resale promised under the second agreement was for consideration equal to sale consideration. Averments in plaint and evidence adduced showed that plaintiffs were ready and willing to perform contract only as per first resale agreement. It was held that plaintiffs were not entitled to decree of specific performance.[2]

Reconveyance or mortgage An agreement of reconveyance is an executory contract and it can be the subject matter of a suit for specific performance of a contract. But a mortgage by conditional sale is an executed contract where the question of specific performance does not arise. So in a suit for specific performance of a contract of sale the plea that in effect and in substance it was a mortgage by conditional sale is a good defence. Similarly the plea that in substance it was loan is also a good defence.

Turning to the question whether the agreement purported to be an agreement of reconveyance is or is not a mortgage by conditional sale, s. 58(*c*), the Transfer of Property Act is material.

Section 58(*c*) of the Transfer of Property Act runs as follows:

> 58(*c*). *Mortgage by conditional sale*. Where, the mortgagor ostensibly sells the mortgaged property—
>
> on condition that on default of payment of the mortgage money on a certain date the sale shall become absolute, or
>
> on condition that on such payment being made the sale shall become void, or

21 *Raj Kishore* v *Prem Singh* AIR 2011 SC 382.

1 *Sri Brahadambal Agency* v *Ramaswamy* AIR 2002 Mad 352. See also *Mostt. Dularo Devi* v *Mostt. Asturna Devi* AIR 2012 Pat 16.

2 *Bal Krishna* v *Bhagwan Das* AIR 2008 SC 1786.

on condition that on such payment being made the buyer shall transfer the property to the seller,

the transaction is called a mortgage by conditional sale and the mortgagee a mortgagee by conditional sale:

Provided that no such transaction shall be deemed to be a mortgage, unless the condition is embodied in the document which effects or purports to effect the sale.

The proviso to s. 58(*c*) has been explained by the Apex Court which lays down that a transaction shall not be a mortgage by conditional sale unless the condition of repurchase is embodied in the impugned deed. But the converse is not true. So even if when the condition of repurchase is embodied in the deed itself it may be a sale out and out with a condition of reconveyance.[3] Proviso appended to s. 58(*c*) is clear and unambiguous. A legal fiction is created thereby that the transaction shall not be held to be a mortgage by conditional sale, unless a condition is embodied in the document which effects or purports to effect the sale. Where two documents are executed, the transaction in question would not amount to a mortgage by way of conditional sale. In a case of this nature, ordinarily the same would be considered to be a deed of sale coupled with an agreement of reconveyance.[4]

Thus, a mortgage by conditional sale must be evidenced by one document whereas a sale with a condition of retransfer may be evidenced by more than one document. A sale with a condition of retransfer is not a mortgage. It is not a partial transfer. By reason of such a transfer all rights have been transferred reserving only a personal right to the seller, and such a personal right would be lost, unless the same is exercised within the stipulated time.[5] A distinction exists between a mortgage by way of conditional sale and a sale with condition of purchase. In the former the debt subsists and a right to redeem remains with the debtor but in case of the latter the transaction does not evidence an arrangement of lending and borrowing and, thus, right to redeem is not reserved thereby.[6]

As held in an MP case in absence of any word in a sale deed which suggests or purports to suggest that the transferor ostensibly sold the property on condition that in default of payment of the consideration (loan) on a certain date the sale shall become absolute, or on condition that on such payment being made the sale shall become void, or that on such payment being made the buyer shall retransfer the property to the seller the document

3 *Chunchun Jha* v *Ebadat Ali* AIR 1954 SC 345; (1955)1 SCR 174; 1954 SCJ 469. *Simrathmull* v *Nanhalingaih* AIR 1963 SC 1182 at p. 1184; 1962 Supp (3) SCR 476.

4 *Manjabai Krishna Patil* v *Raghunath Revaji Patil* (2007)12 SCC 427.

5 *Bishwanath Prasad Singh* v *Rajendra Prasad* (2006)4 SCC 432.

6 *Tulsi* v *Chandrika Prasad* (2006)8 SCC 322.

in question cannot, by any stretch of imagination, be treated as a document of mortgage by conditional sale.[7]

One *P* executed a document in favour of defendant. It was in the form of a sale deed but it contained stipulation that defendant should reconvey the property to *P* on his repaying the amount after five years and before the end of seventh year. The amount was ₹4,000. It was held that there was several circumstances to indicate that the document was a transaction of mortgage by conditional sale and not a sale with a condition for retransfer. In the first place, the condition for repurchase was embodied in the same documents; the transaction was ₹4,000 while the real value of the property was ₹8,000. In the second place, the *patta* was not transferred to the first defendant after the execution of the document by the plaintiff. The *kist* for the land was also continued to be paid by and after his death, by his sons. Lastly, the consideration for reconveyance was ₹4,000 the same amount as the consideration for the original transaction.[8]

In *Vidhyadhar* v *Manikak Rao*,[9] the document was headed as "mortgage by conditional sale". It was in favour of defendant for a sum of ₹1,500 out of which ₹700 were paid at home while ₹800 was paid before the Sub-Registrar. A further stipulation in the deed was that the aforesaid amount of ₹1,500 would be returned to the defendant on or before 5th March 1973 and the property would be reconveyed to the another defendant. Having regard to the circumstances of the case and also the fact that the condition of repurchase is contained in the same document by which the mortgage was created in favour of defendant the deed in question was held to be nothing but a mortgage by conditional sale.

The question is one of determination of the real character of the transaction to be ascertained from the provisions of the deed viewed in the light of the surrounding circumstance. The circumstance that the transaction as phrased in the document is ostensibly a sale with a right of repurchase, the appearance being laboriously maintained that the interest conveyed was an absolute one or that the right of repurchase granted was one in which time was of the essence, is not decisive. Oral evidence of intention is not admissible in interpreting the covenants of the deed but evidence to explain or even to contradict the recitals as distinguished from the terms of the document may, of course, be given. Evidence of contemporaneous conduct is admissible as a surrounding circumstance but not the subsequent conduct of parties.[10] If the condition of retransfer is not embodied in the sale deed, the transaction cannot be regarded as mortgage.[11]

7 *Ramjan Khan* v *Baba Raghunath Dass* AIR 1992 MP 22.

8 *P.L. Bapuswami* v *N. Pattay Gaundar* AIR 1966 SC 902; (1966)2 SCR 918.

9 AIR 1999 SC 1441; (1999)3 SCC 573; JT 1999(2) SC 183.

10 *Bhaskar Waman Joshi* v *Shrinarayan Rambilas Agarwal* AIR 1960 SC 301; (1960)2 SCR 117; 1960 SCJ 327; (1960)2 SCA 189.

11 *Swarnalata* v *Chandi Charan* AIR 1984 Cal 130; (1984)1 Cal LJ 204.

In *Thamboli Raman Lal Mothilal* v *Ghanchi Chinanlal Kesharlal*,[12] Their Lordships of the Supreme Court pointed out that having regard to the nice distinction between a mortgage by conditional sale and the sale with an option to repurchase, one should be guided by the terms of the document alone without much help from the case law. Their Lordships found that the nomenclature of the document was hardly conclusive and much importance should not be attached to the nomenclature since it is the real intention of the parties which requires to be gathered. In the instant case, the document was treated as a deed of conditional sale. The executant in the document took a sum of ₹5,000 in cash. The purpose was to pay miscellaneous debts and domestic expenses and business. A further clause in the document was to the effect that the executor shall pay the amount within a period of five years and in case he fails to pay, neither he nor his heirs or his legal representatives would have any right to take back the said property. All the above clauses were clearly consistent with the express intention of making the transaction a conditional sale with an option for re-purchase. It was held that the said document was not a mortgage by conditional sale but only a sale with an option for repurchase.[13]

When a document which has to be construed as to whether it is a sale with condition of repurchase or a mortgage by conditional sale squarely falls within the definition of mortgage by conditional sale the presumption may be that the document is a mortgage by conditional sale and the onus will be upon the defendant to displace.[14]

Reconveyance or loan A document on the face of it may appear to be a simple agreement for reconveyance but from surrounding circumstances it may be shown to be a loan. This plea of its being a loan may defeat a claim for specific performance. A transaction intended to be a mortgage, but evidence by a sale deed and a separate agreement to repurchase or reconveyance, though cannot, in law, be a mortgage in view of proviso to s. 58(*c*) of the Transfer of Property Act, it may still amount to a "loan in substance".[15]

Mushir Mohamed Khan (died) by LRs v *Smt. Sajeda Bano*[16] is an important decision which raises some basic questions of law. One *H* executed a deed of sale in respect of his house in favour of the appellant *M* for a sum of ₹1,000 only and few days later, the appellant *M* purchaser executed an agreement in favour of *H* seller agreeing to re-convey the house if the amount of ₹1,000 was paid back to him within a period of two years and

12 AIR 1992 SC 1236; 1993 Supp (1) SCC 295; JT 1992(2) SC 525.

13 *Padmashri S.M. Swamy* v *Gowramma* AIR 1993 Kant 208; *Ismail Nadhabhai Khatri* v *Mujibai* AIR 1994 Guj 8.

14 *Madhu Lal* v *Dhonga Mondal* AIR 1983 Pat 60; 1982 Pat LJR 456.

15 *Banku Behari* v *Kalyani Devi* AIR 1967 Cal 351.

16 AIR 2000 SC 1085; (2000)3 SCC 536; JT 2000(2) SC 609.

H seller also executed a rent note in favour of the purchaser *M* on the same day and was paying the rent. There were those three documents—(1) deed of sale; (2) agreement to reconvey; and (3) rent agreement. Under the proviso to s. 58(*c*) of the Transfer of Property Act, the transaction shall not be deemed to be a mortgage unless the condition for retransfer is embodied in the document itself. In the case of hand, the condition for reconveyance was not in the deed of sale. A separate agreement has been entered into between the parties for reconveyance and on the same day the vendor has executed a rent deed in favour of the purchaser and has been paying rent. All the three documents were almost contemporaneous. The High Court came to the conclusion that the prohibition contained in the proviso to s. 58(*c*) of the Transfer of Property Act would operate only in respect of "mortgage by conditional sale" but not in respect of any other mortgage and recorded a finding that the transaction between the parties was a usufructuary mortgage. Having thus found the transaction to be a mortgage, the High Court while reversing the judgment passed by the trial court and the lower appellate court, decreed the suit of the plaintiff for redemption. The Supreme Court after considering all the circumstances of the case found that the amount of ₹1,000 for which the property was sold by the plaintiff in favour of the defendant did not represent the true market value of the property neither on the date on which the deed of sale was executed nor on the date of hearing of the appeal before the Supreme Court. For, the plaintiff offered to pay a sum of ₹1 lakh to the defendant while the defendant made a counter offer of ₹1.5 lakhs. Finally, the Supreme Court, in order to do justice between the parties, directed that the order of the High Court shall be set aside on payment of ₹2 lakhs by the purchaser to the seller within three months from the date of the judgment of the Supreme Court and in case the amount was not paid the appeal shall stand dismissed with costs and the judgment of the High Court for redemption shall stand confirmed. Their Lordships also expressed their concern on the increasing tendency to enter into such transactions in order to deprive the debtor of his right of redemption within the prescribed period of limitation. Their Lordships pointed out that very often, the mortgagee in the place of getting the mortgage deed executed in lieu of loan, obtains an agreement to sell in his favour from the mortgagor so as to bring pressure on the mortgagor by seeking to enforce specific performance to enable the mortgagee to obtain possession of the property for an amount smaller than the real value of the property.

The above observations of Their Lordships of the Supreme Court are poignantly pertinent. The proviso to s. 58(*c*) of the Transfer of Property Act provides that no such transaction shall be deemed to be a mortgage unless the condition is embodied in the document which effects or purports to effect the sale, has done more harm than good. The borrower who is in dire need of money is always at the receiving end and when he enters into a mortgage by conditional sale, it is not possible for him to insist upon the condition for reconveyance incorporated in the mortgage. This gives an unconscionable advantage to the mortgagee who turns round and says that this is not a mortgage but a sale with condition for reconveyance. The deletion of the above proviso to s. 58(*c*) of the Transfer of Property Act is therefore eminently desirable.

This plea is not hit by s. 92, Evidence Act, because under the proviso (6) to s. 92, Evidence Act a party who asserts the transaction to be loan may prove how the document is related to existing circumstances, extrinsic evidence to determine the effect of an instrument is permissible if there is a doubt as to its true meaning.[17] Where a sale with an agreement for repurchase is contained in two separate documents oral evidence that the transaction was intended to be a mortgage is clearly inadmissible under s. 92, Evidence Act. But the question is to be judged on the documents in the light of surrounding circumstances and evidence, if any, in this later behalf, that is, evidence to show how or in what manner to the disputed transaction or the language of the document was related to existing facts will be clearly admissible under the proviso (6) to s. 92 of the Evidence Act. In determining the real nature of the transaction, the surrounding circumstances, true value of the property at the time of the proposed sale and the question of possession immediately after the sale would be relevant.[18]

Reconveyance or honourable pledge In *Rajabu Fathima Bhuhari* v *S.V. Ramkrishna Mudaliar*,[19] the memorandum read:

> "24.3.1959
>
> This is to record the gentleman's understanding between *SVR* and *AMB* that *B* will see to it that in case the purchase amounts as per the sale deeds in favour of *AMB* are repaid within three years from this date the properties will be reconveyed to *SVR* who will also have to pay in addition to sale-price 10% thereof as solatium of the actual amount spent on improvements if any.
>
> Sd/- *NI, VSR* and *K*"

This was sought to be enforced as an agreement of reconveyance.

Rejecting this, the court *held*—,

> "The aforesaid memo is stated to be a 'Gentleman's understanding'. In *COD*, 'Gentleman's agreement' is defined as an agreement resting on gentleman's honour and not a formal contract...................
>
> "The caption of the memorandum itself shows that it is a record of the purpose and intention of the parties concerned which they pledge themselves to fulfil, but such an arrangement is not an enforceable legal document.

17 *Godhara Electric Corpn.* v *State of Gujarat* AIR 1975 SC 32; (1975)1 SCC 199; (1975)2 SCR 42.

18 *Manindra Nath Bose* v *Manindra Lal Gupta* AIR 1955 NUC (Cal) 233; ILR (1956)1 Cal 59.

19 AIR 1973 Mad 70 (DB).

...... The court's duty is to implement the intention of the parties when the essential term of the contract have been agreed upon. In our opinion, the essential terms of the contract relating to reconveyance not having been specifically agreed to between the parties, the suit for specific performance cannot be enforced."[20] "If what passed between them was but treaty or negotiation, or an expectation of contract, or an arrangement between them of an honorary nature, no specific performance can be had."

Plea of estoppel to resist specific performance "Estoppel" is a rule of equity.[21] Estoppel arises when, in consequence of some previous act or statement to which he is either party or privy, a person is precluded from showing the existence of a particular state of facts. Estoppel is based on the maxim, "*Allegans contraria non est audiendus*", and is that species of *praesumptio juris et de jure* where the fact presumed is taken to be true, not as against all the world, but as against a particular party, and that only by reason of some act done: it is in truth a kind of *argumentum ad hominem*.[1]

A person who has expressly made a verbal representation, on the faith of which another has acted, shall not afterwards be allowed to contradict his former statement, in order to profit by that conduct which he has induced. Whenever an attempt is made in the course of legal proceedings to violate this principle, the law replies in the words of the maxim *allegans contraria non est audiendus*, and, by applying the doctrine of estoppel therein contained, prevent the unjust consequences which would otherwise ensure.[2] The expression *allegans contraria non est audiendus* literally means he is not to be heard who alleges things contradictory to each other. By application of this principle a man shall not be permitted or "blow hot and cold" with reference to the same transaction, or insist, at different times, on the truth of each of two conflicting allegations, according to the promptings of his private interest.[3]

To bring the case within the scope of estoppel there must be (*a*) representation by a person or his authorised agent to another in any form—a declaration, act or omission; (*b*) the representation must have been of the existence of a fact and not of promise *de futuro* or intention which might or might not be enforceable in contract; (*c*) the representation must have been meant to be relied upon; (*d*) there must have been belief on the part of the other party in its truth; (*e*) there must have been action on the faith of that declaration, act or omission, that is to say, the declaration, act or omission must have actually caused another to act on the faith of it, and to alter his former position to his prejudice or detriment; (*f*) the

20 *Rose & Frank Co.* v *J.R. Crompton & Bros. Ltd.* [1924] All ER Rep 245 at p. 255 and Fry on *Specific Performance of Contracts*, 6th Ed., p. 129, para 277.
21 *Turner Morrison & Co. Ltd.* v *Hungerford Investment Trust Ltd.* (1972)1 SCC 857.
1 Best on *Evidence*, 10th Ed., p. 451.
2 Broom on *Legal Maxims*, 12th Ed., p. 217.
3 Broom on *Legal Maxims*, 12th Ed., p. 115.

misrepresentation or conduct or omission must have been the proximate cause of leading the other party to act to his prejudice; (*g*) the person claiming the benefit of estoppel must show that he was not aware of the state of things. If he was aware of the real state of affairs or had means of knowledge, there can be no estoppel; (*h*) only the person to whom representation was made or for whom it was designed can avail himself of it. A person is entitled to plead estoppel in his own individual character and not as representative of his assignee.[4]

The question whether a defendant who has executed a contract for sale on the footing that he has independent title to the disputed property which he had agreed to sell, is estopped from taking the plea that the property belongs to Hindu undivided family. There the defendant represented that he as vendor was owner of the disputed property to the extent of 16 annas share. There was no evidence whatsoever that the property was held by Hindu undivided family. In the agreement sought to be specifically performed by the plaintiff there was no whisper as to the property being of HUF. The defendant was never assessed as the *karta* of the HUF, neither was the property shown as that of HUF. The defendant admitted further that he had purchased this property in his own name from the compensation claims arising out of the properties left by him in Pakistan. It was held that the contract was specifically performable and he was estopped from claiming the property to be of HUF.[5]

Pre-emption or right of first refusal In *Bishan Singh* v *Khazan Singh*,[6] the Supreme Court defined the characteristics of a right of pre-emption as follows: (1) The right of pre-emption is not a right to the thing sold but a right to offer of a thing about to be sold. This right is called the primary or inherent right. (2) The pre-emptor has a secondary right or a remedial right to follow the thing sold. (3) It is a right of substitution but not of repurchase, that is the pre-emptor takes the entire bargain and steps into the shoes of the original vendee. (4) It is a right to acquire the whole of the property sold. (5) Preference being the essence of the right the plaintiff must have a superior right to that of the vendee or the person substituted in his place. (6) The right being a very weak right can be defeated by all legitimate methods such as the vendee allowing the claim of a superior or equal right being substituted in his place.

However in later case of *Bhau Ram* v *Baij Nath*[7] the Supreme Court, while upholding the Constitutional validity of the right of pre-emption

4 *Chhaganlal Keshavlal Mehta* v *Palel Narandas Haribhai* AIR 1982 SC 121 at p. 125; (1982)2 SCR 166; (1982)1 SCC 223. See also *Rukmini Devi* v *Mihir Bala* AIR 1977 Cal 161; (1977)1 Cal LJ 125; 81 CWN 481.

5 *Chand Rani Mehra* v *Om Shankar Mehera* AIR 1987 Del 194.

6 AIR 1958 SC 838 at p. 841; 1959 SCR 878.

7 AIR 1962 SC 1476; 1962 Supp (3) SCR 724.

among co-sharers under Art. 19(1)(*f*) of the Constitution (since deleted and such provision is now in Art. 300A, Constitution), held that the law conferring the right of pre-emption on account of vicinage imposed an unreasonable restriction on the fundamental right and so was void.

For distinction between pre-emption and option see *Pritchard* v *Briggs*.[8]

The right is however not hit by the rule of perpetuity. In the words of the Supreme Court, reading s. 14 along with s. 54 of the Transfer of Property Act it is manifest that a mere contract for sale of immovable property does not create any interest in the immovable property and therefore the rule of perpetuity cannot be applied to a convenant of pre-emption even though there is no time-limit within which the option has to be exercised.[9]

Incomplete or inchoate contract Where the contract is incomplete or inchoate, no claim for specific performance can be enforced and this would be a valid defence in a suit for specific performance.[10]

Contingent contracts Section 31 of the Contract Act defines a contingent contract as a contract to do or not to do something, if some event, collateral to such contract, does or does not happen. The point to note is that the uncertain event on the happening of which the contract is conditional must be collateral to the contract and must not form part of the consideration. The condition may be a condition precedent or a condition subsequent.

"Where defendant's performance depends on the consent or approval of one not a party to the contract who is free to withhold his consent, specific performance of the contract will not be decreed where it does not appear that such consent or approval has been or can be obtained, or where it appears that such consent or approval is withheld or refused or has become impossible... The mere fact that a contract or transfer sought to be specifically enforced is subject to the approval of a public agency whose discretion is not subject to control by the court, is not a bar to a decree compelling a party to execute the documents necessary for the consummation of the contract or transfer and to apply to the public agency for its approval. On the other hand, where the public agency fails or refuses to consent to the transfer, the court will not grant specific performance of the contract",[11] in

8 [1980]1 All ER 294.

9 *Rambaran Prosad* v *Ram Mohit Hazra* AIR 1967 SC 744 at p. 749 approving *Ali Hossain Miya* v *Raj Kumar Haldar* AIR 1943 Cal 417 (FB); *Aulad Ali* v *Ali Athar* AIR 1927 All 170 (FB) and *Chinna Munuswami Nayudu* v *Sagalguna Nayudu* AIR 1926 Mad 699 and overruling *Nobin Chandra Soot* v *Nabab Ali Sarkar* (1901)5 CWN 343; *Gopi Ram* v *Jeot Ram* AIR 1923 All 514.

10 For further discussion, *see* under the heading Contracts concluded & completed and Contracts incomplete or incohate in Part 2, Chapter 1 at p. 67.

11 *Corpus Juris Secundum*, vol. 81, at pp. 410-411 quoted *Golab Ray* v *Muralidhar* AIR 1964 Ori 176 (DB).

which case it was held on facts that since the revenue officer had refused his permission, specific performance cannot be decreed. See also *Narain Pattro* v *Aukhoy Narain Manna*[12] where the certificate guardian was given permission to sell at higher rates only, it was held that the original buyer could not claim specific performance since the permission did not extend to his contract. *Motilal* v *Nanhelal*[13] where specific performance was ordered since the parties had not brought any evidence on record to show that the permission may be refused.

If the condition is a condition precedent, the contract will not be enforced: see *Rudra Das Chakravarti* v *Kamakhya Narayan Singh*[14] (execution of a mining lease where the right to mining depended upon the grant of a licence which in its turn depended on the decision of an independent agency); *Kripal Das Jivraj Mal* v *Manager, Encumbered Estates*[15] (sale of specified area of land depending upon the agreement of other co-sharers of the vendor who not being parties to the contract could frustrate the agreement by not agreeing); *Govind Laxman* v *Harichand Mancharam*[16] (bargain being conditional on certain suits being decided in a particular way).

When a contract for transfer of a fragmented piece of land to be implemented on repeal of an Act which prevented fragmentation, it was held to be void because the contingency was of an uncertain nature.[17]

In a case, the vendor had agreed to sell his half share in the property in dispute, but the sale deed was agreed to be executed after a month of the partition of the property and separation of his share. To get the property partitioned and his share separated was an obligation undertaken by the vendor for the benefit of the vendee. It was not a condition precedent without the happening of which no obligation to transfer the share could arise. The vendor having failed to get his share separated, the vendee was entitled to get the same done after the completion of the sale through court, which right had been given to him under the contract. If the sale was of a specified portion, then the situation might have been different. The sale here being of the unspecified share, it could not be said that the contract was a contingent one and the vendee was not entitled to enforce it without the share of the vendor having been separated.[18]

Failure of a contingent contract is due to non-happening of an anticipated event. Whereas impossibility is due to happening of an unanticipated event.[19]

12 ILR (1885)12 Cal 152.
13 AIR 1930 PC 287.
14 AIR 1925 Pat 259.
15 AIR 1936 Sind 26.
16 AIR 1919 Bom 154.
17 *Parvathamma* v *Uma* AIR 2011 Kant 58.
18 *Harbakhsh Singh Gill* v *Ram Rattan* AIR 1988 P&H 60; (1987)91 Punj LR 185.
19 *Gian Chand* v *York Experts* (2015)5 SCC 609. See also *Nandkishore Lalbhai Mehta* v *New Era Fabrics (P) Ltd.* (2015)9 SCC 755; AIR 2015 SC 3796.

When a contingent contract failed because permission of authority not granted, it was anticipated in the contract as a prerequisite to its performance. Thus, consequent restoration of parties to the position in which they were before the contract was held proper.[20]

A contingent contract becomes enforceable when the event on which depends the specific performance happens (*vide* s. 32, the Contract Act). Once the event happened, the contingent contract ripens into an absolute one.[1] In a Supreme Court case certain disputes and differences arose between the sons after the death of their father. The younger brother was contemplating legal proceedings against the elder brother. The mother intervened. The idea of legal proceedings was dropped because the mother gave a letter to younger brother stating that their father wanted to give him ₹50 lakhs and that the mother would give him the money or the balance in the event of default by the elder brother. In effect the elder brother did not pay. It was held s. 25, Contract Act did not hit the contract. Even assuming the letter brought forth a contingent contract within the meaning of s. 31, Contract Act, under s. 32, Contract Act such a contract became enforceable by law on the failure of the elder brother to pay the part of the specified sum.[2]

A party to a contract may waive a condition if it is for his exclusive benefit, but where the condition is fundamental to the enforceability of the agreement as a whole, it is not open to the party to waive it unilaterally.[3]

In a Canadian case,[4] it has been held that it is not open to a party unilaterally to waive a condition precedent so as to enable him to obtain specific performance. Thus where the purchaser agreed to buy land subject to the condition that he would buy a parcel of the adjacent land, specific performance was refused in the absence of that purchase.[5]

Contract depending on sanction of third party There was an agreement for sale which contained a clause to the effect that the vendor was to obtain the sanction of the Chief Commissioner for transfer of the site on which the building was constructed within two months. Such sanction was necessary on account of a condition in the ground lease. It was held that such a contract does not remain inchoate unless and until such sanction is obtained, when there is nothing to suggest that the application for sanction is likely to be rejected. So far as the parties to the agreement are concerned,

20 *SAIL* v *Tycoon Traders* (2015)5 SCC 767.

1 *N.P. Ogeti Balayya* v *K.V. Srinivasayya Setti Sons* AIR 1954 SC 26.

2 *Commissioner of Wealth Tax* v *Vijayaba Dowger Maharani* AIR 1979 SC 982; (1979)2 SCC 213; (1979)3 SCR 545; (1979)2 SCJ 325.

3 *Heron Garage Properties Ltd.* v *Moss* [1974]1 All ER 421.

4 *O'Reilly* v *Marketers Diversified Inc.* (1969) SCR 741.

5 *Barnett* v *Harrison* [1975]57 DLR (3rd) 225; *Gay-Wood-Hall Development Ltd.* v *Wilkes* [1972]23 DLR (3rd) 505; cf. *Dennis* v *Evans* [1972]27 DLR (3rd) 680.

the agreement is a complete agreement. The mere fact that sanction of the Chief Commission is to be obtained before the sale does not make the agreement incomplete and is not a bar to the grant of a decree for specific performance. If the Chief Commissioner does ultimately refuse sanction to the sale, the plaintiffs will not be able to enforce their decree but, as far as the court is concerned, there is no reason for refusing the decree.[6]

As held in a case in a suit for specific performance of a contract of sale and alternatively for refund of consideration, if the performance depends upon volition of a person not party to the suit, a decree for specific performance should not be granted, the person referred to being a landlord.[7] A somewhat different view was taken in a Calcutta case when the question was whether an agreement to sublet certain lands where the consent of the landlord was required to sublet was specifically performable. It was held that the fact that the landlord eventually would not consent is no bar to grant of decree of specific performance.[8] In an Allahabad case the question again arose in connection with an agreement to sell on the sanction of the Collector under s. 7(3) of the UP Encumbered Estates Act. The question only arose in connection with the execution of a decree for specific performance but it was held that it was for the party and not the court to move the Collector to grant sanction to execute a deed.[9]

This view has been followed in an MP case where there could not be effected any sale without the permission of the Government. Such contract was held specifically performable.[10]

The question was specifically raised in a Gujarat Full Bench case.[11] The question was whether a conditional decree for specific performance, subject to the condition of the plaintiff obtaining exemption from the State Government under cl. (*b*), sub-sec. (1) of s. 20 of the Urban Land (Ceiling and Regulation) Act 1976 can or cannot be passed, Gujarat Full Bench held that the passing of a conditional decree for specific performance of the obligation of the holder to transfer vacant land in excess of ceiling limit held by him subject to exemption being obtained under s. 20 is permissible.[12]

A conditional decree for specific performance after obtaining the consent of any authority under any law is permissible. In *Anjali Das* v *Bidyut Sarkar*,[13]

6 *C.L. Katial* v *Mrs. C.W.V. Madden* AIR 1963 Punj 136 at p. 137 approved by Supreme Court in *C.W. Wati Madden* v *C.L. Katil* AIR 1964 SC 978; (1963)2 SCWR 215; (1964)2 SCR 495; (1964)2 SCJ 824.

7 *Punjraj* v *Kalusa* AIR 1927 Nag 233.

8 *Kumar Gokul Chandra Law* v *Haji Muhamma Din* AIR 1938 Cal 136.

9 *Hakim Enayat Ullah* v *Khalil Ullah Khan* AIR 1938 All 432.

10 *Nimar Industrial Corporation* v *M.P. Electricity Board* AIR 1973 MP 281 (DB).

11 *Shah Jitendra Nanalal* v *Patel Lallubhai* AIR 1984 Guj 145 (FB).

12 *Shah Jitendra Nanalal* v *Patel Lallubhai* AIR 1984 Guj 145 at p. 149.

13 AIR 1992 Cal 47.

a decree for specific performance was passed subject to the approval of the cooperative society for the sale of the flat in its building. Where it was contended that possession of the property could not be given to the plaintiff without permission from the Land Development Officer, it was held that such permission was not a condition precedent for grant of a decree for specific performance. If, after the grant of a decree for specific performance, the Land Development Officer refuses to grant permission for the sale, the decree holder may not be in a position to enforce the decree, but for reason of that possibility, the decree cannot be refused.[14] A conditional decree for specific performance can be granted making it subject to exemption being obtained under s. 20 of the Urban Land (Ceiling and Regulation) Act 1976 or any other Statute or relief can be moulded requiring the defendant to obtain permission or consent.[15] The defendant cannot avoid such an agreement on the ground that any such similar permission has not been obtained,[16] nor on the ground that permission has been granted but not in the manner expected by the defendant.[17] A contract for sale of property under attachment subject to court's approval cannot be specifically enforced after the court has refused permission. An agreement to allot and sell flats on the 13th floor of the building if the 13th floor was sanctioned by the local authority, could not be specifically enforced when the authority declined the sanction.[18] The fact that the plaintiff is a foreign citizen is not an absolute bar for purchasing immovable properties in India; any objection about compliance of the Foreign Exchange Regulation Act 1973 (now Foreign Exchange Management Act 1990) does not prevent a decree being passed and the question of permission by the Reserve Bank of India can be raised at the stage of execution of the decree.[19]

Time when essence of contract Section 55, the Contract Act provides—

> "When a party to a contract promises to do a certain thing at or before a specified time, or certain things at or before specified times, and fails to do any such thing at or before the specified time, the contract, or so much of it as has not been performed, becomes voidable at the option of the promisee, if the intention of the parties was that time should be of the essence of the contract."

In a contract relating to sale of immovable property if time is specified for payment of the sale price but not in regard to the execution of the sale

14 *Ajit Prashad Jain* v *N.K. Widhani* AIR 1990 Del 42; *Soni Lalji Jetha* v *Soni Kalidas Devchand* AIR 1967 SC 978; (1967)1 SCR 873; *K. Raheja Constructions* v *Alliance Ministers* AIR 1995 SC 1768; 1995 Supp (3) SCC 17; (1995)3 SCJ 54.

15 *Manzoor Ahmed* v *Gulam Hassan Aram* AIR 2000 SC 191; (1999)7 SCC 703; JT 1999(8) SC 34.

16 *Raghunath Roy* v *Jogeshwar Prasad Sharma* AIR 1999 Del 383.

17 *Rameshwar Swarup* v *Saroj Tyagi* (1998)7 SCC 456; AIR 1998 SC 3389.

18 *Baij Nath* v *Ansal & Saigal Props. P. Ltd.* AIR 1993 Del 285.

19 *Ajit Prasad Jain* v *N.K. Widhani* AIR 1990 Del 42.

deed, time will become the essence only with reference to payment of sale price but not in regard to execution of the sale deed. Normally in regard to contracts relating to sale of immovable properties, time is not considered to be the essence of the contract unless such an intention can be gathered either from the express terms of the contract or impliedly from the intention of the parties as expressed by the terms of the contract.[20] In a contract for sale of immovable property, normally it is presumed that time is not the essence of the contract. Even if there is an express stipulation to that effect, the said presumption can be rebutted. It is well settled that to find out whether time was the essence of the contract, it is better to refer to the terms and conditions of the contract itself.[21] Clear condition in the contract that purchasers would have to definitely deposit balance by date stipulated in contract for sale was held that time was essence of contract.[22]

A vendor under mortgage debt with bank agreed to sell the property to clear the bank loan. It was specifically expressed in the agreement that the vendee shall pay balance sale consideration to bank to clear the mortgage debt within a stipulated day and it was further mentioned that the agreement stand cancelled if balance sale consideration is not paid within that time. It is held that the time is essence of contract.[1] The trial court which passed the decree has ample power to extend time to deposit balance sale consideration.[2]

Commenting upon s. 55 of the Contract Act, the Supreme Court said, "It is not merely because of specification of time at or before which the thing to be done under the contract is promised to be done and default in compliance therewith, that the other party may avoid contract. Such an option arises only if it is intended by the parties that time is of the essence of the contract. Intention to make time of the essence, if expressed in writing, must be in language which is unmistakable; it may also be inferred from the nature of the property agreed to be sold, conduct of the parties and the surrounding circumstances at or before the contract. Specific performance of a contract will ordinarily be granted, notwithstanding default in carrying out the contract within the specified period, if having regard to the express stipulations of the parties, nature of the property and the surrounding circumstances, it is not inequitable to grant the relief. If the contract relates to sale of immovable property, it would normally be presumed that time was not of the essence of the contract. Mere incorporation in the

20 *Saradamani Kandappan* v *S. Rajalakshmi* (2011)12 SCC 18; AIR 2011 SC 3234.

21 *N. Srinivasa* v *Kuttukaran Machine Tools Ltd.* (2009)5 SCC 182.

22 *A.K. Lakshmipathy* v *Rai Saheb Pannalal H.L. Charitable Trust* (2010)1 SCC 287; AIR 2010 SC 577.

1 *Besto Brite Steels Pvt. Ltd., Chennai* v *V. Muthu Krishnan* AIR 2018 Mad 97.

2 *V.M. Kothandaraman* v *S. Deivanai* AIR 2018 Mad 276.

written agreement of clause imposing penalty in case of default does not by itself evidence an intention to make time of the essence."[3]

In the Supreme Court case it was clarified that "it is settled law that the fixation of the period within which the contract has to be performed does not make the stipulation as to time the essence of the contract. When a contract relates to sale of immovable property it will normally be presumed that the time is not the essence of the contract." This case is also the authority for the proposition that the parties may if they so like indicate in unmistakable terms that the time is the essence of the contract.[4]

Therefore in respect of sale of property it must be accepted that time will not be treated to be of essence with regard to contract relating to sale of immovable properties but this presumption will give way to proof of a contrary intention by express words or by the nature of the transaction. Application of this rule would indicate that where the parties have expressly stipulated in their contract that the time fixed for performance must be strictly complied with, the courts will infer an intention to the contrary and would treat time as of the essence of the contract. This presumption would, however, stand rebutted where the circumstances of the contract or the nature of the subject matter indicate that the fixed date must be strictly complied with, e.g. the purchase of a lease hold house for immediate occupation; the purchase of business land or premises such as a public house as a going concern, the option for the purchase of property etc.[5]

When time is of the essence of a contract is a question of fact and the decision of this depends on the entire relevant facts on record of the case, the real test is the intention of the parties. Generally in the context of immovable properties time is not the essence of the contract. But this general principle is subject to the exceptions as may arise on the facts of a given case wherein the parties may make time the essence of the contract even in cases relating to immovable property. The intention of the parties has to be found out on the basis of the material on a record.[6]

3 *Gomathinayagam Pillai* v *Palaniswami Nadar* AIR 1967 SC 868; (1967)1 SCR 227 relying on *Jamshed Khodaram Irani* v *Burjorji Dhunjibai* AIR 1915 PC 83; *Narayanan Nair* v *Zacharia Kuriakose* AIR 1991 Ker 152; *Rakha Singh* v *Santokha* AIR 1976 HP 66 at p. 67; *Raj Rani Bhasin* v *Kartar Singh Mehta* AIR 1975 Del 137 at p. 144 (DB) (held time was of essence); *Dipnarain Singh* v *Dinanath Singh* AIR 1981 Pat 69 at pp. 72-73; *Pakharsingh* v *Kishansingh* AIR 1974 Raj 112; *Sambhunath Chakravarthy* v *Sushma Sinha* AIR 1980 Cal 5; *Mahadeo Prosad* v *Narain Chandra* (1920)24 CWN 330 (mere presence of forfeiture clause without more not indicative of the condition that time was the essence of the contract).

4 *Govind Prosad Chaturvedi* v *Hari Dutt Shastri* AIR 1977 SC 1005; (1977)2 SCR 877; (1977)2 SCC 539.

5 *Suraj Singh* v *Nathi Bai* AIR 1990 MP 323 at pp. 324-325.

6 *Nanak Builders* v *Vinod Kumar Alag* AIR 1991 Del 315 at p. 316.

When the seller of property was in need of money, only short-term extension was allowed, because paying the price constituted time as of the essence.[7] In case of construction contracts, the time of completion would be of the essence when special features exist.[8]

In cases of a contract for the sale of immovable property, time is not of the essence of the contract unless expressly stipulated at the time of the contract or there are circumstances disclosed sufficiently to displace ordinary presumption that in a contract for sale of immovable property, time is not the essence of the contract when initial stipulated time of three months subsequently is reduced to one month, even then it cannot be spelt that time was the essence of contract of transfer.[9]

However, the normal initial presumption of time not ordinarily being of the essence in case of sale of immovable property, is not statutory nor is it absolute and irrebuttable and circumstances of a given contract may clearly negative it.[10]

In a contract with fixed time frame, involvement of additional work admitted by the parties, it was held that parties could not be expected to go into a fresh round of negotiations and reference terms of contract.[11]

But where the object of the contract is commercial enterprise, the court would be strongly inclined to hold time to be essential.[12] Even so, it is a question of intention that has to be gathered from various circumstances.[13]

When under the agreement for sale of land for ₹20,000 a sum of ₹13,000 was paid as advance and the purchaser had to pay ₹5,000 on or before a particular date and take possession and conclude the sale within six months thereafter, it was held that time was not the essence of the contract except in regard to the payment of ₹5,000 agreed to be paid on or before that particular date.[14]

7 *Coromandel Indag Products (P) Ltd.* v *Ganuda Chit & Trading Co. P. Ltd.* (2011)8 SCC 601.

8 *Mc Dermott International Inc.* v *Burn Standrd Co. Ltd.* (2006)11 SCC 181. See also *Nevilal Rohita Construction (P) Ltd.* v *State of Bihar* AIR 2005 Pat 190.

9 *Ram Kishan* v *Bhabi Chand* AIR 1988 Del 20 at p. 22. But see *Badni Nisha* v *Yogendra Prasad Sinha* AIR 2006 Pat 71.

10 *Bal Saroop Daulat Ram* v *Lakhbir Singh Kirpal Singh* AIR 1964 Punj 375 (DB).

11 *Venkatesh Construction Co.* v *Karnataka Vidyuth Karthane* AIR 2016 SC 553; (2016)4 SCC 119.

12 *Sriram Cotton Pressing Factory* v *K.E. Narayanaswami Naidu* AIR 1965 Mad 352 at p. 355 (DB).

13 *A.P. State Electricity Board* v *Patel & Patel* AIR 1977 AP 172 following *Mahabir Prasad Rungta* v *Durga Dutta* AIR 1961 SC 990; (1961)3 SCR 639; (1961)1 SCJ 569.

14 *K.M. Jose* v *Anantha Bhat* AIR 1987 Kant 173; ILR (1986) Kant 4031; (1987)1 Kant LJ 16.

Time will be of essence in such contracts as contracts relating to reversionary interest,[15] contracts for sale of land to be used directly for purposes of trade and commerce, (*e.g.* mines) or contracts for things which are subject to fluctuations in value, as, for example, contracts relating to patents.[16]

Time will be essence of contract in case of contract for reconveyance. It all depends however on facts of the case.[17]

Thus, the legal position in this regard has been explained in *Chand Rani* v *Kamal Rani*[18] where the principle was outlined in the following words:

> It is a well-accepted principle that in the case of sale of immovable property, time is never regarded as the essence of the contract. In fact, there is a presumption against time being the essence of the contract. This principle is not in any way different from that obtainable in England. Under the law of equity which governs the rights of the parties in the case of specific performance of contract to sell real estate, law looks not at the letter but at the substance of the agreement. It has to be ascertained whether under the terms of the contract the parties named a specific time within which completion was to take place, really and in substance it was intended that it should be completed within a reasonable time. An intention to make time the essence of the contract must be expressed in unequivocal language.

Even if time is not the essence of the contract, the court may infer that it is to be performed in a reasonable time: (*i*) from the express terms of the contract; (*ii*) from the nature of the property; and (*iii*) from the surrounding circumstances as, for example, the object of making the contract. The intention to treat time as the essence of the contract may however be evidenced by circumstances which are sufficiently strong to displace the normal presumption that time is not the essence in contract for sale of land.[19] However, it is interesting to note that the distinction between contracts relating to immovable properties and other contracts was not drawn by s. 55 of the Contract Act (or any other provisions of the Contract Act or the Specific Relief Act 1963). The courts in India made the said distinction, by following the English law evolved during the nineteenth century. Time is not of the essence of the contracts relating to immovable

15 *Levy* v *Stogdon* [1899]1 Ch 5.

16 *Payne* v *Banner* [1846]15 LJ Ch 227, contracts relating to shares, *Sparks* v *Liverpool Waterworks Co.* [1807]13 Ves 428; *Campbell* v *London and Brighton Rly. Co.* [1846]5 Hare 519; *Koritschoner's Claim* [1907]98 LI 127; *Hare* v *Nicoll* [1966]1 All ER 285 (CA); contract relating to house for immediate residence, *Tilley* v *Thomas* [1867]3 Ch App 61.

17 *Nathu Singh* v *Jagdish Singh* AIR 1992 All 174; *Raj Kishore* v *Prem Singh* AIR 2011 SC 382.

18 (1993)1 SCC 519.

19 *Gomathinayagam Pillai* v *Palaniswami Nadar* AIR 1967 SC 868; (1967)1 SCR 227.

properties; and that notwithstanding default in carrying out the contract within the specified period, specific performance will ordinarily be granted, if having regard to the express stipulation of the parties, nature of the property and surrounding circumstances, it is not inequitable to grant such relief. [20]

However, noticeable point in this regard is that the principle that time is not of the essence of contracts relating to immovable properties took shape in an era when market values of immovable properties were stable and did not undergo any marked change even over a few years (followed mechanically, even when value ceased to be stable). As a consequence, time for performance, stipulated in the agreement was assumed to be not material, or at all events considered as merely indicating the reasonable period within which contract should be performed. The assumption was that grant of specific performance would not prejudice the vendor defendant financially as there would not be much difference in the market value of the property even if the contract was performed after a few months. This principle made since during the first half of the twentieth century, when there was comparatively very little inflation, in India. But the present era is that of galloping inflation and prices of immovable properties have increased steeply, by leaps and bounds. The reality arising from this economic change cannot continue to be ignored in deciding cases relating to specific performance. The steep increase in prices is a circumstance which makes it inequitable to grant the relief of specific performance where the purchaser does not take steps to complete the sale within the agreed period, and the vendor has not been responsible for any delay or non-performance. A purchaser can no longer take shelter under the principle that time is not of essence in performance of contracts relating to immovable property, to cover his delays, laches, breaches and "non-readiness". The precedents from an era, when high inflation was unknown, holding that time is not of the essence of the contract in regard to immovable properties, may no longer apply, not because the principle laid down therein is unsound or erroneous, but the circumstances that existed when the said principle was evolved, no longer exist.[1]

A correct perspective relating to the question whether time is not of the essence of the contract in contracts relating to immovable property, is given by the Supreme Court in *K.S. Vidyanadam* v *Vairavan*[2] the Supreme Court observed:

> It has been consistently held by the courts in India, following certain early English decisions, that in the case of agreement of sale relating to immovable property, time is not of the essence of the contract unless specifically provided to that effect. ... in the case of urban properties in India, it is

20 *Indira Kaur* v *Sheo Lal Kapoor* (1988)2 SCC 488.
1 *Saradamani Kandappan* v *S. Rajalakshmi* (2011)12 SCC 18.
2 (1997)3 SCC 1.

well-known that their prices have been going up sharply over the last few decades—particularly after 1973. ...

We cannot be oblivious to the reality—and the reality is constant and continuous rise in the values of urban properties—fuelled by large-scale migration of people from rural areas to urban centres and by inflation. ... Indeed, we are inclined to think that the rigor of the rule evolved by courts that time is not of the essence of the contract in the case of immovable properties—evolved in times when prices and values were stable and inflation was unknown—requires to be relaxed, if not modified, particularly in the case of urban immovable properties. It is high time, we do so.

It is now well-settled that laws, which may be reasonable and valid when made, can, with passage of time and consequential change in circumstances, become arbitrary and unreasonable.[3] It is, therefore, submitted that there is an urgent need to revisit the principle that time is not of the essence in contracts relating to immovable properties and also explain the current position of law with regard to contracts relating to immovable property made after 1975, in view of the changed circumstances arising from inflation and steep increase in prices.

Readiness and willingness It is incumbent on the plaintiff in a suit for specific performance to plead and prove with satisfactory evidence[4] that he is and has always been ready and willing to perform his part of the contract. Failure to do so is a good defence in an action for specific performance. Consequently, the decree passed by the court may be set aside if the pleadings are not in the conformity with the mandatory Or. 6, r. 3, CPC, cl. 3 of Form 47 in Appendix A.[5]

The words "readiness and willingness" cannot be put in a strait jacket formula. These are to be determined from the entirety of the facts and circumstances relevant to the intention and conduct of the party concerned. In absence of specific plea by the opposite party, it is a mandate of the statute that the plaintiff has to comply with s. 16(*c*) of the Specific Relief Act 1963 and when there is non-compliance with the statutory mandate, the court is not bound to grant specific performance but to dismiss the suit. It is also clear that readiness to perform must be established throughout the relevant paints of time.[6] But, for the compliance with s. 16(*c*) of the Act it is not necessary for the plaintiff to aver in the same words used in the section, *i.e.* ready and willing to perform the contract. Absence of the specific words in the plaint would not result in dismissal of the suit if

3 *Rattan Arya* v *State of T.N.* (1986)3 SCC 385.
4 *Nanjappan* v *Ramasamy* (2015)14 SCC 341.
5 *Padmakumari* v *Dasayyan* (2015)8 SCC 695.
6 *J.P. Builders* v *A. Ramadas Rao* (2011)1 SCC 429.

sufficient fact and evidence are brought on record to satisfy the court the readiness and willingness to perform his part of the contract.[7]

Doctrine of business efficacy The principle of business efficacy is normally invoked to read a term in an agreement or contract so as to achieve the result or the consequence intended by the parties acting as prudent businessmen. Business efficacy means the power to produce intended results. The classic test of business efficacy was proposed by Bowen, LJ in *Moorcock*.[8] This test requires that a term can only be implied if it is necessary to give business efficacy to the contract to avoid such a failure of consideration that the parties cannot as reasonable businessmen have intended. But, only the most limited term should then be implied—the bare minimum to achieve this goal. If the contract makes business sense without the term, the courts will not imply the same. The following passage from the opinion of Bowen, LJ in *Moorcock* sums up the position:

> "... In business transactions such as this, what the law desires to effect by the implication is to give such business efficacy to the transaction as must have been intended at all events by both parties who are businessmen; not to impose on one side all the perils of the transaction, or to emancipate one side from all the chances of failure, but to make each party promise in law as much, at all events, as it must have been in the contemplation of both parties that he should be responsible for in respect of those perils or chances."

In *Shirlaw* v *Southern Foundries*,[9] the observation made is quite worthy of notice;

> "Prima facie that which in any contract is left to be implied and need not be expressed is something so obvious that it goes without saying; so that, if, while the parties were making their bargain, an officious bystander, were to suggest some express provision for it in their agreement, they would testily suppress him with a common 'Oh, of course!'"

Similar observation can be found in *Trollope and Colls Ltd.* v *North West Metropolitan Regl. Hospital Board*:[10]

> "An expressed term can be implied if and only if the court finds that the parties must have intended that term to form part of their contract: it is not enough for the court to find that such a term would have been adopted by the parties as reasonable men if it had been suggested to them: it must have been a term that went without saying, a term *necessary* to give business efficacy to the contract, a term which, although tacit, formed part of the contract which the parties made for themselves."

7 *Biswanath Ghosh* v *Gobinda Ghosh* (2014)11 SCC 605; AIR 2014 SC 1582.
8 [1889] LR 14 PD 64 (CA).
9 [1939]2 KB 206; [1939]2 All ER 113 (CA).
10 [1973]1 WLR 601; [1973]2 All ER 260 (HL).

However, the business efficacy test should be applied only in cases where the term that is sought to be read as implied is such which could have been clearly intended by the parties at the time of making of the agreement.[11]

Principle of mutuality Mutuality is often said to be a condition of a specific performance. The principle of mutuality depends on two assertions which may be called positive and negative mutuality. The positive mutuality may be exemplified by the vendor of land who can obtain specific performance even though damages would usually be an adequate remedy, because the purchaser is entitled to specific performance and it would be unfair to deny the vendor what is granted to the purchaser. The negative mutuality involves denial of specific performance to a plaintiff, because it would not be available to the defendant.[12] "Thus, where a party who undertakes to render personal services or to perform continuous duties cannot claim specific performance, the remedy is, for that reason, not available against him, and for the same reason a minor cannot get specific performance."[13] Even in America mutuality of obligation or contract is essential to the right to the remedy of specific performance and such relief will be denied in the case of contracts not mutually binding on both parties since in such case the requisite mutuality of obligation is lacking.[14] A contract may not contain an express promise to perform, but it may be implied from the terms thereof so as to give it requisite mutuality and the payment by such party of part of the consideration is a recognition of his obligation giving mutuality of obligation to the contract.

Want of mutuality The doctrine of mutuality means that one party to the contract could not be held bound to that contract when he could not enforce it against the other. The test of mutuality lies in finding out whether the contract is enforceable by either party. In *Mir Sarwarjan* v *Fakhruddin Mahomed Chowdhury*,[15] the Judicial Committee made the application of doctrine of mutuality to specific performance of a contract as settled in India. In a later decision in *Sri Kakulam Subrahmanyam* v *Kurra Subba Rao*,[16] the Privy Council held that where the mother of a minor as guardian entered into a contract for sale which was for the benefit of the minor, the guardian was competent to enter into such a contract. There was a conflict of opinion among various High Courts. The Legislature has now set at rest the controversy by enacting sub-sec. (4) of s. 20 of the Specific Relief Act

11 *Satya Jain* v *Anis Ahmed Rushdie* (2013)8 SCC 131; AIR 2013 SC 434.
12 Cheshire, Fifoot & Furmston's *Law of Contract*, 17th Ed., p. 798.
13 Chitty on *Contracts*, 32nd Ed., vol. 1. para 27-051.
14 *Corpus Juris Secundum*, vol. 81, §15, pp. 728-729.
15 ILR (1907)34 Cal 163.
16 AIR 1948 PC 95.

1963 doing away with the doctrine of mutuality. There is no scope for contending that the doctrine of mutuality will defeat a claim for specific performance.

Insolvency The commission of an act of insolvency by the plaintiff may prevent him from enforcing a contract for sale either as a purchaser or as vendor, because in the former case, he may not be able to pay the money and in the latter case, he may not be capable of conveying the property. The insolvency of a party does not necessarily result in such an incapacity to perform a contract so as to entitle the other party at once to treat it as broken and to claim damages.[17] The receiver may disclaim an onerous contract or may perform what the insolvent was neglecting to perform at the time when he was bound to perform the same. Insolvency has therefore no other effect on the contract other than to put the receiver in the place of the insolvent.

It is only when the insolvency of a party is declared or notified to the other, it can be inferred that there is no intention on his part to perform the contract, that the other is absolved from performance.[18]

Frustration of contract Section 56 of the Contract Act provides—

"An agreement to do an act impossible in itself is void.

"A contract to do an act which, after the contract is made, becomes impossible, or, by reason of some event which the promisor could not prevent, unlawful, becomes void when the act becomes impossible or unlawful.

"Where one person has promised to do something which he knew, or, with reasonable diligence, might have known, and which the promisee did not know, to be impossible or unlawful, such promisor must make compensation to such promisee for any loss which such promisee sustains through the non-performance of the promise."

Interpreting this provision in *Satyabrata Ghose* v *Mugneeram Bangur & Co.*,[19] the Supreme Court held that according to the Indian Law, which is embodied in s. 54 of the Transfer of Property Act, a contract for sale of land does not of itself create any interest in the property which is the subject matter of the contract. The obligations of the parties in a contract for sale of land are, therefore, the same as in other ordinary contracts, and, consequently, the doctrine of frustration is applicable to contracts for sale of land in India. Further, the word "impossible" has not been used in the

17 *Currimbhoy & Co. Ltd.* v *L.A. Creet* AIR 1930 Cal 113; ILR (1930)57 Cal 170.
18 Re, *Ex. P. Carnforth Heamatite Iron Co.* 4 Ch D 108; *Morgan* v *Bair* (1874-75) LR 10 CP 15. See Dutt on *Contract,* 11th Ed., p. 445.
19 AIR 1954 SC 44; 1954 SCR 310; 1954 SCJ 1.

sense of physical or literal impossibility. The performance of an act may not be literally impossible but it may be impracticable and useless from the point of view of the object and purpose which the parties had in view, and if untoward event or change of circumstances totally upsets the very foundation upon which the parties rested their bargain, it can very well be said that the promisor finds it impossible to do the act which he promised to do.

Inability by a financial corporation to pay interest on its bonds is not the same as an impossibility of performance.[20] However, an agreement of lease as contrasted with an agreement to lease creates a demise *in praesenti* and is not within the purview of the doctrine of frustration which can only be applied to executory contracts.[1] Disappointed expectations do not lead to frustrated contracts.[2]

Where pending hearing of second appeal, the suit land is vested in the State, the court would take into account the position as prevailing then and refuse specific performance, if the land is no longer available.[3]

For a brilliant analysis of the doctrine readers may refer to an English decision.[4]

Frustration of contract with an indemnity clause—enforceability There is an implied condition in ordinary contract that the parties shall be exonerated in case, before the breach the performance becomes impossible on account of physical causes or legal prohibitions.

There may be an indemnity clause in contract. In a case a dealer in export of silver had entered into agreement with State Trading Corporation for purpose of exporting silver to a foreign buyer and had made all arrangements to perform the contract. Meanwhile the Export (Control) Fifteen Amendment Order (1979) came into force which imposed a complete ban on export of silver including pre-ban contracts. The agreement between the dealer and the State Trading Corporation contained an indemnity clause according to which in case the contract with foreign buyer could not be performed the dealer undertook to indemnify the State Trading Corporation. It was held in the circumstances of the case that (*i*) even though the contract to export silver related to pre-ban period,

20 *H.P. State Cooperative Bank Ltd.* v *U.P. State Financial Corp.* AIR 2016 HP 29.

1 *H.V. Rajan* v *C.N. Gopal* AIR 1975 SC 261; (1975)4 SCC 302; *Dhruv Dev Chand* v *Harmohinder Singh* AIR 1968 SC 1024; (1968)3 SCR 339; *Sushila Devi* v *Hari Singh* AIR 1971 SC 1756; 1971 (Supp) SCR 671; (1971)2 SCC 288; *Shyam Kumari* v *Ejaz Ahmad Ansari* AIR 1977 All 376 (DB); *Thomas* v *Moram Mar Baselions* AIR 1979 Ker 156.

2 *Pearl Cycle Industries Ltd.* v *A.N. Kaul* AIR 1964 Punj 482.

3 *Shiam Sunder Lal* v *Durga* AIR 1966 All 185.

4 *National Carriers Ltd.* v *Panalpina (Northern) Ltd.* [1981]1 All ER 161 (HL).

the court would not interfere with the Government order prohibiting export of silver. (*ii*) Even if the foreign buyer claims damages from State Trading Corporation for breach of contract due to ban on export of silver, the State Trading Corporation would not be allowed to enforce the indemnity clause in the contract against the exporting dealer in view of the equitable considerations.[5]

Doctrine of frustration Section 56 of the Indian Contract Act 1872 is based on the English rule of frustration of contract. In *Satyabrata Ghose* v *Mugneeram Bangur Co.*[6] the Supreme Court has indicated the scope and effect of s. 56 of the Act. As to the basis of the doctrine it was held by the Supreme Court that the essential idea upon which the doctrine is based is that of impossibility of performance of the contract; in fact impossibility and frustration are often used as interchangeable expressions. The changed circumstances make the performance of the contract impossible and the parties are absolved from the further performance of it as they did not promise to perform an impossibility. The doctrine of frustration is only a special case of the discharge of contract by an impossibility of performance arising after the contract was made. *Force majeure* clause can be invoked when it pertains to the contractual obligation that has perportedly become impossible of performance.[7] "*Force majeure*" is governed by the Contract Act 1872. Insofar as it is relatable to an express or implied clause in a contract it is governed by Chapter III dealing with the contingent contracts, and more particularly, s. 32 thereof. Insofar as a *force majeure* event occurs *de hors* the contract, it is dealt with by a rule of positive law under s. 56 of the Contract Act.[8]

In *Ganga Saran* v *Ram Charan Ram Gopal*,[9] Fazal Ali, J in speaking about frustration said: "It seems necessary for us to emphasise that so far as courts in this country are concerned, they must look primarily to the law as embodied in ss. 32 and 56 of the Indian Contract Act 1872." In *Joseph Constantine S.S. Line Ltd.* v *Imperial Smelting Corpn. Ltd.*[10] Lord Wright stated that in ascertaining the meaning of the contract and its application to the actual occurrences "the court has to decide, not what the parties actually intended, but what as reasonable men they should have intended. The court personifies for this purpose the reasonable man." A contract does

5 *Union of India* v *C. Damani* AIR 1980 SC 1149 at p. 1150; 1980 UJ (SC) 706; 1980 (Supp) SCC 707.

6 AIR 1954 SC 44; *Superintendence Company of India* v *Krishan Murgai* AIR 1980 SC 1717.

7 *Markled Vanaspati & Allied Industries* v *Union of India* (2007)7 SCC 679.

8 *Energy Watchdog* v *CERC* (2017)14 SCC 80; (2018)1 SCC (Civ) 133; (2017)2 CPR 387 (SC).

9 AIR 1952 SC 9 at p. 11; *Naithani Jute Mills* v *Khyaliram Jagannath* AIR 1968 SC 522.

10 [1942] AC 154 at p. 189.

not become frustrated only because one of the many possible ways of performance has become illegal or impossible.[11] There is no general liberty reserved to the courts to absolve a party from liability to perform his part of contract merely because an account of an uncontemplated turn of events, the performance of the contract may become onerous.[12]

Impossibility of performance of a contract can be an excuse to pay damages for non-performance.[13] A contract becomes void under s. 56 of the Contract Act where the performance of the contract is made impossible by the destruction of the specific thing essential to the performance where *A* agrees to let out his music hall on a particular date, the contract becomes void if the hall is destroyed by fire before the appointed day.[14] Municipal authorities directed the contractor to stop work in some blocks and in compliance therewith the contractor stopped the work. It has been held that the contractor cannot be faulted when he refused to carry out any constructional work in violation of stop work notice. Besides, plea of alleged self-induced frustration was not proved.[15]

Doctrine of impossibility The court has to consider and understand the scope of application of the doctrines of *lex non cogit ad impossibilia* (the law does not compel a man to do what he cannot possibly perform); *impossibilium nulla obligatio est* (the law does not expect a party to do the impossible); and *impotentia excusat legem* in the qualified sense that there is a necessary or invincible disability to perform the mandatory part of the law or to forbear the prohibitory. These maxims are akin to the maxim of Roman law *nemo tenetur ad impossibilia* (no one is bound to do an impossibility) which is derived from common sense and natural equity and has been adopted and applied in law from time immemorial. Therefore, when it appears that the performance of the formalities prescribed by a statute has been rendered impossible by circumstances over which the persons interested had no control, like an act of God, the circumstances will be taken as a valid excuse.[16] Thus, where the law creates a duty or charge, and the party is disabled to perform it, without any fault on his part, and has no control over it, the law will in general excuse him. Even in such a circumstance, the statutory provision is not denuded of its mandatory character because of the supervening impossibility caused therein.[17]

11 *Twentshe Overseas Trading Co. Ltd.* v *Uganda Sugar Factory Ltd.* AIR 1945 PC 144.
12 *Continental Construction Co. Ltd.* v *State of M.P.* AIR 1988 SC 1166.
13 *I.F.C.I. Ltd.* v *Connanore Spg. & Wvg. Mills Ltd.* AIR 2002 SC 1841.
14 *Taylor* v *Coldwell* [1863]3 B&S 826.
15 *M.D. Army, W.H.O.* v *Sumangal Services Pvt. Ltd.* AIR 2004 SC 1344.
16 *Chandra Kishore Jha* v *Mahavir Prasad* (1999)8 SCC 266; AIR 1999 SC 3558; *Hira Tikkoo* v *UT, Chandigarh* (2004)6 SCC 765; AIR 2004 SC 3649; *HUDA* v *Dr. Babeswar Kanhar* (2005)1 SCC 191; AIR 2005 SC 1491.
17 *State of M.P.* v *Narmada Bachao Andolan* (2011)7 SCC 639.

Test of "radically different" The modern approach to the doctrine of frustration has been well put in the celebrated *Sea Angel's* case.[18] According to this test, the application of the doctrine of frustration requires a multi-factorial approach. Among the factors which have to be considered are the terms of the contract itself, its matrix or context, the parties' knowledge, expectations, assumptions and contemplations, in particular as to risk, as at the time of the contract, at any rate so far as these can be ascribed mutually and objectively, and then the nature of the supervening event, and the parties' reasonable and objectively ascertainable calculations as to the possibilities of future performance in the new circumstances. Since the subject-matter of the doctrine of frustration is contract, and contracts are about the allocation of risk, and since the allocation and assumption of risk is not simply a matter of express or implied provision but may also depend on less easily defined matters such as "the contemplation of the parties", the application of the doctrine can often be a difficult one. In such circumstances, the test of "radically different" is important: it tells us that the doctrine is not to be lightly invoked; that mere incidence of expense or delay or onerousness is not sufficient; and that there has to be as it were a break in identity between the contract as provided for and contemplated and its performance in the new circumstances.

Acquisition of property agreed to be transferred—frustration of contract The property agreed to be transferred may be acquired by Government exercise of its power of eminent domain. The question then crops up whether or not the contract is frustrated thereby putting in the process an embargo on right of specific performance. What happens there is that for the property compensation payable in lieu thereof gets substituted. On the other hand in consolidation proceedings the party loses all rights in the original holding and new rights are created in the land allotted to him in lieu thereof. In view of this even if the contract may not now be capable of being performed specifically yet the plaintiff can still seek relief by proceeding against the amount awarded as compensation for the land agreed to be sold. It is not correct to say, therefore, that due to acquisition the contract itself gets frustrated.[19]

Contract of sale Vendor-defendant was holding suit property under hire-purchase from A.P. Industrial Infrastructure Corporation (APIIC) which had executed registered sale deed in favour of plaintiff-vendee. Title of vendor was not disputed. Provisions of s. 17 of the Specific Relief Act 1963 are not attracted. Contract would be specifically enforceable.[20]

18 *Edwinton Commercial Corpn.* v *Tsavliris Russ (Worldwide Salvage & Towage) Ltd.* 2007 EWCA Civ 547; [2007]2 Lloyd's Rep 517 (CA).

19 *Nathu Singh* v *Jagdish Singh* AIR 1992 All 174.

20 *Andhra Graphite (P.) Ltd.* v *Jobing Syndicate* AIR 2011 NOC 245 (AP).

Trustee—contract of sale One trustee alone of several trustees cannot enter into a contract of transfer. The defence that other co-trustees having not joined in the contract, the contract is unenforceable is a good defence. The law governing the execution of trusts is well settled. In the case of a private trust, where there are more trustees than one, all must join in the execution of the trust. The concurrence of all is in general necessary in a transaction affecting the trust property, and a majority cannot bind the trust estate. In order to bind the trust estate, the act must be the act of all. They constitute one body in the eye of law, and all must act together. It follows as a necessary corollary, that where there are several trustees they must act unanimously in making a sale or a contract of sale in respect of trust property, unless it is provided otherwise by the terms of the trust deed. In exercising the power of sale, as in the exercise of other powers, a trustee cannot therefore, properly delegate the performance of the acts which he ought personally perform. Although a trustee may listen to the opinions and wishes of others, he must exercise his own judgment. Thus a trustee for sale of property cannot leave the whole conduct of the sale to his co-trustees. The reason for this is that the settlor has entrusted the trust property and its management to all the trustees, and the beneficiaries are entitled to the benefit of their collective wisdom and experience. Consequently, sale of trust property effected without the concurrence of any trustee is of no legal effect and cannot be enforced.[1]

Registered deed of reconveyance—effective dates of transfer Section 47 of the Registration Act lays down that a registered document shall operate from the time which it would have commenced to operate if no registration thereof had been required or made, and not from the time of registration. Thus a sale deed is operative from the date of its execution even though its registration may be effected subsequently.[2] A legal fiction is employed by s. 47 of the Registration Act 1908 by which registration of the document shall relate back to the date of the execution of the document. Thus, for example, in a case, even though registration had been done subsequent to the filing of suit, it related back to the date of execution of the sale deed, which was prior to institution of the suit.[3] Even if the sale price is not paid to the vendor on the date of the execution of the agreement, it does not invalidate the document.[4] Normally, ownership and title to the property will

1 *H.E.H. The Nizam's Jewellery Trust*, in re AIR 1980 SC 17; (1979)4 SCC 602; (1980)1 SCR 459.

2 *K.J. Nathan* v *S.V. Maruthi Rao* AIR 1965 SC 430; (1964)6 SCR 727; (1964)2 SCJ 671; *Gayatri Prasad* v *Board of Revenue* 1973 All WR 606; *Ramnarain Chaube* v *Basdeo Misra* AIR 1934 All 70; *Union Bank Ltd.* v *Ram Rati* AIR 1954 All 595.

3 *Har Narain* v *Mam Chand* (2010)13 SCC 128.

4 *State of Kerala* v *C.C. Refineries* AIR 1968 SC 1361; (1968)3 SCR 556; *Chandrashanker* v *Abhla Mathur* AIR 1952 Bom 56; *Md. Bashir Khan* v *Kulsum Bibi* AIR 1927 All 545; *S. Arunachalam* v *Sivan Perumal Asari* AIR 1970 Mad 226.

pass to the purchaser on registration of the sale deed with effect from the date of execution of the sale deed. But this is not an invariable rule, as the true test of passing of property is the intention of parties. Though registration is *prima facie* proof of an intention to transfer the property, it is not proof of operative transfer if payment of consideration (price) is a condition precedent for passing of the property.[5] Explaining the scope of s. 47, Registration Act, Calcutta High Court held:

(*i*) Provisions of s. 47 of the Registration Act will apply where the successive transfers relate to the same property and there is no contest against any third party.

(*ii*) When the right of pre-emption as in Muslim law or under s. 26F of the Bengal Tenancy Act, arises only out of a valid, complete and *bona fide* sale, provisions of s. 61 and not of s. 47, will be attracted. The registration of the document, which is essential to complete a valid sale, will be complete when, on presentation for registration of the document and admission of execution thereof, the formalities enjoined under ss. 59, 60 and 61(1) are complied with.

(*iii*) In cases where after the date of execution of a document of transfer but before its registration, there are subsequent deeds of transfer in respect of the same property, such documents even if registered earlier than the transfer deed referred to above, will not prevail over such earlier deed which takes effect from its execution.

(*iv*) Similarly on the execution of a transfer deed in respect of a property but before its registration, there is an attachment of the same property, and the transfer deed is subsequently registered attachment will not prevail over the said deed which also takes effect from its execution.

(*v*) A deed of gift duly executed and accepted by the donee cannot be revoked by the donor as absence of registration during the permissible period does not suspend the gift.[6]

However, during the interregnum period of execution of the deed and its registration, the purchaser cannot project himself as the owner of the said property prior to the completion of registration of the deed of sale as per the Registration Act.[7]

Attestation distinguished from execution Attestation testifies/certifies the genuineness of the document. Attestation and execution are different acts, one following the other. Execution includes delivery and signing of the

5 *Kaliaperumal* v *Rajagopal* (2009)4 SCC 193; AIR 2009 SC 2122; (2009)77 AIC 167 (SC).

6 *State of West Bengal* v *Nimai Chand Kundu* AIR 1978 Cal 347; 82 CWN 743.

7 *Arun Bhusan Guha* v *Amal Roy* (2009)2 CHN 752.

document in the presence of the witness and also the whole series of acts or formalities which are necessary to render the document valid. Attestation of sale deed is imperative. Where the *animus* to attestation is totally absent, it is settled law that the document may be admissible but probative value of the entries contained therein may still be required to be examined in the facts and circumstances of a particular case.[8]

Deed—construction of If the words are express and clear, effect must be given to them and any extraneous enquiry into what was thought or intended is ruled out. If, however, there is ambiguity in the language employed then it is permissible to look to the surrounding circumstances to determine what was intended.[9]

> "It is no doubt true that in the matter of interpretation of documents with which they are couched the writing which produces the instrument often takes precedence in the matter of the understanding of the true meaning of the document. But a well set exception is always carved out to this accepted norm. If such an instrument is contemporaneous in point of time with other documents and if those two sets of documents have been understood and acted upon by parties in a particular manner then even though the letters and writing of such document may *prima facie* give a particular meaning to it, yet the same has to be read in conjunction with such contemporaneous documents and be interpreted in the light of subsequent conduct of the authors of the said documents. The best and the surest mode of construing an instrument is to read in the sense which would have been applied when it was drawn up."

The court also observed that though the principle *contemporanea exposition est optima et fortissima in lege* cannot as a matter of course be adopted in the interpretation of statutes by referring to contemporaneous events which led to the passing of the statutes, yet the intention of the parties, when they wrote a document, which is in the midst of other documents, might be gathered and further elucidated by the conduct they have pursued. As has been said by modern authorities "the rule appears to be that, however general the words of an ancient grant may be, it is to be construed by evidence of the manner in which the thing granted has always been possessed and used; for so the parties thereto must be supposed to have intended." As each case has to be decided on its own facts, it cannot be laid down with precision that the language deployed in an instrument should govern in all circumstances and for all times notwithstanding the fact the parties who had occasion to refer to it intended that it should be understood in a specified way, if there is such evidence of supervening conduct by the parties, then notwithstanding the express nature of the

8 *D.R. Rathna Murthy* v *Ramappa* (2011)1 SCC 158.
9 *Chunchun Jha* v *Ebadat Ali* AIR 1954 SC 345; (1955)1 SCR 174.

words used in an instrument, such surrounding circumstances might be taken into consideration in order to understand the legal effect of the words used by the parties in the instrument.[10]

It may be useful to recall the settled law that in ascertaining the true nature of a deed the instrument is to be considered as a whole and the intention of the parties has to be ascertained by the terms thereof and not the extraneous circumstances or evidence.[11]

The nomenclature of a deed and the amount of stamp paid on it though relevant is not conclusive on the question of construction.[12] Extrinsic evidence to determine the effect of an instrument is permissible if there is a doubt as to its true meaning.[13]

Intention of the parties can be gone into even when the terms of the deed are not ambiguous.[14] Despite the recital in the document styled as "leave and licence agreement" and that such document will not have the effect of creating a tenancy, it is open to the court to find out on a consideration of the entire terms and the conditions of the document and also the surrounding circumstances attending the execution of such document, its true legal effect and to conclude it to be lease agreement.[15]

In construing deeds which speak by themselves, but which speech is likely to affect some parties to it, the court should take the precaution of seeing that the document is not only technically proved but that the recitals therein are also true. The courts ought not to, as a matter of course, adopt the recitals as true if a genuine doubt by reason of the circumstances and the evidence let in this case arises and which would prompt the court to require a much better standard of proof of the recitals rather than accepting the recitals as such without any further expatiation of the same. In such cases where the courts are compelled to probe the realities of the situation and the truth of the recitals, the court's jurisdiction to buttress such recitals has been recognized consistently by our court and the Supreme Court. Such recitals may be telling and forcible but, yet, they might require further proof for acceptance by a court of law.[16]

10 *Mangalam Pillai* v *C.S. Appavoo Udayar* AIR 1976 Mad 360 at p. 363 (DB).

11 *Prem Agnani* v *Sub-Registrar, Bangalore* AIR 1975 Kant 1 (SB); *Banwarilal* v *Union of India* AIR 1978 Gau 123; *Sitaram* v *Board of Revenue* AIR 1979 All 301; 1979 All LJ 871 (FB); *G. Cariappa* v *Leila Sinha Roy* AIR 1984 Cal 105; 88 CWN 83; (1984)1 CHN 84.

12 *Thayyil Mammo* v *Kolliath Ramunni* AIR 1966 SC 337; (1966)1 SCJ 138.

13 *Godhara Electric Corporation* v *State of Gujarat* AIR 1975 SC 32; (1975)1 SCC 199; (1975)2 SCR 42.

14 *Shankar* v *Arun* 84 CWN 817 at p. 819; (1980)2 Cal LJ 470 at p. 475.

15 *Ratnakar Ramrao* v *Abdul Karim Jailanisaheb* (1978)2 Kant LJ 158.

16 *Manickathammal* v *Nallasami Pillai* AIR 1977 Mad 83 at pp. 85-86 (DB).

Often, in courts, sale deeds are filed where the consideration is recited as received, whereas it is not received as a matter of fact. That is why there is also a lien in favour of the vendor for the unpaid consideration. Specific evidence of a convincing nature must be adduced to show that a sale deed reciting the payment of consideration was really executed for no consideration and that no consideration was intended to be paid. No doubt, a piece of evidence tending to show that, will be recital of the receipt of the consideration when no consideration has, as a matter of fact, been paid or recited. But such a recital will not be conclusive. A court has to go into the whole evidence and come to its own conclusion.[17]

Further requirements and proofs for specific performance In a suit for specific performance of contract, the plaintiff has to prove that he wants to rely upon the contract and that for the performance of the contract he made a demand for such performance by the defendant. Mere evidence that the plaintiff made repeated demands for execution and registration without specifying when or at what point of time he made the demand is of no value. Moreover, mere demand for execution and registration to a servant of the defendant cannot in law be a demand from the defendant himself.[18] Further, if the plaintiff omits to plead some material fact, he will not be allowed to give evidence of that fact at the trial and if by inadvertence some evidence has been led in respect of such a fact, it will not be looked into.[19]

Likewise, if the defendant merely denies the factum of the contract and does not allege that the contract is not enforceable in law, he will be held bound by his pleadings and will be precluded from raising the question of legality or validity of the contract.[20]

The vendee is under a duty to purchase stamps and have a draft sale deed prepared and to submit the same to the vendor.[1]

Limitation Article 54 of the Limitation Act 1963 prescribes a three-year limit for filing a suit for specific performance of a contract.[2] The time is to run from the date fixed for the performance or if no such date is fixed when the plaintiff has notice of the refusal of the performance. The meaning of

17 *Official Receiver of Salem* v *Chinna Goundan* AIR 1957 Mad 630 at p. 631 *per* Panchapkesa Ayyar, J.

18 *Manick Lal Seal* v *K.P. Chowdhury* AIR 1976 Cal 115 at p. 117.

19 *Nirmala* v *Kumode* AIR 1976 Gau 58 at p. 60 (DB).

20 *Bhupal* v *Man Chand* AIR 1973 All 543 at p. 546 following *Kalyanpur Lime Works* v *State of Bihar* AIR 1954 SC 165; 1954 SCR 958; 1954 SCJ 99.

1 *Pakharsingh* v *Kishansingh* AIR 1974 Raj 112 at p. 115 (see also s. 55(1) of the T.P. Act and *Ma Hnit* v *Maung Po Pu* AIR 1919 PC 124; *Ardeshir H. Mama* v *Flora Sassoon* AIR 1928 PC 208).

2 *Shantaben* v *Hasmukhbhai Bhailalbhai Patel* AIR 2013 Guj 193.

the expression 'date fixed for the performance' is to be understood in correct perspective. Though the word 'date' is used in Art. 54, it should not be taken that a particular date should be specifically stated in the agreement. In fact, even if the time of performance cannot be ascertained at the time of agreement itself, if it could be ascertained at the time of performance, it may be said to be a case where the date is fixed for the performance of the contract. For example, an agreement to execute a sale deed after 'saguvalichit' is given can be construed as an agreement where date is fixed. Further, the date that can be fixed with reference to a future event which is certain to happen is the date on which such event takes place.[3] An agreement to execute a sale after 'saguvalichit' was given was held to be a contract in which date was fixed.[4] When the date for performance is fixed, irrespective of the question as to whether the time is the essence of contract or not, limitation would begin to run from the date fixed.[5]

In a case the seller was under a contractual obligation to file an application for obtaining permission from the competent authority in terms of the provisions contained in s. 27 of the Urban Land (Ceiling and Regulation) Act 1976, and agreement of sale deed was to be performed within a period of six months from the date of obtaining of permission from the competent authority in terms of s. 27 of the Urban Land (Ceiling and Regulation) Act 1976, and the purchaser who was sending notices to the seller from time to time to make the said application, immediately after the declaration of said s. 27 as *ultra vires* the Constitution by Supreme Court called upon the seller to perform his part of contract within one month from the date of receipt of the notice. It was held that the limitation would begin to run from the date after expiry of one month from date of receipt of the said notice. Further in any event, the buyer was at least entitled to six months period from the date of the agreement and even if the period of limitation was computed from that date the suit having been instituted within a period a three years from the said date the same would not be barred by limitation in terms of Art. 54 of the Limitation Act 1963.[6] For scope of this Article see *Sumerchand Hukum Chand* v *Hukumchand Mathuradas*,[7] *Manicklal Seal* v *K.P. Chowdhury*,[8] *Suryanarayana Murthy* v *Appana Veerraju*,[9] *Sambu Natha Chakravarty* v *Sushma Sinha*,[10] *K. Kallaiah* v *Ningegowda*,[11] dissenting

3 *K. Venkoji Rao* v *M. Abdul Khuddur Kureshi* AIR 1991 Kant 119 at p. 123.
4 *Hutehegowda* v *H.M. Basaviah* AIR 1954 Mys 29.
5 *Mahaboob Pasha* v *Sayed Zaheeruddin* AIR 1988 Kant 83; ILR (1987) Kant 2830.
6 *Triloki Vishwakarma* v *Zaitun Nisa* AIR 1992 Pat 40.
7 AIR 1965 MP 177 (DB).
8 AIR 1976 Cal 115.
9 AIR 1980 AP 32.
10 AIR 1980 Cal 5.
11 AIR 1982 Kant 93.

from *Lakshmi Narayan Reddiar* v *Singaravelu Naicker*,[12] *Shiv Hiraf Mining Industries* v *State of Maharashtra*,[13] and *Baruna Giri* v *Rajakishore*.[14]

Suit for specific performance—limitation An agreement to sell did not contain any fixed date for performance. Agreement itself was denied by defendants. Suit was filed within few months of receipt of notice about execution of sale deed in favour of third party. Suit for specific performance of agreement to sell was not barred by limitation.[15]

The original agreement had "fixed date" for performance. Plaintiffs remained silent on receipt of a letter subsequently from defendants with request for postponement of performance to future date without fixing any further date for performance. Plaintiffs by their act of forbearance and not insisting on performance forthwith accepted the postponement of performance. Time for performance stood extended. The case was covered by second part of Art. 54 of the Limitation Act 1963. Plaintiffs realized that there was refusal to perform, when they were forcibly evicted from the godown. The suit was filed within the period of limitation which was to be counted from the date of refusal.[16]

Limitation of a suit for declaration, permanent injunction and possession is 12 years under Art. 65 of the Limitation Act. Such limitation is not 3 years under s. 54.[17]

In terms of Art. 54 of the Limitation Act, suit for specific performance of a contract is required to be filed within three years from the date fixed for the performance. However, in the event no specific date for the performance, within a period of three years from the date when the plaintiff notices the refusal.[18]

Court-fees A suit for specific performance of a contract for granting lease together with a prayer for putting the plaintiff in possession of the suit property should be valued under s. 7(*xii*)(*c*) of s. 7 of the West Bengal Court-fees Act 1970. Section 7(*xii*)(*a*) of s. 7 states that in suits for specific performance of a contract of sale should be valued according to the amount of consideration. So, if a part of a contract is already performed and contract of separate part is sought to be enforced in a suit and a separate amount of consideration is fixed for the said part, the plaintiff is to pay court-fee on

12 AIR 1963 Mad 24.
13 AIR 1983 Bom 82 (DB).
14 AIR 1983 Ori 107 (DB).
15 *Sugani* v *Rameshwar Das* AIR 2006 SC 2172; see *Pancharan Dhara* v *Monmatha Nath Maity* AIR 2006 SC 2281 (time to file suit shall be deemed to run only when plaintiff had notice that performance had been refused).
16 *S. Brahmanand* v *K.R. Muthugopal* AIR 2006 SC 40.
17 *Ghewarchand* v *M/s. Mahendra Singh* AIR 2018 SC 4857; (2018)10 SCC 588.
18 *Himmatlal* v *Rajratan Concept* (2018)3 MP LJ 235; AIR 2018 MP 197.

the distinct part in the contract in respect of which he seeks specific performance.[19] Differing from this Patna decision it has been held in *T. Gangadharaswamy* v *Dowlatram*,[20] that when specific performance of contract is sought to be enforced only in part, *i.e.* in respect of only one of the items of property covered by the agreement—there the defendant had already performed the contract in respect of other item—then too court-fee is to be paid on the whole agreement and not on the basis of the value of only one item. The plaintiff requests the court to give effect to the arrangement which he entered into, but desires that in effecting the conveyance only the property described in the plaint should be conveyed and possession in respect thereof should be given. As the court will in any event have to declare the original arrangement entered into and only on that basis should give relief to the plaintiff, the suit will have to be valued on the consideration mentioned therein.

In an Allahabad case under the corresponding provision in the UP Court-fees Act *R* entered into an agreement of sale of property belonging to two brothers, *B* and *M*. The agreement was executed by *B* for himself as also on behalf of *M*. The agreement was a composite one. Later *M* sold his share to a third party and the plaintiff *R* filed a suit of specific performance of *B*'s share. It was held as the agreement is a composite one the plaintiff is to pay court-fee on the entire sum agreed as sale consideration not half.[21]

Suit for specific performance and possession As provided in s. 22 of the Specific Relief Act no relief of possession can be granted to a plaintiff in a suit for specific performance unless the plaintiff in addition to the prayer for specific performance of the contract also prays for recovery of possession. It has further been provided that at any stage of the proceeding court may allow an amendment to include the prayer for possession. Relief of possession can be granted only if it is specifically prayed for.[22] Relief can also be given if such prayer is present by necessary implication from the nature of relief claimed for.[1]

As held in *Kartick Chandra Pal* v *Dibakar*,[2] when a contract is to be specifically enforced, it simply means simply that when the parties do not agree to perform the contract mutually; the intervention of the court will do all such things as the parties would have been bound to do had this been done without the intervention of the court. A sale of property after payment of the consideration and upon due execution of the deed of sale presupposes

19 *Thakur Prasad Singh* v *Janki Devi* AIR 1967 Pat 281; 1966 BLJR 644.
20 AIR 1975 Kant 203; ILR (1975) Kant 891; (1975)2 Kant LJ 35.
21 *Radhey Shyam Bhargava* v *Biharilal Gupta* (1985)1 Cur Civ Cas 563 (All).
22 *Lavinder Kumar Sharma* v *Pramod Kumar* AIR 2011 P&H 30.
1 *Excel Dealcomm (P) Ltd.* v *Asset Reconstruction Co. (India) Ltd.* (2015)8 SCC 219.
2 AIR 1952 Cal 362.

and requires the vendor to put the purchaser in possession of the property. The court when allowing the prayer for specific performance vests the executing court with all the powers which are required to give full effect to the decree for specific performance. The Supreme Court in *Babulal* v *Hazarilal Kishori Lal*,[3] approvingly referred to this passage. The ratio of this decision is that the relief of possession is dormant but alive in every suit for specific performance. The relief of possession in effect and in substance is ancillary to the main relief of specific performance of contract. So, the plaint can be amended at any stage to include the relief of possession. So much so that, this relief for possession can be granted even by executing court, because the court when allows a prayer for specific performance it gives to the executing court full power to give full effect of the decree of specific performance.[4] Where the court allowed the plaintiff's prayer for specific performance of the contract which itself incorporated a clause for delivery of possession and the decree contained a direction upon the judgment-debtor to sell the suit property to the plaintiff in terms of the agreement it would necessarily be taken to embody a mandate to fulfil all the terms including the term of delivery of possession. The fact that the decree was silent with regard to the prayer for possession would be immaterial. In such a case the principle that a prayer made in the plaint not being allowed, must be deemed to have been refused would not apply.[5]

A son either married or unmarried has no legal right to live in the house which is selfacquired property of his father. He can live in that house upto the time his father allows him to reside there. Merely because the father have allowed him to live in that house so long as his relation with parents are cordial. If a suit for possession is filed by the father against his son, he is entitled to a decree for possession.[6] Evidence on record shows that the plaintiff was in prior possession of suit premises and permitted his son and daughter-in-law to stay in suit property. Plaintiff is entitled to recover possession of suit premises.[7] Where a prospective buyer, being in possession of the suit property pursuant to part performance of agreement for sale, filed a suit for specific performance but the suit was dismissed, it was held that once suit for specific performance filed by the prospective buyer is dismissed, his possession becomes unauthorized and illegal, and the protection of s. 53A of the Transfer of Property Act would not be available. Consequently, the seller, in such an eventuality, is entitled claim back the possession from the prospective buyer on the ground of ownership.[8]

3 AIR 1982 SC 818; (1982)1 SCC 525.
4 *S.S. Rajabathar* v *N.A. Sayeed* AIR 1974 Mad 289; (1974)1 Mad LJ 166; 87 Mad LW 271.
5 *Debabrata Tarafdar* v *Biraj Mohạn Bardhan* AIR 1983 Cal 51.
6 *Sachin* v *Jhabbu Lal* AIR 2017 Del 1.
7 *Sanjay Jairam Shinde* v *Jaivam Sony Shinde* AIR 2017 Bom 22.
8 *Revanasiddayya* v *Gangamma* (2018)1 SCC 610.

Separate court-fee for relief of possession—need of A suit for getting a sale deed executed and registered by the defendant by way of specific performance of a contract for sale and for possession of the property contracted to be sold falls under s. 7(*x*)(*a*) and not under s. 7(*v*) or 7(*vi*), Court Fees Act 1870. The mere fact that possession is claimed would not entitle the court to ignore the essential character of the suit for specific performance and to regard it as one for possession which cannot be decreed unless and until the plaintiff gets specific performance of the contract.[9] In a suit for specific performance there is no question of primary and secondary relief, and both the execution of the conveyance and delivery of possession are essential reliefs. Further, without getting a conveyance it is not possible to get possession.[10] In such a suit the relief for specific performance is the main relief and the relief of possession is ancillary to it. But they do not form distinct subjects within the meaning of s. 17 of the Court Fees Act 1870. Court-fee is therefore payable under s. 7(*x*) of the Court Fees Act.[11]

In *Asit Chowdhury* v *Prafulla Bose*,[12] there was an agreement of sale for ₹60,000 and the plaintiff was put to possession in pursuance of the agreement of sale. But later the defendant dispossessed the plaintiff who sued for recovery of possession. It was held that an objective standard being available the suit should be valued at ₹60,000. It is not clear from the decision rendered by S.N. Sanyal, J if it was a suit for specific performance of contract of sale and for recovery of possession. But presumably the relief of recovery of possession was there, for a mere agreement of sale does not create any title. It may not also be a suit for specific performance because according to the recent trend of decisions s. 53A, T.P. Act can also be invoked by one *qua* plaintiff. Be that as it may, had it been a suit for specific performance of contract and recovery of possession, the suit would have immediately attracted the ratio of the *S.B.* case,[13] and no separate court-fee would have been payable for recovery of possession. But the ultimate decision in *Asit Chowdhury's* case[14] is correct because at any rate the plaintiff was to pay court-fee on the value of the consideration agreed. In an AP case,[15] the suit was for specific performance of a contract of lease and possession of demised premises (vacant site) with structures built thereon. Under the terms of the agreement sought to be specifically enforced the structures which would be built by the defendant was to be given possession of along with the demised premises. It was held that it is quite apparent and

9 *Muljibhai* v *Bai Chanchal* AIR 1945 Bom 81; 46 Bom LR 731.
10 *Gudia Dullabho Sahu* v *Cinni Adinarayana* AIR 1937 Mad 831.
11 *Dhiraj Bala Karia* v *Jethia Estate* AIR 1983 Cal 166; (1982)2 Cal LJ 225; (1983)1 Civ LJ 377 (SB).
12 AIR 1984 Cal 366; (1984)1 CHN 41.
13 *Dhiraj Bala Karia* v *Jethia Estate* AIR 1983 Cal 166; (1982)2 Cal LJ 225.
14 AIR 1984 Cal 366.
15 *Ahmed Bin Mohammed Meera* v *A. Devaji Rao* (1980)1 Andh WR 422.

natural that in the process of enforcement of the agreement possession of the said structures is only ancillary or incidental to the main relief of performance of agreement of lease. So no separate court-fee is payable for possession of the structures. A suit for specific performance of a contract of sale of land and for possession thereof with *mesne profits* impleading the vendor and a subsequent transferee from him who was in possession falls under s. 7(*x*)(*a*) of the Court-Fees Act 1870.[16]

The Tamil Nadu Court Fees and Suits Valuation Act 1955 which has repealed the Court Fees Act 1870 has made the position clear. Under s. 42 of the Tamil Nadu Act, in a suit for specific performance, whether with or without possession, fee shall be payable in the case of a contract for sale, computed on the amount of consideration, in the case of a contract of mortgage, computed on the amount agreed to be secured by the mortgages, in the case of a contract of lease, computed on the aggregate amount of the fine or premium, if any, and on the average of the annual rent agreed to be paid, in the case of a contract of exchange on the amount of consideration, or as the case may be on the market value of the property sought to be got in exchange and in other cases where the consideration for the promise sought to be enforced has a market value, computed on such market value, or where such consideration has no market value, at the rates specified in s. 50.

Defence to action for calls on shares or specific performance A person who is induced to take shares by misrepresentation in a prospectus may obtain relief on an application to rectify the register of members by remaining his name from it and claim for the return of money with interest. Such a person may set up the defence of misrepresentation to an action for calls on shares registered in his name, if he has commenced proceedings for rectification or given some undertaking to commence them within a reasonable time after he has discovered the misrepresentation or if the shares are forfeited. To an action for specific performance of agreement to take shares or debentures, the usual defences in such an action are available.[17]

In this connection it is apposite to refer to Fry on *Specific Performance*, 6th Ed., Part III where the Jurist-Judge has catalogued and discussed the defences available in a suit for specific performance as follows:

(*i*) Incapacity to contract

(*ii*) Non-conclusion of to contract

(*iii*) Incompleteness of the contract

16 *K.P. Tiwari* v *Baiju* AIR 1954 Pat 24; ILR (1954)22 Pat 269.

17 Halsbury's *Laws of England*, 4th Ed., vol. 7, para 238.

(*iv*) Uncertainty of the contract

(*v*) Want of fairness in the contract

(*vi*) Hardship of the contract

(*vii*) Inadequacy of the consideration

(*viii*) Want of mutuality in the contract

(*ix*) Illegality of the contract

(*x*) Contracts *ultra vires*

(*xi*) Statute of frauds and part performance

(*xii*) Formalities required in contracts by corporations

(*xiii*) Misrepresentation

(*xiv*) Fraud

(*xv*) Mistake

(*xvi*) Incapacity of the court to perform part of the contract

(*xvii*) Defect in the subject matter of the contract

(*xviii*) Want of a good title

(*xix*) Failure of the consideration

(*xx*) Default on the part of the plaintiff

(*xxi*) Acts in contravention of the contract

(*xxii*) Non-performance of conditions

(*xxiii*) Incapacity of the defendant to perform his part of the contract

(*xxiv*) Rescission of the contract

(*xxv*) Lapse of time

Though the decisions quoted thereunder are of the courts in England, they have much bearing in the interpretation and application of the provisions of the Specific Relief Act which is based primarily on the law of England.

CHAPTER 4

Jurisdiction and Powers of Court

PART I

Substituted Performance of Contract

Introduction A strong contract enforcement system is essential for the smooth flow of trade and commerce, and for developing confidence of investors. Globally the approach to contract law remedies are either: (*i*) compelling performance, by holding parties to their contract through grant of specific performance and injunctive reliefs, or (*ii*) compensating for loss and damages caused by breach of contract, with specific performance being in the nature of exception rather than the rule. The latter approach has been preferred in India under the Specific Relief Act 1963.[1] The remedy in Indian law has been equitable and parties cannot claim it as a matter of right although it is lawful but such discretion should be exercised judicially and prudently.[2] The purpose of contract remedies is to place a disappointed promisee in as good a position as he would have enjoyed had his promisor performed. Contract law has two methods of achieving this "compensation goal": requiring the breaching party to pay damages, either to enable the promisee to purchase a substitute performance, or to replace the net gains that the promised performance would have generated; or requiring the breaching party to render the promised performance.[3]

Legal and equitable rights Equity is defined as a set of legal principles, entitled by their intrinsic superiority to supersede the older law.[4] Equitable remedies are adverted to soften the rigidity of legal rules to fill up the gaps

1 Report of the Expert Committee on the Specific Relief Act 1963, p. 3.

2 *Shivaji Yallappa Patil* v *Ranajeet Appasaheb Patil* (2018)16 SCC 725; (2019)1 SCC (Civ) 692; AIR 2018 SC 1961.

3 Alan Schwartz, *The Case for Specific Performance*, The Yale Law Journal, vol. 89, p. 271.

4 Henry Maine, *Ancient Law*, 1950, Ch. III, p. 36 (World Classics).

legal system inheres with a view to obviate the chances of gravest injustice that may be caused to the litigants by strict application of such legal rules. Equity is thus a body of rules or principles which form an appendage to the general rules of law, or a gloss upon them. In origin at least, it represents the attempt of English legal system to meet a problem which confronts all legal systems reaching a certain stage of development. In order to ensure the smooth running of society it is necessary to formulate general rules which work well enough in the majority of cases. Sooner or later, however, cases arise in which, in some unforeseen set of facts, the general rules produce substantial unfairness. When this occurs, justice requires either an amendment of the rule or, if the rule is not freely changeable, a further rule or body of rules to mitigate the severity of the rules of law. This new body of rules (or "equity") is therefore distinguishable from the general body of law, not because it relates necessarily to a different subject-matter, but merely because it appears at a later stage of legal development.[5] The *locus classicus* on equity was statement of Sir Nathan Wright, LJ in *Lord Dudley and Ward* v *Lady Dudley*:[6]

> "Equity is no part of the law, but a moral virtue, which qualifies, moderates, and reforms the rigour, hardness, and edge of the law, and is an universal truth; it does also assist the law where it is defective and weak in the Constitution (which is the life of the law) and defends the law from crafty evasions, delusions, and new subtleties, invested and contrived to evade and delude the common law, whereby such as have undoubted right are made remediless: and this is the office of equity, to support and protect the common law from shifts and crafty contrivances against the justice of the law. Equity therefore does not destroy the law, nor create it, but assist it."

However, the legal rights differ from equitable rights, albeit they are not rivals or competitors. The exercise of legal rights depends upon the enforcement of legal rules made by the legislature. But, the equitable rights are exercisable at the discretion of the Court. A court of law cannot exercise its discretionary jurisdiction *de hors* the statutory law. Its discretion must be exercised in terms of the existing statute. In England, the court of equity exercises jurisdiction in equity. The courts of India do not possess any such exclusive jurisdiction. The courts in India exercise jurisdiction both in equity as well as law but exercise of equity jurisdiction is always subject to the provisions of law. If exercise of equity jurisdiction would violate the express provisions contained in law, the same cannot be done. Equity jurisdiction can be exercised only when no law operates in the field.[7]

5 Paton, *The Text Book of Jurisprudence*, 4th Ed. 1972, p. 230; Lee, *Elements of Roman law*, 4th Ed. 1956, pp. 10, 11; Snell's *Equity*, 31st Ed. 2005, p. 4.
6 [1705] Prec Ch 241 at 244.
7 *Shiv Kumar Sharma* v *Santosh Kumari* (2007)8 SCC 600.

In *Shamsu Suhara Beevi* v G. *Alex*[8] the Supreme Court, while dealing with a matter relating to grant of compensation by the High Court under s. 21 of the Specific Relief Act in addition to the relief of specific performance in the absence of prayer made to that effect, either in the plaint or amending the same at any later stage of the proceedings to include the relief of compensation in addition to the relief of specific performance, observed:

> "..... Grant of such a relief in the teeth of express provisions of the statute to the contrary is not permissible. On equitable considerations court cannot ignore or overlook the provisions of the statute. Equity must yield to law."

Another example in this connection is the law of limitation. Law of limitation may harshly affect a particular party but it has to be applied with all its rigour when the statute so prescribes and the courts have no power to extend the period of limitation on equitable grounds. However, many of the principles of English equity have taken statutory form in India and have been incorporated in occasional provisions of various Indian statutes such as the Indian Trusts Act, the Specific Relief Act, Transfer of Property Act etc. and where a question of interpretation of such equity based statutory provisions arises, courts would be justified in seeking aid from the equity source.[9]

Law prior to amendment Section 20 of the Specific Relief Act 1963 preserves judicial discretion to courts as to decreeing specific performance. The court should meticulously consider all facts and circumstances of the case. The court is not bound to grant specific performance merely because it is lawful to do so. The motive behind the litigation should also enter into the judicial verdict. The court should take care to see that it is not used as an instrument of oppression to have an unfair advantage to the plaintiff.[10] Granting of specific performance is an equitable relief, though the same is now governed by the statutory provisions of the Specific Relief Act 1963. These equitable principles are nicely incorporated in s. 20 of the Act. While granting a decree for specific performance, these salutary guidelines shall be in the forefront of the mind of the court.[11] Thus, the provision of s. 20 of the Specific Relief Act 1963 was discretionary before it was amended in 2018 by the Specific Relief (Amendment) Act 2018. After its amendment, it is no longer discretionary. Application of s. 20 of the Act after amendment in 2018 is strictly controlled by the language it has used. Section 20 has introduced the concept of 'substituted performance of contract'. Now, it is a legal right and not equitable one.

8 (2004)8 SCC 569.

9 *Bai Dosabai* v *Mathuradas Govinddas* (1980)3 SCC 545.

10 *Parakunnan Veetill Joseph's Son Mathew* v *Nedumbara Kuruvila's Son* 1987 Supp SCC 340; AIR 1987 SC 2328.

11 *A.C. Arulappan* v *Ahalya Naik* (2001)6 SCC 600.

Background to the Specific Relief (Amendment) Act 2018 The World Bank released the *Ease of Doing Business* rankings and the rank of India therein was 163. The World Bank pained a very dismal picture of India in enforcing contracts and ease of doing business. Generally speaking, the legal regime in India dealing with enforcing contracts is consisted of the Indian Contract Act 1872 and the Specific Relief Act 1963. The former lays down the general principles governing contracts and awarding damages in case of breach of contract, whereas the latter deals with specific performance of contract based on equitable principles. The Specific Relief Act 1963, as mentioned above, provides for specific performance as a discretionary relief by the courts if the court is satisfied that the damages would be inadequate compensation for the breach of contract. Though the specific performance is the remedy available for the breach of contract, yet the award of damages has been the usual and normal remedy for breach of contract in lieu of or at times in addition to the performance of contract.[12]

Need for substituted performance of contract Before the amendment of Act in 2018, the general rule was awarding of damages for the breach of contract. However, compelling specific performance of the contract in breach of contract was the exception. Thus, the image of the legal regime was that in case of contractual breaches, parties embroiled in long drawn litigations only for the purpose of determining the quantum of damages. Therefore, if the parties take years to claim damage, and not the specific performance of the contract, it is but natural that India would hardly be an "investment friendly destination". Thus, to obviate the problem and to fine-tune the system of enforcement of contract, the Government of India appointed a six members expert committee to examine the entire system of enforcement of contract so as to suggest measures to overcome the bottlenecks in ensuring India an investment hub. The expert committee submitted its report to the Government of India and on the basis of the report of the expert committee; the Parliament passed the Specific Relief (Amendment) Bill 2017 which, *inter alia*, amended s. 20 of the Act wherein the Courts had discretion in awarding specific performance. By way of amendment, entire provision of s. 20 of the Act was replaced by a new provision. The newly-replaced provision of s. 20 has introduced a new concept of "substituted performance of contract" generally prevalent in civil law system. This is also known as "right to cover". According to the newly-introduced concept of "substituted performance of contract", the party has the option to arrange for performance of contract by a third party or his own agency to recover the costs from the party who has defaulted or breached the contract. But, the rider is that the loss can be claimed only after the performance of the contract by either a

12 World Bank Report, Doing Business 2018, (31st October 2017), 11.3.1.

third party or by the own agency of the party. Thus, the legislative intention in enacting this provision is aimed at ensuring the performance of contract as a primary rule rather than awarding damages for the breach of contract.

Amended provision of s. 20 of the Act The Specific Relief Act 1963 has been recently amended by the Specific Relief (Amendment) Act 2018. By way of amendment, the remedy of *substituted performance* has been introduced by the Parliament. Earlier the principle relating to damages was applied by Courts to mitigate the loss suffered by a party due to the breach of contract, yet the legislature has given statutory recognition under the amended provision of s. 20 of the Act, though the statutory remedy is available as an option to the party who has suffered breach. Thus, s. 20 now gives an option to an aggrieved party to get the contract performed by a third party, if other party of the contract breaches the contract. This aspect was not in the earlier law and in case of breach the court has the discretion to award damages. However, it is submitted that the newly-introduced provision in s. 20 of the Act poses no problem to get the unfinished work done through third party so far as private parties to contract are concerned. In such cases, the unfinished work would be completed by involving another contractor. But, the situation gets complicated in case of Government contract or in a contract where one of the parties is Government, since in case of a Government contract the formalities prescribed are in addition to those contained in the Contract Act.[13] Thus, to get the unfinished work done in a Government contract, due care is required to be taken.

Analysis of s. 20 of the Specific Relief Act after amendment Section 20 of the Specific Relief Act 1963 as amended by the Amendment Act 2018 reads as follows:

> (1) Without prejudice to the generality of the provisions contained in the Indian Contract Act 1872 (9 of 1872), and, except as otherwise agreed upon by the parties, where the contract is broken due to non-performance of promise by any party, the party who suffers by such breach shall have the option of substituted performance through a third party or by his own agency, and, recover the expenses and other costs actually incurred, spent or suffered by him, from the party committing such breach.
>
> (2) No substituted performance of contract under sub-sec. (1) shall be undertaken unless the party who suffers such breach has given a notice in writing, of not less than thirty days, to the party in breach calling upon him to perform the contract within such time as specified in the notice, and on his refusal or failure to do so, he may get the same performed by a third party or by his own agency:

13 See, Article 299 of the Constitution of India.

Provided that the party who suffers such breach shall not be entitled to recover the expenses and costs under sub-sec. (1) unless he has got the contract performed through a third party or by his own agency.

(3) Where the party suffering breach of contract has got the contract performed through a third party or by his own agency after giving notice under sub-section (1), he shall not be entitled to claim relief of specific performance against the party in breach.

(4) Nothing in this section shall prevent the party who has suffered breach of contract from claiming compensation from the party in breach.

A cursory look at the newly replaced provision of s. 20 of the Act denotes that the scheme of s. 20 as it was before amendment has been entirely altered. Earlier, s. 20 deals with specific performance of contract as a discretionary relief, but now the thrust is on performance of contract either by the party who has suffered breach or through a third party. Therefore, the shift in the legislative thinking is noticeable. By amending s. 20, the legislature as sought to inculcate a kind of feeling in the business community that the performance of contract will be the rule and therefore where the party in breach or default has refused or failed to perform the contract, the innocent party has the option to get the contract performed through a third party or by his own agency. After the amendment, the Courts have been divested of the discretionary power to award damages in lieu of performance of contract where the contract is breached. Further, the party who has suffered breach of contract may claim costs and expenses for getting the contract performed by either third party or his own agency. However, there is one rider under sub-sec. (3). It says that where the party suffering breach has got the contract performed through a third party or by his own agency after giving notice under sub-sec. (1), he shall not be entitled to claim relief of specific performance against the party in breach.

Notice It is incumbent upon the party, who has suffered breach, to serve a notice to the party who has defaulted or breached, of not less than 30 days, calling upon him to perform the contract within such period of time as specified in the notice. If the party in breach, after getting such notice, refuses or fails to perform the contract within the specified period, the party who has suffered may get the contract performed by a third party or by his own agency. Thus, before exercising the option of substituted performance of contract, the party who has suffered breach is required to give notice to the party in default.

Section 20 of the Act whether prospective or retrospective The Amendment Act is silent as to whether the amended provision is prospective or retrospective in nature. Of the various rules guiding how a legislation has to be interpreted, one established rule is that unless a contrary intention appears, a legislation is presumed not to be intended to have a retrospective operation. The idea behind the rule is that a current law should govern current activities. Law passed today cannot apply to the events of the past. If we do something today, we do it keeping in view the law of today and in force and not tomorrow's backward adjustment of it. Our belief in the nature of the law is founded on the bedrock that every human being is entitled to arrange his affairs by relying on the existing law and should not find that his plans have been retrospectively upset. This principle of law is known as *lex prospicit non respicit*: law looks forward not backward.[14] A retrospective legislation is contrary to the general principle that legislation by which the conduct of mankind is to be regulated when introduced for the first time to deal with future acts ought not to change the character of past transactions carried on upon the faith of the then existing law.[15] There is a presumption against the retrospective operation of a statute and further a statute is not to be construed to have a greater retrospective operation than its language renders necessary, but an amending Act which affects the procedure is presumed to be retrospective, unless the amending Act provides otherwise.[16] The provision of s. 20 of the Act is not procedural in nature and it is also not a part of procedural law. Thus, according to the established rule of interpretation, any amendment to a statute is presumed to be prospective unless it is provided otherwise by the amending Act directly or by necessary implication. However, the amendment in procedural law is always retrospective unless provided otherwise by the amending Act. Thus, it is submitted that the amended provision of s. 20 is prospective and not retrospective in its application. No such intendment of retrospectivity is discernible in the amendment provision of s. 20 of the Act. Therefore, the pending cases at the time of the amendment will be decided with reference to the section as it stood prior to its amendment in 2018.

English law The rule of the common law is that, where a party sustains a loss by reason of a breach of a contract, he is, so far as money can do it, to be placed in the same situation, with respect to the damages, as if the contract had been performed.[17] The first principle of contract of damages is that, as far as possible, he who has proved a breach of bargain to supply what he contracted to get is to be placed, as far as money can do it, in as good a situation as if the contract had been performed. The fundamental basis is thus compensation for pecuniary loss naturally flowing from the breach; but this first principle is qualified by a second, which imposes on a plaintiff the duty of taking all reasonable steps to mitigate the loss consequent on the breach, and debars him from claiming in respect of any part of the

14 *CIT* v *Vatika Township (P) Ltd.* (2015)1 SCC 1.
15 *Phillips* v *Eyre* [1870] LR 6 QB 1.
16 *Shyam Sunder* v *Ram Kumar* (2001)8 SCC 24; AIR 2001 SC 2472.
17 [1848]1 Ex 850 at 855; 154 ER 363 at 365.

damage which is due to his neglect to take such step.[18] In English law, this principle is known as '*doctrine of mitigation*'. The doctrine is based on the principle that there must be just allocation of burdens and benefits between the plaintiff and the defendant.

Vicarious performance A contracting party can in the case of many contracts enter into an arrangement by which some other person may perform for him, as far as he is concerned, the obligations of the contract, and the other contracting party will be obliged to accept that performance if it is performance in accordance with the terms of the contract. The contracting party will, however, be liable for any breach that may happen, and the other contracting party is not bound or indeed, entitled to sue the substituted person for breach of contract, although there may, of course, be a remedy in tort, e.g. where the substituted person negligently damages or causes the loss of goods entrusted to him. This is technically known as vicarious performance, and it is "quite a mistake to regard that as an assignment of the contract: it is not.[19] However, the promisor cannot substitute for the agreed performance anything different, even though the substituted performance might appear to be better than, or at least equivalent to, the agreed performance.[20]

Doctrine of mitigation in Indian law Mitigation of loss is a principle engrafted in s. 73 of the Contract Act. It enacts the formula for calculation of damages, for breach of contract. The principle of mitigation obliges the non-defaulting party to take steps and see that the damage is minimized.[1] The principle of mitigation of loss does not give any right to the party who is in breach of the contract but it is a concept that has to be borne in mind by the court while awarding damages.[2] The correct statement of law in this behalf is to be found in Halsbury's *Laws of England*[3] which runs as under:

> "*Plaintiff's duty to mitigate loss.* The plaintiff must take all reasonable steps to mitigate the loss which he has sustained consequent upon the defendant's wrong, and, if he fails to do so, he cannot claim damages for any such loss which he ought reasonably to have avoided."

Again, in para 1194 at p. 478 the following statement occurs under the heading *Standard of conduct required of the plaintiff*:

> "The plaintiff is only required to act reasonably, and whether he has done so is a question of fact in the circumstances of each particular case, and

18 *Westinghouse Electric & Manufacturing Co. Ltd.* v *Underground Electric Railways Co of London Ltd.* [1912] AC 673 at p. 689.
19 Chitty on *Contracts*, 27th Ed., p. 987.
20 Chitty on *Contracts*, 28th Ed., vol. 1, para 22, p. 1098.
1 *Hans Raj Ghai* v *Lt. Governor* ILR (2009)1 Del 179.
2 *M. Lachia Settv and Sons Ltd.* v *Coffee Board* (1980)4 SCC 636.
3 Halsbury's *Laws of England*, 4th Ed., vol. 12, para 1193, p. 477.

> not a question of law. He must act not only in his own interests but also in the interests of the defendant and keep down the damages, so far as it is reasonable and proper, by acting reasonably in the matter... In cases of breach of contract the plaintiff is under no obligation to do anything other than in the ordinary course of business, and where he has been placed in a position of embarrassment the measures which he may be driven to adopt in order to extricate himself ought not to be weighed in nice scales at the instance of the defendant whose breach of contract has occasioned the difficulty...."

Explanation to s. 73 of the Contract Act provides that in estimating the loss or damage arising from a breach of contract, the means which existed of remedying the inconvenience caused by the non-performance of the contract be taken into account. Thus, the explanation implies that if the seller of goods or services defaults, the buyer may have to get the goods and services elsewhere and even by some additional cost. Therefore, while calculating the loss or damage arising from the breach of the contract and fixing damages, *the additional cost* can be taken in to account. The *explanation* thus, in essence, provides the remedy of substituted performance of contract, though the express provision for substituted performance of contract has been made for the first time in any legislation.

Section 40 of the Contract Act and substituted performance Section 40 of the Contract Act provides that if it appears from the nature of the case that it was the intention of the parties to any contract that any promise contained in it should be performed by promissor himself, such promise must be performed by the promissor himself. *In other cases, the promissor or his representative may employ a competent person to perform it.* Thus, where *A* promises to pay *B* a sum of money, *A* may perform this promise, either by personally paying the money to *B*, or by causing it be paid to *B* by another; and, if *A* dies before the time appointed for payment, his representative must perform the promise, or employ some person to do so.

Concept of substituted performance is a modification of doctrine of mitigation The concept of substituted performance of contract as enacted by s. 20 of the Specific Relief Act is a modification of the doctrine of mitigation. The introduction of the concept in s. 20 is for the first time in a common law jurisdiction. However, the change brought about in the existing law by way of the Amendment Act of 2018 is aimed at encouraging and enforcing the performance of contract. It is submitted that the parties to a contract will not now, as a general rule, resort to litigation after breaching contracts. The introduction of the concept of substituted performance of contract will put to an end the problem of lop-sided compensation. It has now settled the position of law that performance of contract is the rule either by the party himself or otherwise. That apart, the new law provides that damages would be awarded in addition to specific performance. This will also be a kind of deterrent against practice of breaching the contract. Thus, the legislative intent in enacting s. 20 is to bring about a paradigm shift in the matter of performance of contract.

Timely completion of contract India is a fast developing country. Therefore, timely completion of contract is a must, in particular, where the contract involves public utility. Earlier, the law was discretionary and as a result the courts used to award damages in case of breach of contract. The specific performance of contract was an exception. This has resulted in delaying the completion of several infrastructure projects due to long-drawn litigation. The ultimate loss was to the developing economy. But, now, with the amendment in s. 20 and thereby doing away with of the discretionary jurisdiction of the court, such large infrastructure projects would be completed with time. Section 20A has been added by the Specific Relief (Amendment) Act 2018 in this regard by the Parliament.

Section 20A of the Specific Relief Act This is a newly-added provision. It debars the court to grant injunction in a suit under this Act involving a contract relating to an infrastructure projects specified in Schedule, where granting injunction would cause impediment or delay in the progress or completion of such infrastructure project. However, infrastructure project means the category of projects and infrastructure Sub-sectors specified in the Schedule. Moreover, s. 41 of the Act has also been amended to provide that the court cannot grant injunction if it would impede or delay the progress or completion of any infrastructure project or interfere with the continued provision of relevant facility related thereto or services being the subject matter of such project.[4] It is submitted that though the inclusion of provision debarring the courts to grant injunctions as noted above may be with an avowed object of encouraging performance of contracts in infrastructure projects and infusing confidence in the parties to contract that the completion of large infrastructure projects would not be delayed because of issuance of injunction by the courts, there is every possibility that the courts may refuse injunction in some *bona fide* cases. However, the amended provisions are aimed at keeping the Specific Performance Act at par with the changes taking place in the field of economic growth in India and abroad so that the age-old provisions may not act as stumbling blocks in *ease of doing business in India*.

Special Courts Section 20B of the Act contemplates establishing of Special Courts. The State Government, in consultation with the Chief Justice of the High Court, shall designate, by notification published in the Official

4 Section 41(*h-a*) as *inserted* vide the Specific Relief (Amendment) Act 2018 with effect from 1.10.2018.

Gazette, one or more Civil Courts as Special Courts within the local limits of the area to exercise jurisdiction and to try a suit under this Act in respect of contracts relating to infrastructure projects. Thus, Civil Courts may be designated as Special Courts for the purposes of disposing of suits involving contracts relating to infrastructure projects. However, it is submitted that the creation of Special Courts by way of amendment in the Act may affect the jurisdiction of the Courts under the Commercial Courts Act 2015 as there is every possibility of overlapping of jurisdiction between the Special Courts under the Specific Relief Act and the Commercial Courts under the Commercial Courts Act 2015 particularly where the suit involves contracts relating to infrastructure projects, construction, etc.

Concept of right to recover The amendment of s. 20 of the Act has given statutory recognition to the concept of 'right to recover' in contract which permits an aggrieved party in case of a breach of contract to get the contract performed by third party and recover at the same time the expenses, cots or loss for such substituted performance of contract from the party who has breached the performance of contract. However, the remedy of substituted performance of contract does not in any way debar the aggrieved party to claim damages for breach of contract. Section 20 emphasizes that right to recover the loss from the defaulting party must be limited to costs actually incurred, spent or suffered by the aggrieved party.

Power to engage experts After the amendment in the Specific Relief Act in 2018, the Court is now empowered to engage experts under s. 14A of the Act where the court considers it necessary to get expert opinion to assist it on any specific issue involved in the suit, it may engage one or more experts and direct to report to it on such issue and may secure attendance of the expert for providing evidence, including production of documents on the issue. This will add to the ability of the court to deal with the technical issues involved in a suit for specific performance of contract concerning construction, development or contract involving public utility. The court may require or direct any person to give relevant information to the expert or to produce, or to provide access to, any relevant documents, goods or other property for his inspection. Such opinion or report given by the expert shall form part of the record of the suit. Taking the assistance of the expert by the courts is not new to Indian legal system. Section 45 of the Evidence Act provides for taking assistance of an expert when the court thinks of forming an opinion upon a point of foreign law, or of science, or art, or as to the identity of handwriting or finger impressions. Section 26 of the Arbitration and Conciliation Act 1996 empowers the arbitral tribunal to appoint one or more experts to report to it on specific issues to be determined by the arbitral tribunal. Sensing the need for such provision of expert evidence, the Expert Committee on the Specific Relief Act has recommended that courts should have the power to summon expert evidence not only on the facts but also on technical/scientific issues. In India, the Evidence Act and CPC do not have specific provisions authorizing courts to summon expert evidence so as to enable the court to seek expert assistance at its own instance on complex technical/scientific issues requiring specialized knowledge/expertise from the experts in various fields. Considering the growing number of transactions involving complex or technical issues requiring specific technical or scientific understanding or knowledge, in addition to the authority to take evidence on facts, for effective redressal of the disputes, it would be appropriate to make provisions in the Act empowering the courts to examine experts in the relevant fields. This would assist the court in appropriately determining the issues in expeditious and efficient manner.[5]

Part II

Nature and Limit of Remedy

Prior to the amendment of the Specific Relief Act in 2018, the jurisdiction to decree of specific performance prior to amendment was discretionary, and the court was not bound to grant such relief because it was lawful to do so. All the same, the discretion must have been exercised in a reasonable manner guided by sound judicial principles and not arbitrarily. If these principles were not observed, the judgment might be upset in appeal. Section 20(1), Specific Relief Act prior to the amendment provided that "the jurisdiction to decree specific performance is discretionary and the court is not bound to grant such relief merely because it is lawful to do so, but the discretion of the court is not arbitrary but sound and reasonable, guided by judicial principles and capable of correction by a court of appeal". Thus the relief of specific performance was discretionary.[6] This discretion was, however, to be exercised in a judicial manner and could not be arbitrary.[7] Under s. 20 of the Specific Relief Act the relief of specific performance of contract was discretionary but not arbitrary. The cases providing for a guide to courts to exercise discretion one way or the other are only illustrative, they are not exhaustive.[8] Relief of specific performance of an agreement of sale was a discretionary relief. An agreement was contingent upon eviction of tenant. There was nothing to show that tenant was evicted from disputed premises at any point of time. Court was not bound to grant decree of specific relief only on proof of execution of agreement. Plaintiff was not entitled to relief of specific performance.[9]

5 Report of the Expert Committee on the Specific Relief Act 1963, 2016, p. 67.

6 *Maya Wanti* v *Kaushalya Devi* (1990)3 SCC 1.

7 *Nanak Builders* v *Vinod Kumar Goel* AIR 1991 Del 315 at p. 319; *Ajit Prashad Jain* v *N.K. Widhani* AIR 1990 Del 42; *Narayana Pillai* v *Kunju Amma* AIR 1990 Ker 177; *Zarina Siddiqui* v *A. Ramalingam* (2015)1 SCC 705; *K. Prakash* v *B.R. Sampath Kumar* AIR 2015 SC 9.

8 *Satya Narayana* v *Yellojirao* AIR 1965 SC 1405; (1965)2 SCR 221; *K. Sambasiva Rao* v *P. Bangaru Raju* AIR 1985 AP 393 at p. 398.

9 *Rajendra Kumar Jha* v *Manohar Lal Soni* AIR 2018 Chh 144.

Reiterating the principle in a case, the High Court of Andhra Pradesh observed:

> "It is not obligatory to decree specific performance. It is always one of discretion. The discretion has to be exercised carefully with circumspection, on sound and reasonable grounds guided by judicial principles. The court has first to consider whether the plaintiff has established the case. His conduct during, at and from the date of contract till date of suit bears great relevance. He must come to the court with clean hands. If his conduct is tainted with falsity of the case or unworthy of acceptance, equity denies him the relief. If he is entitled to the relief then it is the duty of the court to consider the defence of the defendant. If the defence cuts at the case of the plaintiff, in that eventuality also specific performance could be denied."[10]

The agreement for sale between vendor and vendee was found to be contingent depending upon fulfilment of all three conditions. One of the conditions was the settlement with the labour and labour agreeing with the sale contemplated. Refusal to give consent by labour of vendor of the said agreement for sale amounted to non-fulfilment of condition of sale. Vendor thus as stipulated was not bound to complete the sale. It has been held by the Supreme Court that purchaser as condition of agreement would be entitled to refund the amount of earnest money along with interest @18% per annum.[11]

A vendee entered into an agreement to sale upon payment of earnest money-vendor did not execute the sale deed within stipulated period. Vendee approached the vendor for original document of title and encumbrance certificate but the vendor failed to provide such documents. Readiness and willingness on the part of the vendee was proved and the vendee is entitled to relief of specific performance.[12]

Possession of suit property was not given to plaintiff/purchaser at the time of execution of the agreement. Area of land agreed to be sold was not clear and final. Thus plaintiff cannot be said to have done substantial acts or suffered losses due to expenditure in constructions etc., in consequence of contract capable of specific performance. It has been held in facts and circumstances of the case that it would be equitable, just and proper to direct defendant/vendor to pay back amount of earnest money with interest @ 18% per annum to the plaintiff.[13] Even otherwise the plea of alternative relief of refund of earnest money and damages cannot be itself be a bar to claim the decree of specific performance.[14]

10 *G. Rosaiah* v *C. Balarami Reddy* AIR 1989 AP 179.

11 *Nandkishore Lalbhai Mehta* v *New Era Fabrics P. Ltd.* AIR 2015 SC 3796; *V. Muthusami* v *Angammal* AIR 2002 SC 1279.

12 *Gajendran* v *Thangavel* AIR 2018 Mad 39; (2018)2 Mad LJ 129.

13 *Hemanta Mondal* v *Ganesh Chandra Naskar* AIR 2015 SC 3757.

14 *P.C. Varghese* v *Devaki Amma Balambika Devi* (2005)8 SCC 486.

Similarly, prior to amendment in s. 20 of the Act, in a suit of specific performance long years after the institution of suit (here 21 years) if the intending purchaser relinquished part of the total immovable property mentioned in the agreement, court was justified in its discretion to refuse the relief of specific performance.[15] Specific performance of agreement of sale in respect of a share of property owned jointly cannot be refused on the ground that the property will have to be partitioned. Nor it can be refused on the ground that the properties agreed to be sold are scattered at different places.[16] The question whether the performance of a contract would involve hardship on the defendant was to be determined with reference to the circumstances existing at the time of the contract, unless the hardship had resulted from any act of the plaintiff subsequent to the contract [s. 20(2) & *Expls.* 1 & 2 (unamended provision of s. 20)].

The old law was that the doctrine of mutuality would no longer be available to the defendant and the court would not refuse the decree merely on the ground that the contract was not enforceable at the instance of the other party [s. 20(4)].[17]

The ordinary rule, before the amendment in s. 20, was that specific performance should be granted. It ought to be denied only when equitable considerations pointed to its refusal and circumstances showed that damages would constitute an adequate relief.[18] Whether on certain facts the equitable relief prayed for should or should not be granted was a question of law and the second appellate court would be competent to interfere in the matter, if the order was wrong.[19] To avail relief of specific performance, parties need to plead and prove that all the statutory requirements which are prescribed provisions of the Act are fulfilled. Then the court is entitled to exercise its discretion to grant or refuse the relief of specific performance.[20]

He who seeks equity can be put on terms to ensure that equity is done to the opposite party even while granting the relief. The final end of law is justice and so the means to it too should be informed by equity.[21] But, now the equitable considerations do not control the jurisdiction of the Court under s. 20 of the Act. The law which was equitable has been done away with by way of amendment in s. 20 in 2018 and a new concept of substituted performance of contract has been instituted.

15 *Harnam Kaur* v *Jagtar Singh* AIR 1992 Punj 138.

16 *Kartar Singh* v *Harjinder Singh* AIR 1990 SC 854; (1990)3 SCC 517; JT 1990(1) SC 253.

17 *Nanak Builders and Investors* v *Vinod Kumar Alagh* AIR 1991 Del 315.

18 *Prakash Chandra* v *Angadlal* AIR 1979 SC 1241; (1979)4 SCC 393.

19 *Vuppalapati Butchiraju* v *Rajah Sri Ranga Satyanarayana* AIR 1967 AP 69 [reversed on another ground in (1969)2 SCWR 200].

20 *Kamal Kumar* v *Premlata Joshi* AIR 2019 SC 459.

21 *K. Kalapana Saraswathi* v *P.S.S. Somasundram Chettiar* AIR 1980 SC 512.

Expounding the scope of s. 20(2) and (3) prior to amendment in 2018, Jagannatha Shetty, J said in *Ranganayakamma* v *N. Govinda Narayan*,[22] "the illustrations given under sub-secs. (2) and (3) of s. 20 of the Specific Relief Act, in which a court could refuse specific performance are not exhaustive and there may be a broad band of different cases in which also the court may deny relief to the plaintiff. The relief may vary with the circumstances of individual cases judged by the familiar standard of the reasonable man.

> "The Legislature in the first place has given the discretion to courts; and secondly, it is emphasized that the discretion is required to be exercised on sound and reasonable basis guided by judicial principles. Thirdly, it is provided that the decision should be capable of correction by a Court of Appeal. The latter two aspect are always implied and need not be stated when the power is conferred upon courts. The purpose of restating these principles, as we understand, was to discourage a tendency to subject a case to 'legal strait-jacket', and to ensure that Judges are not led into the trap of legalism on the validity of the agreement. Judges cannot approach the matter with a mind sentimental to the rights of the parties, but must take into account the relative hardships in granting or refusing the relief prayed for."

Specific performance—equitable relief Explaining the nature of specific performance as equitable relief prior to amendment in 2018, it was observed by Andhra Pradesh High Court:

> "By its very nature an equitable relief requires the person claiming it to be fair, reasonable and trustworthy. A plaintiff would disentitle himself from claiming such relief if he has flouted the terms of very agreement which he seeks to enforce with impurity. A person cannot be permitted to reap the benefits of a transaction partly through his unilateral acts and to approach a court of law for the balance of it. A plaintiff in a suit of such nature must prove his *bona fide*, before he seeks the assistance of the court to compel the other person to perform his part of the obligation."[23]

As far as the specific performance as equitable relief under s. 20 prior to its amendment in 2018 is concerned, the discretion to grant or not to grant of the equitable relief for specific performance also depends upon the conduct of the parties.[1] The discretion to grant specific performance should not be refused arbitrarily but should be exercised on sound principles of law capable of correction by an appellate court.[2]

22 AIR 1982 Kant 265 at p. 268.

23 *Puvvada Chiranjeeva Rao* v *Busi Koteswara Rao* AIR 2012 AP 17.

1 *Zarina Siddiqui* v *A. Ramalingam* alias *R. Amarnathan* AIR 2015 SC 580.

2 *L.M. David* v *L.C. Arogiaswamy* AIR 1996 SC 2814; *K. Prakash* v *B.R. Sampat Kumar* AIR 2015 SC 9; *Shamsher Singh* v *Rajinder Kumar* AIR 2014 SC 2253.

Thus, specific performance of a contract which was an equitable relief within the discretion of the court prior to the Specific Relief (Amendment) Act 2018, the plaintiff who seeks equity must come with clean hands. Where he does not come with clean hands or where he is guilty of fraud or forgery or other malpractices, he cannot be given any relief by way of specific performance. Even so the conduct must be such as results in prejudicing the interests of the defendants or giving an unfair advantage to the plaintiff. But, now the position is different. The amendment has introduced in s. 20 a new concept and it is "*substituted performance of contract*".

It is an important condition under the old law that a party who desires specific relief must come with clean hands as otherwise specific performance would be refused.[3] In *Ganesh Shet* v *Dr. C.S.G.K. Setty*,[4] Their Lordships of the Supreme Court have pointed out that the circumstances referred to in sub-secs. (2) to (4) of s. 20 in regard to the exercise of discretion in granting a decree for specific performance are not exhaustive. The discretion has to be exercised in accordance with the principles of justice, equity and good conscience and fairness to both the parties.[5] Specific performance ought not to be granted where it would generate injustice.[6] It is needless to point out that the use of discretion depends upon the facts and circumstances of each case.[7] In *Bibi Jaibunisha* v *Jagadish Pandit*[8] it was held that time was not always the essence of the contract unless the agreement specifically stipulates and there are special facts and circumstances in support thereof. In *K.S. Vidyanandam* v *Vairavan*,[9] Their Lordships held that the total inaction on the part of the purchaser for 2$^1/_2$ years in violation of the terms of the agreement coupled with substantial rise in price of the property rendered inequitable the relief of specific performance to the purchaser. Jeevan Reddy, J speaking for the Bench, observed that the court should look at all the relevant circumstances including the time-limit specified in the agreement and determine whether its discretion to grant specific performance should be exercised. His Lordship pointed out that in the case of urban properties in India it was known that prices have been going up sharply over the last few decades, particularly after 1973. Following the

3 *Lourdu Mary David* v *Louis Chinnayya Arokyasamy* (1996)5 SCC 589; AIR 1996 SC 2814; JT 1996(7) SC 499.
4 (1998)5 SCC 381; AIR 1998 SC 2216; JT 1998(4) SC 181.
5 *Kanshi Ram* v *Om Prakash Jawal* (1996)4 SCC 593; AIR 1996 SC 2150; JT 1996(4) SC 733; *Suryanarayanan Upadhyaya* v *Ram Roop Panday* AIR 1994 SC 105; 1995 Supp (4) SCC 542.
6 *Kallithil Sridharan* v *Komath Pandyala Prasanna* (1996)6 SCC 218; JT 1996(8) SC 40.
7 *S. Rangaraju Naidu* v *S. Thiruvarakkarasu* AIR 1995 SC 1769; 1995 Supp (2) SCC 680.
8 (1997)4 SCC 481; JT 1997(2) SC 750.
9 AIR 1997 SC 1751; (1997)3 SCC 1; JT 1997(2) SC 375.

1973 Arab-Israeli war which set in inflationary trend all over the world particularly affected the countries like us who imported our bulk requirement of oil. The learned Judge pointed out "we are inclined to think that the rigour of the rule evolved by the court that time is not of the essence of the contract in the case of immovable properties—evolved in time when prices and values were stable and inflation was unknown—requires to be relaxed, if not modified, particularly in the case of urban immovable properties. It is high time we do so." In that case, the property in suit was a house in Madurai which is one of the major cities of Tamil Nadu. The suit agreement was in December 1978 and six months period specified therein for completing the sale expired in June 1979. The plaintiff issued a notice only on 11th July 1981 and in the meanwhile the price has gone up. Their Lordships were inclined to accept the case of the defendant that the value of the house property in Madurai Town had risen often and this must have induced the plaintiff to wake up after 2½ years and demand specific performance. The total inaction on the part of the plaintiff for about 2½ years is clear violation of the terms of the agreement coupled with substantial rise in prices brought about a situation where according to Their Lordships it was inequitable to give the relief of specific performance to the plaintiff.

We shall now refer to some decisions of the Supreme Court where Their Lordships have exercised their extraordinary discretionary jurisdiction, prior to amendment in 2018, in order to render that real and substantial justice for which courts of law exist. It is, however, submitted that the principles laid down in the following cases would not applicable to the cases that would be initiated after the coming into effect of the Specific Relief (Amendment) Act 2018.

In *Kanshi Ram* v *Om Prakash Jawal,*[10] there was an agreement for sale of a plot of land admeasuring 100 sq. yards in New Delhi for a sum of ₹16,000 and a sum of ₹2,000 was paid as advance. As the vendor failed to execute the deed of sale, the purchaser filed a suit for specific performance and claimed in the alternative damages in the sum of ₹12,000. The court below granted the decree of specific performance. In the appeal by special leave, the counsel for the appellant contended that the appellant was prepared to pay a sum of ₹10 lakhs as damages though the respondent/plaintiff had claimed ₹12,000 only as damages in the alternative. The Supreme Court found that there was no justification for interference with the decree granted by the courts below. But having regard to the facts and circumstances of the case, particularly the rise in price of the property during the pendency of the suit, the Supreme Court got into equity jurisdiction and considered the order of specific performance unrealistic and unfair, inequitable and unjust. Accordingly, they directed the appellant/defendant to pay to the

10 AIR 1996 SC 2150; (1996)4 SCC 593; JT 1996(4) SC 733.

respondent/plaintiff a sum of ₹10 lakhs as compensation within a period of three months and in case of default, the decree for specific performance would stand confirmed.

There was an agreement for sale of joint property which was executed by some of the defendants. Sister and her husband, being interested in the property were not joined as defendants. Property was already mortgaged with co-operative bank. Under the agreement vendors agreed to make good marketable title and to execute proper conveyance by joining necessary person so as to convey absolute title or to redeem any charge or encumbrance. Plaintiff-purchaser was always ready and willing to perform its obligation and discharged mortgage with bank by paying amount three times the amount of agreed consideration with clear understanding that all the defendants would thereafter execute the sale deed. In the facts and circumstances of the case grant of decree to the extent of share of some of defendants in favour of plaintiff was held to be justified and the Supreme Court declined to interfere with it.[11]

In *Gobind Ram* v *Gian Chand*,[12] the appellant agreed to sell the disputed property to the Respondent for a sum of ₹16,000 and received a sum of ₹1,000 as earnest money. As the appellant failed to execute the deed of sale within the stipulated time, the Respondent filed a suit for specific performance. The suit was decreed and the Respondent deposited the balance of consideration of ₹15,000 in the trial court. The appeal filed by the appellant before the High Court was dismissed. However, to mitigate the hardship of the appellant and as the Respondent agreed to pay some more amount, the High Court directed the Respondent to deposit a further sum of ₹1 lakh which the Respondent deposited in the Registry of the High Court. In the Appeal by Special Leave before the Supreme Court, the only contention advanced was that instead of a decree for specific performance compensation may be awarded. The Supreme Court while accepting the clear finding of the High Court that the Appellant tried to wriggle out of the contract because of escalation in prices and that the Respondent had not taken undue or unfair advantage over the appellant, it would be inequitable and unjust to deny the Respondent the decree for specific performance. However, to mitigate the hardship of the appellant, Their Lordships directed the Respondent to deposit a further sum of ₹3 lakhs within four months with the Registry of the Supreme Court and this amount has to be paid to the appellant on his delivering possession of the suit property to the Respondent within six months from the date of the deposit.

11 *Syscon Consultants (P) Ltd.* v *Primella Sanitary Prod. P. Ltd.* AIR 2016 SC 4564.
12 AIR 2000 SC 3106; (2000)7 SCC 548; (2000)6 Supreme 580.

In *Shanta Bai* v *Giriji Bai*,[13] the agreement for sale was entered into in 1975 and the sale amount was ₹6,000. In a suit filed by the plaintiff for specific performance it was contended that since considerable period of time had elapsed since the execution of the agreement for sale and prices had gone up, the discretionary relief for specific performance ought not to have been granted by the courts below. It was admitted by both the parties before the Supreme Court that the market price of the property had gone up many times and consequently the Supreme Court, while confirming the decree for specific performance, directed the Respondent/Plaintiff to pay a further sum of ₹30,000.

In *V. Muthusamy (dead) by L.Rs.* v *Angammal*,[14] the Supreme Court has held that specific performance being a discretionary relief, the court has to look into the comparative hardship. Where the subsequent purchaser was a *bona fide* purchaser for a value without notice and was in possession by investing considerable sum for improvement, Their Lordships held that a decree for specific performance would cause considerable hardship and directed the refund of the advance of ₹3,000 to the plaintiff with interest @12% from the date of suit till payment.

In *Nirmala Anand* v *Advent Corporation Pvt. Ltd.*,[15] the plaintiff was found ready and willing to purchase the flat, but there was heavy escalation of price in the interregnum. The Supreme Court, while holding that neither delay or escalation in price is a ground to deny the relief of specific performance, in order to mitigate the hardship of the vendor, the vendee was directed to pay a further compensatory amount. Their Lordships held that this was not a principle of universal application and would depend upon the facts and circumstances of each case.

In *Maria Angelina (deceased)* v *A.G. Balkis Bibee*,[16] the Supreme Court held that in the absence of any plea by the defendant of hardship if the plaintiff was given a decree for specific performance, the plea cannot be entertained for the first time in the appeal and Their Lordships refused to interfere with the decree for specific performance.

Plaintiff's claims not bona fide In a case initiated prior to the Specific Relief (Amendment) Act 2018, if the plaintiff's claim is not *bona fide*, he would not be entitled to the decree for specific performance.[17] When the plaintiff's witness was not ironical to the defendant, evidence of witness would not be discarded merely because the witness is classmate of defendant.[18]

13 (2001)5 Supreme 395.
14 AIR 2002 SC 1279.
15 AIR 2002 SC 2290.
16 AIR 2002 SC 2385.
17 *Kamireddi Sattiaraju* v *Kandamusi Boolaeswari* AIR 2007 NOC 540 (Mad).
18 *Boddu Satyavathi* v *Boddu Ramakrishna Rao* AIR 2007 NOC 220 (HP).

A mere omission to mention agreement to sell in the sale deed was no ground to hold that agreement for sale was not executed in favour of subsequent transferee.[19]

Relevant consideration for granting and refusing specific performance—moulding of relief Defendant made false statements denying execution of agreement and withholding evidence. Defendant was not entitled to ask court to exercise discretion in his favour and refuse specific performance. Suits remained pending in different courts. There was phenomenal increase in price during the period of pendency of cases. Plaintiff was granted decree of specific performance on condition for payment of ₹15 lacs in addition to amount already paid.[20]

Grant of decree for specific performance—principles enunciated The principles governing the grand of specific performance of contract was considered by the Supreme Court in *K. Prakash* v *B.R. Sampath Kumar*[21] and it was held that "the court's jurisdiction to grant decree of specific performance is discretionary but not arbitrary. Discretion must be exercised in accordance with the sound and reasonable judicial principles. Normally when the trial court exercises its discretion in one way or other after appreciation of entire evidence and materials on record, the appellate court should not interfere unless it is established that the discretion has been exercised perversely, arbitrarily or against judicial principles. It is true that under s. 20 of the Specific Relief Act 1963 a party is not entitled to get a decree for specific performance merely because it is lawful to do so. Nevertheless, once an agreement to sell is legal and validly proved and further requirements for getting such a decree are established, then the court has to exercise its discretion in favour of granting relief for specific performance."[22]

Similarly, finding in criminal proceedings cannot be conclusive, proof of fact, *i.e.* existence of agreement to grant decree without, independent finding by civil courts. Agreement for sale was allegedly executed on a quarter sheet of paper and not on proper stamp paper. No opinion of experts regarding execution of documents was sought for. The said document cannot be believed. Thus no relief of specific performance can be granted in favour of the plaintiff.[23]

Therefore, the court is not bound to grant the relief of specific performance merely because it is lawful to do so. Section 20(1) of the

19 *Ram Prakash* v *Baddal Hussain* AIR 2007 All 212.

20 *Zarina Siddiqui* v *A. Ramalingam* AIR 2015 SC 580. See *Nirmala Anand* v *Advent Corporation (P.) Ltd.* (2002)8 SCC 146; AIR 2002 SC 3396 (in exercise of discretion court may impose reasonable condition including payment of additional amount by one party to the other while granting or refusing decree of specific performance).

21 AIR 2015 SC 9.

22 *K. Prakash* v *B.R. Sampath Kumar* AIR 2015 SC 9.

23 *K. Nanjappa* v *R.A. Hameed* AIR 2015 SC 3389.

Specific Relief Act 1963, indicates that the jurisdiction to decree specific performance is discretionary. Yet, the discretion of the court is not arbitrary but is "sound and reasonable", to be "guided by judicial principles". The exercise of discretion is capable of being corrected by a court of appeal in the hierarchy of appellate courts. Sub-section (2) of s. 20 contains a stipulation of those cases where the court may exercise its discretion not to grant specific performance.[1] It is, however, to be noted that the principles stated here would be applicable to the cases initiated prior to the amendment of s. 20 of the Act whereby a comprehensive change has been brought out by introducing a new concept of *'substituted performance of contract'* in place of the specific performance of contract.

Judicious exercise of discretion Before the amendment in 2018 it was a well-settled law that the power to order specific performance of contract was discretionary and parties cannot claim it as a matter of right although it was lawful but such discretion should be exercised judicially and prudently.[2]

Agreement incapable of specific performance The jurisdiction to order specific performance of contract was based on the existence of a valid and enforceable contract. Where a valid and enforceable contract has not been made, the court would not make a contract for them. Specific performance would not be ordered if the contract itself suffers from some defects which makes the contract invalid or unenforceable. The discretion of court will not be there even though the contract is otherwise valid and enforceable. Where a plot in question is not transferable for a period of ten years, an agreement to sell such plot is not an enforceable contract. Order of High Court decreeing such suit in spite of noticing the said fact was held to be not proper.[3]

A lease agreement provides for exercise of option of renewal before expiry of lease. Option exercised was contrary to terms of lease agreement. Clauses of renewal requiring fixation of terms and conditions for renewal period of lease mutually or in alternative through village Mukhia and Panchas are uncertain and incapable of specific performance. There was no mutual consent for renewal. Suit by lessee sought for specific performance of the alleged agreement of renewal on his alleged right of option of renewal was dismissed. There was no interference with the judgment by the Supreme Court.[4]

An agreement to sell itself neither creates any interest in the land nor does it amount to sale under s. 54 of the T.P. Act. It simply enables the intending buyer to claim specific performance of that agreement only.[5]

1 *Jayakantham* v *Abaykumar* (2017)5 SCC 178.
2 *Shivaji Yallappa Patil* v *Ranajeet Appasaheb Patil* (2018)16 SCC 725.
3 *Satish Kumar* v *Karan Singh* AIR 2016 SC 737.
4 *Shanti Prasad Devi* v *Shankar Mahto* AIR 2005 SC 2905.
5 *Balwant Vithal Kadam* v *Sunil Baburai Kadam* AIR 2018 SC 49; (2018)2 SCC 82.

In a suit specific performance was sought for by the plaintiff against vendor. The land in question was belonging to third party. The land was mutated in favour of the third party on the basis of will and the property was in possession of third party. Specific performance cannot be granted to plaintiff against the vendor.[6]

Bar of civil court jurisdiction A suit for specific performance of agreement of sale of agricultural lands was resisted by defendant's son on the plea that the lands were jointly owned as members of joint family. Suit lands were exclusively recorded in the name of the defendant's father. Son on attaining majority and fully aware of execution of agreement of sale raised the plea of joint ownership, but he did not make any attempt to get their names jointly recorded in revenue papers under s. 49 of the U.P. Consolidation of Holdings Act 1954. Thus, the son was barred from raising the plea of joint ownership before the civil court. It is a question of title exclusively within the jurisdiction of revenue authorities. The agreement of sale executed by the father is binding on sons.[7]

A contract is the licence which is always revokable as licensee has no right or interest. In such a case of revocation of permission the only remedy available is to sue for damages and not for enforcement of licence or contract. Thus, a suit filed for enforcement of licence or contract is barred by s. 14(1)(*c*)[8] of the Specific Relief Act 1963.[9]

Contract of personal service—maintainability of suit When an employee whose services are terminated pleads that such termination is in violation of statutory rules governing his employment, an action for declaration that termination is invalid and that he is deemed to continue in service is maintainable and will not be barred by s. 14 of the Specific Relief Act 1963.[10] But now the position has been changed with the amendment of s. 20 by the Specific Relief (Amendment) Act 2018 (w.e.f. 1.10.2018).

Declaration and permanent injunction in service matter In a private employment there was no written contract. The employee was not complying with the order of the transfer and sought declaration that the transfer was illegal and she would continue to be in service and was entitled to all emoluments. She also sought permanent injunction restraining employer from holding enquiry against her. It was held that if such relief granted would amount to enforcing contract of personal service which is barred under the law. Such relief cannot be granted by civil court.[11]

6 *Baxis Singh* v *Sukhdev Singh (Dead) through LRs.* AIR 2018 SC 2157.
7 *Narender Singh* v *Jai Bhagwan* AIR 2005 SC 582.
8 After the amendment in 2018, s. 14(1)(c) is now s. 14(*d*).
9 *Bharat Petroleum Corporation Ltd.* v *Khaybar Transport Pvt. Ltd.* AIR 2011 All 131.
10 *State Bank of India* v *S.N. Goyal* AIR 2008 SC 2594; see also *Apollo Tyres Ltd.* v *C.P. Sebastian* AIR 2009 SC (Supp) 2174; *Pearlite Liners Pvt. Ltd.* v *Manorama Sirsi* AIR 2004 SC 1373.
11 *Pearlite Liners Pvt. Ltd.* v *Manorama Sirsi* AIR 2004 SC 1373.

Possibility of injury to third party The possibility of injury to the interest of third party does not, by itself, disentitle the plaintiff from specific performance but it depends upon the facts and circumstances of each case which will be considered by the court in the exercise of its discretion. The court may properly exercise discretion to decree specific performance, in any case where the plaintiff has done substantial acts or suffered losses in consequence of a contract capable of specific performance.[12]

Unfair advantage—ground for refusal of relief of specific performance The law is thus stated in Halsbury's *Laws of England*:[13]

> "The court's discretion to grant specific performance is not exercised if the contract is not "equal and fair". Even though no fraud, duress or undue influence such as to justify rescission is shown, the court may still not enforce the contract if it would not be consistent with equity and good conscience to do so."

Section 20(2)(*a*), the Specific Relief Act 1963, prior to its amendment in 2018, *inter alia* provided that when the granting of decree of specific performance entails giving to the plaintiff an undue advantage over the defendant, the relief may be refused.[14]

'Unfair advantage' is not a term of art. Where the plaintiff approaches to victimise the defendant who was thus tricked into entering the contract, the plaintiff can be said to be taking unfair advantage, otherwise mere inadequacy of price is no ground to refuse specific performance.[15]

Unfair advantage arises from the terms of the contract or from the conduct of the parties or from other circumstances contained in the contract. The conduct of the purchaser/tenant in not paying the rent from the date of the agreement and claiming the arrears of rent to be adjusted to the sale consideration was held unacceptable and the claim for specific performance was rightly rejected.[16]

Terms of agreement to sell gave unfair advantage to plaintiff purchaser. Amount of earnest money was received at the time of agreement differently stated in agreement and receipt. Defendants also look the plea that they took only loan of ₹85,000 and mortgaged their land as security and were tricked into putting their thumb impressions on purported agreement of sale. Refusal of relief of specific performance of agreement was held to be proper.[17]

12 *Shivaji Yallappa Patil* v *Ranajeet Appasaheb Patil* (2018)16 SCC 725.
13 4th Ed., vol. 44(1), para 863.
14 *Bal Krishna* v *Bhagwan Das* AIR 2008 SC 1786; see also *N. Balasubramaniam* v *Rajeswari* AIR 2011 Mad 2970 (no unfair advantage to the plaintiff or undue leadership to the defendant shown, specific performance of sale-agreement allowed).
15 *M.S. Madhusoodhanan* v *Kerala Kanmudi Pvt. Ltd.* AIR 2004 SC 909.
16 *Shoba Viswanathan* v *D.P. Kingsley* (1996)1 LW 721 (Mad).
17 *Shamsher Singh* v *Rajinder Kumar* AIR 2014 SC 2253.

The question whether relief of specific performance of contract of the purchase of immovable property should be granted or not always depends on the facts and circumstances of each case and the court would not grant such a relief if it gives the plaintiff an unfair advantage over the defendant.[18] As held in a Calcutta case the relief by way of specific performance being discretionary under s. 20, prior to its amendment in 2018, the plaintiff must come to court with clean hands. If in a suit for specific performance of a contract, the plaintiff does not come with clean hands, as where he is guilty of fraud or some other malpractice, he may ordinarily get no relief by way of specific performance undoubtedly, a contract is to be judged as at the time at which it was entered into, and is fair when made, the fact that it has become too hard by the force of subsequent circumstances, or changing events, will not necessarily prevent its specific performance. Nevertheless, if it is seen that the contract itself is not fair and is one-sided, the court may refuse to enforce the contract.[19]

An absentee owner who lived abroad engaged a broker to look for a prospective buyer. The broker settled with the plaintiff for a sum of ₹45,000 only and out of that the broker received ₹2,000 only. The fact that value of real property was fast rising was carefully concealed from the absentee owner. The broker was not authorised to enter into a binding contract with any third party. His function was to look for the best buyer. By attempting to compel the absentee owner to sell the property, the plaintiff virtually was trying to get an unfair advantage over the absentee owner-defendant. The suit for specific performance failed.[20]

If the plaintiff's conduct has the effect of overreaching the defendant and putting him to any loss, the plaintiff would certainly be disentitled to the equitable relief.[1] In a case along with a contract of sale of a house there was a contemporaneous agreement that the vendee would be given possession of ground floor and vendor after the sale would remain at the first floor as the tenant. Vendee however all along lived in the ground floor and this fact he suppressed in his suit for specific performance. It was held that the vendee having suppressed the oral agreement and having suppressed all along the fact of his being in possession at the ground floor he obtained unfair advantage over the vendor in so many years, his claim for specific performance should be rejected.[2]

18 *Sandhyarani Sarkar* v *Sudha Rani* AIR 1978 SC 537; (1978)2 SCC 116; *Bal Krishna* v *Bhagwan Das* AIR 2008 SC 1786.

19 *Sunil Chandra Ghosh* v *Hemendra Kumar Deb* AIR 1985 Cal 233.

20 *John* v *Chandy Philip* AIR 1988 Ker 122.

1 *Vuppalapati Butchiraju* v *Rajah Sri Ranga Satyanarayana* AIR 1967 AP 69 reversed on other grounds in (1969)2 SCWR 200.

2 *Padma Rani Sikdar* v *Karuppur Shaw* AIR 1989 NOC 22 (Cal); (1988)1 CHN 258.

When the plaintiff forges the signature of the defendant in the application for permission under the Urban Land (Ceiling Regulation) Act 1976 he is not entitled to decree for specific performance of contract in equity.[3]

The conduct of a party which puts the other party in a disadvantageous position, though it does not amount to waiver may in certain circumstances preclude it from obtaining a decree for specific performance.[4] *Held* on facts that there was nothing in the conduct of the plaintiff to disentitle him to the relief, even though he had sought execution of the decree refusing specific performance but allowing refund of earnest money, since he had throughout been maintaining that he did not accept the decree. In a case the defendant agreed to sell property within three years from the date of agreement for a sum of ₹5,000 only, and the plaintiff executed pronote for ₹4,900. So virtually all the consideration had been paid except a sum of ₹100 only. The plaintiff delayed and the defendant sold the same to third party. When the suit for specific performance was filed by the plaintiff, the pronote had been already barred by time. The plaintiff did not deposit the sum of ₹5,000. His stand was that he was to pay only ₹100 towards the sale consideration, rest was already paid and that he was not responsible for the pronote being barred by limitation. The court held that to decree the suit for specific performance is to give him an undue advantage and so the suit must fail.[5]

A contract for sale by the mother of the coparceners all of whom were minors for necessity and for the benefit of the family, will not be enforced by the court if the circumstances transpire to show that the enforcement would be unjust and detrimental to the interest of the minors, particularly when the sale seems to be a distress sale and the value of the property had considerably increased.[6]

Section 20, Specific Relief Act, prior to its amendment in 2018, preserved judicial discretion to courts as to decreeing specific performance. The court should meticulously consider all facts and circumstances of the case. The court is not bound to grant specific performance merely because it is lawful to do so. The motive behind the litigation should also enter into the judicial verdict. The court should take care to see that it is not used as an instrument of oppression to have an unfair advantage to the plaintiff.[7]

3 *Rabindra Nath Sahu* v *Maya Devi* AIR 1991 Pat 192.

4 *Mademsettu Satyanarayana* v *G. Yelloji Rao* AIR 1965 SC 1405 relying on *Lindsay Petroleum Co.* v *Prosper Armstrong Hurd* (1874)5 PC 221 and *Caesar Lamare* v *Thomas Dixon* [1873]6 HL 414 at p. 423; *Ramesh Chandra Chandiok* v *Chunilal Sabharwal* AIR 1971 SC 1238; (1970)3 SCC 140.

5 *Narayana Pillai* v *Kunju Amma* AIR 1990 Ker 177.

6 *E. Venkatakrishna Reddy* v *Minor Amara Babu* (1971)2 MLJ 466; *Kallathil Sridharan* v *Komath Pandyala Prasanna* (1996)6 SCC 218; JT 1996(8) SC 40.

7 *P.V. Joseph's son Mathew* v *N. Kuruvila's Son* AIR 1987 SC 2328.

In this case the owner of the property agreed to sell the same to C and the latter paid advance. On the death of the owner his heirs sold the entire suit property to *M* on receiving full consideration. Subsequent to the execution of the said sale deed in favour of *M* the father-in-law of the deceased owner got an assignment of the agreement of sale. It was evident from the facts and circumstances that the agreement to sell in favour of *M* was not obtained to defraud C from his legitimate rights, if any under the agreement to sell in his favour. It was evident that C had implied consent in executing the subsequent documents. C was not allowed a decree of specific performance.[8]

Where the plaintiff puts up a false plea that he had paid a certain amount, he is not entitled to the equitable relief of specific performance.[9] Likewise, if the conduct of the plaintiff shows that he was unwilling to buy the property and was insisting on production of documents which were irrelevant and not as per the terms of the contract, he would not be entitled to specific performance. Of course, if such a demand is made through a mistake and the mistake is corrected in time, this will not disqualify him.[10] An English Court, however, saw nothing wrong in the conduct of the plaintiff where he and another agreed that the other should stay away from the auction and as a result of this the plaintiff bought the property of the defendant cheaply.[11]

Specific performance may be denied where the plaintiff is guilty of suppressing relevant facts, even though he may be under no duty to disclose them and the suppression may not constitute a fraud [within the meaning of s. 17 of the Contract Act].[12] Specific performance is denied for suppression of material fact of vendee's possession over suit property on date of filing of suit. If suppression of material fact is not proved, decree of specific performance should be granted.[13] But silence is not suppression. In *Dyster* v *Randall & Sons*[14] the purchaser was allowed specific performance of the contract entered into by an agent on his behalf without disclosing the identity of the purchaser, even though if the vendor had known this, he would not have sold the property to the purchaser. Again, when the defendant had no knowledge that a scheme for irrigation by digging a channel was in

8 *P.V. Joseph's son Mathew* v *N. Kuruvila's Son* AIR 1987 SC 2328; 1987 Rajdhani LR 567; (1987)2 UJ (SC) 449.

9 *Kommisetti Venkatasubbayya* v *Karamsetti Venkateswarlu* AIR 1971 AP 279 following *Subbarayudu* v *Tatayya* 1973 Mad WN 1158 and the Judgment of Supreme Court in *V. Piothi Raju* v *V. Butchi Raju* in AC No. 1976 (N) of 1966, delivered on 17.7.1969; see also *M. Veera Raghaviah* v *M. China Veeriah* AIR 1975 AP 350 (DB).

10 *Raj Rani* v *Kartar Singh* AIR 1975 Del 137 at p. 142 (DB).

11 *Harrop* v *Thompson* [1975]2 All ER 94.

12 *Beyfus* v *Lodge* [1925] Ch 350.

13 *Smt. P. Leelavathi Nagendra* v *G. Ravi Pullaiah* AIR 2018 Hyd 8.

14 [1926] Ch 932.

progress which had increased the value of the land to a considerable extent. But the plaintiff who had knowledge of it had suppressed it from the defendant and the price was also inadequate. It was also found in that case that the defendant wound up his business at Chidambaram and went away to his native place, that at the time of entering into the agreement he was not aware of the existence of a scheme for irrigation was in progress. In these circumstances, it was held that the parties were not at equal footing, and the plaintiff was aware and the seller being ignorant of the real value of the land sold. The bargain was oppressive and unconscionable and that it was not appropriate to grant the relief of specific performance.[15]

Specific performance may also be refused if the defendant was intoxicated when he entered into the contract though the plaintiff had not drawn him in to a drink,[16] or if the contract involves breach of a prior agreement, *e.g.* a covenant in a lease prohibiting subletting[17] or if the agreement shows a higher price than that agreed upon in order to deceive prospective mortgagees.[18]

Execution of a sale agreement by owner was not proved and that agreement was found to be unregistered. No attempt was made by vendee to discharge burden by examining handwriting expert. No document was produced to prove that the members in whose favour alleged agreement was executed and have relinquished their possession in favour of vendee. There was no proof of payment of earnest money at the time of execution of the suit agreement. No specific performance can be granted.[19]

Relief of specific performance of contract—not proper Plaintiff wanted to purchase flat of defendant. Intention of parties was to be enforceable only when MOU was actually signed by them. MOU was not ultimately signed by parties. Thus, there was no concluded contract. Plaintiff was not, therefore, entitled to relief of specific performance of contract.[20]

Suit was based on agreement allegedly entered into between parties two years before institution of suit. Eviction suit was instituted against vendee in the same year in which agreement was allegedly entered into. Parties were in litigation since then. No date or sitting was disclosed in plaint to show the finalisation of negotiation amongst evidence of witnesses over preparation of document as well as conduct of parties. Vendor since time of filing of written statement denied her presence regarding the alleged deed of agreement. It was incumbent upon vendee to have got signatures properly verified or

15 *Ramakrishna* v *Palaniappa* AIR 1963 Mad 17.
16 *Malins* v *Freeman* [1837]2 Keen 25.
17 *Warmington* v *Miller* [1973]2 All ER 372.
18 *Zimmerman* v *Letkeman* [1977]79 DLR (3rd) 508.
19 *Lakshmi Sreenivasa Co-operative Building Society* v *Puvvada Rama (Dead) by LRs.* AIR 2018 SC 3580; (2018)9 SCC 251.
20 *Rohit A. Kapadia* v *Perviz J. Modi* AIR 2016 Bom 181.

compared by handwritten expert. Thus, failure by vendee on that score disentitled any relief of specific performance of contract to vendee.[21]

Signatures and thumb impressions of persons were alleged to be not of the owners of the suit properly affixed on agreement. Suit property being joint family property and there being no division among coparceners, vendors were trying to venture to alienate part of suit property without consent of the other owners of the property. Merely because vendee was ready and willing to perform her part of the contract was not sufficient to grant equitable relief to her as she failed to establish to be the full-fledged owner of the property concerned. Thus, grant of decree of specific performance was not proper.[1]

Delay While in England mere delay or laches may be a ground for refusing to give a relief of specific performance, in India, mere delay without such conduct on the part of the plaintiff as would cause prejudice to the defendant does not empower a court to refuse such a relief. But as in England, so in India, proof of abandonment or waiver of a right is not a pre-condition necessary to disentitle the plaintiff to the said relief, for if abandonment or waiver is established, no question of discretion on the part of the court would arise. But waiver is contractual and may constitute a cause of action; it is an agreement to release or not to assert a right. It is not possible or desirable to lay down the circumstances under which a court can exercise its discretion against the plaintiff. But they must be such that the representation by or the conduct or neglect of the plaintiff is directly responsible in inducing the defendant to change his position to his prejudice or such as to bring about a situation when it would be inequitable to give him such a relief.[2]

21 *Bibi Mehrum Nissa* v *Md. Ehsanul Haque* AIR 2016 Pat 76.

1 *K. Bhudamma* v *Smt. Vidyadevi* AIR 2016 Hyd 200.

2 *Satyanarayana* v *Yellojirao* AIR 1965 SC 1405; (1965)2 SCR 221 relying on *Dawson's Bank Ltd.* v *Nippon Menkwa Kabushiki Kaisha* AIR 1935 PC 79 at p. 82, affirming [1964]1 An WR 312, referring to *Nawab Begum* v *A.H. Creet* 27 All 678; *Chamarti Suryaprakasarayulu* v *Arardhi Lakshminarasimha* AIR 1914 Mad 462; *Rameshwar Prasad Sahi* v *Anandi Devi* AIR 1960 Pat 109, approving *Jadu Nath Gupta* v *Chandra Bhusan* AIR 1932 Cal 493 and *Gosthe Behari* v *Omiyo Prosad* AIR 1960 Cal 361 and holding that *Watson* v *Reid* 39 ER 91; *Eads* v *Williams* 43 ER 671; *Clegg* v *Edmondson* 114 RR 336; *Lehmann* v *McArthur* [1868]3 Ch App 496 and *Emile Erlanger* v *New Sombrero Phosphate Co.* [1878]2 AC 1218 have no application in India. See also *Gangabai* v *Srinivasa Rao* AIR 1971 AP 293; *Moram Venkataratnam* v *Gothi Mukkala Jagananadh Raju* (1971)2 AP LJ 57 (DB); *Mir Abdul Hakeem* v *Abdul Mannan* AIR 1972 AP 178 at p. 184 (DB); *Eswari Amma* v *M.K. Korah* AIR 1972 Mad 339 at pp. 344-345 (DB); *Jamshed Khodaram* v *Burjorji Dhunjibhai* AIR 1915 PC 83; *Arjuna Mudaliar* v *Lakshmiammal* AIR 1949 Mad 265; *Sankaralinga* v *Ratnasami* AIR 1952 Mad 389; *T. Venkata Subrahmanyam* v *Vishwanadharaju* AIR 1968 AP 109; *Jitendra Nath Roy* v *Maheswari Bose* AIR 1965 Cal 45 (DB); *Faujmal* v *Nathulal* AIR 1965 Raj 115; *Hamsammal* v *P.V. Thakkar* AIR 1982 Mad 108 (DB); *Manick Lal* v *K.P. Chowdhury* AIR 1976 Cal 115.

Subsequent rise in price will not be treated as hardship entitling refusal of decree of specific performance unless the plaintiff is guilty of conduct, disentitling him from specific performance *viz.*, delay or inaction.[3] The plaintiff cannot be penalised for lapse of time and consequent rise in prices.[4] But in some cases, even where there has been no fault on the purchaser the courts have directed him to deposit additional amount in order to mitigate the hardship of the vendor.[5]

As Art. 54, Limitation Act prescribes a period of three years from the date fixed thereunder the specific performance of a contract, it follows that mere delay without more extending upto the said period cannot be a reason for court to exercise its discretion against giving a relief of specific performance.[6]

In this case contention was to the effect that Art. 54, the Limitation Act is in two parts prescribing separate time-limits. The first part is three years from the date fixed for the specific performance of the contract and the second part refers to the period of limitation as three years from the date when the plaintiff has notice that performance is refused and that part is applicable only in a case where the date is not fixed for the performance of the agreement in the agreement itself. In the said case, the learned counsel urged, the agreement dated 30th September 1965 itself prescribes that date of performance as six months from the date of the agreement and that period of six months expired on 31st March 1966. The last date for filing the suit, therefore, expired on 31st March 1969. Thus, under the first part of Art. 54 itself, the suit was barred by limitation. It was alternatively contended that, even if the agreement dated 30th September 1965 should be held to have not fixed the date for performance of the contract still the suit is barred by limitation, as the appellant refused to perform his part of the contract, as indicated in a letter. The period of limitation therefore ended on 10th September 1978 whereas the suit was filed on 9th March 1981. It was, therefore, submitted that, in either view, the suit filed by the respondent for specific performance of the agreement dated 30th September 1965 was barred by limitation. This contention was repelled because cl. (1) of the agreement, on which reliance was placed did not stipulate any date fixed for the performance of the contract. All that is stated there was that the respondent would select one acre on one side of 13 acres plot described in the schedule within six months from the date of the agreement and the

3 *K.S. Vaidyanathan* v *Vairavan* AIR 1997 SC 1751; (1997)3 SCC 1; JT 1997(2) SC 375.

4 *Kochu Thambu Rowther Hassan Kutti* v *Peer Mohamed Pudhumalaiyar Rowther* AIR 2000 Ker 17.

5 *Gobind Ram* v *Gian Chand* AIR 2000 SC 3106; (2000)7 SCC 548.

6 *Satyanarayana* v *Yellojirao* AIR 1965 SC 1405; (1965)2 SCR 221; *K. Sambasiva Rao* v *P. Bangaru Raju* AIR 1985 AP 393 at p. 398.

respondent would get the same measured and partitioned immediately after the selection and the respondent should be put in physical possession of one acre so selected. The period of six months within which the respondent may select one acre of land cannot be considered to be the period stipulated for the performance of the contract by the appellant. Apart from the above provision in cl. (1), it was not in dispute that the agreement dated 30th September 1965 did not as such provide or stipulate any date for the performance of the contract. The first part of Art. 54, has, therefore, no application. For the application of the second part, what is crucial is the date when the respondent has notice that performance is refused and it is from that date the period of three years limitation runs. The letter by the defendant did not convey any notice. So Art. 54 second part too did not apply.[7]

Relying on the Supreme Court case *Satyanarayana* (ibid) it is held the delay in bringing the suit for specific performance of contract is no ground to refuse relief when the suit is filed within limitation.[8]

Even so, the doctrine of laches in courts of equity is not an arbitrary or technical doctrine. Where it would be practically unjust to give remedy either because the party has by his conduct done that which might fairly be regarded as an equivalent to a waiver of it, or where by his conduct and neglect, he has, though perhaps not waiving that remedy, put the other party in a situation in which it would not be reasonable to place him if the remedy were afterwards to be asserted; in either of these cases, lapse of time and delay are most material.[9]

Delay in filing the suit, non-enquiry regarding the property to be sold and non-inspection of the same shows that the plaintiff is not entitled to specific performance.[10]

Where delay not amounting to a bar by any statute of limitation is pleaded as a defence to a suit for specific performance, the validity of the defence must be tried upon the principles substantially equitable. The two circumstances which are always important in such cases are: (1) the length of the delay, and (2) the nature of the act done during the interval, which might affect either party and cause a balance of justice or injustice in taking the one course or the other so far as it relates to the remedy.[11]

7 *K. Sambasiva Rao* v *P. Bangaru Raju* AIR 1985 AP 393 at pp. 396 397; (1985)2 Cur CC 666.
8 *T.K. Santha* v *A.G. Rathnam* AIR 1990 Ker 69.
9 *Lindsay Petroleum Co.* v *Hurd* LR (1874)5 PC 221 at p. 239 cited with approval in *Jiwan Lal* v *Brij Mohan* AIR 1973 SC 559; (1973)2 SCR 230; (1972)2 SCC 757. (On facts held there was no delay).
10 *K. Bhaskaran Nair* v *Habeeb Mohammed* AIR 2002 Ker 308.
11 *Lyndsay Petroleum Company* v *V. Hurd* LR (1874)5 PC 221.

If due to delay of the plaintiff in bringing his action for specific performance, the delay being unreasonable and the grant of relief to the plaintiff will prejudice the rights of the defendant, the relief will not be granted.[12] Delay will deprive specific performance if coupled with supervening circumstances which alter the situation and create right, title or interest in third parties validly.[13] So also where the defendant has altered his position to his detriment.[14]

The circumstances always important in such cases are the length of the delay and the nature of the acts done during the interval which might affect either party and cause a balance of justice or injustice in taking the one course or other. Delay has two aspects. It may lead to a change in the thing sold or it may imply acquiescence so as to bar a plaintiff's remedy. It is very important to keep these two things separate when the consequences of delay have to be considered in a given case.[15]

Waiver But if waiver or abandonment is proved, specific performance will be refused.[16] In this context the true meaning of the term waiver should be elucidated. Waiver is the abandonment of a right in such a way that the other party is entitled to plead the abandonment by way of confession and avoidance if the right is thereafter asserted, and is either express or implied from conduct. It may sometimes resemble a form of election, and sometimes be based on ordinary principles of estoppel, although, unlike estoppel, waiver must always be an intentional act with knowledge.[17] Waiver is an intentional relinquishment of a known right. There can be no waiver unless the person against whom the waiver is claimed had full knowledge of his rights and of facts enabling him to effectual action for the enforcement of such rights.[18]

Waiver means abandonment of a right and it may be either express or implied from the conduct, but its basic requirement is that it must be an intentional act with knowledge.[19]

12 *Jiwan Lal* v *Brij Mohan Mehra* AIR 1973 SC 559; (1973)2 SCR 230; (1972)2 SCC 757; *Motilal Jain* v *Ramdasi Devi* AIR 2000 SC 2408; (2000)6 SCC 420; JT 2000(8) SC 59.

13 *Tandra Venkata Subramanian* v *Vegesena Viswanatha Raju* AIR 1968 AP 190; *Deenanath* v *Chunnilal* AIR 1975 Raj 69; *Motilal Jain* v *Ramdasi Devi* AIR 2000 SC 2408; (2000)6 SCC 420; JT 2000(8) SC 59.

14 *K. Sambasiva Rao* v *P. Bangaru Raju* AIR 1985 AP 393.

15 *Damacharia Venkata Seshaiah* v *Damacharla Venkayya* AIR 1974 AP 193 at pp. 195-196 (DB) (waiver not proved).

16 *Lekh Singh* v *Dwarkanath* AIR 1929 Lah 249; *R.H. Skinner* v *Veronica Skinner* AIR 1930 Lah 1004; *Rahmath Unnissa Begum* v *Shimoga Co-operative Bank Ltd.* AIR 1951 Mys 59; *Purshottam Sava* v *Kunverjie Devji* AIR 1954 Sau 104; *Gosthe Behari Sadhukhan* v *Omiyo Prosad Mullick* AIR 1960 Cal 361; *Ramswarup Singh* v *Mahabir Mahton* AIR 1960 Pat 235; *Sriram Cotton Pressing Factory P. Ltd.* v *Narayanaswami Naidu* AIR 1965 Mad 352.

17 Halsbury's *Laws of England*, 4th Ed., vol. 16, para 1471 at p. 992.

18 *Associated Hotels* v *Ranjit Singh* AIR 1968 SC 933; (1968)2 SCR 548.

19 *Motilal Padampat Sugar Mills* v *State of UP* AIR 1979 SC 621; (1979)2 SCR 641.

All the same, delay as a defence in a suit for specific performance should be specifically pleaded and if the point is not taken, it will not be allowed in second appeal.[20] It is most fundamental that a party giving up an issue in trial court cannot raise the same in appeal.[1]

In *Dr. Jiwan Lal* v *Brij Mohan Mehra*[2] cl. (6) of the agreement of sale read:

> "In the event of the above premises, which is the subject matter of sale, not being vacated by the income-tax authorities or its being subsequently requisitioned by the Government prior to the registration of the sale deed, the vendor shall refund to the purchaser the sum of ₹10,000 received by the vendor as earnest money plus interest at the rate of 6 per cent per annum."

The premises were requisitioned by the Government. The vendor contended that the contract had come to an end. But the vendees contended that they waived the condition and were entitled to specific performance. *Held*, cl. (6) was inserted in the agreement for the exclusive benefit of the vendees and not for the benefit of the vendor as well as the vendees. Where a stipulation is for the exclusive benefit of one contracting party and does not create liabilities against him, he can waive it unilaterally.[3]

In any case specific performance is not a prize to be awarded by equity to the zealous and denied to the indolent.[4]

Enforcement of contract against consent decree The court would not decree a suit for specific performance against a consent decree duly recorded by a competent court.[5] A suit for specific performance of contract based on consent decree is not barred by s. 47, CPC. Consent decree is nothing but an agreement between the parties superimposed with the seal of the court and the specific performance of such agreement can always be sought by filing substantive suit.[6]

20 *Mir Abdul Hakeem Khan* v *Abdul Mannan Khadri* AIR 1972 AP 178 at p. 183 (DB) relying on *Mokund Lall* v *Chotay Lall* 10 Cal 1061 and *Peer Mahomed* v *Mahomed Ebrahim* 29 Bom 234.

1 *Sukhlal* v *Deepchand* AIR 1954 Raj 58; *Mahadeo Patnaik* v *Dula De* (1968)34 Cut LT 1360; *Jamuna* v *Polayya* AIR 1977 Ori 119; *Indra Prokash Karnani* v *J.K. Merchants* AIR 1977 NOC 234 (Cal); *S.K. Fathima Bi* v *V. Chalapathy* AIR 1978 AP 401; *Bipin* v *Rudranarayan* AIR 1978 Ori 203; *Mahadev* v *Basudev* AIR 1981 Cal 9; *Songadh Group Gram Panchayat* v *Raman Lal* AIR 1984 Guj 140 (FB).

2 AIR 1973 SC 559; (1973)2 SCR 230; (1972)2 SCC 757.

3 *Hawksley* v *Outram* [1892]3 Ch 359 at p. 376 and *Morrell* v *Studd & Millington* [1913]2 Ch 648 at p. 660.

4 *Lazard Bros. & Co. Ltd.* v *Fairfield Properties Co. (Mayfair) Ltd.* [1977]121 SJ 793.

5 *G. Jayashree* v *Bhagwandas S. Patel* (2009)3 SCC 144 (155).

6 *Adetia Das Remedios* v *Anand Giri Keni* AIR 2005 Bom 421.

Willingness When a purchaser is willing to perform his part of contract, he must be entitled to relief of specific performance.[7] It is *inte se* between mother and son where the issue of *benami* can arise but not in respect of third person, such as the appellant.[8]

When the defendant is illiterate, burden lies on the plaintiff to prove that the defendant had put his thumb impression after knowing the contents of agreement of sale.[9]

Hardship The law is thus stated in Halsbury's *Laws of England:*[10]

> "Specific performance may not be ordered where the performance would involve, even without any impropriety on the part of the plaintiff, great hardship to the defendants, so much so, that it would not be unreasonable and harsh to grant equitable relief. Such hardship may be apparent on the face of the contract, or latent and the result of collateral matters in which event the court is more likely to refuse performance."

Section 20, the Specific Relief Act[11] specified under what circumstances hardship can be taken into consideration in refusing relief of specific performance. Section 20(2)(*b*) provided that it was where the specific performance would entail hardship on the defendant which he did not foresee, whereas its non-performance would involve no such hardship on the plaintiff. It was not possible to enumerate the different circumstances which constitute a hardship. Specific performance can be refused on the ground that plaintiff on his own has even quantified the actual amount to which he is entitled to in the event of grant of alternative relief to him. Mere rise in price subsequent to the date of the contract or inadequacy of price is not to be treated as a hardship entailing refusal of specific performance of contract. The hardship involved should be collateral to the contract. In sum it is not just one factor or two, that is relevant for consideration. But it is the sum total of various factors which is required to enter into the judicial verdict. Every decree for specific performance may entail some inconvenience to the parties against whom such a decree is passed. However that is not a circumstance constituting hardship within the meaning of that expression employed in s. 20(2)(*b*)[12] of the Specific Relief Act.[13]

7 *Swarnendu Dasgupta* v *Sadhana Banerjee* AIR 2015 Cal 46; *Naurjala* v *Mahesh Kumar* AIR 2011 HP 47.
8 *Sher Singh* v *Ishan Singh* AIR 2015 P&H 20.
9 *Ayithi Appalaraidu* v *Petla Papamma* AIR 2011 AP 172 (180).
10 4th Ed., vol. 44(1), para 869.
11 Prior to its amendment by the Specific Relief (Amendment) Act 2018.
12 *Ibid.*
13 *K. Venkoji Rao* v *M. Abdul Khuddur Kureshi* AIR 1991 Kant 119; *Syscon Consultants Pvt. Ltd.* v *Primella Sanitary Prod. Pvt. Ltd.* AIR 2016 SC 4564.

In *Sarika Rani* v *Deepak Raj*[14] the trial court as well as the First Appellate Court decreed the suit for specific performance of an agreement for sale, but the High Court upset the concurrent findings holding that the second defendant was a *bona fide* purchaser and that the defendant-vendor would suffer hardship as a result of the decree for specific performance. The second defendant had not even entered into the witness box in support of his claim that he was a *bona fide* purchaser. The Supreme Court held that the High Court ought not to have upset the findings of the first two courts in the Second Appeal and the question of hardship which has not been raised by the defendant should not have been gone into. The judgment of the High Court in the Second Appeal was set aside and that of the trial court restored.

In *A.S. Arulappan* v *Smt. Ahalya Naik*[15] the Supreme Court pointed out that the jurisdiction to decree specific performance was discretionary and the court should consider various circumstances to decide whether such relief was to be granted. If under the terms of the contract the plaintiff got an unfair advantage over the defendant and if the defendant would be put to undue hardship which he did not foresee at the time of the agreement, it was inequitable to grant specific relief and the court could desist from granting the decree to the plaintiff. There in that case, the plaintiff had advanced a sum of ₹42,000 as early as 1st May 1977. She had also parted with ₹4,000 subsequently. While denying her the relief of specific performance on the ground that it would cause hardship to the defendant, the Supreme Court directed that the plaintiff was entitled to refund of a total sum of ₹46,000 with interest at 14% from the date of payment till the date of realisation and created a charge on the suit property.

Simply because the vendor has been residing in the house he agreed to transfer is no ground to refuse relief to vendee no matter the decree of specific performance may entail hardship to the vendor.[16]

While considering the question of hardship, the court will consider the comparative hardships to the parties.[17] As the grant of relief of specific performance is discretionary, the courts should keep in view the hardship which is likely to cause to the other party while exercising this discretionary power.[18]

> "The question of the hardship of a contract is generally to be judged of at the time at which it is entered into. If it be then fair and just and not

14 (2001)4 Supreme 510.

15 (2001)5 Supreme 730.

16 *Yohannan* v *Hari Krishnan Nair* AIR 1992 Ker 49.

17 *V. Muthusami* v *Angammal* AIR 2002 SC 1279; *K. Narendra* v *Riviera Apartments (P.) Ltd.* AIR 1999 SC 2309.

18 *Deralsals* v *Ibrahimsab* AIR 2005 SC 1940.

productive of hardship, it will be immaterial that it may by the force of subsequent circumstances or change of events have become less beneficial to one party, except where these subsequent events have been in some way due to the party who seeks the performance of the contract. For whatever contingencies may attach to a contract or be involved in the performance of either part, they have been taken upon themselves by the parties to it. It has been determined that the reasonableness of a contract to be judged of at the time it is entered into, and not by the light of subsequent events and ...... the same principle applies in considering the fairness of a contract."[19]

The hardship contemplated under cl. (*b*) of sub-sec. (2) of s. 20[20] may be hardship or oppression arising from the terms of the agreement itself or from circumstances existing at the time of entering into it. This has been so clarified by *Explanation* (2) there under. The mere loss or inconvenience resulting from the enforcement of a lawful bargain however onerous should not be regarded as hardship in this context. Inadequacy of prices is not also a ground to be considered, unless the purchaser stands in a fiduciary position to the vendor or fraud entered into the agreement. Lack of knowledge of the real value of the property to be sold on the part of the vendor is not also a ground for refusal. Prehaps, a combination of these coupled with some other circumstances following from the enforcement of the agreement or collateral to it may persuade the court towards refusal provided those hardships were not foreseen by the vendor. In a case a lady, a graduate who used to manage her invalid husband's property with eyes wide open entered into contract of sale. On making all relevant enquiries bargaining price was fixed. It was held that decree for specific performance cannot be denied on the ground that she was unaware of the real nature and potentiality of the property.[21]

Fry in his treatise on *Specific Performance of Contracts*,[1] has stated:

"It would seem that, in considering the hardship which may flow from the execution of a contract, the Court will consider whether it is a result obviously flowing from the terms of the contract, so that it must have been present at the time of the contract to the minds of the contracting parties, or whether it arises from something collateral and so far concealed and latent, as that it might not have been thus present to their minds. It is obvious that a far higher degree of hardship must be present in the former than in the latter class of cases, for it to operate on the discretion of the Court."

See *Ranganayakamma* v *N. Govinda Narayan*[2] following these principles, the court refused specific performance of the contract.

19 Fry on *Specific Performance of Contract*, 6th Ed., p. 199.
20 Prior to its amendment by the Specific Relief (Amendment) Act 2018.
21 *T.K. Santha* v *A.G. Rathnam* AIR 1990 Ker 69.
1 6th Ed., para 425, p. 203.
2 AIR 1982 Kant 265.

In *Kuthumumaraswami Goundan* v *Ranga Rao*[3] the court observed that the mere fact that the defendant entered into a losing bargain or one where plaintiff will reap great gains is clearly not enough ground to deprive the plaintiff of the benefit of his contract. However, wide the jurisdiction of the court may be to grant succour to persons who have been victimised, there is no power to grant relief to a person whose only complaint is that the bargain is foolish and improvident. If the court were to strike down a bargain on the ground that it was not wise on the part of one of the contracting parties to have entered into it, it would be assuming an overriding power to interfere with the freedom of contract.[4]

Even so, subsequent events which have been induced by the conduct of the plaintiff will be relevant.[5]

However, a subsequent rise in price is not relevant and does not furnish any basis for refusing the relief of specific performance.[6]

Likewise, where a purchaser not without notice does some improvement on the land, he cannot be heard to say that the specific performance will cause hardship to him. The injury or hardship is self-induced and the defendant cannot set up his own wrong against the plaintiff to defeat his claim.[7]

The vendor agreed to sell to the prospective vendee who sued for specific performance of contract of sale but the vendor already built on the disputed land godowns and other costly structures. The decree of specific performance was to result in special hardship to the vendor. He was, therefore, directed to pay present value of the disputed land instead of executing sale deed in vendee's favour.[8]

The hardship contemplated under s. 20(2)(*b*)[9] of the Specific Relief Act must be such that the defendant could not foresee, i.e. from something which was not present in the mind of the contracting parties at the time of the contract. Thus where during the pendency of a suit for specific performance of an agreement for sale of a family property the daughters in

3 ILR (1964)2 Mad 500.
4 *Mountford* v *Scott* [1975]1 All ER 198 at pp. 200, 201 (CA).
5 *Moram Venkataratnam* v *Gothi Mukhala Jagannadha Raju* (1971)2 APLJ 57 (DB).
6 *Badruddin* v *Tufail Ahmed* AIR 1963 MP 31 at p. 35; *S.P. Narayanaswami Pillai* v *Dhanakoti Ammal* AIR 1967 Mad 220 at p. 224 following *Sankaralinga* v *Ratnaswami* AIR 1952 Mad 389 at 392; *Mir Abdul Hakeem* v *Abdul Mannan* AIR 1972 AP 178 at p. 184 (DB); *Abdul Satar* AIR 1970 Guj 12 at p. 24; *Chatterbhuj Goel* v *Gurpreet Singh* AIR 1983 P&H 406 at p. 415.
7 *D.V. Sashaiah* v *D. Venkayya* AIR 1974 AP 193 at p. 198 (DB); *T. Venkata Subrahmanyam* v *V. Viswanadha Raju* AIR 1968 AP 190 and *Haradhan Debnath* v *Bhagabati Dasi* AIR 1914 Cal 137.
8 *Damacheria Anjaneyulu* v *Damacheria Venkata Seshaiah* AIR 1987 SC 1641; (1987)2 Guj LH 182; (1987)2 Land LR 570.
9 Prior to its amendment by the Specific Relief (Amendment) Act 2018.

the family got a right to a share by virtue of the Andhra Pradesh Amendment of the Hindu Succession Act, it was held that their right was subject to the agreement.[10] In *K. Narendra* v *Riviera Apartments P. Ltd.*[11] *K* agreed in 1997 with *R* for construction of a multi-storeyed building on *K*'s land. The amount agreed upon was paid and possession of part of the land was also handed over to *R*. After the Urban Land (Ceiling and Regulation) Act 1976 came into force, *K* could construct on the land only in terms of the scheme framed under that Act, which contained conditions restricting the constructed area and requiring that any person could hold only one dwelling unit in the scheme. Specific performance was refused *inter alia* on the ground that the performance of the contract would involve such hardship on *K* as he did not foresee. The doctrine of comparative hardship has been statutorily recognized in India under s. 20(2)(*b*)[12] of the Specific Relief Act. However, by the Specific Relief (Amendment) Act 2018, the position of law with regard to hardship as mentioned in the earlier law has been altered.

In *V. Muthusamy (dead) by LRs* v *Angammal*,[13] the Supreme Court following its earlier decision in *K. Narendra's* case,[14] held that defendants 3 to 6 were *bona fide* purchasers for value without notice of the agreement for sale and a decree for specific performance of the contract for sale would involve hardship on the purchasers-defendants 3 to 6 and no hardship should be caused to the plaintiff and he could be compensated by a decree of compensation and accordingly directed defendants 3 to 6 to return to the plaintiff the advance amount of ₹3,000 with interest at 12%. In *Yohannan* v *Harikrishnan Nair*,[15] the court refused to exercise the discretion not to enforce specific performance of agreement for sale of a house on the ground that hardship would be caused to the vendor by vacating the house. It was held that it cannot be found that such hardship was not foreseen when the contract was entered into so as to bring the case within the ambit of cl. (*b*) of s. 20(2)[12] of the Act. Mere non-availability of alternative accommodation to the vendor will not be a ground for grant of specific performance to the purchaser of the house.[16] Where, however, there is a term in the agreement for sale that the transferor shall execute the deed of sale of the house when alternative accommodation is available to him, the specific performance cannot be sought without waiting for a reasonable time.[17]

The Supreme Court dealing with Explanation 2 of s. 20 of the Act prior to its amendment observed, "Explanation 2 requires that the issue as to

10 *Vanimisadti Anil Kumar* v *Jayavarappu Krishnamurthy* AIR 1995 AP 105.
11 AIR 1999 SC 2309; (1999)5 SCC 77; JT 1999(4) SC 428.
12 Prior to its amendment by the Specific Relief (Amendment) Act 2018.
13 AIR 2002 SC 1279.
14 AIR 1999 SC 2309; (1999)5 SCC 77; JT 1999(4) SC 428.
15 AIR 1992 Ker 49.
16 *Mt. Ford* v *Scott* [1975] Ch 258.
17 *Deokabai* v *Uttam* 1994 Mah LJ 11 (SC).

whether the performance of a contract involves hardship on the defendant has to be determined with reference to the circumstances existing at the time of the contract, except where the hardship has been caused from an act of the plaintiff subsequent to the contract".[18]

Plea of hardship In a suit for specific performance, a plea of hardship has to be raised initially. Such plea cannot be entertained for the first time in appeal by way of SLP, more so, when there are concurrent findings that the plaintiff was ready and willing to perform his part of the contract has been recorded by the lower courts.[19]

Inadequacy of consideration Explanation 1 to s. 20(2)[20] of the Act makes it clear that mere inadequacy of consideration or the mere fact that the contract is onerous to the defendant or improvident in its nature, shall not be deemed to constitute an unfair advantage within the meaning of cl. (*a*) or hardship within the meaning of cl. (*b*).[21]

Specific performance cannot be refused for mere inadequacy of consideration. Even assuming that the sale consideration is inadequate, that cannot be a ground for denying specific performance.[22] Nor can increase in price of property be a ground for refusing the decree of specific performance.[1] Short of undue influence or duress, an agreement between the parties cannot be rendered nugatory on the ground that consideration is not adequate.[2] Though it is not possible to enumerate exhaustively the circumstances which constituted either unfair advantage or hardship, there are certain circumstances which have been held to constitute unfair advantage or hardship. Where the defendants are admittedly illiterate agriculturists and indebted to plaintiff for a long time, these circumstances coupled with inadequacy of consideration will disentitle the plaintiff from claiming specific performance.[3] Even in cases where price is grossly inadequate, the courts require an additional dose of proof that by reason of a design by the avaricious purchaser, the vendor had been victimised.[4] In *Smt. Harbans Atma Singh* v *Ramesh Kumar*[5] the suit agreement was for a sum of ₹2,90,000. The defendant who has got a plot allotted by the Chandigarh Administration out of the defence quota has spent ₹4.5 lakhs

18 *Jayakantham* v *Abaykumar* (2017)5 SCC 178.
19 *Beemaneni Maha Lakshmi* v *Gangumalla Appa Rao* (2019)6 SCC 233.
20 The provision has been amended by the Specific Relief (Amendment) Act 2018.
21 *Surjeet Singh* v *Kartar Singh* AIR 1988 Punj 53; 1987 Punj LR 184.
22 *C.C. Karthiyayini Amma* v *T.V.G. Namboodri* 1996 AIHC 5291 (Ker).
1 *K.M. Madhava Krishnan* v *S.R. Swami* AIR 1995 Mad 318; *S.V.R. Mudaliar* v *Rajabu F. Buhari* AIR 1995 SC 1607; (1995)4 SCC 15.
2 *Vijaya Minerals Pvt. Ltd.* v *Bikash Chandra Deb* AIR 1996 Cal 67.
3 *Manak Chand* v *Puran* AIR 1960 MP 235.
4 *Rengasami Gounder* v *Periamuthu Gounder* 1977(1) MLJ 231 (DB).
5 AIR 1986 P&H 14.

to put up a construction to save the plot from resumption. In such a case, it would cause considerable hardship to the defendant if the suit was decreed for specific performance.

Escalation in price cannot be a defence in a suit for specific performance.[6] Subsequent rise in price will not be treated as hardship entitling refusal of the decree for specific performance.[7] Unless the plaintiff is guilty of conduct disentitling him from specific performance, *viz.*, delay or inaction.[8] The plaintiff cannot be penalised for lapse of time and consequent rise in price.[9]

Plaintiff is not disentitled to get the decree for specific performance by mere fact that there is stipulation in the agreement about the refund of money in the event of defaulting to perform the agreement by the vendor.[10]

Inadequacy of consideration is no ground to refuse relief to the plaintiff vendee.[11] Inadequacy of consideration does not generally operate as unfair advantage, nor as a ground to refuse relief of specific performance of contract. In a case the defendant agreed to sell the disputed property to the plaintiff and the stipulated time for execution of sale deed was extended up to time of the plaintiff's getting orders from Government for exemption of stamp duty and permission from competent authority for the sale and purchaser of urban property. The defendant-vendor kept on receiving substantial sums from plaintiff. While matter was pending for consideration of Government the defendant issued notice stating that price of property had gone up and that he had sufficiently waited for completion of sale. It was also stated that on account of long delay the plaintiff had lost right to purchase property and contract for sale had been terminated. At that stage Government informed that request for exemption could not be complied with. The plaintiff wrote that he was willing to pay stamp duty and register sale deed and was ready and willing to perform his part of contract. But the defendant issued reply notice saying that agreement of sale had already been cancelled. Hence, the suit came to be filed by plaintiff for specific performance of contract. It was held, at the time when contract was entered into, price for

6 *Namazi* v *Central Chinmaya Mission* AIR 1988 Mad 84; 100 LW 582; *P. Laxmi Ammal* v *S. Laxmi Ammal* AIR 1991 Mad 137; *Satya Jain* v *Anis Ahmed Rushdie* AIR 2013 SC 3784.

7 *S.V.R. Mudaliar* v *Rajabu F. Buhari* AIR 1995 SC 1607; (1995)4 SCC 15; JT 1995(3) SC 614.

8 *K.S. Vaidyanathan* v *Vairavan* AIR 1997 SC 1751; (1997)3 SCC 1; JT 1997(2) SC 375; *Saradamani Kandappan* v *S. Rajalakshmi* AIR 2011 SC 3234; *Swaran Singh* v *Swaran Kaur* AIR 2004 P&H 242.

9 *Kochu Thambu Rowther Hassan Kutti* v *Peer Mohamed Pudhumalaiyar Rowther* AIR 2000 Ker 17; *Babulal Agarwal* v *Jothi Srivatsava* AIR 2000 MP 83; *Gobind Ram* v *Gian Chand* AIR 2000 SC 3106; (2000)7 SCC 548; *Laxman Tatyaba Kankate* v *Smt. Taramati Harishchandra Dhatnak* AIR 2010 SC 3025.

10 *Laxman Ram* v *Krishna Ram* AIR 2007 Raj 84.

11 *Yohannan* v *Harikrishan Nair* AIR 1992 Ker 49.

property was adequate. Due to some supervening circumstances namely, grant of exemption from provisions of urban land ceiling and payment of stamp duty there was delay and merely because during this period there was escalation in prices, the inadequacy of price could not constitute an unfair advantage. Thus, delay could not be put against plaintiff so as to deny him right of specific performance on grounds that such relief is discretionary.[12]

Though mere inadequacy of consideration would not entitle the court to refuse to grant a decree for specific performance,[13] the court will refuse the decree where the bargain appears to be so hard as to be unconscionable.[14]

In fact, the only exception is where the inadequacy of consideration is so gross as of itself to prove fraud or imposition on the part of the purchaser.[15] Likewise, if the price named in the agreement is far beyond its value, the court will not decree specific performance.[16]

Specific performance may not be decreed where the sale price was to be settled by named persons, if the court sees reason to believe that the price subsequently fixed by these persons is considerably below the real value of the property,[17] where specific performance was decreed because there was no proof of fraud, mistake, collusion or miscarriage.

Inequitable to enforce specific performance—section 20(2)(c)[18] A court of equity is not bound to decree specific performance, even though the buyer is ready and willing to perform his part of the contract. If the agreement for sale was, in circumstances of great distress and tension for the vendor, where his life was insecure and the property was agreed to be sold at an adequate price, the court will not order specific performance and compensation for breach of contract will be sufficient. Where the plaintiff was already in possession as a mortgagee and creditor and sought to enforce the agreement for sale of the same ancestral property against a widow and minor sons of the deceased vendor who, on mistake, executed the agreement without any legal necessity, or in circumstances of indebtedness to the plaintiff, it was held that enforcing specific performance

12 *N.B. Namazi* v *Central Chinmaya Mission Trust* AIR 1988 Mad 84; (1987)100 Mad LW 582; (1987)2 Mad LJ 317.

13 *Lalji* v *Ramji* AIR 1978 All 212.

14 *Haradhan Debnath* v *Bhagabati Dasi* AIR 1914 Cal 137; *Sukumar Bysack* v *Sushil Kanta Banerjee* AIR 1972 Cal 207; see also *Callaghan* v *Callaghan* [1841]8 Cl & Fin 374 (HL) (transaction in the nature of gift rather than a sale); *Cockell* v *Taylor* [1851]15 Beav 103 (case of great undervalue coupled with the illiteracy and humble circumstances of the defendant).

15 *Borell* v *Dann* 67 ER 181.

16 *Day* v *Newman* 30 ER 36; *Falcke* v *Gray* [1859]4 Drew 651.

17 *Parken* v *Whitby* 37 ER 1142 *cf.*, however, *Weeks* v *Gallard* [1869]21 LT 655 and *Collier* v *Mason* 53 ER 613.

18 The provision has been amended by the Specific Relief (Amendment) Act 2018.

was inequitable.[19] Though mere pecuniary difficulties would afford no excuse, courts have taken into consideration cases of extreme hardship arising after the formation of the contract. Thus in *Patel* v *Ali*,[20] where the vendor's circumstances, had disastrously changed due to illness which left her disabled and bankruptcy of her husband, specific performance of the contract for sale of her house was refused after a lapse of four years. In *Tribhuvan Dutt Tripathy* v *Ramji Tiwari*,[1] the plaintiffs induced the defendant to enter into an agreement for sale with a stipulation that it was their responsibility to get successful performance of another agreement entered by other person in favour of the defendant's son. Since the parties had contemplated performance of both the agreements together and the plaintiffs failed to prove that they had discharged the responsibility as stipulated in the agreement to ensure due performance of the contemporaneous agreements, it was inequitable to grant any relief to them. Where an agreement itself provided an option for the defendant either to pay off the money advanced by the plaintiff for discharge of various debts and retain the property or to sell the property, specific performance for the sale of the property should be refused.[2]

A money lender took a promissory note from the defendant for the money due to him and on the same day the defendant executed an agreement for sale of his property for the discharge of the same promissory note. Though the suit was decreed for specific performance by the courts below, the Supreme Court interfered and granted a decree for money only since the plaintiff had asked for an alternative relief for recovery of the money with interest.[3] Even if it is assumed that the agreement for sale was consciously executed, the materials on record indicated that such an agreement was obtained as a security for the money advanced by the plaintiff and the money that was advanced by the plaintiff was a loan, in the circumstances, specific performance was refused.[4] Generally, the courts will not compel the defendant to do an act which would necessitate a breach by the defendant of a contract with the third party or would compel the defendant to do that which he is not lawfully competent to do.[5]

One of the grounds on which the court may decline to decree specific performance is where it would be ireguitable to enforce specific performance. Where the object of agreement was construction of residential houses for the weaker sections of society on the excess land, but those houses could

19 *Harmit Singh* v *Surjeet Kaur* AIR 2000 Raj 289.
20 [1984] Ch 283.
1 AIR 1991 All 268.
2 *B.R. Mulani* v *Dr. A.B. Aswathanarayana* AIR 1993 SC 1318.
3 *S. Rangaraju Naidu* v *S. Thiruvarakkarasu* AIR 1995 SC 1769; 1995 Supp (2) SCC 680.
4 *Sitaram Lal* v *Jameshwar Das* AIR 1995 Ori 260.
5 Fry on *Specific Performance*, 6th Ed., p. 194.

not be constructed in view of existing master plan, held it would be wholly ireguitable to enforce specific performance of such contract.[6]

Doctrine of mutuality To explain what the doctrine of mutuality stands for the following extract from Jowitt's *Dictionary of English Law*, p. 1215 may be extracted: In every agreement the parties must, as regards the principal or essential part of the transaction, intend the same thing; that is, each must know what the other is to do; this is called mutuality of assent.

In a simple contract arising from agreement, it is sometimes of the essence of the transaction that each party should be bound to do something under it: this requirement is called mutuality; thus, an agreement by *A* to refer a question between himself and *B* to arbitration is not enforceable unless *B* also agrees to be bound by the award; and an agreement by *C* with *D* to learn a trade is not binding unless there is also an undertaking by *D* to teach him. This may be called mutuality of obligation. As stated in Black's *Law Dictionary*: "mutuality of contract" means that "the agreement of both parties to a contract to be bound in some way".[7]

The doctrine of mutuality means that the contract must be enforceable by each party against the other. It does not mean that right for right there must be a corresponding clause. A contract may contain series of clauses and covenants which form the total bargain between the parties and each of them is the consideration for the other. Mutuality in this context does not mean equality and exact arithmatical correspondence. It means that each party to the contract must have the freedom to enforce his rights under the contract against the other.[8]

Section 20(4) enacted that the court shall not refuse to any party specific performance of a contract merely on the ground that the contract was not enforceable at the instance of the other party. Even before this, the accepted position was that it did not apply to unilateral contracts, because in such cases the party seeking to enforce the promise had already performed his obligations and there could not be any question of enforcing the contract against him.[9]

The doctrine of mutuality also did not apply where the defendant himself was at fault, or where only one party had signed the memorandum of agreement, or where the trustee had purchased trust property or where

6 *H.H.M. Shantidevi P. Gaikwad* v *Sanjebhai Haribhai Patle* AIR 2001 SC 1462; (2001)5 SCC 101.

7 10th Ed. 2014.

8 *Dasarath* v *Satyanarayan* AIR 1963 Cal 325.

9 *Shree Ram* v *Ratanlal* AIR 1965 All 83; *Rakhama Sitaram Ghadge* v *Laxman Sitaram Ghadge* AIR 1960 Bom 105 and *Fazaladdin Mondal* v *Panchanan Das* AIR 1957 Cal 92.

the defendant might be deemed to have waived his right. A plea of mutuality cannot be raised in appeal if it is not mentioned in the written statement.[10]

Even so, the language used in s. 20(4)[11] does not justify the inference that the doctrine of mutuality has been completely thrown out of consideration. The use of the word 'merely' clearly shows that it does not exclude the consideration of mutuality along with other consideration.[12] So, where an agreement for sale of property was unilaterally executed by the vendor and towards a sale consideration a pronote, liable to become time barred, was executed by the vendee and the pronote had become time barred on the expiry of the term fixed for execution of sale deed, there was no mutuality of parties and the agreement could not be termed as a contract in the circumstances of case and specific performance could not be granted.[13] When the document is not properly executed such document cannot be believed.[14]

The agreement of reconveyance if executed subsequently to the sale is not void on the ground of absence of mutuality and is specifically enforceable.[15]

Specific performance not ordered—when (American law) A promise will not be specifically enforced if the character and magnitude of the performance would impose on the court burdens in enforcement or supervision that are disproportionate to the advantage to be gained from enforcement. Similarly, a promise to render personal service will not be specifically enforced.[16]

Compensation in Lieu of Substitution of Specific Performance

Compensation is the payment of damages, or any other out that a court orders to be done by a person who has caused injury to another.[17] Compensation to some extent is a matter of guess work.[18] Section 21(1) says that in a suit for specific performance of a contract, the plaintiff may also claim compensation for its breach, either in addition to, or in substitution of, such performance. But in awarding compensation the court shall observe

10 *Darbara Singh* v *Harpal Singh* 1994(I) CCC 905 (907).
11 The provision has been amended by the Specific Relief (Amendment) Act 2018. The provision will be applicable to the cases under the previous law.
12 *Than Singh* v *Barelal* AIR 1974 MP 24 at p. 26 (DB); *Pradeep Kumar* v *Gwalior Improvement Trust* AIR 1978 MP 179 (case remanded).
13 *Narayana Pillai* v *Kunju Amma Thankamma* AIR 1990 Ker 177.
14 *K. Nanjappa* v *R.A. Hameed* alias *Ameersab* AIR 2015 SC 3389.
15 *Dave Ramshanker Jivatram* v *Bai Kailasgauri* AIR 1974 Guj 69 at p. 72 relying on *Rakhama Sitaram Ghadge* v *Laxman Sitaram Ghadge* AIR 1960 Bom 105.
16 *Restatement of the Law,* Second Series, Contract 2d., vol. 3, §366, 367.
17 Black's *Law Dictionary,* 10th Ed. 2014.
18 *K. Narendra* v *Riviera Apartments (P) Ltd.* AIR 1999 SC 2309.

the principles specified in s. 73 of the Indian Contract Act 1872 [s. 21(4)]. Even if the court finds that the case is not fit for specific performance but the defendant is guilty of breach of contract, the court shall award him compensation if the plaintiff is otherwise entitled to compensation for the breach[19] [s. 21(2)]. Likewise, even in a case where the court is inclined to grant specific performance but finds that it is not sufficient to satisfy the justice of the case, it shall award compensation [s. 21(3)]. But in either case the plaintiff must have claimed the compensation [s. 21(5)]. If he has not claimed the compensation, he will be allowed to amend his plaint at any stage of the proceedings on such terms as may be just for including a claim for such compensation [Proviso to s. 21(5)]. The court is not debarred from exercising this jurisdiction, even if the contract has become incapable of specific performance [Expl. to s. 21].

In a case the defendant agreed to sell his agricultural land to plaintiff who was a non-agriculturist. The clauses in the agreement provided that the defendant had to obtain permission to sell the land under the Tenancy Act and to get land converted to non-agricultural user. The plaintiff paid ₹10,000 out of a total of ₹22,000 which was the sale price, as earnest money. The defendant did not take step for obtaining permissions and on one or the other pretext tried to rescind the contract. It was held that mere applying for conversion to non-agricultural land is not enough and the defendant is guilty of breach of contract and is liable to pay damages.[20]

Compensation There was nothing to show that the defendant has breached agreement which has resulted in the plaintiff's suffering from an injury for which it is entitled to claim compensation or damages. Thus, the plaintiff is not entitled to compensation. However, the plaintiff is entitled to refund of the earnest money with interest @ 12% p.a.[1]

Though the mere fact that price of the properties have risen is no ground to refuse specific performance, where the plaintiff claimed an alternative relief, the court would be justified in giving damages.[2] Where in an agreement for sale, the sale requires permission of a third party, the permission is refused and the third party is not amenable to the jurisdiction of the court, damages can be awarded.[3] Where specific performance is refused by the defendant, the plaintiff may claim compensation without claiming specific performance of contract.[4]

19 *S. Abdul Khader* v *Abdul Wajed* (2008)9 SCC 522; *Bhagwan B. Kedari* v *Dwarkanath K. Bagare* AIR 2005 Kant 108.
20 *Shantabai* v *Manakchand* AIR 1988 Bom 82; 1988 Mah LR 732.
1 *Sewa International* v *Kalawati Mathrani* AIR 2016 NOC 163 (Del).
2 *Kanshiram* v *Om Prakash Jawal* AIR 1996 SC 2150; *Jamila Khatton* v *Ram Nivas Gupta* AIR 1998 All 138.
3 *Golab Ray* v *Muralidhar Modi* AIR 1964 Ori 176; *Bishambhar Nath Agarwal* v *Kishan Chand* AIR 1998 All 195.
4 *Naturam* v *Ulluk Chand* AIR 1926 Cal 1041.

An agreement to sell a house by all co-owners except one was made. Suit for specific performance by plaintiff purchaser was instituted. Co-owner, not a party to an agreement to sell, claimed to purchase shares of other co-owners. Counsel for plaintiff gave consent to such purchase by co-owner, not party to agreement, at a reasonable market value within a stipulated period. Valuation of property was agreed to by both the parties. Order passed to execute the sale deed in favour of the said co-owner is a consent order. No appeal lies from such order. It is well settled that the value of property escalates in urban areas very fast and it would not be equitable to grant specific performance after a lapse of long period of time.[5] An order for payment of amount may be made against the plaintiff seeking specific performance, to be paid for the purposes of balancing equities, or for catering to the rise in prices.[6]

It is for the plaintiff to make his election.[7] It is, however, not open to a party to a contract, who has once elected to accept the breach, assuming there was a breach on the part of the other side to cancel that election, and treat the contract as if it were subsisting.[8] The two reliefs of specific performance or damages in lieu of or in substitution of specific performance are not mutually destructive and the suit cannot be said to be barred by unamended s. 14(1).[9] But since such claim postulates a privity of contract, the subsequent purchaser cannot be held liable for damages or compensation, for to make him liable would be nothing short of enforcing a charge upon the property purchased by him which is illegal.[10]

It is settled that the provisions of s. 55(6)(*b*) of the T.P. Act apply not only to a completed conveyance where the seller does not deliver the property sold to the buyer, but also to executory contracts of sale where the seller in breach of the contract transfers the property and delivers it to a third person. It follows that a buyer who fails to get delivery of the property under the contract is entitled unless it is shown that he had improperly declined to accept delivery to a charge on the property against the seller and all persons claiming under him to the extent of the seller's interest therein for the amount of any purchase money property paid in anticipation of the delivery of the property and for interest on such amount. Yet s. 55(6)(*b*) creates a charge only. For enforcement of the charge, the relevant provision is s. 100 of the Transfer of Property Act, and, therefore, the statutory charge created by s. 55(6)(*b*) for refund of prepaid purchase price cannot

5 *Vimaleshwar Nagappa Shet* v *Noor Ahmed Sheriff* AIR 2011 SC 2057.
6 *Satya Jain* v *Anis Ahmed Rushdie* AIR 2013 SC 434.
7 *Gopi Nath Sen* v *Bahadurmul Dulichand* AIR 1979 Cal 203.
8 *K.S. Sundaramayyar* v *K. Jagadeesan* AIR 1965 Mad 85 at p. 86 (DB).
9 *Pasumarti Ramulu* v *Nuthi Anantha Ramulu* AIR 1966 AP 70 at p. 72.
10 *Jhandoo* v *Ramesh Chandra* AIR 1971 All 189 at p. 192.

be enforced against the property in the hands of a subsequent transferee for valuable consideration without notice of charge.[11]

Compensation must be pleaded and proved, and must be distinct from an order granting costs.[12]

Waiver Where the vendee accepts the refund of his deposit knowing fully well that the vendor has cancelled the contract, the mere conditional acceptance by the use of the words 'without prejudice' to his rights under the contract cannot in any manner derogate from the fact that he has acquiesced in the breach of the contract and that it amounts to waiver of his right to enforce the contract.[13] What was of importance was what the vendee did and not what he said.[14]

See also *George Henry Davenport* v *H.M. Queen*[15] assuming a forfeiture had accrued it was waived by the receipt of rent, notwithstanding the conditional acceptance following *Croft* v *Lumley*[16] where money is paid and received as rent under a lease, a mere protest that it is accepted conditionally and without prejudice to the right to insist upon a prior forfeiture, cannot countervail the fact of such receipt,[17] payment made by lessee accepted by the lessor as rent but kept in suspense account subject to payment by the lessee of the remaining amount. *Held* that such a qualification did not make the payments anything else than payments of rent and that the lessor had thereby waived his right to insist on re-entry,[18] (conditional acceptance of rent by the lessor after default involving a forfeiture is nonetheless a waiver), and *Chotu Mia* v *Mst. Sundri*[19] (where after the forfeiture of the lease, the lessee remits certain amount to lessor as rent and the lessor accepts it only as damages for use and occupation, the acceptance of the payment must be deemed to be as rent and operates as a waiver of the forfeiture).

This was the position under the old law. The new provision contained in proviso to sub-sec. (1) to s. 21 makes it obligatory on the court to grant

11 *Abhey Ram* v *Umrao Singh* 1979 All LJ 1309 relying on *Deep Chandra* v *Mohd. Saijad Ali Khan* AIR 1951 All 93 and *Ahmedabad Municipal Corpn.* v *Haji Abdul Gafur* AIR 1971 SC 1201; (1971)1 SCC 757 and observing that *Hari Bapuji* v *Bhagu Sadhu* AIR 1937 Bom 142; *Abdul Hamid Khan* v *Mohd. Ali* AIR 1952 Bom 67 and *Nawal Kishore* v *Municipal Board, Agra* AIR 1943 All 115 (FB).

12 See for an order granting substantial costs after refusing specific performance—*Rattan Lal* v *S.N. Bhalla* AIR 2012 SC 3094.

13 *H.G. Krishna Reddy & Co.* v *M.M. Thimmiah* AIR 1983 Mad 169 at p. 183 (DB).

14 *Deo d. Morecraft* v *Meux* [1824]1 Car & P 347.

15 [1878]3 AC 115.

16 [1858]6 HLC 672.

17 *Kali Krishna Tagore* v *Fazle Ali Chowdhury* 9 Cal 843.

18 *Satyanarayana* v *Venkataramamurthy* AIR 1935 Mad 454.

19 AIR 1945 Pat 260 (FB).

amendment of plaint to include the relief for compensation or refund of the earnest money, even if the claim was barred by limitation at the time the amendment was sought, the discretion being confined only to terms on which the amendment is to be allowed.[20] In *Jagadish Singh's* case, the Supreme Court has held that the court should allow an amendment at any stage of the proceedings and the plaintiff should not be prevented from adding a plea of compensation in lieu of or in addition to that of specific performance of the contract.

Alternative relief An alternative relief under s. 21 doesn't debar or plaintiff from asking for specific relief,[21] on the ground that the plaintiff has, on his own, quantified the actual amount to which he is entitled to in the event of the grant of alternative relief to him.[1] When plaintiff prayed for alternative remedy also of refund of earnest money and damages and suit been not filed with promptitude though within limitation period, decree for specific performance is not justified.[2] Where the plaintiff claim is in accord with the provisions of s. 21, hereby because the plaintiff claims damages in suit for specific performance of contract as alternative relief, it cannot be said that he is not entitled to the main relief of specific performance of the contract.[3]

Alternative remedy of compensation Under s. 21(5) of the said Act, no compensation can be awarded in a suit for specific performance of a contract unless such a claim for compensation has been made in the plaint. If such claim has not been made in the plaint, the court shall at any stage of the proceedings allow the plaintiff to amend the pleadings on such terms as it deems fit to include a claim for compensation. The proviso to s. 21(5) of the said Act is couched in mandatory form and it stipulates that the court shall at any stage of the proceedings allow the plaintiff to amend the plaint.[4]

Compensation for delay In a suit for specific performance claim for compensation was made on the ground that balance sale price was deposited and there was delay in completion of the contract. But there was no pleading nor any evidence as to loss or damage caused to the plaintiff. The plaintiff did not also quantum of damages. Thus, decree for compensation cannot be granted.[5]

20 *Manohar Dhundhiraj Joshi* v *Jhunnulal Hariram Yadao* 1983 Mah LJ 369; *Jagdish Singh* v *Natthu Singh* AIR 1992 SC 1604; (1992)1 SCC 647; JT 1991(5) SC 400.

21 *P.C. Varghese* v *Devaki Amma Balambika Devi* AIR 2006 SC 145; (2005)8 SCC 486; *Raj Kumar Sharma* v *Pushpa Jaggi* AIR 2006 Del 156; but see *Best Sellers Retail (India) Pvt. Ltd.* v *Aditya Birla Nuro Ltd.* AIR 2012 SC 2448.

1 *K. Venkoji Rao* v *M. Abdul Khuddur Kureshi* AIR 1991 Kant 119.

2 *Janila Khatoon* v *Ram Niwas Gupta* AIR 1998 All 138.

3 *Motilal Jain* v *Ramdasi Devi* AIR 2000 SC 2408.

4 *Praveen* v *Hanuman* (2018)4 Mah LJ 837.

5 *Nalini Sheela* v *Subramaniyan Chettiar Shanmughom* AIR 2011 Ker 82.

Amendment to incorporate claims for compensation and possession at any stage On plaintiff's failure in suit for specific performance when he sues for specific performance only, he cannot be allowed refund of consideration because of bar of s. 22, Specific Relief Act, but court may direct the plaintiff to amend the plaint and on plaintiff's so doing may direct refund of consideration. The court is to permit such amendment at any stage of the proceeding in view of s. 22, Specific Relief Act.[6]

As to amendment to convert a suit for specific performance to one for compensation for breach of contract, s. 22(1) and proviso to it s. 22(2) give a long rope to the plaintiff to so amend. It reads: (1) Notwithstanding anything to the contrary contained in CPC 1908, any person suing for the specific performance of a contract for the transfer of immovable property may, in an appropriate case, ask for—

(*a*) ....

(*b*) any other relief to which he may be entitled, including the refund of any earnest money or deposit paid or made by him, in case his claim for specific performance is refused.

Proviso to s. 22(2) states:

Provided that where the plaintiff has not claimed any such relief in the plaint, the court shall, at any stage of the proceeding, allow him to amend the plaint on such terms as may be just for including a claim for such relief. But sometimes, amendment might not be necessary.[7]

The proviso to s. 22(2) permits the plaintiff to amend the plaint *at any stage of the proceeding*. The words under *italics* deserve close scrutiny. Section 22 enacts a rule of pleading that in order to avoid multiplicity of proceedings the plaintiff may claim a decree for possession in a suit for specific performance, even though strictly speaking, the right to possession accrues only when suit for specific performance is decreed. The expression "in appropriate case" in s. 22(1) only indicates that it is not always incumbent on the plaintiff to claim possession or partition or separate possession in a suit for specific performance of a contract for the transfer of immovable property because the relief for specific performance of the contract of sale embraces within its ambit not only the execution of the sale deed but also possession over the property agreed to be conveyed. Therefore, s. 22(2), Specific Relief Act provides for amendment of plaint *at any stage of the proceeding*. The word 'proceeding' is a comprehensive term and generally speaking means a prescribed course of action for enforcing a legal right. It

6 *Sahida Bibi* v *Golam Mohammad* AIR 1983 Cal 216; *Vishwanathan* v *Ramakrishna Chettiar* (2002)1 LW 415 (Mad).

7 *Hemchand* v *Kanilal* AIR 1987 Raj 117; *Krishnamurthy Gounder* v *Venkatakrishnan* AIR 2012 Mad 105.

includes a prescribed mode in which a judicial business is conducted. It includes even an execution proceeding. So, amendment is permissible even in execution stage.[8] Thus it is open to a plaintiff to convert by amendment his case for specific performance into a claim for damages for breach of contract, for such an amendment does not amount to altering the cause of action or the nature of the suit. The cause of action in a suit for specific performance or damage is the breach of the contract and, therefore, when, in lieu of specific performance, damages are asked for the cause of action continues to be the breach of the contract and one relief which is impossible of performance on account of the defendant's conduct is substituted by the alternative relief asked for,[9] specific performance becoming impossible due to *pendente lite* conduct of the defendant. But where the plaintiff is not ready to perform his part under the contact, the question of granting relief by way of damages in lieu of, or in substitution of, specific performance is a matter resting entirely with the court, and parties have nothing to do with it.[10]

In a suit for specific performance of contract, relief of possession and partition does not introduce a new cause of action nor changes the nature of the suit as such would be allowed by the court.[11] In view of s. 22(1)(*a*), a decree for partition and separate possession of property can be granted in addition to a decree for a specific performance of contract.[12] Relief for possession in favour of successful plaintiff in a suit for specific performance cannot be considered as a separate and distinct one.[13] The relief of possession can be granted even at the appellate stage.[14]

In *Rameshwar Nath* v *Uttar Pradesh Union Bank Ltd.*,[15] a view that a proceeding envisaged in s. 22 includes an execution proceeding was taken. It is a term giving the widest freedom to a Court of Law so that it may do justice to the parties in the case. Execution is a stage in the legal proceedings. It is a step in the judicial process. It marks a stage in litigation. It is a step in the ladder. In the journey of litigation there are various stages, one of them is execution.

> "The expression in sub-sec. (1) of s. 22 'in an appropriate case' is very significant. The plaintiff may ask for the relief of possession or partition or

8 *Babu Lal* v *Hazarilal Kishori Lal* AIR 1982 SC 818; (1982)3 SCR 94; 1982 All LJ 345; (1982)1 SCC 525.

9 *Rajendra Nath Saha* v *Saraswati Press Ltd.* AIR 1952 Cal 78; *Gopal Debjibhai Patel* v *Rishal Singh* AIR 1982 Ori 242.

10 *Gopi Nath Sen* v *Bahadurmal Dulichand* AIR 1979 Cal 203.

11 *T. Aswani Desai* v *D. Koundenya* AIR 2007 NOC 463 (AP).

12 *P.C. Varghese* v *Devaki Amma Balambika Devi* AIR 2006 SC 145; (2005)8 SCC 486; *Ansal Props and Ids Pvt. Ltd.* v *Anand Nath* AIR 1990 Del 151.

13 *In re: Kalipada Santra* 1994(II) CCC 161.

14 *Babu Lal* v *Hazari Lal Kishori Lal* AIR 1982 SC 818.

15 AIR 1956 All 586.

separate possession 'in an appropriate case'......... In view of Or. 2, r. 2 of Civil Procedure Code some doubt was entertained whether the relief for specific performance and partition and possession could be combined in one suit; one view being that the cause of action for claiming relief for partition and possession could accrue to the plaintiff only if he acquired title to the property on the execution of a sale deed in his favour and since the relief for specific performance of the contract for sale was not based on the same cause of action as the relief for partition and possession, the two reliefs could not be combined in one suit.

"Similarly, a case may be visualized where after the contract between the plaintiff and the defendant the property passed in possession of a third person. A mere relief for specific performance of the contract of sale may not entitle the plaintiff to obtain possession as against the party in actual possession of the property. As against him, a decree for possession must be specifically claimed for such a person is not bound by the contract sought to be enforced. In a case where exclusive possession is with the contracting party, a decree for specific performance of the contract of sale *simpliciter*, without specifically providing for delivery of possession, may give complete relief to the decree-holder. In order to satisfy the decree against him completely he is bound not only to execute the sale deed but also to put the property in possession of the decree-holder. This is in consonance with the provisions of s. 55(1) of the Transfer of Property Act which provides that the seller is bound to give, on being so required, the buyer or such person as he directs, such possession of the property as its nature admits. There may be circumstances in which a relief for possession cannot be effectively granted to the decree-holder without specifically claiming relief for possession, *viz.*, where the property agreed to be conveyed is jointly held by the defendant with other persons. In such a case the plaintiff in order to obtain complete and effective relief must claim partition of the property and possession over the share of the defendant. It is in such cases that a relief must be specifically pleaded."

Amendment of plaint seeking recovery of possession of a property beyond the jurisdiction of the court Relief of possession is inherent in relief of specific performance.[16] Section 22 empowers the plaintiff in a suit for specific performance to amend the plaint to include the relief for possession "in an appropriate case". But s. 22 does not seek to interfere with the jurisdiction of the court and "in an appropriate case" a claim for possession and ancillary reliefs can be sought by way of amendment in order to avoid multiplicity of proceedings. When the decree for possession could not have been asked for in the original plaint, as the court would be incompetent to try a suit for

16 *Velayuda Chetti* v *Kumaraswami Chettiar* AIR 1920 Mad 933; *Krishnaji Babaji Haral* v *S.M. Wangi* AIR 1925 Bom 181; *B.V. Shariff* v *Naran Kanji* AIR 1932 Bom 595; *Y.A. Kader* v *Muthulakshmi Ammal* AIR 1992 Mad 208.

land and the Legislature in enacting s. 22 did not override cl. 12 of the Letters Patent. As such, the expression "in an appropriate case" must necessarily mean and refer to a case where the plaintiff was competent to make a claim for possession and to seek other ancillary reliefs, to avoid multiplicity of proceedings. It is not the intention of the Legislature to give jurisdiction to a court which had none and it would be a travesty of justice to allow a prayer for possession to be brought into the pleadings in this circuitous manner while admittedly the original court lacked jurisdiction to do so and the plaintiff knew well of his limitations.[17]

The court also gave this additional reason based on s. 28(3). "Sub-section (3) of s. 28 clearly contemplates that if the purchaser or lessee pays the purchase money or other sum which he is ordered to pay under the decree, the court may on application made in the same suit, award the purchaser or lessee such further relief as he may be entitled to. Clause (*b*) of sub-sec. (3) of s. 28 contemplates the delivery of possession or partition and separate possession of the property on the execution of such conveyance or lease. Sub-section (4) of s. 28 bars the filing of a separate suit for any relief which may be claimed under this section."[18]

In *Johnson* v *Agnew*,[19] Lord Wilberforce dealt with the question as to on what date the damages ought to be assessed, and held that where the vendors have acted reasonably in pursuing the remedy of specific performance, the date on which that remedy becomes aborted (not by the vendors' fault), should logically be fixed at the date on which damages should be assessed. It was also observed that there was no warrant for the court awarding damages differently from common law damages. The general principle for the assessment of damages is compensatory, *i.e.* that the innocent party is to be placed so far as money can do, in the same position as if the contract had been performed. Where the contract is one of sale, this principle normally leads to assessment of damages as at the date of the breach, a principle recognized and embodied in the Sale of Goods Act. But this is not an absolute rule; if it follows it would give rise to injustice, the court has power to fix such other date as may be appropriate in the circumstances. In case where a breach of a contract for sale has occurred and the innocent party reasonably continues to try to have the contract completed, it would appear most logical and just rather than tie him to the date of the original breach, to assess damages as at the date when (otherwise than his default) the contract is lost.[20]

17 *Raj Kumar* v *Benoy Kumar* AIR 1985 Cal 328.
18 *Dhiraj Bala Karia* v *Jethia Estate Pvt. Ltd.* AIR 1983 Cal 166 (FB).
19 [1979]1 All ER 883 (HL).
20 *Ogle* v *Earl Vane* [1867] LR 2 QB 275 affd LR 3 QB 272; *Hickman* v *Haynes* [1875] LR 10 CP 598 and *Radford* v *de Froberville* [1978]1 All ER 33.

Refund of consideration In a suit for specific performance of contract of sale where the plaintiff has been found to have given some earnest money then even if not prayed for court can order refund of the sum to plaintiff if and when the suit is dismissed.[1] It is because of s. 70, Contract Act which is based on two essential conditions namely (*i*) a benefit must have been lawfully conferred; and (*ii*) the act must have been done by a person not intending to do it gratuitously and the person for whom it is done must have been really benefited by it. The language of s. 70 is quite wide and can be applied at the discretion of the court to enable the court to do substantial justice. If that is the true meaning of s. 70 of the Contract Act, on the finding that the plaintiff did pay the money to the defendant and the defendant obtained benefits out of the said money by way of saving the house in question, even if the plaintiff's suit for specific performance fails, there cannot be any justification to deny the plaintiff the relief of refund of the money which he had paid to the defendant and the defendant had obtained sufficient advantage out of the said money. The plaintiff when prayed for putting the plaintiff in possession of property pursuant to lease deed and also prayed for any other fit and proper relief which the plaintiff is entitled to under law and equity the court could direct refund of the money received under the deed.[2] In a Vendee's suit for refund of advance paid, the grantum of loss sustained by the vendor resulting from the breach of contract has no relevance.[3]

Defendant proved that he never intended to sell property and the agreement was by way of security for loan amount received by him. Court can grant relief of refund of amount paid by plaintiff. Provisions of s. 22 of the Specific Relief Act 1963 empowers the court to "grant any other relief". It will take into its fold the relief of return of amount received by defendant from plaintiff.[4]

In such a case, the plaintiff is also entitled to return of the amount paid by him together with interest on that amount. If the contract, for no fault of the plaintiff, becomes impossible of performance, s. 21 enables award of compensation in lieu of and in substitution of specific performance.[5]

In *Oakacre Ltd.* v *Claire Cleaners (Holdings) Ltd.*,[6] the plaintiff issued a writ on 29th February 1980 for seeking specific performance of his

1 *Gouri Shankar* v *Fakir Mohan* AIR 1989 Ori 201.
2 *Gouri Shankar* v *Fakir Mohan* (supra).
3 *Vemcharla Padmavathamma* v *Shantilal* AIR 2006 NOC 519 (AP).
4 *Laxman Haraklal* v *Ukhaji Zinga Mahajan* AIR 2011 Bom 159.
5 *Jagdish Singh* v *Natthu Singh* AIR 1992 SC 1604; (1992)1 SCC 647; *Matadyn Agarwal* v *Syed Abdul Razach* AIR 1997 AP 103; *K. Narendra* v *Riviera Apartments Pvt. Ltd.* AIR 1999 SC 2309; (1999)5 SCC 77; *Urmila Devi* v *Deity, Mandir Shree Chamunda Devi Through Temple Commissioner* AIR 2018 SC 640; (2018)2 SCC 284.
6 [1981]3 All ER 667.

contract dated 19th April 1978 and in the alternative relief by way of damages in addition to or in lieu of specific performance. After the issue of the writ, however, the defendant conveyed the land. There was no question of specific performance; but the plaintiff continued its action for damages for delay in completing the bargain.[7] The contractual date of completion was found to be 4th March 1980 and at law the action would be dismissed since the writ was issued earlier on 29th February. The question was whether damages could be recovered in such a situation.

Answering the question in the affirmative, Judge Mervyn Davis, QC held he would not consider the damages claimed in the case as a claim at law isolated and apart from the specific performance claim. Since the action was originally properly constituted as a specific performance action, he would consider the whole case. The action was started in good faith as a specific performance action with a claim for damages in addition or in lieu. It was not started as a claim for damages and nothing more. Within the framework of a specific performance action, the court may award damages for delay in completion despite the fact that the action was instituted before the contractual date of completion. (Inquiry into damages ordered).

Other relief in addition to specific performance The question of grant of alternative relief under cl. (*b*) of s. 22(1) would arise only in case the plaintiff's claim for specific performance is refused.[8] Section 22 enumerates the powers of the court to grant certain other reliefs in addition to the relief of specific performance of a contract for the transfer of immovable property. The plaintiff may in an appropriate case also ask for possession, or partition and separate possession of the property. Even if his claim for specific performance fails, he may ask for any other relief to which he may be entitled, including the refund of the earnest money and deposit, if any. But as under s. 21, he must ask for these reliefs specifically. If he does not do so, the court will not grant him any relief, though the court shall allow him to amend his plaint for the inclusion of these reliefs.[9]

In a case *A* filed a suit for specific performance of contract in respect of a property contracted to be sold by *B*. The suit was filed against *B*'s widow and daughters. But later an amendment was sought for, to show that the defendants were not the legitimate children of *B*. This amendment was not necessary to decide the real question in controversy and was rejected.[10]

In a suit for specific performance of contract, the plaintiff by way of amendment sought for partition, and the amendment was rejected as being

7 *Raineri* v *Miles* [1980]2 All ER 145.

8 *Lavinder Kumar Sharma* v *Parmod Kumar* AIR 2011 P&H 30.

9 *Adcon Electronics (P) Ltd.* v *Daulat* (2001)7 SCC 698; AIR 2001 SC 3712. See also *Rajesh Kumar Choudhari* v *Darshansingh Sardar* AIR 2011 Chh 179.

10 *Ansal Properties and Ind. Pvt. Ltd.* v *Anand Nath* AIR 1990 Del 151.

barred by limitation. The learned Judge did not elaborate how claim for partition became time barred. But usually partition has recurring cause of action, secondly, the learned Judge glossed over the proviso to s. 22(2), Specific Relief Act which provides specifically that plaintiff may be permitted to amend to include such relief *at any stage of the proceeding*. The words under *italics* are eloquent enough to show the incorrect approach of the learned Judge.[11]

Refusal of relief In appropriate case court has power to grant refund of part of advance paid. Section 22(1)(*b*) *inter alia* permits the plaintiff to seek any other relief to which he may be entitled including refund of earnest money or deposit paid or made by him, in case his claim for specific performance is refused.

But when no such prayer has been made the court is not entitled to grant him a refund of advance.[12] Alternative relief of refund of money paid to the seller is allowed with interest.[13] Section 22 enables the court to take into its fold the relief of return of the amount lent.[14]

In *Debabrata Tarafder* v *Biraj Mohan Bardhan*,[15] the plaintiff had filed a suit for the specific performance of the agreement for sale and for the delivery of possession. The trial court passed the decree, but the decree was silent about the delivery of possession. Objection was taken at the execution stage that the decree could not be executed on account of bar of s. 22(2) and on the principle that prayer made in plaint not being allowed must be deemed to have been refused. *Held*, whether a particular prayer has been allowed or not is a matter of construction of the decree in the light of the judgment and any silence in that regard in the decree would not necessarily lead to the conclusion that it had been disallowed, and that where delivery of possession is a part of the agreement between the parties in a suit for specific performance of such an agreement, the prayer for specific performance necessarily contemplates specific performance of the entire agreement including the agreement to deliver possession and an omission on the part of the plaintiff-purchaser to make an express prayer in that regard would not necessarily bring in the bar under sub-sec. (2) of s. 22 of the Specific Relief Act. However, since the indemnity clause was not contemplated by the agreement, it would have to be deleted from the draft conveyance.

The expression 'any stage of the proceeding' will include an appeal from the original decree,[16] (Plaintiff directed to amend his plaint to claim refund

11 *Ansal Properties* v *Anand Nath and Ind. Pvt. Ltd.* v *Anand Nath* AIR 1990 Del 151.
12 *Suraj Singh* v *Nathi Bai* AIR 1990 MP 323 at p. 326.
13 *Sarita Dokania* v *Krishna Dey* (2014)13 SCC 522.
14 *Laxman Harakal* v *Ukhaje Zinga Mahajan* AIR 2011 Bom 159.
15 AIR 1983 Cal 51 (DB).
16 *Sahida Bibi* v *Sk. Golam Muhammad* AIR 1983 Cal 216 (DB).

of earnest money with interest @ 6% p.a. within a specified time, failing which suit to stand dismissed).

Unless the plaintiff gets a decree of specific performance in his favour, he does not get a right to possession at the interlocutory stage.[17] An appellant could accept the decree of trial court directing refund of part consideration, and yet prefer an appeal against that decree for claiming specific performance.[18]

Relief of possession need not be specifically asked for when the contracting vendee is already in possession. Relief of possession would be implied in the decree for specific performance. The question of amendment of plaint would not arise.[19] Section 22 is not retrospective.[20]

Bar to sue afresh for damages after dismissal of suit of specific performance of contract As provided in s. 24, Specific Relief Act if the plaintiff fails in his suit for specific performance of his contract or part thereof, he shall be debarred from suing for compensation for breach of the contract, but without in any way losing his right to sue for any other relief to which he may be entitled by reason of such breach.

The upshot of this provision read with s. 22 is that in a suit for specific performance the plaintiff may as alternative relief pray for damages, he even may pray so by way of amendment at any stage of the proceeding including execution stage or appellate stage. If the plaintiff does not do so, after the dismissal of suit for specific performance he is debarred from suing afresh for damages for breach of the contract or part thereof. He is however free to sue for any other relief arising from breach of contract.

This provisions may be compared with Or. 2, rr. 1, 2, CPC which stand as follows:

> Rule 1. *Frame of suit.* Every suit shall as far as practicable be framed so as to afford ground for final decision upon the subjects in dispute and to prevent further litigation concerning them.
>
> Rule 2. *Suit to include the whole claim.* (1) Every suit shall include the whole of the claim which the plaintiff is entitled to make in respect of the cause of action; but a plaintiff may relinquish any portion of his claim in order to bring the suit within the jurisdiction of any court.
>
> (2) *Relinquishment of part of claim.* Where a plaintiff omits to sue in respect of, or intentionally relinquishes, any portion of his claim, he shall not afterwards sue in respect of the portion so omitted or relinquished.
>
> (3) *Omission to sue for one of several reliefs.* A person entitled to more than one relief in respect of the same cause of action may sue for all or any of such

17 *Purshottam Vishindas Raheja* v *Life Insurnace Corporation of India* AIR 1982 Bom 523.
18 *Ramesh Chandra Chandiok* v *Chuni Lal Sabharwal* AIR 1971 SC 1238.
19 *Hemchand* v *Karilal* AIR 1987 Raj 117.
20 *Mahender Nath Gupta* v *Moti Ram Rattan Chand* AIR 1975 Del 155.

reliefs; but if he omits, except with the leave of the court, to sue for all such reliefs, he shall not afterwards sue for any relief so omitted.

Explanation. For the purposes of this rule an obligation and a collateral security for its performance and successive claims arising under the same obligation shall be deemed respectively to constitute but one cause of action.

Plaintiff's fresh suit claiming damages for breach of contract after dismissal of suit for specific performance is virtually barred not only by s. 24, Specific Relief Act but also by Or. 2, r. 2, CPC.

Every suit, Or. 2, r. 2 lays down should include the whole of the claim the plaintiff is entitled to make in respect of the same cause of action unless he is permitted to relinquish a part in order to bring a suit thereon later. Effect of omission to leave out a part of claim arising out of the same cause of action is fatal to any further suit thereon. Omission to sue for one of several reliefs arising out of the same cause of action without the leave of the court is similarly fatal to any subsequent suit on such left out relief in view of the bar under Or. 2, r. 2(2), CPC.

In connection with the bar of Or. 2, r. 2, CPC the following tests have been laid down by the Supreme Court: (1) the correct test in cases falling under Or. 2, r. 2 is whether the claim in the new suit is in fact founded on a cause of action distinct from that which was the foundation for the former suit; (2) the cause of action means every fact which will be necessary for the plaintiff to prove, if traversed in order to support his right to the judgment; (3) if the evidence to support the two claims is different than the causes of action are also different; (4) the cause of action in the two suits may be considered to be the same if in substance they are identical; (5) cause of action has no relation to defence that may be set up by the defendant nor does it depend upon the character of the relief prayed for by the plaintiff. It refers to the media upon which the plaintiff asks the court to arrive at a conclusion in his favour.[1] The provision of Or. 2, r. 2 applies to cases where a plaintiff omits to sue a portion of the cause of action on which the suit is based either by relinquishing the cause of action or by omitting a part of it. The provision has no application to cases where the plaintiff bases his suit on separate and distinct cause of action and chooses to relinquish one or the other of them. In such case it is open to the plaintiff to file a fresh suit on the basis of a distinct cause of action which he may have so relinquished.[2]

1 *Kewal Singh* v *Lajwanti* AIR 1980 SC 161 at p. 163; (1980)1 SCJ 486; (1980)1 SCC 290; see also *K. Palaniappa* v *Valliammal* AIR 1988 Mad 156 at p. 159 quoting *Sher Ali* v *Torap Ali* AIR 1942 Cal 407.

2 *Kewal Singh* v *Lajwanti* AIR 1980 SC 161; (1980)1 SCJ 486; (1980)1 SCC 290; (1980)1 Ren LJ 167.

Limitation for suit for refund The limitation for a suit for refund of earnest money is three years from the date of dismissal of the suit for specific performance, under Art. 47 of the Limitation Act 1963.[3]

Where contract provides for payment of liquidated damages Explaining the term "liquidated damages" Halsbury[4] lays down:

> The parties may agree by contract that a particular sum is payable on the default of one of them, and, if the agreement is not obnoxious as a 'penalty' such a sum constitutes "liquidated damages" and is payable by the party in default.

The court must find out whether the payment stipulated is in truth liquidated damages or penalty. The essence of a penalty is a payment of money stipulated as *in terrorem* of the offending party; the essence of liquidated damages is a genuine covenanted pre-estimate of damage.[5]

At times a contract may itself provide for the payment of liquidated damages in the event of its breach. Question arises whether in such a case, it would be possible to sue for specific performance. Section 23 provides the answer. It says that even in such a case, the court will order specific performance, if, having regard to the terms of the contract and other attending circumstances, it is satisfied that the sum was named only for the purpose of securing performance of the contract and not for the purpose of giving to the party in default an option of paying money in lieu of specific performance. But if the court orders the specific performance, it will not also order the payment of the sum named in the contract.

Section 23 contains a comprehensive statement of the principles on which the presence of a term in a contract specifying a sum of money to be paid for a breach of the contract has to be construed. Where payment is an alternative to carrying out the other terms of the contract, it would exclude, by the terms itself, specific performance of the contract to convey a property.[6]

Mere mention in the agreement of a liquidated sum to be paid in case of default is no ground for denying specific performance.[7] A contract is specifically enforceable under s. 23 where a contract provides for liquidated

3 *Munni Babu* v *Koer Kamla Singh* AIR 1923 All 321; *Amma Bibi* v *Udit Narain* ILR 31 All 68; 19 MJ 295; *Udit Narain* v *Minnatulla* ILR 25 All 618.

4 Halsbury's *Laws of England*, 4th Ed., vol. 12, para 1109, p. 415.

5 *Dunlop Pneumatic Tyre* v *New Garage* [1915] AC 79.

6 *M.L. Devender Singh* v *Syed Khaja* AIR 1973 SC 2457; (1974)1 SCR 312; (1973)2 SCC 315.

7 *Shakuntala Devi* v *Mohanlal A.R. Jain Market* AIR 1994 Raj 259; *Manzoor Ahmed Magray* v *Gulam Hassan Aram* AIR 2000 SC 191; *P. D'Souza* v *Shondrilo Naidu* AIR 2004 SC 4472.

damages, but doesn't indicate the option that it is in the alternatives.[8] It is for the party resisting specific performance to show why it should not be granted.[9]

When the default clause in the contract provided, *inter alia*, that "the individual who commits the default shall pay the other individual ₹100 as damages, and in addition this contract shall become void". In that case it was held: "The cause merely states the disability of the defaulting party who claims specific performance of the contract under s. 24(*b*) of the Specific Relief Act and does not extend the disability to enforce the contract to the other party and further that the party who brought about the default cannot take advantage of his own wrong and prevent the other party from claiming specific performance."[10]

When it was provided in the agreement that in the event of not performing the agreement of sale, the defendant could have the sale agreement cancelled provided the defendant gave the plaintiff a sum of ₹5,001 in addition to the sum of ₹5,001 already received from the plaintiff. The default clause was provided in respect of the default committed both by the plaintiff and the defendant in the agreement, that is, in case the defendant committed default, he was liable to return the money with another sum of ₹5,001 and if the plaintiff committed default, she had to forfeit the advance paid and that it could not be said that the default clause was only in the case of the default committed by the defendant and not by the plaintiff. It was held that for this default clause the relief of specific performance cannot be negatived.[11]

Fry on *Specific Performance of Contracts,*[12] says:

> "There are three types of such contracts: (1) where the sum mentioned is strictly a penalty—a sum named by way of securing the performance of the contract as the penalty is a bond; (2) where the sum named is to be paid as liquidated damages for a breach of the contract; and (3) where the sum named is an amount the payment of which may be substituted for the performance of the act at the election of the person by whom the money is to be paid or the act done.
>
> "Where the stipulated payment comes under either of the two first mentioned heads, the court will enforce the contract, if in other respects it can and ought to be enforced, just in the same way as a contract not to do a particular act, with a penalty added to secure its performance, or a sum named as liquidated damages, may be specifically enforced by means of an injunction against breaking it.

8 *Kirpal Singh* v *Kartaro* AIR 1980 Raj 212.

9 *Nawab* v *Humam Din* AIR 1925 Lah 605.

10 *Kandasami Chettiar* v *Shanmugha Thevar* AIR 1949 Mad 302; (1948)2 Mad LJ 356; 61 Mad LW 642.

11 *Ramani Ammal* v *Sushil Ammal* AIR 1991 Mad 163 at pp. 169-170.

12 Fry, *Treatise on the Specific Performance of Contracts*, 6th Ed., p. 65.

"On the other hand, where the contract comes under the third head, it is satisfied by the payment of the money and there is no ground for the court to compel the specific performance of the other alternative of the contract.

"The jurisdiction of the court to decree specific relief is discretionary and must be exercised on sound and reasonable grounds 'guided by judicial principles and capable of correction by a court of appeal'. This jurisdiction cannot be curtailed or taken away by merely fixing a sum even as liquidated damages, ... The court has to determine on the facts and circumstances of each case before it, whether specific performance of a contract to convey a property ought to be granted.

"It is immaterial that the stipulated payment under the terms of the contract could be viewed as one for payment of liquidated damages. The question would still remain whether the courts are relieved by the agreement between the parties of the duty to determine on the facts of a particular case, whether damages, specified or left unspecified, would really afford adequate compensation to the party which wants a conveyance of immovable property as agreed upon. The fact that the parties themselves have provided a sum to be paid by the party breaking the contract does not, by itself, remove the strong presumption contemplated by the use of the words 'unless and until the contrary is proved'. The sufficiency or insufficiency of any evidence to remove such a presumption is a matter of evidence. The fact that the parties themselves specified a sum of money to be paid in the event of its breach is, no doubt, a piece of evidence to be considered in deciding whether the presumption has been repelled or not. But it is nothing more than a piece of evidence. It is not conclusive or decisive."

In *Manzoor Ahamed Magray* v *Gulam Hussain Aram*[13] which came up on appeal from the judgment of the High Court of Jammu & Kashmir, the agreement for sale itself provided a default clause to the effect that in case of non-fulfilment of the agreement, the defaulting party shall pay to the other an amount of ₹10,000 as damages and shall be bound to pay the same in view of s. 23 of the Jammu & Kashmir Specific Relief Act. It was therefore contended that the decree for specific performance was not required to be granted. The learned Judges of the Supreme Court referred to Fry on *Specific Performance*, 6th Ed., p. 65. The Supreme Court finally held that the perusal of the terms of the contract indicated that the stipulation for damages was made only for the purpose of securing due performance of the contract and not for the purpose of giving an option of paying money in lieu of specific performance. Consequently the Supreme Court confirmed the decree for specific performance.

13 AIR 2000 SC 191; (1999)7 SCC 703; JT 1999(8) SC 34.

In *Nazir Ahmed Imamudin Raza* v *Gulam Mustafa Faukat*,[14] the agreement for sale provided that the defendant vendor was to obtain permission of the competent authority under the Prevention of Fragmentation and Consolidation of Holdings Act, which he failed to obtain. The agreement provided that if permission was not obtained, the vendor shall repay the earnest money with damages. The suit for specific performance was however decreed and the decree was challenged before the Supreme Court on the ground that the plaintiff having opted for an election, he was disentitled to the relief for specific performance. The Supreme Court held that no question of exercising the option for election arose and the decree for specific performance did not call for any interference.

Is the grant of alternative relief by the trial court a bar to appeal against the denial of the main relief in a suit for specific performance?

In *Sakkhubai Ammal* v *Babu Reddiar*,[15] which came up for consideration, the plaintiff sued for specific performance of an agreement for sale and in the alternative for the refund of a sum of ₹8,001 both under the agreement for sale. The learned trial court denied to the plaintiff the relief of specific performance, but granted a decree for refund of the sum of ₹8,001 with interest at 6% p.a. The plaintiff preferred an appeal before the High Court stating that she ought to have been granted the relief of specific performance. Holding that the appeal is incompetent, the High Court observed as follows:

> "As the choice of the reliefs is always with the plaintiff who is the *dominus litis* in a litigation he could seek for grant of one relief, seek for more than one independent relief or ask for alternative reliefs. If he asks for the last of such reliefs, then he is placing the relief so sought for by him on a par with each other and if the court trying the subject matter grants him one relief, then it follows that he has the benefit of the relief and he cannot throw overboard such a benefit with a design or motive or to further his own cause by seeking umbrage in an appellate court and ask for the relief not granted to him, which, as already stated he, only asked for in the alternative. Alternative is an expression which indicates a choice of a person and if that choice is exercised by him, then he cannot afterwards blow hot and cold and seek for reliefs as he desires by throwing overboard the benefits which he has secured on a full trial in the trial court. This would be encouraging, as we said, the whims and fancies of a litigant. We are therefore of the view that having regard to the trend of decisions here and elsewhere, and on the basic reasonable principle that a man cannot approbate and reprobate, this appeal is not maintainable."

14 (2001)5 Supreme 444.
15 (1977)1 MLJ 311.

The learned Judges of the Madras High Court have purported to follow the decision of the Supreme Court in *Ramesh Chandra Chandyok* v *Chunnilal Sabbharwal (dead) by LRs.*[16] In the case before the Supreme Court, the plaintiff claimed specific performance of an agreement for sale and in the alternative for the refund of ₹7,500 being the amount of earnest money paid by him and ₹15,000 as damages. The trial court found that the plaintiffs were not ready and willing to pay the balance of consideration and denied them the relief of specific performance. It however granted them a decree for ₹7,500 being part payment of the consideration. The plaintiff preferred an appeal before the High Court. The appeal was dismissed by the High Court. The matter came before the Supreme Court by Special Leave. Their Lordships of the Supreme Court found that there was nothing to indicate that the plaintiff did not have the necessary funds to pay the balance of consideration and were not disentitled to a decree for specific performance. It was contended before the Supreme Court that since an alternative relief has been granted to the plaintiffs, they were not entitled to a decree for specific performance. The Supreme Court observed:

> "It is true that the appellant could not accept satisfaction of the decree of the trial court and yet prefer an appeal against that decree. That may well have brought them within the principle that when the plaintiff has elected to proceed in some other manner than for specific performance, he cannot ask for the latter relief. ....
>
> "This illustrates the rule that a party cannot approbate and reprobate at the same time. These propositions are so well known that no possible exception can be taken to them. In the present case, however, the above rule cannot apply because the appellants had by consistent and unequivocal conduct, made it clear that they were not willing to accept the judgment of the trial court as correct. ......
>
> "We are unable to hold that the conduct of the appellants, which is always an important element for consideration, was that it precluded them from obtaining a decree for specific performance."

Accordingly the Supreme Court reversed the judgment and decree of the courts below and granted the plaintiff the main decree for specific performance. The learned Judges of the Madras High Court have relied upon the earlier portion of the observations of the Supreme Court and held that the plaintiff in *Sakkhubai's* case was not entitled to file an appeal against the denial of the main relief for specific performance. Evidently, the learned Judges of the Madras High Court have not referred to the subsequent passage in the judgment of the Supreme Court and particularly the *ratio decidendi* in the case before the Supreme Court where Their Lordships

16 AIR 1971 SC 1238; (1971)2 SCR 573; (1970)3 SCC 140.

accepted the appeal, reversed the judgment of the courts below and decreed the suit for specific performance.

The law is now well settled that where a plaintiff who is denied the main relief and is given an alternative relief, is entitled to prefer an appeal against the denial of the main relief provided that he has not accepted the alternative relief or taken any benefit thereunder.

Specific performance of agreement to sell Suit was for specific performance of agreement to sell. Defence was that time was the essence of the contract and there was express stipulation to that effect. Consequences of non-performance within time were also stipulated in the contract obligation. Obligation to get permission for sale of part of suit land declared surplus was placed on purchaser, but he was unable to get permission within time. Vendor had right to cancel the contract and raised defence that time was of essence of contract. Decree for specific performance could not be granted. In a discretionary relief for specific performance the plaintiff must come with clean hands. Plaintiff suppressed the fact that vendor had returned earnest money on the ground of efflux of time to perform contract, but plaintiff refused to accept it and demanded from vendor to return the earnest money at the rate of 24% interest from the date of payment till realisation. It was held that the conduct of plaintiff disentitles him to get relief of specific performance.[17]

The defendant No. 1, the vendor, agreed to sell suit premises free from all encumbrances and also to deliver title deeds to the purchaser-plaintiff. The vendor received the amount from the plaintiff but failed to carry out his obligations under the agreement. The plaintiff issued legal notice to the vendor to perform his obligations on coming to know about the sale of premises by him to his tenant, defendant No. 2. The plaintiff filed the suit for specific performance. Evidence on record including the evidence of two attesting witnesses on behalf of the defendants showed that the signatures of the vendor on agreement to sell in favour of defendant No. 2 did not tally with signatures on agreement to sell in favour of the plaintiff. Plea that the defendant No. 2 was in possession of suit premises for past couple of years and performance of contract in favour of the plaintiff would cause hardship to her was of no consequence, as s. 20(2)(*b*) of the Specific Relief Act 1963 would not be applicable in the facts of the case as she was put to notice by the plaintiff in eviction proceedings.[18]

Agreement to sell thika tenancy A suit for specific performance of agreement to sell thika tenancy was instituted. The transfer of thika tenancy was prohibited by the West Bengal Thika Tenancy (Acquisition and Regulation) Act 1981—which came into force during the pendency of the suit. Thus,

17 *Citadel Fine Pharmaceuticals* v *Ramaniyam Real Estate P. Ltd.* AIR 2011 SC 3351.
18 *Sargunam* v *Chidambaram* AIR 2005 SC 1420.

agreement to sell became impossible of performance. Decree for specific performance passed after the 1981 Act was liable to be set aside. Plea that right accrued by an agreement entered into under the Act still subsists was held to be untenable.[19]

Agreement to sell and specific performance Agreement to sell was made in respect of rented property to tenant. Relief of specific performance cannot be denied on the ground that price of immovable property is on rise.[20] However, a decree of specific performance cannot be rescinded because prices of land have increased overtime.[21]

Specific performance of shares of private company Subject to restriction that public should not be invited to subscribe to shares, a holder of shares in a private company may agree to sell his shares to a person of his choice. Such agreement is specifically enforceable under s. 10 of the Specific Relief Act 1963.[22] It has been held by a long line of authority that shares in a private limited company would come within the phrase "not easily obtainable in the market".[1]

Contract for sale life estate Life estate holder agreed to sell full rights in property to plaintiff after obtaining permission from the court to sell full rights. Agreement was entered with a view to saving the property from coercive sale for public dues. Vendor filed a suit for permission and waited for two years to obtain permission. Thereafter, the agreement and selling only life interest to third party was terminated. Such action cannot be said to have committed breach of agreement. The vendee plaintiff was not entitled to a decree for specific performance of part of the contract when terms evinced segregation of interest.[2]

Contract of sale—entitlement to Vendees failed to prove that they had tendered entire sale consideration. Vendor retained the power of repudiating sale for non-payment of sale price within a reasonable time. Vendees had not paid sale consideration before repudiation and cancellation of sale deed. Sale deed in favour of vendees would not convey any title to them and hence after lawful repudiation they would not be entitled to claim performance.[3]

Agreement of sale Defendant failed to execute sale deed on the plea that the property in question was joint family property and agreement was result of

19 *Rozan Mian* v *Tahera Begum* AIR 2007 SC 2883.

20 *P.S. Ramakrishna Reddy* v *M.K. Bhagyalakshmi* AIR 2007 SC 1256.

21 *Kumar Dhirendra Mallick* v *Tivoli Park Apartments* (2005)9 SCC 262.

22 Section 10 of the Specific Relief Act 1963 has been *substituted* by the Speciic Relief (Am.) Act 2018, (w.e.f. 1.10.2018).

1 *M.S. Madhusodhanan* v *Kerala Kaumudi Pvt. Ltd.* AIR 2004 SC 909.

2 *H.P.A. International* v *Bhagwandas Fatch Chand Daswani* AIR 2004 SC 3858.

3 *Janak Dulari Devi* v *Kapildeo Rai* AIR 2011 SC 2521.

forcible execution. Existence of coparcenary had not been established. Partition had already taken place. Plaintiff is entitled to decree.[4]

Agreement of sale signed by vendor only All agreements of sale are bilateral contracts as promises are made by both, the vendor agreeing to sell and the purchaser agreeing to purchase. It cannot be said that unless agreement is signed by both the vendor and the purchaser, it is not a valid contract. Even an oral agreement to sell is valid. If so, a written agreement signed by one of the parties, if it evidences such an oral agreement will also be valid. Moreover, in India, an agreement of sale signed by the vendor alone and delivered to the purchaser, and accepted by the purchaser, has always been considered to be a valid contract. In the event of breach by the vendor, it can be specifically enforced by the purchaser. There is, however, no practice of purchaser alone signing an agreement of sale. Where the evidence showed that there was concluded contract, even though the draftsman who prepared the agreement might have used a format intended for execution by both vendor and purchaser clearly demonstrated that it was intended to be executed by the vendor alone and consequently it was held that the decree for specific performance was rightly granted. It was more so, when the vendee had performed her part of contract.[5]

Agreement of sale—breach of contract—clause providing damages Vendor failed to produce original documents and redeemed mortgage in respect of suit property. Sale deed could not be executed. In such case the question of the vendee's readiness and willingness to perform her part of obligations under the contract would not arise. The vendor sought extension of time for registration of sale deed. Time was thus not the essence of the contract. The vendor cannot turn round and plead that the time was the essence of the contract and the vendee was not ready and willing to perform her part of contract. Though there was a clause in the agreement providing for damages in case of breach, yet existence of such clause cannot make suit for specific performance as not maintainable. A distinction between liquidated damage and penalty may be important in common law but as regards equitable remedy the same does not play any significant role. Moreover, there is no binding precedent to the effect that in all cases where there had been escalation of prices, court should either refuse to pass a decree on specific performance of contract or direct the plaintiff to pay a higher sum.[6]

Bar of suits for compensation Section 27 of the Specific Relief Act bars the plaintiff's right to sue for compensation for breach of contract after the dismissal of his suit for specific performance. But it does not bar his right

4 *Hardeo Rai* v *Shakuntala Devi* AIR 2008 SC 2489.
5 *Aloka Bose* v *Parmatma Devi* AIR 2009 SC 1527.
6 *P. D'Souza* v *Shondrito Naidu* AIR 2004 SC 4472.

to sue for any other relief. There is no bar for a fresh suit for possession or partition and separate possession or for refund of earnest money or deposit. These reliefs may be granted in a suit for specific performance, if asked for, and if not asked for, a separate suit will lie.

Under s. 27, the plaintiff can sue for rescission where the causes of unlawfulness of the contract are not apparent and where the defendant is more to blame than the plaintiff.[7] This section is a statutory recognition of the equitable doctrine of *pari delicto*.[8]

Awards and testamentary direction Section 25 of the Specific Relief Act 1963 corresponds to s. 30 of the repealed Act of 1877. At that time, there was no enactment in force in India on the subject of arbitration. Subsequently in 1889, the Indian Arbitration Act was passed. The Arbitration Act 1940 has made elaborate provisions dealing with arbitration. So, the scope of s. 30 of the Specific Relief Act of 1877 has been confined by s. 25 of the new Act to awards which are not governed by the Arbitration Act of 1940 (now the Arbitration and Conciliation Act 1996).

Under the English law, the testamentary direction to execute a settlement operates by way of trust and is not considered under the heading Specific Relief, though the court does in the course of administration of estates and otherwise, direct them to be specifically carried out. All equitable jurisdictions rest on the power of issuing specific orders. The Provision has been amended by the Specific Relief (Amendment) Act 2018. By way of amendment reference to the Arbitration Act 1940 is replaced by the Arbitration and Conciliation Act 1996.

Rectification of instruments Section 26 of the Specific Relief Act 1963 enables the court to rectify any contract or other instrument in writing which through fraud or mutual mistake of the parties, does not express their real intention. But in order thus to procure the rectification of the contract, the proof must be clear, irrefragable and strongest possible.[9] To establish a right to rectification of documents, it is necessary to show that there has been either fraud or mutual mistake; under the terms of the section, it is necessary that the court should find it clearly proved that there was fraud or common mistake. The mistake may arise out of an error of the plaintiff's advisors or a mistake made by the writer while reducing the contract into writing or by sheer negligence. A suit lies for rectification in a deed of sale on the ground of mutual mistake in the description of the property[10] or mistake in stating the price of the property.[11]

7 *J.W. Thomas* v *Hanuman Prasad* AIR 1929 All 837.
8 *Kamarbai* v *Badrinarayan* AIR 1977 Bom 228.
9 Fry on *Specific Performance*, 6th Ed., p. 373.
10 *Natarajan Asari* v *Pechi Muthu Asari* AIR 1972 Mad 192.
11 *Maung Pe Gyi* v *Hakim Ali* AIR 1924 Rang 235.

The question of rectification does not arise when the description of the property is wrong, yet the identity of property is not in doubt.[12] The word "instrument" used in this section has a very wide connotation and includes every document by which any right or liability is or purports to be created, transferred, limited, extended, extinguished or recorded. A decree, an award, a will, a promissory note and various types of documents fall within the provisions of this section. In *Commissioner of Income Tax* v *Kamla Town Trust*[13] a trust was created for the workmen which included amenities like hospitals, schools, temples. The trust deed was sought to be rectified to bring it in conformity with its real intention of creating a public charitable trust alleging mistake attributed to a misunderstanding of the draftsman. The suit was decreed. The Income Tax authorities refused to accept the same. In the proceedings from such order of the Income Tax Officers, it was held by the Supreme Court that the civil court was competent to grant the relief of rectification and that the Income Tax authorities, not being party to the rectification proceedings, could not challenge the competency of the civil court to conduct such proceedings. An acknowledgment of debt is an instrument which can be rectified if the conditions of the section are satisfied. If a mistake creeps into a decree due to mutual mistake of the parties, a suit will lie to set it aside. It is on a similar footing as a compromise decree. An agreement can be rectified on the ground of mistake even after the court has passed the judgment.[14] Thus where a mutual mistake in a deed of mortgage in the description of the property was reproduced in the decree, and the sale of property in execution was not effected, the mortgage deed and the decree could be rectified.[15]

An instrument may not be rectified under this section if the rectification would prejudice the right acquired by third parties in good faith for valuable consideration *viz.*, a subsequent encumbrancer.[16] Rectification sought and ordered pending suit for the same immovable property will be subject to the doctrine of *lis pendens*.[17] Rectification is a discretionary remedy. Laches may defeat a claim for rectification. An aggrieved party should seek the assistance of the court under this section without unreasonable delay. But mere laches is no bar to a suit for rectification on the ground of mutual mistake if the rights of third parties have not intervened. Failure to rectify a deed of sale does not extinguish the title to the property which was really sold but was not properly described in the deed due to mistake. This section

12 *Madhorao Narayanrao* v *Deepchand* AIR 1927 Nag 259.
13 AIR 1996 SC 620; (1996)7 SCC 349; JT 1995(8) SC 364.
14 *Rikhiram Pyarelal* v *Ghasiram* AIR 1978 MP 189.
15 *Ubadrashta Latchayya* v *Gudaparti Sitamma* AIR 1927 Mad 1144; *Noordin Ismailji* v *Md. Umar* AIR 1940 Bom 321.
16 *Madan Mohan Prasad* v *Sital Prasad* AIR 1921 Pat 226.
17 *Khalil Nahak* v *Hadu Nahak* AIR 2006 Ori 131.

is an enabling one.[18] The fact that the plaintiff did not choose to avail himself of it cannot deprive him of the rights which he has acquired under the deed of sale. The same principle applies in the case of a defendant who can successfully resist the suit on the ground that the property in his deed of sale was wrongly described though he has not filed any suit for rectification.[19] Title may be established in a suit without rectification and even though the relevant rectification is barred by time. This is because the relief of rectification is ancillary to the relief in such a case.[20] Rectification will not be ordered where fraud or mistake has not been pleaded.[1]

There was an agreement to sell property. Notice was served by the purchaser to the seller for execution of sale deed. Reply by the seller was that he had agreed to sell only 5 cents of land. Concurrent findings of court were in favour of the purchaser that the agreement was to sell 5 cents plus some structures specified therein. Section 26 is not applicable as there was no ambiguity in deed. No interference in concurrent findings of courts was made by the Supreme Court. Suit for specific performance was held to be rightly decreed.[2]

Decree to the effect that State was estopped from claiming kist amounts as per bids of plaintiffs in view of non-implementation of policy of State expressed in budget speech to ban sale of toddy purporting to rectify part of contract only as regards payment of list is unsustainable.[3]

Section 26 of the Specific Relief Act 1963 has limited application and is applicable only where it is pleaded and proved that through fraud or mutual mistake of the parties, the real intention of parties is not expressed in relation to an instrument. Such rectification is permissible only by the parties to the instrument and by none else.[4]

However, s. 26 of the Act does not empower the plaintiff in a suit to seek direction from the Court upon the defendant to rectify a sale agreement under Or. 6, r. 17 of the CPC.[5]

Rescission after decree of specific performance The relief for rescission of a contract is discretionary.[6] The court retains control over the decree even

18 *Bala Prasad Asaram* v *Asmabi* AIR 1954 Nag 328.

19 *S.N. Palanivelappa Goundan* v *Nachappa Goundan* AIR 1919 Mad 247; *Lakshmi Narayanan* v *Md. Begam* AIR 1952 Nag 90.

20 *Tetali Sooramma* v *Korvqri Venkayya* AIR 1938 Mad 589.

1 *State of Karnataka* v *K.K. Mohandas* AIR 2007 SC 2917.

2 *Subhadra* v *Thankam* AIR 2010 SC 3031.

3 *State of Karnataka* v *K.K. Mohandas* AIR 2007 SC 2917.

4 *Joseph John Peter Sandy* v *Veronica Thomas Rajkumar* AIR 2013 SC 2028.

5 *Smt. Fakkirawwa* v *Ashok* ILR (2014) Kar 4675; (2015)1 Kant LJ 474; (2015)2 ICC 760; (2015)2 CCC 66.

6 *Chanda* v *Rattni* AIR 2007 SC 1514.

after the decree has been passed and the decree is sometimes described as preliminary decree.[7] Application for rescission must be filed in the same court as the suit itself.[8] No statutory form is prescribed for making application of rescission.[9] A default is a condition precedent to an application for rescission of the contract by the vendor under this provision.[10]

The court can extend time fined in the decree for payment of money.[11] The extension of time does not amount to modification of decree. Correctness of order extending time cannot be challenged in execution proceeding.[12] The power to extend time is inbuilt in s. 28 itself.[13] Section 28(1) speaks of decree in general and, lovers decree of both kinds. Even if the decree is conditional, the court has power to extend time for deposit of balance of sale consideration.[14] But such extension should be within reasonable limits.[15] An order rescinding sale agreement under s. 28 is decree, appeal and not resision lies.[16]

By virtue of s. 20 of the Contract Act, any novation, rescission and alteration of a contract can be made only bilaterally. A deed of cancellation will amount to rescission of contract and if the issue in question is viewed from the application of s. 62 of the Contract Act, any rescission must be only bilaterally.[17]

Parties rescinding to do equity Section 30 enables the courts to make compensation to the party as justice may require.[18] If a purchaser seeks rescission, a court of equity can take account of profit he has made, and make allowance for any deterioration in the property.[19] A party, claiming restoration of benefit received must prove value of that benefit.[20]

Cancellation of instruments

When cancellation may be ordered Section 31 of the Specific Relief Act lays down that if a written instrument is void or voidable against any party and

7 *Rajendra Kumar* v *Kuldeep Singh* AIR 2014 SC 1155; *CVRM Ramaswami Chettiar* v *AKRMMCT Chidambaran Chettiar* AIR 1954 Mad 1040; *M. Mohd. Aslam* v *CNA Gowthaman* AIR 2003 Mad 248.

8 *Raman Kutty Gupta* v *Avara* AIR 1994 SC 1699.

9 *P.K. Bhattacharjee* v *M.N.V. Bhattacharjee* AIR 1973 Cal 439.

10 *Hungerford Investments Trust Ltd.* v *Haridas Mundhra* AIR 1971 Cal 182.

11 *Chanda* v *Rattni* AIR 2007 SC 1514.

12 *Prisun Prasad Mishra* v *Kamla Kant Jha* AIR 1972 Pat 322.

13 *Chithambaran Ponnappan* v *Viswambaran* AIR 2001 Ker 205; *Amar Nath Jain* v *Ram Prakash Dhir* 1987 Punj LJ 280.

14 *Prime Promoters Pvt. Ltd.* v *Aroop Kumar Chatterjee* AIR 1999 Cal 186.

15 *K. Balary* v *B. Milliah* (1996)2 CCC 495 (AP).

16 *N.V.S.M. Anandrale* v *K.T. Santhana Krishnan* AIR 2010 Mad 204.

17 *Satya Pal Anand* v *State of M.P.* (2015)15 SCC 263; (2015)155 AIC 129 (SC).

18 *Hamida Bibi* v *Nanha Mal* AIR 1933 All 371.

19 *Spence* v *Crawford* [1939]3 All ER 271 (HL).

20 *Govindram Seksaria* v *Edward Rodbone* AIR 1948 PC 56.

he has a reasonable apprehension that such instrument, if left outstanding, may cause him serious injury, he may sue to have it adjudged void or voidable and the court may, in its discretion, so adjudge it and order it to be delivered up and cancelled. The functioning of equity is not merely remedial but also preventive of injuries. If an instrument ought not to be used or enforced, it is against conscience for the party holding it to retain it, since he can only retain it for some sinister purpose.[1] In a suit to set aside a *kobala*, *A* was unable to prove that the executant understood the nature of the document or that consideration was paid, the court set aside the *kobala*.[2] A deed of sale executed by an illiterate woman for a nominal consideration much below the market value was held liable to be cancelled on the ground of fraud by the purchaser.[3] The relief of cancellation is permissive and not obligatory, as is suggested by the words "may sue" and therefore the court may ignore a void instrument which is a nullity. A person affected by a void instrument can very well ignore the same and file a suit seeking substantive relief which may be available to him without seeking any declaration that the document is void or any consequential relief of its cancellation.[4]

Where an instrument is altogether null and void, the plaintiff may ignore it, if he is in possession of the property and need not bring a suit for cancellation; and if he is out of possession, still he need not seek cancellation and may sue directly for possession.[5] But where a defendant assailed a deed of settlement in a suit for partition alleging fraud and misrepresentation, he can do so only by filing a separate suit for cancellation under s. 31.[6] The relief by way of cancellation of an instrument may be claimed not only by a party to the instrument, but also by any person against whom the instrument is void or voidable.[7] The word "person" in s. 31 is wide enough and includes persons seeking derivative title from the seller.[8] Under certain circumstances, a sham transaction can also be treated as void at the instance of some persons and those persons may approach the appropriate authority for getting it so adjudged and for its cancellation under s. 31.[9]

Section 31 of the Specific Relief Act 1963 thus, refers to both *void* and *voidable* documents. It provides for a discretionary relief. When a document

1 Banerjee's *Law of Specific Relief*, 13th Ed., p. 675.
2 *Abhimanya Biswas* v *Abdul Sk.* AIR 1981 Cal 444.
3 *Mahiruddin Borbhuiya* v *Rythunnessa* AIR 1998 Gau 12.
4 *Sanjay Kaushish* v *D.C. Kaushish* AIR 1992 Del 118.
5 *Khata Chinna Eswara Reddi* v *Kukkala Reddigari Venkatachalamma* AIR 1954 Mad 83.
6 *Kasi Reddi Ramayamma* v *Kasi Reddi Rama Rao* AIR 2000 AP 29.
7 *Suraj Ket Prasad* v *Chandra Mal* AIR 1934 All 1071.
8 *Md. Moorul Joda* v *Bibi Raifunnisa* (1996)7 SCC 767; JT 1995(9) SC 256; (1996)1 Supreme 242.
9 *Keshav Orichandra* v *Laxmi Dhar Nayak* AIR 1993 Ori 1.

is valid, no question arises of its cancellation. When a document is *void ab initio*, a decree for setting aside the same would not be necessary as the same is *non est* in the eye of the law, as it would be a nullity.[10]

Cancellation or setting aside of a registered sale deed by registering authority by invoking administrative power is not permissible even if in allegation of impersonation or fraud is alleged.[11]

Presumption A registered document carries with it a presumption that it was validly executed. It is for the party challenging the genuineness of the transaction to show that the transaction is not valid in law.[12]

Void document General power of attorney (GPA) was alleged to have been executed by plaintiff. It was proved that on the alleged date of execution of GPA she was in SCU in critical condition. Sale deed was executed in favour of defendant on the strength of the said GPA only 12 years after date of its execution. No explanation was offered by defendant for that. Plaintiff denied execution of the GPA and signature thereon. No person who witnessed the execution of the GPA has been examined. Defendant also failed to prove passing of any consideration under the sale agreement. Defendant played fraud in the guise of the GPA and as such the same is vitiated by fraud. It was held that the GPA was a void document and the sale deed based on it would be *non est* in the eye of law.[13]

Cancellation of gift deed Gift deed was executed, but due to illiteracy of parties regarding legal requirement of document, it could not be registered. Unregistered gift deed leaves no impact as provided under s. 49 of the Registration Act 1908. Getting gift deed registered later is obviously to obviate concurrent decrees of two courts. It is impermissible. Gift deed executed by donor was held to be valid and cannot be cancelled.[14]

Cancellation of sale deed A sale deed was executed by practising fraud and undue influence. Burden of proving good faith of transaction would be on the beneficiary. Where burden is not discharged, executants are not bound by the sale deed. Sale deed is liable to be cancelled.[15]

A sale deed executed by a person who was not of a sound mind at the time of execution of the deed is liable to be cancelled.[16] Sale deed executed

10 *Prem Singh* v *Birbal* (2006)5 SCC 353.
11 *Kusum Lata* v *State of UP* AIR 2018 All 210.
12 *Jamila Begum* v *Shami Mohd.* (2019)2 SCC 727.
13 *Ramachandra Monoppa Kallihal* v *Sunanda Tukaram Koparde* AIR 2016 Kar 140.
14 *Sumit Kumar* v *Naresh Kumar* AIR 2016 Utr 72.
15 *Naib Singh* v *Gurdev Kaur* AIR 2011 NOC 382 (P&H).
16 *Chacko* v *Mahadevan* AIR 2007 SC 2967; *Ram Lal Mandal* v *Satya Narayan Mandal* AIR 2012 Pat 189; *Kapoorchand* v *Municipal Board, Sagwara* AIR 2006 Raj 160.

by power of attorney holder after death of the donee is not legal and liable to be cancelled.[17]

Sale deed cannot be nullified by executing a deed of cancellation; even by consent or by agreement between purchaser and vendor a sale deed cannot be annulled. Power to cancel a deed vests with a court and it cannot be exercised by vendor of a property. BDA cannot determine the validity of sale deed. It cannot execute a cancellation of a deed unilaterally.[18]

A sale deed cannot be annulled as cancelled unilaterally by vendor by executing a deed of cancellation. Deed of cancellation cannot be accepted for registration. Cancellation of sale deed can be ordered only under s. 31 of the Specific Relief Act 1963.[19]

In a suit for cancellation of sale deed, plaint was returned on the ground of non-compliance of s. 80, CPC. In such case Registering authorities need not be made parties to the suit. It is the duty of the court to send copy of its decree for cancellation to office where sale deed was registered. Issuance of notice under s. 80, CPC is not necessary in this regard. Return of plaint for want of notice is illegal.[20]

Sale deed was executed when transferor was suffering from alcoholic psychosis. Fact of mental illness was proved by medical certificate. Deed in question also showed that valuable land was sold at very paltry amount. Sale being by a person who was not of sound mind is liable to be set aside. Unsoundness of mind of transferor is a finding of fact. Thus, no interference is permissible in second appeal.[21]

The land in question without any reason, necessity and basis was transferred by registering a sale deed. Suit for cancellation of that sale deed was filed. Such case is triable by Civil Court and not by Revenue Court.[22]

What instruments may be partially cancelled Section 32 provides for partial cancellation of an instrument. Where *A* draws a bill on *B* who endorses it to *C* by whom it appears to be endorsed to *D* who endorses it to *E* and *C*'s endorsement is forged, *C* is entitled to have such endorsement cancelled leaving the bill to stand in other respects. [Illustration to s. 40 of the repealed Act of 1877].

A sale of joint property made by one point owner without consent of other joint-owners can be cancelled to the extent of shares of those joint-owners who did not consent to the sale.[23]

17 *Prahlad* v *Laddevi* AIR 2007 Raj 166.
18 *K. Raju* v *Bangalore Development Authority* AIR 2011 NOC 341 (Kar).
19 *Latif Estate Line India Ltd.* v *Hadeeja Ammal* AIR 2011 Mad 66 (FB).
20 *Achanta Chaya Devi* v *State of Telangana* AIR 2018 Hyd 148.
21 *Chacko* v *Mahadevan* AIR 2007 SC 2967.
22 *Hasti Cement Pvt. Ltd., Jodhpur* v *Sandip Charan* AIR 2018 Raj 143.
23 *Karodi* v *Dasai* AIR 2008 All 100.

Adjustment of equities Section 33(1) provides that on adjudging the cancellation of the instrument, the court may require the party to whom such relief is granted, to restore, so far as may be any benefit which he may have received from the other party and to make any compensation to him which justice may require.

Section 33(2) similarly provides for compensation to defendant that where the defendant successfully resists any suit for specific performance on the ground that the instrument is voidable or void.

A sale was made for the benefit of the minors and those minors subsequently filed suit for possession of the property. The sale was set aside on the ground that it was not binding on the minor. Under this circumstances, it was held that equities are to be worked out by paying compensation adequately to the purchaser.[1] The burden of proving law much of the consideration was actually applied for the benefit of the minor, lies on the transferee.[2] A minor who is seeking to set aside the sale deed, cannot claim interference of court without making restitution.[3]

This decision was distinguished in an AP case where by deed of settlement life estate was granted for executor and his wife and the remainders vested to children to be born to them. But sale of property was effected by the executor absolutely and it was not for the benefit of the children. The purchasers were *bona fide* purchasers for value and they effected improvements. They were not to be blamed in any way. They, however, sought to be compensated when the suit was decreed in favour of the children. The sale was absolutely void and the purchasers were not allowed to be compensated.[4]

The court has no doubt the discretion to order restoration of consideration money, but there must be very strong circumstances in the case to enable the court to find that there is an equity in favour of the defendant.[5] Where the defendant has been in possession of the land in suit for last 12 years and has been enjoying all its produce and has been sufficiently compensated, nothing further can reasonably be demanded of the plaintiff as compensation to the defendant. So also no compensation is payable where a contract is without consideration; where the bond executed by the minor was subsequently incorporated as consideration for another bond executed by him on attaining majority, the other party brought a suit on the basis of the later bond, it was held that no compensation was payable as there was no

1 *Venkama* v *Chisty* AIR 1951 Mad 399.
2 *Mansaram Das* v *Ahmad Hosain Pradhan* AIR 1917 Cal 235.
3 *Padinhare Veetil Madhavi* v *Pachikaran Veetil Balakrishnan* AIR 2010 Ker 111.
4 *Pulibandla Venkata Subbanna* v *D. Chinna Panayya* AIR 1969 AP 34.
5 *Guru Siddha Swamy* v *Parawa* 44 Bom 175.

consideration for the later bond and the bond executed during minority having been void.[6]

The provisions contained in s. 33 are also applicable to instruments that are *ab initio* void and need no cancellation.[7] The section applies to voidable instruments also.[8] As also to the case of a transaction or instrument declared to be void[9] and also to cases where the plaint has not specifically sought the cancellation. In *Pravin Jethalal Kamdar* v *State of Maharashtra*,[10] which was confirmed by the Supreme Court in *State of Maharashtra* v *Pravin Jethalal Kamdar*,[11] the plaintiff had executed a deed of sale in favour of the Government, after it had exercised its option of pre-emptive purchase under the Urban Land Ceiling Act. This provision of that Act was struck down by the Supreme Court. The plaintiff sought possession of the property. Although the sale was void *ab initio*, and there was no necessity to cancel the same, the plaintiff was held entitled to a declaration that it was so and for possession subject to his returning the amount to the consideration to the Government.

Declaration of status or right Section 34 of the Specific Relief Act empowers the court to make a declaration that any person is entitled to any legal character or to any right as to any property, against any person denying or interested to deny his title to such character or right provided that no court shall make any declaration where the plaintiff being able to seek further relief than a mere declaration of title omits to do so. The declaratory decree cannot be obtained as a matter of absolute right. The court has a discretion to grant it or not on a review of all the facts and circumstances of the case.[12] A declaration under s. 34 helps to perpetuate and strengthen the testimony regarding the title of the plaintiff so that adverse attacks on it may not weaken it.[13] It seeks to clear what is doubtful and which is necessary to make clear. It prevents future litigation by removing an existing cause of controversy. It gives remedy to a person against all persons who not only claim an adverse interest to his own, but against all those who may do so and it is intended that all such claims may once and for all be determined in one suit.[14] A declaration to enforce a contract of personal service can be granted in appropriate cases of public servants who have been dismissed from service in contravention of Art. 311 of the Constitution.[15] Where the

6 *Ram Sarup* v *Brij Mohan* AIR 1938 Oudh 14.
7 *Pravin Jethalal Kamdar* v *State of Maharashtra* AIR 1996 Bom 280.
8 *Dhattiporal Hanumantha* v *Kondrakota Sitaramayya* AIR 1939 Mad 106 (FB).
9 *Muppudathi Pillai* v *Krishnasamy Pillai* AIR 1960 Mad 1.
10 AIR 1996 Bom 280.
11 AIR 2000 SC 1099; (2000)3 SCC 460; JT 2000(3) SC 29.
12 *Prithvi* v *Gunan* 17 Cal 933 (PC).
13 *Nilimabose* v *Santhosh Kumar Ghosh* AIR 1997 Cal 202.
14 *T.S. Palaniappa Mudaliar* v *Syed Gulam Ghouse* AIR 1928 Mad 489.
15 *Executive Committee of Uttar Pradesh State Warehousing Corporation* v *Chandra Kiran Tyagi* AIR 1970 SC 1244; (1970)2 SCR 250; (1969)2 SCC 838.

service is under a statute, it cannot be determined arbitrarily and a declaration can be issued.[16] Where the service rules neither expressly nor by implication take away the jurisdiction of civil courts, the remedy under this section is not barred and a suit for declaration can be filed to adjudicate the order passed by a disciplinary authority.[17] A tenant, has under the Transfer of Property Act or Rent Control legislation, an interest in the demised premises which would fall within the expression "property" and can sue for declaration and consequential reliefs, in respect of his interest in the tenanted peroperty.[18]

The proviso to s. 34 is intended to avoid multiplicity of suits and to obtain a decision once for all. It therefore lays down that where the plaintiff is entitled to some consequential relief directly flowing from the right or title the declaration of which he seeks in the suit, he cannot ask for a mere declaration without asking for consequential relief as well. This constitutes the essential difference between this section and ss. 37 and 38 of the Act. There is no such restriction put on injunction and the court may grant an injunction as a substantive relief without any prayer for any declaration.[19] The proviso is mandatory and enjoins the court not to give a declaratory decree where the plaintiff omits to seek further relief in a case falling under this section. The further relief must flow from the relief of declaration and if the further relief is remote and having no connection with the cause of action accrued in favour of the plaintiff, then, there is no need for further relief and the proviso to s. 34 will not be a bar.[20] Where the proviso is attracted, the court should, instead of dismissing the suit, give the plaintiff an opportunity to amend the plaint so as to add a prayer for consequential relief.[21] Supreme Court has held that it is a well settled rule of practice not to dismiss the suit automatically, but to allow the plaintiff to make necessary amendments if he seeks so to do. Supreme Court has further laid down that this objection that the further relief should have been asked for, should be raised at the earliest point of time, so that in such an event it may be open to the plaintiff to ask for necessary amendment to comply with the provisions of s. 42 (now s. 34 of the Specific Relief Act).[22] An amendment may be allowed even where the plaintiff's rights have been affected by the happening of the events subsequent to the filing of the suit, but no action of the

16 *Bool Chand* v *Chancellor, Kurukshetra University* AIR 1968 SC 292; (1968)1 SCR 434; 1968 SLR 119.

17 *Ramendra Krishna Biswas* v *State of Tripura* (1999)1 SCC 472; AIR 1999 SC 294; JT 1998(8) SC 402.

18 *Ratnabala Dasi* v *Ratan Singh Bare* AIR 1990 Cal 26.

19 *Indumathiben* v *Union of India* AIR 1969 Bom 423.

20 *Sheafali Roy* v *Hero Jaswant Das* AIR 1992 All 254.

21 *Deo Kuer* v *Sheo Prasad Singh* AIR 1966 SC 359; (1965)3 SCR 655.

22 *Rukhmabi* v *Lakshmi Narayan* AIR 1960 SC 335; (1960)2 SCR 253; 1960 SCJ 433. See also *Kalyan Singh* v *Vakil Singh* AIR 1990 MP 295.

defendant pending the suit should be allowed to affect or prejudice the right of the plaintiff. Such amendments may not be allowed where it has become time barred.[23]

A mere suit for declaration would lie where a declaration is sought against the Government, as a declaration of the appellant's right by the court was sure to be respected and carried out by the Government.[24]

Where the plaintiff seeks a mere declaration the court fees payable would usually be a small fixed amount. Any further relief sought would attract a court fee based on the valuation of such a relief. As pointed out by Sir Lawrance Jenkims, it is a common fashion to attempt evasion of court fee by casting the prayers of the plaint into a declaratory shape. Where evasion is successful, it cannot be touched, but the device does not merit encouragement or favour.[1]

Suit for declaration In the suit for declaration of title and possession, the respondent-plaintiffs could succeed only on the strength of their own title and not on the weakness of the case of the appellant-defendants. The burden is on the respondent-plaintiffs to establish their title to the suit properties to show that they are entitled for a decree for declaration.[2]

Where the suit property has been acquired and vested in the Government on the culmination of the proceeding under the Land Acquisition Act 1894 and the proceeding was also not challenged by the plaintiff within the reasonable time, it was held that suit for declaration is not maintainable in such a situation. Indeed, no declaration of title over the suit land could be claimed or/and granted by the civil court and nor any suit of such nature could be filed in the civil court in the light of the background facts that the land has been acquired by the Government.[3]

Right to seek partition is a recurring cause of action and a person may file another suit for partition even after having withdrawn the first suit without any liberty as the principle of *res judicata* would not apply as the subsequent suit shall be based on the different cause of action. Similarly, if a co-sharer who is denied his title as a co-sharer, if files a suit for declaration of title and permanent injunction with no intention to get the property separated, he may file the suit for declaration of title and permanent injunction without seeking further relief for partition. A co-sharer cannot be compelled to file a suit for partition even if he is not interested in separation of the property by metes and bounds.[4]

23 *Munilal* v *Oriental Fire and General Insurance Company Ltd.* AIR 1996 SC 642.
24 *Sri Raji Saragnaya Kumarakrishna Yachendra Bahadurgaru* v *Province of Madras* AIR 1945 Mad 5.
1 *Deokali Koer* v *Kedarnath* ILR (1912)39 Cal 704.
2 *Jagdish Prasad Patel* v *Shivnath* (2019)6 SCC 82.
3 *Y.P. Sudhanva Reddy* v *Karnataka Milk Federation* (2018)6 SCC 574.
4 *Karelal* v *Gyanbai* (2018)3 MP LJ 709; AIR 2018 NOC 894.

A declaration that a person is known by two different names or that two different names refer to the same individual is a relief that falls within s. 34 of the Specific Relief Act, since it relates to a question of his legal character. Legal character signifies the status in society of the person seeking declaration. The name of a person is the integral part of the identity of a person and hence a component of his legal status. If that is disputed, the aggrieved is entitled to seek declaration of that right. It is also clear that even if it does not directly fall within the ambit of s. 34 of the Specific Relief Act, the power of the court is not restricted to the cases that are specifically referred to in the Act and power is conferred on the court to act independently of s. 34 of the Act.[5]

The plaintiff in a suit for declaration and possession alleged that the plaintiff was forcefully dispossessed by the defendant. Revenue record shows that the defendant is Bhumiswami in respect of suit property. Since the defendant was in possession of the suit property under her own right, order of court decreeing the suit in favour of the plaintiff was not proper.[6]

In appropriate circumstances the buyer may obtain a declaration out of his legal rights against the seller. A declaration may be made before any breach of contract has occurred and may guide the parties for implementation of contract whose performance is spread over a long period.[7] If it would serve a useful purpose, the court may in its discretion make a negative declaration, e.g. to the effect that the claimant is not liable to the defendant in respect of certain matter.[8] In case of a declaration of indemnity the buyers would be entitled to recover from the sellers damages. But in one case[9] the Court of Appeal has said that the proper course in such situation is for the court to reserve the head of damages.

The suit was for declaration of title that the plaintiff were the owners of the suit land and the defendant had no right, title and interest therein. The plaintiffs' further claim was for prohibitory injunction against the defendant. The plaintiffs based their claim of ownership on several documents which proved exclusively their superior title over the respondents. It has been held by the Supreme Court that the appeal involved substantial question of law and the High Court should have admitted the appeal by framing substantial question of law arising in the case and then after giving notice to the plaintiffs for its final hearing as provided in s. 100 of the Code of Civil Procedure 1908 should have decided the appeal finally on merits. The High

5 *Dr. Mohammed Sabir* v *A.P. Mumthaz* AIR 2019 Ker 178.

6 *Surajbai Galiyna Solanki Bhil* v *Roopa Nevji Dabhar Bhil* AIR 2011 MP 160.

7 *Speltabile Consorzib Veneziano di Armamento & Navigasizone* v *Northumberland Shipbuilding Co. Ltd.* [1919]121 LT 628.

8 *Messier* v *Dowty Ltd. Sabena SA* [2006]1 WLR 2040 (CA).

9 *Trans Trust Sprl* v *Danubian Trading Co. Ltd.* [1952]2 QB 297. See also *Deeny* v *Gooda Walker Ltd.* (No. 3) [1995]4 All ER 280.

Court has committed jurisdictional error when it dismissed the appeal *in limine* stating that it only involves question of fact and therefore the impugned order is liable to set aside.[10]

Plaintiff wanted declaration of his right and title on basis of purchase and he prayed for decree of confirmation of possession on basis of title. No question of suit being barred by limitation can arise when all the defendants of suit admitted the claim of the plaintiff by specific pleadings. Title over property retained by mortgagor was later on sold with right of redemption to the plaintiff. Action of the principal defendants in getting their names mutated in records of rights clouded the title of the plaintiff. Plaintiff needed to institute suit to get his title declared. Clouding of plaintiff's right, title and interest by making alleged erroneous mutation entries shall constitute cause of action in suit.[11]

Discretion of court and alternative relief The proviso to s. 34 of the Act of 1963 prohibits the court from making/granting the declaration as sought if the plaintiff though being in a position to seek further relief than mere declaration omits to do so. Whether the court is precluded from making/granting the declaration as sought in the light of the proviso to s. 34 of the Act of 1963 can be determined from the plaint averments and documents filed along with the plaint.[12] But the proviso would operate only in respect of "a further relief" which would be necessary to give full effect to the relief of declaration of title and no other relief can be brought under the proviso to s. 34 of the Act. The restriction imposed under proviso to s. 34 of the Act would come into play when there is an omission to sue for further relief/reliefs which would give full effect to the relief of declaration of title and without which the declaration sought to be granted would be incomplete and ineffective to a certain extent. A distinction should be drawn based on the requirement under s. 34 of the Specific Relief Act and the proviso attached to it based on the purpose in which the declaration was sought and when the purpose or the declaration found to be incomplete or ineffective to an extent, due to the non-grant of a relief which ought to have been raised alone can be brought under the purview of proviso to s. 34 of the Act. Otherwise, there is no necessity or need to ask for any further relief than a mere declaration.[13]

Suit for declaration relating to personal service Suit for declaration was instituted that the plaintiff was senior to the defendants and promotion to

10 *Haryana State* v *Gram Panchayat Village Kalehri* (2016)4 CHN (SC) 51; (2016)6 SCALE 157.

11 *Golap Chandra Kalita* v *Haren Kolita* AIR 2016 Gau 179.

12 *Prakash G. Goyal* v *Sayyed Ayaz Ali* (2018)5 Mah LJ 830; (2019)194 AIC 420; (2019)1 ICC 213.

13 *Gopakumar* v *Kamalakshy Purushothaman* 2019 AIR CC 2840.

the defendants was illegal. Plea by defendant corporation was that promotion was as per merit-cum-seniority. The issue as to mode/manner of promotion was not framed. Question whether promotion was as per merit-cum-seniority though vital was not decided even in second appeal. Matter was remanded by the Supreme Court for decision of such question.[14]

Declaration as to right of Watan property Trial court decided that "V" failed to prove that he was the adopted son of deceased Watandar and he had no right, title or interest in the suit lands as Watandar. In subsequent proceedings before the Sub-Divisional Officer, the issue was whether "V" was the adopted son of deceased Watandar and having hereditary interest in any inferior village waton under the Watan Abolition Act 1958. It was held by the Supreme Court that such question regarding adoption involving declaration as to status of a person cannot be decided by Collector but by Civil Court.[15]

Adverse possession Mere fact that possession was handed over to defendant in part performance of contract is not enough to non-suit plaintiff. Thus, plaintiff is entitled to relief of recovery of possession.[16]

Defendants as trespassers Plaintiff files a suit for possession on the allegation that the defendants are trespassers. Defence was part performance. Payment receipts were produced by defendants which were admitted by plaintiff. Construction of boundary wall by defendants was also admitted. Plaintiff did not give time as to accrual of cause of action. Finding that omission was purposeful and intentional was proper and denial of relief to plaintiff was justified.[17]

Declaration of title Mere fact that probate of will was granted by competent court in respect of property does not bar civil court for declaration of title and permanent injunction in respect of self same property. Probate court is not competent to decide title or whether the property was joint ancestral property.[18]

When in a suit for declaration of title it was claimed by the plaintiff that the suit property was purchased from the defendant and the suit property never belonged to Shiromani Gurdwara Prabandhak Committee (Gurdwara Committee) inasmuch as in the absence of notification, the property cannot be the property of the Gurdwara Committee. In such a case it was for the plaintiff who had filed the suit for the declaration of the title to prove that his vendor acquired right, title or interest over the suit property either

14 *H.S.E.D. Corporation Ltd.* v *Seema Sharma* AIR 2009 SC 2592.
15 *Ramchandra Dagdu Sonavane* v *Vithu Hira Mahar* AIR 2010 SC 818.
16 *Lakshmi* v *Karuppathal* AIR 2011 Mad 192.
17 *Swarn K. Jain* v *Ravi Mahajan* AIR 2008 SC 2101.
18 *Kanwarjit Singh Dhillon* v *Hardyal Singh Dhillon* AIR 2008 SC 306.

under the general law of succession or tenancy law and he failed to prove the same. Moreover, the entries in the revenue records by itself cannot prove the title to the property unless it is supported by other evidence.[19]

In a suit for declaration of title, the fact was the father of the plaintiffs and defendant were real brothers. The suit house was in two parts and in its back portion defendant was living. There was no evidence that the father of the plaintiffs either purchased the suit property or it was his exclusive property. Plaintiff fails to produce any cogent material or clear documentary evidence. So exclusive title of the plaintiff was not proved and accordingly plaintiffs are not entitle to any relief.[20]

Plaintiff sought declaration of title over suit property and injunction restraining the defendants from interfering with his possession. Failure by the plaintiff to prove his title with suspicious documents was apparent. Documents produced by him showed the grant of permission to construct boundary wall. This cannot establish title, because a tenant or lessee can seek such permission. Plaintiff, being a Mayor and corporator was in a position to obtain such documents. There was no proof that the land was given by way of grant to him. The Supreme Court held that the plaintiff was not entitled to the relief claimed.[21]

Plaintiff and his predecessors in interest had been in possession of land since 1859. Order of Settlement Commissioner was that in absence on record of lease executed by the State predecessor-in-interest of plaintiff should be deemed to be permanent lessee. Order became final. Dismissal of suit by giving contradictory findings regarding title of plaintiff only on the basis of entries in revenue records that suit land was Nazul land was liable to be set aside.[22]

Appellant in *Mehar Chand Das* v *Lal Babu Siddique*,[23] was admitted a tenant of plaintiff-respondent. He was, therefore, in possession. Mere suit for declaration without claiming relief of possession is not tenable.

Suit for declaration—defendant not signatory to the deed in question
In a suit filed by the plaintiff for a declaration on the basis of the registered sale deed, it is always open for the defendant, who is a stranger to the sale deed, to raise a plea that the sale deed was void, fictitious, collusive or not intended to be acted upon and/or not binding to him. Thus, without even challenging the (sale) deed by way of behalf of independent proceedings, in a suit filed by the plaintiff seeking a declaration that he has become the owner pursuant to the registered sale deed, it is always open for the

19 *Dalip Singh* v *Sikh Gurdwara Prabhandak Committee* AIR 2004 SC 137.
20 *Tukaram* v *Raghunath (deceased) through LRs. Ladkibai* AIR 2019 MP 36.
21 *Prabhakar Adsule* v *State of M.P.* AIR 2004 SC 3557.
22 *Narain Prasad Agarwal* v *State of M.P.* AIR 2007 SC 2349.
23 AIR 2007 SC 1499.

defendant, who is stranger to the sale deed, to raise a plea that either the sale deed is not binding to him or the same was without consideration or it was a nominal sale deed or void or fictitious, for that matter, collusive and not intended to be acted upon.[24]

Suit for declaration after acquisition Declaratory decree of ownership of property under s. 34 after the acquisition proceeding has attained finality is not permissible.[1]

Suit for declaration of title—Locus standi A suit was instituted for declaration of title by daughter and collateral of owner in possession. In the event of death of owner in possession an ancestral property of agricultural land would devolve upon his four daughters and not upon collateral. Thus, collateral has no *locus standi* to file the suit.[2]

Suit for declaration of title—Amendment of plaint Plaintiff/appellant sought to add names in the category of plaintiff and sought also more necessary amendments in plaint. The said amendments ought to have been allowed by High Court. Therefore, finding recorded by High Court on substantial question of law without going into amended plaint, was held liable to be set aside. Matter was remitted back to the High Court to decide the said substantial question of law afresh after taking into consideration relief sought for by plaintiff/appellant by amending plaint.[3]

Suit for declaration of sale of property as null and void Purchaser of the property admitted that the suit property was recorded in the names of three brothers. No document on record was produced to prove that the property was partitioned orally. Thus, the sale deed executed by one co-sharer would be null and void. Other co-sharers were entitled to permanent injunction restraining the vendor co-sharer from interfering into their possession.[4]

A property belonging to a minor was allegedly sold by its mother without permission of court. Minor on attaining majority filed a suit for the declaration of the sale deed as null and void. In such case limitation is three years under Art. 60 of the Limitation Act 1963.[5]

Declaration as to termination of service is void. Challenging the order of termination passed by the employer, the employee filed a suit for declaration that the termination was *ab initio* void. The decree was silent about monetary

24 *Thulasidhara* v *Narayanappa* (2019)6 SCC 409.
1 *Y.P. Sudhanva Reddy* v *Karnataka Milk Federation* (2018)6 SCC 574.
2 *Gulkandi* v *Dhikkal* AIR 2016 P&H 73.
3 *Mahila Ramkali Devi* v *Nandram* AIR 2015 SC 2270.
4 *Kailashchandra* v *Padamsingh* AIR 2016 MP 30.
5 *Malatilata Mishra* v *Keshab Chandra Mahapatra* AIR 2018 Ori 10.

benefits. It was held by the Supreme Court that the employee was not entitled to previous salary.[6]

Declaration of title and recovery of possession The suit property, a shop, was situated just adjoining the property owned by the temple. The plaintiff filed documents like the decision of the Charity Commissioner recording that the temple was not the owner of the property and rent note and account book showed the receipt of rent by the plaintiff from the tenant inducted by him in the said shop. The temple failed to produce oral or documentary evidence to prove its title. Attornment by the tenant in favour of the temple was also invalid. Thus, it was held that the plaintiff on the basis of documents filed would be entitled to recover possession and arrears of rent.[7]

Tenant was running a school on property which is claimed to have been acquired by an oral gift. But tenant failed to prove oral gift and also delivery of possession. Tenant did not get mutation done, nor did the tenant inform educational authorities. Payment of rent even after termination of tenancy was not explained. Construction of large number of structures without objection by owner would not confer title. In absence of *animus possidendi*, claim for title by prescription is not tenable. Title not being proved decree for recovery of possession passed against him was proper.[8]

A suit for declaration of title was made on the basis of oral partition. Plaintiff relying on mutation entry which was only indicates entry of her name as to 1/3rd undivided share after death of her husband. Plaintiff have no absolute right to execute sale deed in favour of third plaintiff. Defendant being widow entitled to share equal to that of her sons. Defendant is not a party to the sale deed executed by first plaintiff in favour of the third plaintiff. Such sale deed cannot bind defendant's interest in that property. Plaintiffs are entitled to declaration to extent of their share in suit property.[9]

Declaratory decree vis-a-vis the doctrine of res judicata The principle of *res judicata* belongs to the domain of procedure. When the decision relates to the jurisdiction of a court to try an earlier proceeding, the principle of *res judicata* would not come into play. If the earlier declaratory decree which is sought to be made the basis of *res judicata* is delivered by a court without jurisdiction or is contrary to the existing law at the time the issue comes up for reconsideration such earlier declaratory decree cannot be held to be *res judicata* in a subsequent case unless, of course, protected by any special enactment.[10]

6 *Rajasthan State Road Transport Corpn.* v *Shyam Bihari Lal Gupta* AIR 2005 SC 3476.
7 *R.V.E. Venkatachala Gounder* v *A.V. & V.P. Temple* AIR 2003 SC 4548.
8 *Kamakshi Builders* v *Ambedkar Educational Society* AIR 2007 SC 2191.
9 *Basavanthappa* v *Basavanneppa* AIR 2018 Kant 119.
10 *Shakuntla Devi* v *Kamla* (2005)5 SCC 390.

Suit for eviction and recovery of possession Ownership was claimed by defendant on suit property by way of adverse possession. Documents on record showed that the suit property was owned by grandmother of plaintiff. After the death of the grandmother municipal records showed that plaintiff was a successor in interest/title over the suit property. Claim by defendant of his being possession in land was since 1948. It was belied considering his date of birth. It was not possible for a boy of 11 years old to establish adverse possession. Wife of defendant admitted that suit property came in the ownership of grandsons of the original owner after her death. Thus, adverse possession by defendant was not established. Plaintiff was entitled to decree of recovery of possession.[11]

Suit land was given to predecessors of plaintiff by Royal farman. Names of predecessors of plaintiff were recorded in Khasra Pahani which is basic record of rights prepared by Board of Revenue. Suit land was recorded therein as "self cultivated". Land was being brought under survey settlement as self-cultivated land which is beyond the purview of the Jagir Abolition Act. There was no explanation how suit land got suddenly recorded as Government land. Possession of plaintiff was not denied by Government. Title and possession were proved, plaintiff was, therefore, held to be entitled to decree claimed.[12]

Suit for declaration of title—tenability Property under mortgage was sold by the mortgagor to plaintiff. Property was subsequently purchased by mortgagee in execution of money decree passed against mortgagor in respect of some other loan. Suit was filed by plaintiff-purchaser against mortgagee for declaration and possession. It was held that the suit was not maintainable as plaintiff claimed through mortgagor.[13]

Burden of proof—suit for declaration of title In a suit for declaration of title and possession, the plaintiff could succeed only on the strength of their own title and not on the weakness of the case of the defendant. The burden is on the plaintiff to establish his title to the suit properties to show that he is entitled for a decree for declaration.[14] Plaintiff claimed to have derived title to suit property by virtue of auction sale and sale certificate issued by the Municipal Corporation. Burden of proof of the facts contained in the plaint would on the plaintiff. The defendant can set up nullity of title as defence even though the suit for that purpose was not made. There was no necessity to challenge it by way of substantive suit. Evidence on record showed that the auction sale was contrary to the Municipal Corporation

11 *Shanti Devi* v *Dr. Rahul Khanna* AIR 2016 Utr 110.
12 *Government of Andhra Pradesh* v *Pratap Karan* AIR 2016 SC 1717.
13 *Rukmani Ammal* v *Jagdeesa Gounder* AIR 2006 SC 276.
14 *Jagdish Prasad Patel* v *Shivnath* (2019)6 SCC 82.

Act. Finding recorded by the court on that basis cannot be interfered with as held by the Supreme Court.[15]

A person asserting his title over a property, required to prove as on what basis, he acquired right, title and interest over the property. If he fails to produce relevant documents to prove title, he is not entitle to declaration of title in his favour.[16]

Onus of proof—revenue record, no proof of title Onus to prove title to the suit property lies on the plaintiff. He cannot succeed on weakness of defendant's case. In a suit for declaration of title revenue records are not proof of title. Plaintiff relied on family settlement in absence of suit land for which no explanation was given by plaintiff. Title of plaintiff to suit land became doubtful. Decreeing suit by finding weakness in evidence of defendant was held to be improper.[17]

Failure to claim further relief Suit was instituted by the holder under an agreement to sell against the trespasser. The reliefs claimed were the declaration of title, restoration of possession and injunction. It was held that it could not be said to be non-tenable for failure to claim specific performance, because it was not a relief which could be claimed against the defendant-trespasser. The plaintiff proved the contract for sale entered between him and his vendor and he was put in possession by his vendor. The defendant trespasser was unable to prove any right to possession or better right than the plaintiff. Thus, it was held further that the plaintiff's possession had to be protected and he was entitled to a declaration that he was the owner of the property.[18]

Suit for declaration and injunction Property under possession of plaintiff was ancestral property which consisted of two portions. Defendant, a neighbour used second portion as passage and open space for ingress and egress without having right to do so. Plaintiff has right to protect the title in respect of ancestral property. Plaintiff can restrain defendant from using second portion of property. Defendant was injuncted from using second portion of plaintiff's property as passage and open space.[19]

A suit for declaration of title of a joint family property was instituted. The property was partitioned amongst four brothers. Disputed property was in the share of one of the brothers, but sale deed of that property was executed by another brother. The purchaser cannot confer any title on that property.[20]

15 *Bajranglal Shivchandrai Ruia* v *Shashikant N. Ruia* AIR 2004 SC 2546.
16 *Shankar Dev Pandey* v *Sukhlal Ribai Pando* AIR 2018 Chh 42.
17 *Union of India* v *Vasavi Co-op. Housing Society Ltd.* AIR 2014 SC 937.
18 *Ramesh Chand Ardawattya* v *Anil Panjwani* AIR 2003 SC 2508.
19 *Muthyalappa Chinnobanna* v *Smt. Pallakka Hanumnathappa* AIR 2016 Kar 160.
20 *Santosh Kumar Tiwari* v *Smt. Meena Bai* AIR 2018 Chh 167.

Limitation to suit claiming joint ownership Joint owners inherited suit. Inheritance never remains in abeyance. Passage of time does not extinguish right of co-owner. Suit claiming joint co-ownership cannot be held to be barred by limitation on ground of failure of joint owner to challenge mutation within a period of three years.[21]

Power to do justice under Article 142 of the Constitution Plaintiff claimed to have perfected title by adverse possession and consequently claimed declaration of title and injunction. Suit was dismissed as plaintiff was found to be in unauthorised occupation for years. Plaintiff then offered to purchase the suit land at market rate. The Supreme Court to do justice under Art. 142 of the Constitution allowed him to purchase the said suit property.[22]

Discretion to grant specific performance In case of specific performance of contract, the court has to exercise discretion. Conducts of the parties are relevant factors for exercise of discretion. The court has to consider the entire conduct of the parties in relation to the subject matter and in case of any disqualifying circumstances the court will not grant the relief prayed for.[23]

Effect of declaration A declaration granted by the court under this Chapter, is binding only on the parties to the suit and persons claiming through them and where any of the parties are trustees, on the persons for whom, if in existence at the date of declaration, such parties would be trustees [*vide* s. 35].

Section 35 applies only to a suit for declaration.[24] A declaration granted to an employee of his permanent employment does not bind the person appointed in his place after his termination.[1] By virtue of s. 35, declaration given under s. 34 is binding between the parties. It is a declaration *in personam* and not *in rem*.[2]

When no time for payment or deposit is fixed in the decree for specific performance the law implies a reasonable time within which the contract is to be performed. Then it should be performed within reasonable time. Reasonable time depends upon the facts and circumstances of each case.[3]

Injunction in suit for specific performance Agreement of sale does not create any title or interest in favour of the vendee in view of s. 54, Transfer of Property Act. As to one who seeks to get the property by transfer of the property subsequent to the earlier agreement of sale s. 19(*b*) of the Specific Relief Act provides that specific performance of contract may be enforced

21 *Ram Singh* v *Baldev Singh* AIR 2016 P&H 146.
22 *Birbal* v *Haryana State* AIR 2014 SC 3772.
23 *M.P. Mathur* v *D.T.C.* AIR 2007 SC 414.
24 *N.M. Dagli* v *Hasibhai Manibhai Patel* AIR 1980 Bom 123.
1 *Shiv Kumar Tiwari* v *Jagat Narain Rai* AIR 2002 SC 211; (2001)10 SCC 11.
2 *S.N.P. Shipping Services Pvt. Ltd.* v *World Tanker Carrier Corpn.* AIR 2000 Bom 34.
3 *Kanhaiyalal Porwal* v *Mulla Abdul Hussain* 1984 MP LJ 377; AIR 1985 MP 24.

against any person claiming under the vendor by a title arising subsequently to the contract, except a transferee for value who has paid his money in good faith and without notice of the original contract. Sometimes temporary injunction is asked for to restrain the prospective vendor from dealing with property or making any construction or for any allied reliefs. In order to entitle interim injunction in a suit it is incumbent upon the plaintiff to show that he has a *prima facie* case and further that balance of convenience lies in the grant of *ad interim* injunction prayed for otherwise irreparable injury would be occasioned to him. In a suit for specific performance of the agreement of sale of housing plot the agreement showed that the defendant had entered into an agreement of sale of plot in dispute to the plaintiff for a total consideration of ₹6,60,000 and in pursuance thereof a sum of ₹51,000 was paid by plaintiff to the defendant as earnest money. These facts were not denied by the defendant. It had been categorically stated by the plaintiff in his plaint that he was willing to perform his part of the contract and had been contracting the defendant for completing the further formalities in this behalf but without any result. In such situation, the plaintiff must be held to have established a *prima facie* case in his favour for the grant of *ad interim* injunction restraining the defendant from dealing with the plot in dispute in any manner whatsoever and making construction thereon and the plaintiff will be entitled to an order of temporary injunction.[4] Injunction may also be granted at the instance of the plaintiff restraining the defendant-vendor from completing a sale in favour of a third party in a pursuance of a contract by the main contracting defendant and that third party.[5]

Injunction restraining defendant from transferring the suit property to any third party in a suit for specific performance may be allowed although such a transfer to a third party may be hit by *lis pendens* enacted in s. 52, Transfer of Property Act. It is granted because such third party transferee may be a *bona fide* purchaser for value without notice of prior contract and further he may by expending a large sum make improvement of the suit property. Then, equity may stand in the plaintiff's setting at naught the subsequent transfer.[6]

In this context it may be appropriate to recall that every positive obligation, that is every obligation, to perform an act, necessarily involves an obligation not to perform other inconsistent acts. Sometimes the parties expressly agree that particular inconsistent acts will not be performed, but more generally it is necessary to resort to matters of implication. In either case

4 *Vijay Kumar* v *Mahi Pal* AIR 1987 Del 345; (1987)5 IJ Rep 319.

5 *Kailash Nath & Associates* v *Badri Pershad Seth* AIR 1982 NOC 132 (Del). See also *Terai Tea Co. Ltd.* v *National Kedia* AIR 2012 Cal 43 (no concluded contract is proved and as such no interim injunction granted).

6 *Muktakeshi Dawan* v *Haripada Mozumdar* AIR 1988 Cal 25; 91 CWN 1094; (1988)1 Cur Civ Cas 981 (Cal).

any inconsistent act may be restrained, if it is appropriate to do so. So, for example where specific performance is sought of an agreement to transfer a particular property a court of equity will, in an appropriate case will enjoin the carrying out of the acts that would necessarily prevent the transfer of that property as agreed.[7]

Injunction cannot be granted once the period of contract is over.[8] A direction to the plaintiff in whose favour temporary injunction has been granted, or undertake to pay to the defendant an amount if the plaintiff lost the case, is without jurisdiction.[9]

It may be recalled that s. 52, Transfer of Property Act does not render a transfer made during the pendency of suit of specific performance absolutely void. It means only that if a suit is pending in which any right to immovable property is directly or substantially in question, that property cannot be transferred or otherwise be dealt with by any party to such suit so as to affect the rights of any other party to that suit and if such a transfer takes place the subsequent transferee will be bound by the ultimate decree that may be passed. So, s. 52, T.P. Act *propria vigore* does not warrant granting an injunction to fetter any transfer *lis pendens*. And if in a suit for specific performance court finds that the plaintiff has no *prima facie* case, rejection of prayer of temporary injunction is not exceptionable.[10]

Laying down the principles to be kept in view in granting or refusing temporary injunction in such a matter a Rajasthan case observes: Utmost care, attention and alertness should be exercised by the court in dealing with a suit for specific performance of a contract in which temporary injunction under Or. 39, r. 1 or r. 2 is also prayed for. The court should as a first step, scrutinise the plaint to find out if it contains averments spelling out a negative term or obligation undertaken by the defendant, agreeing to refrain from or not to do a particular thing. If the plaintiff does not allege that the defendant had entered into an agreement involving a negative term this means that the plaint does not disclose a cause of action for specific performance of a negative term of the contract. The court must further keep in view that s. 38, Specific Relief Act which lays down that a perpetual injunction may be granted to the plaintiff to prevent the breach of an obligation existing in his favour. It further enjoins that when such obligation arises from a contract, the court shall be guided by the rules and provisions contained in Chapter II which deals with specific performance of contract. In a suit based on contract involving a negative term, the court

7 Spry on *Principles of Equitable Remedies*, 3rd Ed., p. 431.

8 *Municipal Council, Udaipur* v *Mahendra Kumar* AIR 2008 SC 2507; (2008)12 SCC 771.

9 *Vinod Shah* v *Devinder Bajaj* 2010 AIR SCW 4860.

10 *Agarwal & Co.* v *State of Rajasthan* (1986)2 Cur Civ Cas 217 (Raj).

is prohibited by s. 14, Specific Relief Act from granting injunction if compensation in money would afford adequate relief for its breach.[11]

In suit for specific performance of contract of sale the plaintiff who was guilty of laches, not ready throughout to perform his part of contract is not entitled to restrain the contractee from transferring the contracted land to a third party.[12]

In a case defendant agreed to supply to the plaintiff green leaves. Alleging that the defendant in breach of the said agreement started supplying substandard green leaves which were unfit for producing tea and that the defendant also failed and neglected to supply the minimum quantity of 10,000 kgs. of green leaves as per terms and conditions of the agreement sued for specific performance of the alleged agreement, permanent injunction restraining the defendant from selling the goods to other parties and also for temporary injunction. The court while deciding the question whether to grant temporary injunction or not cannot while dealing with the issue whether the agreement in question has been breached and if so, has it caused irreparable injury to the plaintiff, decide that the grant of mandatory injunction would not be an appropriate relief since while coming to such finding the court would bring itself within the confines of specific performance. It was further held that in deciding the injunction matter the court cannot prejudge the main issue.[13]

When the plaintiff has a clear title supported by documents and a defendant without any claim on the title merely denies the title of the plaintiff, it would not amount to raising of cloud over the title of the plaintiff and it would not be necessary for the plaintiff to sue for declaration and suit for injunction would be sufficient.[14]

Suit for declaration and injunction Suit for declaration and injunction was instituted without seeking for possession. Entries in record of rights will not help to prove possession. Evidence shows possession and enjoyment, either symbolic or actual by the father of the plaintiff. Plaintiff also produced tax paid receipts. No contra evidence was produced by defendant to prove his possession. Thus, question seeking consequential relief by plaintiff for possession does not arise. Suit is liable to be decreed.[15]

Sale deed was executed by Corporation in favour of vendee. Tenant had no right to challenge the transaction between vendee and corporation. Sale

11 *Lucky Minmate* v *State of Rajasthan* AIR 1982 NOC 213 (Raj); 1981 Raj LW 646; 1981 WLN 316.

12 *Jyotsnamoyee Devi* v *Narayan Ch. Pal* (1988)1 Cur Civ Cas 5 (Cal).

13 *Kalyan Mukherjee* v *Rahut Syndicate* AIR 1992 Cal 1.

14 *Laxman Bisan Uke* v *Ashok Ishwar Shinde* (2018)4 Mah LJ 151; (2018)4 Bom CR 105.

15 *K. Jagadishwar* v *Sharada* AIR 2011 Kar 148.

was valid. The vendee was entitled to relief of declaration and injunction from dispossession.[16]

Suit for bare injunction Husband plaintiff purchased suit property in the name of his wife. According to s. 3(2) of the Benami Transactions (Prohibition) Act 1988 presumption is in favour of defendant that the property belongs to her. In absence of any prayer for declaration of title, suit framed is untenable. Besides, an injunction suit *per se* cannot be converted into suit for declaration. Hence husband is not entitled to injunction.[17]

Injunction restraining possession in a suit for specific performance Contract of sale does not create any title to the proposed vendee. So a transferee under a sale deed cannot be prevented by injunction from enjoying possession of property under transfer at the instance of a person having only a previous agreement of sale in his favour.[18] Injunction restraining the defendants from interfering with possession of plaintiff who has sued for specific performance can be granted when the agreement sought to be enforced recites the delivery of possession to the plaintiff. This injunction can be granted under the inherent power.[19] Following the Bombay view Rajasthan High Court restrained the defendant of a specific performance suit from transferring suit property and making construction thereon during pendency of the suit to any third party.[20] It held that there is no justification in treating such a suit as one under s. 53A, TP Act and to refuse relief of injunction. In a suit *A* in whose favour *B* executed an agreement of sale sued and prayed that subsequent transferee *C* be restrained from preventing entry of *A*. It was pointed out that the agreement of sale does not create any interest. The registered conveyance by *B* to *C* must be interpreted as one whereby *C* has entered into possession. Here *A* is not entitled to injunction.[21]

In a case plaintiff prayed for temporary injunction on doctrine of part performance under s. 53A, TP Act alleging that defendant executed an agreement of sale and put him into possession. The defendant alleged that the agreement of sale is a manufactured document, injunction was refused.[1]

Bare suit for injunction when contractee entered into possession A person who enters into possession lawfully on the basis of agreement of sale can maintain a suit for injunction *simpliciter* to restrain the contractor from transferring

16 *K. Krishna* v *A.N. Paramkusha Bai* AIR 2011 AP 165.
17 *Govindammal* v *Murugesan* AIR 2011 Mad 235.
18 *Jiwan Dass* v *Narain Dass* AIR 1981 Del 291.
19 *Venkat Dharaji* v *Vishwanath* AIR 1983 Bom 413; 1983 Mah LJ 284 dissenting from *Krishnamoorthy Kounder* v *Paramjasiva Kounder* AIR 1981 Mad 310.
20 *Rama Devi* v *Sagner Co-operative* AIR 1987 Raj 143; 1986 Raj LR 1018.
21 *Sujan Charan Lenka* v *Pramila Mohanty* AIR 1986 Ori 74; (1985)2 Ori LR 335.
1 *U.N. Sharma* v *Puttegowda* AIR 1986 Kant 99; ILR (1986) Kant 171.

the land agreed to be transferred to a third party without adding a prayer for specific performance of the agreement. It was more so when plaintiff had issued notices after notices to defendant expressing his readiness and willingness to pay the balance of the amount and also that nothing transpired subsequently which made that lawful agreement unlawful by the occurrence of any subsequent event.[2]

Ownership of plaintiff's plot was not disputed. Defendants have threatened to invade plaintiff's right to enjoy his plot or have been trying to breach an obligation existing in favour of the plaintiff. Suit for injunction *simpliciter* without praying for declaration is maintainable.[3]

It is not correct to say that s. 53A, Transfer of Property Act, embodying the doctrine of part performance can be invoked only by the defendant. It can also be invoked by a plaintiff so long he uses it as a shield. So, a plaintiff may sue for injunction to restrain the defendant on the plea of part performance provided, however, the requisite conditions for calling in aid the section are fulfilled.[4]

The right conferred by s. 53A, Transfer of Property Act is a right available to the defendant to protect his possession. It imposes a statutory bar to the transferor. It confers no active title to the transferee.[5] Plaintiff's right to invoke the doctrine of part performance was emphasised in *Babu Ram* v *Basdeo*,[6] which held the equitable doctrine of part performance is available to the plaintiff not only where he is physically in possession of the property on the date of the suit but also where he physically has been found to have been illegally dispossessed by some person claiming under the transferor. The intention that unless the transferee is in possession he cannot invoke s. 53A, TP Act if accepted would reduce the utility of the provision to a naught, because a powerful transferor or a person claiming under him would be able to defeat the provisions by forcibly dispossessing the transferee and leading him to a court as plaintiff. Such a course and the result would not be conducive to the interest of an orderly social order.

Specific performance and injunction Both specific performance and injunction developed historically as equitable and not as common-law remedies. Despite the effects of the Judicature Act reforms this had three results which are

2 *Laxman Pandu Khadke* v *Pandharinath* AIR 1988 Bom 296; 1988 Mah LR 444.
3 *Smt. Prembai* v *Ghanshyam* AIR 2011 MP 1.
4 *Akram Mea* v *Secunderabad Municipal Corporation* AIR 1957 AP 859; *Chaitan Das* v *Murali Dalai* AIR 1971 Ori 41; *S.F. Munuswami* v *Erusa Goundar* AIR 1975 Mad 25; (1974)1 Mad LJ 497; 57 Mad LW 291 contra *Amrao Singh* v *Sanatan Dharma Sabha* AIR 1985 Punj 195; 1984 Punj LJ 542.
5 *Garaj Narain Singh* v *Babulal Khemka* AIR 1975 Pat 58; 1974 BLJR 757; *Conceicoa Antonio Fernandez* v *Dr. Arfano* AIR 1975 Goa 27.
6 AIR 1982 All 414.

relevant even today.[7] The first is that injunction and specific performance are regarded as secondary remedies. The primary is the common-law response of damages. Secondly, neither specific performance nor injunction are available as of right. They remain ultimately as discretionary remedies, if any of such remedies is granted, this will be available on such terms as the court thinks fit. Thirdly, although in most cases the equitable remedies of specific performance and injunction exist as parallel remedies to those available at common law, there are not a few situations where the equitable remedies are not available, but common law ones are or *vice versa*.

Specific performance generally takes the form of an order by the court to the defendant to perform his contractual obligation which includes an arbitration award. The order operates *in personam* and breach of it is a contempt, opening the defendant to a number of penalties including fines, imprisonment and sequestration.[8]

Specific performance and insolvent defendant In this regard Goulding, J in *Golfstraum*[9] states: "[C]ommercial life would be subjected to new and unjust hazards if the court were to decree specific performance of contracts normally sounding only in damages simply because of a party's threatened insolvency."

Specific performance (American law) Specific performance and injunction are alternative reliefs to the award of damages for enforcing contracts. Specific performance is limited to the enforcement of contractual duties only. But injunction as a remedy is used in many fields of law.[10]

Necessary and proper party for suit for specific performance Against a necessary party there must be a right to some relief in respect of the matters involved in the proceeding in question; it must not be possible to pass an effective decree in the absence of such party. The test for determining the effectiveness of decree is whether the decree can be executed without the presence of the party in question as regards the property sought to be decreed in favour of the plaintiff.[11] Only such persons are necessary parties who have interests in the subject matter of the suit and who are likely to be affected.[12]

7 Prof. Neil Andrews, Prof. Malcolm Clarke, Prof. Andrew Tettenborn, Prof. Graham Virgo, *Contractual Duties: Performance, Breach, Termination and Remedies*, 2011 Ed., para 27-002.

8 *Ibid*, para 27-007.

9 [1985]2 All ER 669 at p. 674.

10 *Restatement of the Law*, Second Series, Contracts 2d., vol. 3, p. 162.

11 *Benaras Bank* v *Bhagwan Das* AIR 1974 All 18; *Deputy Commissioner, Hardoi* v *Rama Krishna* AIR 1953 SC 521; 1954 SCR 506; ILR (1954)1 All 168; *Jivandas* v *Narbadabai* AIR 1959 Cal 519; *Badshah* v *Board of Revenue* AIR 1962 MP 12; *Hardeva* v *Ismail* AIR 1970 Raj 167; *S.C. Law* v *K.S. Roy* AIR 1974 Cal 274; *Panne Khushali* v *Jeewanlal* AIR 1976 MP 148; *Hitkarini Sabha* v *D. Mangal Wadi* (1988)1 Cur Civ Cas 469 (MP).

12 *Ram Sharan* v *Mahipatrao* AIR 1987 MP 29; 1987 Jab LJ 115; 1987 Cur Civ Cas LJ (MP) 34.

Thus in a suit for specific performance of a contract of sale a person not a party to the agreement of sale but claiming to be a joint-owner of the subject matter of the suit is neither a necessary nor a proper party and is not entitled to be impleaded in the suit.[13]

Strangers who claim adverse to the title of the defendant-vendor alleging that they are co-owners of the property sought to be sold are not necessary parties nor proper parties.[14] In a suit for specific performance of contract by *A* against *B*, *A* claiming that whatever interest *B* had must pass to *A*, *B*'s sister claimed herself to have a share in the property, held *B*'s sister is not a necessary party.[15] When *X* files a suit for specific performance against *Y*, *Y*'s coparcener who claims that *Y* cannot transfer the property as it is not beneficial to the family can be impleaded as a party, for then it cannot be said the coparcener by his joinder seeks a decision on his or his vendor's title only.[16] A suit by one joint promisee for specific performance of contract is tenable on impleading other promisee as co-defendant on their refusal to sue as plaintiff.[17] When *A* has sued *B* for specific performance of contract of sale, *C* who claims to have entered into another contract with *B* during the pendency of suit cannot be impleaded, he being not a necessary party.[18] When *A* enters into a contract of sale with *B*, in suit by *B* for specific performance *C* claiming that the property is joint property of *A* and *C* cannot be impleaded.[19] In a case *A* filed a suit for specific performance of contract of sale against *B* (the promisor) and *C*, the subsequent transferee. But meanwhile *D* pre-empted the property from *C*. It was held in the suit for specific performance *D* is not a necessary party, nor *D* can claim himself to be added as a defendant.[20] But person claiming under earlier agreement of sale and in possession is a necessary party even when neither possession nor injunction is prayed for.[21]

In a suit for specific performance when the plaintiff has been put into possession of the property regarding which agreement of sale had been entered into and he had already paid the entire sale price to the *karta* of the coparcenary family, the coparceners are not necessary parties.[1]

13 *Krishan Lal* v *Tek Chand* AIR 1987 Punj 197; 1986 Punj LJ 629; (1986)90 Punj LJ 616; ILR (1987)2 P&H 85.
14 *Panna Khushali* v *Jeewanlal* AIR 1976 MP 148; 1976 Jab LJ 84; (1976)1 MPLJ 170.
15 *Rasiklal* v *Natverlal* AIR 1975 Guj 178; (1975)16 Guj LR 533. See also *Jugraj Singh* v *Jaswant Singh* AIR 1971 SC 761; (1971)1 SCR 38.
16 *Atul Sharma* v *Gurinder Sinha* AIR 1984 Punj 365; 1984 Rev LR 283.
17 *Ponnuswami Gounder* v *Rama Boyan* AIR 1979 Mad 130; *Nirmala* v *Sudarshan* AIR 1980 Cal 258; (1980)1 Cal LJ 11.
18 *Mohammadbhai* v *Trustees, Cal. Improvement* AIR 1984 Cal 219.
19 *Ram Bilash Pandey* v *Jai Narayan* AIR 1984 Pat 218.
20 *Gourhari* v *Bimal Kumar* 88 CWN 1067.
21 *Bala Narasimha* v *Ganga Putra Co-op.* AIR 1984 AP 166 contra *Rasiklal* v *Natverlal* AIR 1975 Guj 178.
1 *Aman Behal* v *Arun Kansal* AIR 1987 P&H 52; (1986)2 Land LR 302; 1986(1)89 Punj LR 608; 1986 Rev LR 247; 1986 Rec Laws 89.

In a decree for specific performance of contract of sale when the contracted property had been transferred to subsequent transferee, the decree must direct the vendor to execute the deed and in that deed the subsequent transferee must join.[2] In such suits not only subsequent transferee but also their vendor is a necessary party.[3]

In suit for specific performance of contract of sale, possession too should be prayed for. If not so prayed, the plaint may be amended to include the prayer at any stage. So, if one co-sharer contracts to sell a property, the other co-sharer in possession is at least a proper party. Such a co-sharer may get himself impleaded in the suit for specific performance.[4]

Thus in a suit for specific performance of contract of sale by *A* against *B*, the purchaser in auction sale in a decree against *B*—the auction sale being held during the pendency of the suit for specific performance is a proper party.[5]

Joinder of parties coming under subsequent agreement of sale in pending suit of specific performance Order 1, r. 10(2), CPC empowers the court to strike out the name of any party to the suit or to implead any one as a party in the suit. It however does not empower to substitute a party for another.

Order 1, r. 10(2), CPC stands as follows:

> Rule 10(2). *Court may strike out or add parties.* The court may at any stage of the proceedings, either upon or without the application of either party, and on such terms as may appear to the court to be just, order that the name of any party improperly joined, whether as plaintiff or defendant, be struck out, and that the name of any person who ought to have been joined, whether as plaintiff or defendant, or whose presence before the court may be necessary in order to enable the court effectually and completely to adjudicate upon and settle all the questions involved in the suit, be added.

As held by the Punjab High Court in a suit for specific performance of a sale-agreement a person coming under subsequent sale-agreement in respect of the same property should not be added as a party under Or. 1, r. 10 of the Code of Civil Procedure since unlike a purchaser he had no interest in the property and addition of such a person as party will result is misjoinder of parties.[6] In an identical fact situation Calcutta High Court too came to an identical view.[7] In that suit of Calcutta High Court the suit

2 *Dwarka Prasad Singh* v *Harikant Prasad Singh* AIR 1973 SC 655; (1973)2 SCR 1064; (1973)1 SCC 179.
3 *Khadir Saheb* v *Amin Saheb* AIR 1981 Kant 89.
4 *B. Mahboob Ali* v *B. Subhan Saheb* (1986)1 Andh LT 67 (NRC).
5 *Raj Singh* v *Ram Nivas* AIR 1977 All 104.
6 *Manmohan Singh* v *Sat Narain* AIR 1971 Punj 400.
7 *Mohammadbhai Sk. Mohsinbhoy* v *Trustees Calcutta Improvement Trust* AIR 1984 Cal 219.

filed by the plaintiffs against defendant No. 3 was for a declaration that the plaintiffs were entitled to specific performance of an agreement for sale of the suit property upon payment of the balance sum of the purchase money to the defendant Nos. 1 and 2, who had acquired the property under the Land Acquisition Act. The plaintiffs purchased the property at an auction sale held by the defendant No. 1, who admittedly had a statutory right of pre-emption to purchase the land in the event of the defendants Nos. 1 and 2 deciding to sell the same. The petitioner herein sought to be added as a party defendant to the proceedings by reason of the fact that during the pendency of the said suit an agreement for sale of the suit premises was entered upon between himself and the defendant No. 3, the owner of the suit property, under which agreement he claimed to have paid a certain amount to defendant No. 3. It was held that the petitioner is neither a proper nor a necessary party who is required to be joined in the proceedings and the proceedings between the plaintiff and the defendants can be effectively and completely disposed of in his absence. The prayer of the petitioner for being added under Or. 1, r. 10(2), CPC was thus rejected.[8]

Suit for specific performance Agreement to sell provided obligation on vendors to get suit property registered as Rubber Estate and to obtain licence for planting rubber plants. Plaintiff was always ready and willing to perform his part. Vendors-defendants failed to obtain registration and licence from Rubber Board. Plaintiff was held to be entitled to decree for specific performance.[9]

There was an agreement to sell land. It was contended by the defendant-appellant that there has been considerable increase in price of the land in question. Though it may be true, it cannot be a ground for denying the decree of specific performance to the respondent. The Supreme Court did not find any reason to interfere with the concurrent findings of facts and law as stated in the judgment under appeal.[10]

Impleadment of legal heirs In a suit for specific performance, after death of original vendor, his legal heir if impleaded under Or. 22, r. 4, CPC he cannot go beyond the stand taken by the original vendor. But if he impleaded under Or. 1, r. 10, CPC he would be entitled in his individual capacity to take his own stand.[11]

Order of performance The order of performance of reciprocal promises does not depend upon the order in which the terms of the agreement are reduced into writing. The order of performance should be expressly stated or provided, that is, the agreement should say only after performance of obligations of

8 *Mohammadbhai Sk. Mohsinbhoy* v *Trustees Calcutta Improvement Trust* AIR 1984 Cal 219.

9 *Silvey* v *Arun Varghese* AIR 2008 SC 1568.

10 *Laxman Tatyaba Kankate* v *Taramati Harishchandra Dhatrak* AIR 2010 SC 3025.

11 *Labh Singh* v *Pal Singh* AIR 2019 P&H 17.

vendors, the purchaser will have to perform his obligations. The failure of the purchaser to pay the balance sale consideration within time fixed clearly amounted to breach of contract. As the time for payment was the essence of the contract; the vendors were justified in determining the agreement for sale. The rejection of prayer for specific performance was, therefore, proper.[12]

DECREES

Decree—effect of Decree means a formal expression of an adjudication which the court conclusively and finally determines the rights of the parties with regard to all or any of the matters in controversy in the suit.[13] A sale crystallises in favour of a party to an agreement of sale on the date when a decree for specific performance is passed in his favour and does not date back to the date on which the agreement of sale is entered into between the parties.[14]

Neither a contract of sale nor a decree passed on that basis for specific performance of contract gives any right of title to the decree-holder and the right and title passes to him only on the execution of the deed of sale either by the judgment-debtor himself or by the court itself if he fails to execute the sale deed. It is idle to contend that a valuable right had accrued to the plaintiff merely because a decree for specific performance has been passed against the defendant.[15]

The court which passes the decree for specific performance retains control over the proceedings even after the decree, as the decree is in the nature of a preliminary decree.[16] The apex court in a later decision held that decree made in a suit for specific performance of contract of sale of immovable property calling upon the purchaser to deposit the balance of consideration within the time stipulated in the decree with super added condition that in the event of default the suit would stand dismissed is not a preliminary deceee.[17] If the matter is under appeal, the court will take into account the events and changes in the law occurring during the pendency of the appeal in order to do complete justice between the parties and to

12 *Saradamani Kandappan* v *S. Rajalakshmi* AIR 2011 SC 3234.

13 *Deep Chand* v *Land Acquisition Officer* (1994)4 SCC 99; AIR 1994 SC 1901; *Chandi Prasad* v *Jagdish Prasad* (2004)8 SCC 724.

14 *Gurdial Singh* v *Sewa Singh* AIR 1974 Punj 18; 1973 Rev LR 54; *Ishar* v *Maluk Singh* AIR 1977 Punj 38.

15 *Babu Lal* v *Hazarilal Kishori Lal* AIR 1982 SC 818; (1982)3 SCR 94; (1982)1 SCC 525.

16 *Hungerford Investment Trust Ltd.* v *Haridas Mundhra* AIR 1972 SC 1826; (1972)3 SCR 690; (1972)3 SCC 684 approving *Pearisundari* v *Hari Charan* ILR (1888)15 Cal 211; *Someshwar Dayal* v *Widow of Lalman* AIR 1958 All 483; *Tribeni Tewary* v *Ramratan* AIR 1959 Pat 460 and *Anandilal* v *Gunendra* AIR 1966 Cal 107.

17 *Sandhyarani Sarkar* v *Sudha Rani Devi* AIR 1978 SC 537; (1978)2 SCR 839; (1978)2 SCC 116.

avoid futile decree. But where a decree has been passed, the right obtained by a party under the decree will not be allowed to be defeated by delay in the disposal of the appeal against the decree, if it is possible to save the decree by moulding it to conform to the statutes subsequently coming into force.[18]

Nature of a decree for specific performance A suit for specific performance does not come to an end on passing of a decree and the court which has passed the decree for specific performance retains the control over the decree even after the decree has been passed. The decree for specific performance has been described as a preliminary decree. It can be annulled. The power under s. 28 of the Act is discretionary and the court cannot ordinarily annul the decree once passed by it. Although the power to annul the decree exists yet s. 28 of the Act provides for complete relief to both the parties in terms of the decree. The court does not cease to have the power to extend the time even though the trial court had earlier directed in the decree that payment of balance price to be made by certain date and on failure the suit to stand dismissed. The power exercisable under this section is discretionary.[19]

Decree when property conveyed to subsequent transferee with notice In a decree for specific performance of contract of sale when the contracted property had been transferred to subsequent tansferee, the decree must direct the vendor to execute the deed and in that deed the subsequent transferee must join.[20] Where the property is in the possession of the subsequent transferee with notice, the proper form of decree is to direct specific performance of the contract between the parties to the contract and direct the subsequent transferee to join in the conveyance so as to pass on the title which resides in him to the plaintiff. He does not, of course, join in any special covenants made between the plaintiff and his vendor, all he does is to pass on his title to the plaintiff.[21]

Delivery of possession order in decree for specific performance Under s. 22, Specific Relief Act 1963 a person suing for specific performance of contract may ask for possession, or partition and separate possession of property in addition to such performance or any other relief to which he may be entitled including refund of earnest money or deposit paid or made to him in case his claim for specific performance is refused. No relief of possession or refund of earnest money or deposit can be granted by the court unless it has been specifically claimed. But when court has omitted to give relief of

18 *Pasupuleti Venkateswarlu* v *Motor and General Traders* AIR 1975 SC 1409; (1975)3 SCR 958; (1975)1 SCC 770; *Rameshwar* v *Jot Ram* AIR 1976 SC 49; (1976)1 SCR 847; (1976)1 SCC 194; *Bai Dosabai* v *Mathuradas Govinddas* AIR 1980 SC 1334; (1980)3 SCR 762; (1980)3 SCC 545.

19 *Chanda* v *Rattni* (2007)14 SCC 26.

20 *Dwarka Prosad* v *Harikant* AIR 1973 SC 655; (1973)3 SCC 803.

21 *Durga Prasad* v *Deep Chand* AIR 1954 SC 75; 1954 SCR 360; 1954 SCJ 23 relying on *Kafiladdin* v *Samiraddin* AIR 1951 Cal 67 and the English Practice.

delivery of possession in the decree, executing court can recover possession to the decree-holder.[1] In appropriate case the High Court may modify the earlier decree and grant possession in appeal.[2] This Supreme Court decision pinpointing the words "in an appropriate case" occurring in s. 22(1), Specific Relief Act observed that it is not always incumbent on the plaintiff to claim possession or partition or separate possession in a suit for specific performance of contract for the transfer of immovable property. Besides the proviso to s. 22(2), Specific Relief Act provides for amendment of plaint on such terms as may be just for including a claim for such relief 'at any stage of the proceedings'. This Supreme Court decision was relied on and analysed by a Calcutta Special Bench case which ultimately held that the relief for possession in favour of a successful plaintiff in a suit for specific performance of contract of sale is not a separate or distinct relief. The same is only an ancillary or consequential one. The Special Bench held that for relief of possession in a suit for specific performance no separate court-fee is payable.[3]

Rescission of contracts—(ss. 27 to 30) Section 27 lays down that any person interested in a contract may sue to have it rescinded and such rescission may be adjudged by the court in any of the following cases *viz.*, (*a*) where the contract is voidable or terminable by the plaintiff, and (*b*) where the contract is unlawful for causes not apparent on its face and the defendant is more to blame than the plaintiff. The court may however refuse to rescind the contract (*a*) where the plaintiff has expressly or impliedly ratified it, or (*b*) where owing to change of situation the parties cannot substantially be restored to the position in which they stood when the contract was made or (*c*) when third parties have during the subsistence of the contract acquired rights in good faith without notice and for value, or (*d*) where only a part of the contract is sought to be rescinded and that part is not severable from the rest of the contract. But remedy by way of rescission is not confined to persons named as parties to a contract. It is open to any person, who though not named as a party to the contract, is interested in the contract or whose interest are affected by it. Thus any member of a joint Hindu family is entitled to rescind a contract entered into by the manager. The remedy is also available for legal representatives, heirs and other assigns provided that the original party has not, by his own conduct, disentitled himself to the relief. Rescission will be refused where the plaintiff has expressly or impliedly ratified the contract.[4] So also where the parties cannot

1 *Narayana Pillai* v *Ponnuswami* 1978 Ker LT 512; *Debabrata* v *Biraj Mohon* 1982 East LR 427 relying on *Babulal* v *Hazarilal* AIR 1982 SC 818; (1982)3 SCR 94; (1982)1 SCC 525.

2 *Babu Lal* v *Hazarilal Kishori Lal* AIR 1982 SC 818; (1982)3 SCR 94; 1982 All LJ 345; (1982)1 SCC 525.

3 *Dhiraj Bala Karia* v *Jethia Estate* AIR 1983 Cal 166; (1983)1 East LR 41; 87 CWN 13; (1982)2 Cal LJ 225; (1982)2 CHN 282.

4 *Rangasamy Goundar* v *Nachiappa Gounder* AIR 1918 PC 196.

be substantially restored to their original position; that is where *restitutio in integrum* is impossible. Similarly there will be no rescission where the rights of the third parties have intervened.[5]

Composite order of specific performance and condition that in default to deposit consideration suit is to be dismissed—propriety A decree in a suit for specific performance of contract is in the nature of a preliminary decree, and having regard to s. 28, Specific Relief Act 1963, which constitutes the statutory crystallization of the legal position in that behalf the court has no jurisdiction to provide that if the plaintiff committed default in making the deposit within the time stipulated in the decree, the suit shall stand dismissed. In this view of the matter the Division Bench deleted the default clause in appeal.[6]

In appeal against the decision the Supreme Court it is held that the condition that the suit will be dismissed on non-payment of sale price could not be imposed in the light of the provisions of s. 28, Specific Relief Act.[7] Later, the Supreme Court disapproved the passing of such a composite order although on a different reason and in a different context.[8]

Decree vis-a-vis original contract In *Saudagar Singh* v *Nazeer*,[9] Megarry, V.C. observed that (1) when an order for the specific performance of a contract for the sale of land is made, the contract continues to exist and is not merged in the order,[10] though it does not necessarily mean that the exercise of the rights that it confers and remains unaffected by an order for specific performance of that contract; (2) by applying to the court for an order of specific performance, and obtaining it, the applicant puts it into the hands of the court how the contract is to be carried out. As the court is seized of the matter and has made an order, the working out, variation or cancellation of that order is essentially a matter for the court. The continued existence of the contract is one thing, its working out is another; and (3) though the order is made, of course, by reference to the rights of the parties under the contract; yet, when made, it is the provisions of the order and not of the contract which regulate how the contract is to be carried out. Provisions in the contract as to the deduction of title, the preparation and delivery of conveyance, the mode and date of completion and many other matters must all yield to any directions on these matters which are given or under the decree for specific performance.

5 *Nirmal Singh* v *Gejo Mihan Singh* AIR 1997 P&H 260.
6 *K. Saraswathi* v *P.S.S. Somasundaram Chettiar* (1977)2 Mad LJ 68 reviewed in *Resham Singh* v *Manmohan Singh* AIR 1985 Punj 103; *Kedarnath* v *Kanwal Bhatia* AIR 1998 P&H 86.
7 *K. Kalpana Saraswathi* v *P.S.S. Somasundaram Chettiar* AIR 1980 SC 512; (1980)2 SCR 293; *Yeshwant Sri Pati Patil* v *Balkrishna* (1988)1 Cur Civ Cas 715 (Bom).
8 *Chinnamarkathian* v *Ayyavoo* AIR 1982 SC 137; (1982)2 SCR 146; (1982)1 SCC 159.
9 [1978]3 All ER 817.
10 *Austins of East Ham Ltd.* v *Macey* [1941] Ch 338.

Till a decree for specific performance is obtained, the vendor or the purchaser from him is entitled to the full enjoyment of the property. In fact, even if a decree for specific performance is obtained and no sale deed is actually executed, it cannot be said that any interest in the property has passed.[11]

Specification of date for depositing purchase money or other sum in the decree Order 20, r. 12A, CPC introduced by CPC (Amendment) Act 1976 stands as follows:

> 12A. *Decree for specific performance of contract for the sale or lease of immovable property*. Where a decree for the specific performance of a contract for the sale or lease of immovable property orders that the purchase-money or other sum be paid by the purchaser or lessee, it shall specify the period within which the payment shall be made.

This rule obligates the court to specify in the decree the date by which purchase-money or other sum is to be paid by the purchaser or the lessee.

Post-decree reliefs to plaintiffs If the purchaser or the lessee pays the purchase-money or other sum which he is ordered to pay under the decree within the period referred to in s. 28(1) the court may, on application made in the same suit, award the purchaser or the lessee such further relief as he may be entitled to, including in appropriate cases, all or any of the following reliefs, namely, (*a*) the execution of a proper conveyance or lease by the vendor or the lessor; (*b*) the delivery of possession, or partition and separate possession, of the property on the execution of such conveyance or lease [s. 28(3)]. It is also provided that no separate suit shall lie where any of the said reliefs can be claimed under the above provision.[12] Where delay is due to defendant's conduct, the plaintiff may also be entitled to damages.[13]

If it becomes impossible to enforce the decree, the plaintiff is not precluded from pursuing his remedy at law.[14]

Fixation of time for deposit of balance consideration in decree and appeal—effect In suit for specific performance when lower court while granting decree directs the plaintiff to deposit the balance of consideration within a period, say two months; and when the decree is affirmed by the High Court, these two months should be reckoned from the decree of High Court.[15] But the Punjab High Court held otherwise. In that case the trial court granted one month's time to decree-holder to deposit the sale price.

11 *Jiwan Dass* v *Narain Dass* AIR 1981 Del 291; *Govinda Chandra Ghose* v *Provabati Ghose* AIR 1956 Cal 147 and *S. Ramalingam Pillai* v *G.R. Jagadammal* AIR 1957 AP 960.

12 *Babu Lal* v *Hazari Lal Kishori Lal* AIR 1982 SC 818; (1982)3 SCR 94; (1982)1 SCC 525.

13 *Eastan* v *Brown* [1981]3 All ER 278.

14 *Johnson* v *Agnew* [1979]1 All ER 883.

15 *Hindurao* v *Yeshwant Laxman* AIR 1983 Bom 60; 1982 Mah LJ 794.

The appeal against the decree was dismissed, but the appellate court did not mention any time for depositing the sale price. It was held decree-holder can deposit the sale price one month after the appellate decree till the judgment-debtor raised objection under s. 28, Specific Relief Act rescinding the contract.[16]

Extension of time to deposit balance of consideration after decree The power of the court to extend the time for compliance with an order of court even though time originally fixed by the court may have expired stands preserved in s. 148, CPC which stands as follows:

> 148. *Enlargement of time.* Where any period is fixed or granted by the Court for the doing of any act prescribed or allowed by this Code, the Court may, in its discretion, from time to time, enlarge such period not exceeding thirty days in total, even though the period originally fixed or granted may have expired.

In a case suit was decreed on 29th September 1988 with direction to deposit the balance of consideration within 30 days. No deposit was made within the said period. The application dated 30th January 1989 for grant of time to deposit the balance of consideration was rejected on the ground that court became *functus officio*. It was held that the court has jurisdiction to extend time if sufficient cause is shown. Further party should not suffer for negligence of his advocate.[17]

There is no doubt that in a conditional decree for specific performance of the nature contemplated in s. 28(1), Specific Relief Act 1963 the court would have the power to grant an extension of time for payment fixed under decree.[18] Doubtlessly court retains power to extend time before it expires.[19] Sometimes a time is fixed in default of which the suit is to be automatically dismissed. Supreme Court in decreeing such types of orders held: where a period is fixed or granted by the court for doing an act prescribed or allowed by Code, the court may in its discretion from time to time enlarge such period even though the period originally fixed or granted may expire. If a court in exercise of the jurisdiction can grant time to do a thing, the jurisdiction to grant time would inhere in its ambit of the jurisdiction to extend time initially fixed by it. Passing of a composite order would be acting in disregard of the jurisdiction, in that while granting time simultaneously the court denies to itself the jurisdiction to extend time. If the court by its own act denies itself the jurisdiction to do so, it would be denying to itself the jurisdiction which in the absence of a negative provision

16 *Amar Nath Jain* v *Ram Parkash Dhir* AIR 1988 NOC 20 (P&H); (1987)91 Punj LR 490.

17 *Ram Narayan Mondal* v *Maniklal Sadhu* AIR 1991 Cal 388 relying on *Tapan Chatterjee* v *Kalyani Devi* AIR 1985 Cal 243; *K. Kalpana Saraswathi* v *P.S.S. Somasundaram Chettiar* AIR 1980 SC 512; (1980)2 SCR 293; (1980)1 SCC 630.

18 *Babulal* v *Jagannath* (1970)72 Bom LR 835.

19 *Nikhil Kr. Saha* v *Hedayat Ali Molla* AIR 1983 Cal 401; 86 CWN 766; (1983)1 CHN 395.

it undoubtedly enjoys.[20] When court passes a conditional order allowing petition on payment of costs with the direction that non-payment of cost by the date fixed would entail dismissal of petition, but cost is not deposited by the date fixed, nor the court rejects the petition by a specific order, court does not become *functus officio*. It can grant time for payment of costs.[1]

The court does not cease to have power to extend the time even though the trial court had earlier directed in the decree that payment of balance price be made by a certain date and on failure the suit to stand dismissed.[2] Time may be extended even though the application is made after the time fixed for payment in the decree has expired.[3] The court which passed the decree can give extension of time even where the decree has merged with the decree of the High Court and even after the expiry of time given by the decree.[4] The court has power to extend the time for any type of decree whether preliminary or final.[5] Time may be extended even though time has been fixed in the decree itself or even in a consent decree.[6] But time for payment of the price may not be extended where the decree-holder has made considerable unexplained delay—in this case there was a delay of five years—in depositing the amount, without having sought extension of time in the meanwhile.[7] However in *Ouseph* v *Devassy*[8] the purchaser paid the balance of price 15 years after the agreement, that is ten years after the decree but one day before the vendor applied for rescission. The delay in depositing the amount was condoned and the application for rescission dismissed because the vendor had received large part of the price at the time of the agreement, the purchaser had been in possession throughout and the vendor had not proved any demand for the balance.

Section 148 of the Code of Civil Procedure empowers the court to deal with events that might arise subsequent to an order, for the purpose of enlarging the time for payment even though peremptorily fixed.[9] In the Supreme Court case a Division Bench of High Court allowed an appeal on condition that appellant would pay the deficit court-fee within a specified

20 *Chinnamarkathian* v *Ayyavoo* AIR 1982 SC 137; (1982)1 Mad LJ (SC) 17; (1982)2 SCR 146; *Kedarnath* v *Kanwal Bhatia* AIR 1998 P&H 86.

1 *Muniammal* v *Sakkubai* AIR 1988 Mad 241; (1987)100 Mad LW 1191; (1988)1 Cur Civ Cas 595.

2 *Kedarnath* v *Kanwal Bhatia* AIR 1998 P&H 86.

3 *Ram Narayan Mondal* v *Maniklal Sadhu* AIR 1991 Cal 388.

4 *Bisun Prasad Mishra* v *Kamla Kant Jha* AIR 1972 Pat 322.

5 *Prime Promoters Pvt. Ltd.* v *Aroop Kumar Chatterjee* AIR 1999 Cal 186.

6 *V.S. Palanisamy Chettiar* v *C. Alagappan* AIR 1999 SC 918; (1999)4 SCC 702; JT 1999(1) SC 216.

7 *V.S. Palanisamy Chettiar* v *C. Alagappan* AIR 1999 SC 918; (1999)4 SCC 702; JT 1999(1) SC 216.

8 AIR 2001 Ker 104.

9 *Mahanth Ram Das* v *Ganga Das* AIR 1961 SC 882; (1961)3 SCR 763 followed in *Dulhin Jibuchli* v *Sitaram Sharma* AIR 1983 Pat 336; 1983 BBCJ (HC) 327.

time and further directed that appeal would stand dismissed if the deficit court-fee was not paid within the time given. No Division Bench was sitting on that date and on the last day before the time granted expired, the appellant filed a petition for extension of time. Such extension of time should be granted. This Supreme Court decision was relied on in several cases which held court has power to extend time under s. 148, CPC even after the time fixed by decree or order expired.[10] In both the latter cases an *ex parte* decree was to be set aside on payment of a cost on a date peremptorily fixed in default of which the Misc. Case was to be dismissed. It was held even then time may be extended. Similar is the view of M.P. High Court[11] and of Allahabad High Court.[12] In a similar situation Kerala High Court held otherwise.[13] But another Kerala High Court case held such power exists even after the expiry of period originally fixed.[14] Time for payment of deficit court-fee even after the conditional order made on that behalf worked out by expiry of time was extended. This power to extend time exists particularly when the default has been caused by default of the court.[15] Time may thus be extended for payment when possession is decreed on payment, time of payment being not fixed saying that in default, the suit would be dismissed.[16]

Extension of time for deposit for consideration when time fixed by consent In a Calcutta case by compromise decree the plaintiff agreed to pay to the defendant a given sum within a particular period of time. At the instance of the plaintiff this time was extended by the court.[17] In this case Calcutta High Court relied upon a Supreme Court case which clearly laid down the principle of law that when the parties entered into a compromise and invited the court to make an order in terms of the compromise which the court did, the time for deposit stipulated by the parties became the time allowed by the court and thus it gives the court the jurisdiction to extend time in appropriate cases. Of course time

10 *Lakshmi Bala Chanak* v *Brojendra Nath* AIR 1971 Cal 243; *New Bangasree Bastralaya* v *Ramanlal Phurna* (1976)1 Cal LJ 634 contrary view expressed in *Tarapada* v *Nepal* AIR 1965 Cal 354 being held to be no longer good law; *Nikhil Saha* v *Heabyet Ali* 86 CWN 766; *Akbar Ali* v *Abdul Wahab* AIR 1977 J&K 36 (contra *Mr. Mohd.* v *Nair Singh* AIR 1970 J&K 33); *Maruti Vishnu* v *Bapu Keshav* AIR 1970 Bom 398; *Shankar* v *Parwatibai* AIR 1976 Bom 241 (contrary view in *L.P. Jain* v *Nand Kumar* AIR 1961 Bom 254 being held to be no longer a good law); *Andhra Rice Mills* v *B. Chanchiah* (1968)2 Andh LT 115; *Periaswami Asari* v *President, Illupur Panchayat* AIR 1973 Mad 250; (1973)1 Mad LJ 244; *Yashola* v *Narayanan* (1996)11 SCC 228; (1996)7 Supreme 378.

11 *Budhulal* v *Chhotelal* AIR 1977 MP 1 (FB).

12 *Gobardhan Singh* v *Barsati* AIR 1972 All 246; 1972 All LJ 169.

13 *S.M. Bhatta* v *A. Beary* AIR 1973 Ker 185; ILR (1972)2 Ker 642.

14 *Janaki Amma* v *Krishnan* 1978 Ker LT 463.

15 *Debi Prosad* v *Deb Kumar* AIR 1981 Cal 254; 85 CWN 911.

16 *Surai Singh* v *Rajnarain Lal* AIR 1984 Pat 155.

17 *Mangala Ghosh* v *Rabindra Nath* AIR 1987 Cal 307.

would not be extended ordinarily, nor for the mere asking. It would be granted in rare cases to prevent manifest injustice.[18]

As to extension of time fixed by consent, Punjab High Court has added a new dimension. Consent decree being essentially a contract with the seal of the court superimposed thereon, the court is entitled to relieve a party from a penal clause, if there be any, under s. 74, Contract Act. So if the consent decree stipulates that on non-payment of instalment the plaintiff-decree holder would be entitled to oust the defendant-tenant and get possession, such a clause is in the nature of a penalty and court can relieve a party from such a clause. The ratio of the decision cannot be accepted without a criticism. A consent decree is not merely a contract between the parties but is one with *court's command superadded to it*. Having once solemnised the contract by its seal, can the court hold a term as penal? Can the court both approbate and reprobate? The said Punjab decision does not answer these questions.[19] The Supreme Court in a case of *Sova Ray* v *Gostha Behari Dey*,[20] settled two questions. First, the true import of the words "penal clause", secondly, whether time in a consent decree can be extended by mere asking. In a partition decree on compromise plaintiff's 1/3rd share was declared. It was however further agreed that half of the plaintiffs, i.e. 1/6th share, would go to the defendant No. 9 provided he paid a sum of ₹40,000 to the plaintiffs by a particular date, failing payment within time, the decree passed by the trial court would stand confirmed as per terms of the compromise. According to the agreement the sum of ₹40,000 was to be paid in two instalments; the first instalment of ₹10,000 by 31st July 1979 and the remaining amount of ₹30,000 by 28th February 1980. The first instalment was paid within time but the remaining amount was not paid. The defendant No. 9 made a grossly belated prayer for extending the time for deposit the second instalment. The Supreme Court held the clause is not penal in nature. The expression 'penalty' is an elastic term with different shades of meaning but it always involves an idea of punishment. The impugned clause in that case did not involve infliction of any punishment: it merely deprived the defendant No. 9 of a special advantage in case of default. The Supreme Court further held that assuming the High Court had power to extend the time, was not justified in allowing the prayer of the defendant No. 9 permitting him to make a grossly belated payment. Even where such a power exists it is not to be exercised liberally. The Supreme Court followed the following observation of an earlier Supreme Court case: "Of course, time would not be extended ordinarily, nor for the mere asking. It would be granted in rare cases to prevent manifest injustice.

18 *Pariyakkal* v *Dakshyani* AIR 1983 SC 428; (1983)2 SCR 467; (1983)2 SCC 127.
19 *Mehru* v *Mohonlal* AIR 1985 Punj 143; 1985 Punj LJ 37; (1985)1 Cur Civ Cas 444; (1985)1 Cur LJ (Civ & Cr) 56; (1985)1 Land LR 327.
20 AIR 1988 SC 981; (1988)3 SCR 287; (1988)2 SCC 134.

True, the court would not rewrite a contract between the parties but the court would relieve against a forfeiture clause".[1]

Delay in deposit for no fault of party In law there is a maxim "*Actus Curiae Neminem Gravabit*" which means that act of court should do no harm to a litigant. The pre-emption money under Or. 20, r. 14, CPC is directed to be deposited within specified time. But when because of the transfer of presiding officer, no one having taken his charge when party deposits pre-emption money not on the specified dates but later, the party should not suffer. The title would pass to the pre-emptor the moment the deposit is made.[2]

This Supreme Court case indeed relates to a decree of pre-emption but the principles emanating from this decision can be applied in respect of a decree of specific performance of contract in view of the maxim *ubi eadem ratio ibi idem jus* (like reasons doth make like laws). As stated in Broom: The law consists, not in particular instances and precedents, but in the reason of law; for "reason is the life of law".[3]

To defendant Where in a suit for specific performance for the sale or lease of immovable property a decree has been made, but the purchaser or the lessee fails to make payment of the purchase money or other sum which the court has ordered him to pay within the period allowed by the decree, or such further period as the court may allow, the vendor or the lessor may apply to the court to have the contract rescinded, and on such application the court may rescind the contract either as regards the party in default, or altogether, as the justice of the case may require [s. 28(1)]. If the court rescinds the contract, it shall direct the purchaser or the lessee to restore the possession of the property to the vendor or the lessor, and where the possession has been taken by the vendee or the lessee, may, in addition, direct the payment of all rents and profits which have accrued in respect of that property from the date on which possession was so obtained by the purchaser or the lessee until restoration of the possession to the vendor or the lessor. But if the justice of the case so requires, the court may also direct the vendor or the lessor to refund any sums paid by the vendee or lessee as earnest money or deposit in connection with the contract [s. 28(2)].

But it has been held that the power under s. 28 is discretionary[4] and the court could not exercise its power on flimsy grounds and annul the decree passed by it. A clear case of default has to be found out in order to give relief of rescission of contract so as to nullify the decree of specific performance.[5]

1 *Periakkal* v *Sm. Dalbhyani* AIR 1983 SC 428; (1983)2 SCR 467.
2 *Bhoop* v *Matadin Bhardwaj* AIR 1991 SC 373; 1990 Supp (3) SCR 410; (1991)2 SCC 128.
3 Broom's *Legal Maxims*, 12th Ed., p. 106.
4 *Chanda* v *Rattni* AIR 2007 SC 1514.
5 *Bisun Prasad Mishra* v *Kamla Kant Jha* AIR 1972 Pat 322 at p. 325.

In a decree for specific performance, time given for depositing money is an incidental direction and can be extended by the trial court and not by the executing or the appellate court.[6] When the time for payment of money is extended, it does not mean a modification of the decree. The court has also power under s. 148 of the CPC to extend the time even after its expiry.[7]

In *Sarupi* v *Har Gian*,[8] the Punjab High Court held, when the court fixes the time for the deposit of the sale price, this is move for the purpose of convenience rather than in compliance with any provision of law. The decree for specific performance of the contract for sale is not a final decree of the character that completely debars the court from fixing or extending the time for deposit of the purchaser money ...... The matter as to grant of time to deposit the purchase-money is purely discretionary. Fixation of time for payment of purchase-money is not a part of the controversy between the parties in suit for specific performance and does not determine any rights of the parties. As such, it does not partake the nature of a decree. The time can be extended even at the back of the vendor. At best, the vendor has a right to move for the rescission of the contract. The decree as such does not lapse automatically.[9]

But where the decree provided that "Defendant shall execute a sale deed in respect of the suit land in favour of the plaintiff. The plaintiff shall deposit in court the costs for execution and registration of the sale deed within one month from this date. In case the plaintiff fails to deposit the costs as aforesaid, the suit shall stand dismissed", the decree was a self-operative final decree and it is impossible to apply the provisions of s. 28.[10] The same view was taken in *Sushila Devi* v *Mohd. Shafi*.[11]

Even so, where the vendee deposits the money in a wrong court owing to a *bona fide* mistake, he cannot be penalised.[12]

Section 29 of the Specific Relief Act provides for the grant of alternative relief to the plaintiff suing for specific performance if the contract cannot be specifically enforced. Hence, a party suit for specific performance may, in the alternative sue for rescission of the contract, but the converse is not

6 *M.V. Kshirsagar* v *B.K. Jadhav* AIR 1970 Bom 398.

7 *Mahanth Ram Das* v *Ganga Das* AIR 1961 SC 882; (1961)3 SCR 763; (1962)1 SCJ 427.

8 AIR 1975 P&H 231.

9 *Rajan Patro* v *Akur Sahu* AIR 1959 Ori 74.

10 *Bhujangrao Ganpati* v *Sheshrao Rajaram* AIR 1974 Bom 104 at p. 105 following unreported judgment of the Division Bench in C.A. No. 3964 of 1958 delivered on 19.8.1959 and dissenting from *Babulal* v *Jagannath* (1970)72 Bom LR 835. (See also *Mahanth Ram* v *Ganga Das* AIR 1961 SC 882 which while interpreting s. 148, CPC said that "conditional decrees" were excluded from the ambit of s. 148 and *Bhutanath Das* v *Sahadeb Chandra Panja* AIR 1962 Cal 485).

11 1982 All LJ 478.

12 *Sarupi* v *Har Gian* AIR 1975 P&H 231 following *Nazar Singh* v *Munshi Singh* AIR 1971 Punj 42.

true and a person suing for rescission cannot in the alternative sue for specific performance.[13] Thus where a party to the contract commits an anticipatory breach of the contract, the other party to the contract may treat the breach as putting end to the contract and sue for damages, but in that event he cannot ask for specific performance.[14]

Section 30 of the Specific Relief Act enables the court to do equity when a contract is rescinded. If rescission is to be granted, both parties must be restored to *status quo* ante. If a purchaser seeks rescission the court of equity can take account of any profit he has made and make an allowance for any deterioration in the property.[15] A party claiming restoration of benefit received must prove the value of that benefit. Where the court has ordered rescission of a decree of specific relief, it can order refund of advance of all purchase prices and such an order may be passed not only against the vendor but also against third parties who had purchased the property with the knowledge of the agreement and who had undertaken liability to repay the amount paid by the plaintiff to the vendor.[16] The section enables the court to pay compensation to the parties as justice may require.

Execution of decree Relevant provisions are contained in Rules 31 (decree for specific movable property), 32 (decree for specific performance), 34 (decree for execution of document or endorsement of negotiable instrument), 35 (decree for immovable property) and 36 (decree for delivery of immovable property when in occupancy of tenant), of Or. 21 of the Code of Civil Procedure.

In the matter of execution of a decree for specific performance when there is no dispute as to the identity of the property, technical plea of misdescription of boundaries does not stand in the execution.[17]

In a case the plaintiff sued for a declaration that he was the owner and not tenant of the defendant. It ended in a compromise decree whereby the defendant agreed to execute and register a deed of reconveyance. For default in so doing no separate suit is necessary, nor it lies. The matter pertains to execution. The decree may be put to execution.[18]

Service of draft deed of transfer on the judgment of suit for specific performance Judgment-debtor of a suit for specific performance when allows the decree to go by default, *i.e.* does not execute the transfer deed in favour of decree-holder Or. 21, r. 34, CPC provides the procedure to be adopted by the decree-holder.

13 *Premraj* v *DLF Housing & Construction P. Ltd.* AIR 1968 SC 1355; (1968)3 SCR 648; *Roop Chand Chaudhari* v *Ranjit Kumari* AIR 1991 P&H 212.

14 *Jawaharlal Wadha* v *Haripada Chakrobarty* AIR 1989 SC 606; 1988 Supp (3) SCR 513; (1989)1 SCC 76.

15 *Erlanger* v *New Sombrero Phosphate Co.* [1878]3 AC 1218.

16 *Vasudeo Harchand Kolhe* v *Bhaulal Nadaqrsingh Rajput* AIR 1994 Bom 127.

17 *Kassim Beevi* v *Meeranchi Mytheen Beevi* AIR 1987 Ker 226.

18 *Bishambhar Agarwal* v *Kishan Chand* AIR 1990 All 65; (1989)3 Cur Civ Cas 518.

Order 21, r. 34 reads as follows:

34. *Decree for execution of document, or endorsement of negotiable instrument.* (1) Where a decree is for the execution of a document or for the endorsement of a negotiable instrument and the judgment-debtor neglects or refuses to obey the decree, the decree-holder may prepare a draft of the document or endorsement in accordance with the terms of the decree and deliver the same to the Court.

(2) The Court shall thereupon cause the draft to be served on the judgment-debtor together with a notice requiring his objections (if any) to be made within such time as the Court fixes in this behalf.

(3) Where the judgment-debtor objects to the draft, his objections shall be stated in writing within such time, and the Court shall make such order approving or altering the draft, as it thinks fit.

(4) The decree-holder shall deliver to the Court a copy of the draft with such alterations (if any) as the Court may have directed upon the proper stamp-paper if a stamp is required by the law for the time being in force; and the Judge or such officer as may be appointed in this behalf shall execute the document so delivered.

(5) The execution of a document or the endorsement of a negotiable instrument under this rule may be in the following form, namely:

" C.D., Judge of the Court of

(*or as the case may be*), for *A.B.*, in a suit by *E.F.*, against *A.B.*", and shall have the same effect as the execution of the document or the endorsement of the negotiable instrument by the party ordered to execute or endorse the same.

(6) (*a*) Where the registration of the document is required under any law for the time being in force, the Court, or such officer of the Court as may be authorised in this behalf by the Court, shall cause the document to be registered in accordance with such law.

(*b*) Where the registration of the document is not so required, but the decree-holder desires it to be registered, the Court may make such order as it thinks fit.

(*c*) Where the Court makes any order for the registration of any document, it may make such order as it thinks fit as to the expenses of registration.

The most important part of the procedure is service of draft deed of transfer on the judgment-debtor or judgment-debtors, where the judgment-debtor does not appear despite notice under Or. 21, r. 34(2), CPC the provision as to transmission of draft deed to the judgment-debtor must be held to be directory and non-compliance therewith would not vitiate the sale deed executed under the order of the court unless the judgment-debtor is able to show that prejudice was caused to him by the draft deed not being served upon him and opportunity thereby being denied to him to file objection against it.[19]

19 *Darshan Kaur* v *Gurdial Singh* AIR 1990 Punj 231; 1990 Punj LJ 136 but see *P. Venkanna Chetty* v *B. Apparao Naidu* AIR 1959 AP 666.

Stamp duty on a deed of sale executed as per decree of specific performance
The question has come up for consideration as to the quantum of stamp duty payable on a deed of conveyance executed as per the decree for specific performance either by the defendant or by the court. This question has assumed some importance in Tamil Nadu as the stamp duty on conveyance is not only heavy but is based on not the price agreed upon between the parties but on the market value of the property and the market value is determined by the Registration authorities on the basis of the guideline value issued by the Government which very often has no relevance to the actual market price. In *A.V. Varadaraju* v *Selvaraju Muthayammal & Thulasimani*[20] there was a decree for specific performance to execute a deed of sale for ₹12,000. On the failure of the defendant to execute the deed of sale, the court executed the deed and sent it for registration on payment of stamp duty on the sum of ₹12,000. The Registering authority claimed that the market value was ₹50,000 and insisted on payment of stamp duty on that amount and for production of Income Tax certificate. The District Munsif accepted the contention of the Registering authority. But the High Court on revision, set aside the order of the District Munsif and held that the stamp duty is payable only on the sum of ₹12,000 for which the decree has been passed. In *Jayaraman* v *Revenue Divisional Officer, Salem,*[1] Venkataswamy, J, (then of the Madras High Court), held the same view and followed the decision rendered in *A.V. Varadaraju* v *Selvaraju Muthayammal & Thulasimani.*[2] The matter came up before Madras High Court in *S.P. Padmavathy* v *State of Tamil Nadu.*[3] The deed was executed for a sum of ₹2,79,000 as per the decree for specific performance, but the Registering authority demanded stamp duty on a sum of ₹7,06,312.50 as the market value and called for an additional stamp duty of ₹56,077. The Bench held that in the case of an instrument of conveyance executed pursuant to the decree of specific performance passed by the civil court in which there is no allegation of deliberate under-valuation or lack of *bona fides* in valuing the subject of transfer with a view to evade payment of appropriate stamp duty, the mere fact that there is a time gap between the agreement for sale and the execution of the deed is not sufficient for the registering officer to invoke s. 47A of the Stamp Act (Madras Amendment) and claim additional stamp duty and consequently the order of the registering officer was quashed. In *Narayanasamy Naicker* v *District Collector, Chengalpattu District,*[4] the same view has been taken by a learned single Judge of the Madras High Court.

20 (1996)2 LW 716.
1 (1996)2 LW 179.
2 (1996)2 LW 716.
3 (1997)2 LW 979.
4 (1998)3 LW 254.

Part Three

Specific Performance of Statutory Obligation

CHAPTER 1

Restitution

Restitution—concept of The concept of restitution is a common law principle and it is a remedy against unjust enrichment or unjust benefit. The core of the concept lies in the conscience of the court which prevents a party from retaining money of or some benefit derived from another which he has received by way of erroneous decree of court. Such remedy in English law is generally different from a remedy in contract or in tort and falls within a third category of common law remedy which is called *quasi*-contract or restitution.[1] From the concept of restitution one thing emerges that the obligation to restitute lies on the person or the authority that has received unjust enrichment or unjust benefit.[2] A person is enriched if he has received a benefit and similarly a person is unjustly enriched if the retention of the benefit would be unjust. The word "benefit" denotes any form of advantage.[3] The concept of restitution is basically founded on the idea that when a decree is reversed, law imposes an obligation on the party who received an unjust benefit of the erroneous decree to restitute the other party for what the other party has lost during the period the erroneous decree was in operation. Thus the court while granting restitution is required to restore

1 *State of Gujarat* v *Essar Oil Ltd.* AIR 2012 SC 1146; (2012)3 SCC 522.

2 *See* Halsbury's *Laws of England*, 4th Ed., vol. 9, p. 434; see also 5th Ed., vol. 88, para 1 (The path to recognise the law of restitution was recognised in 1991 by the House of Lords), see *Lipkin Gorman (a firm)* v *Karpnale Ltd.* [1992]4 All ER 512 (HL).

3 See *Restatement of the Law of Restitution* by American Law Institute, p. 12.

the parties as far as possible to their same position as they were in at the time when the court by its erroneous action displaced them.[4]

The juristic foundation of restitution can be traced to a third category of law, namely quasi-contractual relationships.[5] Section 144, CPC is founded on the equitable principle that one who has taken advantage of a decree of a court should not be permitted to retain it, if the decree is reversed or modified.[6] Section 144, CPC is not the fountain source of restitution; it is rather a statutory recognition of a pre-existing rule of justice, equity and fair play. That is why it is often held that even away from s. 144 the court has inherent jurisdiction to order restitution so as to do complete justice between the parties.[7] Thus, it is the duty of the court under s. 144, CPC to "place the parties in the position which they would have occupied but for such decree or order or such part thereof as has been varied, reversed, set aside or modified. ..." Nor indeed does this duty or jurisdiction arise merely under the said section. It is inherent in the general jurisdiction of the court to act rightly and fairly according to the circumstances towards all parties involved.[8] In *Alexander Rodger* v *Comptoir D'Escompte de Paris*,[9] Cairns LC, observed as under:

> One of the first and highest duties of all courts is to take care that the act of the court does no injury to any of the suitors and when the expression, "the act of the court" is used, it does not mean merely the act of the primary court, or of any intermediate court of appeal, but the act of the court as a whole from the lowest court which entertains jurisdiction over the matter up to the highest court which finally disposes of the case.

Section 65 of the Contract Act which is based on equitable doctrine, provides for the restitution of any benefit received under a void agreement or contract and, therefore, mandates that any "person" which obviously would include a party to the agreement, who has received any advantage under an agreement which is discovered to be void or under a contract which becomes void, has to restore such advantage or to pay compensation for it, to the person from whom he received that advantage or benefit.[10]

Restitution—meaning The word 'restitution' is not defined in the Code of Civil Procedure 1908, though s.144 of the Code embodies the doctrine of

4 *State of Gujarat* v *Essar Oil Limited* (2012)3 SCC 522; AIR 2012 SC 1146; see *Lal Bhagwant Singh* v *Sri Kishen Das* AIR 1953 SC 136; *Binayak Swain* v *Ramesh Chandra Panigrahi* AIR 1966 SC 948.

5 Sections 69 and 70 of the Indian Contract Act 1872 recognize the principle of restitution.

6 *Zafar Khan* v *Board of Revenue* 1984 Supp SCC 505.

7 *Indore Development Authority* v *Shailendra* (2018)3 SCC 412.

8 *Jai Berham* v *Kedar Nath Marwari* (1921-22)49 IA 351; AIR 1922 PC 269.

9 (1871) LR 3 PC 465; 17 ER 120.

10 *Tarsem Singh* v *Sukhminder Singh* (1998)3 SCC 471; AIR 1998 SC 1400.

restitution. In its etymological sense, it means restoring to a party on the modification, variation or reversal of a decree or order, what has been lost to him in execution of decree or order of the court or in direct consequence of a decree or order.[11] In law, the term 'restitution' means:

> "A body of substantive law in which liability is based not on tort or contract but on the dependent's unjust enrichment."[12]

The word 'restitution' was used in the earlier common law to denote the return or restoration of a specific thing or condition. In modern legal usage, its meaning has frequently been extended to include not only the restoration or giving back of something to its rightful owner, but also compensation, reimbursement, indemnification, or reparation for benefits derived from, or for loss or injury caused to another. As a general principle, the obligation to do justice rests upon all persons, natural and artificial; if one obtains the money or property of others without authority, the law, independently of express contract, will compel restitution or compensation.[13] Thus, any civilized system of law is bound to provide remedies for cases of what has been called unjust enrichment or unjust benefit, that is, to prevent a man from retaining the money of, or some benefit derived from, another which it is against conscience that he should keep.[14] The principle of restitution has been statutorily recognized in s. 144, CPC. Section 144, CPC speaks not only of a decree being varied, reversed, set aside or modified but also includes an order on a par with a decree. The scope of the provision is wide enough so as to include therein almost all the kinds of variation, reversal, setting aside or modification of a decree or order. The interim order passed by the court merges into a final decision.[15] Section 70 of the Contract Act also embodies the principle of restitution. What s. 70 prevents is unjust enrichment and it applies as much to individuals as to corporations and Government.[16]

Restitution vis-a-vis disgorgement Like restitution, disgorgement is also an equitable remedy. It aims at preventing unjust enrichment. It is a gain-based remedy. In the realm of securities law, disgorgement plays the same role as the principle of restitution plays in civil law. Among the equitable power of a court is the power to grant restitution and disgorgement.[17] Thus, being an equitable remedy, it may be tailored in each individual case, to reach the ends of justice and equity.[18] Disgorgement is an equitable monetary

11 *Zafar Khan v Board of Revenue, U.P.* 1984 Supp SCC 505; AIR 1985 SC 39.
12 Black's *Law Dictionary*, 10th Ed.
13 *American Jurisprudence* 2d, vol. 66, Am Jur 2d.
14 *Fibrosa v Fairbairn* [1942]2 All ER 122; [1943] AC 32.
15 *South Eastern Coalfields Ltd. v State of M.P.* (2003)8 SCC 648.
16 *State of W.B. v B.K. Mondal and Sons* 1962 Supp (1) SCR 876; AIR 1962 SC 779.
17 *Curtis Mfg. Co. v Plasti-Clip Corp.* 888 F Supp 1212; 104 (DNH 1994).
18 George E. Palmer, *The Law of Restitution* § 2.12, at 158 (1978).

remedy "designed to deprive a wrongdoer of his unjust enrichment and to deter others" from future violations.[19]

Both disgorgement and restitution are look-alike and are equitable in nature. However, restitution is the giving back of wealth received by a defendant from a claimant, which must be given back or restored because it amounts to an unjust enrichment at the claimant's expense. Disgorgement is the giving up to a claimant of a gain made by a defendant, as a consequence of a wrongdoing committed against the claimant, but received from a third party.[20]

Restitution and unjust enrichment Unjust enrichment is basic to the subject of restitution, and is indeed approached as a fundamental principle thereof. They are usually linked together, and restitution is frequently based upon the theory of unjust enrichment. However, although unjust enrichment is often referred to or regarded as a ground for restitution, it is perhaps more accurate to regard it as a prerequisite, for usually there can be no restitution without unjust enrichment. It is defined as the unjust retention of a benefit to the loss of another or the retention of money or property of another against the fundamental principles of justice or equity and good conscience. A person is enriched if he has received a benefit, and he is unjustly enriched if retention of the benefit would be unjust. Unjust enrichment of a person occurs when he has and retains money or benefits which in justice and equity belong to another.[1]

Meaning of 'benefit' A person confers benefit upon another if he gives to the other possession of or some other interest in money, land, chattels, or performs services beneficial to or at the request of the other, satisfies a debt or a duty of the other or in a way adds to the other's security or advantage. He confers a benefit not only where he adds to the property of another but also where he saves the other from expense or loss. Thus the word "benefit" therefore denotes any form of advantage.[2]

Restitution provision Statutory provision relating to restitution is contained in s. 144, CPC which compels the party to restore the advantage he gained over his adversary on the strength of a judicial verdict later found wrong.

19 Federal Trade Commission, *Policy Statement on Monetary Equitable Remedies in Competition Cases 2003*, Federal Register, vol. 68, No. 149, 4th August 2003.

20 R.B. Grantham and C.E.F. Rickett, *Disgorgement for unjust enrichment?* Cambridge Law Journal, 62(I), March 2003, pp. 159-180.

1 *Rameshwar* v *State of Haryana* (2018)6 SCC 215 referred to *Indian Council For Enviro-Legal* v *Union of India* AIR 1996 SC 1446; see also *Nelson* v *Larholt* [1948]1 KB 339.

2 *State of Gujarat* v *Essar Oil Ltd.* (2012)3 SCC 522; *Restatement of the Law of Restitution* by American Law Institute, 1937, St. Paul, p. 12.

Section 144, CPC is not exhaustive of the principle of restitution and where a case does not fall within the strict terms of this section, the court in exercise of its discretion may grant or refuse the relief under its inherent power.[3] It incorporates only a part of the general law of restitution.[4] The power of court to grant restitution is not confined to the cases covered by the provisions of s. 144, CPC, it extends also to cases which do not come strictly within this section. The reason is that a court has an inherent power under s. 151 of the Code irrespective of this section to order restitution.[5] On account of the discharge and satisfaction of the decree under appeal, the appellate court does not become *functus officio* and the benefits, if any, which can flow to the applicants from the appellate order must be given to him by applying the principles of restitution under s. 144, CPC.[6] If a person purchases property in court auction with the knowledge of pending appeal against the decree cannot resist restitution.[7]

A peep into history The law of restitution had its origin in the old forms of action, particularly the action of *Indebitatus Assumpsit*[8] which was developed in the seventeenth century. The function of this action was to enable the claimant to recover a sum of money from the defendant after the claimant had established that the defendant owed a debt to the claimant which the defendant had promised to repay. Although the essential feature of the action was that a debt was owed by the defendant, the promise of repayment was required to enable the action to be accommodated within the system of formal pleading which existed at the time. Although initially the defendant's promise to repay the claimant had to be proved expressly, increasingly it was implied from the circumstances of the case, so that the promise became a fiction.[9] In India, the Code of Civil Procedure 1882, for the first time introduced in s. 583 a provision for restitution, by declaring that when a party entitled to any benefit, by way of restitution or otherwise, under a decree passed in an appeal desires to obtain execution of the same, he shall apply to the court which passed the decree against which the appeal was preferred and such court shall proceed to execute the decree passed in

3 *Gangadhar* v *Raghubar Dayal* AIR 1975 All 102 (FB).
4 *Kavita Trehan* v *Balsara Hygiene Products Ltd.* (1994)5 SCC 380.
5 *Kannappa Mudaliar* v *Ayyaswami Gounder* (1998)1 CTC 33.
6 *Sagarmal Panch* v *Chief Judicial Magistrate, Puri* AIR 1989 Ori 158 (FB).
7 *Chinnamal* v *P. Arumugham* AIR 1990 SC 1828.
8 The Latin phrase means 'being indebted' or 'to have undertaken a debt', (https://definitions uslegal.com).
9 Graham Virgo, *The Principles of Law of Restitution*, 2nd Ed., 2006, p. 19 (Oxford); For detailed analysis of the history of restitution, see Jackson's *The History of Quasi-Contract in English Law*, (Cambridge: Cambridge University Press), 1936. See also Baker, *The History of Quasi-Contract in English Law' in Restitution: Past, Present and Future*, Eds. Cornish, Nolan, O'Sullivan and Virgo, Ch. 3 and Ibbetson, *A Historical Introduction to the Law of Obligations*, (Oxford: Clarendon Press), 1999, Part IV.

appeal, according to the rules stipulated for execution of decrees in suits. It also indicated in sufficiently clear terms that an application for restitution therein was in substance an application for execution of an appellate decree. At one stage, it was thought that no suit could be brought for the relief and restitution proceedings had to be commenced by an application for execution of the decree and that such proceedings had to be regulated by the rules providing for the execution of the decrees in suit.[10] However, the Code of Civil Procedure 1908 replaced s. 583 of the previous Code by s. 144. It is more comprehensive than s. 583 of the Code of 1882. The Privy Council while explaining the scope and ambit of s. 144, CPC observed in *Jai Berham* v *Kedar Nath Marwari*,[11]

> "It is the duty of the Court under s. 144 of the Civil Procedure Code to place the parties in the position which they would have occupied but for such decree or such part thereof as has been varied or reversed. Nor indeed does this duty or jurisdiction arise merely under the said section. It is inherent to the general jurisdiction of the Court to act rightly and fairly according to the circumstances towards all parties involved."

Scope of restitution A party who has wholly or in part performed his part of the contract and has not received the agreed counter-performance in full may be entitled to restitution in respect of his own performance. Where it consists of a payment of money, the payer will seek to get it back, where it consists of some other benefit, he will claim recompense or *quantum meruit* in respect of it. An action will lie to recover back money paid under a contract or a purported contract. The ground for restitution is unjust impoverishment of a party or unjust enrichment of the other party, and the relief or measure of restitution is restoring what is lost to the impoverished party, or, correspondingly, returning of the advantage by the unjustly enriched party. If either of these is caused by an order of the court, which is varied, modified or reversed in appeal, revision or any other proceeding, such restitution takes the statutory shape of s. 144 of the Code. In either case, the principle commands that the party successful in getting the original decree or order varied, modified or reversed, ought to be placed in the same situation in which it would have been, had the original decree or order not been passed against it. Correspondingly, the unsuccessful party will have to return the advantage gained by it as a result of the original order. There is, however, no particular way of achieving this. The actual order that may have to be passed towards such restitution depends on a host of factors, such as (*i*) what the excluded party (or the successful party) would have made and (*ii*) what the party under obligation (or the unsuccessful party) might reasonably have made, had the original decree or order not been

10 *Prog Narain* v *Kamakhia Singh* 19 MLJ 599 (PC).
11 AIR 1922 PC 269.

there or would have been there in the same form as the varied or modified decree or order. In any event, the endeavour, it is important to remember, is to do real justice as between the parties.[12]

In order to be entitled to restitution, the order or the decree need not be varied or reversed in an appeal or revision by a superior court. Such restitution would be available even where the order of the decree is valid in any other proceedings like review or under Or. 9, r. 13, CPC. The words "varied or reversed" in s. 144, CPC have been used having regard to the effect or result of the proceedings set out.[13] It is submitted that the word 'reversal' is not defined in the Code and no special meaning for the purpose of s. 144 has been given. Therefore, the ordinary meaning of the word has to be taken into consideration while understanding the meaning of the word 'reverse' under s.144 of the CPC. Ordinarily, the word 'reverse' means "to undo or make void". The word 'reverse' should be given wider meaning so far as s.144 of the CPC is concerned. It is further submitted that from the scheme of the provision in s.144 of the CPC, restricted meaning of the term should not be resorted to. Similar view has been expressed by the Calcutta High Court also.[14] Likewise, the term 'party' as used in s. 144 should be given wider meaning. Because, it is clear that it is not confined only to the original parties to the suit but applies also to persons who would become subsequently concerned.[15]

The object of s. 144 is to provide a speedy and simple remedy for any party who has suffered by reason of an erroneous decree made by a court of first instance and it does not apply to a case where the court has to decide questions of conflicting rights under different decrees which may be very complicated.[16]

However, mere allegation that plaintiff got in to possession unlawfully is not sufficient and, therefore, cannot be the basis for restitution.[17]

Recovery of money paid

(1) *Total failure of consideration* A contracting party can recover back money paid under a contract if there is total failure of consideration. It means that no part of the performance for which he bargained was done.[18] In *Fibresa Spolka Akeyina* v *Fairbairn Lawson Combe Barbour Ltd.*[19] a buyer of goods

12 *Bhikchand* v *Shamabai Dhanraj Gugale* (2018)181 AIC 402.
13 *Forgetech Pvt. Ltd* v *Sayee Industries* (1993)2 LW 342 (Mad).
14 *Jagat Bandhu Shaw* v *Ram Nagina Pandey* 1978 CHN 214; AIR 1977 Cal 281.
15 *Kadirvelu Chettiar* v *Kempu Chettiar* ILR (1941) Mad 498; (1940)52 LW 816; AIR 1941 Mad 315.
16 *Ashutosh Nandi* v *Kundal Kamini Dasi* (1928-29)33 CWN 908; AIR 1929 Cal 814.
17 *Begum Janammal* v *Selva Arasu* AIR 1988 Mad 174.
18 *Stoczina Glanska SA* v *Latvian Shipping Co.* [1998]1 WLR 574 (the test is whether performance has been rendered, not whether performance has been received).
19 [1943] AC 32; [1942]2 All ER 122 (HL).

recovered back an advance payment when frustration had prevented the delivery of any part of goods. Lord Simon in that context defined the meaning of "consideration" which is as follows: "In the law relating to the formation of contract, the promise to do a thing may often be the consideration, but when one is considering the law of failure of consideration and of the *quasi*-contractual right to recover money on that ground it is, generally speaking, not the promise which is referred to but the performance of the promise."[20]

(2) ***Partial failure*** When there is a partial failure of consideration, the general rule is that there is no right to recover back a proportionate part of money paid. For example, if *A* employed *B* for a lump sum paid in advance to paint *A*'s house, and *B* abandoned the job before it was finished, *A* could not recover back any part of the payment. The right to recover back money paid on account of failure of consideration is said to be restricted to cases in which the failure is "total". One reason for this requirement is that *A* has already his remedy in damages. It is because *A* had made a bad bargain by paying *B* more than *B*'s performance was worth. If *B* had done nothing after receiving the advance payment, *A*'s right to recover the payment could be justified on the ground that *B* would be unjustly enriched if he were allowed to keep money paid to him for nothing but a broken promise.[1]

(3) ***Money paid under a void contract*** The general rule is that when money paid under a void contract, money can be recovered back;[2] but there are differences of opinion as to the legal basis of the rule.[3] Where money was paid under a void contract, the payment will often be made in the mistaken belief that the contract was valid. Such a mistake was not formerly a ground on which the payer was entitled to the return of his money since the mistake was one of law and it had been held that there was no right to recover back money paid under the mistake of law as opposed to mistake of fact. But this view has been overruled by the House of Lords in *Kleinwort Benson Ltd.* v *Lincoln CC.*[4]

Restitution—genesis of principle The basic principle underlying the restitution is "*actus curaie neminem gravabit*" which means that the act of the court should not result in harm to a litigant.It enables the party to relegate to the original position, blotting out the changed situation pursuant to the wrong order. The party wronged is retrieved and restored to the position prevailing at the earlier stage prior to the passing of the initial order.[5] It is the first

20 *Fibresa Spolka Akeyina* v *Fairbairn Lawson Combe Barbour Ltd.* [1943] AC 32; [1942]2 All ER 122 (HL) at p. 48.

1 Treitel, *The Law of Contract,* 14th Ed., para 22-004.

2 See s. 65 of the Indian Contract Act 1872.

3 Treitel, *The Law of Contract,* 11th Ed., p. 1058.

4 [1999]2 AC 349. See *Nurdin & Peacock Plc.* v *DB Ramsden & Co. Ltd.* [1999]1 All ER 941.

5 *Syed M.M. Rizvi* v *Subhash Singh* (2014)105 ALR 405.

and highest duty of all courts to take care that the act of the court does no injury to a suitor.[6] In *Lal Bhagwant Singh*[6] a compromise decree on an application by the judgment debtor under the United Provinces Agriculturist Relief Act 1934 was modified and an instalment decree for a reduced amount was passed with a condition, that in case of default of three instalments the amended decree for the whole amount would be executable. On appeal by the decree holder the original compromise decree was restored. During the pendency of judgment debtor's further appeal which was eventually allowed and by which the amended instalment decree was restored, judgment debtor's property was purchased by the decree holder and taken possession of in execution of the original compromise decree. It was held that judgment debtor is entitled to restitution.[7] In almost an identical situation purchase money was allowed to be recovered in a restitution proceeding.[8] The real basis for the power of court to order restitution is that a person who has obtained benefit under an order of court which is subsequently found to be wrong should not be allowed to retain the benefit which he had obtained under the wrong order. In a Kerala case the plaintiff filed a suit for redemption of a mortgage; defendant however had made some improvement on the mortgaged property. The suit was decreed but the plaintiff appealed contending that he is not liable to pay the value of improvement. Second appeal ended in a remand order directing the trial court to ascertain the value of improvement. Defendant filed an application for restitution alleging that plaintiff had no right to get possession without paying the value of the improvement. The trial court ordered that the plaintiff is to deposit certain sum being cost of improvement. It was held that this order being passed on an application for restitution is appealable, revision is not tenable.[9] Interest can also be allowed by way of restitution.[10] So far as the case where s. 144, CPC can be brought to operation court is under an obligation to grant restitution.[11] The court cannot order conditional restitution.[12]

6 *Lal Bhagwant Singh* v *Sri Kishan Das* AIR 1953 SC 136; 1953 SCR 559; 1953 SCJ 188; 1953 SCC 539; 1953 All LJ 249; *Binayak Swain* v *Ramesh Chandra Panigrahi* AIR 1966 SC 948; (1966)3 SCR 24 followed in *Shatrugna Badri Singh* v *Mange Mir Singh* AIR 1972 Del 212; *Ganesh Pershad* v *Adi Hindu Social Service League* AIR 1975 AP 310; *S.M. Deshmukh* v *Ganesh Krishnaji Khare* AIR 1975 Bom 82; ILR (1975) Bom 533; *Pappu Reddiar* v *P.S.V.R. Ramanatha Iyer* AIR 1963 Mad 45 (FB).

7 *Lal Bhagwant Singh* v *Sri Kishan Das* AIR 1953 SC 136; 1953 SCR 559; 1953 SCJ 188; 1953 SCA 722; 1953 All LJ 249; *Binayak Swain* v *Ramesh Chandra Panigrahi* AIR 1966 SC 948; (1966)3 SCR 24.

8 *Ramlakhan* v *Biharilal* 1970 MPLJ (Notes) 48.

9 *Govinda Pillai* v *Padmanabha Pillai* AIR 1987 Ker 32.

10 *Lucy Kochuvareed* v *P. Mariappa Goundar* AIR 1979 SC 1214; (1979)3 SCR 58.

11 *Devi Ram Chand* v *S.V. Bastikar* AIR 1968 Bom 57; ILR (1967) Bom 945 relying on *Binayak Swain* v *Ramesh Chandra Panigrahi* AIR 1966 SC 948; (1966)3 SCR 24; *State of A.P.* v *Manick Chand* AIR 1973 AP 27; (1972)2 Andh LT 23.

12 *Khemchand Sharma* v *Padmolochan Panda* AIR 1974 Ori 29; (1973)1 Cut WR 530; 39 Cut LT 435.

Restitution under s. 151 of CPC Restitutionary claims are to be found in equity as well as at law. Restitutionary law has many branches.[13] In India, apart from the statutory provisions for restitution, the Civil Court has inherent power to order restitution. The jurisdiction to make restitution is inherent in every court and will be exercised whenever the justice of the case demands. It will be exercised under inherent powers where the case did not strictly fall within the ambit of s. 144.[14] However, the power vested under s. 151 being discretionary and to be used to do real and substantial justice to the parties, must be exercised fairly, reasonably and objectively but not arbitrarily.

Restitution by executing court The court which passes the decree may order for restitution. But, the question is whether an executing court can order restitution, if situation so arises. The Supreme Court in *Mohijibhai* v *Manibhai*[15] observed that the application for restitution under s. 144, CPC is an application for the execution of a decree. The Andhra Pradesh High Court relying on *Mohijibhai* (supra) held that it that being so, obviously the execution court has jurisdiction to order for the restitution.[16] However, it is submitted that the view taken by the Andhra Pradesh High Court in *Nallapati* (supra) is contrary to the law laid down by the Supreme Court. The Supreme Court held that restitution could be ordered by the court, which passed the decree or order and that the court to which the decree has been transferred for execution could not order the restitution.[17]

Appeal against the order of restitution The court is empowered to order restitution under s. 144 of the CPC. However, the case which is not covered under s. 144 restitution may be ordered under s. 151 of the CPC. Courts have armed themselves under s. 151 with powers of restitution in the interests of justice which do not fall within the four corners of s. 144. Order 43 of the Code provides for appeals from orders. Appeals would seem to lie from orders made under s. 144 of the Code on the footing that the determination of a question under this section amounts to a decree and is appealable as such.[18] But, situation would be different when the order for restitution is passed under s. 151 of the CPC. There is a cleavage of opinions amongst different High Courts. The views of Nagpur High Court[19]

13 Goff & Jones, *The Law of Restitution*, 4th Ed., p. 3.
14 *Nallapati Pandu Ranga Rao* v *Vempati Venkateshwar Rao* (2015)2 ALT 177; 2015(4) Andh LD 54.
15 AIR 1965 SC 1477.
16 *Mohammed Abdul Sattar* v *Mrs. Shahzad Tahera* 2012 AIR CC 1270; (2012)2 ALT 230.
17 *Neelathupara Kummi Seethi Koya Phangal* v *Montharapalla Padippua Attakoya* AIR 1994 SC 1591.
18 *Gulam Mohamed Allarakha* v *Akbarbhai Sheikh Abdeallibhai* 1982 Mah LJ 757.
19 *Sheonandanlal* v *Gopal Babaji* 1943 NLJ 172; AIR 1943 Nag 172.

and Calcutta High Court[20] are that the order of restitution passed under s. 151 is appealable. However, the views of High Courts of Madras,[1] Punjab,[2] Patna[3] and Bombay[4] are that no appeal will be maintainable against the order of restitution passed under s. 151 of the CPC. It is submitted that the views of High Courts of Madras, Patna, Punjab and Bombay are correct as the right to appeal is not an inherent right. It is the creature of the Statute. It has to be specifically provided for by the Statute itself. If the Statute does not provide for any right to appeal, no appeal can be entertained. Since the CPC does not provide for appeal from the order of restitution passed under s. 151 of the CPC or under Or. 43 thereof, no appeal is maintainable against the order of restitution passed under s. 151 of the CPC.

Person entitled to apply There was dispute amongst legal heirs of a deceased applicant and deponent who claimed to be the legatee under the Will executed by the deceased. Question as to the entitlement to restoration of possession of suit property has to be resolved between the petitioners and the respondent who is already impleaded as a party to the proceedings and who claims to be the sole legatee under the Will of the deceased and entitled to the possession under s. 144, CPC. The Supreme Court held that there would be no interference with the judgment passed on the application for restitution in a review petition under Art. 137 of the Constitution of India.[5] A party entitled to restitution can pursue his application for restitution even though he sold away his interest in the meantime.[6]

Subsequent purchasers and doctrine of restitution Purchasers may include the decree-holder, *bona fide* stranger purchaser, or innocent purchaser. In *Binayak Swain* v *Ramesh Chandra Panigrahi*[7] where in execution of an *ex parte* decree the property of the judgment-debtor was purchased by the decree-holder. The decree was set aside in appeal and the case remanded for fresh disposal. The Supreme Court held that the judgment-debtor was entitled to restitution even though ultimately after fresh disposal a decree was passed in favour of the decree-holder. The court observed that the principle of the doctrine of restitution is that on the reversal of a decree the law imposes an obligation on the party to the suit who received the benefit of the erroneous decree to make restitution to the other party for what he has lost. This obligation arises automatically on the reversal or modification

20 *Gopal Laskar* v *Harihar Mukherjee* AIR 1948 Cal 37; *Sasikanta Acharjee* v *Jalil Baksh* AIR 1931 Cal 779.
1 *Sayyed Usman Saheb* v *Vegisena Sivaramaraju* AIR 1950 Mad 463.
2 *Kaku Singh* v *Gobind Singh* AIR 1959 Punj 468.
3 *Ramanandan* v *Jagannath* AIR 1958 Pat 547.
4 *Mangilal Kajodimal* v *Shankar Shravan Nikam* (1956)58 Bom LR 107.
5 *Dev Dutta* v *Sohan Lal* (2000)9 SCC 200.
6 *Smt. Dayawati* v *Champa Ram* 1976 All LJ 694.
7 AIR 1966 SC 948.

of the decree and necessarily carries with it the right to restitution of all that has been done under the erroneous decree; and the court in making restitution is bound to restore the parties so far as they can be restored to the same position they were in at the time when the court by its erroneous action had displaced them.

But, in *Zain-Ul-Abdin Khan* v *Mohd. Asghar Ali Khan,*[8] the distinction was made between the the decree-holders who come in and purchase under their own decree which is afterwards reversed on appeal and the *bona fide* purchasers who come in and buy at the sale in execution of a decree to which they are not parties and at a time when the decree is a valid decree and when this order for sale is a valid order. It was held that the sales in favour of *bona fide* purchasers who were not parties to the decree at a time when the decree was valid would be protected. The dictum of Privy Council was followed by Calcutta High Court.[9] The High Court observed:

> "The Court as a matter of policy has a tender regard for honest purchasers at sales held in execution of its decrees though the sales may be subsequently set aside, where those purchasers are not parties to the suit and the decree has not been passed without jurisdiction. But the same measure of protection is not extended to purchasers who are themselves the decree-holders; nor can the purchasers from such decree-holders claim that the Court owes them any duty...."

However, the distinction between a stranger who purchases at an auction sale and an assignee from a decree-holder purchaser at an auction sale is quite clear. But, the High Courts of Patna[10], Madras[11] and Kerala[12], however, appear to have equated an assignee from a decree-holder auction-purchaser with a stranger auction-purchaser on the basis that an assignee from a decree-holder auction-purchaser has to be considered as a *bona fide* purchaser for value who should not be allowed to suffer on account of the mistakes or irregularities committed in a court of law. It is, however, humbly submitted that the views of the aforesaid High Courts do not appear to be correct in as much as an assignee of a decree-holder auction-purchaser stands in no better position than his assignor.[13] This view was upheld by the Supreme Court also.[14]

It was held by the Supreme Court that persons who purchase at a court auction who are strangers to the decree are afforded protection by the court

8 *Zain-Ul-Abdin Khan* v *Mohd. Asghar Ali Khan* ILR (1888)10 All 166; (1887)15 IA 12.
9 *Satis Chandra Ghose* v *Rameswari Dasi* AIR 1915 Cal 363; 20 CWN 665.
10 *Gopi Lal* v *Jamuna Prasad* AIR 1954 Pat 36.
11 *S. Chokalingam Asari* v *N.S. Krishna Iyer* AIR 1964 Mad 404.
12 *Parameswaran Pillai Kumara Pillai* v *Chinna Lakshmi* 1970 Ker LJ 450.
13 *Abdul Rahman* v *Sarat Ali* AIR 1916 Cal 710; 20 CWN 667.
14 *Padanathil Ruqmini Amma* v *P.K. Abdulla* (1996)7 SCC 668.

because they are not in any way connected with the decree. Unless they are assured of title; the court auction would not fetch a good price and would be detrimental to the decree-holder. The policy, therefore, is to protect such purchasers. This policy cannot extend to those outsiders who do not purchase at a court auction. When outsiders purchase from a decree-holder who is an auction-purchaser clearly their title is dependent upon the title of decree-holder auction-purchaser. It is a defeasible title liable to be defeated if the decree is set aside. A person who takes an assignment of the property from such a purchaser is expected to be aware of the defeasibility of the title of his assignor. He has not purchased the property through the court at all. There is, therefore, no question of the court extending any protection to him. The doctrine of a *bona fide* purchaser for value also cannot extend to such an outsider who derives his title through a decree-holder auction-purchaser. He is aware or is expected to be aware of the nature of the title derived by his seller who is a decree-holder auction-purchaser.[15]

Judgment per incuriam and doctrine of restitution A per *incuriam* judgment is a judgment which has been rendered without taking into account the statutory provision and the same cannot be considered to be a binding precedent.[16] Thus, the question is where the decision is rendered per *incuriam*, can the doctrine of restitution be made applicable?[17] In the case of a mere erroneous judgment of a court the principle of *"actus curiae"* cannot be invoked. However, in *South Eastern Coalfields Ltd.* v *State of M.P.*,[18] it was held that the doctrine of *actus curiae neminem gravabit* is not confined in its application only to such acts of the court which were erroneous; the doctrine is applicable to all such acts as to which it can be held that the court would not have so acted had it been correctly apprised of the facts and the law. It is the principle of restitution which is attracted.

Restitution—conditions For application of restitution three conditions are to be satisfied; (1) the restitution sought must be in respect of a decree or order which had been varied or reversed; (2) the party applying for restitution must be entitled to benefit under a revising decree or order; and (3) the relief claimed must be properly consequential on the reversal or variation of decree or order.[19] Or in other words: (1) there must be an erroneous judgment; (2) the benefit of this erroneous judgment has been received by one party; and (3) the erroneous judgment has been reserved. When *X* files a suit for a declaration only, fails in trial court but succeeds in appeal, but meanwhile

15 *Padanathil Ruqmini Amma* v *P.K. Abdulla* (1996)7 SCC 668.
16 *Union of India* v *Manik Lal Banerjee* (2006)9 SCC 643.
17 *State of Gujarat* v *Essar Oil Ltd* (2012)3 SCC 522.
18 (2003)8 SCC 648.
19 *Ganesh Pershad* v *Adi Hindu Social Service League* AIR 1975 AP 310; (1974)1 Andh LT 405; (1975)1 Andh WR 203.

he is dispossessed, after the success of appeal he cannot pray for restitution, for the other side did not derive any benefit from the erroneous judgment.[20]

In *Banchhanidhi's* case,[1] the Orissa High Court held that following conditions must be fulfilled for application of the principles of restitution:

(*i*) There must be an erroneous judgment;

(*ii*) Benefit of that erroneous judgment must have been received by a party to the record;

(*iii*) The party claiming restitution must show that as a consequence of the error in the judgment or decree; a party received the benefit; and

(*iv*) The erroneous judgment was reversed in appeal.

Relying on the principles laid down in *Banchhanidhi* (supra), the Orissa High Court refused restitution in *Md. Jakir* v *Murarilal Agarwalla*.[2] In *Md. Jakir* (supra), the suit was filed for specific performance of contract by the plaintiff against defendant No. 1 and for a declaration that the alleged sale deed in favour of defendant No. 2 by defendant No. 1 was illegal and inoperative. Plaintiff obtained *ex parte* decree but could not obtain the benefit of being in possession of the suit premises. In the meantime, the said *ex parte* judgment was reversed. Defendant No. 2 did not lose possession of the premises because of the said erroneous judgment and in addition to all this even the judgment by which the earlier judgment has been reversed has declared that the sale in favour of defendant No. 2 by defendant No. 1 is invalid. In this view of this, it was held that the provisions of s. 144 of the CPC have no application.

When a decree is appealed against and the suit eventually abates, the decree is set at naught and the parties may be restituted to the same position as they occupied before the suit being filed.[3] Although restitution is mandatory on existence of the conditions for the applicability of the section,[4] and court cannot order conditional restitution,[5] yet the court acting under s. 144, CPC retains jurisdiction to refuse to direct restitution and pass some other order which appears to him equitable and just.[6] In a

20 *Banchhanidhi Das* v *Bhanu Sahuani* AIR 1974 Ori 148; ILR (1973) Cut 498; 39 Cut LT 731.

1 *Banchhanidhi Das* v *Bhanu Sahuani* AIR 1974 Ori 148.

2 *Md. Jakir* v *Murarilal Agarwalla* AIR 1988 Ori 178.

3 *Lakhpati Singh* v *Raghunath Singh* AIR 1974 All 479; 1974 All LJ 430.

4 *Binayak Swain* v *Ramesh Chandra Panigrahi* AIR 1966 SC 948; (1966)3 SCR 24; *State of A.P.* v *Manik Chand* AIR 1973 AP 27; (1972)2 Andh LT 23; *Jadh Singh* v *Joginder* 1978 Rev LR 440.

5 *Khem Chand* v *Padmalochan* AIR 1974 Ori 29; (1973)1 Cut WR 530; 39 Cut LT 435.

6 *Lal Bhagwant Singh* v *Sri Kishan Das* AIR 1953 SC 136; 1953 SCR 559; 1953 SCJ 188; 1953 SCA 722; 1953 All LJ 249; *Pappu Reddiar* v *P.S.V. RamnathIyer* AIR 1963 Mad 45.

case as a result of fraud played the House Rent Controller ordered eviction, it was held the House Rent Controller can set aside the order and restore possession to the heirs of the tenant ordered to be evicted. Even the new tenant inducted by the landlord within four days from the eviction to overreach the order of the court was also evicted.[7]

A party who is not directly a party in the proceeding reversing or setting aside the earlier decree can also pray for restitution.[8] A party who has not appealed may have restitution on the decree being reversed in appeal.[9] A stranger however is not entitled to restitution.[10] Thus when an owner dispossessed sues for recovery of possession and if his appeal is allowed but meanwhile the land stands vested, the owner cannot get restitution against State.[11]

Thus if in a suit for declaration or injunction the trial court by an *ad interim* order directs the defendant to deposit in court certain sums for payment to plaintiff till the disposal of the suit and on appeal the amount is ordered to be refunded, the defendant can under s. 144, CPC get the amount.[12]

Application for restitution is not confined to reversal of decree by appellate or revisional court but also includes reversal in writ proceedings.[13]

When there is no decree or order to be reversed s. 144, CPC goes out of the way. In a case a money decree provided that in case the amount could not be recovered from *A*, it could be recovered from *B*. Sale of *A's* property in execution was set aside. But decree-holder already had withdrawn money. It was held remedy of auction purchaser lay in Or. 21, r. 93, CPC and not in a proceeding for restitution as there was no decree to be reversed.[14]

Provisions of restitution apply only where the decree is varied or reversed and not where the decree has merely become inexecutable due to intervening circumstances such as enforcement of law. Thus when certain villagers in a suit filed in representative capacity have obtained possession in execution

7 *B. Lilavati* v *Dandubala* AIR 1979 NOC 63 (AP).
8 *Gangadhar* v *Raghubar Dayal* AIR 1975 All 102; 1974 All LJ 151.
9 *B. Yamuna Bai* v *Lade Venkoba Rao* AIR 1976 AP 46.
10 *Laxmi Chand* v *Sundrabai* AIR 1952 Nag 275.
11 *Mathura Prosad Missir* v *Fulmati* AIR 1977 NOC 173 (Pat).
12 *Martand Ramchandra Potdar* v *Dattatraya Ramchandra Potdar* AIR 1975 Bom 237; 77 Bom LR 239.
13 *Dangalia* v *Deshraj* AIR 1974 MP 49; 1973 Jab LJ 768; 1973 MPLJ 796; 1973 MPWR 505. This decision may require reconsideration in view of the *Explanation* added to s. 141 by the CPC (Am.) Act 1976, whereby the procedures prescribed by the Code do not apply to writ proceedings. But the ratio of the decision may be supported on the ground that restitution may also be granted *ex debito justitiae* apart from the provisions contained in s. 144 of the Code. For a contrary view in respect of the scope of restitution see *Syed Ajaz Ali* v *Md. Rafiq* AIR 1974 All 178 (*ibid*).
14 *Vijaya Devi* v *Ram Swarup* AIR 1975 All 229.

of the decree passed in the suit, but later an enactment is passed rendering such decree inexecutable keeping the validity of the decrees intact, no restitution can be ordered.[15] The provision of restitution does not apply independently of the consequence of decree reversed. Thus if a judgment debtor voluntarily sells an immovable property to decree-holder to meet the decretal dues in a money decree where the immovable property was not the subject matter of the decree, on reversal of the decree he is not entitled to restitution.[16] Section 144, CPC does not apply when no benefit has accrued to the opposite party on the strength of subsequently reversed or varied decree or order. When a party has got a benefit but not on the strength of such a decree or order, s. 144 does not apply. Thus when plaintiff's suit for declaration of title and permanent injunction against the defendant has failed up to highest court, the defendant cannot invoke s. 144, CPC to compel the unsuccessful plaintiff to demolish the structure he raised.[17]

When in execution of *ex parte* decree a tenant is evicted and landlord inducts a new tenant who takes the premises *bona fide,* he cannot be ejected on reversal of earlier decree, for, being a tenant, the second tenant can protect his possession under usual Rent Control Protection clause.[18] Section 144, CPC would not be attracted.[19]

Section 144, CPC applies only when any benefit has accrued to the adversary on the strength of a decree or order subsequently varied or reversed or set aside or modified. Where there is no allegation that plaintiff got possession through a decree or order, the provision of restitution cannot be invoked.[20] Possession when is lost by physical force of opposite party, remedy does not lie in proceeding for restitution.[1]

Restitution, however, can be granted against a *bona fide* purchaser in execution sale when the decree on the basis of which sale was held, is reversed.[2]

Decree-holder when after obtaining possession sells the suit property to third party, even then on reversal of decree the third party purchaser is bound to restitute the possession to the successful party.[3] Where an outsider

15 *Khyali Ram* v *Mast Ram* AIR 1977 HP 41.
16 *Purshottam Bhagwant Sulakhe* v *Suryakant Gopal Sulakhe* AIR 1978 Bom 303.
17 *Begam Janammal* v *Selva Arasu* AIR 1988 Mad 174.
18 *Sham Lal Dhingra* v *Jaswant Kaur* AIR 1980 Del 171.
19 See also *Binayak Swain* v *Ramesh Chandra* AIR 1966 SC 948.
20 *Begum Janammal* v *Selva Arasu* AIR 1988 Mad 174.
1 *Sunampudu K. Reddy* v *Pallam Reddy* AIR 1980 NOC 99 (AP).
2 *Abdul Ghani* v *Mahendra* AIR 1979 All 106; *Chinnammal* v *Arumugham* AIR 1990 SC 1828; (1990)1 SCR 78; (1990)1 SCC 513.
3 *Kamal Ch. Dutta* v *Ram Chandra Goala* AIR 1980 Gau 19.

purchases a property from a decree-holder auction-purchaser, it is a defeasible title liable to be defeated if the decree is set aside. A person who takes an assignment of the property from such a purchaser, is expected to be aware of the defeasibility of the title of his assignor. If such a person lost his possession as a result of an order being passed in restitution, he cannot maintain a suit based on his title since he had no title to the property.[4] An application for restitution is the only remedy for refund of purchase money paid by auction-purchaser on the order of sale being set aside at the objection of judgment-debtor.[5] In *Upendra* v *Jayanti*,[6] the applicant for restitution did not press his petition on the clear understanding that the original suit would be taken up for hearing on setting aside the *ex parte* decree in pursuance of which possession was delivered but the opposite party adopted dilatory tactics delaying the disposal of suit, it was held he can renew his prayer for restitution. When a tenant who gets into possession of premises on the basis of an order for temporary injunction withdraws the suit, he is bound to restore possession of the premises to the landlord.[7] Confirming the decision of the High Court of Delhi, the Supreme Court observed that after getting the order of injunction the plaintiff disturbed the *status quo* as on the date of the suit and sold away the defendant's goods and converted them into money and that upon dismissal of the suit, the interlocutary order stood set aside and whatever was done to upset the *status quo* was required to be undone to the extent possible.[8] When an appeal was dismissed for default the interim order of stay was also vacated. The plaintiff executed the decree for eviction and got possession. When the order of dismissal was set aside, the defendant is entitled to order for restoration of the appeal. The interim order of stay also got restored.[9]

Right of auction-purchaser to apply for restitution An assignee from a decree-holder auction-purchaser cannot be equated with a *bona fide* purchaser for value without notice. The distinction between a stranger who purchases at auction and assignee from a decree-holder purchaser at an auction sale is quite clear. Persons who purchase at a court auction who are strangers to the decree are afforded protection by the court. When an outsider purchases from a decree-holder who is an auction-purchaser, his title is dependent upon the title of the decree-holder auction-purchaser. Thus, an assignee from a decree-holder auction-purchaser is liable to restitute on reversal of the decree.[10]

4 *Padanathil Rukmini Amma* v *P.K. Abdullah* AIR 1996 SC 1204; (1996)7 SCC 668; JT 1996(1) SC 381.
5 *Ram Chandra* v *Munir* (1978)4 All LR 285; 1978 All LJ 171.
6 (1980)2 Cal LJ 484.
7 *Bhaurao* v *Sanitribai* AIR 1991 Bom 55.
8 *Kavitha Trahan* v *Balsara Hygiene Products Ltd.* AIR 1995 SC 441; (1994)5 SCC 380.
9 *K.N. Krishnappa* v *T.R. Gopalakrishan Setty* AIR 1997 Kant 152.
10 *Padanathil Rugmini Amma* v *P.K. Abdulla* AIR 1996 SC 1204.

Bona fide purchaser's right is not to be affected by restitution proceedings but it is distinguished in situations, when (1) the court is considering an interim order of stay on such sale during the pendency of the main issues, and (2) sale consideration has been partly paid and delivery has not been taken by the third party purchaser.[11]

Restitution to trespasser Section 144 of the CPC does not say that a person would be entitled to restitution simply because the decree is set aside or varied or reversed. The condition under which the person would be entitled to restitution is that he must be on the date of application a person "entitled to benefit by way of restitution or otherwise". The section clearly says that restitution would not come as a matter of course either on variation or on reversal of the decree; but the person must also be entitled to any benefit by way of restitution. Thus, for example, if a suit is instituted against a trespasser and the plaintiff gets a decree against the trespasser and finally that decree is reversed will the trespasser be entitled to restitution? He will not be entitled to restitution for the simple reason that he is not entitled to benefit by way of restitution. He has no right to be restituted to the property. If he has none, he cannot be said to be entitled to the benefit of restitution.[12] In this connection, the observation of Lord Atkin in *S.N. Banerji's* case is worth noting;

> "that justice does not require such a preposterous conclusion as they (trespassers), should be put back in a position which they have no right to occupy..."[13]

But, where there is a competition between two trespassers, possession plays an important role. Thus, if the plaintiff and defendant are both trespassers then, the defendant who is in possession can, ordinarily, maintain an application for restitution on the basis of his prior possession in respect of the disputed property.[14]

The party applying for restitution must be entitled to benefit. It cannot be granted to a trespasser.[15]

Restitution—competent court to make The court which passed the decree is entitled to order restitution. The meaning of the term "court which passed the decree or order" has been explained in the *Explanation* to s. 144(2). In view of cl. (*a*) of the *Explanation* to s. 144, when decree of lower court is

11 *Woods Beach Hotels Ltd.* v *Mabusa Urban Co-operated Bank of Goa Ltd.* (2009)13 SCC 748.
12 *Mahadeo Prosad Shaw* v *Calcutta Dyeing and Cleaning Co.* AIR 1961 Cal 70.
13 *S.N. Banerji* v *Kuchwar Lime and Stone Co. Ltd.* AIR 1941 PC 128.
14 *Mathura Prasad Missir* v *Most. Fulmati Kuer* 1976 PLJR 416.
15 *Ramji Seth* v *Zohra* AIR 1983 NOC 154 (All); 1983 All CJ 322.

reversed by High Court and reversal affirmed by Supreme Court, not Supreme Court but the trial court is entitled to order restitution.[16]

Provisions of restitution under s. 144 apply to courts only and not to authorities or tribunals. In the absence of an express provision an authority or tribunal cannot order restitution *ex debito justitiae.*[17] For the purpose of restitution, however it is immaterial that the court passing the initial order had no jurisdiction to entertain the litigation initially.[18] Rent Controller having all the powers of civil court may order restitution if not under s. 144 but under inherent power.[19]

In a subsequent decision in *T. Sivasankaran* v *H.K.N. Kacharlal Sowcar,*[20] a Division Bench of the High Court of Madras analysed the law *in extenso* with reference to the power of the Rent Controller under the Tamil Nadu Buildings (Lease and Rent Control) Act 1960 [hereinafter referred to as the "Tamil Nadu Act"], in the matter of execution and pointed out that it was a cardinal principle of law that the acts of court should not be allowed to work injury on the suitor—*actus curiae neminem gravabit*—an act of court shall prejudice no man. Their Lordships held that s. 18 of the Tamil Nadu Act 1960 created a fiction that every order passed by the Rent Controller shall be executed as if such an order was an order of a civil court, and for that purpose the Controller was given all the powers of a civil court, the application for restitution was only an application in execution and consequently, the Rent Controller, in terms of s. 18, has got the power to entertain the execution petition at the instance of the landlord who obtains an order of eviction and he will have equally the power to entertain a petition for restitution, when the order of eviction passed against the tenant is reversed. Their Lordships further held that s. 144, CPC is not exhaustive and the power to direct restitution is inherent in the court itself and rests on the principle that a court of justice is under a duty to repair the injury done to a party by its act and that the right of a party to have restitution and the duty of the court to give him the restitution do not rest on the provisions of s. 144, CPC which defines the procedure only by enacting that an application for restitution is to be made in the court of first instance. It is therefore obvious that the power of a court to order restitution is not confined to s. 144 of the CPC but also extends to the exercise of inherent power under s. 151 of the CPC.

16 *State Bank of Sourashtra* v *Chittaranjan* AIR 1980 SC 1528; 1980 All LJ 654; (1980)1 SCC 516; *Neelathupara Kummi Seethi Koya Phangal* v *Montharapalla Padippua Attakoya* AIR 1994 SC 1591; 1994 Supp (3) SCC 760.
17 *Syed Ajaz Ali* v *Md Rafiq* AIR 1974 All 178; 1974 All 1 (HC); 1974 All LJ 165.
18 *Deepchand* v *Jhando* AIR 1982 Del 24; (1981)20 Del LT 149; (1981)2 Ren CJ 673.
19 *T.K. Sundaram* v *Balraj* AIR 1983 Mad 225; 96 Mad LW 235; (1983)1 Mad LJ 220; 1982 TNLJ 297.
20 AIR 1984 Mad 37; (1984)1 MLJ 155 (DB).

In *Mahaveer Electric Corporation* v *B. Ashok Kumar*[1] the High Court of Madras dealt with the power of the Rent Controller with regard to restitution vis-a-vis the provisions of the Tamil Nadu Buildings (Lease and Rent Control) Act 1960. The question was whether the Rent Controller was competent to pass order of redelivery of the tenanted premises after demolition of the old structure and reconstruction of new building. The High Court observed that the right granted under the Tamil Nadu Buildings (Lease and Rent Control) Act 1960 is not a common law right as enunciated by the Transfer of Property Act. But it is only a statutory right created under the said enactment. The purpose of the said Act is only to give protection from eviction. The rights conferred under the statute cannot be extended to a person from whom the building has been recovered. It is also very difficult to extend the benefit of the Act to a new building, which was not at all let out to any tenant. When the Act itself is not applicable to the building in question, it will not be possible for this court to make this Act applicable and grant redelivery to the petitioner. The redelivery by itself implies that what is to be redelivered is something which was delivered, when what was delivered is not there, the redelivery is impossible. Thus, redelivery was not allowed by the High Court, though the Rent Controller was found competent to pass such order of redelivery.

The point is covered by a direct decision of the Supreme Court in *Bholanath Varshney (dead) through LRs* v *Mulk Raj Madhan*.[2] In that case, the landlord instituted the suit for eviction against the tenant under the Transfer of Property Act after giving due notice under s. 106 of the said Act. He contended that the building was constructed in 1974 and as 10 years had not elapsed since then, the Uttar Pradesh Urban Buildings (Regulation of Letting, Rent and Eviction) Act 1972 did not apply to it. The trial court dismissed the suit holding that the above Act applied. On appeal, learned District Judge held that on the date of the institution of the suit the building was less than 10 years old and hence the Act was inapplicable. The High Court held that as the suit building completed 10 years of its existence during the pendency of the suit, the Act would apply and therefore the tenant could be evicted only on one or more grounds mentioned in the Uttar Pradesh Urban Buildings (Regulation of Letting, Rent and Eviction) Act 1972. Reversing the above said judgment of the Allahabad High Court, the Supreme Court held that the law applicable on the date of the institution of the suit alone governs the suit and the mere fact that the statutory period of 10 years expires during the pendency of the suit/appeal/revision, and accordingly the Act does not become applicable.

Following the aforesaid decision, it has been held by the High Court of Madras in *G. Srinivasan* v *K. Kanchana*,[3] that the right of the parties has

1 (1997)2 CTC 107; 1997 AIHC 1301.
2 AIR 1994 SC 1664; (1994)2 SCC 127; JT 1994(1) SC 181.
3 1996 TNLJ 488.

to be decided as on the date of suit and any change of circumstances thereafter will not affect the right of the parties to get possession and even if the exemption period is over during the pendency of the litigation, the plaintiff is entitled to get possession pursuant to a decree in a civil suit and need not move the Rent Controller under the Rent Control Act. If the reasoning of the learned single Judge that as a new building has come into existence after the presentation of the application for eviction under the Tamil Nadu Act of 1960 and restitution cannot be granted, is accepted, it would open the flood gates of fraud and the landlords who take delivery of possession under an *ex parte* order, can demolish the building, put up a new one and face the court with a *fait accompli* and resist successfully the application for restitution.

The second reasoning of the learned single Judge is that the old demised premises is no longer in existence, that a new building has come into existence, new tenants have been inducted and two shops had been sold to the respondents and hence it is not possible to order restitution and re-delivery. The same view has been taken by the same learned single Judge in *Anjuman-E-Palah-Millan Dharul Hifaz by its Trustees* v *Mohammed Obaidullah*,[4] where the landlord took possession of the premises under an order under s. 11(4) of the Tamil Nadu Buildings (Lease and Rent Control) Act 1960 and inducted a new tenant before the order for eviction was finally reversed. The learned single Judge held that as the new tenant has been in possession for three years, he cannot be dispossessed and re-delivery could not be ordered. It is submitted with due deference to the learned Judge, that the induction of new tenants into a building or the sale of the building or portion thereof to others cannot be a bar to order restitution and re-delivery since such transfers are affected by the doctrine of *lis pendens*.

In *Gurjoginder Singh* v *Jaswant Kaur*,[5] the premises was occupied by another tenant. The Supreme Court held that the new tenant was liable to be evicted and possession restored to the original tenant. Even the construction of a new building has been held to come under the provisions of s. 52 of the Transfer of Property Act. In *Mohammed Ismail* v *Ashiq Hussain*,[6] the High Court of Allahabad has held that the words "otherwise dealt with" in s. 52 of the Transfer of Property Act are general and can include the raising of construction wrongfully and on the application of the rule of equity, no party can be permitted to take advantage of such an act committed during the pendency of the suit. To hold otherwise, would be to put a premium on fraud and it would be possible for a landlord to get *ex parte* orders of eviction behind the tenant, obtain possession, induct new tenants, put up a new construction and drive the original tenant into a helpless situation.

4 (1997)1 MLJ 378.
5 1994 All CJ 688 (SC).
6 AIR 1970 All 648.

No doubt, in *Mahavir Electric Corporation* v *B. Ashok Kumar*[7] the old demised premises is no longer in existence and the question of re-delivery presents some difficulty, but this circumstance cannot render the original tenant helpless and the court powerless. It is the duty of the court to ensure that no litigant goes back with the feeling that he was prejudiced by an act of the court. In *B. Gangadhar* v *B.G. Rajalingam,*[8] which was a suit for declaration and recovery of possession, the defendant constructed shops and inducted tenants into possession during the pendency of the suit. The Supreme Court held that the executing court would be justified to order removal of construction made *pendente lite* so that the decree for possession or eviction, as the case may be, is effectively and completely executed and delivery of possession given to the decree-holder expeditiously. In any event, the original tenant is entitled to adequate compensation and the executing court which has the power to mould the relief according to the circumstances of the case, is competent to award adequate compensation. In both the above cases, the original tenant had been left in the lurch.

Court to grant restitution It was held that restitution cannot be granted by the Supreme Court in an appeal filed against reversal of decree by High Court.[9] The court of first instance mentioned in the section really means the court which is competent to set matters right by granting restitution in the manner and to the extent that is proper under the circumstances of the case.[10] Reiterating the position of law, the Supreme Court observed that the limitation for restitution under the Limitation Act is 12 years. It is for the executing court to decide whether the restitution petition, if any filed, is within the limitation or not. It is only the court which passed the original decree, which can order restitution. Restitution cannot be granted by the Supreme Court.[11] The High Court hearing an appeal from a decree, by which the suit for cancellation of sale deed was dismissed, cannot be treated to be the court of first instance, to pass an order for restitution.[12]

When a decree has been reversed which attained finality restitution should not be refused.[13]

Restitution under inherent power The courts have power to order restitution under inherent power even in cases not covered by s. 144, CPC.[14] And

7 1997 AIHC 1301 (Mad).
8 (1996)1 LW 145 (SC).
9 *State Bank of Saurashtra* v *Chitranjan Rangnath* AIR 1980 SC 1528.
10 *C.S. Ratanchand* v *Multanmull* AIR 1964 Mys 117.
11 *Vijay Singh* v *Shanti Devi* (2017)8 SCC 837.
12 *LRs. of Tej Singh* v *Gomati Devi* (2015)3 RLW 1925.
13 *Rajendra Singh* v *Prem Mai* AIR 2007 SC 3057; (2007)11 SCC 37.
14 *Rasu Moopanar* v *T.K. Ram Murthy Iyer* (1967)1 Mad LJ 287; 80 Mad LW 42; *Martand Ramchandra Potdar* v *Dattatraya Ramchandra Potdar* AIR 1975 Bom 237; 77 Bom LR 239; *Gangabai* v *Raghuvir Dayal* AIR 1975 All 102.

such order is appealable.[15] This inherent power so far as that of High Court is concerned has been recognised.[16] Thus when a decree-holder on misrepresenting the court that *ex parte* decree authorises the court to put him to possession, gets possession, on setting aside the *ex parte* decree, the ejected defendant can get restitution under inherent power of court.[17]

If the partners of a firm were in possession of the property of the defendants as their clearing and forwarding agent, there cropped up a dispute about commission amount and a suit was filed and the goods were sold on the basis of an interim order of the court in the suit. Eventually the suit was found to be not maintainable as the firm was not registered. Through s. 144, CPC in terms did not apply, under inherent power the court directed restitution.[18]

A wrong order should not be perpetuated by keeping it alive and respecting it and that in exercise of inherent power, the courts have power to apply the principles of restitution to myriad situation not strictly falling within the terms of s. 144, CPC.[19] When interim orders passed have been reversed by the final adjudication of the case, the successful party can demand restitution of benefit earned by the party or for compensation of which he has lost.[20]

This inherent power cannot go to an inordinate length. So when the court grants restitution to a tenant evicted by execution of decree, merely because the tenant has appealed against the decree, it is not legal.[1]

The court has ample jurisdiction and is perfectly justified in passing an order of mandatory injunction under s. 151, CPC for the restoration of the possession to the aggrieved party, in case such a party had been dispossessed in disobedience of the order of injunction. The court can in the exercise of its inherent power pass such order for ends of justice as would undo the wrong done to the aggrieved party.[2] If the plaintiff had taken the law in his own hands and has sought to dispossess the defendant, the court may pass appropriate order for restoration. Such an order by the court may be an exercise of its inherent power under s. 151 or s. 94 and need not be covered under cls. (*b*) and (*c*) of r. 1, Or. 39.[3]

15 *Meheran Bibi* v *Sk. Razek* AIR 1978 Cal 365.

16 *Pandrangi Lingeswara Rao* v *Pukkipatli Venkata Subbarao* (1966)2 Andh WR 144; *Subhas Chandra* v *Bodhi Raj* AIR 1969 J&K 8; *Ramlakhan* v *Biharilal* 1970 MPLJ (Notes) 48.

17 *Babaji Charan* v *Laxmipriya* AIR 1982 NOC 117 (Ori); 51 Cut LT 137; ILR (1980)2 Cut 571.

18 *Jagdish Raj Kohli* v *Lekhraj Suri* AIR 1982 J&K 2.

19 *South Eastern Coalfields Ltd.* v *State of MP* (2003)8 SCC 648.

20 *Atma Ram Property (P) Ltd.* v *Federal Motors (P) Ltd.* (2005)1 SCC 705.

1 *Kavita Trehan* v *Balsara Hygiene Products* AIR 1992 Del 92.

2 *Kailash Chand Gupta* v *Rukam Singh Yadhav* AIR 1998 MP 310.

3 *Harish Chandra Narayan Mourya* v *Rajendra Prasad Darshai Varma* 1997 AIHC 2588 (Bom).

Where a suit challenging the defendant's title and praying for declaration of possession is decreed by the trial court but is dismissed by the Privy Council, the defendant will not be entitled to get possession by way of restitution under ss. 144 and 151, CPC if his title to the property has been extinguished by twelve years' adverse possession by the plaintiff.[4]

Restitution in L.A. Act proceeding When enhanced compensation in an appeal under the Land Acquisition Act is refused and the respondent claimant has already realised the enhanced compensation and interest thereon, then no matter whether or not appellate court has directed to refund, the State is entitled to refund the sum refused in appeal along with proportionate interest and solatium thereon.[5]

Restitution—a proceeding in execution A proceeding for restitution is a proceeding in execution.[6]

As such limitation for application for restoration of possession under s. 144, CPC is governed by Art. 136 and not by Art. 128, Limitation Act.[7]

It is not necessary for restitution that a succession certificate should be brought. The benefit lost is not a debt. So to have the benefit restored no succession certificate is necessary.[8] Application for restitution being an application for execution, when an amount is deposited by appellant as per stay order of appellate court, and the decree is reversed in appeal, application for restitution of the amount deposited should be filed in the trial court,[9] being an execution proceeding restitution can be obtained by an application, not by a separate suit.[10]

Abatement of restitution in miscellaneous case As restitution application is one for execution, Or. 22, r. 12, CPC applies and the application does not abate. But if during appeal from an order of restitution, the petitioner or O.P. dies, the appeal does abate just as it occurred in appeal against orders

4 *Narayan Patil* v *Puttabai* AIR 1945 PC 5.
5 *State of Punjab* v *Kartar Singh* AIR 1986 P&H 312; ILR (1986)1 P&H 328; 1985(2) 88 Punj LR 683; (1986)1 Land LR 562.
6 *Mahji Bhai Mohan Bhai Barot* v *Patel Manibhai Gokalbhai* AIR 1965 SC 1477; (1965)2 SCR 436; 1965 All LJ 525; *Macbool Alam Khan* v *Mst. Khodeja* AIR 1966 SC 1194; (1966)3 SCR 476; *Kusum Samal* v *Banamali Rout* AIR 1974 Ori 105; (1973)2 Cut WR 1139; 39 Cut LT 1031; *Martand Ramchandra Potdar* v *Dattatraya Ramchandra Potdar* AIR 1975 Bom 237; 77 Bom LR 239; *Gangadhar* v *Raghubar Dayal* AIR 1975 All 102; *Subhas Kumar* v *Sheobalak* AIR 1975 Pat 307; *Math Sauna* v *Kedarnath* AIR 1977 All 115; *Dharam Nath* v *Hari Dusadh* AIR 1977 Pat 204; *Purshottam* v *Suryakant* AIR 1978 Bom 303; *Nafis Ahmad* v *Abdul Rahim* AIR 1979 All 63; *Attra* v *Ram Singh* (1984)1 Ren CJ 494 (Punj).
7 *Nafis Ahmad* v *Abdul Rahim* AIR 1979 All 63; *Attra* v *Ram Singh* (ibid).
8 *Kashi Mahammad* v *Mukhu Sahib* 1971 Ker LJ 217.
9 *Math Sauna* v *Kedar Nath Chanbe* AIR 1977 All 115.
10 *Math Sauna* v *Kedar Nath Chanbe* (ibid).

in execution proceedings.[11] It is apposite to mention that although a proceeding for restitution is an execution proceeding, an adjudication under s. 144 is a decree [*vide* s. 2(2), CPC] and thus is appealable.

Reversal or variation of decree in revision The decisions are unanimous on the point that in view of the word "appeal" being deleted in present s. 144, which word occurred in s. 583 of (old) CPC 1882 restitution should be ordered on reversal of decree in revision by superior court. The position is now clear by s. 144(1) which has now substituted "varied or reversed" by the words "varied or reversed in any appeal, revision or other proceeding ....". The principle is that if a person is placed in possession of property by an order of court and that order is set aside such person is under an obligation to restore possession to aggrieved party. He cannot object to restitution on the ground that he had delivered possession to a third party in the meantime.[12] The words "varies or reversed" in s. 144, CPC have been used having regard to the effect or result of the proceedings set out. Therefore, the term 'reversal' cannot be interpreted to exclude setting aside of a decree or order in a proceeding like the present one under Or. 9, r. 13, CPC.[13]

On reversal of a decree of eviction a tenant dispossessed in execution of eviction-order may be restituted to possession.[14] When by a decree a decree-holder is entitled only to symbolical delivery of possession of a tenanted premises, but mistakenly he gets *khas* possession, the tenant can be restituted to possession if he attorns to the decree-holder.[15]

Restitution applies to 'order' Restitution applies to order also apart from cases of reversion or of variation of a decree.[16] Section 2(14) of the CPC defines 'order' to mean "the formal expression of any decision of a Civil Court which is not a decree".

No revision from order under s. 144, CPC No revision lies from an order on an application falling under s. 144, CPC, for such an order is appealable as a decree.[17]

Reversal in a proceeding under Or. 9, CPC Even when a decree is reversed or set aside in a proceeding under Or. 9, CPC restitution can be ordered.[18]

11 *Surendra Patnaik* v *Dasarath* AIR 1960 Ori 14; *Kusum Samal* v *Banamali Rout* AIR 1974 Ori 105; (1973)2 Cut WR 1139; 39 Cut LT 1031.

12 *Ramratan* v *Mathura Prasad* AIR 1971 MP 69; 1970 MPLJ 963; 1970 Jab LJ 907.

13 *Forgetech Pvt. Ltd.* v *Sayee Industries* (1993)2 LW 342; (1994)1 BC 662.

14 *T. Sivasankaran* v *H.K.N. Kacharlal* AIR 1984 Mad 37; 96 Mad LW 618; (1981)1 MLJ 155; *T.K. Sundaram* v *Balraj* AIR 1983 Mad 225; 1982 TNLJ 297.

15 *Panchayati A.B.U. Nirman* v *Rameswar Mandal* AIR 1984 Pat 95; 1984 Pat LJR 79.

16 *Ram Chandra* v *Munir Ahmed* (1978)4 ALR 285; 1978 All LJ 171.

17 *Maqbool Alam Khan* v *Mt. Khodaija Begum* AIR 1949 Pat 133.

18 *S.M. Deshmukh* v *Ganesh Khare* AIR 1975 Bom 82; 75 Bom LR 405; 1974 Mah LJ 628; *Allahabad Theatres* v *Pandit Ram Sajiwan Mishra* AIR 1949 All 730; ILR (1949) All 313; *Jagat Bandhu* v *Ram Nagina* AIR 1977 Cal 281; *Khusi Md.* v *Subhash*

The contrary view primarily proceeded on the view that when a decree is set aside in a proceeding under Or. 9, CPC the decree is not varied or reversed but only superseded. That was the view in *Gopal Paroi's* case.[19]

Section 144 has been so amended to bring within its fold cases even when the decree is varied, set aside or modified in any appeal, revision or other proceedings. The contrary view thus stands superseded.

No restitution of money or property—when A minor cannot recover the money paid under a voidable contract unless there is a total failure of consideration. In *Steinberg* v *Scala (Leeds) Ltd.*,[20] a minor applied for shares in a company but repudiated after allotment. She thus avoided liability for future calls, but her claim for the return of money already paid was rejected as there was no total failure of consideration; because she had got the very shares she bargained for. Property transferred under a marriage settlement would also be irrecoverable once the marriage had taken place. But where a minor had agreed to enter into a partnership and paid a deposit of £100, to be forfeited if he had failed to execute the partnership deed, and no partnership deed was executed, because the minor repudiated, it was held that he could get his deposit back as there was a total failure of consideration.[21] An adult can recover the money paid if there has been a total failure of consideration.[22]

Earnest money It means a deposit paid prospective buyer to show a good faith intention to complete the transaction and ordinarily forfeited if the buyer defaults.[1] Vendor have an imperfect title of land in question. Plea of vendor that the vendee could have filed suit for specific performance. Termination of that agreement by vendee on account of incapacity of vendor to execute the agreement of sale. Once no agreement survives, there is no requirement for plaintiff to file the suit for specific performance. Thus suit for recovery of earnest file the suit for specific performance. Thus suit for recovery of earnest money under s. 7 is maintainable.[2]

Liability for restitution Liquor licence-holders challenged the creation of the sole distributorship. Interim order was passed that in case licence-holders

---

70 CWN 1027; *Upendra* v *Jayanti* (1980)2 Cal LJ 484; *Fatima Khatoon* v *Swarup Singh* 88 CWN 773; AIR 1984 Cal 257; (1984)1 Cal LJ 517 contra *Gopal Paroi* v *Swarna Bewa* AIR 1931 Cal 14; 34 CWN 707; *Kundan Kishanlal* v *Board of Revenue* AIR 1972 All 184; 1971 All WR 632; *Tailor Sathar Khan* v *Sk. Ahammad Sahab* (1986)1 Andh LT 477; (1986)2 Cur Civ Cas 473 (the head note of CCC case is confusing).

19 *Gopal Paroi* v *Swarn Bewa* AIR 1931 Cal 14.

20 [1923]2 Ch 452.

21 *Corpe* v *Overton* [1833]10 Bing 252; see *Everett* v *Wilkins* [1874]29 LT 846.

22 Treitel, *The Law of Contract,* 11th Ed., p. 548.

1 Black's *Law Dictionary*, 9th Ed.

2 *Lokesh* v *Rameshwar Tyagi* AIR 2018 P&H 56.

lose, they shall compensate the sole distributor. One licence-holder withdrew the appeal and was doing business in contravention of monopoly created by taking advantage of unclear legal position. Licence-holder was directed to compensate sole distributor.[3] Restitution is an equitable principle. Court must see that litigant does not go back with the feeling that he was prejudiced by act done on the faith of the court's order. If settlement in Bhopal Gas Diaster case is set aside, Union Carbide Corporation will be entitled to restitution of the entire amount deposited with interest.[4]

Reversal of decree in separate proceeding Superseding a large number of decisions taking a contrary view the amended s. 144, CPC makes it clear that the section applies also to cases when decree is set aside or modified in any suit instituted for the purpose. The view stands in the line of *T. Subbarayadi* v *Shetti*.[5]

Possession through time barred execution case—restitution Restitution is permissible even when delivery of possession is found to be in pursuance of an execution proceeding time barred.[6]

It is apposite in this context to extract a few lines from a decision rendered by the Apex Court, namely, s. 3, Limitation Act only bars the remedy, but does not destroy the right which the remedy relates to. Only exception in which the right becomes barred by limitation is when the right is destroyed. For example under s. 27, Limitation Act a suit for possession of any property becomes barred by limitation when the right to property itself is destroyed. Except in such case the right subsists.[7]

Restitution against tenant inducted bona fide When on eviction of a tenant in execution of an *ex parte* decree for eviction, another tenant who was unware of the litigation was inducted and the earlier decree for eviction subsequently reversed, the evicted tenant cannot have the possession restored to him when the tenant subsequently inducted opposes as he will be entitled to protection under the relevant provision of the Rent Control Legislation interdicting eviction of tenant. To such a case s. 144, CPC would not apply.[8] But in *Mangilal* v *Kailash Chand*[9] the landlord evicted a tenant in execution of an eviction-decree despite stay of execution by the High Court. Thereafter the evicted tenant sought for being restituted to possession. Meanwhile the landlord let out the premises to another tenant who opposed

3 *K.T. Venkatagiri* v *State of Karnataka* AIR 2003 SC 1819.
4 *Union Carbide Corpn.* v *Union of India* AIR 1992 SC 248.
5 AIR 1917 Mad 239; *Sarnalata Dasi* v *Manmohan Modak* AIR 1973 Cal 140; 75 CWN 927.
6 *Vaidehi Kuar* v *Banshu* AIR 1979 All 413.
7 *Punjab National Bank* v *Surendra Prosad Sinha* AIR 1992 SC 1815; (1992)2 SCR 258.
8 *Shamlal Dhingra* v *Jaswant Kaur* AIR 1980 Del 171.
9 *Mangilal* v *Kailash Chand Sharma* AIR 1982 Raj 269.

his eviction on the ground of his being a *bona fide* transferee of interest, for value. But it was held the lower court allowed the landlord to evict erroneously despite the stay order and here restitution was ordered under the inherent power. Here the newly inducted tenant cannot oppose the eviction.

In *Gurjoginder Singh* v *Jaswant Kaur,*[10] the tenant was evicted under an *ex parte* order which was subsequently set aside and restoration of possession was directed. The premises in question was found occupied by another tenant in the meantime. It was held that the new tenant was liable to be evicted and possession to be restored to the original tenant.

When the proceedings for eviction against the tenant is without the jurisdiction, the tenant having been dispossessed by such eviction decree, is entitled to the restitution.[11]

Restitution for erroneous delivery of possession despite stay of execution in appeal When executing court delivers possession to decree-holder after execution being stayed by appellate court but before the stay order being communicated to the executing court, the possession to judgment-debtor may be restored.[12] When stay order is passed subsequently possession cannot be restored to judgment-debtor.[13] Proceeding in ignorance of stay order is not a nullity.[14] But it is not that the court must restore possession, for then *Explanation* to Or. 41, r. 5 laying down that stay order would be effective from the date of its communication would lose all its importance.[15]

Even if the appeal has been filed but no stay of execution is ordered, the execution court can execute the decree and grant possession to the decree holder.[16] However, the execution of the decree during pendency of the appeal would, thus, be subject to the restitution of the property in the event the appeal is allowed and the decree is set aside.[17]

Restitution of rent to tenant If a person on filing a suit against tenant withdraws rent deposited by him but subsequently it is found in appeal reversing the decree that he had no *locus standi* to sue, the tenant is entitled to get back the rent under s. 144, CPC.[18]

10 (1994)2 SCC 368; 1994 All CJ 688 (SC).
11 *Amrit Varsha Hindi Dainik* v *Bihar State Agri-Marketing Board* AIR 2000 Pat 192.
12 *Mulraj* v *Murti Raghu Nathji Maharaj* AIR 1967 SC 1386; (1967)3 SCR 84; *Mangilal* v *Kailash Chand Sharma* AIR 1982 Raj 269, but see *Paikamma* v *Maroti* AIR 1983 Bom 363; 1983 Mah LJ 589.
13 *Paikamma* v *Maroti* (ibid).
14 *Mulraj* v *Murti Raghu Nathji Maharaj* AIR 1967 SC 1386; (1967)3 SCR 84; *S. Sathiya Narayan* v *B.B. Kanyalal* AIR 1983 Mad 264; 1983 TNLJ 196.
15 *Deepchand* v *Krishan Datt* AIR 1980 Punj 150.
16 *Inder Chand Jain* v *Motilal* (2009)14 SCC 663.
17 *Ibid.*
18 *S. Algiriswami Naidu* v *C. Ammal* AIR 1982 Mad 384; (1982)2 Mad LJ 22.

Forceful dispossession and restitution A tenant may be evicted by the landlord but that must be done according to the due process of law and not by vandalism. If a tenant is, thus dispossessed, he has got remedy to be restored to his previous possession under the order of the court and such order, the court is competent to pass under s. 151, CPC. In such a case, recourse to s. 144 would not be proper. But, at the same time, the well-defined power of the Court under s. 151 may be taken recourse to.[19] Thus, where the question of restitution is involved and s. 144, CPC does not cover that case, there in the interest of justice, the court may exercise its inherent power under s. 151, CPC for restoration of possession of the petitioner as *ante*.[20]

Restitution against heir, transferee, tenant, etc. The word "parties" in s. 144 also includes representative of a party. So a judgment-debtor can proceed against original decree-holder as also his assignee. The fact that he has not chosen to proceed against original decree-holder would not take away his right.[1] It can also be claimed against *bona fide* stranger purchaser for value.[2] If some of the heirs of deceased O.P.—judgment-debtors are not brought on record or not served with notice under Or. 21, r. 22, CPC, even then restitution may be ordered.[3] Decree-holder when obtains possession under *ex parte* decree but that is reversed by appellate court, restitution is to be ordered even if the decree-holder sells it to any third person.[4]

Restitution may be ordered against a transferee or legal representatives no matter whether they have been joined in the suit or not.[5] Transferee of property during pendency of appeal is liable to restore possession, his transfer being hit by s. 52, T.P. Act.[6] Tenant inducted *pendente lite* is liable to be evicted in restitution proceeding.[7]

Transferee from decree-holder—restitution against—on decree being set aside A combined reading of ss. 47, 144, Or. 21, rr. 97 to 103, CPC and s. 52, T.P. Act shows that any transfer of possession of immovable property during the pendency of a suit which involves any right to such property, would be

19 *Kartick Chandra Boroye* v *Kashi Nath Mondal* (1997)1 CHN 360; Cal LT 1997(2) HC 126.

20 *Mrs. Kabita Tehran* v *Baldara Hygiene Product Ltd.* AIR 1995 SC 441.

1 *Payre Chand* v *Ashrafunnissa Begum* AIR 1975 AP 228; *Jagadish Lal Arora* v *M.E. Periera* AIR 1977 Del 12.

2 *Dayawati* v *Champa Ram* AIR 1977 NOC 117 (All); 1976 All WC 423.

3 *Kamala Dutta* v *Ballyganj Estates* AIR 1974 Cal 75; 77 CWN 839.

4 *Ganesh Pershad* v *Adi Hindu Society Service League* AIR 1975 AP 310; (1974)1 Andh LT 405; (1975)1 Andh WR 203.

5 *Sukhan Singh* v *Uma Shankar Misir* AIR 1935 All 65; *Samarji Singh* v *Director of Consolidation, U.P.* AIR 1975 All 82.

6 *Narayan Laxman* v *Vishnu Woman* AIR 1967 Bom 117; *Mohan Rice Mills* v *Hazarika* AIR 1957 Assam 111.

7 *Manik Chand S. Shah* v *Gangadhar Sankar Shete* AIR 1961 Bom 288; *Shankar Lal* v *Ramkrishna* AIR 1976 All 250; (1976)2 All LR 25.

incapable in law of affecting the rights that flow in relation to the property from a decree that may be passed in the suit. It is also evident that where a defendant has been deprived of the possession of the property in execution of a decree for such possession and the decree was eventually set aside, the party who is deprived of possession is entitled to the possession being restored to him unless the justice of the cause points to the contrary; and then the party that has taken the benefit is under an obligation to restore possession and the court is fully empowered, as indeed obliged, to order restitution by evicting not only the party which has taken the advantage but all those whose possession is relatable to such a party. In such cases the transferee from the party, who obtained the advantage, or a further transferee from such a transferee, would be within the reach of the court irrespective of whether such transferee or transferees were acting in good faith and without any knowledge of the earlier proceedings.[8] In an Allahabad case on an *ex parte* decree being passed, the decree-holder who obtained possession sold the same to respondent. Later the *ex parte* decree was set aside. It was found that respondent was not a *bona fide* purchaser. On the premises it was held that the judgment-debtor is entitled to restitution, the decree-holder should be directed to refund the consideration to the respondent.[9]

Restitution in respect of property demolished The doctrine of frustration embodied in s. 56, Contract Act which renders contract void by reason of the impossibility of performance of the act required on account of some event which the promisor could not prevent would not apply in case of a lease. The rights of parties after a lease is granted do not rest on contract.

In a case in execution of a decree of redemption of mortgage a tenant under the mortgagee was dispossessed. Through a proceeding under Or. 21, r. 100, CPC the possession of the tenant was ordered to be restored. But meanwhile the building in which tenant was in possession was demolished by Municipality. It was held that even if the building has been demolished, the tenant is entitled to restoration, not only of the vacant site but of the superstructure to be raised by the mortgagor on it.[10]

No restoration of suit under s. 144 Under ss. 144 and 151 of the CPC, the decree declared by Civil Court null and void cannot be restored. Section 144 of the CPC permits restitution of status and not restoration of suit.[11]

Person not party to appeal The suit was instituted by the sole legatee for possession of the suit house challenging the allegation made by his mother in favour of the 1st defendant who in the meantime mortgaged it to the 3rd defendant. The suit was decreed. The appeal was preferred by the 3rd

8 *Jagadish Lal Arora* v *M.E. Periera* AIR 1977 Del 12.
9 *Sheo Shampat* v *Keshonath* (1979)5 All LR 219 (HC).
10 *Amir Chand* v *Chunilal* AIR 1990 Punj 345; (1990)2 Ren LR 137.
11 *Neela Bai* v *Bhupendra Rajput* (2006)44 AIC 912.

defendant only against that decree and it was allowed holding that the suit house was not the self-acquired property of the plaintiff's father and that the alienation was voidable but not void. On the question whether the 1st defendant who did not carry the matter by way of an appeal was entitled to restitution, it was held that the 1st defendant was entitled to possession till such time the alienation in his favour was avoided.[12] A claimant whose claim to attached property is allowed can apply for restitution.[13]

Interest by way of restitution As far back as 1871 the Judicial Committee in *Rodger* v *Comptoir D'Escompte de Paris*,[14] made it clear that interest is a part of normal relief given in restitution. Lord Atkin in *L. Guran Ditta* v *T.R. Ditta* observed that the duty of the court when awarding restitution under s. 144 of the Code is imperative. It shall place the applicant in the position in which he would have been if the order had not been made: and for this purpose the court is armed with powers (the "may" is empowering, not discretionary) as to *mesne* profits, interest and so forth.[15]

In *ONGC* v *Assocn. of Natural Gas Consuming Inds.*,[16] agreements for supply of gas were entered into between the ONGC and different industries. The agreement stipulated the price, mode of payment and also the interest payable in case of delay in payment. After the expiry of the term of the agreement ONGC proposed that the contract should be renewed but at the enhanced price. The purchaser challenged the increase in the price of gas as fixed. By an interim order the court directed ONGC to supply gas at the old rate. The escalation in price made by ONGC was found to be valid by court. ONGC made claim for interest which was disputed by the purchasers. It was held that ONGC was entitled to claim interest from the purchasers for the delayed payment of the principal amount.

Writ proceedings and s. 144, CPC Writ proceedings under Art. 226 of the Constitution have been held to be proceedings before a Civil Court and that by virtue of s. 141, CPC the provisions of the Code can be applied to such proceedings. According to this view an application under s. 144, CPC will lie where an order under Art. 226 is reversed in appeal.[17] Where the relief sought for in the writ petition was rejected by the court in spite of the interim directions granted initially, the position as on the date of challenge of the impugned proceedings should be restored while restoring the same the disadvantages that are likely to be caused to the aggrieved person should not be ignored.[18]

12 *B. Yamuna Bai* v *L. Venkaba Rao* AIR 1976 AP 46.
13 *Krishna Gopal* v *Gokul Prasad* AIR 1970 All 261 (FB).
14 (1871) LR 3 PC 465.
15 (1935)37 Bom LR 162; AIR 1935 PC 12; (1935)68 Mad LJ 168.
16 AIR 2001 SC 2796.
17 *Regional Food Controller* v *Hazari Mal* AIR 1967 All 272.
18 *Kavali Roller Flour Mills Pvt. Ltd.* v *A.P. Electricity Board, Hyderabad* AIR 2004 NOC 247 (AP).

It needs mention that s. 144 of the Code falls under Part XI under the chapter captioned as 'Miscellaneous'. Section 141 of the Code defines 'miscellaneous proceeding'. It provides that the procedure provided in this Code in regard to suits shall be followed, as far as it can be made applicable, in all proceedings in any court of civil jurisdiction. It is submitted that after the amendment[19] in the Code in 1976, and with the insertion of *Explanation*[20] in s.141 of the CPC, the application of s. 144 is now barred to writ proceedings. But, judicial trends, after the amendment in 1976, seem to be that though s. 144 is not applicable directly to writ proceedings, yet the underlying principle of the doctrine of restitution will apply to such proceedings. The recent trends are, however, in favour of application of the principle of restitution to interim orders passed in writ proceedings. Thus, it is not permissible for a party to file a writ petition, obtaining certain orders during the pendency of the petition and withdraw the same without getting proper adjudication of the issue involved therein and insist that the benefits of the interim orders or consequential orders passed in pursuance of the interim order passed by the writ court would continue. The benefit of the interim relief automatically gets withdrawn/ neutralized on withdrawal of the said petition. In such a case concept of restitution becomes applicable otherwise the party would continue to get benefit of the interim order even after losing the case in the court.[1]

Essence of restitution The essence of the restitution proceedings contemplated under s. 144 of the CPC is that the party should have been disabled to pursue further in working out his rights or enjoy the property due to wrong decree or order and on reversal of such decree or order he should be reinstated to the original position and consequential reliefs by way of costs or damages or otherwise should be given.[2] The essence of the law of restitution is whether a claimant can claim a benefit from the defendant. Restitutionary remedies are distinct from those which are traditionally available in contract or in tort. In *Fibrosa Spolka Akeyjina* v *Fairbairn Lanson Combe Barbour Ltd.*[3] Lord Wright says: "It is clear that any civilized system of law is bound to provide remedies for cases of what has been called unjust enrichment or unjust benefit, that is, to prevent a man from retaining the money of, or some benefit derived from, another which it is against conscience that he should keep." The House of Lords has recognized the restitutionary remedies where the defendant has been unjustly enriched at the expense of the claimant.[4]

19 Act 104 of 1976, s. 47 (w.e.f 1.2.1977).

20 *Explanation.* In this section, the expression "proceedings" includes proceedings under Order IX, but does not include any proceeding under Article 226 of the Constitution.

1 *Kalabharati Advertising* v *Hemant Vimalnath Narichania* (2010)9 SCC 437; *Abhimanyoo Ram* v *State of U.P.* (2008)17 SCC 73.

2 *Lal Ahammed* v *Shaik Abdul Sammad Saheb* (1983)2 AP LJ 139.

3 [1942]2 All ER 122; [1943] AC 32 at p. 61.

4 *Lipkin Gorman (A Firm) Ltd.* v *Karpnale* [1991]2 AC 548; *Dentsche Morgan Grenfell Group Plc* v *IRC* [2006] UKHL 49; [2007]1 AC 558.

Theoretical basis of restitution[5] There are two main theories relating to the basis of restitution. The first is unjust enrichment according to which the law of restitution is equated with the unjust enrichment principle so that restitutionary remedies are available where the defendant has been unjustly enriched at the expense of the claimant. The second is a composite theory whereby restitutionary remedies are available either where the defendant has been unjustly enriched or where the defendant has profited from the commission of a relevant wrong or where the defendant has interfered with the claimant's proprietary rights.

Ultra vires demands by a public authority Money paid by a subject to a public authority in the form of taxes or other levies paid pursuant to an *ultra vires* demand by the authority is *prima facie* recoverable by the subject as of right. The claimant is not recovered to prove in such a case that he was mistaken in paying the money, nor that the money was paid as a result of pressure or duress exercised by the public authority. But the claimant must prove that the payment was made to a public authority in response to (and sufficiently connected with) an apparent statutory requirements to pay tax or some other import which in fact or in law is not lawfully due.[6]

Defences and bars to restitution The following are the defences and bars to restitution:

(1) Restitution will be denied where the defendant cannot be restored to his original position.

(2) The claimant is estopped.

(3) The defendant is a *bona fide* purchaser.

(4) Public policy precludes restitution.

Restitution is denied where the benefit was conferred—(*a*) as a valid gift; (*b*) pursuant to a valid common law, equitable or statutory obligation owed by the claimant to the defendant; (*c*) by the claimant while performing an obligation owed to a third party; (*d*) in submission to an honest claim, under process of law or compromise of a disputed claim; and (*e*) by the claimant acting voluntarily or officiously.

There are other defences available to restitutionary claims.[7] These are—(*a*) illegality; (*b*) incapacity; and (*c*) limitation.

5 Chitty on *Contracts*, 32nd Ed., vol. 1, para 29-009.

6 Halsbury's *Laws of England*, 5th Ed., vol. 88, para 458. See *Woolwich Building Society* v *IRC (No. 2)* [1992]3 All ER 737 (HL); *Deulsche Morgan Grenfell Group Plc.* v *Inland Revenue Commrs.* [2007]1 All ER 449; *British Steel Plc.* v *Customs and Excise Commrs.* [1997]2 All ER 366 (CA).

7 Halsbury's *Laws of England*, 5th Ed., vol. 88, para 565.

Chapter 2

Possessory Suit

General The word 'possession' is used in various contexts and phrases, for example, in the phrase "actual possession" or "to take possession" or "interest in possession" or "estate in possession" or "entitled in possession".[1] Legal possession may mean that possession which is recognized and protected as such by law. Legal possession is ordinarily associated with *de facto* possession; but legal possession may exist without *de facto* possession, and *de facto* possession is not always regarded as possession in law. A person who, although having no *de facto* possession, is deemed to have possession in law is sometimes said to have constructive possession.[2] Further, possession of the past is one thing, and the right to remain or continue in future is another thing. It is the latter which is usually more in controversy than the former, and it is the latter which has seen much abuse and misuse before the courts.[3] Possession is flexible term and is not necessarily restricted to mere actual possession of the property. The legal conception of possession may be in various forms. The two elements of possession are the corpus and the animus. A person though in physical possession may not be in possession in the eye of the law, if the animus be lacking. On the contrary, to be in possession, it is not necessary that one must be in actual physical contact. To gain the complete idea of possession, one must consider:

(*i*) the person possessing,

(*ii*) the things possessed, and

(*iii*) the persons excluded from possession.[4]

1 Halsbury's *Laws of England*, 4th Ed., vol. 35, para 1214 at p. 735.
2 *B. Gangadhar* v *B.G. Rajalingam* (1995)5 SCC 238.
3 *Maria Margarida Sequeira Fernandes* v *Erasmo Jack de Sequeira* (2012)5 SCC 370; AIR 2012 SC 1727.
4 *Sham Lal* v *Rajinder Kumar* (1994)30 DRJ 596.

As explained by Salmond, possession is a very vital relationship which needs protection under every system of jurisprudence. Salmond says, "the continuing exercise of a claim to the exclusive use of a thing constitutes the possession of it." All things we need to use and consume must be in our possession. It is, therefore, the most basic relationship between men and things. Sections 5 to 8 of the Specific Relief Act 1963 deal with recovery of possession of properties. Section 5 provides that a person entitled to possession of specific immovable property may recover it by a suit under the Code of Civil Procedure. Section 6 provides for a special and expeditious remedy for recovery of possession of immovable property by way of a summary suit. Sections 7 & 8 deal with the recovery of movable properties. As pointed out by the Supreme Court the provisions in the Specific Relief Act is founded more on public policy than on jurisprudence.[5]

Section 5 lays down the general proposition of law that a person who has a right to the possession of any specific immovable property may recover the same by instituting a suit in the manner prescribed in the Code of Civil Procedure. If the statute provides for the applicability of the Code, there cannot be any doubt whatsoever that all the relevant provisions thereof shall apply.[6] The expression "person entitled to the possession" means having a right to possession. This right to possession may arise by contract, by inheritance or by prescription. Mere possessory title is enough.[7] A possessory title is good against everyone who does not have a better title and such a possessory title is heritable and transferable.[8] Thus, to recover possession, the plaintiff must show a better title in himself than in the defendant. *Pari causa potior est conditio possidentis* [every man can keep what he possesses unless someone can prove that he has a better title] is a well-known dictum. But the person claiming relief on the basis of prior possession must show juridical possession; he must not be a mere servant or a deputee or an appointee for the benefit of his employer.[9] Or a mere licensee or a custodian,[10] unless the licence is coupled with a grant and the licensee is put in possession of the land,[11] or the person is occupying in a mere ministerial capacity, *viz,* a son occupying the room of a father's house.[12] As pointed out in *Tamizuddin* v *Ashrub Ali*,[13] a non-occupancy

5 *Krishna Kishore* v *Govt. of Andhra Pradesh* AIR 1990 SC 2292; (1991)1 SCC 184; 1990 Supp (2) SCR 8.

6 *Shanshu Suhara Beevi* v *G. Alex* (2004)8 SCC 569; *Hardes Ores (P) Ltd.* v *Hede & Company* (2007)5 SCC 614; *D.D. Mahasabha Jaipur* v *Mahant Ram Niwas* AIR 2008 SC 2187.

7 *Somnath* v *Raju* AIR 1970 SC 846; (1970)2 SCR 869; (1969)3 SCC 129.

8 *Phiraya Lal Kapoor* v *Jayarani* AIR 1997 Raj 230.

9 *Soba* v *Ram Pat Paul* AIR 1957 All 394.

10 *Manbahal Roy* v *Ram Gulam Pandey* AIR 1927 All 633.

11 *Sita Ram* v *Jaganath* 67 Ind Cas 322.

12 *Nritto Lal Mitter* v *Rajendro Narain Deb* ILR (1895)22 Cal 562.

13 ILR (1904)31 Cal 647 (FB).

raiyat dispossessed from his holding may bring a possessory action under this section. He has sufficient right and title to his land being a tenant of land to maintain an action on his title and his remedy is not restricted to s. 6 of the Act. A tenant who is wrongfully dispossessed can seek to recover the possession from his own landlord under s. 5 of the Specific Relief Act on the basis of his possessory title.[14]

Where there is merely an interference with plaintiff's lawful possession or threat of disposition, it is sufficient to sue for an injunction simpliciter.[15]

However, no suit for possession is maintainable once the land has been acquired under the Land Acquisition Act 1894.[16] A possessory title is good against everyone who does not have a better title.[17] Thus, even a trespasser cannot be dispossessed without there being a decree from the appropriate Civil Court and it is no part of the statutory duty of the police to evict alleged unlawful occupier as well as to put someone in possession.[18] For the purpose of s. 6 of the Act, the suit to recover joint possession is also maintainable.[19]

Conduct of the parties In a suit under s. 5 or s. 6 of the Specific Relief Act 1963, the Court must not confine itself to the consideration of the terms of contract. It must look to the conduct of the parties.[20]

Restitution of possession to dispossessed by summary suit A decree in summary suit for restoration to possession aims at compelling the unauthorized dispossessor to restore possession to dispossessed, if the suit is instituted within six months from the dispossession and the dispossession is effected without the consent of plaintiff and otherwise than in due course of law, the relevant statutory provision is contained in s. 6, Specific Relief Act.

Thus, a bare reading of the above-said provision shows that a person who has been illegally dispossessed of his immovable property may himself or through any person claiming through him recover such possession by filing a suit within six months from the date of dispossession. In such a suit, the entitlement of the plaintiff to recover possession of property from which he claims to have been illegally dispossessed has to be adjudicated independently of the question of title that may be set up by the defendant in such a suit. In fact, in a suit under s. 6, the only question that has to

14 *Nasir Singh* v *Bajoram* AIR 1969 J&K 9 (FB); *Lallo Yashwant Singh* v *Rao Jagadish Singh* AIR 1968 SC 620; (1968)2 SCR 203.

15 *Anathula Sudhakar* v *P. Buchi Reddy* AIR 2008 SC 2033; (2008)4 SCC 594.

16 *Market Committee, Hodal* v *Sukhdevi* (2016)1 SCC 290.

17 *Dandapani Sahu* v *Budhuram Lohar* (2007)54 AIC 666.

18 *Bikash Roy* v *State of West Bengal* (2008)1 CHN 554; (2008)65 AIC 790; (2008)4 ICC 794; (2008)1 Cal LJ 395.

19 *Ashutosh Das* v *Sushma Rani Das* (1995)3 Gau LR 292.

20 *Mira Rani Dutta* v *Snehalata Saraf* (2003)4 CHN 128 (Cal).

be determined by the Court is: (1) whether the plaintiff was in possession of the disputed property; (2) he had been illegally dispossessed there from on any date within six months prior to the filing of the suit? This is because s. 6(2) prescribes a period of six months from the date of dispossession as the outer limit for filing of a suit. As the question of possession and illegal dispossession there from is the only issue germane to a suit under s. 6, a proceeding there under, naturally, would partake the character of a summary proceeding against which the remedy by way of appeal or review has been specifically excluded by sub-sec. (3) of s. 6. Sub-section (4) also makes it clear that an unsuccessful litigant in a suit under s. 6 would have the option of filing a fresh suit for recovery of possession on the basis of title, if any.[1]

Object of possessory suit The object behind possessory suit envisaged in s. 6, Specific Relief Act is to discourage persons taking law into their own hands and is based and founded by public policy. It is a summary remedy available to the person in possession of immovable property when he is dispossessed otherwise than in due process of law. A suit under s. 6 of the Specific Relief Act is not maintainable against the State and after expiry of six months from the date of dispossession. It does not operate as a bar to institution of a suit for recovery of possession on the basis of title.[2] A proceeding under s. 6 of the Specific Relief Act is intended to be a summary proceeding, the object of which is to afford an immediate remedy to an aggrieved party to reclaim possession of which he may have been unjustly denied by an illegal act of dispossession. Question of title or better right of possession does not arise for adjudication in a suit under s. 6 where the only issue required to be decided is as to whether the plaintiff was in possession at any time six months prior to the date of filing of the suit.[3] It is an additional mode of relief provided under the Specific Relief Act and it cannot be said to affect the relief available under the civil law.[4] But, akin to s. 53A of the Transfer of Property Act, this provision can be employed only as a shield and not as a sword. It does not empower the trespasser or rival owner to take forcible possession and thereafter plead insulation from immediate ouster by the real owner who can reasonably prove his previous possession, actual or legal.[5]

Possessory suit—adjudication of title In a possessory suit under s. 6 the court's power is limited in granting restoration of possession only. Court

1 *ITC Ltd.* v *Adarsh Coop. Housing Society Ltd.* (2013)10 SCC 169; (2012)118 AIC 96 (SC).
2 *Sobhabati* v *Lakshmi Chand* AIR 1984 Ori 171; (1984)1 Ori LR 560; *Kausalya* v *Padmanav* AIR 1987 Ori 28.
3 *Mohd. Mehtab Khan* v *Khushumma Ibrahim* AIR 2013 SC 1099.
4 *Mohit Ch. Saikia* v *Md. Lal Mian,* (2006)3 Gau LR 112; (2006)43 AIC 487; (2006)3 Gau LR 435; (2006)4 CCC 411.
5 *Avtar Singh* v *Sarla Gupta* (2004)2 CCC 413.

cannot adjudicate title, nor can order removal of structure on suit land, if any.[6]

Section 6 of the Specific Relief Act dealt with 'suit-by person dispossessed of immovable property'. Object of s. 6 of the Specific Relief Act is to afford an immediate remedy to an aggrieved party to reclaim possession of which he may have been unjustly denied by an illegal act of dispossession.[7]

In a possessory suit plaintiff can succeed by proving continuous possession prior to dispossession. Plaintiff is not to establish tilte.[8] The pleadings and documents establish title to a particular property and possession is in question, it will be for the person in possession to give sufficiently detailed pleadings, particulars and documents to support his claim in order to continue in possession.

Therefore, for obtaining relief of recovery of possession on the basis of possessory title in the land, the plaintiff is required to plead and prove that he was in possession over the land and was subsequently dispossessed. Unless the plaintiff avers in the plaint and proves that he has been dispossessed subsequently, he is not entitled to relief of recovery of possession on the basis of possessory title.[9]

It would be imperative that one who claims possession must give all such details as enumerated hereunder:

(*a*) Who is or are the owner or owners of the property;

(*b*) Title of the property;

(*c*) Who is in possession of the title documents;

(*d*) Identity of the claimant or claimants to possession;

(*e*) The date of entry into possession;

(*f*) How he came into possession—whether he purchased the property or inherited or got the same in gift or by any other method;

(*g*) In case he purchased the property, what is the consideration; if he has taken it on rent, how much is the rent, license fee or lease amount;

(*h*) If taken on rent, license fee or lease—then insist on rent deed, license deed or lease dead;

(*i*) Who are the persons in possession/occupation or otherwise living with him, is what capacity; as family members, friends or servants, etc.;

6 *Madan Singh* v *Taiyab Hussain* AIR 1990 Gau 85; *Ramachandra* v *Damodar* AIR 2007 SC 2577; *Parasa Range Rao* v *Mathe Sanjeeva Rao* AIR 2006 AP 366.

7 *Mohd. Mehtab Khan* v *Khushunmaq Ibrahim* AIR 2013 SC 1099.

8 *Daulat Singh* v *Tulsi Ram* AIR 1990 MP 348.

9 *Manjit Singh* v *Shanti Devi* (2010)15 SCC 578.

(*j*) Subsequent conduct, i.e. any event which might have extinguished his entitlement to possession or caused shift therein; and

(*k*) Basis of his claim that not to deliver possession but continue in possession.[10]

The plaintiff may not have absolute title to suit property. Thus a tenant wrongfully dispossessed by his landlord may invoke s. 6, Specific Relief Act. This principle is deducible from a Supreme Court decision which held that all that s. 6, Specific Relief Act provides is that a person, even if he is a landlord cannot take the law in his own hands and forcibly evict a tenant after the expiry of lease. Section 6, Specific Relief Act frowns upon forcible dispossession without recourse to law but does not at the same time declare that the possession of the evicted person is a lawful possession. Referring to r. 13 of the Madras Cinemas (Regulation) Rules the Supreme Court held that a tenant on the expiry of lease cannot be said to continue in lawful possession of the property against the wishes of the landlord if such a possession is not otherwise protected statutorily.[11]

A person in possession over land without any lawful title has right to exclude all except the rightful owner. So, on the basis of long possession a plaintiff albeit without title can get a decree of eviction against rank trespasser.[12] In possessory suit, it was held that proof of title is unnecessary.[13]

In *S.R. Ejaz* v *Tamil Nadu Handloom Weavers' Co-op. Society,*[14] the appellant was forcibly dispossessed by the respondent Co-operative Society pending suit filed by the respondent for eviction of the appellant. The appellant gave a complaint before the police, made representation to the higher authorities and also filed a writ. As he could not get any relief, he filed a suit under s. 6 of the Specific Relief Act within the statutory period of six months. The respondent Co-operative Society pleaded that it took possession with the consent of the appellant. The suit was dismissed. The appellant filed a Civil Revision Petition before the High Court and the High Court remanded the matter for fresh disposal. The appellant took up the matter to the Supreme Court. Their Lordships held that the plea of the respondent that the appellant surrendered possession cannot be accepted, and allowed the appeal and directed the respondent to restore possession to the appellant.

Where a licensee has been forcibly dispossessed, he may either pursue his remedy under s. 64 of the Easements Act or under this provision.[15] In

10 *Maria Margarida Sequeria Fernandes* v *Erasmo Jack de Sequeria (Dead) through L.Rs.* AIR 2012 SC 1727.

11 *M.C. Chokalingam* v *Manickavasagam* AIR 1974 SC 104; (1974)1 SCC 48; (1974)1 SCWR 196; (1974)2 Mad LJ 27.

12 *E. Mangulu* v *Paddi Sriramulu* (1974)1 Cut WR 568.

13 *R. Rasen* v *P. Lustom* AIR 1974 Gau 66; 1973 Ass LR 297.

14 AIR 2002 SC 1152.

15 *M.S. Baliga* v *Mangalore City Corporation* AIR 1998 Kant 76.

Krishna Ram Mahale v *Shobha Venkatarao*,[16] the Supreme Court, while dealing with eviction of a licensee by the owner after the expiry of licence, laid down the law as follows—

> "It is well-settled law in this country that where a person is in settled possession of property, even on the assumption that he had no right to remain on the property, he cannot be dispossessed by the owner of the property except by recourse to law."

A real owner is entitled to defend illegal occupation of his property and is entitled to throw him out during the "act and process of trespassing".[17] But where possession of such a person has been peaceful, long, anterior or accomplished and settled, although with no right to remain in possession, he cannot be ousted or dispossessed by the owner except "in due course of law".[18] When the land has already been acquired under notification of the Land Acquisition Act and compensation paid to the land-losers then suit for possession is not maintainable.[19] Though the landlord is entitled to possession of land from his tenant on the expiry of the period of tenancy, yet, if the tenant holds over, he cannot dispossess him on his own authority and if he does so, it is competent to the tenant to sue the landlord for protection under this section. The Indian law does not recognize in the landlord a right of extra-judicial re-entry.[20]

In a suit under s. 6 of the Act, the status of the parties is immaterial.[1]

"Possessio contra omnes valet praeter eur cui ius sit possessionis" It means that a person who has possession has a good title against all those who have a better title.[2]

Nature of possessory suit A suit under s. 6 of the Specific Relief Act is like a summary trial inasmuch as the enquiry is confined to finding out the possession and dispossession within a period of six months prior from the date of the suit ignoring the question of title.[3] The enquiry under s. 6 of

16 AIR 1989 SC 2097; (1989)4 SCC 131; JT 1989(3) SC 489.
17 *Lalloo Yeshwant Singh* v *Rao Jagadish Singh* AIR 1968 SC 620; (1968)2 SCR 203; *Krishna Ram Mahale* v *Shobha Venkatarao* AIR 1989 SC 2097; (1989)4 SCC 131; *Hemchand Jain* v *Anil Kumar* AIR 1993 Del 99; *Nabe Kishore Sahu* v *East India Arms Company* AIR 1998 Ori 95.
18 *Hemchand Jain* v *Anil Kumar* AIR 1993 All 99; *Nabe Kishore Sahu* v *East India Arms Company* AIR 1998 Ori 95.
19 *Mkt. Commtt. Hodal* v *Sukhdevi* AIR 2016 SC 2226.
20 *Patil Exhibitors Pvt. Ltd.* v *Corporation of the City of Bangalore* AIR 1986 Kant 194; *Munshiram* v *Delhi Administration* AIR 1968 SC 702; (1968)2 SCR 455; *East India Hotels Ltd.* v *Syndicate Bank* 1992 Supp (2) SCC 29; JT 1991(6) SC 112.
1 *Sweet Home Co-Operative Housing Society Ltd.* v *Himanshu Khurana* (2011)1 Mah LJ 494; (2011)3 Bom CR 168; (2011)1 AIR Bom R 677.
2 *Rame Gowda* v *M. Varadappa Naidu* (2004)1 SCC 769.
3 *Parikshit Dutta* v *Bijoy Kumar Agarwal* (2017)2 Gau LR 505.

the Act by the Court is limited in nature. Thus, for instance, where a person is put, following a proceeding under s. 145, CrPC, in possession of a plot of land, such dispossession of the plaintiff not being *otherwise than in due course of law*, no suit under s. 6 of the Specific Relief Act, in such a case, can be maintained. In fact, even if it is found, in such a suit under s. 6 of the Specific Relief Act, that the plaintiff had been in possession of the suit land and yet the defendant has been put in possession of the land in due course of law by way of an order passed under sub-sec. (4) of s. 145, CrPC. The plaintiff cannot be put into possession of such a land by the civil court by evicting the defendant there from, for, in a suit under s. 6 of the Specific Relief Act, the civil court cannot decide or hold that the proceeding under s. 145, CrPC was illegally drawn and/or the declaration of possession thereof in favour of the defendant was illegal or incorrectly given. If, in a given case, the defendant has been put into possession of the suit land following the proceeding under s. 145, CrPC, the remedy lies in instituting a suit either for the plaintiff's declaration of rights, title and interest over such a property under s. 34 of the Specific Relief Act or in instituting a suit, under s. 5 of the Specific Relief Act, seeking declaration of his possession over such a plot of land and recovery of possession thereof. To put it differently, in a suit under s. 6 of the Specific Relief Act, until the time a civil court finds that a person has been dispossessed *otherwise than in due course of law*, he cannot be put into possession of the plot of land, which such a person claims to have been in possession of.[4] However, it keeps the relative titles of parties intact and they are not affected by any decision which may be reached.[5]

Suit for possession Suit for possession was filed on the basis of possessory title. Plaintiff need not establish his title. It is enough if long-standing peaceful possession is proved.[6]

Settled possession It is the settled possession or effective possession of a person without title which would entitle him to protect his possession even as against the true owner. The concept of settled possession and the right of the possessor to protect his possession against the owner has come to be settled by a catena of decisions.[7]

In *Munshi Ram* v *Delhi Admn.*,[8] it was held by the Supreme Court that no one, including the true owner, has a right to dispossess the trespasser

4 *Karuna Kanta Barman* v *Ramesh Baishya* (2006)3 Gau LR 790.
5 *Pandhari Shamrao Kolhe* v *Meerabai* 1980 Mah LJ 39.
6 *Sanwal Ram* v *Ramjan* AIR 2016 Chh 48 relying on *Prataprai N. Kothari* v *John Braganza* (1999)4 SCC 403; AIR 1999 SC 1666; *Rame Gowda* v *M. Varadappa Naidu* (2004)1 SCC 769; AIR 2004 SC 4609.
7 *Rame Gowda* v *M. Varadappa Naidu* (2004)1 SCC 769; *Ram Rattan* v *State of U.P.* (1977)1 SCC 188; 1977 SCC (Cri) 85.
8 AIR 1968 SC 702; (1968)2 SCR 455; 1968 CrLJ 806.

by force if the trespasser is in settled possession of the land and in such a case unless he is evicted in the due course of law, he is entitled to defend his possession even against the rightful owner. But merely stray or even intermittent acts of trespass do not give such a right against the true owner. The possession which a trespasser is entitled to defend against the rightful owner must be settled possession, extending over a sufficiently long period of time and acquiesced to by the true owner. A casual act of possession would not have the effect of interrupting the possession of the rightful owner. The rightful owner may re-enter and reinstate himself provided he does not use more force than is necessary. Such entry will be viewed only as resistance to an intrusion upon his possession which has never been lost. A stray act of trespass, or a possession which has not matured into settled possession, can be obstructed or removed by the true owner even by using necessary force.

But, in *Puran Singh* v *State of Punjab*,[9] it was made clear by the Supreme Court that it is difficult to lay down any hard-and-fast rule as to when the possession of a trespasser can mature into settled possession. The "settled possession" must be (*i*) effective, (*ii*) undisturbed, and (*iii*) to the knowledge of the owner or without any attempt at concealment by the trespasser. The phrase "settled possession" does not carry any special charm or magic in it; nor is it a ritualistic formula which can be confined in a strait-jacket. An occupation of the property by a person as an agent or a servant acting at the instance of the owner will not amount to actual physical possession. The Supreme Court laid down the following tests which may be adopted as a working rule for determining the attributes of "settled possession":

(*i*) that the trespasser must be in actual physical possession of the property over a sufficiently long period;

(*ii*) that the possession must be to the knowledge (either express or implied) of the owner or without any attempt at concealment by the trespasser and which contains an element of *animus possidendi*. The nature of possession of the trespasser would, however, be a matter to be decided on the facts and circumstances of each case;

(*iii*) the process of dispossession of the true owner by the trespasser must be complete and final and must be acquiesced to by the true owner; and

(*iv*) that one of the usual tests to determine the quality of settled possession, in the case of culturable land, would be whether or not the trespasser, after having taken possession, had grown any crop. If the crop had been grown by the trespasser, then even the true owner, has no right to destroy the crop grown by the trespasser and take forcible possession.

9 (1975)4 SCC 518; 1975 SCC (Cri) 608.

Thus, where a person is in settled possession of the property, his possession cannot be disturbed even if it be assumed that his possession is without title and he had no right to remain in possession. Injunction can be issued to the extent of restraining the defendant from forcibly dispossessing the plaintiff without following the due course of law.[10] A person without title but in "settled" possession, as against mere fugitive possession, can get back possession if forcibly dispossessed or rather, if dispossessed otherwise than by due process of law.[11]

Suit for declaration of title and possession Claim was based on patta granted to plaintiff. Defendant, on the other hand, claimed to be permanent ryots under the T.N. Estates Lands Act 1908. Existence of patta was proved; but plaintiff was unable to prove nature of rights conferred on him. Course adopted by court to proceed to determine status of plaintiff was to describe plaintiff as *mirasidar* in views of rent receipts issued by plaintiff as *Ekabogam Mirasidar* was held to be justified by the Supreme Court.[12] Suit property was belong to female Hindu who died intestate. Property would revert back to heirs of her father. Her stepsisters are entitled to share in that property as co-owners and they are already in possession of that property. Suit for declaration and joint possession is maintainable.[13]

Suit property was donated to Congress Committee. All India Congress Party constructed "Congress Bhavan" on a part of the property. There was a split in congress party. Party led by Indira Gandhi was declared by the Election Commission as Indian National Congress and owner of all properties belonging to Congress. Plea by defendant Janta Dal was that the decision of Election Commission would not confer title on Plaintiff Congress Party. It has been held by the Supreme Court that the plea of defendant was not tenable when Election Commission applied the test of majority declared that the party led by Indira Gandhi was true Congress and owner of property. Furthermore, when decision of Election Commission was upheld by the Supreme Court. Defendant though in possession had no right over properties, lease deeds executed by them had no legal effect. Thus, the suit was liable to be decreed. Defendant was given time to vacate property.[14]

Limitation for suit for possession and declaration The limitation for filing a suit for possession on the basis of title is 12 years and, therefore, merely because one of the reliefs sought is of declaration that will not mean that the outer limitation of 12 years is lost. In a suit filed for possession based

10 *Zoo Authority of Karnataka, Mysore* v *Anand* 1999 AIHC 3630; (1999)2 CCC 396.
11 *Sopan Sukhdeo Sable* v *Asstt. Charity Commr.* (2004)3 SCC 137.
12 *Ambikapathi Ammal* v *Sri Kandaswamy Koil* AIR 2015 SC 1871.
13 *Sukhwinder Kaur* v *Rajwant Kaur* AIR 2018 P&H 199.
14 *Janatha Dal Party* v *The Indian National Congress* AIR 2014 SC 1062.

on title the plaintiff is bound to prove his title and pray for a declaration that he is the owner of the suit land because his suit on the basis of title cannot succeed unless he is held to have some title over the land. However, the main relief is of possession and, therefore, the suit will be governed by Art. 65 of the Limitation Act 1963. This Article deals with a suit for possession of immovable property or any interest therein based on title and the limitation is 12 years from the date when possession of the land becomes adverse to the plaintiff.[15]

Suit for possession by person wrongfully dispossessed Plaintiffs purchased suit land by registered sale deed. Plaintiffs being registered owners, burden is on defendants to prove their long possession. Defendants failed to prove the same. Point of time of dispossession within six months prior to the date of filing of suit was proved by plaintiffs. Thus plaintiffs were entitled to restoration of possession. If dispossession was by illegal means, then also, plaintiffs were entitled to the relief under s. 6 of the Specific Relief Act 1963 irrespective of time of six months of dispossession.[16]

Suit against Government Section 6(2)(*b*) of the Act bar suit against the Government. Thus, where the petitioner was dispossessed from the shop room constructed on land of a Government authority and there is a clear finding that the shop room was constructed illegally without approval of the local authority and that too on Municipal land. Therefore, a suit for recovery of possession is not maintainable, against the Government under cl. (*b*) of s. 6(2) of the Specific Relief Act.[17]

Tenant by sufferance A tenant by sufferance is a tenant who continues in possession without the consent or acquiescence of the lessor. But, the situation would be different where there is consent or acquiescence on the part of the lessor to continue in possession. In case of a statutory tenant the possession is protected.[18] However, the tenant by sufferance has juridical possession and as a result thereof he is entitled to an injunction.[19] The possession of such tenant cannot be said to be unlawful.[20] The possession of tenant by sufferance should be protected by Courts.[21]

15 *Sopanrao* v *Syed Mehmood* (2019)7 SCC 76.
16 *Gordhan Singh* v *Kanhaiyalal* AIR 2016 Raj 112.
17 *Ali Mahammad Bepari* v *Chairman of Bilasipara Town Committee* (2015)2 Gau LR 18.
18 *Ganga Dutt Murarka* v *Kartik Chandra Das* (1) AIR 1961 SC 1067; *Rhawanju Lakhanshi* v *Himatlal Jamnadas Dani* (2) (1972)1 SCC 388; AIR 1972 SC 819; *Badrilal* v *Municipal Corporation of Indore* (3) (1973)2 SCC 388; AIR 1973 SC 508.
19 *Sri Balaji Trading Company* v *Veeraswamy Srinivasan* 1980(1) Andh WR 28.
20 *M.C. Chockalingam* v *V. Manickavasagam* (1974)1 SCC 48.
21 *Mogllipuvvu Annapurnaiah* v *Maiampati Narasimha Rao* (1982)1 APLJ 130.

Caretaker's suit (Gratuitous possessee) The watchman, caretaker or a servant employed to look after the property can never acquire interest in the property irrespective of his long possession. The watchman, caretaker or a servant is under an obligation to hand over the possession forthwith on demand. According to the principles of justice, equity and good conscience, the courts are not justified in protecting the possession of a watchman, caretaker or servant who was only allowed to live into the premises to look after the same.[22] An occupation of the property by a person as an agent or a servant at the instance of the owner will not amount to actual physical possession.[1] The possession of a servant or agent is that of his master or principal as the case may be for all purposes and the former cannot maintain a suit against the latter on the basis of such possession.[2] A man may hold an object without claiming any interest therein for himself. A servant though holding an object holds it for his master. He has, therefore, merely custody of the thing and not the possession which would always be with the master though the master may not be in actual contact of the thing. It is in this light in which the concept of possession has to be understood in the context of a servant and a master.[3] Thus, a suit by an agent or by the servant under s. 6 against the master would not be maintainable.[4]

Nature of pleadings Whenever pleadings and documents established title to a particular property and possession is in question, it will be for the person in possession to give sufficiently detailed pleadings, particulars and documents to support his claim in order to continue in possession.[5]

The provisions of s. 14 of the Limitation Act are applicable to suit failed under s. 6 of the Specific Relief Act.[6]

Dispossession The possession contemplated in s. 6 of the Act is not mere actual physical possession but it will also include constructive possession and a person, who is deprived of his constructive possession, can also maintain a suit under the said section. In the case of a landlord and tenant the landlord is in possession of the demised land or building through his tenant and when the tenant, who is in physical possession is dispossessed, either the tenant who is in physical possession or the landlord who is in possession of the property let out, through his tenant, can maintain a suit in his own name, under s. 6 of the Act.[7] There must be total dispossession

22 A. *Shanmugam* v *Ariya Kshatriya Rajakula Vamsathu Madalaya Nandhavana Paripalanai Sangam* (2012)6 SCC 430.
1 *Puran Singh* v *State of Punjab* (1975)4 SCC 518; 1975 SCC (Cri) 608.
2 *Mahabir Prasad Jain* v *Ganga Singh* (1999)8 SCC 274.
3 *Sham Lal* v *Rajinder Kumar* (1994)30 DRJ 596.
4 *Akila* v *Nisar* (2012)91 ALR 103; (2012)3 All LJ 16; AIR 2012 All 93.
5 *Maria Margaride Sequeria Fernandes* v *Erasmo Jack de Sequeria* AIR 2012 SC 1727.
6 *Pratapsing Ganpatrao Kadam* v *Maruti Reghunath Todkar* AIR 2003 Bom 11.
7 S. *Ramakrishnan* v *Thangamuthu Nattar* (1991)2 LW 36; (1991)1 Mad LJ 16.

from the actual physical possession of the land and mere trespassing into the land in one occasion would not be suffice to attract the provision of s. 6 of the Specific Relief Act. A mere isolated act of trespass over the property is not coming within the purview of definition of dispossession in terms of s. 6 of the Specific Relief Act.[8]

Dispossession in excess of property decreed Where the petitioner alleges that he was dispossessed in execution proceeding in excess of the land decreed by the Court, it was held that suit under s. 6 of the Act is not maintainable. But, the proper remedy would be to take recourse to s. 47 of the CPC to file objection before the executing Court.[9] It is well settled that when a sale in execution of a decree is impugned on the ground that it is not warranted by the terms thereof, that question could be agitated, when it arises between parties to the decree, only by an application under s. 47 of CPC and not in a separate suit.[10]

Limitation for possessory suit Section 6, Specific Relief Act provides that if, the plaintiff is dispossessed without his consent and except in due course of law can sue for restoration of possession and he must do it within six months from the date of dispossession. This special rule of the limitation prevails over the general law of limitation contained in the Limitation Act 1963. The dispossessed plaintiff has also the option to bring a regular title suit for declaration of title and recovery of possession wherein Art. 65 of the Limitation Act 1963 is applicable.[11]

Therefore in possessory suit under s. 6, Specific Relief Act, absence of finding that the plaintiff was dispossessed within six months preceding the filing of suit renders the decree liable to be set aside.[12] A suit for possession under s. 6 filed beyond six months of his dispossession is not maintainable.[13] However, where a suit was not filed within six months as required under s. 6 of the Act because of the pendency of the proceedings under s. 145, CPC which ultimately ended in dismissal with liberty to file a fresh suit for possession and consequently the suit under the section was filed immediately, the Supreme Court held that the suit was filed in time under s. 6 of the Act.[14]

Suit for possession—maintainability without prayer for declaration of title Suit was filed by plaintiff for possession based on title on strength of sale

8 *Tapan Kr. Mani* v *Ashutosh Mahato* (2002)4 CHN 16; (2002)1 ICC 646.
9 *Jagdish Kumar* v *VIIth Additional Civil Judge, Kanpur Dehat* (2007)54 AIC 606.
10 *Merla Ramanna* v *Nallaparaju* (1955)2 SCR 938; AIR 1956 SC 87.
11 *Chandra Bhan Prasad* v *Mohanlal* AIR 1987 Cal 322.
12 *Subal Chandra* v *Manmohan Moral* AIR 1991 NOC 106 (Gau).
13 *Tirumala Tirupati Devasthanam* v *K.M. Krishnaiahy* AIR 1998 SC 1132; (1998)3 SCC 331; JT 1998(2) SC 231.
14 *Biharilal* v *Bhuri Devi* AIR 1997 SC 1879; (1997)2 SCC 279; JT 1996(11) SC 585.

deed executed in her favour by sole surviving successor of one of the deceased sons of deceased owner. Main plea of defendant was that she was an adopted daughter of deceased widow of deceased owner who was in possession of property as widow's estate before it was sold to plaintiff. Defendant was unable to prove adoption. Plea did not *prima facie* put any cloud over plaintiff's title. Suit for possession simpliciter without declaration of title was held to be maintainable.[15]

Suit for possession—maintainability Land in question was already acquired by notification under ss. 4 and 6 of the Land Acquisition Act 1894 (now ss. 11 and 19 of the Right to Fair Compensation and Transparency in Land Acquisition, Rehabilitation and Resettlement Act 2013) and compensation was also paid to the respondents in the instant appeal. In such circumstances order decreeing suit for possession was held to be not proper especially when land had already been acquired.[16] Therefore, to avail of relief in such summary proceeding, the person concerned must prove his "previous possession" and "wrongful dispossession". The question of proving wrongful dispossession will naturally arise if and only if the "previous possession" is proved. It is only persons who were in "possession" who can sue under this section. If the previous possession of the person claiming relief under this section is itself in dispute, the court should attribute possession to the person with better title.[17]

Mandatory injunction in possessory suit In a suit under s. 6 of the Act, there is no bar to the grant of the relief of mandatory injunction on an application under Or. 39, rr. 1 & 2, CPC if the relief sought through the application is the same which is prayed for in the suit itself. However, the Court would be slow and circumspect while granting such a relief because the said relief can be granted only in those discerning few cases where the Court comes to the conclusion that a grave injustice would be done to the petitioner in case such a relief is not granted. If the Court is of the view that the opposite party has got no legs to stand upon and non-granting of the injunction would result in injustice to the petitioner then the Court would not hesitate in coming to the rescue of such a petitioner.[18] Where the plaintiff who was in possession of the suit schedule property was unlawfully dispossessed by the act of the defendants and the defendants demolished the wall and interfered with his peaceful possession the suit by the plaintiff for possession of the suit house and also for mandatory injunction to construct the wall damaged by the defendants would be maintainable under

15 *Muddasani Venkata Narsaiah* v *Muddasani Sarojana* AIR 2016 SC 2250.

16 *Mkt. Commtt Hodal* v *Sukhdevi* AIR 2016 SC 2226.

17 *Tajul Islam* v *Shariyatullah Mansoorali Sheikh* (1994)2 Mah LJ 1191; 1995 AIHC 1911.

18 *Uttam Singh* v *Raghubir Singh* ILR (1997)1 Del 674; (1997)69 DLT 302; 1998 AIHC 1463.

s. 6, Specific Relief Act and question of seeking declaration of title would not arise in such a suit.[19]

Appeal against interim order Order passed under s. 6 of the Specific Relief Act is not appealable and any interim order passed in the said suit is also not appealable.[20] But, an order passed under Or. 39, rr. 1 & 2, CPC in proceeding under s. 6 of the Act may be challenged in appeal under Or. 43, r. 1, CPC and therefore, the contention that an appeal in suit under s. 6 of the Act is not maintainable cannot be accepted for simple reason that the suit is not yet finally decided nor there is decree and/or final order is passed.[1] However, it must be noted that since the decree passed under s. 6 of the Act is not appealable, no order passed in execution of any decree passed under s. 6 of the Act to which Or. 21, r. 103, CPC applies shall be subject to appeal.[2]

Can a suit for injunction based on title be converted into a suit under s. 6 of the Specific Relief Act? In *Nagar Palika Jind* v *Jagat Singh*[3] the plaintiff filed a suit for an injunction restraining the Respondent Municipal Committee from interfering with his possession of the suit property. The Municipal Committee resisted the claim on the ground that the plaintiff was neither the owner of the land nor was he in possession. The trial court came to the conclusion that the plaintiff failed to prove that he was the owner or that he was in possession of the suit land and dismissed the claim. The first Appellate Court found title in and possession with the plaintiff, allowed the appeal and decreed the action. The second appeal filed on behalf of the defendant Municipal Committee was dismissed. The Supreme Court held in favour of the defendant/appellant on both the questions of title and possession. Faced with such a situation, the Counsel for the plaintiff/respondent took a stand that even if he had failed to prove his title, the suit should be treated as one based on possession and dispossession in terms of s. 6 of the Specific Relief Act 1963. The Supreme Court rejected the contention and observed that the plaintiff never alleged that he had been dispossessed by the appellant Municipal Committee; on the other hand he claimed to be the owner of the land in question and asserted that he was in possession as owner and sought for a permanent injunction restraining the appellant from interfering with his possession. In such a case, Their Lordships held that the principle of s. 6 of the Specific Relief Act could not be applied.

19 *Girajawwa* v *Basawwa* AIR 1991 Kant 51.
20 *Suresh Saggar* v *Vijay Saggar* AIR 2010 P&H 104.
1 *Rajeshree Pravin Sonawane* v *Arvind Kumar Fatechand* (2014)2 Mah LJ 580; (2014)2 Bom CR 111.
2 *Raghunath R. Shingate* v *Jayant Gajanan Pathak* (2011)6 Mah LJ 799; (2012)1 Bom CR 301; (2012)110 AIC 299; (2012)1 ICC 971; (2011)6 AIR Bom R 199; 2011 AIR CC 3385.
3 AIR 1995 SC 1377; (1995)3 SCC 426; JT 1995(3) SC 281.

In *East India Hotels Ltd.* v *Syndicate Bank,*[4] East India Hotels Ltd. which owned the Hotel Oberoy Towers situated in Nariman Point, Bombay, took a loan for its construction from the plaintiff Syndicate Bank and as an integral part of the bargain, the Hotel entered into an agreement of leave and licence in favour of the Bank for a period of 12 years with an option for renewal for another period of 12 years. After the expiry of the period of 12 years, the Hotels rejected the request of the bank for renewal and caused a notice to the Bank to the effect and to hand over possession, but the Bank did not deliver possession and continued to be in possession of the premises. A disastrous fire broke out in the premises as a result of which the plaintiff Bank and other shops were seriously affected. The plaintiff vacated the premises and delivered possession to the Hotels on the alleged understanding that possession will be re-delivered to the Bank after renovation. But the defendant Hotels did not re-deliver possession, whereupon the Bank filed a suit under s. 6 of the Specific Relief Act for recovery of possession. Their Lordships Kasliwal, J and K. Ramaswamy, J who constituted the Bench of the Supreme Court, differed on the interpretation of the provisions of s. 6 of the Specific Relief Act. Justice Kasliwal held that the only prohibition under the provisions of s. 6 was not to use force or any unlawful means for dispossessing the person in possession. The possession of the licensee, according to the learned Judge, remaining in occupation after the expiry of the term of licence was no better than that of a trespasser and if the true owner came into possession of the premises without using any force or on account of fire or other act of *vis major,* it would not be in the interest of justice to grant a decree for possession in favour of the licensee under s. 6 of the Act. Ramaswamy, J differed from his learned brother and held that the expression "due course of law" in s. 6 means such an exercise of the powers of duly constituted Tribunal or court in accordance with the procedure established by law under such safeguards for the protection of individual rights. According to the learned Judge, even a landlord under colour of title, cannot dispossess a person in occupation except in due course of law, and if the person dispossessed expresses *animus possidendi,* he was entitled to the relief under s. 6. In view of this difference of opinion, the matter was placed before the learned Chief Justice for constituting a larger Bench. Meanwhile in *R.P. Bhupal Prasad* v *State of Andhra Pradesh,*[5] the question was whether possession of the site taken on lease by a lessee of the theatre after the termination of the lease in contravention of the terms of the lease, and despite the absence of acquiescence by the lessor was lawful, came up for consideration before a Bench of the Supreme Court consisting of

4 1992 Supp (2) SCC 29; JT 1991(6) SC 112.
5 (1995)5 SCC 698; AIR 1996 SC 140; JT 1995(6) SC 258.

K. Ramaswamy, J and B.L. Hansaria, J In the said decision, the observation of K. Ramaswamy, J in *East India Hotels Ltd.* v *Syndicate Bank* referred to above, was quoted with approval.

Similarly in another decision in *Annamallai Club* v *Government of Tamil Nadu*,[6] which was considered by another Bench consisting of K. Ramaswamy, J and G.B. Pattnaik, J the observation of K. Ramaswamy, J in *East India Hotels Ltd.* v *Syndicate Bank* was quoted with approval. But the conflict of opinion between Kasliwa, LJ and Ramaswamy, J in *East India Hotels Ltd.* v *Syndicate Bank*,[7] referred to above does not seem to have been decided yet.

Similarly, where the plaintiff-tenant filed the suit initially for permanent injunction when his right for possession was threatened by the landlord-defendant and subsequently amended the plaint for recovery of possession soon after he was forcibly evicted from the suit property despite the existence of interim order of injunction, it was held that such amendment of the plaint and suit for restoration of possession is maintainable in a civil court.[8]

Receiver in possessory suit The provisions of Or. 40, r. 1, CPC empower the civil court to appoint a receiver if the court considers it just and convenient. It is a salutary provision empowering the court to do justice between the parties pending final decision of the suit and such powers are necessary even in a suit instituted under s. 6 of the Specific Relief Act. Consequently, a receiver under Or. 40 , r. 1, CPC in a suit under s. 6 of the Specific Relief Act can be appointed.[9]

But a different view has been expressed in an Orissa case which held that admitted dispossession of the plaintiffs is the basis for a suit under s. 6 of the Act. When a person is dispossessed from property, there is no scope for declaration of possession. The necessary prayer, therefore is for recovery of possession. Appointment of a receiver or permanent injunction is not a necessary relief in such a suit.[10]

Injunction against the decree passed under s. 6 of the Act Section 6(4) of the Act does not bar any person to bring a regular suit founded upon his title in respect of the immovable property and to recover possession thereof even though a suit instituted under sub-sec. (1) of s. 6 of the said Act has been decreed against him. A regular suit for title and recovery of possession is maintainable in view of the language of sub-sec. (4) of s. 6 of the said Act

6 AIR 1997 SC 3650; (1997)3 SCC 169.

7 1992 Supp (2) SCC 29; JT 1991(6) SC 112.

8 *Kamarapu Veera Laxmi* v *Vemula Krishna Murthy* (1999)1 APLJ 271; (1999)2 ALD 400; *Samir Sobhan Sanyal* v *Tracks Trade Pvt. Ltd.* (1996)4 SCC 144; AIR 1996 SC 2102.

9 *Meghji Jetha* v *Kalyanji Nanji* AIR 1987 Bom 273 at p. 275; (1987)89 Bom LR 107.

10 *Gangadhar Somarath* v *Honu Majhi* AIR 1988 Ori 141.

and the legislature did not intend to give the proceedings under s. 6(1) of the said Act the character of finality. The defeated party can bring a suit for declaration of his title and for recovery of possession and it is his duty in the subsequent suit to prove his title. If the plaintiff in the subsequent suit is in possession, that is, the decree passed in the earlier suit not yet having been executed against him, he can pray for maintenance of *status quo* and the court in the subsequent suit can pass an order restraining the defendants of the subsequent suit from disturbing the possession of the plaintiff in the said suit.[11] Sub-section (4) of s. 6 of the Specific Relief Act is only enabling provision to file a suit and recover possession. It cannot by any implication whatsoever be construed as to create a bar from seeking temporary injunction. The person who has been in possession of the property is certainly entitled to seek the relief of temporary injunction pending the regular suit filed for title though he has suffered a decree under Specific Relief Act instituted by the opposite party.[12]

Injunction to trespasser against true owner A trespasser can seek restoration of possession under s. 6 of the Specific Relief Act. But, so far as the question of seeking injunction by the trespasser is concerned, it does not depend upon s. 6 of the Act. It is required to be decided with reference to the general principles applicable to grant or refusal of injunction.[13] In *Mahadeo Savlaram Shelke v Pune Municipal Corporation,*[14] it was held by the Supreme Court that a trespasser could not seek injunction against the true owner. Different High Courts have also laid down the same proposition,[15] although there are some contrary decisions[16] to the effect that till evicted by due process of law, a trespasser is entitled to injunction against the true owner. However, it is respectfully submitted that the contrary decisions holding that the trespasser is entitled to get injunction even against the true owner runs counter to the decision of the Supreme Court in *Mahadeo Savlaram Shelke* (supra), and are, therefore, not binding.

11 *Kalidas Mondal* v *Abdul Hossein* (2003)3 CHN 1; (2004)13 AIC 668; (2003)3 ICC 118; Cal LT 2003(3) HC 253; (2004)2 CCC 266.

12 *A.N. Paramkusha Bai* v *K. Krishan* (1999)3 AP LJ 465; *P. Venkateswarlu* v *A. Venkateswara Rao* (1) (1988)1 AP LJ 39.

13 *D.T.T.D.C.* v *D.R. Mehra & Sons* (1996)37 DRJ 183 (DB); (1996)62 DLT 234 (DB); AIR 1996 Del 351.

14 (1995)3 SCC 33; JT 1995(2) SC 504.

15 *Hoshiar Singh* v *Gaon Sabha* (1988)36 DLT 428; *K.V. Narayan* v *S. Sharana Gowda* AIR 1986 Karn 77; *Alamelu Achi* v *Ponnaiah* AIR 1962 Mad 149; *Biswabam Pvt. Ltd.* v *Santosh* AIR 1964 Cal 235; *Bishni* v *Bahadur Singh* AIR 1980 All 209; *Padmanabha* v *Thkomas* AIR 1989 Ker 188.

16 *Bhawani Investments Ltd.* v *Shree Properties* (1987)32 DLT 397; *Moyilivarapu Annapurnaih* v *Melampati Narsimha Rao* AIR 1982 AP 253; *Patil Exhibitors (Pvt.) Ltd.* v *The Corporation of the City of Bangalore* AIR 1986 Kant 194; *Bhola Nath* v *Maharao Raja Saheb Bundi State of Rajasthan* AIR 1984 All 60; *Geeta* v *Ashok Kumar* (1982)84 Punj LR 291.

Section 145, CrPC vis-a-vis s. 6 of the Specific Relief Act In a suit under section 6 of the Specific Relief Act, the limited enquiry, which is required to be made by the civil court, is confined to the question as to whether the plaintiff had been in possession of the immovable property, which is the subject-matter of the suit, and if he had been in possession thereof, whether he had been dispossessed there from, without his consent, *otherwise than in due course of law* and, further, whether such dispossession had taken place not later than six months before institution of the suit. If any of the conditions, indicated hereinbefore, is found absent, the plaintiff's suit must fail. Logically, therefore, when a person is put, following a proceeding under s. 145, CrPC, in possession of a plot of land, such dispossession of the plaintiff not being *otherwise than in due course of law*, no suit under s. 6 of the Specific Relief Act, in such a case, can be maintained. In fact, even if it is found, in such a suit under s. 6 of the Specific Relief Act, that the plaintiff had been in possession of the suit land and yet the defendant has been put in possession of the land in due course of law by way of an order passed under sub-sec. (4) of s. 145, CrPC, the plaintiff cannot be put into possession of such a land by the civil court by evicting the defendant there from, for, in a suit under s. 6 of the Specific Relief Act, the civil court cannot decide or hold that the proceeding under s. 145, CrPC was illegally drawn and/or the declaration of possession thereof in favour of the defendant was illegal or incorrectly given. If, in a given case, the defendant has been put into possession of the suit land following the proceeding under s. 145, CrPC, the remedy lies in instituting a suit either for the plaintiff's declaration of rights, title and interest over such a property under s. 34 of the Specific Relief Act or in instituting a suit, under s. 5 of the Specific Relief Act, seeking declaration of his possession over such a plot of land and recovery of possession thereof. To put it differently, in a suit under s. 6 of the Specific Relief Act, until the time a civil court finds that a person has been dispossessed *otherwise than in due course of law*, he cannot be put into possession of the plot of land, which such a person claims to have been in possession of.[17]

Possessory suit—elements to be proved by the plaintiff To succeed in a summary suit for restitution to possession under s. 6, Specific Relief Act, the plaintiff is to establish the following namely; (*a*) that he was in exclusive possession over the disputed property; (*b*) that the disputed property is an immovable property; (*c*) that the plaintiff was dispossessed within six months from the date of the suit; (*d*) that the dispossession was effected without the consent of the plaintiff; (*e*) that the dispossession aforesaid was effected otherwise than in due course of law; (*f*) that the dispossession is by one other that the Government.

17 *Karuna Kanta Barman* v *Ramesh Baishya* (2006)3 Gau LR 790.

Actions under s. 6 are not to be burdened with issues of title or claims to ownership, howsoever indistinctly. In other words, the Court must only see whether the plaintiff was in possession, and not whether he/she should have been in possession.[18]

Impressing upon the need of proof of exclusive possession a Punjab case held that unless the plaintiff proves his exclusive possession prior to dispossession, his suit is liable to fail. If he succeeded in establishing his joint possession (here with his brother), such joint possession with his brother can be restored to him.[19]

But it may be found that s. 6 has used the expression "any person". The expression is eloquent enough to show that if one of several persons entitled to possession, remains in exclusive possession by arrangement with others who too are entitled to possess, may sue under s. 6, Specific Relief Act.[20]

Legal representatives of deceased respondent established their title to suit property before Civil Judge and High Court in second appeal. It was proved to be ancestral property of the deceased. Finding recorded by High Court was held to be valid being supported by cogent reasons. There was no miscarriage of justice and as such there would be no interference. Further, since appellant Municipality denied title of property to the deceased, no question of their adverse title over the same would arise.[1]

Persons having juridical possession are entitled to protection of possession under s. 6 of the Act. Thus, a tenant cannot be forcibly ousted from the tenanted property even after the tenancy has terminated. If such a tenant is forced out of tenancy without following the due course of law, recourse can be had to s. 6 of the Act. But, if such a tenant, without following s. 6 of the Act, reoccupies the tenancy forcefully, his possession thereafter in the tenanted property would not be termed as juridical possession. Therefore, any subsequent dispossession of such tenant would not give him the benefit of s. 6 of the Act.[2]

Any question pertaining to title or interest over the land cannot be gone into by the court in deciding the suit under s. 6 of the Specific Relief Act. As a matter of fact; the Court would not have any jurisdiction to entertain or decide any issues pertaining to title and interest over the land while deciding a suit filed under s. 6 of the Specific Relief Act.[3]

To sum up following principles can be culled out that govern the suit of a possessory title as contemplated under s. 6 of the Specific Relief Act:

18 *Roop Lalwani* v *Sunita Lalwani* (2014)4 HCC (Del) 130.
19 *Hakam Singh* v *Banta Singh* AIR 1989 NOC 10 (P&H).
20 *Nirjivandas Madhavdas* v *Mohomed Ali Khan Ibrahim Khan* ILR (1880)5 Bom 208.
1 *City Municipal Council, Bhalki by its Chief Officer* v *Gurappa* AIR 2015 SC 3826.
2 *K. Krishna* v A.N. *Paramkusha Bai* (2012)2 ICC 804 (AP).
3 *Narayan Chandra Dey* v *Swarnalatasonowal* (2015)3 Gau LR 474.

(1) That the plaintiff should be in prior possession of the suit property as prior possession is prima facie a proof of title.
(2) To maintain a possessory suit, title is immaterial and irrelevant.
(3) Such a suit is maintainable against a third party and not the person who claims himself to be the owner of the suit property.
(4) If it is filed against a person who claims itself as owner, the plaintiff has to establish a better title.
(5) Suit of possessory title has to be filed before the expiry of six months from dispossession.
(6) If a suit is filed after the expiry of six months it is obligatory upon the plaintiff to establish a better title.[4]

Defence in possessory suit When the suit is filed under s. 6 of the Act for possession, the sole consideration for the Court is possession. The scope of enquiry is thus limited to possession within six months immediately preceding the date of filing of the suit. In such a suit, the defendant cannot set up a defence of title in himself. The only defence that can legitimately be set up is antecedent possession.[5] It is no defence in such a suit that the plaintiff was in possession illegally, or that he did not have title, or that title vested with the defendants.[6]

Interim restoration The Court has ample power under s. 6 of the Specific Relief Act, to grant interim relief by directing to restore the possession which existed immediately before filing of the suit, i.e. before the alleged act of removal of unlawful means. It is true that there is no express provision of granting interim relief for recovery of possession. Section 6 of the Act provides for suit by person dispossessed of immovable property. It is a special and speedy remedy for a particular kind of grievance, viz. to replace in possession, a person who had been evicted from immovable property of which he had been in possession otherwise than by due process of law. The plaintiff is only required to prove his previous possession and if he succeeds in doing so, he would be entitled for a decree for restoration of possession from the defendant who has dispossessed him. The object is to check the tendency of recovery of possession of property by taking law in hand. Limitation for filing the suit is six months. In a case where there is sufficient material on record to show that the plaintiff was in previous possession and he has been dispossessed unlawfully, grave injustice would be caused if such a person is told that the Court is not competent to grant immediate interim relief by way of restoration of possession. The Court which has

4 *Jagmal v Municipal Corporation of Delhi* ILR (2003)1 Del 581.
5 *Kanakadhara Constructions v K. Jhansi Laxmi Bai* (2005)3 APLJ 206; (2006)39 AIC 957; (2005)6 ALD 805; (2005)6 ALT 679; (2006)1 CCC 138.
6 *Roop Lalwani v Sunita Lalwani* (2014)4 HCC (Del) 130.

ultimate power to pass decree for possession has necessarily power to give such relief by interim order unless it is prohibited. There is no prohibition under s. 6 of the Act to grant interim relief. The Apex Court in *Savitri* v *Govind Singh*[7] held that every Court must be deemed to possess by necessary intendment all such powers as are necessary to make its orders effective. It is of course true that such power is to be exercised by the Court with great care and caution and only in the rare and exceptional case. The plaintiff is required to show more than just *prima facie* case that he was in lawful possession of the subject premises just before he was evicted unlawfully. Thus, the court has power under s. 6 of the Act to grant interim relief by directing restoration of possession pending disposal of the suit.[8]

Without consent Section 6 of the Specific Relief Act has no application where the plaintiff had been dispossessed peacefully and with his consent.[9] Taking possession of the property of a limited company with the consent of the Directors and not with the consent of the company in its General Body Meeting, did not make the dispossession as one "without his consent" and therefore does not fall within this section.[10] In the same way, where after the lessor refused to extend the lease and sought to take possession at the termination of the lease and the lessee gave vacant possession by removing his things, the latter could not resort to proceed against him under s. 6 of the Specific Relief Act.[11] The act of dispossession and not the discontinuance of possession, if without consent, attracts s. 6 of the Act. Thus, where the tenant had given the premises to the landlord for the marriage of the landlord's son, s. 6 did not apply for recovery of the premises from the landlord.[12]

Otherwise than in due course of law A person is said to be dispossessed "otherwise than in due course of law" if he is dispossessed by another acting on his own authority and without the intervention of a court of law. The words "due course of law" are not merely equivalent to the word "legally", for a thing which is perfectly legal may still be by no means a thing done "in due course of law". For example, a quiet possession cannot be disturbed by force relying on terms in a lease deed drawn in conformity with the statutory provisions.[13] The expression "due course of law" means regular, normal process and effect of law operating on a matter which has been laid before it for adjudication which would ordinarily be by way of a civil suit

7 AIR 1986 SC 984.
8 *Ramesh Devchand Pala* v *Jayantkumar Gordhandas Madani* AIR 1998 Guj 120.
9 *Anant Bahadur Singh* v *Ashtabhuja Bax Singh* AIR 1960 All 227.
10 *Shri Onama Glass Works Ltd.* v *Ram Harak Pandey* AIR 1966 MP 282.
11 *Neyveli Lignite Corpn. Ltd.* v *K.S. Narayana Iyer* AIR 1965 Mad 122; *Chinna Pillai* v *Govindaswami Naidu* AIR 1969 Mad 191.
12 *Sukhjeet Singh* v *Sirajunnissa* AIR 2001 MP 59.
13 *Chinna Pillai* v *Govindasamy Naidu* AIR 1969 Mad 191.

including a process arising out of proceeding under this section. Possession obtained in execution proceedings.[14] Revenue proceedings or, for example, proceedings under s. 145, CrPC, would also be one in due course of law, but not where the person dispossessed was not a party to the proceedings.[15] Thus, where a landlord made a complaint in the tenant's absence to the Police seeking breaking open a locked demised premises alleging that some foul smell emitted from there, the Chief Judicial Magistrate permitted breaking open the locks and the Police handed back the premises to the landlord, it was held possession was taken by the landlord otherwise than in due course of law and the tenant was entitled to possession under this section.[16]

The courts in India have viewed with askance any process other than strict compliance of law as valid in dispossessing a person in occupation of immovable property against his consent. The reason is obvious that it aims to preserve the efficacy of law and peace and order in the society.[17]

Failure in possessory suit—remedy Section 6(3), Specific Relief Act interdicts an appeal against or review of an order or decree in possessory suit under s. 6(1) of the Act. But in view of s. 6(4) of the Act a regular title suit to recover possession is not barred. An order passed in execution of decree in a suit under s. 6, Specific Relief Act can also be challenged by a regular suit, there cannot be any bar to file a separate regular suit challenging an order in execution.[18]

Though no appeal lies against a decree in a suit under s. 6 of the Specific Relief Act, by virtue of s. 6(3) of the Act it has been held that the party aggrieved by the decree may seek revision by the High Court under s. 115, CPC.[19] Ordinarily, the High Court will not interfere in revision as there is remedy by way of a suit.[20] But the High Court may interfere in exceptional cases where the case is clear and the parties ought not to be driven to a regular suit, where the decree was contrary to s. 6 of the Specific Relief Act or where the suit under this provision was dismissed without trial under a misapprehension of the scope of the provision.[1] The High Court however

14 *Muralidhar* v *Jayanti Prasad* AIR 1932 All 703; *Sagar Mahila Vidyalaya* v *Pandit Sadasivarao Harshe* AIR 1991 SC 1825; (1991)2 SCR 906; (1991)3 SCC 588.

15 *LRs of Ganesh Mal* v *Velaram* AIR 2000 Raj 76.

16 *Bannasilal Kejrimal* v *Sajjan Kumar Jalam* AIR 2000 NOC 26 (Gau).

17 *East India Hotels Ltd.* v *Syndicate Bank* 1992 Supp (2) SCC 29.

18 *Jamaluddin* v *Asimullah* AIR 1974 All 69.

19 *Mahaboob Pasha* v *Viswanatha Chetty* AIR 1994 Kant 350.

20 *Subbarayadu* v *Pandivi Satyanandam* AIR 1933 Mad 609; *Anima* v *Ajay Kumar* (2000)4 SCC 119; 2000(10) SRJ 480; *City Municipal Council, Bhalki* v *Gurappa* AIR 2015 SC 3826.

1 *Neyveli Lignite Corporation Ltd.* v *Narayana Iyer* AIR 1965 Mad 122; *Chinna Pillai* v *Govindaswami Naidu* AIR 1969 Mad 191; *Kousalya* v *Padmanav Padhee* AIR 1987 Ori 28; *Mahaboob Pasha* v *Viswanatha Chetty* AIR 1994 Kant 350; *Ajodhiya Prasad Belihar Sao* v *Ghasiram Premsai Nai* AIR 1937 Nag 326.

will not re-appreciate the evidence in such a revision.[2] In *Vanitha M. Khanolkar* v *Pragna M. Pai*,[3] it was held that the statutory provisions contained in s. 6(3) of the Specific Relief Act barring an appeal, cannot cut across the constitutional power of the High Court. Even the power flowing from the paramount charter under which the High Court functions would not get excluded unless the statutory enactment concerned expressly excludes appeals from the Letters Patent. No such bar is discernible from s. 6(3) of the Act. It could not seriously be contended by the learned counsel for the respondents that if cl. 15 of the Letters Patent is invoked, the order would not be appealable. Consequently in Their Lordships' view on the clear language of cl. 15 of the Letters Patent which is applicable to the Bombay High Court, the appeal to the Division Bench was maintainable against the order passed by the learned single Judge of the High Court exercising original jurisdiction. In *East India Hotels Ltd.* v *Syndicate Bank*,[4] it was held by the Supreme Court that the remedy of judicial review under Art. 136 of the Constitution is plenary and is not hedged with the bar of appeal or review prescribed by s. 6 of the Specific Relief Act. The contention of the counsel for the respondents before the Supreme Court that it could not review the decision of the High Court was held to be *ex facie* desperate and was rejected.

In *Ashok Nagar Welfare Association* v *R.K. Sharma*,[5] an interesting case came up before Their Lordships of the Supreme Court. A suit under s. 6 of the Specific Relief Act was filed in the Original Side of the High Court of Delhi. It was found that ultimately care was not exercised by the concerned officer of the court in checking up whether summons were duly served and whether there was a case for effecting substituted service and whether the mandatory provisions as to the service of summons were complied with. The entire picture was not placed before the court which readily accepted the report of the Deputy Registrar and proceeded on the basis that service was complete and the defendant failed to respond to the summons. Consequently the learned Single Judge passed an *ex parte* decree. On appeal, the Division Bench of the High Court, after going through the above facts, set aside the *ex parte* decree. In the Special Leave Petition, the learned Judges of the Supreme Court held that if such a decree is allowed to remain it would have resulted in miscarriage of justice. They refused to shut their eyes on the ground realities and the factual events and declined to exercise their discretionary power under Art. 136 of the Constitution and interfere with the order of the Division Bench of the High Court.

2 *Padartha Amat* v *Siba Sahu* AIR 1993 Ori 92.
3 AIR 1998 SC 424; (1998)1 SCC 500; JT 1997(9) SC 490.
4 1992 Supp (2) SCC 29; JT 1991(6) SC 112.
5 (2000)8 Supreme 647.

In a case where the plaintiff has been dissatisfied with a decree under s. 6 of the said Act he could immediately institute a suit for declaration of his title and he could claim the available consequential relief. If he has been in possession of the suit property, all that he could pray for was that *status quo* be maintained and an injunction be issued restraining the defendant from dispossessing him.[6] The High Court of Calcutta in *Kalidas Mondal* v *Abdul Hossein*,[7] has held that the defeated party can bring a suit for declaration of his title and for recovery of possession and it is his duty in the subsequent suit to prove his title. If the plaintiff in the subsequent suit is in possession, that is, the decree passed in the earlier suit not yet having been executed against him, he can pray for maintenance of *status quo* and the court in the subsequent suit can pass an order restraining the defendants of the subsequent suit from disturbing the possession of the plaintiff in the said suit. However, in a suit which is filed on the basis of possessory title after the expiry of a period of six months, the defendant can defend himself by proving title and if he proves title, he could remain in possession.[8] However, the decree passed in a summary manner under sub-sec. (1) of s. 6 can be defeated by establishing the legal right of possession based on title over the suit property by filing the suit under sub-sec. (4) of s. 6 of the said Act seems to be the settled legal position.[9]

Distinction between a suit under s. 5 and a suit under s. 6 There is a distinction between a suit instituted under s. 5 and s. 6 of the Specific Relief Act 1963. The remedies available under the provisions of the aforesaid sections are mutually exclusive as in case of suit filed under s. 5 of the said Act, the plaintiff has to bring out a suit for recovery of possession based on title whereas a suit filed under s. 6 of the said Act requires the following conditions to concur namely; person should have been in possession in respect of the immovable property; there is a dispossession other than in due process of law; relief for recovery of possession and the suit must be brought within six months from the date of the dispossession.[10]

Section 5 provides that a person entitled to possession of specific immovable property may recover it in the manner provided by the Code of Civil Procedure that is to say, by a suit in ejectment on the basis of title. Section 6 provides for summary remedy to a person who has, without his

6 *Mohammad Hussain Suleman Shaikh* v *Batukbhai Valjibhai* AIR 1984 Guj 66; *Gouranga Chandra Deb* v *Satish Chandra Dev* AIR 1955 Tripura 13; *Laisram Noyon Singh* v *Miajan Mia* AIR 1969 Manipur 49.

7 (2003)3 CHN 1; (2004)13 AIC 668; (2003)3 ICC 118; Cal LT 2003(3) HC 253.

8 *Tirumala Tirupati Devasthanams* v *K.M. Krishnaiah* (1998)3 SCC 331; AIR 1998 SC 1132.

9 *Manoj* v *Chandrakishore* (2014)2 Mah LJ 758; (2014)1 Bom CR 657; (2014)2 AIR Bom R 599.

10 *Arati Ghosh* v *Kalpana Pathak* (2013)3 ICC 337 (Cal).

consent, been dispossessed of the immovable property otherwise than in due course of law, for recovery of possession without establishing his title provided that his suit is filed within six months from the date of the dispossession. A suit for possession based on title, although possessory title, is maintainable even after the suit under s. 6 is dismissed. The provisions of these two sections are not mutually exclusive. In *Nair Service Society* v *K.C. Alexander*[11] the plaintiff brought a suit for possession of lands alleging possession of the same for 70 years and forcible dispossession by the defendant. The defendant denied forcible dispossession and pleaded that a possessory suit after the expiry of six months was not possible under s. 9 of the Specific Relief Act 1877 (now s. 6). The High Court held in appeal that the plaintiff was in possession before the suit and could maintain a suit based on prior possession without proof of title and therefore could eject the defendant. On appeal, the Supreme Court upheld the decision of the High Court and held that the provisions of these two sections are not mutually exclusive. Hidayatullah, J (as he then was), who delivered the judgment, observed that s. 8 (now s. 5) of the Act did not limit the kinds of suits but only laid down that the Code of Civil Procedure must be followed. This is very different from saying that a suit based on possession alone is incompetent after the expiry of six months. If s. 9 (now s. 6) of the Specific Relief Act is utilized, the plaintiff need not prove title and the title of the defendant does not avail him. Where however the period of six months has lapsed, the question of title can be raised by the defendant and if he does so, the plaintiff must establish a better title or fail. In other words, the right is only restricted to possession only in a suit under s. 6, but does not bar a suit on prior possession within 12 years and the title need not be proved unless the defendant can prove one. The present amended Arts. 64 and 65 of the Limitation Act make the point clear. Article 64 enables a suit to be filed within 12 years from dispossession for possession of immovable property based on possession and not on title, when the plaintiff while in possession of the property had been dispossessed, and Art. 65 provides for a suit for possession of immovable property or any interest therein based on title. The amendment is not remedial but declaratory of the law. The same view has been taken by Their Lordships of the Supreme Court in *Somnath Barman* v *S.P. Raju*[12] independently of the case in *Nair Service Society* v *K.C. Alexander*.[13]

Recovery of possession The writ petition filed for recovery of possession under Art. 226 of the Constitution of India is not permissible, since the alternative remedy is available under s.6 of the Act and if the limitation period provided for the same expires, then the regular suit is the appropriate

11 AIR 1968 SC 1165; (1968)3 SCR 163.
12 AIR 1970 SC 846; (1970)2 SCR 869; (1969)3 SCC 129..
13 AIR 1968 SC 1165; (1968)3 SCR 163.

remedy for the purpose of recovery of possession.[14] Plaintiff claims to be a tenant of suit property but he fails to produce original copy of tenancy agreement. In such case rent receipts is not sufficient to establish prior possession of plaintiff. Landlord filed an eviction suit against heirs of original tenant but not against plaintiff. Plaintiff failed to prove his prior possession at the time of dispossession, he is not entitled to recover possession of suit property.[15]

Applicability of Art. 227 of the Constitution Section 6 of the Specific Relief Act creates a jurisdiction of a summary nature. The two basic elements on consideration of which the Court is required to exercise this jurisdiction are actual possession and the nature of the manner of dispossession. These are elements findings of which are bound to be findings of fact and as such, are not ordinarily liable to interference in exercise of revisional jurisdiction unless such interference is called for on satisfaction of well recognized ratios propounded by authoritative pronouncements. The finding of facts in a suit under s. 6 of the Act is not liable to interference ordinarily under Art. 227 of the Constitution of India.[16]

Construction after dispossession The jurisdiction of the Court under s.6 of the Act is not ousted by the wrong committed by the defendant. Thus, where the defendant after dispossessing the plaintiff in an illegal and forcible manner makes a construction in hasty manner that will not dislodge the plaintiff from invoking s. 6 of the Specific Relief Act and jurisdiction of the court under s. 6 cannot be ousted by the wrong of the defendant in the form of illegal and forcible construction. Otherwise, it would provide a tool in the hands of the defendant to forcibly occupy anybody's property and make a speedy construction. Thus, it cannot be said that in case if the construction is made on the subject-matter of the suit under s. 6 of the Specific Relief Act, the suit will have to be dismissed for want of jurisdiction.[17] Order to remove the construction so made by the defendant cannot be passed in a proceeding under s.6 of the Act.[18]

Second suit for mesne profit or damages Section 7 of the Specific Relief Act 1963 provides that a person entitled to the possession of specific movable property may recover it in the manner provided by the Code of Civil Procedure 1908. Provisions of ss. 6 and 7 of the Act are separate and if a suit is filed under s. 6 for restoration of possession within a period of six

14 *Shanker Tripathi* v *Deputy Inspector General of Police* (2005)61 ALR 82; 2005 All LJ 2814.
15 *Ramesh Chnd Koiri* v *Chandan Koiri* AIR 2018 Cal 314.
16 *In the matter of: Balaram Dey* v *Chaya Dey* (1993)1 CHN 12.
17 *Ramniwas Sharma* v *Jasoda Bai* (2010)87 AIC 489; (2010)2 CCC 319.
18 *Mahabir Prasad Jain* v *Ganga Singh* (1999)8 SCC 274; *Rahmatulla* v *Maftzuilla* AIR 1915 Cal 687.

months, then a second suit filed for claiming damages or *mesne profit* is neither barred by the principle of Or. II, r. 2 and nor barred on the principle of *res judicata* because the scope of two suits are quite different as under s. 6 of the Specific Relief Act a special kind of remedy has been provided under the law to the plaintiff to claim possession under special circumstances when he is dispossessed without following the due process of law. Therefore, the second suit for damages is not barred on the principle of Or. II, r. 2 of the CPC. Though Or. II, r. 2, CPC provides that all causes of action should be joined in one suit, yet this principle is not applicable where two suits of different nature have been filed under ss. 6 and 7 of the Specific Relief Act 1963.[19]

Recovery of specific movable properties Section 7 provides for the recovery of specific movable property by means of a suit under the Code of Civil Procedure. When the court decrees delivery of such property, the decree will also state the amount of money to be paid as an alternative if delivery cannot be had (Or. 20, r. 10 of Code of Civil Procedure). This does not prevent any person entitled to delivery of possession of movable property to sue only for its value. The court may also decree only the value of the property instead of ordering its delivery.

Recovery of specific or ascertained goods The Privy Council[20] held that an order of specific performance could not be made where the seller agreed to supply all the coal that might be required for the buyers' steel work, specific or "ascertained" goods. According to Atkin, LJ, in *Re Wait*[21] "probably means identified in accordance with the agreement after the time the contract of sale is made." In another case[22] the judge ruled that "ascertained" means that the individuality of the goods must be found out, and when it is, then the goods have been ascertained or specific. In England the equitable remedy of specific performance before the Sale of Goods Act 1979 was discretionary and a wide discretion is conferred on the court by s. 52 of the said Act. The discretion of the court relates to (*i*) whether or not to make an order of specific performance, (*ii*) type of goods in question, (*iii*) conduct of both buyer and seller, (*iv*) hardship which an order would inflict on the seller.[23]

Section 8 provides for delivery of specific movable property at the instance of the person entitled to immediate possession from the defendant having possession or control over it in four cases, *viz.*,

19 *Triloksingh* v *Shantilal* (2002)5 MPLJ 471.
20 *Dominion Coal Co. Ltd.* v *Dominion Iron & Steel Co. Ltd.* [1909]AC 293.
21 [1927]1 Ch 606 at p. 630.
22 *Thamas Sack & Bag Co. Ltd.* v *Knowles & Co. Ltd.* [1918]88 LJ KB 585.
23 Benjamin's *Sale of Goods*, 9th Ed., para 17-100.

(*a*) where the defendant holds it as the trustee or the agent of the plaintiff; or

(*b*) if compensation for its loss will not be an adequate relief; or

(*c*) if the actual damage caused by its loss is extremely difficult to ascertain; or

(*d*) when possession has been wrongly transferred from the plaintiff.

Proprietary claims to possession or damages Where the property in goods and right of possession of them has passed to the buyer, he may bring against the seller a proprietary action for goods under the law of torts, viz. proceedings for wrongful interference with the goods seeking an order for the specific delivery of goods or an action for damages for conversion when the seller's detention of goods amounts to denial of the buyer's title to them. In such a case the buyer is better advised to sue the seller for a contractual remedy rather than a remedy in tort, since a claim for certain consequential losses is easier to establish in contract and courts are unwilling to award the buyer a higher measure of damages if he sues in tort rather than in contract. The buyer, by virtue of his immediate right to possession of the goods, may bring a tortious action against a stranger for recovery of full value of the goods from a stranger who converts them by taking them wrongfully out of the possession of the seller.[24]

24 Benjamin's *Sale of Goods,* 9th Ed., para 17-105.

CHAPTER 3

Pre-emption

Introduction The law of pre-emption is, historically speaking, a product of custom of the Mohammedan world. The right of pre-emption was not recognized under the Hindu law.[1] It came to be enforced here after the advent of Mohammedan rule. But the Shia law does not recognize such right.[2] To start with, it was accepted as a part of custom and was applied by the courts, particularly in Northern India, accordingly. It received statutory recognition in s. 22 of the Hindu Succession Act 1956.[3] Literally speaking, the word pre-emption means "to have priority to offer of sale of property over others". Thus seen, right of priority to purchase neighbour's or partner's property can also be the creature of contracts apart from the legal right of pre-emption as conceived under the Mohammedan law. Such contractual right of pre-emption can come into existence under variety of circumstances. Every such contract, however, may not carry with it all the attributes of legal right of pre-emption or its incidents.[4] The right of pre-emption based on consanguinity has been variously described as 'feudal', 'piratical', 'tribal', 'weak', 'easily defeated', etc.[5] Fusing as it does the ties of blood and soil, it cannot be doubted that the right is antiquated and feudal in origin and in character.[6]

Pre-emption is a right of purchasing property before or in preference to other persons.[7] Pre-emption is the right to buy before others.[8] From this standpoint it is encompassed within Specific Relief.

1 *Bhau Ram* v *Baij Nath Singh* 1962 Supp (3) SCR 724; AIR 1962 SC 1476.
2 Mulla, *Principles of Mahomedan Law*, 21st Ed., §249, p. 337.
3 Per B. L. Hansaria, J in *Krishna* v *State of Haryana* (1994)4 SCC 703.
4 *Sunni Masjid and Madrassa Trust* v *Abdul Kadar Usuf Bhabha* 1979 Mah LJ 821.
5 *Kalwa* v *Vasakha Singh* AIR 1982 P&H 480; *Bishan Singh* v *Khazan Singh* AIR 1958 SC 838; 1959 SCR 878.
6 *Krishna Kumar Birla* v *Rajendra Singh Lodha* (2008)4 SCC 300.
7 *P. Jayabaskar* v *Saraswathi* 2000(1) CTC 334 (Mad).
8 Black's *Law Dictionary*, 10th Ed.

This is a right which the adjacent owner of an immovable property possesses to acquire by purchase another property sold to another person. Four classes of persons can claim pre-emption: (*a*) co-sharers in the property; (*b*) participators in easements; and (*c*) owners of adjacent immovable property; (*d*) bargadar under the W.B. Land Reforms Act. The right of pre-emption is in effect, as if in a sale deed the vendee's name is rubbed out and pre-emptor's name inserted in his place. So, in a decree or order of pre-emption direction to require pre-emptee to execute a sale deed in favour of pre-emptor is not called for.[9] Thus, succinctly speaking, the law of pre-emption imposes a limitation or disability upon the ownership of a property to the extent that it restricts the owner's unfettered right of sale and compels him to sell the property to his co-sharer or neighbour as the case may be.[10]

Right of pre-emption—object of It is common knowledge that the right of pre-emption is generally conferred on a co-sharer in the property or on a person who claims some right over the property, *e.g.* a right of way, etc. or on the ground of vicinage, *i.e.* being an owner of the adjoining property. This right may be founded in statute or custom or personal law by which the parties are governed. The sole object of conferring this right on a co-sharer or owner of an adjacent immovable property is to exclude strangers from acquiring interest in an immovable property as a co-sharer or to keep objectionable strangers away from the neighbourhood. This right is purely personal and cannot be transferred to a third party for the obvious reason that it would defeat the very purpose of its conferment.[11] The foundation of the right of pre-emption is the avoidance of the inconveniences and disturbances which would arise from the introduction of a stranger into the land.[12]

The primary object of the law of pre-emption is to prevent a stranger from acquiring property in any area which has been populated by a particular fraternity or class of people.[13]

Nature and scope of right of pre-emption According to Tayabji, the law of pre-emption is personal. It is not territorial, nor an incident of property. A person who is not a native of or domiciled within a locality where pre-emption is enforced by law or custom but who owns lands within the same locality will not necessarily be subject to the law of pre-emption.[14] But, where the statutory right of pre-emption attaches to land it is not a mere personal right.[15] Similarly, where a right of pre-emption is recognized by

9 *Teeja Devi* v *Noratmal* AIR 1976 Raj 95; 1975 Raj LW 269; 1975 WLN 332.
10 *Audh Behari Singh* v *Gajadhar Jaipuria* (1955)1 SCR 70; AIR 1954 SC 417.
11 *Bhoop alleged S/o Sheo* v *Matadin Bhardwaj S/o Lakmi Chand* AIR 1991 SC 373; *Zila Singh* v *Hazari* AIR 1979 SC 1066; (1979)3 SCC 265.
12 *Shri Audh Behari Singh* v *Gajadhar Jaipuria* (1955)1 SCR 70.
13 *Bhau Ram* v *B. Baijnath Singh* AIR 1962 SC 1476.
14 Tyabji's *Muhammadan Law*, p. 670, para 523(*e*).
15 *Bhagwan Das* v *Chet Ram* AIR 1971 SC 369.

statute, it has to be treated as mandatory and not discretionary and the proposition is well-settled by a five-Judge Bench of the Supreme Court in *Shyam Sunder* v *Ram Kumar.*[16] The relevant passage from *Shyam Sunder* (supra) is worth quoting here;

> "The right of pre-emption of a co-sharer is an incident of property attached to the land itself. It is some sort of encumbrance carrying with the land which can be enforced by or against the co-owner of the land. The main object behind the right of pre-emption, either based on custom or statutory law, is to prevent intrusion of a stranger into the family holding or property. A co-sharer under the law of pre-emption has right to substitute himself in place of a stranger in respect of a portion of the property purchased by him, meaning thereby that where a co-sharer transfers his share in holding, the other co-sharer has right to veto such transfer and thereby prevent the stranger from acquiring the holding in an area where the law of pre-emption prevails. Such a right at present may be characterized as archaic, feudal and outmoded but this was law for nearly two centuries, either based on custom or statutory law. It is in this background the right of pre-emption under statutory law has been held to be mandatory and not mere discretionary."

The pre-emptor who claims the right to pre-empt a sale on the date of sale must continue to possess that right till the date of decree. If he loses that right before the passing of the decree, the decree for pre-emption cannot be granted even though he had such right on the date of institution of the suit.[17] However, a right to claim pre-emption is not a right in the estate. It creates an interest in the property. It does not create an interest in succession. If such a right has been created by an agreement, the same can be enforced only in the event any contingency in that behalf takes place. A will is not a transfer for enforcement of a right of pre-emption under a contract. It must be enforced by a suit.[18] It is true that it is a personal right and is not capable of being transferred. And the right of pre-emption being a right of substitution, the vendor also cannot in the garb of a Benamidar pre-empt his own sale.[19] In *A. Razzaque Sajan Sahed Bagwan* v *Ibrahim*[20] the Supreme Court has held that the plaintiff's suit was decreed by the lower court on the ground that the plaintiff being a *Shafi-i-jar* was entitled to claim the right of pre-emption. But in some previous cases the Supreme Court held the law of pre-emption based on vicinage is void, thus the decree of the trial court was set aside denying the plaintiff's right of pre-emption. The object behind the right of pre-emption under ss. 26 and 27

16 (2001)8 SCC 24.

17 *Rikhi Ram* v *Ram Kumar* AIR 1975 SC 1869.

18 *Krishna Kumar Birla* v *Rajendra Singh Lodha* (2008)4 SCC 300.

19 *Sukhnandan Singh* v *Jamiat Singh* (1971)1 SCC 707; AIR 1971 SC 1158.

20 A. *Razzaque Sajan Sahed Bagwan* v *Ibrahim Haj Muhammed Hussain* AIR 1999 SC 2043.

of the Urban Land (Ceiling and Regulation) Act 1976 in favour of the State Government as to prevent concentration of urban land in the hands of a few well-to-do persons and to bring about equitable distribution of urban land amongst the common people. But any urban or urbanisable land with a building or a portion or such building which is within the ceiling area will be transferable without the constraints mentioned in sub-sec. (1) of s. 27 of the said Act.[1] Where the statute requires the court to make an independent valuation of the share transferred, the valuation should be on the basis of prevailing market price and variation in the market rate after transfer to the third party. The valuation should be fair to both the parties, the pre-emptor and the pre-emptee and not like fixing a relative value of different shares as is done in case of partition.[2]

As to the nature of the right of pre-emption the following principles are well settled: (1) The right of pre-emption is not a right to the thing sold or a right to the offer of a thing about to be sold. This right is called the primary or inherent right. (2) The pre-emptor has a secondary right or a remedial right to follow the thing sold. (3) It is a right of substitution but not of re-purchase, *i.e.* the pre-emptor takes the entire bargain and steps into the shoes of the original vendee. (4) It is a right to acquire the whole of the property sold or a share of the property sold. (5) Preference being the essence of the right the plaintiff must have a superior right to that of the vendee or the person substituted in his place. (6) The right being a very weak right it can be defeated by all legitimate methods, such as the vendee allowing the claim of a superior or equal right being substituted in his place.[3] In *Radhakrishnan Lakshminarayan Toshnival* v *Shridhar Ramachandra Alshi*,[4] the Supreme Court repelled the claim that the vendor and vendee by accepting price and transferring possession without registration of deed of sale adopted subterfuge to defeat the right of pre-emption and observed that "there were no equities in favour of a pre-emptor whose sole object is to disturb a valid transaction by virtue of the rights created in him by statute. To defeat the law of pre-emption by any legitimate means, is not fraud on the part of either the vendor or the vendee and a person is entitled to steer clear of the law of pre-emption by all lawful means". Such being the nature of the right, Their Lordships held that it was harsh to claim that its extinction by conduct would amount to statutory illegality or would be opposed to public policy.[5] Right of pre-emption is not a personal right on

1 *Maharao Saheb Bhim Singhji* v *Union of India* AIR 1981 SC 234.

2 *Subol Chandra Modak* v *Gostho Behari Das* 60 CWN 829.

3 *Bishan Singh* v *Khazam Singh* AIR 1958 SC 838; 1959 SCR 878; 1958 SCJ 1234; *Mahabir Prasad* v *Chanda Devi* AIR 1979 All 167; *Chandrup Singh* v *Dataram* AIR 1983 P&H 1; 1982 Rev LR 375; *Sundra* v *Harnam Singh* AIR 1983 P&H 25.

4 AIR 1960 SC 1368; (1961)1 SCR 248; (1961)1 SCJ 215.

5 *Indirabai* v *Nand Kishore* (1990)4 SCC 668; AIR 1991 SC 1055.

the part of the pre-emptor to get the re-transfer of the property from the vendee who has already become the owner of the same. It is true that the right of pre-emption becomes enforceable only when there is sale but the right exists antecedently to the sale, the foundation of the right being the avoidance of inconvenience and disturbance arising from introduction of stranger into the land. The correct legal position is that the statutory law of pre-emption imposes a limitation or disability upon the ownership of a property to the extent that it restricts the owner's right of sale and compels him to sell the property to the person entitled to pre-empt. In other words the statutory right of pre-emption though not amounting to an interest in the land is a right which attaches to the land and which can be enforced against a purchaser by the person entitled to pre-empt.[6]

Where the pre-emptor decree-holder deposits the purchase money within time, title in pre-emptional land accrues to him and assignment of his right in land by the decree-holder does not amount to transfer of mere decree and the assignee is entitled to invoke the decree and obtain possession in view of s. 146, Or. 20, r. 14 and Or. 21, r. 16, CPC.

The statutory right of pre-emption though does not amount to an interest in the land is a right which attaches to the land and can be enforced against the purchaser by the person entitled to pre-empt. Legal representatives therefore can continue the suit on the death of original pre-emptor.[7]

In *Bas Deo Rai* v *Jhagru Rai*[8] it was held that a contract of pre-emption falls within the second part of s. 40 of the Transfer of Property Act and that it can be enforced against all gratuitous transferees and even against transferees for consideration with notice. In *Ram Baran Prasad* v *Ram Mohit Hazra*[9] ruled that except where a contrary intention appears in a contract of pre-emption as in other contracts, assignability is the rule that where there is an assignment the benefit and obligation under the pre-emption agreement would pass to the representatives of the original parties, including the assignees or transferees, subject to the well-known exception that *bona fide* transferees for value without notice would not be affected by obligation. It was further held that the contract is enforceable under whether s. 23(*b*) or s. 27(*b*) of the Specific Relief Act 1877 and under this section [s. 40 of the Transfer of Property Act]. This decision has been affirmed by the Supreme Court in *Ram Baran Prasad* v *Ram Mohit Hazra*.[10]

6 *Zila Singh* v *Hazari* AIR 1979 SC 1066; (1979)3 SCC 265; (1979)3 SCR 222.
7 *Sampuran Singh* v *Jal Kaur* AIR 1973 P&H 320.
8 AIR 1924 All 400; ILR (1924)46 All 333.
9 AIR 1961 Cal 152.
10 AIR 1967 SC 744; (1967)1 SCR 293.

The nature of right of pre-emption was summarized in *Mool Chand* v *Ganga Jal*[11] in the following words:

(*i*) The right of pre-emption is not a right to the thing sold but a right to the offer of a thing about to be sold. This right is called the primary or inherent right.

(*ii*) The pre-emptor has a secondary right or a remedial right to follow the thing sold.

(*iii*) It is a right of substitution but not of repurchase, *i.e.* the pre-emptor takes the entire bargain and steps into the shoes of the original vendee.

(*iv*) It is a right to acquire the whole of the property sold and not a share of the property sold.

(*v*) Preference being the essence of the right, the plaintiff must have a superior right to that of the vendee or the person substituted in his place.

(*vi*) The right being a very weak right, it can be defeated by all legitimate methods, such as the vendee allowing the claimant of a superior or equal right being substituted in his place.

Right of pre-emption to co-sharers In a case under the Punjab Pre-emption Act 1913 the Supreme Court held that the right of pre-emption to a co-sharer is justified and *intra vires*. The court held that the right of pre-emption given to co-sharers is justified as the classification of co-sharers as a class by themselves for the purpose of vesting in them the right of pre-emption is reasonable. The right of pre-emption vested in tenant can also be easily sustained. There can be no denying that the movement of all land reform legislations has been towards enabling the tiller of the soil to obtain proprietary right in the soil so that he may not be disturbed from possession of the land and deprived of his livelihood by a superior proprietor. The right of pre-emption in favour of a tenant granted by the Act is only another instance of a legislation aimed at protecting the tenant. There can be no doubt that tenants form a distinct class by themselves and the right of pre-emption granted in their favour is reasonable and in the public interest.[12] Explaining the decision of *Atam Prakash's* case, the Supreme Court struck down clauses first, secondly and thirdly of s. 15(1)(*b*) of the Punjab Pre-emption Act 1913, as discriminatory and violative of Arts. 14 and 15 of the Constitution. Since the court found certain intrinsic contradictions in the list of relatives covered by those three clauses, it saw no justification for the classification contained in the said provision conferring a right based on consanguinity. At the same time it upheld the right conferred on co-sharers.

11 ILR (1930)11 Lah 258 (FB); AIR 1930 Lah 356.

12 *Atam Prakash* v *State of Haryana* AIR 1986 SC 859; (1986)1 Supreme 628.

Thus the purport of *Atam Prakash's* case was that while co-sharers were entitled to pre-empt, the enforcement of that right on certain kinsfolk based on the rule of consanguinity being a relic of the feudal past could not be tolerated. The court never intended to exclude any specified co-owners from the scope of clause fourthly of s. 15(1)(*b*) of the Punjab Pre-emption Act. Once enforcement of the right of pre-emption in favour of co-sharers was considered to be a reasonable restriction on the right to hold, acquire and dispose of property under Art. 19(1)(*f*) (since repealed and now Art. 300A of the Constitution) the same restriction was held to be valid when tested on the touchstone of Art. 14 or Art. 15 of the Constitution. It could not be said that the purport of the decision in *Atam Prakash's* case was to deny the right of pre-emption to those relative or relatives of the vendor or vendors who were specified in the erstwhile first three clauses of s. 15(1)(*b*) of even if they happen to be co-sharers. The expression 'other co-sharers' was used in the fourth clause of the said provision to ensure that no co-sharer was left out or omitted and not to deny the right to kinsfolk co-sharers covered by the preceding clauses. On a proper construction of clause fourthly after the preceding clauses were held to be unconstitutional the word 'other' preceding the word 'co-sharer' must be deemed to have become redundant.[13]

The right of pre-emption of a co-sharer is an incident of property attached to the land itself. It is some sort of encumbrance carrying with the land which can be enforced by or against the co-owner of the land. The main object behind the right of pre-emption, either based on custom or statutory law, is to prevent intrusion of a stranger into the family holding or property. A co-sharer under the law of pre-emption has right to substitute himself in place of a stranger in respect of a portion of the property purchased by him, meaning thereby that where a co-sharer transfers his share in holding, the other co-sharer has right to veto such transfer and thereby prevent the stranger from acquiring the holding in an area where the law of pre-emption prevails. Such a right at present may be characterized as archaic, feudal and outmoded but this was law for nearly two centuries, either based on custom or statutory law. It is in this background the right of pre-emption under statutory law has been held to be mandatory and not mere discretionary.[14] Co-sharers include brothers.[15]

Pre-emption—estoppel defeating right of pre-emption On referring to right of pre-emption under the Rajasthan Pre-emption Act 1966 the Supreme Court held that the right of pre-emption is a weak right and it can be

13 *Bhikha Ram* v *Ram Sarup* AIR 1992 SC 207; (1992)1 SCC 319; JT 1991(4) SC 199.

14 *Suresh Prasad Singh* v *Dulhin Phulkumari Devi* (2010)6 SCC 441; *Shyam Sunder* v *Ram Kumar* (2001)8 SCC 24.

15 *Karnail Singh* v *Anil Kumar* (1995)2 SCC 9.

defeated by estoppel. Even in Muslim law, which is the genesis of this right, as it was unknown to Hindu law and was brought in wake of Mohammedan rule, it is settled that the right of pre-emption is lost by estoppel and acquiescence. Estoppel is a rule of equity following out of fairness striking on behaviour deficient in good faith. It operates as a check on spurious conduct by preventing the inducer from taking advantage and assailing forfeiture already accomplished. It is invoked and applied to aid the law in administration of justice. But for it great many injustice may have been perpetrated.[16] Referring to the Rajasthan Pre-emption Act 1966 which requires a vendor to serve the notice on persons having right of pre-emption the Supreme Court held that failure to serve the notice as required under the Act does not render the sale made by the vendor in favour of vendee *ultra vires*. The approach that no estoppel could arise unless notice under s. 8 of the Act was given by the seller and pre-emptor should have had occasion to pay to tender price, ignores the fallacy that estoppel need not be specifically provided as it can always be used as a weapon of defence.[17]

Section 8(1) of the West Bengal Land Reforms Act 1955 provides *inter alia* that if a portion or share of a plot of land of a *raiyat* is transferred to any person other than a co-sharer of a *raiyat* in the plot of a land, the *bargadar* in the plot of land or any co-sharer of a *raiyat* in the plot of land may pre-empt the said portion or share of the plot of land transferred. A question arose whether a stranger transferee can be allowed to turn round and plead recitals of the notice of transfer is not correct or whether he would be estopped from so pleading. In *Mohini Mohan Mitra* v *Radha Sundari Dasi*[18] the transferee was held estopped from so pleading and providing that the property sold was not an occupancy holding when there was nothing to show that the landlord applying for pre-emption knew that the tenancy was not an occupancy holding. In that decision it was proved that the transferee made a representation of the fact that the tenancy was an occupancy holding and the petitioners acted on the faith of this representation.

In *Malati Bala Deb Gupta* v *Narendra Chandra Bhattacharjee*,[19] it is said that a transferee is estopped from denying the truth of the recitals of the notice, but plea of estoppel can be defeated if it is shown that the pre-emptor had knowledge of the real state of affairs and the notice did not mislead him. All the cases having been considered in *Shiromoni Prosad Bhakat* v *Raghunandan Prasad Shaw*[20] it has been laid down in order to find

16 *Indira Bai* v *Nand Kishore* AIR 1991 SC 1055; (1990)4 SCC 668; JT 1990(4) SC 163.
17 *Indira Bai* v *Nand Kishore* (ibid).
18 AIR 1935 Cal 481; 39 CWN 1014.
19 AIR 1944 Cal 253; 48 CWN 269; *Sankaracharya Mullick* v *Sk. Sudemani* 49 CWN 580.
20 (1954)58 CWN 612.

an estoppel against a person it must be proved that a representation was made by the person sought to be estopped and that the person seeking to raise the plea acted on the faith of the representation and did so to his prejudice. So, in order to estop the transferee it must be shown that notice under s. 5 of the W.B. Land Reforms Act 1955 contained a representation by the transferee.

All these decisions were referred to in a later Full Bench case.[1] It has been held that a vendee-pre-emptee is estopped from disputing the nature of tenancy and is debarred from contending that the tenancy is else that what has been stated in the notice of transfer, because, purchaser being vitally interested in the transfer it must be presumed that he gave the notice. On this ground the Full Bench distinguished *Shiromoni Prosad's* case. In view of the pronouncement by the Full Bench, it is submitted *Shiromoni Prosad's* case is no longer a good law.

Pre-emption under W.B. Land Reforms Act on transfer of a part of plot of land
Section 8, W.B. Land Reforms Act 1955 deals with right of pre-emption when a part or share of a plot of land is transferred to one who is not a co-sharer of the plot of land.

Section 8 of the W.B. Land Reforms Act stands as follows:

> 8. *Right of purchase by co-sharer or contiguous tenant.* (1) If a portion or share of a plot of land of a *raiyat* is transferred to any person other than a co-sharer of a *raiyat* in the plot of land, the *bargadar* in the plot of land may, within three months of the date of such transfer, or any co-sharer of a *raiyat* in the plot of land may, within three months of the service of the notice given under sub-sec. (5) of s. 5, or any *raiyat* possessing land adjoining such plot of land may, within four months of the date of such transfer, apply to the Munsif having territorial jurisdiction, for transfer of the said portion or share of the plot of land to him, subject to the limit mentioned in s. 14-M, on deposit of the consideration money together with a further sum of ten per cent of that amount:
>
> Provided that if the *bargadar* in the plot of land, a co-sharer of a *raiyat* in a plot of land and a *raiyat* possessing land adjoining such plot of land apply for such transfer, the *bargadar* shall have the prior right to have such portion or share of the plot of land transferred to him, and in such a case, the deposit made by others shall be refunded to them:
>
> Provided further that where the *bargadar* does not apply for such transfer and a co-sharer of a *raiyat* in a plot of land and a *raiyat* possessing land adjoining such plot of land both apply for such transfer, the former shall have the prior right to have such portion or share of the plot of land transferred to him, and in such a case, the deposit made by the latter shall be refunded to him:

1 *Chaitanya Charan Nayak* v *Manik Chandra Nandy* AIR 1972 Cal 520 followed in *Brojendra Nath Mondal* v *Sushil Kr. Sana* (1984)2 Cal LJ 275.

Provided also that as amongst *raiyats* possessing lands adjoining such plot of land preference shall be given to the *raiyat* having the longest common boundary with the land transferred.

(2) Nothing in this section shall apply to—

(*a*) a transfer by exchange or by partition, or

(*b*) a transfer by bequest or gift, or *hiba-bil-ewaz*, or

(*c*) a mortgage mentioned in s. 7, or

(*d*) a transfer for charitable or religious purposes or both without reservation of any pecuniary benefit for any individual, or

(*e*) a transfer of land in favour of a *bargadar*, in respect of such land if after such transfer, the transferee holds as a *raiyat* land not exceeding one acre (or 0.4047 hectare) in area in the aggregate.

Explanation. All orders passed and the consequences thereof under ss. 8, 9 and 10 shall be subject to the provisions of Chapter II-B.

(3) Every application pending before a Revenue Officer at the commencement of s. 7 of the West Bengal Land Reforms (Amendment) Act 1972 shall, on such commencement, stand transferred to, and disposed of by, the Munsif having jurisdiction in relation to the area in which the land is situated and on such transfer every such application shall be dealt with from the stage at which it was so transferred and shall be disposed of in accordance with the provisions of this Act, as amended by the West Bengal Land Reforms (Amendment) Act 1972.

Section 2(6), W.B. Land Reforms Act [since substituted by the W.B. Land Reforms (Amendment) Act 2000] proves that 'holding' means land or lands held by a *raiyat*. In view of s. 2(7) of the Act land encompasses within itself land of every description whether agricultural or non-agricultural. So, s. 8, W.B. Land Reforms Act operates whenever any part or share of agricultural or non-agricultural land is transferred to a stranger.

The first proviso to s. 8(1) provides that in case of competition among a *bargadar* in the plot of land, co-sharer of a *raiyat* and a contiguous tenant for pre-emption, the right to pre-empt of the *bargadar* shall prevail over that of others. The second proviso provides that if no *bargadar* in the plot of land does apply and the competition is confined between a co-sharer of a *raiyat* and *raiyat* of contiguous land, the claim of co-sharer of a *raiyat* shall prevail over the claim of contiguous *raiyat*. The third proviso provides that in case of competition between two contiguous tenants the claim of the tenant having longest common boundary shall prevail over the claim of the other. It is significant that a contiguous tenant is not under any disability in enforcing the right of pre-emption even when the transferee himself is another contiguous tenant even with common boundary longer than that of the applicant. Thus in *Narayan Ch. Ghosh* v *Sanat Kumar Das,*[2] A purchased

2 (1975)2 Cal LJ 79; AIR 1975 Cal 290.

a portion of the plot of land adjoining his land. *B* also held lands adjoining the transferred land and he applied for pre-emption. *A* resisted the claim on the ground that he having adjoining lands with longer common boundary the pre-emption application must fail, S. Dutt, J held that the second proviso does not contemplate a transfer to a person who is already a *raiyat* possessing adjoining lands. It contemplates two rival applicants for pre-emption on the ground of vicinage. So, when a *raiyat* possessing adjoining lands is also a transferee of a portion of a plot of land he cannot resist an application for pre-emption by another *raiyat* holding lands adjoining the disputed lands.

In *Ishan Chandra Ghatak* v *Sashadhar Maity*[3] *T*, a co-sharer *raiyat* in respect of a *jama* consisting of several plots of land including plot No. 579 sold his share in plot No. 579 to *S*. *I* filed an application for pre-emption on the plea that he had lands adjoining the plot of land, a portion of which was sold to *T*. The application was allowed although petitioner's land and land sold was intervened by some portion of land of plot No. 579 because a holding may include only one plot and also several plots. For the success of a pre-emptor on the ground of vicinage it is enough if he owns land contiguous to holding—not necessarily to the very plot sold. A view different from the one expressed in *Narayan Chandra Ghosh's* case has been taken in *Saranan Mondal* v *Bijoy Bhusan Ghosh*[4] laying down that the second proviso to s. 8 would also apply to a case when the pre-emptee and the pre-emptor both are possessing adjoining lands. In effect *Saranan Mondal's* case lays down that (*a*) when pre-emption is applied for on the ground of vicinage, and (*b*) the pre-emptee himself is an owner having longer common boundary than that of the pre-emptor, then the pre-emption application on the ground of vicinage would fail. The pre-emption application in *Saraman Mondal's* case, however, failed as it did not disclose that only a share or portion of the holding (now plot of land) was sold. The observation in respect of the scope of the third proviso to s. 8 was in the nature of obiter observation.

In *Ardhendu Bhusan Haldar (dead) by LRs* v *Smt. Ganga Muni Mondal*[5] Their Lordships were dealing with the right of a pre-emptor under the West Bengal Estates Acquisition Act 1953. A co-owner of a holding sold identifiable plots to two persons under different deeds of sale. Both the transferees acquired title to their identifiable plots and were no co-sharers with their transferor. When the co-owners of the holding sold a third plot to a third person, the transferees of the two earlier plots were held not entitled to claim any right of pre-emption against the third transferor.

Pre-emption sought for exceeding the ceiling limit A question may arise as to whether the court can allow an application for pre-emption where it exceeds

3 (1977)1 Cal LJ 398; AIR 1978 NOC 194 (Cal); 82 CWN 182.
4 AIR 1979 Cal 174.
5 AIR 1990 SC 2240; 1990 Supp (1) SCR 527; (1991)1 SCC 270.

the ceiling limit as provided under s.14M of the West Bengal Land Reforms Act 1955. There was divergence of opinions on this point in different cases. However, the controversy was set at rest by a Division Bench judgment of Calcutta High Court in *Ismail Saikh* v *Fosiuddin Mondal*.[6] It was held by the High Court in *Ismail Saikh* (supra), that the *Munsif* (Civil Court) [now Civil Judge (Junior Division)] is not required to determine the ceiling before making an order of pre-emption. The ratio laid down in *Ismail Saikh* (supra) has been relied upon by Calcutta High Court in *Ayub Khan* v *Mahadeb Dolui*.[7]

Composite application and single deposit for pre-emption by two or more adjoining raiyats In *Sadhan Chandra Samanta* v *Jaladhi Bala*[8] two contiguous *raiyats* made a joint application for pre-emption to pre-empt sale in respect of an adjoining land. They also made a single deposit. Two points were raised, first whether such a joint application is tenable or not; secondly if single deposit by both was tenable. The trial court allowed the application of the contiguous *raiyat* having longest common boundary. Rejecting the objections the High Court held that even if separate applications under s. 8 were filed it would have been necessary to try them analogously. So, joint application by both entails no misjoinder of parties. As to single and composite deposit by both, the court also upheld the same relying on an earlier Division Bench case.[9] Dealing with the self-same issue of seeking right of pre-emption based on a composite application for six separate deeds, it was held that a single composite application under s. 8 of the West Bengal Land Reforms Act 1955, is maintainable in respect of six separate deeds pertaining to the same plot of land executed on various dates, by virtue of the said deeds of sale/transfer being registered on a single date.[10]

Contiguous raiyat or bargadar of different district—pre-emption by Prior to the amendment in the West Bengal Land Reforms Act 1955 in 2000 the concept of 'holding of a *raiyat*' was in vogue. As amended by s. 26(1)(*a*) of the West Bengal Land Holding Revenue Act 1979, the meaning of the term 'holding of a *raiyat*' was 'land or lands held by a *raiyat*' under s. 2(6) of the West Bengal Land Reforms Act 1955. However, it created problem when a *raiyat* was found to have possessed land in different districts of West Bengal, since the definition of 'holding of a *raiyat*' meant land possessed by such *raiyat* in different districts in West Bengal would be taken together to constitute a holding. This position of law with regard to 'holding of a *raiyat*'

6 AIR 1982 Cal 146; (1982)1 CHN 68.
7 (2013)3 CHN 195 (Cal).
8 (1986)1 Cal LJ 170.
9 *Sadhan Ch. Samanta* v *Jaladhi Bala* (1986)1 Cal LJ 170 relying on *Jyotish Ch. Sardar* v *Hiralal Sardar* ILR (1971)1 Cal 213.
10 *Jagannath Dhali* v *Ram Chandra Mandal* AIR 2010 Cal 32.

was criticised by the High Court of Calcutta in *Devendra Nath Karak* v *Rekha Pal*,[11] while dealing with a pre-emption application. The High Court observed:

> "The effect of the amendment is that whether the lands or land held by a *raiyat* can be treated as a unit for assessment of revenue or not, such land or lands will constitute a holding. As for instance, a *raiyat* may have lands in different districts in West Bengal. All his land taken together will constitute a holding".

Similar view was expressed in *Sk. Daiyan Ali* v *Sk. Sekabat Ali*.[12] Thus, if a *raiyat* holds one plot of land in Malda and another plot in Midnapore, both the plots will constitute one holding. So, if a land at Malda is transferred to a stranger of the holding, any *raiyat* having land contiguous to transferor's Midnapore land may invoke the right of pre-emption on the ground of vicinage.

Then again if a *raiyat* has two plots in the district of Malda and one in Bankura all the three plots would constitute one holding, if one Malda-plot is transferred and one *raiyat* having land contiguous to another Malda-plot and another *raiyat* having land contiguous to the Bankura-plot apply for pre-emption and if Bankura plot-holder has longer common boundary than that of Malda plot-holder, then the Bankura-*raiyat*'s claim will prevail in respect of the Malda-plot over the Malda-*raiyat*. Following the same analogy a *bargadar* of different district but in respect of land held by the same *raiyat* may also apply for pre-emption to pre-empt sale in different district whatsoever. For, holding means land or lands held by a *raiyat*. Such lands may situate in different districts. A *bargadar* cultivating land in *A* district can justly be called *bargadar* in the holding, when part of the holding is situate in *B* district.

Therefore, the need was to make necessary amendment in the West Bengal Land Reforms Act 1955 so far as the concept of 'holding' was concerned. The Legislature amended the West Bengal Land Reforms Act 1955 by way of the West Bengal Land Reforms (Amendment) Act 2000 by which the definition of holding was omitted in s. 2(6) of the Act and it was replaced by 'plot of land'. Corresponding amendment was also made in s. 8 of the Act. Thus, after the amendment the right to pre-emption under s. 8 of the Act would be maintainable only when a portion or share of a plot of land of a *raiyat* is transferred to a person other than the co-sharer of a *raiyat* in the plot of land. Thus, now the controversy has been set at rest as the court would not be required to apply the principle of 'holding of a *raiyat*' as it was done away with by the West Bengal Land Reforms (Amendment) Act 2000 with retrospective effect from 7th August 1969.[13]

11 90 CWN 22.
12 Cal LT 1996(2) HC 9.
13 *Sarafat Ali* v *Hossain Ali Mollah* (2002)4 CHN 285.

It may be recalled that according to the phraseology of s. 8, West Bengal Land Reforms Act if any portion or share of a plot of land is transferred to any *raiyat* possessing land adjoining such plot of lands he may apply for pre-emption.

It is the contiguity of the land or pre-emptor, to the plot of land which is material, not whether the pre-emptor's land is contiguous to the transferred land constituting the share or portion of the plot of land.

Adjoining raiyats two or more—effect When a share or portion of a plot of land governed by the W.B. Land Reforms Act is transferred a *raiyat* possessing land adjoining the disputed plot of land can invoke the right of pre-emption under s. 8(1), W.B. Land Reforms Act. The word "a" preceding the collocation of words "*raiyat* possessing land adjoining such plot of land" may be kept in view. The English word "a" also means any. The word "a" has varied meanings and uses. "A" means "one" or "any", but less emphatically than either. It may mean one where only one is intended, or it may mean any one of a great number.

So, if an adjoining plot of land is held by two co-sharer *raiyats* any one of them may invoke the right of pre-emption without impleading the other.

It would be evident from the provision itself that any *raiyat* possessing land adjoining to such plot of land would definitely envisage that any of the co-sharers or any of the *raiyats* having adjoining land and in cases, more than one person being co-owners or co-*raiyats* being adjoining owners can apply under section of the W.B.L.R. Act. Keeping in mind, the purpose and object of ss. 8 and 9 of the W.B.L.R. Act, it is obvious that the provision under s. 13(2) of the General Clauses Act 1897[14] would also have application in the present context.[15]

As to order of pre-emption under s. 8, W.B. Land Reforms Act usually there is no order for delivery of possession to successful pre-emptor. When its predecessor provision in s. 26F, Bengal Tenancy Act 1885 contained categorically a provision to the effect: the court on further application of such applicant or applicants (*i.e.* successful pre-emptor) may place him or them in possession of the property vested in them (*i.e.* the property pre-empted) in s. 26F(7)(*c*), B.T. Act, alike provision is absent in s. 8, W.B. Land Reforms Act. But, it is submitted it entails no change in legal position. For, in view of Or. 20, r. 14(1)(*b*), CPC the executing court should read the mandate of delivery of possession in every order under s. 8, W.B. Land Reforms Act. An order under s. 8, W.B. Land Reforms Act conclusively determines the rights of the parties and therefore is a decree.

14 Section 13(2) of the General Clauses Act 1897 provides that words in the singular shall include the plural, and *vice versa*.

15 *Nasiruddin Sk.* v *Mahasin Ali Khan* (2016)1 Cal LJ 352; (2016)1 CHN 147.

Pre-emption of portion or share of family of undivided dwelling-house
Section 44, Transfer of Property Act does not give a stranger transferee of a dwelling-house belonging to an undivided family a right to joint possession and confers a corresponding right on the other members of the family to deny the right to joint possession to a stranger transferee. Section 4 of the Partition Act is complementary to s. 44, Transfer of Property Act.[16]

Section 4(1) of the Partition Act reads as follows:

> Where a share of a dwelling-house belonging to an undivided family has been transferred to a person who is not a member of such family and such transferee sues for partition, the court shall, if any member of the family being a shareholder shall undertake to buy the share of such transferee, make a valuation of such share in such manner as it thinks fit and direct the sale of such share to such shareholder, and may give all necessary and proper directions in that behalf.

Explaining the scope of s. 4(1) of the Partition Act the Supreme Court held that s. 4(1) of the Partition Act gives a right to a member of the family whose co-sharer has transferred his share, to purchase the transferee's share on a value to be fixed in accordance with law when the transferee filed a suit for partition. But these are valuable rights to the members of the undivided family whatever may be the object or purpose for which they were conferred on such members.[17]

Section 4 of the Partition Act deserves a liberal construction so that its provisions may be applied in such a way as would promote and fulfil the object of the Act, which is to preserve the integrity of the undivided family of the dwelling-house and to enable the members of the family to keep it for themselves as far as possible.[18]

However, giving a liberal interpretation does not mean that the wordings of the section and the clear interpretation thereof be ignored. The relevant wordings are "dwelling-house belonging to an undivided family". Thus it must be a dwelling- house belonging to an undivided family. The further requirement is that the transfer must be to a person who is not a member of "such family". The words "such family" necessarily refers to the undivided family to whom the dwelling-house belongs.[19]

Even if at the time of institution of suit there is one member of the undivided family having an interest in the property which is the

16 *Dorab Cawasji Warden* v *Coomi Sorab Warden* AIR 1990 SC 867 (868); JT 1990(1) SC 199.
17 *Dorab Cawasji Warden* v *Coomi Sarab Warden* (ibid).
18 *Satyabhama De* v *Jatindra Mohan Deb* AIR 1929 Cal 269; *Abu Isha Thakur* v *Dinabandhu Banik* AIR 1947 Cal 426; 51 CWN 639; *Botokrishna Ghosh* v *Akshoy Kumar Ghosh* AIR 1950 Cal 111; 54 CWN 660; *Sunil Kumar* v *Provash Chandra* AIR 1969 Cal 88.
19 *Gautam Paul* v *Debi Rani Paul* (2000)8 SCC 330; AIR 2001 SC 61.

dwelling-house of the undivided family, he has the right to pre-empt under s. 4, Partition Act.[20]

But expressing a different view it has been held that an application under s. 4, Partition Act is not maintainable by a person who at the date of the institution of partition suit is the sole surviving member of the undivided family which owned the property and owned a share in the dwelling-house concerned.[1]

Invocation of s. 4, Partition Act by a co-sharer as a defendant Section 4 of the Partition Act applied not only in the case of a suit by the stranger-purchaser as plaintiff but also, to a case, where the said stranger-purchaser was sued as a defendant for partition.[2] Following these decisions it was held that in a suit filed by a member of the family it cannot be said that the stranger-purchaser being a defendant in a suit for partition, the provision of s. 4 can have no application. The prayer of the defendant to purchase the share of the plaintiff being a major shareholder not being a prayer within the meaning of s. 2 of the Act, certainly s. 3 could not be invoked regarding the claim of pre-emption. Though the plaintiff was not entitled to purchase the share of the defendant under s. 3 he was entitled to pre-empt, the said share under s. 4.[3]

That was the view of Calcutta High Court consistently followed as pointed out in the case.[4] But a note of dissent was introduced in *Netai Das* v *Hari Das*.[5] In this case the Division Bench pointed out that the view of Calcutta High Court was different from not only the views of Bombay and Madras High Court but also from the view expressed by the Allahabad High Court in the case of *Sakhwat Ali* v *Ali Hossain*.[6] In *Netai Das's* case (*supra*) learned judges observed that in order to attract s. 4 of the Partition Act "it must appear to the court that the stranger-transferee has claimed or is claiming partition and separate allotment", and that application of the said section in a case in which the stranger-transferee does not claim or is not claiming partition and separate allotment is unwarranted by the language of the statute. The question ultimately was referred to a Special Bench of Calcutta

20 *Mohiddin Molla* v *Jitendra Nath Karmakar* AIR 1976 Cal 288.

1 *Durgapada Pal* v *Debidas Mukherjee* 77 CWN 734.

2 *Abu Isha Thakur* v *Dinabandhu Banik* AIR 1947 Cal 426; 51 CWN 639; *Haradhone Halder* v *Usha Charan Karmakar* AIR 1953 Cal 292; 96 Cal LJ 168; *Sunil Kumar* v *Provash Chandra* AIR 1969 Cal 88.

3 *Bholanath* v *Sailendra Nath* AIR 1984 Cal 319 at p. 320; (1983)2 CHN 383; (1983)2 Cal LJ 235; 88 CWN 228.

4 *Surendranath Achar* v *Ramchandra Hazra* 75 CWN 195 (see the last part of this heading where on referring to an observation of Supreme Court, the propriety of this view has been questioned.)

5 ILR (1967)2 Cal 301.

6 AIR 1957 All 366 (FB).

High Court where it was held that right of pre-emption under s. 4, Partition Act is available to a co-sharer of an undivided family dwelling-house when he himself files a suit for partition and the stranger-purchaser is arraigned as defendant and irrespective of the fact whether the stranger-purchaser has actually applied for partition or for separate allotment of his share or not. The parties in the suit being interchangeable the right to claim separate allotment is germane in any party be he the plaintiff or the defendant.[7]

The right to relief is not confined to a suit by stranger-transferee. But it is available even in a suit for partition filed by a member for the family.[8]

Expressing a contrary view Allahabad High Court held that s. 4 of the Partition Act does not apply to a suit by a member of the family for possession against a transferee in possession.[9] In this connection it is apposite to extract a few lines from the judgment of Supreme Court which go to suggest that s. 4 can be invoked only when the stranger-transferee has filed a suit for partition. The law declared by the Supreme Court in view of Art. 141, Constitution becomes the law of the land and is binding of all subordinate courts. The Supreme Court has observed "Section 4 of the Partition Act gives a right to a member of the family who has not transferred his share to purchase the transferee's share on a value to be fixed in accordance with law *when the transferee filed a suit for partition.*"[10]

The last words under *italics* above are eloquent enough to show that the apex court meant that s. 4, Partition Act can be invoked if a stranger-transferee sues for partition and not when a co-sharer family member sues for partition and the stranger-transferee figures as a defendant. If the aforesaid words at p. 877, para 25, R.H.C. of the AIR are taken to be the law declared by the Supreme Court it is respectfully submitted that Calcutta and Orissa High Court's views stand superseded and the Allahabad Full Bench view prevails. The High Court at Calcutta tried to interpret the word "sue" in the collocation of words "such transferee sues for partition" as including "to defend". But the apex court by using the words "transferee filed a suit" has scotched that approach.

To sum up the Supreme Court observed that s. 44 of the Transfer of Property Act adequately protects the family members against intrusion by an outsider into the dwelling-house. The only manner in which an outsider can get possession is to sue for possession and claim separation of his share. In that case s. 4 of the Partition Act comes into play. Except for s. 4 of the

7 *Siba Prasad* v *Bibhuti Bhusan* AIR 1989 Cal 35 at p. 40; 92 CWN 513; (1988)1 CHN 1.

8 *Tajpal Khandelwal* v *Purnima Bai* AIR 1976 Ori 62; ILR (1975) Cut 1231; (1975) Cut WR 929.

9 *Sakhawat Ali* v *Ali Hossain* AIR 1957 All 366 (FB).

10 *Dorab Cawasji Warden* v *Coomi Sorab Warden* AIR 1990 SC 867; (1990)1 SCR 332; (1990)2 SCC 117.

Partition Act there is no other law which provides a right to a co-sharer to purchase the share sold to an outsider. Thus before the right of pre-emption, under s. 4, is exercised the conditions laid down therein have to be complied with. One of the conditions is that the outsider must sue for partition. Section 4 does not provide the co-sharer a right to pre-empt where the stranger/outsider does nothing after purchasing the share. In other words, s. 4 is not giving a right to a co-sharer to pre-empt and purchase the share sold to an outsider anytime he/she wants. However, a mere assertion of a claim to a share without demanding separation and possession (by the outsider) is not enough to give to the other co-sharers a right of pre-emption. There is a difference between a mere assertion that he has a share and a claiming for possession of that share. So long as the stranger-purchaser does not seek actual division and possession, either in the suit or in execution proceedings, it cannot be said that he has sued for partition.[11] At the same time, it is not necessary that the stranger-purchaser must file a suit. Even if he moves an execution application for separating his share by metes and bounds, it would be treated to be an application for partition and separate possession.[12] Section 4 of the Partition Act can be pressed into service in a case where final decree has not been passed or even when the final decree has been passed but possession on the basis of such final decree has not been delivered in execution of the final decree for partition.[13]

Undivided dwelling-house belonging to a family The terms "undivided family" and "dwelling-house" in both s. 4 of the Partition Act and s. 44 of the Transfer of Property Act bear the same meaning. The expression undivided stands *qua* the dwelling-house. The family may be divided but in the absence of a document, evidencing partition of the suit house by metes and bounds and on the documentary evidence showing that the property is held by the family co-sharers it must be held that the pre-emptor has shown a *prima facie* case that the dwelling-house belonged to an undivided family consisting of the petitioner himself and his co-sharers. And the petitioner can invoke s. 4 of the Partition Act.[14]

The expression "dwelling-house belonging to an undivided family" in s. 4 means family not divided *qua* dwelling-house. The essence of the matter is that the house itself should be undivided even though the co-sharers have defined shares. As long as there is a dwelling-house which has not been divided *qua* the family it might be said to be a dwelling-house belonging to an undivided family for the purpose of s. 4.[15]

11 *Gautam Paul* v *Debi Rani Paul* (2000)8 SCC 330.
12 *Babu Lal* v *Habibnoor Khan* (2000)5 SCC 662; AIR 2000 SC 2684.
13 *Subhas Mukherjee* v *Ashok Kr. Roy* (1999)2 CHN 261. See also *Ghanteswar Ghosh* v *Madan Mohon Ghosh* AIR 1997 SC 471.
14 *Dorab Cawasji Warden* v *Coomi Sorab Warden* (supra).
15 *Nirupoma Basak* v *Baidyanath Pramanick* AIR 1985 Cal 406.

Once the disputed property is held to be an undivided family dwelling-house partial occupation of the house by tenants would not divest the same of the character of an undivided family dwelling-house.[16] In *Satyendra Kundu* v *Amar Nath Ghosh*[17] the entire two-storeyed house comprising two bed rooms and one small room on each floor excepting one room was given away in tenancy. In *Dulal Chandra Chatterjee* v *Gostha Behari Mitra*[18] the entire house was let out to a tenant and the family shifted elsewhere. In both the cases it was held that the house did not cease to be a dwelling-house. Demise *ipso facto* would not forfeit the character although a permanent lease may forfeit. The test is whether there is still the scope or opportunity of the demised portion being used as a homestead, if necessary, and the further test is whether the co-sharers have finally abandoned the intention to occupy the property as a dwelling-house.[19]

Pre-emption application—averments needed A petition under s. 4, Partition Act should not be read with microscopic scrutiny but in a broader manner. If so read it will be enough if there are averments in the petition to satisfy the requirements of s. 4 of the Partition Act.

Waiver of right of pre-emption for co-sharer's not objecting to sale to stranger Waiver means an intentional relinquishment of known right. Since the right of pre-emption under s. 4 accrues to a co-sharer of the undivided dwelling-house only after a partition suit is filed by the stranger-purchaser, it cannot be said to have been waived after a sale of a share to a stranger-purchaser. Therefore, where a co-sharer transferred his undivided share in the dwelling-house to a stranger-purchaser and the other co-sharers declined to purchase the said share, though it was offered to them before it was purchased by the stranger, and they did not object to the possession of the said share by the stranger the disinclination on the part of the other co-sharers to purchase the share of the co-sharer and their non-objection to the possession of the same by the stranger-purchaser, which were earlier to the filing of the partition suit by the stranger-purchaser, do not amount to a waiver of the right of pre-emption under s. 4 by the other co-sharers which arose upon filing of the partition suit by the stranger-purchaser.[20]

Stranger obtaining possession—effect on co-sharer's exercising right of pre-emption If some of the co-sharers of the undivided dwelling-house have transferred their interest to strangers that will not by itself change the

16 *Kartick Chandra Basu* v *Subal Chandra Mondal* (1989)2 CHN 65; Cal LT (1989)2 HC 110; (1989)1 Cal LJ 439; (1990)1 HLR 20.

17 AIR 1964 Cal 54.

18 AIR 1953 Cal 259.

19 *Kartick Chandra Basu* v *Subal Chandra Mondal* (1989)2 CHN 65; Cal LT (1989)2 HC 110; (1989)1 Cal LJ 439; (1990)1 HLR 20.

20 *Nirupoma Basak* v *Baidyanath Pramanick* AIR 1985 Cal 406.

nature and character of the house and take the case out of operation of s. 4. Until the dwelling-house is completely alienated to strangers it will still be an undivided dwelling-house within the meaning of s. 4. The position of the character of the dwelling-house is to be considered by reference to the date of purchase by the stranger-purchaser and not the date of the partition suit. The right of the members of the family who are shareholders to pre-empt under s. 4 accrues as soon as suit for partition is filed by the stranger to the family and subsist during the pendency of the suit until it is terminated by an effective final decree. The mere fact that the purchaser has obtained possession is not sufficient to defeat the claim of a member of the family under s. 4 unless it can be shown that the purchaser's possession was such that he could be regarded as having become a member of the family but the purchaser must have to be a member of the undivided family at the date of sale. Therefore, the purchase of an undivided share in the property by the stranger and his possession thereof and collection of rent in respect of the portion from the tenants without any objection by the other co-sharers will not change the nature and character of the property even though the possession of the stranger-purchaser may not be wrongful under s. 44, T.P. Act and it would not cease to be a dwelling-house belonging to an undivided family.[1]

Dwelling-house—s. 4, Partition Act A co-sharer can enforce pre-emption against a stranger-purchaser of an undivided dwelling-house.

The expression dwelling-house used in s. 44, Transfer of Property Act and s. 4, Partition Act bear the same meaning. It includes not merely the actual structure or building but also adjacent buildings, cartilage garden, courtyard, orchard and all that is necessary for the convenient occupation of the house but not that which is only for the personal use and convenience of the occupier. The dwelling-house would therefore include the land on which it stands and every appurtenant and accessory which may be deemed necessary to a full and complete enjoyment of the house. It may, in some cases, be difficult to determine with regard to a particular adjacent plot, as to whether or not it is necessary to the enjoyment of a house but the question must be determined upon evidence and plan must be prepared of the entire subject matter of the litigation and the court will determine, on the above principles, how much of any particular adjacent land may be justly treated as included within the dwelling-house.[2]

In a case the plaintiffs brought a suit for partition and pre-emption under s. 4 of the Partition Act 1893, against the defendant, a stranger-purchaser, in respect of the suit property which as alleged in the plaint, was a dwelling-house and homestead, but which could not be prepared for want

1 *Nirupoma Basak* v *Baidyanath Pramanick* AIR 1985 Cal 406.
2 *Kshirode Ghosal* v *Sarada Prasad* (1910)12 Cal LJ 525.

of money and was in a dilapidated state; the roof had caved in, but the walls were standing; but the plaintiffs were using the latrine and the walls and were using the two rooms for stocking hay and straw and were keeping their cattle in the house, although the plaintiffs had constructed a new house on the other side of the road and were themselves living there. These facts were established by the plaintiff's evidence and there was no evidence that the plaintiffs had abandoned the house. It was held that the property in question was a 'dwelling-house' within s. 4 of the Partition Act 1893 and the plaintiffs, therefore, were entitled to pre-emption.[3]

If in fact a house is used for residential purpose by the members of the family, then it can be decisively termed 'a dwelling-house'. A dwelling-house may be tenanted in certain circumstances.

By mere grant of tenancy, a house which is otherwise a residential house of the members of the undivided family owning it, does not cease to be a dwelling-house.[4]

The crucial test of a dwelling-house is that the house must have been meant for residential purposes, though temporarily it might be used for other purposes, according to the exigencies or circumstances. On fact the house in question was not held to be a dwelling-house.[5]

In order to decide whether a house is a dwelling-house or not, it has got to be considered how the house is being used or for what purpose the house is there. Where a small portion of the suit property constitutes a shop, but the defendant, the owner of the dwelling-house inherited it from his father and his other co-sharers have sold their shares to different persons, simply because there is a shop in the suit dwelling-house, the character of the dwelling-house does not change.[6]

Acid test to decide whether a land is encompassed within the definition of dwelling-house is to see if the land is needed for the beneficial enjoyment of the family. The daughter and daughter's son of a co-sharer sold a portion of the land in favour of defendant, a stranger. This plot, a vacant plot having no construction on it was used as a place for study of children, during summer the members of the family used to sit there and sometimes sleep there. It was held the plaintiff is entitled to buy up the share of that plot from the stranger.[7]

Relevant date of valuation—pre-emption under s. 4 of Partition Act In the matter of valuation of the share or portion of the dwelling-house, relevant

3 *Radhaballav Kundu* v *Purna Chandra Singh* (1978)82 CWN 957.
4 *Bhagwati Lal* v *Bhorelal* AIR 1974 Raj 225; 1974 Raj LW 139.
5 *Tejpal Khandelwal* v *Purnima Bai* AIR 1976 Ori 62; (1975)2 Cut WR 929.
6 *Mohiddin Molla* v *Jitendranath Karmakar* AIR 1976 Cal 288.
7 *Purusottam Sutar* v *Chuni Majhi* (1972)1 Cut WR 221.

date for valuation is an important element. The last portion of s. 4(1) of the Partition Act postulates making of valuation of the share to be pre-empted by a member of the family of the dwelling-house undivided. The court has been given the discretion to make valuation in such manner as it thinks fit. The plain meaning of the provision refers to the market value on the date of the suit and not on the date of sale. The sale by the stranger to the co-sharer family member is in the nature of a forced sale, the valuation has to be fixed with great care and caution so as not to cause any hardship to the parties.[8] Relying on *Mt. Sumitra* v *Dhannu*[9] Patna High Court held that s. 4(1) gives an option to any member of the family who is a co-sharer in respect of a dwelling-house a portion whereof has been transferred to a stranger of the family to purchase the share so transferred. On such option being exercised the valuation of such share has to be determined. The crucial date for the purpose of fixing up the valuation of the share of such transferee is the date when option to purchase is exercised by the family member co-sharer.[10] The valuation of the property should be determined as on the date of filing of the suit and not the present market value.[11]

Family The words "such family" necessarily refers to the undivided family to whom the dwelling-house belongs.[12] Family *includes* a group of persons related in blood, who live in one house, or under one head or management. It does not mean a body of persons who can trace their descent from a common ancestor.[13] The term family embraces a collective body of persons in the house or within the cartilage.[14]

Family member—s. 4, Partition Act Section 4, Partition Act is not confined to a Hindu Mitakshara family. It extends to Mahomedan, Christian and other families as well. The family members might have divided their other properties by metes and bounds or there might be severance of joint status amongst them. The family would still be treated as 'undivided' in respect of the dwelling-house if the same has not been divided amongst them by metes and bounds.[15] The expression 'family' has not been defined in the Partition Act. Its meaning is very elastic. No comprehensible formula can be laid down to ascertain its import. A son-in-law coming to a Mahomedan

8 *Bhikari Behera* v *Dharmananda Natia* AIR 1963 Ori 40; ILR (1962) Cut 458; 8 Cut LT 300.

9 AIR 1952 Nag 193(2); ILR (1949) Nag 370; *Subal Chandra* v *Gostha Behari* 60 CWN 829.

10 *Lal Kejriwal* v *Bhawanath Jha* AIR 1977 Pat 5; *Radha Devi* v *Mithilesh Thakur* (2008)4 PLJR 35.

11 *Meena Devi Panch* v *Bina Shukla* (2014)136 AIC 370.

12 *Gautam Paul* v *Debi Rani Paul* (2000)8 SCC 330.

13 *Kartick Chandra Basu* v *Subal Chandra Mondal* (1989)2 CHN 65; Cal LT 1989(2) HC 110; (1989)1 Cal LJ 439; (1990)1 HLR 20.

14 *Khirode* v *Sarada* 12 CLJ 525.

15 *Tejpal Khandelwal* v *Purnima Bai* AIR 1976 Ori 62; (1975) Cut WR 1231.

family visiting his father-in-law occasionally can be regarded as a member of the family.[16] To claim pre-emption the family member must be a co-sharer, *i.e.* must have title to the extent of some fractional share. In an Orissa case although there was partition between two brothers *A&B,* the dwelling-house remained undivided, *A* sold his share to a stranger, *B* was all along alive, *B's* wife, son and daughter sought to invoke s. 4, Partition Act. It was held they are not co-sharers *albeit,* they are family members and they have no *locus standi* to invoke s. 4, Partition Act.[17]

Pre-emption application by a family member co-sharer before final and after preliminary decree On a consideration of the language in s. 4 of the Partition Act, its requirements and its scope and object, it is manifest that any application under s. 4 of the Partition Act should be filed before the final decree is passed. So viewed, the petition of a family member co-sharer under s. 4 of the Partition Act after the preliminary decree and before final decree in the partition suit is entertainable.[18] But, even after co-sharers have become separate in title they can maintain an application for pre-emption. All that is necessary is that the decree for partition must not be fully satisfied.[19] It was also held that pre-emption application is also maintainable even after final decree is passed and at the stage of execution[20] and till the possession is delivered in terms of final decree.[1]

Stranger purchasing a share of the family dwelling-house after passing of final decree—whether pre-emption maintainable If a stranger purchases during the pendency of a suit for partition before the passing of a preliminary decree in that suit or during the pendency of that suit before passing of the final decree or even during the appellate stage from final decree in that suit for partition is subject to the right of pre-emption under s. 4 of the Act, there is no reason why s. 4 of the Act should not be attracted because the stranger-purchaser makes the purchase after the passing of the final decree and in course of the execution proceeding for delivery of possession by metes and bounds in accordance with the final decree. The right conferred by s. 4 of the Act is not lost merely by reason of the fact that the purchaser has obtained possession but only if the possession has been such that the purchaser may be regarded as having become a member of the family.[2]

16 *Ahmad Khan* v *Shaik Nazir* AIR 1971 Ori 284; ILR (1971) Cut 851.
17 *Gita Devi Saragi* v *Madan Mohan Masanta* AIR 1969 Ori 294; 35 Cut LT 562.
18 *Partha Sarathi Ghosh* v *Sulekha Ghosh* AIR 1988 Cal 61; 91 CWN 1197 relying on *Abdul Sattar* v *A. Nawab* AIR 1980 Mad 235.
19 *Bimalendu Chatterjee* v *Sarita Chhyajlani* (2002)1 CHN 145; (2002)1 ICC 1023; (2002)1 Cal LJ 1; (2002)2 ALT (DNC 8.2)8; (2002)1 CCC 309.
20 *Madan Mohan Ghosh* v *Ghanteswar Ghosh* (1991)1 CHN 464; (1991)1 Cal LJ 328.
1 *Subhas Mukherjee* v *Ashok Kr. Roy* (1999)2 CHN 261.
2 *Dilip Gupta* v *Sarada Verma* (1988)1 CHN 394.

Pre-emptor transferring share before implementation of pre-emption Section 4(1), Partition Act gives an option to any member of the family who is a co-sharer in respect of an undivided dwelling-house, a portion whereof has been transferred to one, a stranger to the family, to purchase the share of such transferee. But it may so happen that the pre-emptor co-sharer himself has ceased to be a co-sharer by reason of transfer of his or her share before implementation of the pre-emption. The right of pre-emption of the co-sharer then must be deemed to be lost. In a suit for partition of a dwelling-house brought by a stranger-purchaser a defendant applied for pre-emption under s. 4 of the Partition Act in which application was allowed and a direction was given that a valuation should be made of the share of the plaintiff in the property. It was further directed that on the defendant depositing the amount so ascertained the share of the plaintiff was to vest in the defendant and the suit should stand dismissed. But it so happened that after such order being passed the family member co-sharer sold his own share to another person but reacquired the same. It was held that the said defendant by reason of the intermediate transfer lost his right to pre-empt notwithstanding his reacquisition of the same and the defendant's application for pre-emption was dismissed.[3]

Order of sale—when decree An order of sale under s. 4, Partition Act may or may not contain a direction as to delivery of possession. But in view of s. 8, Partition Act 1893 such an order is deemed to be a decree. Such a decree doubtlessly is executable. Executing court must spell out from the decree a mandate of delivery of possession whether or not such relief is specifically granted.

Right to pre-empt existence till decision essential Right to pre-empt must exist not only at the time of the sale of the land and the date of the application but also at the time of the application being decided.[4]

As held in a case under the Punjab Pre-emption Act under the general law of pre-emption it is firmly established that the decisive date as regards the right of pre-emption to pre-empt the sale was the date of decree. The pre-emptor must continue to possess the right till the date of the decree. If he loses the right before the decree being passed, the decree for pre-emption cannot be granted even though he may have such right on the date of the suit.[5]

3 *Safura Bibi* v *Ram Prasad Shaw* AIR 1977 Cal 207; 81 CWN 446; ILR (1977)1 Cal 4.

4 *Bhagwan Das* v *Chet Ram* AIR 1971 SC 369; (1971)2 SCR 640; *Kalipada Ghosh* v *Dulal Ghosh* 82 CWN 950; (1978)2 Cal LJ 155; *Seikh Abdul Aziz* v *Samidannessa Bibi* (1987)1 Cal LJ 137.

5 *Rikhi Ram* v *Ram Kumar* AIR 1975 SC 1869; (1975)2 SCC 318.

Right of pre-emption under the Hindu Succession Act The relevant provision is contained in s. 22 of the Hindu Succession Act. It reads as follows:

> 22. *Preferential right to acquire property in certain cases.* (1) Where, after the commencement of this Act, an interest in any immovable property of an intestate, or in any business carried on by him or her, whether solely or in conjunction with others, devolves upon two or more heirs specified in class I of the Schedule, and any one of such heirs proposes to transfer his or her interest in the property or business, the other heirs shall have a preferential right to acquire the interest proposed to be transferred.
>
> (2) The consideration for which any interest in the property of the deceased may be transferred under this section shall, in the absence of any agreement between the parties, be determined by the court on application being made to it in this behalf, and if any person proposing to acquire the interest is not willing to acquire it for the consideration so determined, such person shall be liable to pay all costs of or incident to the application.
>
> (3) If there are two or more heirs specified in class I of the Schedule proposing to acquire any interest under this section, that heir who offers the highest consideration for the transfer shall be preferred.
>
> *Explanation.* In this section, "court" means the court within the limits of whose jurisdiction the immovable property is situated or the business is carried on, and includes any other court which the State Government may, by notification in the Official Gazette, specify in this behalf.

Section 22 of the Hindu Succession Act does not apply where the property devolves by survivorship. The section is confined to a devolution of property by inheritance only and that too, where the property devolves upon the heirs specified in Class I of the Schedule.[6] It is not available to the legal heirs of Class I heir against another Class I heir of a common ancestor.[7] A claim under this provision is not sustainable if it is found that the property which is proposed to be transferred, is capable of being partitioned[8] or where the partition has already taken place since partition clothes the respective parties with authority to hold their shares independently and absolutely as their separate properties.[9] In a case, where third party purchaser joins the final decree proceedings for partition of his share, co-sharer can exercise his right of pre-emption without filing a separate suit.[10] The right under s. 22(1) of the Hindu Succession Act can be enforced by a separate suit and not by any application in a partition suit.[11]

6 *Bholanath Rastogi* v *Santhosh Prakash Arya* AIR 1975 Pat 336.

7 *M. Ramasamy* v *S. Duraisamy* (2013)1 LW 412; (2012)6 CTC 564; (2013)121 AIC 957; (2013)2 HLR 110.

8 *Dwijabrata Das* v *Debabrata Das* AIR 1994 Gau 88.

9 *Bhagirathi Chhatoi* v *Adikanda Chhatoi* AIR 1988 Ori 285; (1988)66 CLT 172.

10 *N. Manickam* v *Kanagaraj* (2012)3 CTC 495; (2012)2 LW 739; (2012)117 AIC 502.

11 *A. Bheemamma* v *A Balamma* (2010)85 AIC 773 (AP); AIR 2009 AP 202.

The right of pre-emption is not available in case of transfer of tenancy in agricultural holding.[12] The preferential right to acquire property under the section is confined only to case of devolution of property upon two or more heirs specified in Class I of the Schedule. It is not available when the property has passed on to persons claiming through such heir's.[13] When a transfer has already taken place, the purchaser acquires a joint right in the property subject to the rights of the other heirs in Class I of the Schedule.[14]

Sub-section (2) of s. 22 of the Hindu Succession Act provides for a cheap and speedy remedy for the determination of consideration for which any interest in the property or business of the deceased "may be transferred under this section." Sub-section (2) of s. 22 of the Act does not create any right wholly independent of that created by sub-sec. (1) of s. 22. It is only where the other heirs of the deceased have a preferential right to acquire under sub-sec. (1) of s. 22, that an application for determination of the consideration has to be moved in the court specified in the *Explanation* appended to the section.

Section 22(3) of the Hindu Succession Act lays down that where two or more heirs specified in Class I of the Schedule propose to acquire any interest under this section, that heir who offers the highest consideration for the transfer shall be preferred. The alienation envisaged in the section is not void but only voidable.

The conditions necessary for invoking s. 22 of the Hindu Succession Act are as follows:

(1) An interest in any immovable property of an intestate or in any business devolves upon two or more heirs specified in Class I of the Schedule.

(2) Any one of such heirs proposes to transfer his or her interest in the property or business.

(3) In that case, the other heirs shall have a preferential right to acquire the interest proposed to be transferred.[15]

Explaining the scope of the section an M.P. case held: The title of this section indicates that it concerns itself with preferential right to acquire property in certain cases. In sub-sec. (1) the expression used is "proposes to transfer". Accordingly, when the legislature talks of preferential right to acquire the interest "proposed to be transferred" in sub-sec. (1) of s. 22, it talks of a "contemplated transfer" and not of "concluded transfer" or "transfer

12 *Ram Ratan* v *Chandra Prakash* AIR 2012 Raj 185.
13 *Ganeshappa* v *Krishnamma* AIR 2005 Kant 160.
14 *Arati Das* v *Bharati Sarkar* AIR 2009 Cal 8.
15 N. *Manickam* v *Kanagaraj* (2012)3 CTC 495; (2012)2 LW 739; (2012)117 AIC 502.

already effected". The right to acquire preferentially the interest is conceived as a right exercisable at a stage where one of the heirs of the deceased proposes to transfer his or her interest in the property or business left by the deceased Hindu dying intestate. Acceptance of the contention that s. 22(1) of the Act creates a preferential right to acquire the interest already transferred will involve re-writing thereof. This is not permissible on any established principle of construction of statutes.[16]

The above view expressed by H.G. Mishra, J in *Ghewarwala Jain* v *Hanuman Prasad*,[17] it is respectfully submitted, is not correct. Section 22 of the Hindu Succession Act has not been happily worded and this has led to the above observation of the learned single Judge of the High Court of Madhya Pradesh. In Mulla's *Hindu Law*, it has been stated thus: "The section requires more explicit and stringent language. It does not say how and when the right of preference is to be exercised. It is loosely worded and the expression 'transfer' itself is likely to create some difficulty."[18] If it is construed that the right of pre-emption available to an heir of a deceased Hindu should be exercised before the transfer by the other heir is completed, the transferor heir can surreptitiously transfer his share to a stranger without the knowledge of his co-heirs and thus defeat the provisions of this section. This could never have been the intendment of the Legislature.

A Division Bench of Kerala High Court held the object of sub-sec. (1) is that in cases where by virtue of intestate succession under the Act, any interest in immovable property has devolved upon two or more heirs specified in Class I of the Schedule and any one of such heirs proposes to transfer his interest in the property the other heirs should have a preferential right to acquire the interest which is so proposed to be transferred. The said intention of Parliament can be effectuated only if we consider the section as conferring an enforceable right on the heirs other than the one who proposes to transfer his interest. The section confers on such co-heirs a preferential right to acquire the interest which is proposed to be transferred by the other co-heir. In case the proposed transfer is effected by one of the co-heirs in violation of the right conferred on his co-heirs by sub-sec. (1) the latter cannot certainly be without a remedy because every legal right must necessarily carry with it a remedy for enforcing the same. The remedy of the non-alienating co-heirs, in such circumstances, will be to seek the intervention of the court to enable them to acquire the right which has been transferred away by the other co-heirs in violation of sub-sec. (1) of s. 22. Inasmuch as the section does not provide any special procedure for

16 *Ghewarwala Jain* v *Hanuman Prasad* AIR 1981 MP 250.
17 AIR 1981 MP 250.
18 Mulla's *Hindu Law*, 22nd Ed., p. 1248.

seeking the said remedy the ordinary procedure for enforcement of any civil right has to be resorted to by the co-heirs who wish to enforce their rights under s. 22(1); in other words the remedy is by way of a regular civil suit before the competent court.[19]

In a case where the plaintiff himself has alienated his share in the ancestral property in violation of the conditions of s. 22 of the Hindu Succession Act, he cannot be permitted to claim any benefit under s. 22 of the Hindu Succession Act against the other heirs.[20]

Limitation The preferential right under the provision can be claimed within the stipulated period of limitation. Any claim beyond that period of limitation would be barred.[1] For the purpose of limitation in relation to an application under s. 22 of the Act, Art. 97 of the Limitation Act 1963 would apply.[2]

Pre-emption under State statutes The provisions of pre-emption stand embodied in a few State statutes, *e.g.* Punjab Pre-emption Act 1913, Rajasthan Pre-emption Act 1966, W.B. Land Reforms Act 1955.

Decree in a suit for pre-emption This has been dealt with in Or. 20, r. 14. It lays down the duty of the court when purchase money has not been paid in court. The duties have been laid down in cls. (*a*) and (*b*) of Or. 20, r. 14(1). Direction given in a decree is mandatory. Mere filing of appeal does not suspend the decree and when one fails to deposit in pursuance of the order of trial court his right is lost forever; extension of time by the appellate court being not permissible. If the appellate court stays the decree it is something else.[3] An appellate court on affirming pre-emption decree of lower court is bound to fix a time for deposit of pre-emption money. The omission is an error rectifiable under s. 152, CPC.[4] A decree in terms of Or. 20, r. 14 imposes obligations on both sides and they are so conditioned that performance by one is conditional on the performance by the other. To

19 *Valliyil Sreedevi Amma* v *Subhadra Devi* AIR 1976 Ker 19; *Tarak Das Ghosh* v *Sunil Kumar Ghosh* AIR 1980 Cal 53; *Muralidhar Das* v *Bansidhar Das* AIR 1986 Ori 119; *Bhagirathi Chhatoi* v *Adikanda Chhatoi* AIR 1988 Ori 285; *P.T. Srinivasamurthy* v *P. Leelavathy* AIR 2000 Mad 516; *Kulasekaran Chettiar (died)* v *Meenakshiammal* (2002)2 MLJ 95; (2002)2 LW 294.

20 *Hazi Abdul Jalil* v *Kalipada Das* (2016)3 Gau LR 177.

1 *Ashutosh Chaturvedi* v *Prano Devi* AIR 2008 SC 2171; *J.L. Babu* v *Gowri Shankar* AIR 2009 AP 202.

2 *Tarak Das Ghosh* v *Sunil Kumar Ghosh* (1980)1 CHN 192; AIR 1980 Cal 53.

3 *Naguba Appa* v *Namdev* AIR 1954 SC 50; ILR (1953) Hyd 445; *Sulleh Singh* v *Sohanlal* AIR 1975 SC 1957; (1975)2 SCC 605; *Jagtar Singh* v *Kartar Singh* AIR 1980 Punj 313; *Panni Lal* v *Daya Ram* AIR 1985 Punj 277; (1985)2 Cur Civ Cas 504.

4 *Pratap Kaur* v *Sardara Singh* AIR 1974 Punj 298; *Gian Chand* v *Joginder Singh* AIR 1983 Punj 330.

put it differently the obligations are reciprocal and are interlinked and they cannot be separated. If the defendant by obtaining a stay order from the appellate court relieves himself of the obligation to deliver possession of the properties the plaintiff decree-holder should also be deemed to be relieved of his obligation to deposit the money so long as the stay order continues.[5] Subject to this, in order to be entitled to execute a decree obtained by a successful pre-emptor, he has to show that he has sufficiently complied with the decree he has obtained. If in terms of the decree costs are allowed, he may deduct his costs while depositing the amount so that his suit would stand decreed.[6] If the purchase money had not been paid the decree shall specify a date and on such payment being made title accrues to the pre-emptor.[7] If the court omits to mention the pre-emption value in the preliminary decree and the final decree is also prepared based upon the preliminary decree, it was held that the executing court can invoke s. 151 of the CPC to rectify the final decree.[8]

Execution of pre-emption decree by a purchaser from pre-emptor The question whether the purchaser of land from a pre-emptor who has become the owner in pursuance of a pre-emption decree after complying with the provisions of Or. 20, r. 14, CPC can execute the decree in order to obtain possession of land purchased by him cropped up in Supreme Court. There *N* after obtaining a decree for pre-emption and after complying with the order made simultaneously with the decree for pre-emption, for depositing various amounts sold the land in respect of which the decree was passed to *A* who was duly impleaded as a party in appeal against the pre-emption decree. On *A*'s filing execution application seeking to execute the decree to recover actual possession of the lands purchased by him from *N*, the Supreme Court held: *N* having complied with Or. 20, r. 14, CPC had become the owner of the lands and his legal representatives on his death were rightly substituted in the proceeding. If the sale deed in respect of land on its proper construction would show that the decree itself was assigned obviously the application for execution would be maintainable under Or. 21, r. 16, CPC.[9] But if the appellants did not fall within the four corners of Or. 21, r. 16 because though the land, the subject matter of the decree was sold to appellants, the decree itself was not assigned, they would nonetheless be able to maintain application for execution under s. 146, CPC as persons

5 *Dattatreya* v *Shaikh Mahaboob Shaikh Ali* AIR 1970 SC 750; (1969)2 SCR 514; (1970)1 SCJ 540.
6 *Niranjan Singh* v *Sher Singh* 1971 Rev LR 639.
7 *Jit Singh* v *Ram Murti* 1973 Rev LR 346.
8 *Pratap Kumar Sadhu* v *Manowara Begum* (2013)2 ICC 469 (Cal).
9 *Zila Singh* v *Hazari* AIR 1979 SC 1066; (1979)3 SCC 265 reversing *Hazari* v *Zila Singh* AIR 1970 Punj 215 (FB).

claiming under the decree-holder.[10] In a case the pre-emptor was found entitled to evict a tenant inducted by the pre-emptee.[11]

Non-payment of pre-emption money as decreed—effect The last line of Or. 20, r. 14(1)(*b*), CPC reads that the effect of such non-deposit is that "the suit shall be dismissed". The expression is not "the suit shall stand dismissed". There is a distinction between the total non-deposit within time fixed and its effect on the suit and the partial deposit. According to the provisions of Or. 20, r. 14 suit shall be dismissed if the purchase money is not paid within the time fixed by the decree. The condition of the decree about the dismissal of the suit for non-deposit of purchase money is in these words: "suit shall be dismissed". This would not mean that after the failure of the pre-emptor to deposit the money as conditioned by the decree, the suit is again to be brought before the court for non-compliance with the command of Or. 20, r. 14, CPC. Nor is the court required to do anything after the deposit is made validly within the time fixed. It has not to pass a fresh order for decreeing the suit. Therefore there is no difference between the 'suit shall be dismissed' and 'the suit shall stand dismissed.' Both these expressions mean that the effect of non-compliance with the order is to dismiss the suit unless the pre-emption price is paid within the specified time. Second order of dismissal of suit is not required to be passed for non-deposit of the purchase price. However where a direction is made for deposit of purchase money and the pre-emptor is awarded the costs of the litigation, deposit by the plaintiffs after deducting his own cost from the purchase money would amount to full deposit in terms of the decree.[12]

Payment into court of purchase money and costs—accrual of title to the pre-emptor The words "whose title thereto shall be deemed to have accrued from the date of payment" occurring in r. 14(1)(*b*) of Or. 20, CPC make it clear that immediately on payment of the purchase money on or before the specified date, the title to the property would vest in the pre-emptor without any further documentation. Thus as soon as the amount of purchase money is deposited in court by the decree-holder, the title to the pre-emptional land accrues to him by the fiction of law and he becomes the owner of the said land and the judgment-debtor is under an obligation to deliver possession thereof to him.[13]

Delivery of possession by executing court on pre-emption decree or order A decree of pre-emption in view of Or. 20, r. 14(1)(*b*), CPC must contain, *inter alia*, a direction that on payment of purchase money together

10 *Sanwant Singh* v *Zail Singh* (1986)1 Cur Civ Cas 826 (Punj).
11 *Bindu* v *Kirku* AIR 1988 J&K 1 (FB).
12 *Shyam Sunder Shaw* v *Netai* AIR 1987 SC 1421; (1987)1 UJ (SC) 609.
13 *Bhoop* v *Matadin Bhardwaj* AIR 1991 SC 373; (1991)2 SCC 128; JT 1990(4) SC 594.

with costs, if any, the defendant shall deliver possession to the plaintiff whose title shall be deemed to have accrued from the date of payment of pre-emption money in court.

The right of pre-emption prior to the decree may be weak but after it becomes a vested right, it can only be taken away by a known method of law.[14] The title to the decree-holder accrues from the date of the payment required to be made under a pre-emption decree.[15]

Where the time was given by the trial court to deposit the decretal amount but the same was not complied with, it was held that the direction of the trial court is mandatory and the time cannot be extended by the appellate court.[16] Failure to deposit the purchase money within time prescribed in the decree would tantamount to dismissal of the suit.[17] But, where there is a *bona fide* mistake and a small fraction of purchase money is not deposited due to arithmetical mistake, it was held that the court can in such cases extend the time for depositing the remaining amount under s. 148 of the CPC.[18] However, where the delay is caused by the act of the court, the deposit can be accepted.[19]

Delivery of possession of the property pre-empted being implicit in every decree for pre-emption in favour of the pre-emptor the executing court should read in every such decree the mandate as to delivery of possession no matter whether the decree on the point is specific or not. It is because it is not true that executing court has no power to find out the true effect of decree. Despite the absence of relief of delivery of possession in the decree of title suit the executing court was held to have the power to grant delivery of possession.[20]

Any other interpretation fettering the power of executing court to deliver possession due to absence of such specific direction in the decree would render the adjudication on pre-emption sterile and would hit the maxim *ut res magis valeat quam pareat* (the thing may rather have effect than be destroyed). But, where the petitioner/plaintiff fails to deposit purchase money within time as mentioned in the decree, it will tantamount to dismissal of decree etc.[21]

Originated in custom many years ago and subsequently codified, the law of pre-emption was necessitated for the then village community and society

14 *Shyam Sunder* v *Ram Kumar* (2001)8 SCC 24.
15 *Reshmu* v *Rajinder Singh* (2000)3 SCC 47.
16 *Sulleh Singh* v *Sohan Lal* (1975)2 SCC 505; AIR 1975 SC 1975.
17 *Harnama Singh* v *Harbhajan Singh* 1992 Supp (1) SCC 709; AIR 1992 SC 109.
18 *Johri Singh* v *Sukh Pal Singh* (1989)4 SCC 40.
19 *Bhoop* v *Matadin Bhardwaj* (1991)2 SCC 128; AIR 1991 SC 373.
20 *Biswanath* v *Uttara Bewa* AIR 1988 Ori 9; (1986)62 Cut LJ 112.
21 *Harnama Singh* v *Harbhajan Singh* 1992 Supp (1) SCC 709.

for its preservation, integrity and maintenance of peace and security. However, in modern times, owing to the changed circumstances, the right of pre-emption based on statutes is very much a maligned law and is characterized as feudal, archaic and outmoded, but so long it is statutorily recognized, it has to be given the same treatment as any other law deserves. The main object behind the right of pre-emption, either based on custom or statutory law, is to prevent intrusion of a stranger into the family-holding or property.[22] It is, therefore, submitted that in view of the changed social and economic conditions of present society, rural or urban, the time has come to give a rethink to the existing law of pre-emption to narrow down the ambit of laws of pre-emption, be it statutory, customary or personal, only to co-sharer of immovable property.

22 *Shyam Sunder* v *Ram Kumar* (2001)8 SCC 24.

CHAPTER 4

Injunctions

Introduction Peeping into the hoary past of legal history, certain injunction-like remedies were found to be in vogue. They were called the forerunners or ancestors of injunctions, since they functioned in the ways similar to injunctions. The remedies were the interdict of ancient Roman law, the writs of the English Kings in the period following the Norman Conquest, and the writs of the early English common law courts.[1] The origin of the relief of injunction can be traced to the principles of equity. Etymologically, the term equity is derived from Latin term "aquitas", which means equalizing or levelling. Thus, equity is something which levels down any arbitrary action or preference leading to denial of justice. Traditionally it is founded upon three assumptions:

(*i*) that equity was a matter of grace,

(*ii*) that equity is a matter of conscience, and

(*iii*) equity was enforceable by a process of contempt.

Equitable relief is distinct from the legal relief. Equitable relief is always within the discretion of the Court whereas the legal relief is a matter of right. However, with the enactment of the Specific Relief Act, granting of injunctions has been regulated by the relevant provisions of the Act. That, however, does not mean that the principles underlying the relief of injunction have not been obliterated. They still hold good. Sections 38 to 42 of the Specific Relief Act 1963 now regulate the discretion of the Court. The use of the term 'may' in s. 38 of the Act indicates that the relief is discretionary.

An injunction is a judicial remedy by which a person is ordered to refrain from doing or ordered to do a particular act or thing. It is a remedy of an

1 See generally, J. Story, *Commentaries on Equity Jurisprudence*, 5th Ed., § 866; M. Bigelow, *History of Procedure in England*, 1880, pp. 197-98.

equitable nature and, therefore, acts in personam.[2] Injunction, legally means, a court order commanding or preventing on action.[3] But, as the remedy is an equitable one, it is in principle a discretionary remedy and it may be refused on the ground that its award would cause such particular hardship to the defendant as to be oppressive to him.[4]

An injunction may be permanent (perpetual) or temporary. A permanent injunction is final and conclusive of the facts in the context of which the injunction is granted. A temporary injunction by contrast is granted on a *prima facie* view of the facts and, as the word "temporary" itself indicates, is an interim order pending a final adjudication of the rights of the parties. This distinction is not to be confused with the distinction between a prohibitory or preventive injunction on the one hand and a mandatory injunction on the other. In the first case a party is prevented from doing a particular thing or continuing with a particular action. A mandatory injunction on the other hand commands an act to be done and is provided for under s. 39 of the Specific Relief Act 1963.[5] For claiming injunction plaintiff has to prove *prima facie* case in his favour. If no *prima facie* case is established in favour of plaintiff, injunction cannot be granted.[6] An injunction is, a judicial process by which one who has invaded or is threatening to invade the legal rights of another is restrained from commencing such wrongful act or continuing it. Injunctions are either prohibitory or mandatory. A prohibitory injunction forbids the defendant to do a wrongful act which would be an infringement of some right of the plaintiff, legal or equitable. A mandatory injunction forbids the defendant to permit the continuance of a wrongful state of things that already existed at the time when the injunction is issued. Thus, a mandatory injunction, in effect, calls upon a person to do some positive act, for example, it directs the defendant to pull down the wall that exists. The performance of a mandatory injunction is thus to restore a wrongful state of things to their former rightful order. Injunction as a remedy acts *in personam*. It is not a judgment *in rem*.[7] It cannot be enforced against persons other than the person against whom it is granted, though it may be enforced against the legal representatives of a deceased judgment debtor under s. 50 of the Code of Civil Procedure, and against purchasers *pendente lite* under s. 52 of the Transfer of Property Act.[8]

2 Halsbury'a *Laws of England*, 4th Ed., vol. 24, para 801, pp. 417-418.
3 Black's *Law Dictionary*, 10th Ed. 2014.
4 Chitty on *Contracts*, 33rd Ed. 2018, vol. 1, p. 2033.
5 *State of Haryana* v *State of Punjab* (2004)12 SCC 673.
6 *P. Narsing Rao* v *K. Lalitha* AIR 2018 Hyd 75.
7 *Khushi Ram* v *Lal Man* AIR 1983 Del 78.
8 *Ramachandra Deshbandhu* v *Lakshmana Rao Kulkarni* AIR 2000 Kant 298.

In addition to three basic principles the court, while granting injunction, must take into consideration the conduct of the parties.[9]

Injunction Injunction, an equitable remedy, is essentially negative. The prime form, the prohibitory is just that: forcing a defendant to desist from wrongful conduct or even forbidding him to do so when he has not even started to do wrong; but this latter type, the *quia timet* injunction, will be granted normally only where the danger is both great and imminent. The mandatory injunction is admittedly positive in requiring the doing of some act, but it is essentially negative in that it enforces a negative obligation by forcing a wrongdoer to undo his wrong, as where the infringer of a right of light is obliged to pull down an offending obstruction. Usually the courts are much less ready to grant a mandatory injunction than they would have been to award a prohibitory one before any act is done, especially when the defendant has not acted wittingly or irresponsibly and the cost of the work would be substantial. This is all the more the case when the plaintiff seeks a *quia timet* mandatory injunction (*e.g.* to require preventive measures to sustain a positive obligation of support for land or building). A special form of injunction is the interlocutory or interim one.[10]

Chapter VII of the Specific Relief Act deals with injunctions generally and Chapter VIII deals with perpetual injunctions. Section 36 of the Specific Relief Act lays down that preventive relief is granted at the discretion of the court by injunction temporary or perpetual. Section 37(1) of the Specific Relief Act lays down that temporary injunctions are such as are to continue until a specified time, or until the further order of the court and they may be granted at any stage of a suit and are regulated by the Code of Civil Procedure 1908. Section 37(2) of the Act lays down that a perpetual injunction can only be granted by the decree made at the hearing and upon the merits of the suit, the defendant is thereby perpetually enjoined from the assertion of a right, or from the commission of an act, which would be contrary to the rights of the plaintiff. Order 39, CPC deals with temporary injunction both prohibitory and mandatory.

Perpetual injunctions are regulated by ss. 38 to 42 of the Specific Relief Act 1963. Temporary injunction on the other hand, as provided by s. 37 of the Act, is regulated mainly by the provisions of the CPC. For an order for a temporary injunction under Or. 39, r. 1, CPC the suit need not be one for injunction. For the relief of temporary injunction under r. 2 of Or. 39 the suit has to be one for injunction.[11] In the M.P. case it was held that

9 *Makers Development Services Pvt. Ltd.* v *M. Visvesvaraya Industrial Research and Development Centre* (2012)1 SCC 735; (2012)1 CHN (SC) 97.

10 P.F. Smith & S.H. Bailey on *Modern English Legal System*, Ed. 1984, p. 657; see *Rajendraprasad R. Singh* v *Municipal Corpn. of Bombay* AIR 2003 Bom 392.

11 *Jhummamal* v *Motilal* AIR 1991 MP 199 at p. 202; *Bhinka* v *Charan Singh* AIR 1959 SC 960.

the orders under s. 145(6) of the CrPC are merely temporary police orders made to prevent the breaches of the peace. Such orders passed as a result of an inquiry in summary proceedings decide no question of title and are not conclusive. They are subject to the result of the decision of the competent court entitled to determine the question of right or title to the property and the powers of the civil court are in no way fettered by an order passed under s. 145(6).[12]

Jurisdiction Initially, the Common law courts did not have the jurisdiction to issue injunctions.[13] It was the Court of Chancery where the remedy of injunction was available to those whose wrongs could not be adequately redressed by damages. However, with the enactment of the Common Law Procedure Act, 1854, the common law courts were empowered to grant injunctions in certain cases.[14] The Courts in India exercise jurisdiction both in equity as well as law but exercise of equity jurisdiction is always subject to the provisions of law. If exercise of equity jurisdiction would violate the express provisions contained in law, the same cannot be done. Equity jurisdiction can be exercised only when no law operates in the field.[15]

Nature of relief An injunction is an order of the court directing a party to the proceedings to do or refrain from doing a specified act. It is granted in cases in which monetary compensation affords an inadequate remedy to an injured party. Thus, in one old case, the claimants had been annoyed by the daily ringing of a nearby Church bell at 5:00 am. The parson, Churchwardens and others on behalf of the parish agreed to stop the ringing of the five o'clock bell during the lives of the claimants if they provided the church with a new cupola, clock and bell; and when the bell was wrong in breach of this agreement, the court restrained it by injunction.[16] However, an injunction is not restricted to remedying breaches of contract but will be granted to restrain other wrongs. Indeed the origin of the jurisdiction seems to have been derived from the old, common law writ of prohibition of waste.[17]

Relief akin to injunction In a general sense, though every order of a court which commands or forbids is an injunction, but in its *accepted* legal sense, an injunction is a judicial mandate operating *in personam* by which, upon certain established principles of equity, a party is required to do or refrain

12 *Jhummamal* v *Motilal* AIR 1991 MP 199.

13 Pollack and Maitland, *History of English Law*, 2nd Ed. 1898, pp. 595, 596.

14 Snell's *Equity*, 31st Ed. 2005, p. 381, (Thomson).

15 *Shiv Kumar Sharma* v *Santosh Kumari* AIR 2008 SC 171.

16 Snell's *Equity*, 31st Ed. 2005, p. 379, (Thomson, Sweet & Maxwell); *Martin* v *Martin* (1725)2 P. Wms 266.

17 *Goodeson v Gallatin* [1771]2 Dick 183.

from doing a particular thing.[18] At times, the appointment of receiver operates, in effect, as injunction. But, all orders or directions similar to injunction are not orders of injunction. Thus, for example, a direction to pay money either by way of final or interim order is not considered to be an injunction.[19]

Prohibitory preventive injunctions—limitations Prohibitory injunctions are theoretically available, as with regard to remedies at common law they are inadequate for the protection of the claimant's rights. In addition they are subject to the general discretion of the court and also to general equitable defences, such as laches and acquiescence.[20] So far as a prohibitory injunction is concerned, the test is that of "*balance of convenience and inconvenience*". This rule applies to a prohibitory injunction restraining a defendant from future breaches. But, if the dependent has already broken his contract he may be ordered by mandatory injunction actually to undo the breach.[21]

Prohibitory injunction relating to immovable property The position of law in regard to suit on this point is summarized by the Supreme Court which is as follows:

(*a*) Where a cloud is raised over plaintiff's title and he does not have possession, a suit for declaration and possession with or without a consequential injunction, is the remedy. Where the plaintiff's title is not in dispute or under a cloud, but he is out of possession, he has to sue for possession with a consequential injunction. Where there is merely an interference with plaintiff's lawful possession or threat of dispossession, it is sufficient to sue for an injunction *simpliciter*.

(*b*) As a suit for injunction *simpliciter* is concerned only with possession, normally the issue of title will not be directly and substantially in issue. The prayer for injunction will be decided with reference to the finding on possession. But in cases where *de jure* possession has to be established on the basis of title to property, as in the case of vacant sites, the issue of title may directly and substantially arise for consideration, as without a finding thereon, it will not be possible to decide the issue of possession.

(*c*) But a finding on title cannot be recorded in a suit for injunction, unless there are necessary pleadings and appropriate issue regarding

18 Howard C. Joyce, *A Treatise on the Law Relating to Injunctions*, 1909, s. 1 at pp. 2-3.

19 *Food Corpn. of India* v *Sukh Deo Prasad* (2009)5 SCC 665.

20 *Contractual Duties: Performance, Breach, Termination and Remedies* by Professor Neil Andrews, Prof. Malcolm Clarke, Prof. Andrew Tettenborn and Prof. Graham Virgo, 2011 Ed., para 28-006.

21 Chitty on *Contracts*, 33rd Ed., vol. 1, p. 2034.

title (either specific or implied). Where the averments regarding title are absent in a plaint and where there is no issue relating to title, the court will not investigate or examine or render a finding on a question of title, in a suit for injunction. Even where there are necessary pleadings and issue, if the matter involves complicated questions of fact and law relating to title, the court will relegate the parties to the remedy by way of comprehensive suit for declaration of title, instead of deciding the issue in a suit for mere injunction.

(*d*) Where there are necessary pleadings regarding title and appropriate issue relating to title on which parties lead evidence, if the matter involved is simple and straight forward, the court may decide upon the issue regarding title, even in a suit for injunction. But such cases are exception to the normal rule that question of title will not be decided in suit for injunction. But persons having clear title and possession suing for injunction, should not be driven to the costlier and more cumbersome remedy of a suit for declaration, merely because some meddler vexatiously or wrongfully makes a claim or tries to encroach upon his property. The court should use its discretion carefully to identify cases where it will enquire into title and cases where it will refer to plaintiff to a more comprehensive declaratory suit, depending upon the facts of the case.[1]

Reasons against granting prohibitory injunctions The effect of *Lumley* v *Wagner*[2] and the cases following it is that an injunction to prevent a breach of contract should not be refused on the ground that the breach can be compensated with damages. Because damages may not be regarded as a sufficient remedy for the claimant faced with a threatened breach of a negative stipulation. But in the following cases[3] granting of prohibitory injunction may be refused: (*i*) No adequate purpose would serve. (*ii*) A court would not grant the relief if the precise content of the clause is unclear. (*iii*) There is lack of assurance of counter-performance by the claimant. (*iv*) The court does not retain discretion to refuse when any hardship to the defendant would outweigh the harm that would be suffered by the claimant if refused specific relief of injunction. (*v*) Grant of injunction may affect the defendant's human right. (*vi*) The injunction against a breach of contract is subject to all the general equitable defences, such as laches and the rule that he who comes to equity must do equity.

Injunction sought was not to restrain the party from carrying on trade or business but from using the Trade Mark which is the subject matter of

1 *Anathula Sudhakar* v *P. Buchi Reddy* AIR 2008 SC 2033.

2 [1852]1 De GM & G 604.

3 *Contractual Duties:Performance, Breach, Termination and Remedies*—by Professor Neil Andrews, Prof. Malcolm Clarke, Prof. Andrew Tettenborn and Prof. Graham Virgo, 2011 Ed., paras 28-012–28-020.

dispute. Thus, the provisions of s. 27 of the Indian Contract Act are not attracted.[4]

Principles for grant of a temporary injunction In *Gujarat Bottling Company* v *Coca-Cola Company*[5] Their Lordships of the Supreme Court have laid down the following tests in granting temporary injunctions:

(1) Whether the plaintiff has a *prima facie* case?

(2) Whether the balance of convenience is in favour of the plaintiff?

(3) Whether the plaintiff would suffer an irreparable injury if the prayer for mandatory injunction is disallowed?

The burden is on the plaintiff to establish these three factors concurrently. In a suit for possession of immovable property, the court can grant temporary injunction to ensure observation of *status quo* and to restrain the defendants from wasting, removing, alienating, demolishing, altering, transferring and changing the shape.[6] Interim injunction may also be granted restraining the defendants from transferring and encumbering the property or making any construction thereon pending disposal of the suit for specific performance of the agreement for sale.[7] If a suit for a permanent injunction is not competent, the court will have no jurisdiction to grant an *ad interim* injunction.[8] The court cannot grant by way of interim relief what could not be granted in the main suit itself.[9] In *Gramophone Company India Ltd.* v *Baleswar*[10] where an artiste had a contract to become exclusive artiste of the plaintiff company but he rendered music for another company in breach of agreement and brought out two cassette recordings, it was held that the balance of convenience did not lie in favour of granting an interlocutary injunction restraining the Respondent from selling cassettes as the plaintiff could be adequately compensated in terms of money in case he succeeded in the suit.[11]

In *Multichannel India Ltd.* v *Kavitalaya Productions Pvt. Ltd.*,[12] where the terms of the contract were disputed, the court refused interim injunction on the ground of comparative convenience. But where under a letter of intent for setting up a joint venture the letter was acted upon long time by

4 *Suresh Dhanuka* v *Sunita Mahapatra* AIR 2012 SC 892.
5 AIR 1995 SC 2372; (1995)5 SCC 545; JT 1995(6) SC 3.
6 *Hari Shankar* v *Satya Prakash* AIR 1982 Raj 183.
7 *Vijayakumar Gupta* v *Mahi Pal* AIR 1987 Del 345; *T. Pannerselvam* v *A. Baylis* AIR 1986 Mad 284.
8 *Cotton Corporation of India Ltd.* v *United Industrial Bank Ltd.* AIR 1983 SC 1272; (1983)3 SCR 962; (1983)4 SCC 625; *Lakhmi Chand* v *Sarala Devi* AIR 1988 P&H 146.
9 *Premchand* v *Manakchand* AIR 1997 Raj 198.
10 AIR 1990 Cal 6.
11 *Misra & Co.* v *Hindustan Aeronautics Ltd* AIR 1986 Ori 22.
12 AIR 1999 Mad 59.

the Indian partner and considerable amount spent, properties purchased, permission applied for, staff recruited, the foreign partner of the joint venture was restrained by an injunction from inducting a third party as a joint venture partner or associate.[13] In *Dalpat Kumar* v *Prahlad Singh*,[14] the Supreme Court pointed out that the court should be cautious and must consider the conduct of the plaintiff, probable injuries to either party and where the plaintiff could be adequately compensated when he seeks a temporary injunction in a suit to set aside a decree on the ground of fraud or want of jurisdiction. Where public interest is involved, the court must exercise extra caution. When temporary injunction is sought to prevent public authorities, the question of public policy must also be considered in addition to the other three requirements for a grant of temporary injunction.[15] Similarly where an injunction is applied for to restrain the execution or implementation of any scheme of public utility, public interest is one of the material and relevant considerations weighing with the court.[16] Likewise, in land acquisition proceedings, the court must consider the larger public interest of necessity of rapid acquisition for grant of basic infrastructure facilities for development.[17] In granting injunction in respect of Government contracts, particularly high cost Government projects involving funds from international financial institutions, the likelihood of escalation of cost of the project must be taken into consideration.[18]

In a suit the plaintiff prayed for restraining the defendant from interfering with the peaceful possession of the plaintiff. Failure by either party to prove title would not disentitle the plaintiff who is in "settled possession" to protect his possession. Thus, the grant of injunction was proper.[19]

Plaintiff is in settled possession of allotted sites within contract. A temporary injunction is sought to prevent defendant from forcibly taking back possession of allotted sites. A 3 months' notice to plaintiff by defendant was issued. Defendant cannot be permitted to take back forcible possession of settled sites from plaintiff without taking recourse of law. Defendant terminated the contract and issued notice wrongfully in pursuance of his right reserved in clause of contract. Injunction is liable to be ganted.[20]

13 *Wellmen Hindustan Ltd.* v *NCR Corporation* AIR 1993 Del 32.

14 AIR 1993 SC 276; (1992)1 SCC 719; JT 1991(6) SC 502.

15 *State of Assam* v *M.S. Associates* AIR 1994 Gau 105; *Deputy Managing Director, CESC Ltd.* v *Nabakumar Mondal* AIR 2000 Cal 97.

16 *Mahadeo Savlaram Shelke* v *Pune Municipal Corporation* (1995)3 SCC 33; JT 1995(2) SC 504; *Superintending Engineer* v *Thanga Prasakam* AIR 1999 Mad 365.

17 *Ramnik Lal N. Bhutta* v *State of Maharashtra* (1997)1 SCC 134; AIR 1997 SC 1236.

18 *Asia Foundation and Construction Ltd.* v *Trafalgar House Construction Ltd.* (1997)1 SCC 738; JT 1997(1) SC 309.

19 *Rame Gowda* v *M. Varadappa Naidu* AIR 2004 SC 4609, relied on in *Farhath* v *Noorunissa Begum* AIR 2011 Mad 266.

20 *Pioneer Publicity Corporation Pvt. Ltd.* v *Hooghly River Bridge Commissioners* AIR 2018 Cal 74.

Grant of injunction depends upon the discretion of the court. Exercise of discretion by granting a temporary injunction when there is "no material", or refusing to grant a temporary injunction by ignoring the relevant documents produced, are instances of action which are termed as arbitrary, capricious or perverse. In such cases, the Appellate Court may interfere.[21] It is, however, required to be mentioned that it may not be appropriate for any court to hold a mini-trial at the stage of grant of temporary injunction.[1]

Declaration of Khatedari rights and injunction Claim by successor of erstwhile khatedar after a period of 39 years from the date of confirment of khatedari rights on subsequent khatedar was held to be not maintainable since during the said period khatedari right of erstwhile khatedar or his successors stood extinguished.[2]

Perpetual injunction (ss. 38 to 42) Section 38 of the Specific Relief Act deals with the circumstances in which a perpetual injunction may be granted. Section 41(*b*) of the Act does not qualify the term 'injunction' and therefore, it would comprehend both interim and perpetual injunction.[3] But, the court has no jurisdiction to grant a perpetual injunction restraining a person from instituting a proceeding in a court not subordinate to it.[4] Where the plaintiff alleged an agreement for sale of the suit property but filed the suit only for injunction restraining the defendants from alienating the property, it was held that the plaintiff was not entitled to the grant of injunction, for there was an equally efficacious remedy through a suit for specific performance.[5] Where the registration of trade mark is not transferred in the name of the plaintiff, though he is the proprietor of the trade mark, the plaintiff can be debarred from filing the suit for injunction.[6] In *Weston Electronics Ltd.* v *Weston Industries*[7] where the plaintiff was using the registered trade mark "Western" since 1966, the defendant was restrained from using the similar trade mark.

Suit for perpetual injunction restraining other partners/defendants of the firm from alienating scheduled properties in the plaint. Partnership being partnership-at-will, no injunction can be granted without a prayer for dissolution of the firm and settlement of account.[8] Laws of perpetual injunction are in accordance with justice, equity and good conscience. A

21 *Arshad Zaheer* v *Municipal Corpn. of Greater Mumbai* (2006)5 SCC 282.
1 *Anand Prasad Agarwalla* v *Tarkeshwar Prasad* (2001)5 SCC 568.
2 *Jagannath* v *State of Rajasthan* AIR 2016 Raj 89.
3 *Cotton Corpn. of India Ltd.* v *United Industrial Bank Ltd.* (1983)4 SCC 625.
4 *Cotton Corpn. of India Ltd.* v *United Industrial Bank Ltd.* (supra).
5 *Rajendra Kumar* v *Mahendra Kumar Mittal* AIR 1992 All 35.
6 *Modi Threads Ltd.* v *Som Soot Gola Factory* AIR 1992 Del 4.
7 AIR 1992 Del 340.
8 *Scaria Paul* v *Paracka Industries, Ernakulam District* AIR 2011 Ker 97.

person is not entitled to permanent inunction *ipso facto*, even if possession is established in his favour as relief of perpetual injunction is discretionary.[9]

Where a suit has been filed for declaration of title and permanent injunction, it cannot be said that the suit was for perpetual injunction.[10]

A suit for permanent injunction by a coparcener against the father, a *karta* for restraining him for alienating the house property belonging to the joint Hindu family for legal necessity would not be maintainable because the coparcener had got the remedy of challenging the sale and getting it set aside in a suit subsequent to the completion of the sale.[11] But an injunction may be granted against the *karta* or Manager of a joint Hindu family in a suit by a coparcener where there is apprehension of waste or ouster.[12]

In a suit for specific performance, the appellant was not put in possession of the suit properties in part-performance of the agreement of sale. As per the agreement of sale, she was only entrusted with the suit scheduled properties as a caretaker until possession was given on receipt of the entire sale consideration. As neither the entire sale consideration was paid nor possession delivered, the plaintiff remained merely a caretaker and on cancellation of the agreement of sale by the respondents, the plaintiff became liable to leave the suit scheduled properties as the possession continued to be with the defendants. As the appellant never had "possession" she was not entitled to seek a permanent injunction to protect her possession.[13]

Plaintiff claiming to be ordinary trustees formed a committee of management of trust. Their right to administer and manage the trust is civil right. If such right is invaded or breached, they have cause of action to sue for perpetual injunction. They need not sue for declaration or for possession since there is no cloud on their right.[14]

When the defendants have established their possession over the suit property and plaintiffs have failed to establish their better title than defendants, plaintiffs are not entitled to relief of permanent injunction.[15]

Once the decree of perpetual injunction and mandatory injunction has become final, the judgment-debtor is required to obey the decree. In whatever

9 *Patel Chaturbhai Ghelabhai* v *Patel Manubhai Ghelabhai-DECD* AIR 2018 Guj 184.
10 *Nagar Palika Parishad, Mihona* v *Ramnath* (2014)6 SCC 394.
11 *Sunil Kumar* v *Ram Prakash* AIR 1988 SC 576; (1988)2 SCR 623; (1988)2 SCC 77.
12 *Sunil Kumar* v *Ram Prakash* AIR 1988 SC 576; *Jujhar Singh* v *Giani Talok Singh* AIR 1987 P&H 34; *Kailash Chand* v *Bajrang Lal* AIR 1997 Raj 205.
13 *Saradamani Kandappan* v *S. Rajalakshmi* (2011)12 SCC 18; AIR 2011 SC 3234.
14 *Breach Candy Swimming Bath Trust* v *Dipesh Mehta* AIR 2016 NOC 167 (Bom).
15 *Durga Matha Building Constructions Co-op. Housing Society Ltd.* v *Sada Yellaiah* AIR 2010 AP 231.

form he obstructs, it is liable to removal for violation and the natural consequence is the execution proceedings under Or. 21, r. 32, CPC.[16]

A suit for permanent injunction and declaration by tenant was filed on apprehension that landlord was attempting to deny his right as tenant and to dispossed him without following due process of law. But landlord filed a subsequent suit for eviction. Apprehension of denial of status as tenant and dispossession without following due process of law does not arise. Injunction cannot be granted.[17]

Suit for declaration and permanent prohibitory injunction The appellant in *Milkhi Ram* v *State of HP*,[18] pleaded that the owner of suit property executed gift deed of 4 biswas and not 4 bighas in favour of Education Department as claimed by them and that gift deed produced by them is obtained by fraud. The appellant was unable to prove gift deed of 4 biswas in court and his possession of suit property as non-occupancy tenant. Education Department by cogent documentary and oral evidence was able to prove execution of gift deed in its favour and had also produced record of revenue entries. Thus, it was held that the appellant was not entitled to reliefs of declaration and injunction.

Decree for permanent injunction Decree for injunction is an equitable relief. The courts while passing a decree for permanent injunction would avoid multiplicity of proceedings. The court while•passing such a decree is obligated to consider the statutory provisions governing the same.[19] Even after the death of the judgment debtor, the decree for permanent injunction can be enforced against the legal representative of the judgment-debtor. Section 50 read with Or. 21, r. 32, CPC would be applicable in such cases.[20]

Suit land was jointly owned by parties as co-sharers/co-owners. Injunction was sought by one co-owner against the other co-owner who has been in exclusive possession of joint land not generally permissible. But due to construction raised by defendant co-owner, right of path and free flow of water from house of the plaintiff co-owner was destroyed. Plaintiff was not intending to completely oust defendant from his possession, but sought injunction regarding passage and free flow of water. Thus, injunction restraining defendant from blocking of passage of water was granted.[21]

16 *Jai Dayal* v *Krishan Lal Garg* (1996)11 SCC 588; AIR 1997 SC 3765.
17 *Shankar Lal Prajapat* v *Anjalee Dutta Choudhury* AIR 2018 Meg 4.
18 AIR 2016 HP 215.
19 *Academy of General Education* v *B. Malini Mallya* (2009)4 SCC 256; AIR 2009 SC 1982.
20 *Prabhakara Adiga* v *Gowri* (2017)4 SCC 97.
21 *Kewal Krishan* v *Amrit Lal* AIR 2016 NOC 765 (HP).

In case of waste or ouster an injunction may be granted against the manager of the joint Hindu family at the instance of the coparcener. But, nonetheless a blanket injunction restraining permanently from alienating the property of the joint Hindu family even in the case of legal necessity cannot be granted.[22]

Where as a result of working of the furnace installed in the premises of the defendants, the plaintiff, neighbour and members of his family were worst affected, the plaintiff would be entitled to the permanent injunction restraining the operation of the furnace. No one can be allowed to use his own property in such a manner that it creates a nuisance for his neighbours.[1]

In a case contract of purchase by a minor entered into on his behalf by his mother was found beneficial to the minor. In a suit instituted by the mother for specific performance the vendor was injuncted temporarily from transferring the property to a third party.[2]

The general proposition is well settled that a plaintiff who is not in possession is not entitled to the relief without claiming recovery of possession. Before an injunction is granted it has to be shown that the plaintiff was in possession.[3] Possession when has been obtained by forcible entry, suit by such person for injunction is not tenable.[4] Interim injunction will not be granted unless permanent injunction has been sought.[5] Injunction cannot be granted once the period of contract is over.[6]

Where *A* lets certain arable lands to *B* for the purposes of husbandry, but without an express contract as to the mode of cultivation, and contrary to the mode of cultivation customary in the District *B* threatens to sow these lands with seeds injurious thereto and requiring many years to eradicate, *A* is entitled for injunction to restrain *B* from sowing the lands in contravention of the implied contract to use them in a husband-like manner. [*Illustration K* to s. 44 of the repealed Specific Relief Act 1877]. In *Ranjit Chander Mitter* v *Union of India*[7] it was held that the remedy of a contractor on a wrongful termination of the contract is only damages and granting him an injunction to restrain the termination of the contract would amount to specific performance. Where the contract is by nature

22 *Sunil Kumar* v *Ram Prakash* AIR 1988 SC 576 approving *Shiv Kumar Moot Chand Arora* v *M.C. Jaswant Ram Arora* AIR 1972 Punj 147.
1 *Darshan Ram* v *Nazar Ram* AIR 1989 Punj 253.
2 *Mukesh* v *Deo Narayan* AIR 1987 MP 85.
3 *Thimmaiah* v *Shabira* (2008)4 SCC 182.
4 *Padmanabhan* v *Thomas* AIR 1989 Ker 188.
5 *Ishwarbhai* v *B.H. Mohanlal Nanda* AIR 2002 Guj 328.
6 *Municipal Council, Udaipur* v *Mahendra Kumar* AIR 2008 SC 2507; (2008)12 SCC 771.
7 AIR 1963 Cal 594.

determinable or which would involve constant supervision of the court, the court will not grant an injunction.[8]

It is a well settled principle that the plaintiff who seeks injunction must come to court with clean hands. In *Swet Raj Hansh Co-op. Society* v *Suraj Municipal Corporation*,[9] the plaintiff who is neither the owner of the land nor has obtained sanction for building plans, cannot seek injunction to prevent the local authority from demolishing the structure put up by him contrary to the law. It is also well settled that injunction will be refused when the plaintiff has acquiesced in the injurious act of the defendant for a long period.[10] Acquiescence in an infringement relating to trade mark amounts to consent will be a complete defence.[11] An injunction can be issued to restrain a co-owner trying to convert the portion of the residential building into one suitable for business purposes.[12] Similarly, injunctions can be issued to a co-sharer who prevents the other co-sharers using the common pathway or trying to raise a construction in the joint property.[13] Since s. 44 of the Transfer of Property Act precludes a transferee of a joint owner from claiming joint possession, an injunction can be issued against him from forcing his way into dwelling house.[14]

The possession of a tenant by sufferance is judicial and he is entitled to remain in possession till he is evicted in due course of law. His possession can therefore be protected by an injunction. But a person in wrongful possession is not entitled to injunction against rightful owner to protect unlawful possession.[15] Thus no injunction was issued in favour of the licensee of a liquor shop whose licence was terminated. In *Rev. Joseph Cherian* v *Celin Thomas*,[16] where injunction was sought for by an employee restraining the employer from evicting her from the quarters till her entitlements and retirement dues had been cleared, it was held that her entitlement did not

8 *Airport Authority of India* v *Dilbagh Singh* AIR 1997 Del 340; *Triveni Structurals Ltd* v *New Age Enterprises* AIR 1993 All 78; *Rajasthan Breweries Ltd.* v *Stroh Breweries Company* AIR 2000 Del 450.

9 AIR 1995 Guj 60.

10 *S.N. Sadasiva Chettiar* v *T.K. Subramanian* (1997)1 MLJ 67.

11 *Power Control Appliances* v *Sumeet Machines P. Ltd.* (1994)2 SCC 448; JT 1994(2) SC 70.

12 *Muthu* alias *Vava* v *Amusalu* AIR 1993 Ker 272.

13 *Vasudeva Prabhu* v *Madhava Prabhu* AIR 1993 Ker 68; *Om Prakash* v *Chhaju Ram* AIR 1992 P&H 219; *Rabi Narayan Sundari* v *Susheela Devi* AIR 2000 NOC 18 (Ori).

14 *Dorab Cawasji Warden* v *Coomi Sorab Warden* AIR 1990 SC 867; *Balasubramanian* v *Nagalingam* AIR 1996 Mad 146.

15 *Premji Ratansay Shah* v *Union of India* (1994)5 SCC 547; JT 1994(6) SC 585; *Mahadeo Savlaram Shelke* v *Puna Municipal Corporation* (1995)3 SCC 33; JT 1995(2) SC 504; *Tamil Nadu Housing Board* v *A. Viswan* (1996)8 SCC 259; AIR 1996 SC 3377; *DTTDC* v *Dr. Mehra & Sons* AIR 1996 Del 351.

16 AIR 1999 Ori 93.

give her the right to continue in occupation and was not entitled to any such injunction. In *Shilpa S. Shetty* v *Magna Publications Co. Ltd.*,[17] an injunction was issued restraining publication of articles making allegations against the personal life of an actress, especially when it was not required in public interest. Civil Court has no jurisdiction to grant injunction under the Industrial Disputes Act 1947 to prevent threatened injury on breach of service contract.[18]

Suit for permanent injunction Decree for permanent injunction in mandatory form to demolish construction on encroached land without deciding title of the plaintiff is improper.[19]

Suit for permanent injunction with decree for mandatory injunction directing the defendant to handover the possession does not come within the purview of s. 6 of the Specific Relief Act.[20] Plaintiff's father was tenant in suit property. There is nothing to indicate that the plaintiff is continuing in the same capacity. Plaintiff is unable to establish the possession of suit property. Suit for permanent injunction against true owner is not maintainable.[21]

Injunction was sought for restraining vendor/defendant from alienating suit property. Admittedly property has been acquired by defendant under a Will. Since Will is unprobated, sale deed cannot be executed. Cause of action for a suit for specific performance of contract does not arise. Suit for permanent injunction is maintainable.[22] A suit for restraining defendant from creating any disturbances in possession of plaintiff. If plaintiff's title in property is not in dispute or under any cloud suit for injunction simpliciter is maintainable.[1]

Suit was for permanent injunction against dispossession. Defendant took the plea that she was put in possession under agreement for sole. Appellate court took defendant's case as that of plaintiff and on that basis directed the plaintiff to refund amount received with interest. Direction was set aside.[2]

Plaintiffs were looking after the suit property after the death of its owner. In their absence defendant falsely declared himself as owner of the said property and entered into construction agreement with developer. When

17 AIR 2001 Bom 176.
18 *Premier Automobiles Ltd.* v *Kamlekar Shantaram Wadke* (1976)1 SCC 496; 1976 SCC (L&S) 70.
19 *Gurunath Manohar Pavaskar* v *Nagesh Siddappa Navalgund* AIR 2008 SC 901.
20 *H.V. Vebavyasachar* v *Shivashankar* AIR 2010 SC (Supp) 394; *Bhagwan Swarup Nagar* v *Ram Kishan* AIR 2009 SC (Supp) 127.
21 *Mona Singh* v *Mukesh* AIR 2018 P&H 160.
22 *R. Ramani* v *Shanthi Damodaran* AIR 2011 Mad 60.
1 *Panchanan Das* v *Ramesh Chandra Mishra* AIR 2018 Ori 34.
2 *Ramakrishna Rao* v *Rai Murari* AIR 2008 SC 1182.

original owner protested, construction work on property in question was stopped for sometime. It goes to show that defendants were not sure of their possession as well as title suit property by adverse possession. In this context grant of injunction restraining defendants from interfering with possession of plaintiffs and from proceeding with construction work and to restore possession of suit property in its previous condition was justified.[3]

Finding by trial court was that the plaintiffs failed to prove their possession. Grant of relief to plaintiffs by the court without considering effect of such finding and without recording any finding of possession is illegal.[4]

Suit by licensee for permanent injunction against the licensor restraining him from increasing rent of suit shop. License period had already expired. Suit was not maintainable.[5] Suit for injunction without any relief of possession is maintainable.[6]

Land in question was acquired by the Improvement Trust. The plaintiff claimed himself to be the owner and sought injunction against his dispossession. Both trial court and the High Court by wrongly appreciating evidence on record held that other land and not the land in question was acquired. The decree for permanent injunction was set aside.[7]

Equitable relief of permanent injunction cannot be granted to person who is himself guilty of inequitable conduct. The landlord invoked jurisdiction of tenancy court and sought relief of eviction. Possession was taken in execution petition, but appeal filed by tenant was allowed and restitution of possession to tenant ordered. Landlord cannot seek permanent injunction restraining the tenant from interfering with his possession by challenging jurisdiction of tenancy court to order restitution. Injunction in such case cannot be granted.[8]

Entries made in Government Land Records maintained under the Cantonment Land Manual are conclusive proof of title to land Government Land Record showed that the land in dispute is covered under "old grant". Classification of land also leads to same conclusions. Plaintiff did not produce any document to show title of his predecessor-in-interest. Plaintiff held the said land probably under "old grant" which was resumed by the Central Government. Plaintiff did not possess it as "owner". Therefore, suit by plaintiff for permanent injunction restraining Government from interfering with his possession and title was held that no decree could be passed.[9]

3 *Maria Colaco* v *Alba Flora Herminda D'Souza* AIR 2008 SC 1965.
4 *Thimmaiah* v *Shabira* AIR 2008 SC 1275.
5 *Municipal Council, Udaipur* v *Mahendra Kumar* AIR 2008 SC 2507.
6 *Ved Prakash Rastogi* v *Nagar Palika, Budan* AIR 2008 All 27.
7 *Yamuna Nagar Improvement Trust* v *Khariati Lal* AIR 2005 SC 2245.
8 *Kanchusthabam Satyanarayana* v *Namudri Achutaramaya* AIR 2005 SC 2010.
9 *Union of India* v *Robert Zomawia Street* AIR 2014 SC 2721.

Permanent injunction is an equitable relief. Conduct of plaintiff is relevant. Plaintiff though claimed herself to be joint owner with defendants after having already raised construction over suit land sought injunction without even disclosing this fact. Plaintiff having not approached court with clean hands was not entitled to relief of injunction.[10]

A suit for permanent injunction to prevent any competitor from carrying on same trade cannot be granted.[11]

Suit for permanent injunction restraining mortgagee from interfering with possession of mortgagor was filed. Mortgagor created an usufructuary mortgage in favour of mortgagee by handing over possession. Subsequently mortgagor redeemed mortgage and take back possession. Thereafter the mortgagor continues in possession and exclusive enjoyment of suit property. Mortgagee failed to establish his possession over suit property. Order of the Revenue Authorities proved possession and exclusive enjoyment of property. In such case injunction may be granted.[12]

A watchman or a caretaker or a servant employed to look after the property can never acquire interest of the property irrespective of his long possession. Therefore, they are not entitled to get any order of injunction against the real owner of the property.[13]

Permanent prohibitory injunction It is a settled principle of law that in order to claim prohibitory (temporary or permanent) injunction, it is necessary for the plaintiff to prima facie prove apart from establishing other two ingredients, namely, irreparable loss and injury that his possession over the suit land is "legal".[14] Plaintiff sought injunction against recovery officers on the ground that he has paid his share of tax as co-owner of bus. Plea of defendant co-owner was that he ceased his ownership by alienation of his share and hence was not liable to pay passenger tax. Affidavit filed by defendant in support of his plea was not reliable. It was executed on non-judicial stamp paper, purchased much after date of the execution. Agreement entered between plaintiff and other bus providers also showed that defendant continued to be co-owner at relevant time. Thus, on merits plaintiff was entitled to injunction.[15]

For several years plaintiff was paying house-tax as was found by trial court on the basis of house-tax receipts and extracts of house-tax register.

10 *Kalawati* v *Netar Singh* AIR 2016 HP 85 relying on *M. Gurudas* v *Rasaranjan* (2006)8 SCC 367; AIR 2006 SC 3275.

11 *Gumudu Chittibabu* v *Kotni Narasimha Murty* AIR 2018 Ori 166.

12 *V. Rajendran (Died)* v *K. Chinna Pillai* AIR 2019 Mad 40.

13 *Shammugam* v *Ariya Kashatriay Rajakula Vamsatty Madalaya Nandhavana Paripalanai Sangam* AIR 2012 SC 2010.

14 *Agnigundala Venkata Ranga Rao* v *Indukuru Ramachandra Reddy* (2017)7 SCC 694.

15 *Dev Raj* v *State of Himachal Pradesh* AIR 2016 HP 150.

There was sufficient evidence to prove that plaintiff was in possession of plot in question. Advocate Commissioner's report showed that defendant was found to be in possession of the disputed property. This could not be accepted for being contrary to evidence on record. Plot belonging to defendant was in south of plot in question and house of defendant was situated over that plot. Trial Court decreed suit only in respect of plot in question. The Supreme Court declined to interfere with the said decree.[16]

Law does not permit a person to claim unhindered or unobstructed prospect or view to any building as a matter of right and as such a person is not entitled to claim a decree for permanent prohibitory injunction on the basis of violation of such right.[17]

Suit for permanent injunction against dispossession Plaintiff claimed to be in possession of property in part performance of agreement to sell and claimed to have inducted tenant. Fact that tenant was in possession of suit property was undisputed. Interim injunction was granted against defendant. Reversal of the order on the ground that plaintiff having filed suit for injunction without reserving right to sue for relief of specific performance was not entitled to injunction was held to be improper.[18]

Construction done with the consent of the plaintiff When construction and other development works on the suit property was done with the consent of the plaintiff suit for removal of unauthorised construction and permanent injunction is not maintainable.[19]

Suit for removal of unauthorised construction and permanent injunction Defendant is alleged to have raised construction on public street. Report of B.P.O. certified that defendant made encroachment over disputed street by constructing a part of his house. In all sale deeds the area of the said street of 10 feet width is shown and that evidence is unrebutted. It is proved from evidence on record that there was encroachment. Thus, the judgment and decree passed by the trial court was confirmed by the Supreme Court and the appeal was dismissed.[20]

Suit for permanent injunction without possession Where in a suit for permanent injunction restraining the defendants from interfering with the possession of land in dispute or from raising boundary wall, the plaintiffs fail to prove that they are in possession, the suit is liable to be dismissed only on that ground. The declaration that the plaintiffs are the owners in such case is unwarranted.[21]

16 *Zarif Ahmad* v *Mohd. Farooq* AIR 2015 SC 1236.
17 *Thambi Cheriyan* v *Babu* AIR 2015 Ker 231.
18 *Lakshmi* v *E. Jayaram* AIR 2013 SC 2939.
19 *Suresh Kumar* v *Smt. Om Kalra* AIR 2012 HP 125.
20 *Hari Ram* v *Jyoti Prasad* AIR 2011 SC 952.
21 *Ramji Rai* v *Jagdish Mallah* AIR 2007 SC 900.

Injunction for protection of possessory title In the case of a permanent injunction based on protection of possessory title in which the plaintiff alleges that he is in possession and that his possession is being threatened by the defendant, the plaintiff is entitled to sue for mere injunction without adding a prayer for declaration of his rights.[22]

Mandatory injunction Mandatory injunction which is a form of specific relief has been dealt with in s. 39 of the Specific Relief Act. Mandatory injunction requires the party to do a specific thing and in this sense it is a specific relief.

The principle of moulding of relief could at best be resorted to at the time of consideration of final relief in the main suit and not at an interlocutory stage. There is marked distinction between moulding of relief and granting mandatory relief at an interlocutory stage. As regards the latter, that can be granted only to restore the *status quo* and not to establish a new set of things differing from the state which existed at the date when the suit was instituted.[23]

The plaintiff purchased the property from a vendor who put his servant, the defendant to look after the property and the defendant used to cultivate it and appropriate the benefits therefrom for more than 12 years. The defendant was neither a licensee nor an adverse possessor. The court held after an elaborate discussion of the elements of possession that it was not at all in the possession of the defendant and in such a situation a suit for mandatory injunction is proper relief. Relief of mandatory injunction is a specific relief.[1]

When the owner of an agricultural property sought for removal of electric poles and high tension wires on his land by a decree of mandatory injunction, the trial court granted the decree because despite the objection of the owner of the property the Electricity Board did not seek the permission of the District Magistrate as provided in s. 16, Telegraphs Act. Allahabad High Court reversed the decree observing: Even on the assumption that the view taken by the civil judge about the legality of the action of the Board was correct, which is seriously disputed by the counsel for the Board, it is clear that the grant or otherwise of the discretionary relief of mandatory injunction prayed for by the plaintiff had to be judged, not on the footing that he was entitled to it for the action of the Board was not lawful but, on consideration germane to the grant of the discretionary relief of injunction.[2]

22 *Ramji Rai* v *Jagdish Mallah* (2007)14 SCC 200.
23 *Samir Narain Bhojwani* v *Aurora Properties & Investments* (2018)17 SCC 203.
1 *Patel Naranbhai Jhinabhai* v *Gopaldas Venidas* AIR 1982 Guj 340.
2 *U.P. Electricity Board* v *R. Wheeler* AIR 1983 All 8; 1982 All CJ 297; 1982 All WC 478.

The co-owners held a *ravish* (way) on the first floor accessible through a staircase meant to be jointly used by the parties. The plaintiff, however, disused the *ravish* for many years in coming to the property exclusively used by them. At the time of institution of suit and as a matter of fact long disuse of joint raish, an easy and convenient alternative way for going to the properties, the court refused to entitle the plaintiff the relief of mandatory injunction in respect of the *ravish*.[3]

When despite interim injunction prohibiting the defendant from dispossessing the plaintiff, the defendant dispossesses the plaintiff, he is entitled to be restored to possession in view of subsequent event.[4]

Two elements must be considered before the grant of a mandatory injunction, *viz*, (1) what acts are necessary in order to prevent a breach of obligation, and (2) whether these acts such as the court is capable of enforcing. The plaintiff must show that there has been a breach of obligation, that is a legal obligation, and that it is necessary to maintain the *status quo*.[5] Failure on the part of the defendant to prove his case does not entitle the plaintiff to a decree for mandatory injunction.[6] Where the defendants holding the property of their father under a Will were enjoined upon a duty to provide food, clothing and residence to the widow of the testator, the court granted a mandatory injunction compelling the defendants to perform their obligation.[7] After the termination of the licence, a mandatory injunction could be issued to the licensee to vacate the premises.[8] Where a suit in effect was a suit for possession, the relief should not be denied merely because the plaint is couched in terms of a suit for mandatory injunction.[9] Where a tenant of a shop made a structural change in that he dug the floor deep to put a floor at a lower level, mandatory injunction was granted even where the plaintiff had sought only a prohibitory injunction.[10] A tenant whether on occupancy right or not cannot erect a house upon agricultural holdings for purposes other than agriculture which has the effect of changing the agricultural holdings, mandatory injunction can be issued directing him to remove the building.[11]

Easementary right was acquired by purchasers over suit passage by way of grant. Condition of grant as to manner of use of suit passage jointly by all purchasers and retention of right over passage by vendor was accepted

3 *Inder Lal* v *Abdul Salem* AIR 1983 Raj 57.
4 *Maya Devi* v *Mehria Gram Dal Mill* AIR 1988 Punj 176 relying on *Kanakku Kumara Pillai Tharu* v *Mathevan* AIR 1963 Ker 179 (FB).
5 *R. Lakshmipathi* v *Madras Gymkhana Club* (1996)2 MLJ 573.
6 *Shankar Kumar* v *Mohanlal Sharma* AIR 1998 Ori 117.
7 *Bhagwan Kaur* v *Chetan Singh* AIR 1988 P&H 198.
8 *Prabirendranath Nande* v *Narendranath Nande* AIR 1958 Cal 179.
9 *Santlal Jain* v *Avtar Jain* AIR 1985 SC 857; (1985)2 SCC 332.
10 *Parameshwari Dass Khanna* v *Bhola Nath Parihar* AIR 1981 Del 77.
11 *Ramanathan* v *Zamindar of Ramnad* ILR (1893)16 Mad 407.

by all purchasers. Raising of iron gate and boundary wall by one of the purchasers over suit passage would amount to causation of nuisance and infringement of right of other purchasers and vendor. Thus, injunction was granted against the defendant.[12]

A mandatory injunction commands an act to be done. This command may direct the restoration of *status quo* ante or may direct the performance of a positive act altering the existing state of things.[13] A mandatory injunction like a preventive injunction may be temporary or final.[14]

Interim mandatory injunction An interim mandatory injunction is not a remedy that is easily granted. It is an order that is passed only in circumstances which are clear and the *prima facie* materials clearly justify a finding that the *status quo* has been altered by one of the parties to the litigation and the interests of justice demanded that the *status quo ante* be restored by way of an interim mandatory injunction.[15] Grant of mandatory interim relief requires the highest degree of satisfaction of the court; much higher than a case involving grant of prohibitory injunction.[16] It is rare power to be exercised by the Court.

Mandatory injunction to evict Brother of plaintiff transferred leasehold rights in suit property to plaintiff sister. Plaintiff purchased suit property to become its absolute owner. Respondents, two daughters of plaintiff's brother were allowed to reside in suit in property. Suit was instituted by plaintiff claiming mandatory injunction to evict respondents. Respondents were not claiming to be tenants, but claiming 2/3 share in suit property on the plea that transfer of property by their father to plaintiff was sham. Possession of respondents was permissive and as such the plaintiff was entitled to decree for mandatory injunction to evict respondents. However, since third daughter of plaintiff's brother had been impleaded as LR of plaintiff, she could get benefit of decree only upon her proving either in execution or by filing title suit that she has inherited suit property and is its sole owner.[17]

Specific performance—mandatory injunction Specific performance or a mandatory injunction or order of a court instructing a party to perform its contractual obligations is the exception to the general rules of contract. Parties to a breach of contract suit are often acrimonious. Judicial resources on forcing them to "play nice" rather than just ordering payment of damages and leaving enforcement to the parties are originally equitable devices. This sort of decree is easier to enforce but is sometimes considered a waste of

12 *Jayanti Kar* v *Dillip Kumar Patnaik* AIR 2016 Ori 44.
13 Kerr on *Injunctions*, 6th Ed., p. 40.
14 *State of Haryana* v *State of Punjab* (2004)12 SCC 673.
15 *Kishore Kumar Khaitan* v *Praveen Kumar Singh* (2006)3 SCC 312.
16 *Mohd. Mehtab Khan* v *Khushnuma Ibrahim Khan* (2013)9 SCC 221.
17 *Gowri* v *Shanthi* AIR 2014 SC 2863.

judicial resources if money damages will suffice. Thus, the basic rule is that relief for specific performance is only available when money damages are inadequate to compensate the non-breaching party.[18]

Execution of mandatory injunction The execution of a mandatory injunction is under Or. 21, r. 32(1), of the CPC by attachment of the properties and detention in prison and under Or. 22, r. 32(3) by directing that the act may be done so far as practicable by the decree-holder or some other person appointed by the court.[19] Once a decree for mandatory injunction is passed ordering removal of an obstruction, it is not necessary to file another suit for removal of a new obstruction. Non-compliance of a decree of mandatory injunction is a continuing disobedience of the decree and can be enforced in the execution proceedings of the decree itself by attaching or imprisonment.[20]

Temporary mandatory injunction The power of the court to grant temporary mandatory injunction is also imbedded in s. 39 of the Specific Relief Act. An interlocutory mandatory injunction is generally granted directing the defendants to undo what he might have done in respect of the property after he has come to know about the plaintiff's action seeking to restrain him from doing these acts. But there is no absolute proposition that an interlocutory mandatory injunction can be directed only against actions done by the defendants in bringing change in the situation of the property in dispute with the knowledge of plaintiff's suit. If forcible and unlawful change is effected in the situation of a property by a defendant before the plaintiff could have occasion to file a suit and such a change very adversely or prejudically affects the enjoyments of the property by the plaintiff, nothing should prevent a court in a fit case to issue interlocutory mandatory injunction directing the defendant to undo what he has done, even though without the knowledge of the plaintiff's suit.[1]

Court has power to issue mandatory injunction pending trial,[2] but after notice to the party concerned.[3] Mandatory injunction on an interlocutory application is granted sparingly and that too not to establish a new state of things but to restore the *status quo*.[4] In plaintiff's suit for recovery of

18 George W. Kuney and Robert M. Lloyd, *Contracts: Transactions and Litigation*, 3rd Ed., p. 594.
19 *V.S. Alwar Ayengar* v *Gurusamy Thevar* AIR 1981 Mad 354.
20 *Jai Dayal* v *Krishan Lal Garg* AIR 1997 SC 3765; (1996)11 SCC 588.
1 *Arundhuti Nan* v *P.M. Daryanami* 90 CWN 1028.
2 *Channupati* v *Bobbala* AIR 1977 NOC 257 (AP); (1978)2 Andh WR 138; 1977 Andh LT 242.
3 *Vijay Srivastava* v *Mirhul Enterprises* AIR 1988 Del 140.
4 *Bihar University* v *Rajendra Singh* AIR 1978 Pat 144; 1978 BLJR 326; *Nandan Pictures* v *Art Pictures* AIR 1956 Cal 428; *Dyneshwar* v *Atmaram* AIR 1980 Goa 30; *Maghum Films* v *Golcha Properties* AIR 1983 Del 392; *Pronob Kumar Sarkar* v *Basanti Roy* (1987)1 Cal LJ 60; 91 CWN 665.

possession against a licensee, the defendant alleging himself to be a tenant secured an order of temporary mandatory injunction on the allegation that he was a tenant and the plaintiff-landlord had rendered his bathroom useless. The court directed the plaintiff to restore the bathroom to original conditions. This judgment may deserve some criticism. In a suit by the plaintiff, defendant unless he comes with a case of counter-claim, can pray for injunction if the defendant's claim to relief arises out of the plaintiff's causes of action or is incidental to it.

In *Pranab Kumar Sarkar's* case[5] the plaintiff's suit was for ejectment of a licensee, not ejectment of a tenant. So, the plaintiff's cause of action consisted of the allegation that the defendant had been occupying *qua* licensee, *i.e.* the transaction between the plaintiff's vendor and the defendant created no interest in the defendant on the suit property and further that the licence had been revoked. The defendant's prayer for temporary mandatory injunction to compel the plaintiff to restore the bathroom to original condition was a few miles apart from plaintiff's cause of action. Nor the defendant's prayer was incidental to it. It is not intelligible how the prayer of the defendant was tenable. The principle as to when a defendant is entitled to an injunction in a suit by plaintiff the learned judge has correctly formulated but not followed in practice.

In a Gujarat case temporary mandatory injunction was sought for, for eviction of hutment dwellers from public road where they were living for about 10 years on being thrown out by private individual. There a controversy cropped up namely between fundamental rights to eke out livelihood staying on hutments and the statutory duty to be removed. It was held interim mandatory injunction directing removal of hutments is not justified.[6]

As stated by Spry: A mandatory injunction can only be granted where the plaintiff shows a very strong probability upon the facts that grave damage will accrue to him in future. But a difficulty in accepting this view without qualification is that it does not take account of the cases, where, for example, the apprehended damage to the plaintiff cannot be described as grave, but is nonetheless substantial, and where compliance on the part of the defendant, such as by removing a hoarding, would cause little if any inconvenience. It could hardly be denied that in circumstances such as these a mandatory injunction will ordinarily issue, in the absence of special circumstances such as laches or acquiescence. It hence appears to be preferable to state generally that whenever a substantial injury to the plaintiff is shown, being an injury that might, before it took place, have been enjoined

5 *Pronob Kumar Sarkar* v *Basanti Roy* (1987)1 Cal LJ 60; (1987)1 SCJ 17; 91 CWN 665.

6 *Surat Municipal Corpn.* v *Ramesh Chandra* AIR 1986 Guj 50; 1985 Guj LH 35; see also *Bombay Mineral Employees' Union* v *Bombay Port Trust* (1989)1 Cur Civ Cas 67 (SC).

by a prohibitory injunction if the court thought fit, a mandatory injunction may be granted unless consequent prejudice to the defendant is so disproportionate that course is unjust in all circumstances.[7]

A tenant, a company filed a suit against the landlord for restraining the landlord from interfering with his possession and obtained an interim order of temporary injunction by which *status quo* was directed to be maintained. The plaintiff company appealed and it transpired then that landlord had already dispossessed the tenant. The tenant then filed a fresh suit for recovery of possession and in that suit the court by a temporary mandatory injunction restored the possession of the premises to the plaintiff-tenant. The court held that temporary mandatory injunction can be granted on interlocutory application, even if it means the granting of whole relief prayed for in the suit.[8]

Another Goa decision *Suman Ismail Abdulatif* v *Madan Vawan*,[9] did not agree with the view that a temporary mandatory injunction can be granted only to restore *status quo* and no other. It was held: a mandatory injunction can be issued on an interlocutory application where with a notice of the institution of the suit and the prayer made in the plaint for injunction to restrain the doing of certain act, the defendant does that act and thereby alters the factual basis of the suit-claim. Where the injury is immediate and pressing and irreparable and clearly established by the proofs and not acquiesced in by the plaintiff, a temporary mandatory injunction may be granted, although the act complained of was fully completed before the commencement of the suit. It is not that temporary mandatory injunction can be granted only to restore the *status quo*.[10] A Delhi case too stands in the line.[11]

In a pending suit for ejectment landlord if he so prays should be allowed to injunct tenant's raising construction on premises.[12] Defendant when puts up construction *pendente lite* or after decree, court may order its demolition.[13] Mandatory injunction to stop private nuisance namely emitting smoke from a furnace causing hazard to the health of a neighbour can be granted.[14]

A Division Bench of Calcutta High Court observed it is only in every rare cases that a mandatory injunction is granted on an interlocutory

7 Spry on *Principles of Equitable Remedies*, 3rd Ed., p. 515.
8 *Indian Cable Co.* v *Sumitra Chakraborty* AIR 1985 Cal 248; 89 CWN 559; (1985)1 CHN 428.
9 AIR 1980 NOC 49 (Goa).
10 *Suman Ismail* v *Madan Vawan* AIR 1980 NOC 49 (Goa).
11 *Baldev Raj* v *Savitri* AIR 1982 NOC 40 (Del); 1981 Rajdhani LR 367.
12 *Sri Radha Krishna* v *S.L. Khettry* 88 CWN 507.
13 *Ramrup Rai* v *Gheodhari Kuer* AIR 1980 Pat 197; 1980 BLJR 478.
14 *Achuttan Gopal Nair* v *Sreedharan Nair* (1989)1 Cur Civ Cas 238.

application and instances where such an injunction is granted by means of an *"ad interim"* order pending the decision of the application itself are almost unknown .... it would appear that if a mandatory injunction is granted at all on an interlocutory application, it is granted only to restore the *status quo* and not granted to establish a new state of thing differing from the state which existed at the date when the suit was instituted.[15]

A temporary mandatory injunction can be issued only in case of extreme hardship and compelling circumstances and mostly in those cases when *status quo* existing on the date of the institution of the suit is to be restored.[16]

In a case there was a dispute about granting of licence for collection of carcass, hides and bones of dead animals. The plaintiff respondent filed the suit for permanent injunction against the defendants on the ground that when the plaintiff is entitled to the licence by the Zilla Parishad the defendants are not. The temporary mandatory injunction in favour of the plaintiff was not endorsed by the Allahabad Division Bench as the court did not notice that the defendants had already started collecting carcass, hides and bones of dead animals from before the date of the suit. It was held that if the auction in favour of defendant is bad in law, the necessary arrangement should have been made by the trial court with a view to adjust the equity between the parties at the time of final decision of the suit.[17]

It cannot be said that no mandatory injunction can be granted by the court on an interlocutory application in any circumstances. There is no bar to the court's granting interlocutory relief in the mandatory form though in doing so, the court should act with greatest circumspection and such powers can be exercised only in rare and exceptional cases. Whether or not case comes in the category of 'rare' and 'exceptional' one, is to be judged according to the facts and circumstances surrounding it. A mandatory injunction can be granted on an interlocutory application after notice to the defendant and after hearing the parties. Therefore, where on the evidence on record it was found that the plaintiffs had paid more than 95% of the costs fixed in the agreements in respect of the flats and besides the above said amounts, the plaintiffs had advanced the interest free loans so that the construction can be completed by the defendants and each of them can get possession of the flat booked by them, it was held to be a fit case to issue mandatory injunction directing the defendants to hand over the possession of flats to plaintiffs without any delay.[18]

In *State of Rajasthan* v *Sohani Devi*[19] an interim mandatory injunction was ordered directing the defendants to remove the wall which obstructed

15 *Nandan Pictures Ltd.* v *Art Pictures Ltd.* AIR 1956 Cal 428.
16 *Magnum Films* v *Golcha Properties* AIR 1983 Del 392.
17 *Zilla Parishad Bijnor* v *Pashu Shav Chhedan* AIR 1991 All 18.
18 *Vijay Srivastava* v *Mirahul Enterprises* AIR 1988 Del 140; 1988 Rajdhani LR 7.
19 AIR 1999 Raj 126.

the right of way and which was constructed pending proceedings. Such an order was also granted where forcible dispossession was accomplished immediately before suit, as otherwise a person who has been ousted from the premises by unlawful means will remain outside the premises and continue to face hardship while the wrong-doer will enjoy the building till the culmination of the suit proceedings.[20] But in a suit challenging the order of demolition where the demolition was carried out in good faith and in due process of law, in the absence of any injunction, its reconstruction could not be ordered pending the suit.[1] An interim mandatory injunction has also been granted by civil court by ordering the landlord to reconstruct the demolished wall and to make the premises habitable.[2] So also to restore to a tenant possession surreptitiously taken by the landlord during the continuance of the tenancy and in breach of the direction of the rent laws.[3] In *Sampat Raj C. Shah* v *Lajpat Roy C. Agarwal*,[4] where the plaintiff had given donation to a trust on condition that the hospital of the trust should have a specified name and the said condition appeared in the deed of lease executed in favour of the trust, mandatory injunction was given to the trust to correct the name as specified in the deed. In *Bhupat Lal Govindji* v *Banumathi Dayalal*,[5] the court granted an interim mandatory injunction requiring the defendant/respondent to return possession of the premises to the plaintiff when the defendant, during the interval between the dismissal of the suit and the filing of the appeal, managed to put his lock on the premises. The absence of prayer for a mandatory relief was held not a bar to the grant of such a relief.[6]

Mandamus to compel the Government to discharge statutory obligation The court in exercise of writ jurisdiction can require the Government to comply with any statutory obligation. Thus as many as eighty workmen who had been engaged by a Company though not directly but through contractors; or in other words, the services of the workmen where being utilised by the company, as contract labour. A grievance was made on their behalf to the effect that though engaged as contract labour they were made to discharge duties of perennial nature connected with the business of the company. According to the appellants such engagement of the appellants through the contractor was intended only to deprive them of the ordinary benefits of direct appointment by the company. It was further claimed that such

20 *Ramesh Devchand Pala* v *Jayantkumar Gordhandas Madani* AIR 1998 Guj 120.
1 *Municipal Corporation of Greater Bombay* v *Bishandas Motilal Sharma* AIR 1997 Bom 74.
2 *Govardhan Singh* v *Mulk Raj Singh* AIR 1973 J&K 63.
3 *Indian Cable Company Ltd.* v *Sumitra Chakraborty* AIR 1985 Cal 248.
4 AIR 2000 Guj 67.
5 AIR 1984 Guj 10.
6 *Indian Cable Company Ltd.* v *Sumitra Chakraborty* AIR 1985 Cal 248.

employment of the appellants comes within the prohibition of s. 10 of the Contract Labour (Regulation and Abolition) Act 1970.

The matter referred to the State Government was kept unattended since 1970. So the failure of the State Government to discharge their statutory obligation to exercise the discretion in one way or the other was the subject matter of a complaint. It was wrong to hold that since the statute gave a discretion to the State Government the court could not issue any mandate. The court would not issue a mandate either to issue prohibition or not to do so, but the court was entitled to issue a mandate upon the State Government to discharge their statutory obligation of deciding the complaint one way or the other as required under s. 10, Contract Labour (Regulation and Abolition) Act 1970.[7]

Section 40 of the Specific Relief Act enables the plaintiff in a suit for perpetual injunction or mandatory injunction to claim damages either in addition to or in substitution for such injunction and the court may, if it thinks fit, award such damages. But no relief for damages shall be granted under this section unless the plaintiff has claimed such relief in his plaint; provided that the court shall at any stage of the proceedings allow the plaintiff to amend the plaint seeking damages. The dismissal of the suit to prevent a breach of an obligation existing in favour of the plaintiff shall bar his right to sue for damages for such breach. This is a new provision added in the Act of 1963, but it embodies what has been the accepted principle of law in India. The aim is to prevent multiplicity of suits, compelling the plaintiff to sue for all the reliefs arising from the infringement of his right in the same suit. The conditions for giving damages instead of injunctions are:

(1) injury to the plaintiff's right is small; or

(2) it is one capable of being estimated in money; or

(3) it is one which is capable of being compensated by small money payment; or

(4) the case is one in which it would be oppressive to defendant to grant an injunction.

But these factors are not decisive where the defendant is acting in blatant and calculated disregard of the plaintiff's rights.[8] Damages will also be awarded where grant of injunction would be infructuous, that is, where the licence granted by the defendant in respect of which injunction is sought has been cancelled by the authorities.[9] In *Makhanlal Natta* v *Tridib Ghosh*[10] the court

7 *A.K. Chowdhury* v *State of W.B.* 91 CWN 212.
8 *Jagcard* v *Sawyer* [1995]2 All ER 189.
9 *K.B. Machiah* v *Ajjittira S. Mandana* AIR 1997 Kant 194.
10 AIR 1993 Cal 289.

granted an injunction against the defendant who being an actor agreed to work for one drama company but thereafter entered into an agreement to work for another company. The plaintiff may also seek amendment of the plaint where he wants to seek damages due to the circumstances altered during the pendency of the suit.[11] Amendment may also be allowed even at the appellate stage.[12]

Injunction when refused Section 41 of the Specific Relief Act catalogues the circumstances under which perpetual injunction cannot be granted. Clauses (*a*) and (*b*) of s. 41 make it clear that the injunction is not directed against the court but *in personam* setting at rest the conflict in the decisions of various courts. There was also divergence of judicial view whether this section applies to temporary injunction. This conflict has now been set at rest by the Supreme Court holding that the provisions of the section can be applied where injunctions are sought at an interim stage of the proceedings.[13] The prohibition contained in cl. (*b*) applies to proceedings in a court not subordinate to that from which the injunction is sought. The court of the Tahsildar is not subordinate to a Civil Court and hence s. 41(*b*) stands as a bar for the grant of injunction restraining the Tahsildar from dispossessing the plaintiff. This section does not apply where the court grants injunction is respect of proceedings before itself.[14] Section 41(*b*) will be attracted only when an injunction is sought to restrain the party from instituting or prosecuting any action in a court in India. Thus, in *V/O Tractoro Exports, Moscow* v *Tharapore Company*[15] an injunction was granted restraining a party from proceeding with an arbitration in Moscow. It has been held very unfair to refuse the restraint order in a case where an action in a foreign court would be oppressive in the facts and circumstances of the case making such an imposition necessary or expedient. Thus in *Oil and Natural Gas Corporation* v *Western Company of North America*[16] where the contract was subject to the Indian Arbitration Act 1940 (since repealed and replaced by the Arbitration and Conciliation Act 1996) and to the exclusive jurisdiction of the Indian courts, but the foreign company was seeking to violate the very arbitration clause, on the basis of which the award was given by seeking confirmation of the award in the New York court under the American law, the court held that if the restraint order was not granted,

11 *K.B. Machaish* v *Ajjittira S. Mandana* AIR 1997 Kant 194.
12 *MRK Rao* v *Corporation of City of Bangalore* AIR 1992 Kant 411.
13 *Cotton Corporation of India* v *United Industrial Bank Ltd.* AIR 1983 SC 1272; (1983)3 SCR 962; (1983)4 SCC 625; *Bindu Latha Das* v *Braja Behari Palit* AIR 1993 Ori 86.
14 *Raghavan* v *Sankaran Ezhuthassan* AIR 1993 Ker 178; *Santha* v *Vasu* AIR 1996 Ker 188.
15 AIR 1971 SC 1; (1970)3 SCR 53; (1969)3 SCC 562.
16 AIR 1987 SC 674; (1987)1 SCR 1024; (1987)1 SCC 496.

serious prejudice would be caused and the party violating the very arbitration clause which stipulated the proceedings to be governed by the Arbitration Act 1940 (since repealed and replaced by the Arbitration and Conciliation Act 1996) and the agreement to be governed by the laws of India on the basis of which the award came into existence, will have secured an order enforcing the award from the foreign court in violation of the very clause of the contract. Where a bank sought injunction against a past employee who had allegedly misappropriated large amounts restraining him from alienating his properties when it apprehended that he would dispose of the properties, the suit was held not hit by s. 41(*h*) of the Act.[17] A petroleum products dealer making a partnership without any written consent of the petroleum supplying company as required under the dealership agreement, was held not entitled to injunction restraining the company from stopping of supplies.[18]

An injunction restraining release of electricity connection for tubewell is not proper.[19] A civil court cannot issue mandatory injunction to the Government or Governmental Authorities for initiation of acquisition proceeding.[20] No injunction can be refused when efficacious remedy is available.[1] An injunction cannot be granted when the plaintiff has no personal interest in the matter. The provisions of the Specific Relief Act do not apply to the right conferred on the corporation.[2]

The Recovery of Debts Due to Banks and Financial Institutions Act 1993 creates a Special Tribunal and confers jurisdiction upon Tribunal to decide all claims made by banks and financial institutions. Banks cannot be injuncted from initiating any proceedings for recovery of any money due to them before the Debts Recovery Tribunal. General power of superintendence of High Courts under Arts. 226 and 227 of the Constitution over all Tribunals and other Fora constituted under special enactments does not make Debts Recovery Tribunal, a court subordinate to High Court.[3]

The Court of Small Causes at Bombay is subordinate to the High Court and to a single Judge exercising Original Jurisdiction, therefore, the natural conclusion is that such single Judge in exercise of power under the Original Jurisdiction is empowered to pass an order of injunction restraining a party from prosecuting a suit in the Court of Small Causes at Bombay. Thus, with reference to the provisions of s. 41(*b*) of the Specific Relief Act 1963,

17 *K. Dakshinamoorthy* v *State Bank of India* AIR 2001 Mad 167.

18 *Joginder Pal* v *Hindustan Petroleum Company Ltd.* AIR 1997 P&H 248.

19 *Balkar Singh* v *Baru Ram* AIR 2013 P&H 62.

20 *Hullappa* v *State of Karnataka* AIR 2013 Kant 37; *Geeta Devi* v *Dibru Ram* alias *Ram Rakha* AIR 2004 HP 29.

1 *M. Vijayalakshmi* v *T. Shanmugam* AIR 2011 Mad 88.

2 *Dilip Kaushal* v *State* AIR 2008 MP 324.

3 *Rajshree Sugars & Chemicals Ltd.* v *Axis Bank Ltd.* AIR 2011 Mad 144.

the Small Cause Court constituted under the Presidency Small Cause Courts is subordinate to the Bombay High Court on its Original Side.[4]

Injunctions to perform negative agreement Section 42 provides that where a contract comprises an affirmative agreement to do a certain act coupled with a negative agreement express or implied, not to do certain act, the circumstances that the court is unable to compel the specific performance of the affirmative agreement shall not preclude it from granting an injunction to perform the negative agreement. Where the contract contains both positive and negative covenants, the court in a suitable case, will restrain the breach of the negative covenant with a view to complete the performance of the contract.[5] The principle is, the court should "operate to bind men's consciences, as far as they can be bound, to a true and literal performance of their agreements and it will not suffer them to depart from their contract at their pleasure" as observed by Lord St. Leonards in *Lumly* v *Wagner*.[6] An injunction to forbear need not necessarily be expressed in the negative terms. Thus "A" agrees that he will take all the electric energy he requires from "X" company at a specific price. Read according to its strict affirmative tenure, this is an idle agreement, for, *A* is not bound to take any current at all from "X" company. To make it significant and really operative as intended, it has been held that it must be read as an undertaking by *A* not to take electric energy from any other source of supply which is the only way of reasonable construction.[7] As held in *Taprogge Gesellschaft MBH* v *IAEC, Delhi Ltd.*,[8] if the positive or affirmative agreement cannot be specifically enforced, the negative covenant can be enforced by an injunction under s. 42.

In *Gujarat Bottling Company* v *Coca-Cola Company*,[9] there was a negative agreement by Gujarat Bottling Company not to manufacture, sell, deal or otherwise deal with the products other than those of Coca-Cola Company with whom Gujarat Bottling Company entered into a contract. It was found that Gujarat Bottling Company had not acted in terms of the main agreement and in the suit filed by Coca-Cola Company an interim injunction was granted by the High Court in enforcing the negative covenant and the application by Gujarat Bottling Company to vacate the same was held by the Supreme Court to have been rightly dismissed by the High Court. There was a divergence of judicial opinion as to whether the court can grant

4 *Export Credit Guarantee Corpn. of India* v *Annamma Philips* AIR 2011 Bom 18 (FB).
5 *Niranjan Shankar Golikari* v *Cenutury Spinning and Manufacturing Company Ltd.* AIR 1967 SC 1098; (1967)2 SCR 378.
6 [1843]60 All Eng Rep 368 at 373.
7 *Metropolitan Electric Supply Company* v *Ginder* [1901]2 Ch 799; *Vijaya Minerals P Ltd.* v *Bikash Chandra Deb* AIR 1996 Cal 67.
8 AIR 1988 Bom 157.
9 AIR 1995 SC 2372; (1995)5 SCC 545; JT 1995(6) SC 3.

temporary injunction on terms of s. 42. The High Courts of Calcutta and Delhi have taken a view that the interim order can be passed.[10] The opposite view is held by the High Courts of Madhya Pradesh and Travancore-Cochin.[11] In view of the decision of the Supreme Court in *Gujarat Bottling Company* v *Coca-Cola Company,*[12] it is safe to assume that an order of interim injunction can be granted by the court in terms of s. 42 of the Specific Relief Act.

Mareva injunction 'Mareva' injunction is an established feature of English Law and the English Court has been categorical enough to record that there should not be any hesitation in the matter of such a grant where it appears likely that the plaintiff would recover judgment against the defendant for a certain or approximate sum and there is reason to believe that the defendant has the assets within the jurisdiction to meet the judgment but may deal with the same, so that they would not be available or traceable when the judgment is given against him. One of the basic criteria for the grant of Mareva injunction is that the assets must be located within the jurisdiction to confer jurisdiction on the Court to grant a Mareva injunction. The concept of grant of Mareva injunction is not different from the power of the High Court to grant interlocutory or final order of an injunction and under its general power of jurisdiction to grant an *ex parte* injunction the English Court has developed a principle that the Court has power to restrain the defendant from removing assets from the jurisdiction pending the trial of action whenever it was just and convenient to do so.[13] However, there is a rider to the principle governing issuance of Mareva injunction. The rider is that if the injunction sought is merely to exert pressure on the defendant it would amount to abuse of the jurisdiction.[14] Mareva injunctions are now also known as 'freezing orders'.[15]

In *Allen* v *Jambo Holdings Ltd.*[16] it was observed that there is no difference in principle between commercial actions and actions for personal injuries or other causes of action in regard to the issue of a Mareva injunction. The issue of an injunction depends on the balance of justice and convenience.

The legal basis for a Mareva order is somewhat similar to the rationale for arresting ships in the admiralty jurisdiction.[17]

10 *Vijaya Minerals P. Ltd.* v *Bikash Chandra Deb* AIR 1996 Cal 67; *Frank Simoes Advertising P. Ltd.* v *Hada Leasing and Industry Ltd.* AIR 1988 Del 362.

11 *Mohammed Lathif Choudhury* v *Amritkala Baveja* AIR 1959 MP 309; *Sreedhara Shenoy* v *Thanumalayan* AIR 1973 TC 90.

12 AIR 1995 SC 2372; (1995)1 SCC 200; JT 1994(7) SC 694.

13 *Popular Jute Exchange Limited* v *Murlidhar Ratanlal Exports Ltd.* (2006)4 CHN 381.

14 *Third Chandris Shipping Corporation* v *Unimarine SA* [1979]2 All ER 972.

15 Snell's *Equity,* 31st Ed., p. 416 (Thomson).

16 [1980]2 All ER 502.

17 *Abheya Realtors Private Limited* v *SSIPL Retail Limited* (2010)2 CHN 203.

Anti-suit injunction When a court restrains a party to a suit/proceeding before it from instituting or prosecuting a case in another court including a foreign court, it is called anti-suit injunction. It is a common ground that the courts in India have power to issue anti-suit injunction to a party over whom it has personal jurisdiction, in an appropriate case. This is because courts of equity exercise jurisdiction *in personam*. However, having regard to the rule of comity, this power will be exercised sparingly because such an injunction though directed against a person, in effect causes interference in the exercise of jurisdiction by another court. The courts in India like the courts in England are courts of both law and equity. The principles governing grant of injunction, an equitable relief, by a court will also govern grant of anti-suit injunction which is but a species of injunction.[18] Facts and circumstances are required to be considered before passing an anti-suit injunction.[19] An anti-suit injunction application would fall only under the inherent power of the Court and is consequently covered by precedent law.[20]

The husband through another person filed a petition under s. 13, Hindu Marriage Act against wife at Family Court in India and the wife also filed a petition for divorce on the ground of irretrievable break down of marriage in Foreign Court. There was no record to prove that the husband will suffer grave injustice if proceedings are continued before Foreign Court. In such case anti suit injunction cannot be granted.[21]

Execution of injunction Once a suit is decreed, the interim order, if any, merges into the final order. Thus, any injunction passed during the pendency of the suit merges with the final order when the suit is decreed. In case there is a grievance of non-compliance with the terms of the decree passed in the civil suit, the remedy available to the aggrieved person is to approach the execution court under Or. 21, r. 32, CPC which provides for elaborate proceedings in which the parties can adduce their evidence and can examine and cross-examine the witnesses. The provision of Or. 21, r. 32, CPC applies to prohibitory as well as mandatory injunctions. To put it differently, a person disobeys an order of injunction not only when he fails to perform an act which he is directed to do but also when he does an act which he is prohibited from doing. Execution of an injunction decree is to be made in pursuance of Or. 21, r. 32, CPC as the CPC provides a particular manner and mode of execution and therefore, no other mode is permissible.[22]

18 *Modi Entertainment Network* v *W.S.G. Cricket Pte. Ltd.* (2003)4 SCC 341.
19 *KSL and Industries Ltd.* v *Punjab National Bank* (2014)2 Mah LJ 542; (2014)134 AIC 850; (2015)1 Bom CR 210.
20 *Sandip Shankarlal Kedia* v *Pooja Kedia* (2013)4 Mah LJ 673; (2013)3 AIR Bom R 1380; II(2013) DMC 659.
21 *Dinesh Singh Thakur* v *Sonal Thakur* AIR 2018 SC 2094.
22 *Hungerford Investment Trust Ltd.* v *Haridas Mundhra* (1972)3 SCC 684; AIR 1972 SC 1826; *Kanwar Singh Saini* v *High Court of Delhi* (2012)4 SCC 307.

Compensation for obtaining injunction on insufficient grounds Section 95, CPC provides for a summary remedy to get compensation where a temporary injunction has been granted if such injunction was applied for on insufficient grounds or there were no reasonable or probable grounds for instituting the claim for injunction. The defendant in such a proceeding is simply to present a petition to the court and the court subject to its pecuniary jurisdiction can give compensation up to ₹1000. The remedy under the Code is optional and an injured party can file a regular suit against the applicant for injunction for compensation if he has not already sought relief under the aforesaid provision. Thus this section is an alternative remedy in cases of wrongful obtainment of an injunction and it does not in any way interfere with the principles regulating suits for damages for tort of malicious legal process.[23]

23 *Bank of India* v *Lekhimoni Das* (2000)3 SCC 640; *Bhupendra Nath Chatterjee* v *Trinayani Devi* AIR 1944 Cal 289; 48 CWN 348; *Inder Singh Nihal Singh* v *Chief Commr., Delhi* AIR 1963 Punj 158; 65 Punj LR 33; *K. Syamalambal* v *N. Namberumal Chettiar* (1957)1 MLJ 118; AIR 1957 Mad 156; *Albert Bonnan* v *Imperial Tobacco Co. of India Ltd.* AIR 1929 PC 222; 1929 All LJ 1070; *Basamma* v *Peerappa* AIR 1982 Kant 9.

APPENDICES

APPENDIX 1

The Specific Relief Act 1963

[Act No. 47 of 1963][1]

[13th December 1963

[As Amended by the Specific Relief (Amendment) Act 2018 w.e.f. 1.10.2018]

An Act to define and amend
the law relating to certain kinds of Specific Relief

Prefatory Note The following extract from the Statement of Objects and Reasons is given below:

"This Bill seeks to implement the recommendations of the Law Commission contained in the Ninth Report on the Specific Relief Act, 1877, except in regard to section 42 which is being retained as it now stands. An earlier Bill on the subject introduced in the Lok Sabha on the 23rd December, 1960, lapsed on its dissolution. The notes on clauses, extracted from the Report of the Law Commission, explain the changes made in the existing Act." (*Vide* Gazette of India, Extra., Part II, section 2 dated June 15, 1962).

BE it enacted by Parliament in the Fourteenth Year of the Republic of India as follows—

Part I
PRELIMINARY

1. Short title, extent and commencement. (1) This Act may be called the Specific Relief Act, 1963.

(2) It extends to the whole of India except *[.............].

(3) It shall come into force on such date[2] as the Central Government may, by notification in the Official Gazette, appoint.

---

1 The Act received the assent of President on 13th December, 1963 and published in *Gazette of India*, Extra., Part II, section 1, dated 16th December, 1963.

* The words "except the State of Jammu and Kashmir" *omitted* by Jammu and Kashmir Reorganisation Act 2019 (w.e.f. 31.10.2019).

2 1st March, 1964; *vide* Notification No. S.O. 189, dated 13th January, 1964, *Gazette of India*, Part II, section 3(*ii*), p. 214.

Applicability The provisions of the Specific Relief Act 1963 would not apply to the contracts which are governed by the statutory provisions.[3]

2. Definitions. In this Act, unless the context otherwise requires,—

(*a*) "Obligation" includes every duty enforceable by law;

(*b*) "settlement" means an instrument other than a will or codicil as defined by the Indian Succession Act, 1925 (39 of 1925), whereby the destination or devolution of successive interests in movable or immovable property is disposed of or is agreed to be disposed of;

(*c*) "trust" has the same meaning as in section 3 of the Indian Trusts Act, 1882 (2 of 1882), and includes an obligation in the nature of a trust within the meaning of Chapter IX of that Act;

(*d*) "trustee" includes every person holding property in trust;

(*e*) all other words and expressions used herein, but not defined, and defined in the Indian Contract Act, 1872 (9 of 1872), have the meanings respectively assigned to them in that Act.

3. Savings. Except as otherwise provided herein, nothing in this Act shall be deemed—

(*a*) to deprive any person of any right to relief, other than specific performance, which he may have under any contract; or

(*b*) to affect the operation of the Indian Registration Act, 1908 (16 of 1908), on documents.

Admission of document Section 3(*b*) of the Specific Relief Act 1963 provides that nothing in this Act shall be deemed to affect the operation of the Registration Act 1908 on documents. By admission of an unregistered sale deed in evidence in suit for specific performance as evidence of contract, none of the provisions of the 1908 Act is affected; rather court acts in consonance with proviso to s. 49 of the 1908 Act.[4]

4. Specific relief to be granted only for enforcing individual civil rights and not for enforcing penal laws. Specific relief can be granted only for the purpose of enforcing individual civil rights and not for the mere purpose of enforcing a penal law.

Part II

SPECIFIC RELIEF

Chapter I

RECOVERING POSSESSION OF PROPERTY

5. Recovery of specific immovable property. A person entitled to the possession of specific immovable property may recover it in the manner provided by the Code of Civil Procedure, 1908 (5 of 1908).

3 *Union of India* v *Millenium Mumbai Broadcast Pvt. Ltd.* AIR 2006 SC 2750.

4 *S. Kaladevi* v *V.R. Somasundaram* AIR 2010 SC 1654.

6. Suit by person dispossessed of immovable property. (1) If any person is dispossessed without his consent of immovable property otherwise than in due course of law, he or any person [5][through whom he has been in possession or any person] claiming through him may, by suit, recover possession thereof, notwithstanding any other title that may be set up in such suit.

(2) No suit under this section shall be brought—

(*a*) after the expiry of six months from the date of dispossession; or

(*b*) against the Government.

(3) No appeal shall lie from any order or decree passed in any suit instituted under this section, nor shall any review of any such order or decree be allowed.

(4) Nothing in this section shall bar any person from suit to establish his title to such property and to recover possession thereof.

Relief of possession Plaintiff has to prove his previous possession and dispossession by the defendant otherwise than in due course of law within six months from the date dispossession before filing of the suit. Thus, the sole question for determination is whether the plaintiff was in possession of the disputed property within six months previous to the institution of the suit or not and whether he had been deprived of such possession by the defendant, otherwise in due course of law. If these conditions are fulfilled, the plaintiff is entitled to the decree.[6]

Suit for declaration of title Sole deed and partition deed were executed hardly three years prior to suit. To establish the title it was necessary to trace it to a point beyond a minimum of 12 years before the suit. This became all the more necessary where the plaintiff did not have possession, nor were the revenue entries available to support the ownership or possession of plaintiff and his vendors for a period of 12 years and more, prior to the suit.[7]

Suit for possession

(*a*) Suit land was joint family property. There was a sale by *karta* and his sons in favour of plaintiffs who were put in possession of the suit land. Non-consenting son sold his undivided share in favour of defendants. No suit for partition was instituted either by non-consenting co-parcener nor by defendants. Suit for possession by plaintiff was instituted on the ground that they were dispossessed by the defendants. Legal necessity would not be fact in issue in such suit, and therefore, it was not relevant fact. Mere finding that sale

5 *Inserted* by the Specific Relief (Amendment) Act 2018 (18 of 2018) w.e.f. 1.10.2018.
6 *Sarvesh Kumari Yadav* v *H.C. Ahuja* AIR 2011 Del 61; see also *Kameswar Deka* v *Gajen Deka* AIR 2011 Gau 39 (sole evidence of plaintiff was not relied and as such no decree was passed in favour of plaintiff).
7 *T.K. Mohammed Abubucker* v *P.S.M. Ahamed Abdul Khader* AIR 2009 SC 2966.

was not for legal necessity would not give defendants right to get their share demarcated. Suit was entitled to be decreed.[8]

(*b*) Where forcibly dispossessed tenant reoccupied premises without consent of landlord and without challenging earlier eviction and he delayed in filing suit for possession, he is not entitled to relief of possession.[9]

(*c*) Finding of High Court in regard to title of the plaintiff attained finality. It was for the defendant to prove that they were in possession of the suit property on the basis of hostile title and as such the title of the plaintiff has extinguished. Plaintiff need not file suit for declaration of title to the property.[10]

(*d*) Finding of facts in a suit for possession shows that two incomplete flats were handed over to the plaintiff purchaser by the developer. The plaintiff agreed to construct partition, walls, doors and windows inside the flats. Collapsibles were put by the plaintiff and keys to the flats were with the plaintiff. No agreement between the parties was made under which the plaintiff was obliged to return possession of the flats for completion of work. The developer failed to prove "permissive" possession as alleged. No evidence of transfer of suit flats by the developer to alleged *bona fide* purchasers. Plaintiff proved to be in general possession of flats and the plaintiff was wrongly dispossessed.[11]

Suit for recovery of possession The suit for recovery of possession of the suit premises was instituted on the allegation of taking wrongful and forcible possession by the defendant. The suit was decreed by the trial court, but on appeal to the High Court, the judgment and decree were set aside. The plaintiff-petitioner preferred an appeal to the Supreme Court. It was held that the respondent stating himself to be the tenant of the suit premises and produced rent receipts marked by original landlady and signed by the plaintiff who had admitted his signatures on back portion of the rent receipts. There was no further burden of proof on the respondent to lead additional evidence in proof of writing on rent receipts and their due execution by the deceased landlady. Onus of proof lay on the plaintiff to explain how blank printed rent receipts came to be signed by him on their back portions. No consequential amendment was made in plaint by the plaintiff taking plea of fraud and forgery of rent receipts, nor was there any evidence of forgery led. Thus, the dismissal of the suit by the High Court was proper.[12]

8 *Subodhkumar* v *Bhagwant Namdeorao Mehetre* AIR 2007 SC 1324.
9 *K. Krishna* v *A.N. Paramkusha Bai* AIR 2011 AP 165.
10 *Annakili* v *A. Vedanayagam* AIR 2008 SC 346.
11 *Sudhir Jaggi* v *Sunil Akash Sinha Choudhury* AIR 2005 SC 1243.
12 *Narbada Devi Gupta* v *Birendra Kumar Jaiswal* AIR 2004 SC 175.

Suit for possession by trespasser A trespasser on the land is evicted by one who is not a true owner. The trespasser has a right to file a suit and claim a decree for possession and possessory title alone. He need not prove his ownership. His possessory right holds good against all but the true owner.[13]

Counter-claim—Bombay Court-fees Act 1959 The defendant was unlawfully dispossessed and as such wanted to enforce his statutory right conferred upon him by s. 6 of the Specific Relief Act 1963. Since, relief of counter-claim is like a plaint in a suit, it need not be required to be valued under s. 6(*v*) of the Bombay Court-fees Act 1959.[14]

7. Recovery of specific movable property. A person entitled to the possession of specific movable property may recover it in the manner provided by the Code of Civil Procedure, 1908.

Explanation 1. A trustee may sue under this section for the possession of movable property to the beneficial interest in which the person for whom he is trustee is entitled.

Explanation 2. A special or temporary right to the present possession of movable property is sufficient to support a suit under this section.

8. Liability of person in possession, not as owner, to deliver to persons entitled to immediate possession. Any person having the possession or control of a particular article of movable property, of which he is not the owner, may be compelled specifically to deliver it to the person entitled to its immediate possession, in any of the following cases—

(*a*) when the thing claimed is held by the defendant as the agent or trustee of the plaintiff;

(*b*) when compensation in money would not afford the plaintiff adequate relief for the loss of the thing claimed;

(*c*) when it would be extremely difficult to ascertain the actual damage caused by its loss;

(*d*) when the possession of the thing claimed has been wrongfully transferred from the plaintiff.

Explanation. Unless and until the contrary is proved, the court shall, in respect of any article of movable property claimed under clause (*b*) or clause (*c*) of this section, presume—

(*a*) that compensation in money would not afford the plaintiff adequate relief for the loss of the thing claimed, or, as the case may be;

(*b*) that it would be extremely difficult to ascertain the actual damage caused by its loss.

13 *Ajay Kumar* v *Chanchala Devi* AIR 2011 HP 37 relying on *Somnath Burman* v *Dr. S.P. Raju* AIR 1970 SC 846.

14 *Sushila Uttamchand Jain* v *Rajesh Kumar Prakashchand Jain* AIR 2012 Bom 22.

Chapter II

SPECIFIC PERFORMANCE OF CONTRACTS

9. Defences respecting suits for relief based on contract. Except as otherwise provided herein, where any relief is claimed under this Chapter in respect of a contract, the person against whom the relief is claimed may plead by way of defence any ground which is available to him under any law relating to contracts.

Contracts which can be specifically enforced

[15][**10. Specific performance in respect of contracts.** The specific performance of a contract shall be enforced by the Court subject to the provisions contained in sub-section (2) of section 11, section 14 and section 16.]

11. Cases in which specific performance of contracts connected with trusts enforceable. (1) Except as otherwise provided in this Act, specific performance of a [16][contract shall], be enforced when the act agreed to be done is in the performance wholly or partly of a trust.

(2) A contract made by a trustee in excess of his powers or in breach of trust cannot be specifically enforced.

12. Specific performance of part of contract. (1) Except as otherwise hereinafter provided in this section, the Court shall not direct the specific performance of a part of a contract.

(2) Where a party to a contract is unable to perform the whole of his part of it, but the part which must be left unperformed by only a small proportion to the whole in value and admits of compensation in money, the Court may, at the suit of either party, direct the specific performance of so much of the contract as can be performed, and award compensation in money for the deficiency.

(3) Where a party to a contract is unable to perform the whole of his part of it, and the part which must be left unperformed either—

(*a*) forms a considerable part of the whole, though admitting of compensation in money; or

(*b*) does not admit of compensation in money;

he is not entitled to obtain a decree for specific performance; but the Court may, at the suit of the other party, direct the party in default to perform specifically so much of his part of the contract as he can perform, if the other party—

(*i*) in a case falling under clause (*a*), pays or has paid the agreed consideration for the whole of the contract reduced by the consideration for the part which must be left unperformed and in a case falling under clause (*b*), pays or has paid the consideration for the whole of the contract without any abatement; and

(*ii*) in either case, relinquishes all claims to the performance of the remaining part of the contract and all right to compensation, either for the deficiency

15 *Substituted* by the Specific Relief (Amendment) Act 2018 (18 of 2018) w.e.f. 1.10.2018.

16 *Substituted* by the Specific Relief (Amendment) Act 2018 (18 of 2018), for "contract may, in the discretion of the Court" w.e.f. 1.10.2018.

or for the loss or damage sustained by him through the default of the defendant.

(4) When a part of a contract which, taken by itself, can and ought to be specifically performed, stands on a separate and independent footing from another part of the same contract which cannot or ought not to be specifically performed, the Court may direct specific performance of the former part.

Explanation. For the purposes of this section, a party to a contract shall be deemed to be unable to perform the whole of his part of it if a portion of its subject-matter existing at the date of the contract has ceased to exist at the time of its performance.

13. Rights of purchaser or lessee against person with no title or imperfect title. (1) Where a person contracts to sell or let certain immovable property having no title or only an imperfect title, the purchaser or lessee (subject to the other provisions of this Chapter), has the following rights, namely—

(*a*) if the vendor or lessor has subsequently to the contract acquired any interest in the property, the purchaser or lessee may compel him to make good the contract out of such interest;

(*b*) where the concurrence of other persons is necessary for validating the title, and they are bound to concur at the request of the vendor or lessor, the purchaser or lessee may compel him to procure such concurrence, and when a conveyance by other persons is necessary to validate the title and they are bound to convey at the request of the vendor or lessor, the purchaser or lessee may compel him to procure such conveyance;

(*c*) where the vendor professes to sell unencumbered property, but the property is mortgaged for an amount not exceeding the purchase money and the vendor has in fact only a right to redeem it, the purchaser may compel him to redeem the mortgage and to obtain a valid discharge, and, where necessary, also a conveyance from the mortgagee;

(*d*) where the vendor or lessor sues for specific performance of the contract and the suit is dismissed on the ground of his want of title or imperfect title, the defendant has a right to a return of his deposit, if any, with interest thereon, to his costs of the suit, and to a lien for such deposit, interest and costs on the interest, if any, of the vendor or lessor in the property which is the subject-matter of the contract.

(2) The provisions of sub-section (1) shall also apply, as far as may be, to contracts for the sale or hire of movable property.

Contracts which cannot be specifically enforced

[17][**14. Contracts not specifically enforceable.** (1) The following contracts cannot be specifically enforced, namely—

(*a*) where a party to the contract has obtained substituted performance of contract in accordance with the provisions of section 20;

17 *Substituted* by the Specific Relief (Amendment) Act 2018 (18 of 2018) w.e.f. 1.10.2018.

(*b*) a contract, the performance of which involves the performance of a continuous duty which the Court cannot supervise;

(*c*) a contract which is so dependent on the personal qualifications of the parties that the Court cannot enforce specific performance of its material terms; and

(*d*) a contract which is in its nature determinable.

14A. Power of Court to engage experts. (1) Without prejudice to the generality of the provisions contained in the Code of Civil Procedure, 1908 (5 of 1908), in any suit under this Act, where the Court considers it necessary to get expert opinion to assist it on any specific issue involved in the suit, it may engage one or more experts and direct to report to it on such issue and may secure attendance of the expert for providing evidence, including production of documents on the issue.

(2) The Court may require or direct any person to give relevant information to the expert or to produce, or to provide access to, any relevant documents, goods or other property for his inspection.

(3) The opinion or report given by the expert shall form part of the record of the suit; and the Court, or with the permission of the Court any of the parties to the suit, may examine the expert personally in open Court on any of the matters referred to him or mentioned in his opinion or report, or as to his opinion or report, or as to the manner in which he has made the inspection.

(4) The expert shall be entitled to such fee, cost or expense as the Court may fix, which shall be payable by the parties in such proportion, and at such time, as the Court may direct.]

Persons for or against whom contracts may be specifically enforced

15. Who may obtain specific performance. Except as otherwise provided by this Chapter, the specific performance of a contract may be obtained by—

(*a*) any party thereto;

(*b*) the representative in interest or the principal, of any party thereto:

Provided that where the learning, skill, solvency or any personal quality of such party is a material ingredient in the contract, or where the contract provides that his interest shall not be assigned, his representative in interest or his principal shall not be entitled to specific performance of the contract, unless such party has already performed his part of the contract, or the performance thereof by his representative in interest, or his principal, has been accepted by the other party;

(*c*) where the contract is a settlement on marriage, or a compromise of doubtful rights between members of the same family, any person beneficially entitled thereunder;

(*d*) where the contract has been entered into by a tenant for life in due exercise of a power, the remainderman;

(*e*) a reversioner in possession, where the agreement is a covenant entered into with his predecessor in title and the reversioner is entitled to the benefit of such covenant;

(*f*) a reversioner in remainder, where the agreement is such a covenant, and the reversioner is entitled to the benefit thereof and will sustain material injury by reason of its breach;

[18][(*fa*) when a limited liability partnership has entered into a contract and subsequently becomes amalgamated with another limited liability partnership, the new limited liability partnership which arises out of the amalgamation;]

(*g*) when a company has entered into a contract and subsequently becomes amalgamated with another company, the new company which arises out of the amalgamation;

(*h*) when the promoters of a company have, before its incorporation, entered into a contract for the purposes of the company, and such contract is warranted by the terms of the incorporation, the company:

Provided that the company has accepted the contract and has communicated such acceptance to the other party to the contract.

16. Personal bars to relief. Specific performance of a contract cannot be enforced in favour of a person—

[1][(*a*) who has obtained substituted performance of contract under section 20; or]

(*b*) who has become incapable of performing, or violates any essential term of, the contract that on his part remains to be performed, or acts in fraud of the contract, or wilfully acts at variance with, or in subversion of, the relation intended to be established by the contract; or

(*c*) [1][who fails to prove] that he has performed or has always been ready and willing to perform the essential terms of the contract which are to be performed by him, other than terms the performance of which has been prevented or waived by the defendant.

Explanation. For the purpose of clause (*c*),—

(*i*) where a contract involves the payment of money, it is not essential for the plaintiff to actually tender to the defendant or to deposit in Court any money except when so directed by the Court;

(*ii*) the plaintiff [1][must prove] performance of, or readiness and willingness to perform, the contract according to its true construction.

17. Contract to sell or let property by one who has no title, not specifically enforceable. (1) A contract to sell or let any immovable property cannot be specifically enforced in favour of a vendor or lessor—

(*a*) who, knowing himself not to have any title to the property, has contracted to sell or let the property;

---

18 *Inserted* by the Specific Relief (Amendment) Act 2018 (18 of 2018) w.e.f. 1.10.2018.

1 *Substituted* by the Specific Relief (Amendment) Act 2018 (18 of 2018) w.e.f. 1.10.2018.

(*b*) who, though he entered into the contract believing that he had a good title to the property, cannot at the time fixed by the parties or by the Court for the completion of the sale or letting, give the purchaser or lessee a title free from reasonable doubt.

(2) The provisions of sub-section (1) shall also apply, as far as may be, to contracts for the sale or hire of movable property.

18. Non-enforcement except with variation. Where a plaintiff seeks specific performance of a contract in writing, to which the defendant sets up a variation, the plaintiff cannot obtain the performance sought, except with the variation so set up, in the following cases, namely—

(*a*) where by fraud, mistake of fact or misrepresentation, the written contract of which performance is sought is in its terms or effect different from what the parties agreed to, or does not contain all the terms agreed to between the parties on the basis of which the defendant entered into the contract;

(*b*) where the object of the parties was to produce a certain legal result which the contract as framed is not calculated to produce;

(*c*) where the parties have, subsequently to the execution of the contract, varied its terms.

19. Relief against parties and persons claiming under them by subsequent title. Except as otherwise provided by this Chapter, specific performance of a contract may be enforced against—

(*a*) either party thereto;

(*b*) any other person claiming under him by a title arising subsequently to the contract, except a transferee for value who has paid his money in good faith and without notice of the original contract;

(*c*) any person claiming under a title which, though prior to the contract and known to the plaintiff, might have been displaced by the defendant;

[2][(*ca*) when a limited liability partnership has entered into a contract and subsequently becomes amalgamated with another limited liability partnership, the new limited liability partnership which arises out of the amalgamation;]

(*d*) when a company has entered into a contract and subsequently becomes amalgamated with another company, the new company which arises out of the amalgamation;

(*e*) when the promoters of a company have, before its incorporation, entered into a contract for the purpose of the company and such contract is warranted by the terms of the incorporation, the company:

Provided that the company has accepted the contract and communicated such acceptance to the other party to the contract.

2 *Inserted* by the Specific Relief (Amendment) Act 2018 (18 of 2018) w.e.f. 1.10.2018.

[3][*Substituted performance of contracts, etc.*]

[4][**20. Substituted performance of contract.** (1) Without prejudice to the generality of the provisions contained in the Indian Contract Act, 1872 (9 of 1872), and, except as otherwise agreed upon by the parties, where the contract is broken due to non-performance of promise by any party, the party who suffers by such breach shall have the option of substituted performance through a third party or by his own agency, and, recover the expenses and other costs actually incurred, spent or suffered by him, from the party committing such breach.

(2) No substituted performance of contract under sub-section (1) shall be undertaken unless the party who suffers such breach has given a notice in writing, of not less than thirty days, to the party in breach calling upon him to perform the contract within such time as specified in the notice, and on his refusal or failure to do so, he may get the same performed by a third party or by his own agency:

Provided that the party who suffers such breach shall not be entitled to recover the expenses and costs under sub-section (1) unless he has got the contract performed through a third party or by his own agency.

(3) Where the party suffering breach of contract has got the contract performed through a third party or by his own agency after giving notice under sub-section (1), he shall not be entitled to claim relief of specific performance against the party in breach.

(4) Nothing in this section shall prevent the party who has suffered breach of contract from claiming compensation from the party in breach.

20A. Special provisions for contract relating to infrastructure project. (1) No injunction shall be granted by a Court in a suit under this Act involving a contract relating to an infrastructure project specified in the Schedule, where granting injunction would cause impediment or delay in the progress or completion of such infrastructure project.

Explanation. For the purposes of this section, section 20B and clause (*ha*) of section 41, the expression "infrastructure project" means the category of projects and infrastructure Sub-Sectors specified in the Schedule.

(2) The Central Government may, depending upon the requirement for development of infrastructure projects, and if it considers necessary or expedient to do so, by notification in the Official Gazette, amend the Schedule relating to any Category of projects or Infrastructure Sub-Sectors.

(3) Every notification issued under this Act by the Central Government shall be laid, as soon as may be after it is issued, before each House of Parliament, while it is in session, for a total period of thirty days which may be comprised in one session or in two or more successive sessions, and if, before the expiry of the session immediately following the session or the successive sessions aforesaid, both Houses

3 *Substituted* by the Specific Relief (Amendment) Act 2018 (18 of 2018) w.e.f. 1.10.2018.

4 *Substituted* by the Specific Relief (Amendment) Act 2018 (18 of 2018) w.e.f. 1.10.2018.

agree in making any modification in the notification or both Houses agree that the notification should not be made, the notification shall thereafter have effect only in such modified form or be of no effect, as the case may be; so, however, that any such modification or annulment shall be without prejudice to the validity of anything previously done under that notification.

20B. Special Courts. The State Government, in consultation with the Chief Justice of the High Court, shall designate, by notification published in the Official Gazette, one or more Civil Courts as Special Courts, within the local limits of the area to exercise jurisdiction and to try a suit under this Act in respect of contracts relating to infrastructure projects.

20C. Expeditious disposal of suits. Notwithstanding anything contained in the Code of Civil Procedure, 1908 (5 of 1908), a suit filed under the provisions of this Act shall be disposed of by the Court within a period of twelve months from the date of service of summons to the defendant:

Provided that the said period may be extended for a further period not exceeding six months in aggregate after recording reasons in writing for such extension by the Court.]

21. Power to award compensation in certain cases. (1) In a suit for specific performance of a contract, the plaintiff may also claim compensation for its breach [5][in addition to] such performance.

(2) If, in any such suit, the court decides that specific performance ought not to be granted, but that there is a contract between the parties which has been broken by the defendant, and that the plaintiff is entitled to compensation for that breach, it shall award him such compensation accordingly.

(3) If, in any such suit, the Court decides that specific performance ought to be granted, but that it is not sufficient to satisfy the justice of the case, and that some compensation for breach of the contract should also be made to the plaintiff, it shall award him such compensation accordingly.

(4) In determining the amount of any compensation awarded under this section, the Court shall be guided by the principles specified in section 73 of the Indian Contract Act, 1872 (9 of 1872).

(5) No compensation shall be awarded under this section unless the plaintiff has claimed such compensation in his plaint:

Provided that where the plaintiff has not claimed any such compensation in the plaint, the Court shall, at any stage of the proceeding, allow him to amend the plaint, on such terms as may be just, for including a claim for such compensation.

Explanation. The circumstance that the contract has become incapable of specific performance does not preclude the Court from exercising the jurisdiction conferred by this section.

22. Power to grant relief for possession, partition, refund of earnest money, etc. (1) Notwithstanding anything to the contrary contained in the Code of Civil

5 *Substituted* by the Specific Relief (Amendment) Act 2018 (18 of 2018) w.e.f. 1.10.2018.

Procedure, 1908 (5 of 1908), any person suing for the specific performance of a contract for the transfer of immovable property may, in an appropriate case, ask for—

(*a*) possession, or partition and separate possession, of the property, in addition to such performance; or

(*b*) any other relief to which he may be entitled, including the refund of any earnest money or deposit paid or made by him, in case his claim for specific performance is refused.

(2) No relief under clause (*a*) or clause (*b*) of sub-section (1) shall be granted by the court unless it has been specifically claimed:

Provided that where the plaintiff has not claimed any such relief in the plaint, the Court shall, at any stage of the proceeding, allow him to amend the plaint on such terms as may be just for including a claim for such relief.

(3) The power of the Court to grant relief under clause (*b*) of sub-section (1) shall be without prejudice to its powers to award compensation under section 21.

23. Liquidation of damages not a bar to specific performance. (1) A contract, otherwise proper to be specifically enforced, may be so enforced, though a sum be named in it as the amount to be paid in case of its breach and the party in default is willing to pay the same, if the Court, having regard to the terms of the contract and other attending circumstances, is satisfied that the sum was named only for the purpose of securing performance of the contract and not for the purpose of giving to the party in default an option of paying money in lieu of specific performance.

(2) When enforcing specific performance under this section, the Court shall not also decree payment of the sum so named in the contract.

24. Bar of suit for compensation for breach after dismissal of suit for specific performance. The dismissal of a suit for specific performance of a contract or part thereof shall bar the plaintiff's right to sue for compensation for the breach of such contract or part, as the case may be, but shall not bar his right to sue for any other relief to which he may be entitled, by reason of such breach.

Enforcement of awards and directions to execute settlements

25. Application of preceding sections to certain awards and testamentary directions to execute settlements. The provisions of this Chapter as to contracts shall apply to awards to which [6][the Arbitration and Conciliation Act, 1996 (26 of 1996)], does not apply and to directions in a will or codicil to execute a particular settlement.

Chapter III

RECTIFICATION OF INSTRUMENTS

26. When instrument may be rectified. (1) When, through fraud or a mutual mistake of the parties, a contract or other instrument in writing (not being the articles of association of a company to which the Companies Act, 1956, applies) does not express their real intention, then—

6 *Substituted* by the Specific Relief (Amendment) Act 2018 (18 of 2018) w.e.f. 1.10.2018.

(*a*) either party or his representative in interest may institute a suit to have the instrument rectified; or

(*b*) the plaintiff may, in any suit in which any right arising under the instrument is in issue, claim in his pleading that the instrument be rectified; or

(*c*) a defendant in any such suit as is referred to in clause (*b*), may, in addition to any other defence open to him, ask for rectification of the instrument.

(2) If, in any suit in which a contract or other instrument is sought to be rectified under sub-section (1), the court finds that the instrument, through fraud or mistake, does not express the real intention of the parties, the Court may, in its discretion, direct rectification of the instrument so as to express that intention, so far as this can be done without prejudice to rights acquired by third persons in good faith and for value.

(3) A contract in writing may first be rectified, and then if the party claiming rectification has so prayed in his pleading and the Court thinks fit, may be specifically enforced.

(4) No relief for the rectification of an instrument shall be granted to any party under this section unless it has been specifically claimed:

Provided that where a party has not claimed any such relief in his pleading, the Court shall, at any stage of the proceeding, allow him to amend the pleading on such terms as may be just for including such claim.

Chapter IV

RESCISSION OF CONTRACTS

27. Where rescission may be adjudged or refused. (1) Any person interested in a contract may sue to have it rescinded, and such rescission may be adjudged by the Court in any of the following cases, namely—

(*a*) where the contract is voidable or terminable by the plaintiff;

(*b*) where the contract is unlawful for causes not apparent on its face and the defendant is more to blame than the plaintiff.

(2) Notwithstanding anything contained in sub-section (1), the court may refuse to rescind the contract—

(*a*) where the plaintiff has expressly or impliedly ratified the contract; or

(*b*) where, owing to the change of circumstances which has taken place since the making of the contract (not being due to any act of the defendant himself), the parties cannot be substantially restored to the position in which they stood when the contract was made; or

(*c*) where third parties have, during the subsistence of the contract, acquired rights in good faith without notice and for value; or

(*d*) where only a part of the contract is sought to be rescinded and such part is not severable from the rest of the contract.

Explanation. In this section "contract", in relation to the territories to which the Transfer of Property Act, 1882 (4 of 1882) does not extend, means a contract in writing.

28. Rescission in certain circumstances of contracts for the sale or lease of immovable property, in specific performance of which has been decreed. (1) Where in any suit a decree for specific performance of a contract for the sale or lease of immovable property has been made and the purchaser or lessee does not, within the period allowed by the decree or such further period as the Court may allow, pay the purchase money or other sum which the Court has ordered him to pay, the vendor or lessor may apply in the same suit in which the decree is made, to have the contract rescinded and on such application the Court may, by order, rescind the contract either so far as regards the party in default or altogether, as the justice of the case may require.

(2) Where a contract is rescinded under sub-section (1), the Court—

(*a*) shall direct the purchaser or the lessee, if he has obtained possession of the property under the contract, to restore such possession to the vendor or lessor; and

(*b*) may direct payment to the vendor or lessor of all the rents and profits which have accrued in respect of the property from the date on which possession was so obtained by the purchaser or lessee until restoration of possession to the vendor or lessor, and, if the justice of the case so requires, the refund of any sum paid by the vendee or lessee as earnest money or deposit in connection with the contract.

(3) If the purchaser or lessee pays the purchase money or other sum which he is ordered to pay under the decree within the period referred to in sub-section (1), the Court may, on application made in the same suit, award the purchaser or lessee such further relief as he may be entitled to, including in appropriate cases all or any of the following reliefs, namely—

(*a*) the execution of a proper conveyance or lease by the vendor or lessor;

(*b*) the delivery of possession, or partition and separate possession, of the property on the execution of such conveyance or lease.

(4) No separate suit in respect of any relief which may be claimed under this section shall lie at the instance of a vendor, purchaser, lessor or lessee, as the case may be.

(5) The costs of any proceedings under this section shall be in the discretion of the Court.

29. Alternative prayer for rescission in suit for specific performance. A plaintiff instituting a suit for the specific performance of a contract in writing may pray in the alternative that, if the contract cannot be specifically enforced, it may be rescinded and delivered up to be cancelled; and the court, if it refuses to enforce the contract specifically, may direct it to be rescinded and delivered up accordingly.

30. Court may require parties rescinding to do equity. On adjudging the rescission of a contract, the Court may require the party to whom such relief is granted to restore, so far as may be, any benefit which he may have received from the other party and to make any compensation to him which justice may require.

Chapter V

CANCELLATION OF INSTRUMENTS

31. When cancellation may be ordered. (1) Any person against whom a written instrument is void or voidable, and who has reasonable apprehension that such instrument, if left outstanding, may cause him serious injury, may sue to have it adjudged void or voidable; and the Court may, in its discretion, so adjudge it and order it to be delivered up and cancelled.

(2) If the instrument has been registered under the Indian Registration Act, 1908 (16 of 1908), the Court shall also send a copy of its decree to the officer in whose office the instrument has been so registered; and such officer shall note on the copy of the instrument contained in his books the fact of its cancellation.

32. What instruments may be partially cancelled. Where an instrument is evidence of different rights or different obligations, the Court may, in a proper case, cancel it in part and allow it to stand for the residue.

33. Power to require benefit to be restored or compensation to be made when instrument is cancelled or is successfully resisted as being void or voidable. (1) On adjudging the cancellation of an instrument, the Court may require the party to whom such relief is granted, to restore, so far as may be any benefit which he may have received from the other party and to make any compensation to him which justice may require.

(2) Where a defendant successfully resists any suit on the ground—

(*a*) that the instrument sought to be enforced against him in the suit is voidable, the Court may, if the defendant has received any benefit under the instrument from the other party, require him to restore, so far as may be, such benefit to that party or to make compensation for it;

(*b*) that the agreement sought to be enforced against him in the suit is void by reason of his not having been competent to contract under section 11 of the Indian Contract Act, 1872 (9 of 1872), the Court may, if the defendant has received any benefit under the agreement from the other party, require him to restore, so far as may be, such benefit to that party, to the extent to which he or his estate has benefited thereby.

Chapter VI

DECLARATORY DECREES

34. Discretion of Court as to declaration of status or right. Any person entitled to any legal character, or to any right as to any property, may institute a suit against any person denying, or interested to deny, his title to such character or right, and the Court may in its discretion make therein a declaration that he is so entitled, and the plaintiff need not in such suit ask for any further relief:

Provided that no Court shall make any such declaration where the plaintiff, being able to seek further relief than a mere declaration of title, omits to do so.

Explanation. A trustee of property is a "person interested to deny" a title adverse to the title of some one who is not in existence, and for whom, if in existence, he would be a trustee.

35. Effect of declaration. A declaration made under this Chapter is binding only on the parties to the suit, persons claiming through them respectively, and, where any of the parties are trustees, on the persons for whom, if in existence at the date of the declaration such parties would be trustees.

Part III

PREVENTIVE RELIEF

Chapter VII

INJUNCTIONS GENERALLY

36. Preventive relief how granted. Preventive relief is granted at the discretion of the Court by injunction, temporary or perpetual.

37. Temporary and perpetual injunctions. (1) Temporary injunctions are such as are to continue until a specified time, or until the further order of the Court, and they may be granted at any stage of a suit, and are regulated by the Code of Civil Procedure, 1908 (5 of 1908).

(2) A perpetual injunction can only be granted by the decree made at the hearing and upon the merits of the suit; the defendant is thereby perpetually enjoined from the assertion of a right, or from the commission of an act, which would be contrary to the rights of the plaintiff.

Chapter VIII

PERPETUAL INJUNCTIONS

38. Perpetual injunction when granted. (1) Subject to the other provisions contained in or referred to by this Chapter, a perpetual injunction may be granted to the plaintiff to prevent the breach of an obligation existing in his favour, whether expressly or by implication.

(2) When any such obligation arises from contract, the Court shall be guided by the rules and provisions contained in Chapter II.

(3) When the defendant invades or threatens to invade the plaintiff's right to, or enjoyment of, property, the Court may grant a perpetual injunction in the following cases, namely—

(*a*) where the defendant is trustee of the property for the plaintiff;

(*b*) where there exists no standard for ascertaining the actual damage caused, or likely to be caused, by the invasion;

(*c*) where the invasion is such that compensation in money would not afford adequate relief;

(*d*) where the injunction is necessary to prevent a multiplicity of judicial proceedings.

39. Mandatory injunctions. When, to prevent the breach of an obligation, it is necessary to compel the performance of certain acts which the Court is capable of enforcing, the Court may in its discretion grant an injunction to prevent the breach complained of, and also to compel performance of the requisite acts.

40. Damages in lieu of, or in addition to, injunction. (1) The plaintiff in a suit for perpetual injunction under section 38, or mandatory injunction under section 39, may claim damages either in addition to, or in substitution for, such injunction and the Court may, if it thinks fit, award such damages.

(2) No relief for damages shall be granted under this section unless the plaintiff has claimed such relief in his plaint:

Provided that where no such damages have been claimed in the plaint, the Court shall, at any stage of the proceedings, allow the plaintiff to amend the plaint on such terms as may be just for including such claim.

(3) The dismissal of a suit to prevent the breach of an obligation existing in favour of the plaintiff shall bar his right to sue for damages for such breach.

41. Injunction when refused. An injunction cannot be granted—

(*a*) to restrain any person from prosecuting a judicial proceeding pending at the institution of the suit in which the injunction is sought, unless such restraint is necessary to prevent a multiplicity of proceedings;

(*b*) to restrain any person from instituting or prosecuting any proceeding in a Court not subordinate to that from which the injunction is sought;

(*c*) to restrain any person from applying to any legislative body;

(*d*) to restrain any person from instituting or prosecuting any proceeding in a criminal matter;

(*e*) to prevent the breach of a contract the performance of which would not be specifically enforced;

(*f*) to prevent, on the ground of nuisance, an act of which it is not reasonably clear that it will be a nuisance;

(*g*) to prevent a continuing breach in which the plaintiff has acquiesced;

(*h*) when equally efficacious relief can certainly be obtained by any other usual mode of proceeding except in case of breach of trust;

[7][(*ha*) if it would impede or delay the progress or completion of any infrastructure project or interfere with the continued provision of relevant facility related thereto or services being the subject matter of such project;]

(*i*) when the conduct of the plaintiff or his agents has been such as to disentitle him to the assistance of the Court;

(*j*) when the plaintiff has no personal interest in the matter.

42. Injunction to perform negative agreement. Notwithstanding anything contained in clause (*e*) of section 41, where a contract comprises an affirmative agreement to do a certain act, coupled with a negative agreement, express or implied, not to do a certain act, the circumstance that the Court is unable to compel specific performance of the affirmative agreement shall not preclude it from granting an injunction to perform the negative agreement:

7 *Inserted* by the Specific Relief (Amendment) Act 2018 (18 of 2018) w.e.f. 1.10.2018.

Provided that the plaintiff has not failed to perform the contract so far as it is binding on him.

43. Amendment of Act 1 of 1940. [*Repealed by the Repealing and Amending Act*, 1974 (56 of 1974), *section* 2 *and schedule* 1.]

44. Repeal. [*Repealed by the Repealing and Amending Act*, 1974 (56 of 1974), *section* 2 *and schedule* 1.]

[1][THE SCHEDULE

[*See* sections 20A and 41(*ha*)]

CATEGORY OF PROJECTS AND INFRASTRUCTURE SUB-SECTORS

Sl. No.	*Category*	*Infrastructure Sub-Sectors*
1	2	3
1.	Transport	(*a*) Road and bridges
		(*b*) Ports (including Capital Dredging)
		(*c*) Shipyards (including a floating or land-based facility with the essential features of waterfront, turning basin, berthing and docking facility, slipways or ship lifts, and which is self-sufficient for carrying on shipbuilding/repair/breaking activities)
		(*d*) Inland Waterways
		(*e*) Airports
		(*f*) Railway Track, tunnels, viaducts, bridges, terminal infrastructure including stations and adjoining commercial infrastructure
		(*g*) Urban Public Transport (except rolling stock in case of urban road transport)
2.	Energy	(*a*) Electricity Generation
		(*b*) Electricity Transmission
		(*c*) Electricity Distribution
		(*d*) Oil pipelines
		(*e*) Oil/Gas/Liquefied Natural Gas (LNG) storage facility (including strategic storage of crude oil)
		(*f*) Gas pipelines (including city gas distribution network)

1 *Inserted* by the Specific Relief (Amendment) Act 2018 (18 of 2018) w.e.f. 1.10.2018.

Sl. No.	Category	Infrastructure Sub-Sectors
1	2	3
3.	Water and Sanitation	(a) Solid Waste Management (b) Water supply pipelines (c) Water treatment plants (d) Sewage collection, treatment and disposal system (e) Irrigation (dams, channels, embankments, etc.) (f) Storm Water Drainage System (g) Slurry pipelines
4.	Communication	(a) Telecommunication (Fixed network including optic fibre/wire/cable networks which provide broadband/internet) (b) Telecommunication towers (c) Telecommunications and Telecom Services
5.	Social and Commercial Infrastructure	(a) Education Institutions (capital stock) (b) Sports infrastructure (including provision of Sports Stadia and Infrastructure for Academies for Training/Research in Sports and Sports-relating activities) (c) Hospitals (capital stock including Medical Colleges, Para Medical Training Institutes and Diagnostic Centres) (d) Tourism infrastructure, *viz.* (*i*) three-star or higher category classified hotels located outside cities with population of more than one million; (*ii*) ropeways and cable cars (e) Common infrastructure for industrial parks and other parks with industrial activity such as food parks, textile parks, Special Economic Zones, tourism facilities and agriculture markets (f) Post-harvest storage infrastructure for agriculture and horticulture produce including cold storage (g) Terminal markets (h) Soil-testing laboratories

Sl. No.	Category	Infrastructure Sub-Sectors
1	2	3
		(*i*) Cold chain (including cold room facility for farm level pre-cooling, for preservation or storage of agriculture and allied produce, marine products and meat)
		(*j*) Affordable Housing (including a housing project using at least 50% of the Floor Area Ratio (FAR)/Floor Space Index (FSI) for dwelling units with carpet area of not more than 60 square meters *Explanation.*—For the purposes of this sub-clause, the term "carpet area" shall have the same meaning as assigned to it in clause (*k*) of section 2 of the Real Estate (Regulation and Development) Act, 2016 (16 of 2016).]

APPENDIX 2

The Indian Contract Act 1872

[Act No. IX of 1872]

[25th April, 1872

[RELEVANT PORTION]

Preamble. Whereas it is expedient to define and amend certain parts of the law relating to contracts; it is hereby enacted as follows:

PRELIMINARY

1. Short title. This Act may be called the Indian Contract Act 1872.

Extent, commencement. It extends to the whole of India *[.................]; and it shall come into force on the first day of September, 1872.

Enactment repealed. Nothing herein contained shall affect the provisions of any Statute, Act or Regulation not hereby expressly repealed, nor any usage or custom of trade, nor any incident of any contract, not inconsistent with the provisions of this Act.

2. Interpretation clause. In this Act the following words and expressions are used in the following senses, unless a contrary intention appears from the context:—

(*a*) When one person signifies to another his willingness to do or to abstain from doing anything, with a view to obtaining the assent of that other to such act or abstinence, he is said to make a proposal;

(*b*) When the person to whom the proposal is made signifies his assent thereto, the proposal is said to be accepted. A proposal, when accepted, becomes a promise;

(*c*) The person making the proposal is called the "promisor", and the person accepting the proposal is called the "promisee";

(*d*) When, at the desire of the promisor, the promisee or any other person has done or abstained from doing , or does or abstains from doing, or promises to do or to abstain from doing, something, such act or abstinence or promise is called a consideration for the promise;

(*e*) Every promise and every set of promises, forming the consideration for each other, is an agreement;

* The words "except the State of Jammu and Kashmir" *omitted* by Jammu and Kashmir Reorganisation Act 2019 (w.e.f. 31.10.2019).

(*f*) Promises which form the consideration or part of the consideration for each other, are called reciprocal promises;

(*g*) An agreement not enforceable by law is said to be void;

(*h*) An agreement enforceable by law is a contract;

(*i*) An agreement which is enforceable by law at the option of one or more of the parties thereto, but not at the option of the other or others, is a voidable contract;

(*j*) A contract which ceases to be enforceable by law becomes void when it ceases to be enforceable.

Chapter I

Of the Communication, Acceptance and Revocation of Proposals

3. Communication, acceptance and revocation of proposals. The communication of proposals, the acceptance of proposals, and the revocation of proposals and acceptances, respectively, are deemed to be made by any Act or omission of the party proposing, accepting or revoking, by which he intends to communicate such proposal, acceptance or revocation, or which has the effect of communicating it.

4. Communication when complete. The communication of a proposal is complete when it comes to the knowledge of the person to whom it is made.

The communication of an acceptance is complete,—

as against the proposer, when it is put in a course of transmission to him, so as to be out of the power of the acceptor;

as against the acceptor, when it comes to the knowledge of the proposer.

The communication of a revocation is complete,—

as against the person who makes it, when it is put into a course of transmission to the person to whom it is made, so as to be out of the power of the person who makes it;

as against the person to whom it is made, when it comes to his knowledge.

Illustrations

(*a*) *A* proposes, by letter, to sell a house to *B* at a certain price.

The communication of the proposal is complete when *B* receives the letter.

(*b*) *B* accepts *A*'s proposal by a letter sent by post.

The communication of the acceptance is complete,

as against *A*, when the letter is posted;

as against *B*, when the letter is received by *A*.

(*c*) *A* revokes his proposal by telegram.

The revocation is complete as against *A* when the telegram is despatched. It is complete as against *B* when *B* receives it.

B revokes his acceptance by telegram. *B's* revocation is complete as against *B* when the telegram is despatched, and as against *A*, when it reaches him.

5. Revocation of proposals and acceptances. A proposal may be revoked at any time before the communication of its acceptance is complete as against the proposer, but not afterwards.

An acceptance may be revoked at any time before the communication of the acceptance is complete as against the acceptor, but not afterwards.

Illustrations

A proposers, by a letter sent by post, to sell his house to *B*.

B accepts the proposal by a letter sent by post.

A may revoke his proposal at any time before or at the moment when *B* posts his letter of acceptance, but not afterwards.

B may revoke his acceptance at any time before or at the moment when the letter communicating it reaches *A*, but not afterwards.

6. Revocation how made. A proposal is revoked—

(1) by the communication of notice of revocation by the proposer to the other party;

(2) by the lapse of the time prescribed in such proposal for its acceptance, or, if no time is so prescribed, by the lapse of a reasonable time, without communication of the acceptance;

(3) by the failure of the acceptor to fulfil a condition precedent to acceptance; or

(4) by the death or insanity of the proposer, if the fact of his death or insanity comes to the knowledge of the acceptor before acceptance.

7. Acceptance must be absolute. In order to convert a proposal into a promise, the acceptance must—

(1) be absolute and unqualified;

(2) be expressed in some usual and reasonable manner, unless the proposal prescribes the manner in which it is to be accepted. If the proposal prescribes a manner in which it is to be accepted, and the acceptance is not made in such manner, the proposer may, within a reasonable time after the acceptance is communicated to him, insist that his proposal shall be accepted in the prescribed manner, and not otherwise; but, if he fails to do so, he accepts the acceptance.

8. Acceptance by performing conditions, or receiving consideration. Performance of the conditions of a proposal, or the acceptance of any consideration for a reciprocal promise which may be offered with a proposal, is an acceptance of the proposal.

9. Promises, express and implied. In so far as the proposal or acceptance of any promise is made in words, the promise is said to be express. In so far as such proposal or acceptance is made otherwise than in words, the promise is said to be implied.

Chapter II

Of Contracts, Voidable Contracts and Void Agreements

10. What agreements are contracts. All agreements are contracts if they are made by the free consent of parties competent to contract, for a lawful consideration and with a lawful object, and are not hereby expressly declared to be void.

Nothing herein contained shall affect any law in force in India, and not hereby expressly repealed, by which any contract is required to be made in writing or in the presence of witnesses, or any law relating to the registration of documents.

11. Who are competent to contract. Every person is competent to contract who is of the age of majority according to the law to which he is subject, and who is of sound mind, and is not disqualified from contracting by any law to which he is subject.

12. What is a sound mind for the purposes of contracting. A person is said to be of sound mind for the purpose of making a contract, if, at the time when he makes it, he is capable of understanding it and of forming a rational judgment as to its effect upon his interests.

A person who is usually of unsound mind, but occasionally of sound mind, may make contract when he is of sound mind.

A person who is usually of sound mind, but occasionally of unsound mind, may not make a contract when he is of unsound mind.

Illustrations

(*a*) A patient in a lunatic asylum, who is at intervals of sound mind, may contract during those intervals.

(*b*) A sane man, who is delirious from fever, or who is so drunk that he cannot understand the terms of a contract, or from a rational judgment as to its effect on his interests, cannot contract whilst such delirium or drunkenness lasts.

13. "Consent" defined. Two or more persons are said to consent when they agree upon the same thing in the same sense.

14. "Free consent" defined. Consent is said to be free when it is not caused by—

(1) coercion, as defined in section 15, or

(2) undue influence, as defined in section 16, or

(3) fraud, as defined in section 17, or

(4) misrepresentation, as defined in section 18, or

(5) mistake, subject to the provisions of sections 20, 21 and 22.

Consent is said to be so caused when it would not have been given but for the existence of such coercion, undue influence, fraud, misrepresentation or mistake.

15. "Coercion" defined. "Coercion" is the committing, or threatening to commit, any act forbidden by the Indian Penal Code (XLV of 1860), or the unlawful detaining, or threatening to detain, any property, to the prejudice of any person whatever, with the intention of causing any person to enter into an agreement.

Explanation. It is immaterial whether the Indian Penal Code (XLV of 1860) is or is not in force in the place where the coercion is employed.

Illustrations

A, on board an English ship on the high seas, causes *B* to enter into an agreement by an act amounting to criminal intimidation under the Indian Penal Code (XLV of 1860).

A afterwards sues *B* for breach of contract at Calcutta.

A has employed coercion, although his act is not an offence by the law of England, and although section 506 of the Indian Penal Code (XLV of 1860) was not in force at the time when or place where the act was done.

16. "Undue influence" defined. (1) A contract is said to be induced by 'undue influence' where the relations subsisting between the parties are such that one of the parties is in a position to dominate the will of the other and uses that position to obtain an unfair advantage over the other.

(2) In particular and without prejudice to the generality of the foregoing principle, a person is deemed to be in a position to dominate the will of another—

(*a*) where he holds a real or apparent authority over the other, or where he stands in a fiduciary relation to the other; or

(*b*) where he makes a contract with a person whose mental capacity is temporarily or permanently affected by reason of age, illness, or mental or bodily distress.

(3) Where a person, who is in a position to dominate the will of another, enters into a contract with him, and the transaction appears, on the face of it or on the evidence adduced, to be unconscionable, the burden of proving that such contract was not induced by undue influence shall lie upon the person in a position to dominate the will of the other.

Nothing in this sub-section shall after the provisions of section 111 of the Indian Evidence Act, 1872 (1 of 1872).

Illustrations

(*a*) *A*, having advanced money to his son. *B*, during his minority, upon *B's* coming of age obtains, by misuse of parental influence, a bond from *B*, for a greater amount than the sum due in respect of the advance. *A* employs undue influence.

(*b*) *A*, a man enfeebled by disease or age, is induced, by *B*'s influence over him as his medical attendant, to agree to pay *B* an unreasonable sum for his professional services. *B* employs undue influence.

(*c*) *A*, being in debt to *B*, the money-lender of his village, contracts a fresh loan on terms which appear to be unconscionable. It lies on *B*, to prove that the contract was not induced by undue influence.

(*d*) *A* applies to a banker for a loan at a time when there is stringency in the money market. The banker declines to make the loan except at an unusually high rate of interest. *A* accepts the loan on these terms. This is a transaction in the ordinary course of business, and the contract is not induced by undue influence.

17. "Fraud" defined. "Fraud" means and includes any of the following acts committed by a party to a contract, or with his connivance, or by his agent, with intent to deceive another party thereto or his agent, or to induce him to enter into the contract—

(1) the suggestion, as a fact, of that which is not true, by one who does not believe it to be true;

(2) the active concealment of a fact by one having knowledge or belief of the fact;

(3) a promise made without any intention of performing it;

(4) any other act fitted to deceive;

(5) any such act or omission as the law specially declares to be fraudulent.

Explanation. Mere silence as to facts likely to affect the willingness of a person to enter into a contract is not fraud, unless the circumstances of the case are such that, regard being had to them, it is the duty of the person keeping silence to speak, or unless his silence is, in itself, equivalent to speech.

Illustrations

(*a*) *A* sells, by auction, to *B*, a horse which *A* knows to be unsound. *A* says nothing to *B* about the horse's unsoundness. This is not fraud in *A*.

(*b*) *B* is *A*'s daughter and has just come of age. Here, the relation between the parties would make it *A*'s duty to tell *B* if the horse is unsound.

(*c*) *B* says to *A*—"If you do not deny it, I shall assume that the horse is sound". *A* says nothing. Here *A's* silence is equivalent to speech.

(*d*) *A* and *B*, being traders, enter upon a contract. *A* has private information of a change in prices which would affect *B*'s willingness to proceed with the contract. *A* is not bound to inform *B*.

18. "Misrepresentation" defined. "Misrepresentation" means and includes—

(1) the positive assertion, in a manner not warranted by the information of the person making it, of that which is not true, though he believes it to be true;

(2) any breach of duty which, without an intent to deceive, gains an advantage of the person committing it, or any one claiming under him, by misleading another to his prejudice or to the prejudice of any one claiming under him;

(3) causing, however innocently, a party to an agreement, to make a mistake as to the substance of the thing which is the subject of the agreement.

19. Voidability of agreements without free consent. When consent to an agreement is caused by coercion, fraud or misrepresentation, the agreement is a contract voidable at the option of the party whose consent was so caused.

A party to contract, whose consent was caused by fraud or misrepresentation, may, if he thinks fit, insist that the contract shall be performed, and that he shall be put in the position in which he would have been if the representations made had been true.

Exception. If such consent was caused by misrepresentation or by silence, fraudulent within the meaning of section 17, the contract, nevertheless, is not voidable, if the party whose consent was so caused had the means of discovering the truth with ordinary diligence.

Explanation. A fraud or misrepresentation which did not cause the consent to a contract of the party on whom such fraud was practised, or to whom such misrepresentation was made, does not render a contract voidable.

Illustrations

(*a*) *A*, intending to deceive *B*, falsely represents that five hundred maunds of indigo are made annually at *A*'s factory, and thereby induces *B* to buy the factory. The contract is voidable at the option of *B*.

(*b*) *A*, by a misrepresentation, leads *B* erroneously to believe that five hundred maunds of indigo are made annually at *A's* factory. *B* examines the accounts of the factory, which show that only four hundred maunds of indigo have been made. After this *B* buys the factory. The contract is not voidable on account of *A's* misrepresentation.

(*c*) *A* fraudulently informs *B* that *A's* estate is free from encumbrance. *B* thereupon buys the estate. The estate is subject to a mortgage. *B* may either avoid the contract, or may insist on its being carried out and the mortgage-debt redeemed.

(*d*) *B*, having discovered a vein of ore on the estate of *A*, adopts means to conceal, and does conceal the existence of the ore from *A*. Through *A's* ignorance *B* is enabled to buy the estate at an under-value. The contract is voidable at the option of *A*.

(*e*) *A* is entitled to succeed to an estate at the death of *B*. *B* dies; *C*, having received intelligence of *B's* death, prevents the intelligence reaching *A*, and thus induces *A* to sell him his interest in the estate. The sale is voidable at the option of *A*.

19A. Power to set aside contract induced by undue influence. When consent to an agreement is caused by undue influence, the agreement is a contract voidable at the option of the party whose consent was so caused.

Any such contract may be set aside either absolutely or, if the party who was entitled to avoid it has received any benefit thereunder, upon such terms and conditions as to the Court may seem just.

Illustrations

(*a*) *A's* son has forged *B's* name to a promissory note. *B*, under threat of prosecuting *A's* son, obtains a bond from *A* for the amount of the forged note. If *B* sues on this bond, the Court may set the bond aside.

(*b*) *A*, a money-lender, advances Rs. 100 to *B*, an agriculturist, and, by undue influence, induces *B* to execute a bond for Rs. 200 with interest at 6 per cent per month. The Court may set the bond aside, ordering *B* to repay Rs. 100 with such interest as may seem just.

20. Agreement void where both parties are under mistake as to matter of fact. Where both the parties to an agreement are under a mistake as to a matter of fact essential to the agreement, the agreement is void.

Explanation. An erroneous opinion as to the value of the thing which forms the subject-matter of the agreement, is not to be deemed a mistake as to a matter of fact.

Illustrations

(*a*) *A* agrees to sell to *B* a specific cargo of goods supposed to be on its way from England to Bombay. It turns out that, before the day of the bargain, the ship conveying the cargo had been cast away and the goods lost. Neither party was aware of these facts. The agreement is void.

(*b*) *A* agrees to buy from *B* a certain horse. It turns out that the horse was dead at the time of the bargain, though neither party was aware of the fact. The agreement is void.

(*c*) *A*, being entitled to an estate for the life of *B*, agrees to sell it to *C*. *B* was dead at the time of the agreement, but both parties were ignorant of the fact. The agreement is void.

21. Effect of mistakes as to law. A contract is not voidable because it was caused by a mistake as to any law in force in India; but a mistake as to a law not in force in India has the same effect as a mistake of fact.

Illustration

A and *B* make a contract grounded on the erroneous belief that a particular debt is barred by the Indian Law of Limitation; the contract is not voidable.

22. Contract caused by mistake of one party as to matter of fact. A contract is not voidable merely because it was caused by one of the parties to it being under a mistake as to a matter of fact.

23. What considerations and objects are lawful, and what not. The consideration or object of an agreement is lawful, unless—

it is forbidden by law; or

is of such a nature that, if permitted, it would defeat the provisions of any law; or

is fraudulent; or

involves or implies, injury to the person or property of another; or

the Court regards it as immoral; or

opposed to public policy.

In each of these cases, the consideration or object of an agreement is said to be unlawful. Every agreement of which the object or consideration is unlawful is void.

Illustrations

(*a*) *A* agrees to sell his house to *B* for 10,000 rupees. Here, *B*'s promise to pay the sum of 10,000 rupees is the consideration for *A*'s promise to sell the house, and *A's* promise to sell the house is the consideration for *B*'s promise to pay the 10,000 rupees. These are lawful considerations.

(*b*) *A* promises to pay *B* 1,000 rupees at the end of six months, if *C*, who owes the sum to *B*, fails to pay it, *B* promises to grant time to *C* accordingly. Here, the promise of each party is the consideration for the promise of the other party, and they are lawful considerations.

(*c*) *A* promises, for a certain sum paid to him by *B*, to make good to *B* the value of his ship if it is wrecked on a certain voyage. Here, *A*'s promise is the consideration for *B*'s payment, and *B*'s payment is the consideration for *A*'s promise, and these are lawful considerations.

(*d*) *A* promises to maintain *B*'s child, and *B* promises to pay *A* 1,000 rupees yearly for the purpose. Here, the promise of each party is the consideration for the promise of the other party. They are lawful considerations.

(*e*) *A*, *B* and *C* enter into an agreement for the division among them of gains acquire, or to be acquired, by them by fraud. The agreement is void, as its object is unlawful.

(*f*) *A* promises to obtain for *B* an employment in the public service and *B* promises to pay 1,000 rupees to *A*. The agreement is void, as the consideration for it is unlawful.

(*g*) *A*, being agent for a landed proprietor, agrees for money, without the knowledge of his principal, to obtain for *B* a lease of land belonging to his principal. The agreement between *A* and *B* is void, as it implies a fraud by concealment, by *A*, on his principal.

(*h*) *A* promises *B* to drop a prosecution which he has instituted against *B* for robbery, and *B* promises to restore the value of the things taken. The agreement is void, as its object is unlawful.

(*i*) *A*'s estate is sold for arrears of revenue under the provisions of an Act of the Legislature, by which the defaulter is prohibited from purchasing the estate. *B*, upon an understanding with *A*, becomes the purchaser, and agrees to convey the estate to *A* upon receiving from him the price which *B* has paid. The agreement is void, as it renders the transaction, in effect, a purchase by the defaulter, and would so defeat the object of the law.

(*j*) *A*, who is *B*'s *Mukhtar*, promises to exercise his influence, as such, with *B* in favour of *C*, and *C* promises to pay 1,000 rupees to *A*. The agreement is void, because it is immoral.

(*k*) *A* agrees to let her daughter to hire to *B* for concubinage. The agreement is void, because it is immoral, though the letting may not be punishable under the Indian Penal Code (XLV of 1860).

Void Agreements

24. Agreements void, if considerations and objects unlawful in part. If any part of a single consideration for one or more objects, or any one or any part of any one of several considerations for a single object, is unlawful, the agreement is void.

Illustration

A promises to superintend, on behalf of *B*, a legal manufacturer of indigo, and an illegal traffic in other articles. *B* promises to pay to *A* a salary of 10,000 rupees a year. The agreement is void, the object of *A*'s promise, and the consideration for *B*'s promise, being in part unlawful.

25. Agreement without consideration, void, unless it is in writing and registered, or is a promise to compensate for something done, or is a promise to pay a debt barred by limitation law. An agreement made without consideration is void, unless—

(1) It is expressed in writing and registered under the law for the time being in force for the registration of documents, and is made on account of natural love and affection between parties standing in a near relation to each other; or unless.

(2) It is a promise to compensate, wholly or in part, a person who has already voluntarily done something for the promisor, or something which the promisor was legally compellable to do; or unless.

(3) It is a promise, made in writing and signed by the person to be charged therewith, or by his agent generally or specially authorised in that behalf, to pay wholly or in part a debt of which the creditor might have enforced payment but for the law for the limitation of suits.

If any of these cases, such an agreement is a contract.

Explanation 1. Nothing in this section shall affect the validity, as between the donor and donee, of any gift actually made.

Explanation 2. An agreement to which the consent of the promisor is freely given is not void merely because the consideration is inadequate; but the inadequacy of the consideration may be taken into account by the court in determining the question whether the consent of the promisor was freely given.

Illustrations

(*a*) *A* promises, for no consideration, to give to *B*, Rs. 1,000. This is a void agreement.

(*b*) *A*, for natural love and affection, promises to give his son, *B*, Rs. 1,000. *A* puts his promise to *B* into writing and registers it. This is a contract.

(*c*) *A* finds *B*'s purse and gives it to him. *B* promises to give *A* Rs. 50. This is a contract.

(*d*) *A* supports *B*'s infant son. *B* promises to pay *A*'s expenses in so doing. This is a contract.

(*e*) *A* owes *B* Rs. 1,000, but the debt is barred by the Limitation Act. *A* signs a written promise to pay *B* Rs. 500 on account of the debt. This is a contract.

(*f*) *A* agrees to sell a horse worth Rs. 1,000 for Rs. 10. *A*'s consent to the agreement was freely given. The agreement is a contract notwithstanding the inadequacy of the consideration.

(*g*) *A* agrees to sell a horse worth Rs. 1,000 for Rs. 10. *A* denies that his consent to the agreement was freely given.

The inadequacy of the consideration is a fact which the court should take into account in considering whether or not *A*'s consent was freely given.

26. Agreement in restraint of marriage, void. Every agreement in restraint of the marriage of any person, other than a minor, is void.

27. Agreement in restraint of trade, void. Every agreement by which any one is restrained from exercising a lawful profession, trade or business of any kind, is to that extent void.

Exception 1. *Saving of agreement not to carry on business of which goodwill is sold*. One who sells the goodwill of a business, may agree with the buyer to refrain from carrying on a similar business, within specified local limits, so long as the buyer, or any person deriving title to the goodwill from him, carries on a like business therein:

Provided that such limits appear to the Court reasonable, regard being had to the nature of the business.

28. Agreements in restraint of legal proceedings, void. Every agreement,—

(*a*) by which any party thereto is restricted absolutely from enforcing his rights under or in respect of any contract, by the usual legal proceedings in the ordinary tribunals, or which limits the time within which he may thus enforce his rights; or

(*b*) which extinguishes the rights of any party thereto, or discharges any party thereto, from any liability, under or in respect of any contract on the expiry of a specified period so as to restrict any party from enforcing his rights,

is void to that extent.

Exception 1. *Saving of contract to refer to arbitration dispute that may arise.* This section shall not render illegal a contract, by which two or more persons agree that any dispute which may arise between them in respect of any subject or class of subjects shall be referred to arbitration, and that only the amount awarded in such arbitration shall be recoverable in respect of the dispute so referred.

Exception 2. *Saving of contract to refer questions that have already arisen.* Nor shall this section render illegal any contract in writing, by which two or more persons agree to refer to arbitration any question between them which has already arisen, or affect any provision of any law in force for the time being as to references to arbitration.

Exception 3. [1][*Saving of a guarantee agreement of a bank or a financial institution.* This section shall not render illegal a contract in writting by which any bank or financial institution stipulate a term in a guarantee or any agreement making a provision for guarantee for extinguishment of the rights or discharge of any party thereto from any liability under or in respect of such guarantee or agreement on the expiry of a specified period which is not less than one year from the date of occurring or non-occurring of a specified event for extinguishment or discharge of such party from the said liability.

Explanation. (*i*) In *Exception* 3, the expression "bank" means—

(*a*) a "banking company" as defined in clause (*c*) of section 5 of the Banking Regulation Act, 1949 (10 of 1949);

(*b*) "a corresponding new bank" as defined in clause (*da*) of section 5 of the Banking Regulation Act, 1949 (10 of 1949);

(*c*) "State Bank of India" constituted under section 3 of the State Bank of India Act, 1955 (23 of 1955);

(*d*) "a subsidiary bank" as defined in clause (*k*) of section 2 of the State Bank of India (Subsidiary Banks) Act, 1959 (38 of 1959);

(*e*) "a Regional Rural Bank" established under section 3 of the Regional Rural Banks Act, 1976 (21 of 1976);

(*f*) "a Co-operative Bank" as defined in clause (*cci*) of section 5 of the Banking Regulation Act 1949 (10 of 1949);

(*g*) "a multi-State co-operative bank" as defined in clause (*cciia*) of section 5 of the Banking Regulation Act, 1949 (10 of 1949); and

(*ii*) In *Exception* 3, the expression "a financial institution" means any Public financial institution within the meaning of section 4A of the Companies Act 1956 (1 of 1956)].

29. Agreements void for uncertainty. Agreements, the meaning of which is not certain, or capable of being made certain, are void.

Illustrations

(*a*) *A* agrees to sell to *B* "a hundred tons of oil." There is nothing whatever to show what kind of oil was intended. The agreement is void for uncertainty.

---

1 *Inserted* by Act 4 of 2013 (w.e.f. 18.1.2013).

(*b*) *A* agrees to sell to *B* one hundred tons of oil of a specified description, known as an article of commerce. There is no uncertainty here to make the agreement void.

(*c*) *A*, who is a dealer in coconut oil only, agrees to sell to *B*, "one hundred tons of oil". The nature of *A's* trade affords an indication of the meaning of the words, and *A* has entered into a contract for the sale of one hundred tons of coconut oil.

(*d*) *A* agrees to sell to *B* "all the grain in my granary at Ramnagar". There is no uncertainty here to make the agreement void.

(*e*) *A* agrees to sell to *B* "one thousand maunds of rice at a price to be fixed by *C*". As the price is capable of being made certain, there is no uncertainty here to make the agreement void.

(*f*) *A* agrees to sell to *B* "my white horse for rupees five hundred or rupees one thousand". There is nothing to show which of the two prices was to be given. The agreement is void.

30. Agreements by way of wager, void. Agreements by way of wager are void; and no suit shall be brought for recovering anything alleged to be won on any wager, or entrusted to any person to abide by the result of any game or other uncertain event on which any wager is made.

Exception in favour of certain prizes for horse-racing. This section shall not be deemed to render unlawful a subscription, or contribution, or agreement to subscribe or contribute, made or entered into for or toward any plate, prize or sum of money, of the value or amount of five hundred rupees or upwards, to be rewarded to the winner or winners of any horse-race.

Section 294A of the Indian Penal Code not affected. Nothing in this section shall be deemed to legalize any transaction connected with horse-racing, to which the provisions of section 294A of the Indian Penal Code (XLV of 1860) apply.

Chapter III

Of Contingent Contracts

31. "Contingent contract" defined. A "contingent contract" is a contract to do or not to do something, if some event, collateral to such contract, does or does not happen.

Illustration

A contracts to pay to *B* Rs. 10,000 if *B's* house is burnt. This is a contingent contract.

32. Enforcement of contracts contingent on an event happening. Contingent contracts to do or not to do anything if an uncertain future event happens, cannot be enforced by law unless and until that event has happened.

If the event becomes impossible, such contracts become void.

Illustrations

(*a*) *A* makes a contract with *B* to buy *B's* horse if *A* survives *C*. This contract cannot be enforced by law unless and until *C* dies in *A's* lifetime.

(*b*) *A* makes a contract with *B* to sell a horse to *B* at a specified price, if *C*, to whom the horse has been offered, refuses to buy him. The contract cannot be enforced by law unless and until *C* refuses to buy the horse.

(*c*) *A* contracts to pay *B* a sum of money when *B* marries *C*. *C* dies without being married to *B*. The contract becomes void.

33. Enforcement of contracts contingent on an event not happening. Contingent contracts to do or not to do anything if an uncertain future event does not happen, can be enforced when the happening of that event becomes impossible, and not before.

Illustration

A agrees to pay *B* a sum of money if a certain ship does not return. The ship is sunk. The contract can be enforced when the ship sinks.

34. When event on which contract is contingent to be deemed impossible, if it is the future conduct of a living person. If the future event on which a contract is contingent is the way in which a person will act at an unspecified time, the event shall be considered to become impossible when such person does anything which renders it impossible that he should so act within any definite time, or otherwise than under further contingencies.

Illustration

A agrees to pay *B* a sum of money if *B* marries *C*, *C* marries *D*. The marriage of *B* to *C* must now be considered impossible, although it is possible that *D* may die and that *C* may afterwards marry *B*.

35. When contracts become void, which are contingent on happening of specified event within fixed time. Contingent contracts to do or not to do anything, if a specified uncertain event happens within a fixed time, become void if, at the expiration of the time fixed, such event has not happened, or if, before the time fixed, such event becomes impossible.

When contracts may be enforced, which are contingent on specified event not happening within fixed time. Contingent contracts to do or not to do anything, if a specified uncertain event does not happen within a fixed time, may be enforced by law when the time fixed has expired, and such event has not happened, or, before the time fixed has expired, if it becomes certain that such event will not happen.

Illustrations

(*a*) *A* promises to pay *B* a sum of money if a certain ship returns within a year. The contract may be enforced if the ship returns within the year, and becomes void if the ship is burnt within the year.

(*b*) *A* promises to pay *B* a sum of money if a certain ship does not return within a year. The contract may be enforced if the ship does not return within the year, or is burnt within the year.

36. Agreements contingent on impossible events, void. Contingent agreements to do or not to do anything, if an impossible event happens, are void, whether the impossibility of the event is known or not to the parties to the agreement at the time when it is made.

Illustrations

(*a*) *A* agrees to pay *B* 1,000 rupees if two straight lines should enclose a space. The agreement is void.

(*b*) *A* agrees to pay *B* 1,000 rupees if *B* will marry *A*'s daughter *C*. *C* was dead at the time of the agreement. The agreement is void.

Chapter IV

OF THE PERFORMANCE OF CONTRACTS

Contracts which must be performed

37. Obligation of parties to contract. The parties to a contract must either perform, or offer to perform, their respective promises, unless such performance is dispensed with or excused under the provisions of this Act, or of any other law.

Promises bind the representatives of the promisors in case of the death of such promisors before performance, unless a contrary intention appears from the contract.

Illustrations

(*a*) *A* promises to deliver goods to *B* on a certain day on payment of Rs. 1,000. *A* dies before that day. *A*'s representatives are bound to deliver the goods to *B*, and *B* is bound to pay Rs. 1,000 to *A*'s representatives.

(*b*) *A* promises to paint a picture for *B* by a certain day, at a certain price. *A* dies before the day. The contract cannot be enforced either by *A*'s representatives or by *B*.

38. Effect of refusal to accept offer of performance. Where a promisor has made an offer of performance to the promisee, and the offer has not been accepted, the promisor is not responsible for non-performance, nor does he thereby lost his rights under the contract.

Every such offer must fulfil the following conditions—

(1) it must be unconditional;

(2) it must be made at a proper time and place, and under such circumstances that the person to whom it is made may have a reasonable opportunity of ascertaining that the person by whom it is made is able and willing there and then to do the whole of what he is bound by his promise to do;

(3) if the offer is an offer to deliver anything to the promisee, the promisee must have a reasonable opportunity of seeing that the thing offered is the thing which the promisor is bound by his promise to deliver.

An offer to one of several joint promisees has the same legal consequences as an offer to all of them.

Illustration

A contracts to deliver to *B* at his warehouse, on the 1st March, 1873, 100 bales of cotton of a particular quality. In order to make an offer of performance with the effect stated in this section. *A* must bring the cotton to *B*'s warehouse, on the appointed day, under such circumstances that *B* may have a reasonable opportunity of satisfying himself that the thing offered is cotton of the quality contracted for, and that there are 100 bales.

39. Effect of refusal of party to perform promise wholly. When a party to a contract has refused to perform, or disabled himself from performing, his promise in its entirety, the promisee may put an end to the contract, unless he has signified, by words or conduct, his acquiescence in its continuance.

Illustrations

(*a*) *A*, a singer, enters into a contract with *B*, the manager of a theatre, to sing at his theatre two nights in every week during the next two months, and *B* engages to pay her 100 rupees for each night's performance. On the sixth night, *A* wilfully absents herself from the theatre. *B* is at liberty to put an end to the contract.

(*b*) *A*, a singer, enters into a contract with *B*, the manager of a theatre, to sing at his theatre two nights in every week during the next two months, and *B* engages to pay her at the rate of 100 rupees for each night. On the sixth night, *A* wilfully absents herself. With the assent of *B*, *A* sings on the seventh night. *B* has signified his acquiescence in the continuance of the contract, and cannot now put an end to it, but is entitled to compensation for damage sustained by him through *A*'s failure to sing on the sixth night.

By whom contracts must be performed

40. Person by whom promise is to be performed. If it appears from the nature of the case that it was the intention of the parties to any contract that any promise contained in it should be performed by the promisor himself, such promise must be performed by the promisor. In other cases, the promisor or his representatives may employ a competent person to perform it.

Illustrations

(*a*) *A*, promises to pay *B* a sum of money. *A* may perform this promise, either by personally paying the money to *B*, or by causing it to be paid to *B* by another; and if *A* dies before the time appointed for payment, his representatives must perform the promise, or employ some proper person to do so.

(*b*) *A* promises to paint a picture for *B*. *A* must perform this promise personally.

41. Effect of accepting performance from third person. When a promisee accepts performance of the promise from a third person, he cannot afterwards enforce it against the promisor.

42. Devolution of joint liabilities. When two or more persons have made a joint promise, then, unless a contrary intention appears by the contract, all such persons, during their joint lives, and, after the death of any of them, his representative jointly with the survivor or survivors, and, after the death of the last survivor, the representatives of all jointly, must fulfil the promise.

43. Any one of joint promisors may be compelled to perform. When two or more persons make a joint promise, the promisee may, in the absence of express agreement to the contrary, compel any one or more of such joint promisors to perform the whole of the promise.

Each promisor may compel contribution. Each of two or more joint promisors may compel every other joint promisor to contribute equally with himself to the performance of the promise, unless a contrary intention appears from the contract.

Sharing of loss by default in contribution. If any one of two or more joint promisors makes default in such contribution, the remaining joint promisors must bear the loss arising from such default in equal shares.

Explanation. Nothing in this section shall prevent a surety from recovering, from his principal, payments made by the surety on behalf of the principal, or entitle the principal to recover anything from the surety on account of payment made by the principal.

Illustrations

(*a*) *A*, *B* and *C* jointly promise to pay *D* 3,000 rupees. *D* may compel either *A* or *B* or *C* to pay him 3,000 rupees.

(*b*) *A*, *B* and *C* jointly promise to pay *D* the sum of 3,000 rupees, *C* is compelled to pay the whole. *A* is insolvent, but his assets are sufficient to pay one-half of his debts. *C* is entitled to receive 500 rupees from *A*'s estate, and 1,250 rupees from *B*.

(*c*) *A*, *B* and *C* are under a joint promise to pay *D* 3,000 rupees. *C* is unable to pay anything, and *A* is compelled to pay the whole. *A* is entitled to receive 1,500 rupees from *B*.

(*d*) *A*, *B* and *C* are under a joint promise to pay *D* 3,000 rupees. *A* and *B* being only sureties for *C*. *C* fails to pay. *A* and *B* are compelled to pay the whole sum. They are entitled to recover it from *C*.

44. Effect of release of one joint promisor. Where two or more persons have made a joint promise, a release of one of such joint promisors by the promisee does not discharge the other joint promisor or joint promisors; neither does it free the joint promisor so released from responsibility to the other joint promisor or joint promisors.

45. Devolution of joint rights. When a person has made a promise to two or more persons jointly, then, unless a contrary intention appears from the contract, the right to claim performance rests, as between him and them, with them during their joint lives, and, after the death of any of them, with the representative of such deceased person jointly with the survivor or survivors, and, after the death of the last survivor, with the representatives of all jointly.

Illustration

A, in consideration of 5,000 rupees, lent to him by *B* and C, promises *B* and *C* jointly to repay them that sum with interest on a day specified, *B* dies. The right to claim performance rests with *B*'s representative jointly with *C* during *C*'s life, and, after the death of *C*, with the representatives of *B* and *C* jointly.

Time and place for performance

46. Time for performance of promise, where no application is to be made and no time is specified. Where, by the contract, a promisor is to perform his promise without application by the promisee, and no time for performance is specified, the engagement must be performed within a reasonable time.

Explanation. The question "what is a reasonable time" is, in each particular case, a question of fact.

47. Time and place for performance of promise, where time is specified and no application to be made. When a promise is to be performed on a certain day, and the promisor has undertaken to perform it without application by the promisee, the promisor may perform it at any time during the usual hours of business on such day and at the place at which the promise ought to be performed.

Illustration

A promises to deliver goods at *B*'s warehouse on the 1st January. On that day *A* brings the goods to *B's* warehouse, but after the usual hour for closing it, and they are not received. *A* has not performed his promise.

48. Application for performance on certain day to be at proper time and place. When a promise is to be performed on a certain day, and the promisor has not undertaken to perform it without application by the promisee, it is the duty of the promisee to apply for the performance at a proper place and within the usual hours of business.

Explanation. The question "what is a proper time and place" is, in each particular case, a question of fact.

49. Place for performance of promise, where no application to be made and no place fixed for performance. When a promise is to be performed without application by the promisee, and no place is fixed for the performance of it, it is the duty of the promisor to apply to the promisee to appoint a reasonable place for the performance of the promise, and to perform it at such a place.

Illustration

A undertakes to deliver a thousand maunds of jute to *B* on a fixed day. *A* must apply to *B* to appoint a reasonable place for the purpose of receiving it, and must deliver it to him at such place.

50. Performance in manner or at time prescribed or sanctioned by promisee. The performance of any promise may be made in any manner, or at any time which the promisee prescribes or sanctions.

Illustrations

(*a*) *B* owes *A* 2,000 rupees. *A* desires *B* to pay the amount to *A*'s account with C, a banker. B, who also banks with *C*, orders the amount to be transferred from his account to *A*'s credit, and this is done by *C*. Afterwards, and before *A* knows of the transfer, *C* fails. There has been a good payment by *B*.

(*b*) *A* and *B* are mutually indebted. *A* and *B* settle an account by setting off one item, against another, and *B* pays *A* the balance found to be due from him upon such settlement. This amounts to a payment *A* and *B*, respectively, of the sums which they owed to each other.

(*c*) *A* owes *B* 2,000 rupees. *B* accepts some of *A*'s goods in reduction of the debt. The delivery of the goods operates as a part payment.

(*d*) *A* desires *B*, who owes him Rs. 100, to send him a note for Rs. 100 by post. The debt is discharged as soon as *B* puts into the post a letter containing the note duly addressed to *A*.

Performance of reciprocal promises

51. Promisor not bound to perform, unless reciprocal promisee ready and willing to perform. When a contract consists of reciprocal promises to be simultaneously performed, no promisor need perform his promise unless the promisee is ready and willing to perform his reciprocal promise.

Illustrations

(*a*) *A* and *B* contract that *A* shall deliver goods to *B* to be paid for by *B* on delivery. *A* need not deliver the goods, unless *B* is ready and willing to pay for the goods on delivery.

B need not pay for the goods, unless *A* is ready and willing to deliver them on payment.

(*b*) *A* and *B* contract that *A* shall deliver goods to *B* at a price to be paid by instalments, the first instalment to be paid on delivery.

A need not deliver, unless *B* is ready and willing to pay the first instalment on delivery.

B need not pay the first instalment, unless *A* is ready and willing to deliver the goods on payment of the first instalment.

52. Order of performance of reciprocal promises. Where the order in which reciprocal promises are to be performed is expressly fixed by the contract, they shall be performed in that order; and where the order is not expressly fixed by the contract, they shall be performed in that order which the nature of the transaction requires.

Illustrations

(*a*) *A* and *B* contract that *A* shall build a house for *B* at a fixed price. *A*'s promise to build the house must be performed before *B*'s promise to pay for it.

(*b*) *A* and *B* contract that *A* shall make over his stock-in-trade to *B* at a fixed price, and *B* promise to give security for the payment of the money. *A*'s promise need not be performed until the security is given, for the nature of transaction requires that *A* should have security before he delivers up his stock.

53. Liability of party preventing event on which contract is to take effect. When a contract contains reciprocal promises, and one party to the contract prevents the other from performing his promise, the contract becomes voidable at the option of the party so prevented; and he is entitled to compensation from the other party for any loss which he may sustain in consequence of the non-performance of the contract.

Illustration

A and *B* contract that *B* shall execute certain work for *A* for a thousand rupees. *B* is ready and willing to execute the work accordingly, but *A* prevents him from doing so. The contract is voidable at the option of *B*; and, if he elects to rescind it, he is entitled to recover from *A* compensation for any loss which he has incurred by its non-performance.

54. Effect of default as to that promise which should be first performed, in contract consisting of reciprocal promises. When a contract consists of reciprocal promises, such that one of them cannot be performed, or that its performance cannot be claimed till the other has been performed, and the promisor of the promise last mentioned fails to perform it, such promisor cannot claim the performance of the reciprocal promise, and must make compensation to the other party to the contract of any loss which such other party may sustain by the non-performance of the contract.

Illustrations

(*a*) *A* hires *B*'s ship to take in and convey, from Calcutta to Mauritius, a cargo to be provided by *A*, *B* receiving a certain freight for its conveyance. *A* does not provide any cargo for the ship. *A* cannot claim the performance of *B*'s promise, and must make compensation to *B* for the loss which *B* sustains by the non-performance of the contract.

(*b*) *A* contracts with *B* to execute certain builder's work for a fixed price, *B* supplying the scaffolding and timber necessary for the work. *B* refuses to furnish any scaffolding or timber, and the work cannot be executed, *A* need not execute the work, and *B* is bound to make compensation to *A* for any loss caused to him by the non-performance of the contract.

(*c*) *A* contracts with *B* to deliver to him, at a specified price, certain merchandise on board a ship which cannot arrive for a month, and *B* engages to pay for the merchandise within a week from the date of the contract. *B* does not pay within the week. *A*'s promise to deliver need not be performed, and *B* must make compensation.

(*d*) *A* promises *B* to sell him one hundred bales of merchandise, to be delivered next day, and *B* promises *A* to pay for them within a month. *A* does not deliver according to his promise. *B*'s promise to pay need not be performed and *A* must make compensation.

55. Effect of failure to perform at a fixed time, in contract in which time is essential. When a party to a contract promises to do a certain thing at or before a specified time, or certain things at or before specified times, and fails to do any such thing at or before the specified time, the contract, or so much of it as has not been performed, becomes voidable at the option of the promisee, if the intention of the parties was that time should be of the essence of the contract.

Effect of such failure when time is not essential. If it was not the intention of the parties that time should be of the essence of the contract, the contract does not become voidable by the failure to do such thing at or before the specified time; but the promisee is entitled to compensation from the promisor for any loss occasioned to him by such failure.

Effect of acceptance of performance at time other than that agreed upon. If, in case of a contract voidable on account of the promisor's failure to perform his promise at the time agreed, the promisee accepts performance of such promise at any time other than that agreed, the promisee cannot claim compensation for any loss occasioned by the non-performance of the promise at the time agreed, unless, at the time of such acceptance, he gives notice to the promisor of his intention to do so.

56. Agreement to do impossible act. An agreement to do an act impossible in itself is void.

Contract to do act afterwards becoming impossible or unlawful. A contract to do an act which, after the contract is made, becomes impossible, or, by reason of some event which the promisor could not prevent, unlawful, becomes void when the act becomes impossible or unlawful.

Compensation for loss through non-performance of act known to be impossible or unlawful. Where one person has promised to do something which he knew, or, with reasonable diligence, might have known, and which the promisee did not know, to be impossible or unlawful, such promisor must make compensation to such promisee for any loss which such promisee sustains through the non-performance of the promise.

Illustrations

(*a*) *A* agrees with *B* to discover treasure by magic. The agreement is void.

(*b*) *A* and *B* contract to marry each other. Before the time fixed for the marriage, *A* goes mad. The contract becomes void.

(*c*) *A* contracts to marry *B*, being already married to *C*, and being forbidden by the law to which he is subject to practise polygamy. *A* must make compensation to *B* for the loss caused to her by the non-performance of his promise.

(*d*) *A* contracts to take in cargo for *B* at a foreign port. *A*'s Government afterwards declares war against the country in which the port is situated. The contract becomes void when war is declared.

(*e*) *A* contracts to act at a theatre for six months in consideration of a sum paid in advance by *B*. On several occasions *A* is too ill to act. The contract to act on those occasions becomes void.

57. Reciprocal promise to do things legal, and also other things illegal. Where persons reciprocally promise, firstly, to do certain things which are legal, and, secondly, under specified circumstances, to do certain other things which are illegal, the first set of promises is a contract, but the second is a void agreement.

Illustration

A and *B* agree that *A* shall sell *B* a house for 10,000 rupees, but that, if *B* uses it as a gambling house, he shall pay *A* 50,000 rupees for it.

The first set of reciprocal promises, namely, to sell the house and to pay 10,000 rupees for it, is a contract.

The second set is for an unlawful object, namely, that *B* may use the house as a gambling house, and is a void agreement.

58. Alternative promise, one branch being illegal. In the case of an alternative promise, one branch of which is legal and the other illegal, the legal branch alone can be enforced.

Illustration

A and *B* agree that *A* shall pay *B* 1,000 rupees, for which *B* shall afterwards deliver to *A* either rice or smuggled opium.

This is a valid contract to deliver rice, and a void agreement as to the opium.

* * * * *

Contracts which need not be performed

62. Effect of novation, rescission and alteration of contract. If the parties to a contract agree to substitute a new contract for it, or to rescind or alter it, the original contract need not be performed.

Illustrations

(*a*) *A* owes money to *B* under a contract. It is agreed between *A*, *B* and *C* that *B* shall thenceforth accept *C* as his debtor, instead of *A*. The old debt of *A* to *B* is at an end, and a new debt from *C* to *B* has been contracted.

(*b*) *A* owes *B* 10,000 rupees. *A* enters into an agreement with *B*, and gives *B* a mortgage of his (*A*'s) estate for 5,000 rupees in place of the debt of 10,000 rupees. This is a new contract and extinguishes the old.

(*c*) *A* owes *B* 1,000 rupees under a contract. *B* owes *C* 1,000 rupees. *B* orders *A* to credit C with 1,000 rupees in his books, but C does not assent to the arrangement. *B* still owes *C* 1,000 rupees, and no new contract has been entered into.

63. Promisee may dispense with or remit performance of promise. Every promisee may dispense with or remit, wholly or in part, the performance of the promise made to him, or may extend the time for such performance, or may accept instead of it any satisfaction which he thinks fit.

Illustrations

(*a*) *A* promises to paint a picture for *B*. *B* afterwards forbids him to do so. *A* is no longer bound to perform the promise.

(*b*) *A* owes *B* 5,000 rupees. *A* pays to *B*, and *B* accepts, in satisfaction of the whole debt, 2,000 rupees paid at the time and place at which the 5,000 rupees were payable. The whole debt is discharged.

(*c*) *A* owes *B* 5,000 rupees. *C* pays to *B* 1,000 rupees, and *B* accepts them, in satisfaction of his claim on *A*. This payment is a discharge of the whole claim.

(*d*) *A* owes *B*, under a contract, a sum of money, the amount of which has not been ascertained. *A*, without ascertaining the amount, gives to *B*, and *B*, in satisfaction thereof, accepts, the sum of 2,000 rupees. This is a discharge of the whole debt, whatever may be its amount.

(*e*) *A* owes *B* 2,000 rupees, and is also indebted to other creditors. *A* makes an arrangement with his creditors, including *B*, to pay them, a composition of eight annas in the rupee upon their respective demands. Payment to *B* of 1,000 rupees is a discharge of *B*'s demand.

64. Consequences of rescission of voidable contract. When a person at whose option a contract is voidable rescinds it, the other party thereto need not perform any promise therein contained in which he is the promisor. The party rescinding a voidable contract shall, if he had received any benefit thereunder from another party to such contract, restore such benefit, so far as may be, to the person from whom it was received.

65. Obligation of person who has received advantage under void agreement, or contract that becomes void. When an agreement is discovered to be void, or when a contract becomes void, any person who has received any advantage under such agreement or contract is bound to restore it, or to make compensation for it, to the person from whom he received it.

Illustrations

(*a*) *A* pays *B* 1,000 rupees in consideration of *B*'s promising to marry *C*, *A*'s daughter. C is dead at the time of the promise. The agreement is void, but *B* must repay *A* the 1,000 rupees.

(*b*) *A* contracts with *B* to deliver to him 250 maunds of rice before the 1st of May. *A* delivers 130 maunds only before that day, and none after. *B* retains the 130 maunds after the 1st of May. He is bound to pay *A* for them.

(*c*) *A*, a singer, contracts with *B*, the manager of a theatre, to sing at his theatre for two nights in every week during the next two month, and *B* engages to pay her a hundred rupees for each night's performance. On the sixth night, *A* wilfully absents herself from the theatre, and *B*, in consequence, rescinds the contract. *B* must pay *A* for the five nights on which she had sung.

(*d*) *A* contracts to sing for *B* at a concert for 1,000 rupees, which are paid in advance. *A* is too ill to sing. *A* is not bound to make compensation to *B* for the loss of the profits which *B* would have made if *A* had been able to sing, but must refund to *B* the 1,000 rupees paid in advance.

66. Mode of communicating or revoking rescission of voidable contract. The rescission of a voidable contract may be communicated or revoked in the same manner, and subject to the same rules, as apply to the communication or revocation of a proposal.

67. Effect of neglect of promisee to afford promisor reasonable facilities for performance. If any promisee neglects or refuses to afford the promisor reasonable facilities for the performance of his promise, the promisor is excused by such neglect or refusal as to any non-performance caused thereby.

Illustration

A contracts with *B* to repair *B's* house.

B neglects or refuses to point out to *A* the places in which his house requires repair.

A is excused for the non-performance of the contract, if it is caused by such neglect or refusal.

* * *

Chapter VI

Of the consequences of breach of contract

73. Compensation for loss or damage caused by breach of contract. When a contract has been broken, the party who suffers by such breach is entitled to receive, from the party who has broken the contract, compensation for any loss or damage caused to him thereby, which naturally arose in the usual course of things from such breach, or which the parties knew, when they made the contract, to be likely to result from the breach of it.

Such compensation is not to be given for any remote and indirect loss or damage sustained by reason of the breach.

Compensation for failure to discharge obligation resembling those created by contract. When an obligation resembling those created by contract has been incurred and has not been discharged, any person injured by the failure to discharge it is entitled to receive the same compensation from the party in default, as if such person had contracted to discharge it and had broken his contract.

Explanation. In estimating the loss or damage arising from a breach of contract, the means which existed of remedying the inconvenience caused by the non-performance of the contract must be taken into account.

Illustrations

(*a*) *A* contracts to sell and deliver 50 maunds of saltpetre to *B*, at a certain price to be paid on delivery. *A* breaks his promise. *B* is entitled to receive from *A*, by way of compensation, the sum, if any, by which the contract price falls short of the price for which *B* might have obtained 50 maunds of saltpetre of like quality at the time when the saltpetre ought to have been delivered.

(*b*) *A* hires *B*'s ship to go to Bombay, and there take on board, on the first of January, a cargo, which *A* is to provide, and to bring it to Calcutta, the freight to be paid when earned. *B*'s ship does not go to Bombay, but *A* has opportunities of procuring suitable conveyance for the cargo upon terms as advantageous as those on which he had chartered the ship. *A* avails himself of those opportunities, but is put to trouble and expense in doing so. *A* is entitled to receive compensation from *B* in respect of such trouble and expense.

(*c*) *A* contracts to buy of *B*, at a stated price, 50 maunds of rice, no time being fixed for delivery. *A* afterwards informs *B* that he will not accept the rice if tendered to him. *B* is entitled to receive from *A*, by way of compensation, the amount, if any, by which the contract price exceeds that which *B* can obtain for the rice at the time when *A* informs *B* that he will not accept it.

(*d*) *A* contracts to buy *B*'s ship for 60,000 rupees, but breaks his promise. *A* must pay to *B*, by way of compensation, the excess, if any, of the contract price over the price which *B* can obtain for the ship at the time of the breach of promise.

(*e*) *A*, the owner of a boat, contracts with *B* to take a cargo of jute to Mirzapur, for sale at that place, starting on a specified day. The boat, owing to some unavoidable cause, does not start at the time appointed, whereby the arrival of the cargo at Mirzapur is delayed beyond the time when it would have arrived if the boat had sailed according to the contract. After that date, and before the arrival of the cargo, the price of jute falls. The measure of the compensation payable to *B* by *A* is the difference between the price which *B* could have obtained for the cargo at Mirzapur at the time when it would have arrived if forwarded in due course, and its market price at the time when it actually arrived.

(*f*) *A* contracts to repair *B*'s house in a certain manner, and receives payment in advance. *A* repairs the house, but not according to contract. *B* is entitled to recover from *A* the cost of making the repairs conforming to the contract.

(*g*) *A* contracts to let his ship to *B* for a year, from the first of January, for a certain price. Freights rises, and on the first of January, the hire obtainable for the ship is higher than the contract price. *A* breaks his promise. He must pay to *B*, by way of compensation, a sum equal to the difference between the contract price and the price for which *B* could hire a similar ship for a year on and from the first of January.

(*h*) *A* contracts to supply *B* with a certain quantity of iron at a fixed price, being a higher price than that for which *A* could procure and deliver the iron. *B* wrongfully refuses to receive the iron. *B* must pay to *A*, by way of compensation, the difference between the contract price of the iron and the sum for which *A* could have obtained and delivered it.

(*i*) *A* delivers to *B*, a common carrier, a machine, to be conveyed, without delay, to *A*'s mill, informing *B* that his mill is stopped for want of the machine. *B* unreasonably delays the delivery of the machine, and *A*, in consequence, loses a profitable contract with the Government. *A* is entitled to receive from *B*, by way of compensation, the average amount of profit which would have been made by the working of the mill during the time that delivery of it was delayed, but not the loss sustained through the loss of the Government contract.

(*j*) *A*, having contracted with *B* to supply *B* with 1,000 tons of iron at 100 rupees a ton, to be delivered at a stated time, contracts with *C* for the purchase of 1,000 tons of iron at 80 rupees a ton, telling *C* that he does so for the purpose of performing his contract with *B*. *C* fails to perform his contract with *A*, who cannot procure other iron, and *B*, in consequence, rescinds the contract. *C* must pay to *A* 20,000 rupees, being the profit which *A* would have made by the performance of his contract with *B*.

(*k*) *A* contracts with *B* to make and deliver to *B*, by a fixed day, for a specified price, a certain piece of machinery. *A* does not deliver the piece of machinery at the time specified, and, in consequence of this, *B* is obliged to procure another at a higher price than that which he was to have paid to *A*, and is prevented from performing a contract which *B* had made with a third person at the time of his contract with *A* (but which had not been then communicated to *A*), and is compelled to make compensation for breach of that contract. *A* must pay to *B*, by way of compensation, the difference between the contract price of the price of machinery and the sum paid by *B* for another, but not the sum paid by *B* to the third person by way of compensation.

(*l*) *A*, a builder, contracts to erect and finish a house by the first of January, in order that *B* may give possession of it at that time to *C*, to whom *B* has contracted to let it. *A* is informed of the contract between *B* and *C*, *A* builds the house so badly that, before the first of January, it falls down and has to be rebuilt by *B*, who, in consequence, loses the rent which he was to have received from *C*, and is obliged to make compensation to *C* for the breach of his contract. *A* must make compensation to *B* for the cost of rebuilding the house, for the rent lost, and for the compensation made to *C*.

(*m*) *A* sells certain merchandise to *B*, warranting it to be of a particular quality, and *B*, in reliance upon this warranty, sells it to *C* with a similar warranty. The goods prove to be not according to the warranty, and *B* becomes liable to pay *C* a sum of money by way of compensation. *B* is entitled to be reimbursed this sum by *A*.

(*n*) *A* contracts to pay a sum of money to *B* on a day specified. *A* does not pay the money on that day *B*, in consequence of not receiving the money on that day, is unable to pay his debts, and is totally ruined. *A* is not liable to make good to *B* anything except the principal sum he contracted to pay, together with interest upto the day of payment.

(*o*) *A* contracts to deliver 50 maunds of saltpetre to *B* on the first of January, at a certain price. *B* afterwards, before the first of January, contracts to sell the saltpetre to *C* at a price higher than the market price of the first of January. *A* breaks his promise. In estimating the compensation payable by *A* to *B*, the market price of the first of January, and not the profit which would have arisen to *B* from the sale to *C*, is to be taken into account.

(*p*) *A* contracts to sell and deliver 500 bales of cotton to *B* on a fixed day. *A* knows nothing of *B*'s mode of conducting his business. *A* breaks his promise, and *B*, having no cotton, is obliged to close his mill. *A* is not responsible to *B* for the loss caused to *B* by the closing of the mill.

(*q*) *A* contracts to sell and deliver to *B*, on the first of January, certain cloth which *B* intends to manufacture into caps of a particular kind, for which there is no demand, except at that season. The cloth is not delivered till after the appointed time, and too late to be used that year in making caps. *B* is entitled to receive from *A*, by way of compensation, the difference between the contract price of the cloth and its market price at the time of delivery, but not the profits which he expected to obtain by making caps, nor the expenses which he has been put to in making preparation for the manufacture.

(*r*) *A*, a ship-owner, contracts with *B* to convey him from Calcutta to Sydney in *A*'s ship, sailing on the first of January, and *B* pays to *A*, by way of deposit, one-half of his passage-money. The ship does not sail on the first of January, and *B*, after being, in consequence, detained in Calcutta for some time, and thereby put to some expense, proceeds to Sydney in another vessel, and, inconsequence, arriving too late in Sydney, loses a sum of money. *A* is liable to repay to *B* his deposit, with interest, and the expense to which he is put by his detention in Calcutta, and the excess, if any, of the passage-money paid for the second ship over that agreed upon for the first, but not the sum of money which *B* lost by arriving in Sydney too late.

74. Compensation for breach of contract where penalty stipulated for. When a contract has been broken, if a sum is named in the contract as the amount to be paid in case of such breach, or if the contract contains any other stipulation by way of penalty, the party complaining of the breach is entitled, whether or not actual damage or loss is proved to have been caused thereby, to receive from the party who has broken the contract reasonable compensation not exceeding the amount so named or, as the case may be, the penalty stipulated for.

Explanation. A stipulation for increased interest from the date of default may be a stipulation by way of penalty.

Exception. When any person enters into any bail-bond, recognizance or other instrument of the same nature, or under the provisions of any law, or under the orders of the Central Government or of any State Government, gives any bond for the performance of any public duty or act in which the public are interested, he shall be liable, upon breach of the condition of any such instrument, to pay the whole sum mentioned therein.

Explanation. A person who enters into a contract with Government does not necessarily thereby undertake any public duty, or promise to do an act in which the public are interested.

Illustrations

(*a*) *A* contracts with *B* to pay *B* Rs. 1,000, if he fails to pay *B* Rs. 500 on a given day. *A* fails to pay *B* Rs. 500 on that day. *B* is entitled to recover from *A* such compensation, not exceeding Rs. 1,000, as the Court considers reasonable.

(*b*) *A* contracts with *B* that, if *A* practices as a surgeon within Calcutta, he will pay *B* Rs. 5,000. *A* practises as a surgeon in Calcutta. *B* is entitled to such compensation, not exceeding Rs. 5,000, as the Court considers reasonable.

(*c*) *A* gives a recognizance binding him in a penalty of Rs. 500 to appear in Court on a certain day. He forfeits his recognizance. He is liable to pay the whole penalty.

(*d*) *A* gives *B* a bond for the repayment of Rs. 1,000 with interest at 12 per cent at the end of six months, with a stipulation that, in case of default, interest shall be payable at the rate of 75 per cent, from the date of default. This is a stipulation by way of penalty, and *B* is only entitled to recover from *A* such compensation as the Court considers reasonable.

(*e*) *A*, who owes money to *B*, a money-lender, undertakes to repay him by delivering to him 10 maunds of grain on a certain date, and stipulates that, in the event of his not delivering the stipulated amount by the stipulated date, he shall be liable to deliver 20 maunds. This is a stipulation by way of penalty, and *B* is only entitled to reasonable compensation in case of breach.

(*f*) *A* undertakes to repay *B* a loan of Rs. 1,000 by five equal monthly instalments, with a stipulation that, in default of payment of any instalment, the whole shall become due. This stipulation is not by way of penalty, and the contract may be enforced according to its terms.

(*g*) *A* borrows Rs. 100 from *B* and gives him a bond for Rs. 200 payable by five yearly instalments of Rs. 40, with a stipulation that, in default of payment of any instalment, the whole shall become due. This is a stipulation by way of penalty.

75. Party rightfully rescinding contract, entitled to compensation. A person who rightfully rescinds a contract is entitled to compensation for any damage which he has sustained through the non-fulfilment of the contract.

Illustration

A, a singer, contracts with *B*, the manager of a theatre, to sing at his theatre for two nights in every week during the next two months, and *B* engages to pay her 100 rupees for each night's performance. On the sixth night, *A* wilfully absents herself from the theatre, and *B*, in consequence, rescinds the contract. *B* is entitled to claim compensation for the damage which he has sustained through the non-fulfilment of the contract.

APPENDIX 3

The Registration Act 1908

[Act No. 16 of 1908]

[18th December, 1908

[RELEVANT PORTION]

* * *

Section 17. Documents of which registration is compulsory. (1) The following documents shall be registered, if the property to which they relate is situate in a district in which, and if they have been executed on or after the date on which, Act No. XVI of 1864, or the Indian Registration Act, 1866, or the Indian Registration Act, 1871, or the Indian Registration Act, 1877, or this Act came or comes into force, namely:

(*a*) instruments of gift of immovable property;

(*b*) other non-testamentary instruments which purport or operate to create, declare, assign, limit or extinguish, whether in present or in future, any right, title or interest, whether vested or contingent, of the value of one hundred rupees and upwards, to or in immovable property;

(*c*) non-testamentary instruments which acknowledge the receipt or payment of any consideration on account of the creation, declaration, assignment, limitation or extinction of any such right, title or interest, and

(*d*) leases of immovable property from year to year, or for any term exceeding one year, or reserving a yearly rent;

(*e*) non-testamentary instruments transferring or assigning, any decree or order of a court or any award when such decree or order or award purports or operates to create, declare, assign, limit or extinguish, whether in present or in future, any right, title or interest, whether vested or contingent, of the value of one hundred rupees and upwards, to or in immovable property:

Provided that the State Government may, by order published in the (Official Gazette), exempt from the operation of this sub-section any lease executed in any district, or part of a district, the terms granted by which do not exceed five years and the annual rents reserved by which do not exceed fifty rupees.

*[(1A) The documents containing contracts to transfer for consideration, any immovable property for the purpose of section 53A of the Transfer of Property Act, 1882 (4 of 1882) shall be registered if they have been executed on or after the commencement of the Registration and Other Related Laws (Amendment) Act, 2001, and if such documents are not registered on or after such commencement, then, they shall have no effect for the purposes of the said section 53A].

(2) Nothing in clauses (*b*) and (*c*) of sub-section (1) applies to—

(*i*) any composition deed; or

(*ii*) any instrument relating to shares in a joint stock Company, notwithstanding that the assets of such Company consist in whole or in part of immovable property; or

(*iii*) any debenture issued by any such Company and not creating, declaring, assigning, limiting or extinguishing any right, title or interest, to or in immovable property except in so far as it entitles the holder to the security afforded by a registered instrument whereby the Company has mortgaged, conveyed or otherwise transferred the whole or part of its immovable property or any interest therein to trustees upon trust for the benefit of the holders of such debentures; or

(*iv*) any endorsement upon or transfer of any debenture issued by any such Company; or

(*v*) **[any document other than the documents specified in sub-section (1A)] not itself creating, declaring, assigning, limiting or extinguishing any right, title or interest of the value of one hundred rupees and upwards to or in immovable property, but merely creating a right to obtain another document which will, when executed, create, declare, assign, limit or extinguish any such right, title or interest; or

(*vi*) any decree or order of a Court except a decree or order expressed to be made on a compromise and comprising immovable property other than that which is the subject-matter of the suit or proceeding; or

(*vii*) any grant of immovable property by Government; or

(*viii*) any instrument of partition made by a Revenue-officer; or

(*ix*) any order granting a loan or instrument of collateral security granted under the Land Improvement Act, 1871, or the Land Improvement Loans Act, 1883; or

(*x*) any order granting a loan under the Agriculturists' Loans Act, 1884, or instrument for securing the repayment of a loan made under that Act; or

(*xa*) any order made under the Charitable Endowments Act, 1890 (6 of 1890), vesting any property in a Treasurer of Charitable Endowments or divesting any such Treasurer of any property; or

---

* *Inserted* by Act 48 of 2001, s. 3(*a*) (w.e.f. 24-9-2001).

** *Substituted* by Act 48 of 2001, s. 3(*b*) for "any document" (w.e.f. 24-9-2001).

(*xi*) any endorsement on a mortgage-deed acknowledging the payment of the whole or any part of the mortgage-money, and any other receipt for payment of money due under a mortgage when the receipt does not purport to extinguish the mortgage; or

(*xii*) any certificate of sale granted to the purchaser of any property sold by public auction by a Civil or Revenue-officer.

Explanation.—A document purporting or operating to effect a contract for the sale of immovable property shall not be deemed to require or ever to have required registration by reason only of the fact that such document contains a recital of the payment of any earnest money or of the whole or any part of the purchase money.

(3) Authorities to adopt a son, executed after the 1st day of January, 1872, and not conferred by a will, shall also be registered.

* * *

49. Effect of non-registration of documents required to be registered. No document required by section 17 [or by any provision of the Transfer of Property Act, 1882 (4 of 1882)], to be registered shall—

(*a*) affect any immovable property comprised therein, or

(*b*) confer any power to adopt, or

(*c*) be received as evidence of any transaction affecting such property or conferring such power,

unless it has been registered:

Provided that an unregistered document affecting immovable property and required by this Act or the Transfer of Property Act, 1882 (4 of 1882), to be registered may be received as evidence of a contract in a suit for specific performance under Chapter II of the Specific Relief Act, 1877 (3 of 1877), *[* * *], or as evidence of any collateral transaction not required to be effected by registered instrument.

* *Omitted* by Act 48 of 2001, s. 6 (w.e.f. 24-9-2001).

The Transfer of Property Act 1882

[Act No. 4 of 1882]

[17th February, 1882

[RELEVANT PORTION]

* * *

53A. Part performance. Where any person contracts to transfer for consideration any immovable property by writing signed by him or on his behalf from which the terms necessary to constitute the transfer can be ascertained with reasonable certainty,

and the transferee has, in part performance of the contract, taken possession of the property or any part thereof, or the transferee, being already in possession, continues in possession in part performance of the contract and has done some act in furtherance of the contract,

and the transferee has performed or is willing to perform his part of the contract,

then, notwithstanding that *[* * *] where there is an instrument of transfer, that the transfer has not been completed in the manner prescribed therefore by the law of the time being in force, the transferor or any person claiming under him shall be debarred from enforcing against the transferee and persons claiming under him any right in respect of the property of which the transferee has taken or continued in possession, other than a right expressly provided by the terms of the contract:

Provided that nothing in this section shall affect the rights of a transferee for consideration who has no notice of the contract or of the part performance thereof.

* *Omitted* by Act 48 of 2001, s. 10 (w.e.f. 24.9.2001).

Appendix 5

Plaints and Written Statements of Suits for Specific Performance under the Specific Relief Act 1963

1. Suit for possession under s. 6 of the Specific Relief Act 1963 and other applicable provisions of law valued at Rs. ......

Suit No. .... of ....

In the Court of .... at ....

(Set out cause title)

The plaintiff states as follows:

1. The plaintiff is a neighbour of the defendant. The defendant owns an extensive vacant plot of land.

2. The plaintiff by negotiation entered into an agreement with the defendant for lease of 5 cottahs of the land of defendant adjacent to the plaintiff's residential premises.

3. The defendant executed a lease deed in respect of the said 5 cottahs of land in favour of the plaintiff and also got the said lease deed duly registered with the appropriate authorities. A copy of the Registered lease deed is annexed hereto and marked 'A'.

4. The plaintiff was taken by surprise to receive a notice from the defendant asking the plaintiff to surrender the said lease and vacate the land forthwith. A copy of the said letter/notice is annexed hereto and marked 'B'.

5. The plaintiff duly replied to the said letter/notice of defendant stating that the lease period did not expire and, therefore, there was no breach of the said Lease Agreement and as such, there is no valid reason for the defendant to ask the plaintiff to vacate the leasehold premises.

6. The defendant has been threatening the plaintiff that unless the leasehold land is immediately vacated by the plaintiff and possession handed over to the defendant the plaintiff would be forcibly evicted from the said leasehold land.

7. The defendant is also from time to time threatening the plaintiff that the defendant would forcibly take possession of the said leasehold property unless the plaintiff decides to voluntarily surrender the said leasehold premises.

8. The defendant, in fact, has in breach of the said Lease Agreement and unlawfully with the assistance of rowdy elements tried to forcibly take possession of the leasehold property with all other assets of the plaintiff on .... and the plaintiff duly lodged a complaint with the local Police Station. A copy of the said complaint dated .... is annexed hereto and marked 'C'. The police authorities apparently did not take any action and the plaintiff has not been able to get possession of the leasehold property after the defendant wrongfully took possession thereof.

9. The plaintiff states that the plaintiff is entitled to removal of the defendant from the leasehold premises and to obtain immediate possession of the said lease-hold property and to use the property in accordance with the terms and conditions of the lease deed.

10. The plaintiff is therefore entitled to recovery of the possession of the leasehold premises and to use the same in his favour as the said Lease Agreement is valid for a period of 99 years and the lease period has not expired and further the said lease deed is already registered, valid and enforceable.

11. The plaintiff is entitled to and claims possession of the said leasehold premises wrongfully and forcibly taken possession of by the defendant without any valid and lawful reason. Thus there has been no breach by the plaintiff of the Lease Agreement inasmuch as the lease rentals have been paid regularly by plaintiff and receipts issued to the plaintiff thereof. Copies of such rental receipts for the last twelve months are annexed hereto collectively marked 'D'. The plaintiff is thus entitled to and claims ouster of the defendant from the leasehold premises to giving possession thereof to the plaintiff.

12. The Leasehold property is situate at .... within jurisdiction of this learned court. Further defendant also resides at the aforesaid address within jurisdiction of this learned court. The plaintiff's cause of action also arose at the site of the leasehold property and the defendant also resides both within the jurisdiction of this learned court and as such, this learned court has the jurisdiction to entertain, try and determine this suit.

13. For the purposes of jurisdiction and court fees, the suit is valued at Rs. .... on which requisite court fees in stamps have been duly paid.

The plaintiff, therefore, prays for and claims:

(*a*) Decree for a declaration that forcible and wrongful taking possession of the leasehold premises by the defendant is unlawful and contrary to the terms and conditions of the Lease Agreement;

(*b*) Decree for a declaration that the plaintiff is entitled to have possession of the leasehold premises with a direction to the defendant to make over possession of leasehold premises to plaintiff;

(*c*) Injunction restraining the defendant from entering into the said leasehold premises during the validity period of the said lease agreement;

(*d*) Costs of this suit be paid by defendant to plaintiff;

(*e*) Further and other orders be made and reliefs be granted as to which plaintiff is entitled to in law and in equity.

Verification

I, Mr. F., son of Mr. G, the plaintiff abovementioned, do hereby say that the statements contained in paragraphs 1 to 13 hereinabove are true to my knowledge and to the best of my belief.

Signature of the plaintiff

Signature of plaintiff's Advocate

Affidavit

2. Affidavit in support of the plaint

Suit No. .... of ....

In the Court of .... at ....

(Set out cause title)

I, ... son of .... residing at .... do hereby solemnly affirm and say as follows:

1. I am the plaintiff in the above suit and I know the facts and circumstances of the case as stated in the plaint and I am competent to make this affidavit.

2. I say that the statements made in paragraphs 1, 2 and 3 of the plaint are matters of record and questions of fact.

3. With reference to paragraphs 4 and 5 of the plaint the statements made therein are true to my knowledge.

4. I state that the statements made in paragraphs 6 and 7 of the plaint are true and correct.

5. The statements made in paragraph 8 of the plaint are also true and correct to my knowledge.

6. The statements made in paragraphs 9, 10 and 11 of the plaint are my humble submissions before this Learned Court.

7. With reference to the statements made in paragraphs 12 and 13 of the plaint, these are matters of fact and law.

8. The statements made in paragraphs 1 to 5 of the foregoing affidavit are true to my knowledge based on facts and records and those made in paragraphs 6 and 7 thereof are my submissions to this Learned Court.

Solemnly affirmed
by the said ....
.....................................in the court
House at .... on
this .... day of ....
....

Before me
Magistrate/Notary

Identified by me,
Clerk to ....
Advocate

N.B. : The plaintiff who has verified the plaint has to affirm a separate affidavit proving the facts stated in the plaint as required under s. 26(2) and Or. VI, r. 15(4) of the Code of Civil Procedure 1908, as this is intended to be used as Examination-in-chief of the plaintiff.

3. Suit for specific performance of agreement to sell a property

Suit No. .... of ....

In the Court of .... at ....

(Set out cause title)

The plaintiff states as follows:

1. The plaintiff is a resident of .... within the jurisdiction of this learned court. The defendant No. 1 resides at the same locality where the plaintiff resides and defendant owns a plot of land adjacent to the residence of plaintiff.

2. With intent to construct an Extension Building the plaintiff entered into an agreement with defendant No. 1 for purchase of 3 cottahs of land adjacent to the premises of plaintiff.

3. After negotiation it was agreed by and between the parties herein that the defendant No. 1 would sell 3 cottahs of land adjacent to the plaintiff's premises at a price of Rs. 10,000 per cottah totalling to Rs. 30,000. At the request of the defendant No. 1 the plaintiff paid Rs. 10,000 by way of advance to defendant No. 1 pending execution of Sale Deed.

4. The defendant No. 1 received the advance of Rs. 10,000 as Earnest Money and issued a formal receipt therefore. A copy of receipt is annexed hereto marked 'A'.

5. The plaintiff requested defendant No. 1 to execute the registered Sale Deed and offered to pay the balance of Rs. 20,000 thereafter. The defendant No. 1 assured the plaintiff that the Sale Deed would be prepared and executed and registered very soon, and thereafter possession would be given to the plaintiff.

6. But suppressing all these facts and the binding agreement with the plaintiff, defendant No. 1 illegally entered into an agreement for sale of the said land with defendant No. 2 which fact the plaintiff came to know through a neighbour of the plaintiff.

7. Thereafter plaintiff contacted the defendant No. 1 and complained about his agreement with defendant No. 2 for sale of the same 3 cottahs of leasehold land.

8. But the defendant No. 1 could not give any definite satisfactory reply but only evaded the issue.

9. The plaintiff then anticipating illegal act of defendant No. 1 issued a letter to defendant No. 1 stating that the defendant No. 1 was bound to execute a Sale Deed in favour of plaintiff in respect of said 3 cottahs of land as there has already been an agreement to that effect for which an advance payment of Rs. 10,000 has been made to defendant No. 1 and the defendant No 1 is bound to execute a Registered Sale Deed in respect thereof in favour of the plaintiff. A copy of the said letter was also sent to defendant No. 2 advising not to purchase the said plot of land measuring 3 cottahs from defendant No. 1 as the plaintiff has already purchased the same and had also advanced to defendant No. 1 a sum of Rs. 10,000 (ten thousand) and is also ever ready and willing to pay balance sum of Rs. 20,000 at the time of execution of the Sale Deed. A copy of the letter sent to defendant No. 2 is annexed hereto and marked 'B'.

10. The plaintiff states that the defendant No. 1 is not legally entitled to sell the said property to defendant No. 2 or to any body else excepting the plaintiff and purported Sale Deed for sale of 3 cottahs of land to defendant No. 2 is in clear breach of the agreement with the plaintiff and the same is fraudulent and cannot be sustained.

11. The plaintiff was and is ever ready and willing to perform his part of the said contract and pay balance sum of Rs. 20,000 on the defendant No. 1 executing and registering the Sale Deed.

12. In the facts and circumstances of the case the plaintiff is entitled to and claims specific performance of the contract and a decree directing defendant No. 1 to execute a registered Sale Deed in favour of plaintiff in respect of said 3 cottahs of land on payment by the plaintiff of the balance sum of Rs. 20,000 to defendant No. 1.

13. The plaintiff's cause of action arose at .... within the jurisdiction of this learned court and the immovable landed property being subject-matter of the suit is also situated within the jurisdiction of this learned court.

14. For the purposes of jurisdiction and court fees, the suit is valued at Rs. .... on which requisite court fees in stamp has been paid.

15. No part of the plaintiff's claims is barred by the law of limitation.

The plaintiff, therefore, prays for and claims:

(*a*) Decree for Specific Performance of the said agreement with the defendant No. 1 with direction to defendant No. 1 to execute a Registered Sale Deed in favour of plaintiff regarding 3 cottahs of land adjacent to the premises of plaintiff.

(*b*) Alternatively, a decree for refund of Rs. 10,000 paid as advance by way of Earnest Money with interest @ 17% per annum and cost and damages at Rs. 50,000 being present market value of 3 cottahs of land in the said locality.

(*c*) Injunction restraining the defendant No. 2 from entering into any agreement or purchasing the said 3 cottahs of land from defendant No. 1.

(*d*) Costs of suit be paid by defendant No. 1 to plaintiff.

(*e*) Further and other orders be made and directions be given as to this learned court may deem fit and proper to afford complete relief to the plaintiff.

Verification

I, Mr. A. son of Mr. K. the plaintiff above-named, hereby verify and confirm that the statements contained in paragraphs 1 to 17 hereinabove are true to my knowledge and to the best of my belief.

Signature of the plaintiff

Signature of plaintiff's Advocate

Affidavit (See Form 2)

N.B.: The person who has verified the plaint shall affirm an affidavit proving the facts stated in the plaint as required by s. 26(2) and Or. VI, r. 15(4) of the Code of Civil Procedure 1908. This is intended to be used as an Examination-in-Chief of the plaintiff.

4. Suit for pre-emption

Suit No. .... of .... 20......

In the Court of .... at ......

(Set out cause title)

The plaintiff states:

1. The plaintiff and defendant No. 1 jointly inherited from their late father Mr. C several Bighas of land with two one-storied buildings as described in a schedule annexed hereto marked 'A'.

2. The plaintiff and defendant No. 1 agreed to partition the said property into two portions. One of the terms of the partition was that if either of the parties wanted to sell or dispose of his portion of the land and/or building or any portion thereof the same would be offered first to the other party with three months' time to consider the matter.

3. In violation of the said agreement the defendant No. 1 without the knowledge of the plaintiff sold and transferred 10 cottahs of land out of his share to defendant No. 2 by a deed of sale executed and duly registered for a sum of Rs. 2 lakhs. The said sale is invalid to the knowledge of defendants.

4. The plaintiff after coming to know of the said transaction immediately requested the defendant No. 2 to sell and transfer the said property on receiving the consideration money paid to defendant No. 1 plus 16% by way of interest.

5. The defendant No. 2, however, refused to reconvey the said land purchased from defendant No. 1 without assigning any reason.

6. The plaintiff, therefore, through his lawyer issued a notice to the defendants and requested the defendant No. 2 to reconvey the said property purchased from defendant No. 1 to the plaintiff on payment of the price he paid to defendant No. 1 with interest at 16% per annum from the date of payment till the demand made by the plaintiff for reconveyance of the same to the plaintiff. Defendant No. 2 refused to comply with the request of the plaintiff.

7. The plaintiff's cause of action arose within the jurisdiction of this learned court and the cause of action is continuing from day to day.

8. For the purposes of jurisdiction and court fees the suit is valued at .... on which court fees in stamps have been paid.

The plaintiff, therefore, prays for and claims:

(*a*) Decree against defendant No. 2 for transfer of the land sold by defendant No. 1 to defendant No. 2 in enforcement of plaintiff's right of pre-emption on payment of the consideration money paid by defendant No. 2 to defendant No. 1 plus 16% interest;

(*b*) Receiver;

(*c*) Injunction;

(*d*) Costs;

(*e*) Further and other reliefs.

Verification

I, Mr. A, son of Mr. C, residing at .... do hereby verify and say as follows:

1. I am the plaintiff and I know the facts and circumstances of this case and I am able to depose thereto.

2. The statements in paragraphs 1 to 8 hereinabove are true to my knowledge.

Plaintiff's signature Clerk to Advocate

Plaintiff's Advocate

5. Affidavit in support of the facts stated in the plaint for pre-emption

Suit No. .... of .... 20.......

In the Court of .... at ......

(See FORM 2)

6. Written statement of defendant to the plaint for pre-emption

Suit No. .... of .... 20.......

In the Court of .... at ......

(Set out cause title)

This defendant states:

1. The plaintiff has no valid cause of action against this defendant, the suit is not maintainable and be dismissed with costs.

2. Without prejudice to the aforesaid, this defendant deals with the allegations and contentions contained in the plaint in the following paragraphs.

3. The statement in paragraph 1 of plaint is a matter of record.

4. With reference to paragraph 2 of plaint, the defendant will refer to the deed of partition so as to ascertain the terms and conditions of the partition. This defendant states that there was no condition in the agreement restricting the sale or disposal of a portion of this defendant's property after the said partition.

In the present case, the question of offering first to plaintiff the sale of a portion of the land of this defendant to defendant No. 2 did not and could not arise. By such sale of portion of this defendant's land to defendant No. 2 this defendant has not committed any breach of any term of the agreement. This defendant has not sold his portion of land and/or building but only a portion of this defendant's property which is not prohibited by the agreement of such partition. The alleged right of pre-emption of the plaintiff can apply only to the land attached to the said portion of land belonging to plaintiff.

5. With reference to paragraph 3 of plaint, this defendant states that for such transfer of 10 cottahs of the land to defendant No. 2 the plaintiff cannot enforce his right of pre-emption or the restrictive term in the partition deed. In any event, after the said Partition Deed was executed, this defendant told the plaintiff that for construction of a multistoreyed building this defendant would have to sell a portion of his land. This defendant states that the transfer of 10 cottahs of land to the defendant No. 2 was not in breach of any agreement.

6. With reference to paragraph 4 of plaint, this defendant states that it was only for defendant No. 2 to sell and transfer said property to plaintiff in terms of the offer made by the plaintiff but the plaintiff had no right of pre-emption.

7. With reference to paragraph 5 of the plaint, this defendant states that it was within the lawful right of the defendant No. 2 to refuse to sell his land to the plaintiff.

8. With reference to paragraph 6 of the plaint, this defendant states that the lawyer's notice was contrary to agreement between parties and in any event, it was at the option of defendant No. 2 to re-sell the said property accepting the offer of the plaintiff. The plaintiff then had no legal right for reconveyance of the said land by defendant No. 2 in favour of plaintiff.

9. With reference to paragraph 7 of plaint, this defendant states that the plaintiff has no valid cause of action for this suit and, as such, the suit is not maintainable, and this learned court has no jurisdiction to entertain, try or determine the claims of the plaintiff.

10. The suit be dismissed with costs.

Verification

I, Mr. B, son of Mr. C, residing at .... do hereby verify and say as follows:

1. I am defendant No. 1 and I know the facts and circumstances of this case and I am able to depose thereto.

2. The statements in paragraphs 1 to 10 hereinabove are true to my knowledge.

Defendant's signature — Clerk to the Advocate

Defendant's Advocate

7. Affidavit of the defendant in support of the facts stated in the written statement

Suit No. .... of .... 20.........

In the court of .... at ....

(Set out cause title)

I, ... son of .... aged about .... years, residing at .... do hereby solemnly affirm and state as follows:

1. I am the defendant No. 1 in the instant case and I know the facts and circumstances of the case. I am authorised and competent to make this affidavit on behalf of the defendants and I am able to depose in support of the statements made herein.

2. The statements made in paragraphs 1 and 2 of the written statement are submissions before this Learned Court.

3. The statements made in paragraphs 3 and 4 of the said written statement there are matters of record and also questions of law.

4. The statements made in paragraph 5 of the said written statement are questions of fact and law.

5. The statements made in paragraphs 6 and 7 of the said written statement are questions of law.

6. The statements made in paragraphs 8, 9 and 10 of the said written statement are the humble submissions before the Learned Court.

7. The statements made in paragraphs 1, 3, 4 and 5 of this affidavit are true to my knowledge and belief and those made in paragraphs 2 and 6 hereinabove are my humble submissions before this Learned Court.

Solemnly affirmed by the said	Identified by me, ...
in the Court House at	Clerk to Mr./Ms. ....
on this .... day of.	Advocate
Before me Magistrate/Notary	

Specific Performance

1. Sale of Land

Purchaser versus Vendor

8. Claim by purchaser for specific performance of a contract to sell land with an alternative claim for damages[1]

1. By an agreement in writing, dated ...., the defendant agreed to sell and the plaintiff agreed to buy at the price of Rs. .... a plot of land specified at the foot of the plaint free of all encumbrances.

---

1 *Readiness and willingness.* Averment and proof is necessary under s. 16 of the Specific Relief Act 1963. *Mama* v *Sassoon* (1927-28) LR 55 IA 360, 373, 375; *Narinjan* v *Md. Yunus* AIR 1932 Lah 266. After a bargain of sale has been repudiated by the vendor, the purchaser claiming specific performance can, in the absence of any evidence to the contrary, easily discharge the onus about readiness and willingness by simply showing that he is still ready and willing to carry out his bargain; *Brijmohan* v *Chandrabhagabai* AIR 1939 Nag 173; *Ramakrishnayya* v *Sreeramulu* AIR 1939 Mad 547.

Suit for specific performance, if suit for land within the meaning of clause 12 of the Letters Patent. A distinction must be drawn between a vendor's suit and a purchaser's suit for specific performance. A vendor's suit for specific performance, that is to say, for the purchase prior is not a suit for land; *Land Mortgage Bank* v *Sudurudeen Ahmad* (1892) ILR 19 Cal 358, folld. in *Nagendra Nath* v *Eraligool Co.* (1922) ILR 49 Cal 670; *Velliappa Chettiar* v *Govinda Dass* (1929) ILR 52 Mad 809 (FB); *Sewdayal Ramjeedas* v *Official Trustee of Bengal* (1931) ILR 58 Cal 768, 779. A purchaser's suit for specific performance is a suit for land; *All India Sugar Mills* v *Sardar Sundar Singh* ILR (1937)2 Cal 644.

Specific performance—an equitable relief. A contract to be specifically enforceable must be mutual; *Debendra* v *Lalit Krishna* (1937-38)42 CWN 1090. The relief of specific performance is an equitable relief lying in the discretion of the Court; *Subbarayadu* v *Tatayya* 1937 MWN 1158. See s. 20, Specific Relief Act 1963; *Saukhi Sah* v *Mahamaya* AIR 1934 Pat 518. The court will not decree specific performance of an act which the defendant is not in a position to perform; *Lal Chand* v *Hari Chand* (1938-39) CWN 903.

Specific performance and/or damages. Under s. 21, Specific Relief Act 1963, any person suing for the specific performance of a contract may also claim compensation for its breach, either in addition to, or in substitution of, such performance. If in any such suit the court decides that specific performance ought not to be granted, but that there is a contract between the parties which has been broken by the defendant and that the plaintiff is entitled to compensation for that breach, it shall award him compensation accordingly. If in any such suit the court decides that

2. The said agreement provided, *inter alia*, that Rs. 1,000 should be paid immediately by the plaintiff to the defendant as a deposit in part payment of the purchase money and the remainder on the .... day of .... 20........, on which date the sale should be completed.

3. The plaintiff duly paid the said deposit.

4. A draft conveyance was drawn up and was approved in writing by the parties on ....

5. Thereafter, the said draft conveyance was engrossed and stamped and, on .... 20......., the date fixed for completion of the sale, the plaintiff offered to pay to the defendant Rs. ...., the remainder of the purchase money

---

specific performance ought to be granted, but that it is not sufficient to satisfy the justice of the case, and that some compensation for breach of the contract should also be made to the plaintiff, it shall award him such compensation accordingly.

In determining the amount of any compensation awarded under this section, the court shall be guided by the principles specified in s. 73 of the Contract Act. No compensation shall be awarded under this section unless the plaintiff has claimed such compensation in his plaint; provided that where the plaintiff has not claimed any such compensation in the plaint, the court shall at any stage of the proceeding, allow him to amend the plaint on such terms as may be just, for including a claim for such compensation. The circumstances that the contract has become incapable of specific performance does not preclude the court from exercising the jurisdiction conferred by s. 21 of the Act. Where the vendee on a breach of contract by the vendors claimed a decree for specific performance or in the alternative a refund with interest of the amount of the purchase price paid by him to the vendors but withdrew during the pendency of the suit his claim for specific performance and the vendors did not suffer from the suit, *Held*: that the vendee was not debarred from claiming the refund as the claim sought only *restitutio in integrum* and was not strictly one for damages; *Jaggo Bai* v *Harihar Prasad* AIR 1940 All 41; *Ramakrishnayya* v *Sreeramulu* AIR 1939 Mad 547. Absence of title; *Kisanlal* v *Nandeo* AIR 1943 Nag 299. Imperfect title; *Pundalik* v *Jainarayan* AIR 1949 Nag 83. Partial performance when enforceable; *Krishna* v *Graham* 50 Cal 700 and see *Ramalu* v *Venkatasubba* AIR 1944 Mad 554.

Interest upon deposit. In a suit on breach of contract by the vendor, the vendee is entitled to a claim for interest upon the amount of purchase price paid by him to the vendor and retained by him even after his repudiation of the contract; *Jaggo Bai* v *Harihar* AIR 1940 All 41.

Where no time is fixed for performance. Section 46, Indian Contract Act.

Limitation. Three years, under Article 54, Limitation Act 1963 from the date fixed for the performance, or, if no such date is fixed, when the plaintiff has notice that performance is refused. Even a suit for specific performance of a registered contract comes under this Article; *Srinivasa* v *Rengasami* (1908) ILR 31 Mad 452, 453.

Parties to suit. Sections 15 and 19, Specific Relief Act 1963. Specific performance cannot be enforced against a minor; *Krishna Chandra* v *Rishabha* AIR 1939 Nag 265; Section 16(*a*). Person in possession of property and claiming adversely to vendor and person attaching property are necessary parties; *Shivsankarappa* v *Shivappa* AIR 1943 Bom 27.

Court fee. The Court Fees Act s. 7, cl. X (*a*), according to the amount of the consideration. See *Dullabho* v *Adinarayana* AIR 1937 Mad 881.

Agreement for sale, if compulsorily registrable. It is now settled law that a mere agreement for the sale of immovable property is not compulsorily registrable.

but the defendant failed and neglected to execute the conveyance, whereupon on ...., notice in writing was given by the plaintiff to the defendant requiring him to complete the sale on or before ....

6. On the last mentioned date the plaintiff again offered to pay to the defendant Rs. ...., the remainder of the purchase money. Yet the defendant has not completed the sale.

7. The plaintiff has been and still is ready and willing to perform his part of the said agreement.

8. If the defendant completes the sale, the plaintiff shall claim damage to the extent of Rs. .... which the plaintiff has suffered by reason of the defendant's wrongful refusal to complete the sale in accordance with the terms of the said agreement. The following are the particulars of such damage.

Particulars:

9. If the court does not direct specific performance of the said agreement then the plaintiff shall claim Rs. .... damages made up as follows:

The plaintiff claims—

(1) Specific performance of the said agreement.

(2) Rs. .... damages under paragraph 8 hereof. Alternatively—

(3) Refund of the said deposit of Rs. ...., together with interest thereon at the rate of Rs. .... *per cent. per annum.*

(4) Rs. .... damages, under paragraph 9 hereof.

9. Claim by purchaser for specific performance and/or damages (Another Form)

In the High Court etc.
O. O. Jn.

1. By an agreement in writing, dated .... 20........., it was agreed that the defendant would sell and the plaintiff would buy unencumbered premises No. ...., the particulars whereof are specified in the schedule hereto, upon, *inter alia*, the following terms:

(Here set out the terms)

2. Upon the signing of the said agreement, the plaintiff paid to the defendant the sum of Rs. .... by way of deposit.

3. On ...., the defendant's solicitor delivered to the plaintiff's Advocate the abstract of the defendant's title to the said property.

4. On the said .... 20........, the plaintiff's Advocate forwarded to the defendant's Advocate his requisitions in writing in respect of such title.

5. On .... 20........, the defendant's Advocate delivered to the plaintiff's Advocate, his answers to the said requisitions.

6. On .... 20........., the plaintiff's Advocate forwarded the draft conveyance to the defendant's Advocate for approval. The said draft conveyance has not been returned to the plaintiff or his Advocate.

7. The defendant is wrongfully neglecting and refusing to complete the sale although thereunto requested in writing dated .... and .....

8. The plaintiff has always been and is ready and willing to complete the said purchase in accordance with the terms of the said agreement.

9. If the defendant completes the sale, the plaintiff shall claim damage to the extent of Rs. ...., which the plaintiff has suffered by reason of the defendant's wrongful refusal to complete the sale in accordance with the terms of the said agreement. The following are the particulars of such damages:

Particulars:

10. If the court does not direct specific performance of the said agreement then the plaintiff shall claim Rs. .... damages made up as follows: (Here give particulars).

The plaintiff claims—

(1) Specific performance of the said agreement.

(2) Rs. .... damages under paragraph 9 hereof.

Alternatively—

(3) Refund of the said deposit of Rs. ...., together with interest thereon at the rate of Rs. .... *per cent. per annum.*

(4) Rs. .... damages, under paragraph 10 hereof.

Purchaser versus Vendor and Third-party Purchaser

10. Claim by purchaser for specific performance of contract for sale of property, subsequently sold to third party[2]

1. By a registered agreement dated .... 20........, the defendant A.B. agreed to sell to the plaintiff the house and premises No. .... Road, situate within the local limits of the jurisdiction of the court more particularly described in the schedule hereto, for the price of Rs. .... where of Rs. .... was payable forthwith as earnest money and the balance payable on the .... day of ....

---

2 *Kafiladdin* v *Samiraddin* (1929-30)34 CWN 698, 701 (When subsequently to a contract for sale of a property, the said property is conveyed to a third party who purchases with notice of the contract and a suit for specific performance of the contract succeeds the proper decree to pass is to direct both the original contracting party and the subsequent purchaser to convey the property to the plaintiff).

Court fee. Where the plaintiff not only seeks for specific performance of a contract of sale, but also asks that the defendant may be compelled to execute a conveyance and to deliver possession of the property to him, the suit is in substance one for possession of the property and should be valued under s. 7, cl. (*v*) of the Court Fees Act, according to the value of the subject-matter; *Madan Mohan* v *Gaja Prasad* (1911)14 Cal LJ 159. But see *Ramanujam* v *Sivalingam* (1924) ILR 47 Mad 150 (where it has been held that a suit for specific performance and delivery of possession clearly falls within the description of a suit for specific performance, under cl. x(*a*) and the addition of the prayer for possession makes no difference. The suit cannot be properly described as a suit for possession of property and brought under cl. (*v*) of the Court Fees Act, simply because a prayer for possession is added).

20........, when the sale should be completed. It was also agreed that in these respects time was to be of the essence of the contract.

2. The plaintiff duly paid the said earnest money and, on .... the date fixed for completion of the sale, tendered the balance of the consideration money and called upon the defendant A.B. to transfer the said property by a sufficient instrument, but the defendant A. B., has not done so.

3. The plaintiff has been and still is ready and willing to perform his part of the said agreement.

4. On .... 20......, the defendant A.B. sold the said property to the defendant C.D. who purchased the same with notice of the aforesaid agreement for sale.

5. If the court does not direct specific performance of the said agreement, then the plaintiff shall claim Rs. .... damages made up as follows: (Here give particulars).

The plaintiff claims—

(1) A declaration that he is entitled to specific performance of the agreement dated ....

(2) That the defendants do execute a proper conveyance of the said property to the plaintiff.

(3) Rs. ...., damage for withholding the transfer.

(4) Possession of the said property.

Alternatively—

(5) Refund of the said deposit of Rs. ...., together with interest thereon at the rate of Rs. .... *per cent. per annum.*

(6) Rs. .... damages, under paragraph 5 hereof.

11. Suit for specific performance of contract for sale of painting

Suit No. .... of .... 20......

In the court of .... at ....

(Set out cause title)

The plaintiff states as follows:

1. The plaintiff is a dealer in artistic goods, rare articles and good paintings.

2. The defendant is a painter and artist and he has painted several pictures and portraits and has acquired the reputation as a painter.

3. On and from .... the defendant held an exhibition of his paintings at the Exhibition Hall at .... within the jurisdiction of this learned court.

4. At the said exhibition an open invitation to the public was made to see the exhibition of the paintings of the defendant. The plaintiff had a talk with the defendant No. 1 and in the course of conversation the plaintiff was given to understand that each of the said paintings exhibited was meant for sale.

5. At the exhibition plaintiff selected a painting with a picture painted of a particular God and the plaintiff found that there was some speciality in the painting.

6. The plaintiff had a discussion with the painter, the defendant No. 1 and the plaintiff offered to purchase the said painting and asked for the price. The defendant

after considerable deliberation offered to sell the said painting to the plaintiff at Rs. 2 lakhs. The plaintiff requested the defendant to reduce the price, if possible, but the defendant did not agree.

7. The plaintiff, therefore, had to accept the price asked for by the defendant being Rs. 2 lakhs and issued a cheque then and there and the defendant accepted the same in full satisfaction of the price of the said painting and promised to deliver the same after the exhibition was over which would not take more than three days. With the consent of the defendant the plaintiff put his signature at a convenient place at the back of the painting for identification. The defendant also issued a receipt for Rs. 2 lakhs giving details of the cheque number, date and the banker and gave some indication for identification of the said painting purchased by the plaintiff.

8. After the exhibition was over and before taking back the paintings by the defendant, the plaintiff requested for delivery of the painting.

9. The defendant expressed regret and also apologised and stated that the said painting was sold to another customer for Rs. 3 lakhs who immediately took delivery of the said painting on payment of Rs. 3 lakhs in cash. The defendant offered to return the said cheque which was not encashed. The plaintiff objected to such conduct of the defendant and did not accept such breach of contract and the plaintiff told the defendant that appropriate steps would be taken in the matter. The plaintiff also took the name and address of the purchaser of the said painting which had been purchased earlier by the plaintiff.

10. In view of the breach of contract by the defendant No. 1 and the wrongful act in reselling the said painting which belonged to the plaintiff by purchase of the same, the plaintiff has suffered loss and damages which the plaintiff assesses at Rs. 5 lakhs.

11. The breach of agreement was committed by the defendant No. 1 at .... a place within the jurisdiction of this learned court. The suit is being filed within three months from the date of the said breach by the defendant No. 1.

12. The plaintiff states that the said painting became the property of the plaintiff on and from .... the date on which the price of the painting was paid by cheque to the defendant No. 1.

13. Defendant No. 1 wrongfully sold the said painting which was the property of the plaintiff to defendant No. 2 though the defendant No. 1 had no title to the said painting and as such defendant No. 2 did not acquire any right or title to the said painting.

14. The plaintiff states that the defendant No. 2 took the possession of the said painting belonging to the plaintiff as the custodian and trustee of the plaintiff and is liable to deliver the said painting in good condition to the plaintiff. The defendant No. 2 has not acquired any right title or interest in the said painting which did not belong to defendant No. 1 and defendant No. 1 had no title to the said painting and by sale of the said painting to defendant No. 2, the defendant No. 2 did not get any title to the said painting.

15. In the premises the plaintiff claims return of the said painting by defendant No. 2 and damages for the trouble caused to the plaintiff by wrongful acts of the defendants.

16. The plaintiff's cause of action arose at the address of the defendants where the plaintiff's painting was sold by defendant No. 1 to the plaintiff and resold to defendant No. 2.

17. For the purposes of jurisdiction and court fees the suit is valued at Rs. .... on which court fees in stamps have been paid.

18. The suit is not barred by the law of limitation or by the principle of waiver or acquiescence.

The plaintiff, therefore, prays for and claims:

(*a*) Decree for specific performance of the contract of sale of the said painting and delivery of the painting to the plaintiff;

(*b*) Declaration that defendant No. 2 has not acquired any right title or interest in the said painting which had earlier been sold to the plaintiff;

(*c*) Decree for damages against defendant No. 1 for selling the said painting twice and causing mental agony and pain to the plaintiff and expenses;

(*d*) Receiver be appointed to take immediate possession of the said painting from the premises of defendant No. 2 or wherever the same may be found;

(*e*) Decree for delivery of the said painting to the plaintiff;

(*f*) Costs;

(*g*) Further and other reliefs as the plaintiff is entitled to in law and in equity.

Verification

I, Mr. A, son of Mr. B residing at .... do hereby verify and say as follows:

1. I am the plaintiff and I know the facts and circumstances of this case and I am able to depose thereto.

2. The statements in paragraphs 1 to 18 hereinabove are true to my knowledge.

Plaintiff's signature Clerk to Advocate
Plaintiff's Advocate

12. Affidavit in support of the facts stated in the plaint for specific performance of contract for sale of the painting

Suit No. .... of .... 20.......

In the court of .... at ....

(See FORM 2 *ante*)

13. Written statement of defendant to the plaint for specific performance of contract for sale of painting

Suit No. .... of .... 20......

In the court of .... at ....

(Set out cause title)

11. With reference to paragraph 12 of the plaint, this defendant denies that the painting became the sole property of the plaintiff on and from the date alleged inasmuch as the price of the painting was not paid by the plaintiff as his cheque given by the plaintiff was not encashed even within three days after deposit of said cheque at defendant's bank for collection and credit.

12. With reference to paragraph 13 of plaint, this defendant denies that the said painting was wrongfully resold to defendant No. 2 and it is denied that defendant No. 1 had no clear title to said painting being an unpaid-seller. The said resale was in exercise of the legal rights of the defendant No. 1 as an unpaid seller of the said painting.

13. With reference to paragraph 14 of plaint, this defendant states that the defendant No. 2 paid cash and took delivery of the said painting and he cannot be a custodian or trustee in respect of the said painting. This defendant states that defendant No. 2 is the lawful owner of the said painting and the plaintiff cannot have any valid cause of action against any one of the defendants.

14. With reference to paragraph 15 of plaint, this defendant denies that the plaintiff is entitled to return of the said painting, by the defendant No. 2, or is entitled to claim damages for any alleged trouble caused to him by the said resale of the said painting. It is also denied that the said resale of the said painting by defendant No. 1 to defendant No. 2 was wrongful.

15. With reference to paragraph 16 of the plaint, this defendant denies that the plaintiff has any cause of action against any one of the defendants, and the suit be dismissed with costs, as disclosing no cause of action.

16. With reference to paragraph 17 of the plaint, this defendant does not admit that this learned court has jurisdiction and the question of payment of court fees in stamps is immaterial.

17. With reference to paragraph 18 of plaint, this defendant denies that the suit is not barred by law of limitation or by principles of waiver or acquiescence and this defendant states that the plaintiff has no cause of action for the present suit and the same be dismissed with costs.

Verification

I, Mr. Painter, son of Mr. .... residing at .... do hereby affirm and verify as follows:

1. I am the defendant No. 1 above-named, and I know the facts and circumstances of this case, I am the painter and seller of the said painting, being the subject-matter of this suit and I know the facts and circumstances of this case and I am able to depose thereto.

2. The statements contained in paragraphs Nos. 1 to 17 hereinabove are true to my knowledge.

Signature of Defendant No. 1 Clerk to Advocate

Advocate of Defendant No. 1

14. Affidavit of the defendant in support of the facts stated in the written statement to suit for specific performance, for sale of painting

Suit No. .... of .... 20......

In the court of .... at .....

(See FORM 6 *ante*)

The defendant No. 1 states as follows:

1. The suit is not maintainable, the plaintiff has no valid cause of action and the suit be dismissed with costs.

2. Without prejudice to the aforesaid, but strongly relying thereon, this defendant deals with the allegations and contentions of the plaintiff in the plaint.

3. Save and except what are matters of record, this defendant does not admit the validity and correctness of statements in paragraphs 1, 2 and 3 of the plaint.

4. With reference to paragraph 4 of the plaint, save and except that the paintings could be sold the defendant does not make any admission in respect of anything contained in the said paragraph.

5. The statements contained in paragraph 5 of plaint are true and correct.

6. The statements in paragraph 6 of plaint are substantially correct.

7. With reference to paragraph 7 of the plaint this defendant states that the said sale was on the specific condition that the cheque would be immediately encashed on deposit of the same in the account of defendant No. 1 Mr. Painter.

8. With reference to paragraphs 8 and 9 of plaint, this defendant states that the defendant No. 1 agreed that the said sale would be complete if the said cheque was encashed and/or credited to the account of this defendant within two days of presentation of the said cheque in the account of defendant No. 1. The said cheque was deposited on same day on which the plaintiff handed over the cheque to this defendant but the cheque was not encashed even on expiry of 3 days and in this connection, a certificate from Banker of this defendant is annexed hereto and marked 'A'.

After this non payment of plaintiff's cheque, at the exhibition, another person selected the same painting as the plaintiff sought to purchase and in view of the fact that the plaintiff's cheque was not honoured, till then, and that defendant No. 2 offered Rs. 3 lakhs for the very same painting being Rs. 1 lakh more than the amount plaintiff agreed to pay this defendant agreed to sell the said painting to defendant No. 2 at Rs. 3 lakhs and the transaction was closed immediately. When the plaintiff approached this defendant and wanted delivery of said painting the defendant No. 1 regretted and stated that due to non-encashment of the said plaintiff's cheque this defendant No. 1 sold the very same painting to defendant No. 2 on receipt of cash. The plaintiff wrongfully made accusations against defendant No. 1 since defendant No. 1 repudiated the sale and such repudiation was strictly on legal basis.

9. With reference to paragraph 10 of the plaint, this defendant denies that there has been any breach of contract by this defendant or that the resale of the said painting was wrong or that the plaintiff had suffered loss or damage or that the alleged loss or damages could be assessed at Rs. 5 lakhs. The plaintiff has no cause of action against this defendant.

10. With reference to paragraph 11 of the plaint, this defendant states that in the facts and circumstances of this case, there has been no breach of the agreement. Such breach of agreement was by plaintiff inasmuch as his cheque was not encashed though sent to bank for collection and encashment 3 days earlier. This defendant being an unpaid seller under the law, including the provisions of Sale of Goods Act, the defendant was entitled to resell the very same painting *inter alia*, to the defendant No. 2. The plaintiff has no cause of action for this suit.

17. For the purposes of jurisdiction and court fees the suit is valued at Rs. .... on which court fees in stamps have been paid.

18. The suit is not barred by the law of limitation or by the principle of waiver or acquiescence.

The plaintiff, therefore, prays for and claims:

(*a*) Decree for specific performance of the contract of sale of the said painting and delivery of the painting to the plaintiff;

(*b*) Declaration that defendant No. 2 has not acquired any right title or interest in the said painting which had earlier been sold to the plaintiff;

(*c*) Decree for damages against defendant No. 1 for selling the said painting twice and causing mental agony and pain to the plaintiff and expenses;

(*d*) Receiver be appointed to take immediate possession of the said painting from the premises of defendant No. 2 or wherever the same may be found;

(*e*) Decree for delivery of the said painting to the plaintiff;

(*f*) Costs;

(*g*) Further and other reliefs as the plaintiff is entitled to in law and in equity.

Verification

I, Mr. A, son of Mr. B residing at .... do hereby verify and say as follows:

1. I am the plaintiff and I know the facts and circumstances of this case and I am able to depose thereto.

2. The statements in paragraphs 1 to 18 hereinabove are true to my knowledge.

Plaintiff's signature — Clerk to Advocate

Plaintiff's Advocate

12. Affidavit in support of the facts stated in the plaint for specific performance of contract for sale of the painting

Suit No. .... of .... 20.......

In the court of .... at ....

(See FORM 2 *ante*)

13. Written statement of defendant to the plaint for specific performance of contract for sale of painting

Suit No. .... of .... 20......

In the court of .... at ....

(Set out cause title)

after considerable deliberation offered to sell the said painting to the plaintiff at Rs. 2 lakhs. The plaintiff requested the defendant to reduce the price, if possible, but the defendant did not agree.

7. The plaintiff, therefore, had to accept the price asked for by the defendant being Rs. 2 lakhs and issued a cheque then and there and the defendant accepted the same in full satisfaction of the price of the said painting and promised to deliver the same after the exhibition was over which would not take more than three days. With the consent of the defendant the plaintiff put his signature at a convenient place at the back of the painting for identification. The defendant also issued a receipt for Rs. 2 lakhs giving details of the cheque number, date and the banker and gave some indication for identification of the said painting purchased by the plaintiff.

8. After the exhibition was over and before taking back the paintings by the defendant, the plaintiff requested for delivery of the painting.

9. The defendant expressed regret and also apologised and stated that the said painting was sold to another customer for Rs. 3 lakhs who immediately took delivery of the said painting on payment of Rs. 3 lakhs in cash. The defendant offered to return the said cheque which was not encashed. The plaintiff objected to such conduct of the defendant and did not accept such breach of contract and the plaintiff told the defendant that appropriate steps would be taken in the matter. The plaintiff also took the name and address of the purchaser of the said painting which had been purchased earlier by the plaintiff.

10. In view of the breach of contract by the defendant No. 1 and the wrongful act in reselling the said painting which belonged to the plaintiff by purchase of the same, the plaintiff has suffered loss and damages which the plaintiff assesses at Rs. 5 lakhs.

11. The breach of agreement was committed by the defendant No. 1 at .... a place within the jurisdiction of this learned court. The suit is being filed within three months from the date of the said breach by the defendant No. 1.

12. The plaintiff states that the said painting became the property of the plaintiff on and from .... the date on which the price of the painting was paid by cheque to the defendant No. 1.

13. Defendant No. 1 wrongfully sold the said painting which was the property of the plaintiff to defendant No. 2 though the defendant No. 1 had no title to the said painting and as such defendant No. 2 did not acquire any right or title to the said painting.

14. The plaintiff states that the defendant No. 2 took the possession of the said painting belonging to the plaintiff as the custodian and trustee of the plaintiff and is liable to deliver the said painting in good condition to the plaintiff. The defendant No. 2 has not acquired any right title or interest in the said painting which did not belong to defendant No. 1 and defendant No. 1 had no title to the said painting and by sale of the said painting to defendant No. 2, the defendant No. 2 did not get any title to the said painting.

15. In the premises the plaintiff claims return of the said painting by defendant No. 2 and damages for the trouble caused to the plaintiff by wrongful acts of the defendants.

16. The plaintiff's cause of action arose at the address of the defendants where the plaintiff's painting was sold by defendant No. 1 to the plaintiff and resold to defendant No. 2.

Index

G: SP 47